Just Garret

First published in 2010 by
Liberties Press
Guinness Enterprise Centre | Taylor's Lane | Dublin 8
Tel: +353 (1) 415 1224
www.libertiespress.com | info@libertiespress.com

Distributed in the United States by
Dufour Editions | PO Box 7 | Chester Springs | Pennsylvania | 19425

and in Australia by
James Bennett Pty Limited | InBooks | 3 Narabang Way
Belrose NSW 2085

Trade enquiries to Gill & Macmillan Distribution
Hume Avenue | Park West | Dublin 12
Tel: +353 (1) 500 9534 | Fax: +353 (1) 500 9595
sales@gillmacmillan.ie

ISBN: 978-1-905483-68-6
2 4 6 8 10 9 7 5 3 1
A CIP record for this title is available from the British Library.

Cover design by Sin É Design
Internal design by Liberties Press
Printed by ScandBook

Just Garret

Tales from the Political Front Line

Garret FitzGerald

To my children, Mary, John and Mark, and my grandchildren, whose patience was sometimes strained by my absorption in an attempt to produce this text whilst simultaneously completing, for later publication, a research project in early nineteenth-century history. These tasks completed, I hope to be a more relaxed parent and grandparent in future!

Contents

~: Acknowledgements :~

I should like to acknowledge the patient assistance of Mary Molloy and Annie O'Curry in preparing the manuscript of this book for publication. I also want to acknowledge the forbearance of Liberties Press over the past two years of missed deadlines!

~: Introduction :~

I suppose that in trying to sum up my eighty-four years – to date! – the first thing to say is how very fortunate I've been – in my parents, in my wife, and in my family above all.

But also in my careers:

First, in Aer Lingus, for twelve years, where at an early age I was give an opportunity, together with enthusiastic colleagues, to help to make the company a commercially efficient airline.

Then in UCD, where the conservatism I had inherited from my father was effectively challenged by my 1960s students as well as by my own children, with the result that I became a committed social democrat.

And in that same decade, working closely with the public sector, I learnt to appreciate the commitment of so many public servants to the public good.

In the political party that I chose to join, and in political life generally, I was given an appropriate outlet for the combative side of my nature – a characteristic that had been less welcome in academe!

In my post as Minister for Foreign Affairs, at the very start of Ireland's involvement in the European Union, I was given the opportunity of establishing Ireland's positive role in that new and enlarged context, backed by a remarkable team of able and dedicated diplomats. And – as was also the case in my later role of Taoiseach – I was also given an opportunity to fulfil an early ambition to work with people on both sides of the deeply divided Northern Ireland community for peace and reconciliation in that part of Ireland, where my own ancestral roots lie deep. And also of starting to heal some of the wounds that centuries of a conflicted history had inflicted on our relationship with Great Britain.

Finally, as the seventh Leader of an internationally-recognised Irish Government, I was given an opportunity to serve the Irish people in a most challenging period – in circumstances that were difficult and unpropitious, and which offered less opportunities for job satisfaction than I had found in my earlier life.

However, those difficult years were eased by a very positive relationship with most of my colleagues, and by the chance it gave me to protect the less well-off from the impact of the measures we had to take to save the economy – something which is sadly not being emulated in the current crisis.

And also by the opportunity it gave me to initiate the overdue process of substituting a pluralist society for the narrow single-ethos culture that had perhaps been an inevitable inheritance from the national revolution which had been forced on us in the closing stages of the British imperial system.

In the twenty-three years of retirement which have followed, I have had the opportunity to work with governments of more than a score of countries which have been anxious to learn both from Irish successes and Irish failures; to write a thousand further weekly articles in the *Irish Times* (to which I started contributing fifty-six years ago) on social, economic and political issues, seeking through this channel to inform and influence public policy; to research and publish, through the Royal Irish Academy, material on such historical issues as the geographical pattern of the eighteenth- and nineteenth-century decline of the Irish language and the state of Irish primary education prior to the launching of our national school system in 1831; and to publish five books and over a dozen contributions to others.

Has it all been worthwhile? Yes, although I am constantly aware, and frequently upset, by the recollection of how much more I might have been able to achieve with greater patience and better judgment: the truth is that, after a long life, one tends to be more conscious of one's failures than of one's successes.

However, most Irish people are kind and generous, and I am constantly heartened by the good wishes of people I meet wherever I go. I can testify to the fact that, contrary to what we often say about each other, the Irish are a very warm – and forgiving – people!

PS – Because the variety of my activities over two-thirds of a century must be confusing, I append a map of my various careers.

1

~: Early Childhood :~

When I was two my mother, with the aid of some inheritance from her father, purchased a nineteenth-century house, Fairy Hill, just south of Bray. The house was set in several acres of gardens and lawns, and surrounded on three sides by fields, with two small woods and a complex of stables and outbuildings. The dwelling itself was a substantial two-storeyed building with a bewildering and eccentric internal plan involving five different levels on the ground floor and three on the first floor. The front hall, entered through a double hall door, gave on the right to the living room, which was called 'the study'. On the other side of the hall was a little-used sitting room, opening on to a space used by my eldest brother, Desmond, as a workroom.

Halfway up the main staircase from the back hall was a spacious drawing room that opened, through a conservatory, on to a balcony, with steps down to the walled flower garden at the back of the house. Continuing up another flight of the main stairs, one reached a large landing serving four bedrooms, and a door into the nursery corridor, which had two more bedrooms, as well as the solitary bathroom.

The back hall also gave access to a cloakroom and, up some steps, on the right, to a large dining room, at the end of which was a pantry and a side door to the garden and, on the left, down a couple more steps, the kitchen quarters. The indoor staff comprised a cook and a maid.

Outside the back door from the kitchen was a vegetable and fruit garden, and beside it the stables, with their lofts and mangers and numerous outbuildings, including a cow-shed and a hen-house. The entrance to the house was up a drive running parallel to the road from the gate at the bottom of the hill, with a side gate for pedestrians nearer to the house. The drive widened in front of the house and then swept on up the hill to the stables. Lawns, broken by borders with rose bushes, sloped down in front of the house to a tennis court, which also served as a croquet lawn; below this was a meadow, and beyond that a small but mysterious wood. Through a carefully maintained gap in the trees was a dramatic view of the great houses of Sorrento Terrace on the sea at Dalkey, four miles away.

Between the house and the road, overlooked by the drawing-room windows, was a smaller lawn, surrounded by herbaceous borders, which was used for clock-golf. The path between it and the house, leading through a gate into the walled flower garden, was used as the tradesmen's entrance: otherwise, it would have been necessary to circumnavigate the entire house to reach the kitchen door. All the groceries, and the milk – which came in a huge milk-can, delivered by pony and trap – were delivered through a window into our playroom beside the kitchen.

Weekend meat arrived by post, with a tenpenny stamp I think, from Carlingford, County Louth. Three decades later, I found myself canvassing a vote there for the Senate from the butcher, who had become a county councilor. Later, his son, an elderly parish priest, wrote to tell me how, as a young man, he had brought this and other meat parcels to the post office each week.

On the far side of the house, the drive curving up to the stables was crossed by a wide path, which, from the top of some log steps outside the study window, stretched between yew trees to a gate and stile overlooking the fields and offering a view of the Dublin and Wicklow hills. The Yew Walk, as we called it, was a favourite stroll, with the added attraction for a child that it gave access to the hen-run. The hen-house door in turn provided an easy route to the roofs of the stables, in the valleys of which cigarettes could be safely smoked – as my brother Fergus taught me to do when I was seven. Thereafter for some years I faced the difficult choice between deploying my three-penny pocket money in its entirety on five Players, or reserving a penny for other purposes by slumming it with five Woodbines – until much later, at the age of fourteen, I took a rational decision to divert this expenditure, undertaken only because of peer pressure, into more enjoyable items such as chocolate and ice cream.

In the earlier years, the loft of the stables – no longer used for horses at that time, of course – still housed hay, saved each summer in the meadow below the house. The hay-making was a great occasion each year, and the hay-filled loft was a playground thereafter, so long as the hay lasted. We also at one period raised chickens and ducks for our own consumption, but this experiment ended abruptly after all two-score fowl were killed one night by a marauding fox. I still recall the morning scene of devastation, viewed from the nursery window.

The two small woods offered great scope for Fergus and myself – huts to be built, and trees to be climbed – as did the surrounding fields, rented to local farmers, who grazed sheep and lambs in the early years, and later cows. The cows provided suitably large and immobile targets for bow-and-arrow practice. At one period, the fields also served as a makeshift children's golf course, developed by Fergus.

The gardens and lawns, and their surroundings, gave ample scope for my mother's gardening skills – an enthusiasm which she deployed with the aid of a gardener who lived in the gate-lodge and who, in the early years, when my father still enjoyed a ministerial income, was aided by an under-gardener. Flowers were in profusion: every conceivable shade of sweet pea across the centre of the flower garden, new varieties of violets in a special border in one corner, and roses everywhere. In the neighbouring vegetable garden, fruit and vegetables were grown in quantity: strawberries, raspberries, gooseberries, currants, Japanese winberries plums and greengages, peaches and, in a greenhouse – and never very successfully – grapes from an ancient vine.

An orchard, established by my mother in part of the field beside the vegetable and fruit garden, provided apples and pears in abundance. But soft fruit was the predominant crop – 'crop' being the operative word, for in addition to supplying immediate domestic needs, swollen by relatives from London and Belfast, and sometimes from North America, as well as by large numbers of my parents' and my elder brothers' friends at weekends, the garden provided the raw material for hundreds of pounds of jam and jelly which my mother produced each summer – principally strawberry and raspberry jam, but also plum, damson and greengage jam and raspberry, loganberry, redcurrant and apply jelly. Picking the fruit was less laborious when, especially at weekends, there were many helpers.

Only one thing was lacking from a child's viewpoint: water. Efforts to divine a well near the garage proved fruitless, and there was nowhere to dabble feet or to sail boats – although, of course, the sea at Bray was only a mile or so away. Because my elder brothers were a good deal older than me, they left me much to my own devices, but my next brother, Fergus, faced with having brothers six years older and six years younger than himself, made the best he could of the company of a much younger sibling. He was a romantic and imaginative child. Under his guidance, I learnt how to look after white mice and a grass snake; played cowboys and Indians; re-enacted the legends of King Arthur and the fall of the Bastille; turned the garden paths into a simulacrum of the French railway system; studied astronomy; learned Egyptian hieroglyphics; played airships, with a clothes basket suspended by a rope from the branch of a tree; and made quantities of toffee (trays of which, dyed bright pink with cochineal, tended to be left gathering dust on top of and underneath cupboards).

We also devised and acted out plays. One of these was based on Browning's *King Robert of Sicily*; another was a detective drama written by Fergus. Performances were given after Christmas to an invited audience which included Edward and Christine Longford of the Gate Theatre. One such performance had to be postponed because, for reasons I now forget, I went on strike.

Fergus taught me to type with two fingers and a thumb – an art I have never lost, and never improved upon. At the age of thirteen, he had gained access to the

National Library, where he copied out in a red notebook the grammar, syntax and vocabulary (but only to the letter 'B') of the Quechua language of the Incas of Peru. Wanting a 'fair' copy of this material, and feeling that he had done his share, he required me at the age of seven to type out his notes.

Both my parents typed as well as having shorthand (my father's shorthand notes of the 1930 Imperial Conference remain to be deciphered) and, as they changed typewriters every fifteen years or so, they passed on their older models to their children – with the oldest typewriter going to the youngest child. Thus I undertook Fergus's task on my mother's first typewriter – a very early model indeed, on which the letters came down from above. My mother had purchased it second-hand around 1908. Later I graduated to an early-twentieth-century portable Royal typewriter, which in the late 1950s the makers enthusiastically received as a trade-in, apparently regarding it as a valuable antique needed for their museum. My first typewriter must have been thrown out before I realised its potential worth.

Fergus thus provided me with a wide-ranging supplementary education and rudimentary secretarial training. Other skills – playing bridge and poker, the ability to walk up to seven miles, and the courage to trespass on all surrounding properties – were learnt from an afternoon 'governess', Miss Cuddy, then in her late fifties. By the time I was five, and going to school, Miss Cuddy had replaced an earlier Nurse O'Neill; she remained with me until I went for a year to Coláiste na Rinne at the age of nine.

This somewhat Victorian nursery-type upbringing partly reflected the fact that my mother did not feel able, in her forties and early fifties, to undertake the task of looking after a child full-time. She had spent the previous fifteen years bringing up my three elder brothers – the first ten years having been complicated by her revolutionary activities and by my father's frequent absences in jail, as well as by lack of money. Her health never fully recovered from the physical and nervous illness that followed my birth, although few outsiders realised she had health problems, because of the restless energy with which she tackled the running of a large house and garden, the organisation of endless parties, and incessant letter-writing to relatives and friends around the world, not to speak of skiing and ice skating – until she had a bad fall at the age of fifty-five – as well as occasional tennis.

That my upbringing would be adult-orientated rather than child-orientated became clear to me on my fifth birthday. I was to start school in a couple of months' time, and Nurse was leaving. Mother took me for a walk around the neighbouring lanes; halting at a quiet spot where we sat down on a bank beside the road, she produced some sandwiches, explaining that this was my birthday tea and that I was now too old to have parties on future birthdays. I accepted this philosophically: I wasn't accustomed to seeing much of other children anyway, and was delighted with the generosity and imagination my parents showed at birthday times and

Christmas. I think it was on that birthday that I woke to find erected on the nursery floor a zinc-and-wood playhouse that survived until my children's time. Another gift – at Christmas that year, I think – was a rocking horse, which, after being renovated, is still going strong.

My mother was the product of a middle-class Victorian environment which involved extensive supplementation of parental care by nurses and governesses. She had never been able to afford such luxuries when my elder brothers were young, and it seemed natural to her to take advantage of the recent inheritance from her father by trying to give me the kind of childhood she had herself enjoyed. In fact, she devoted a lot of time to my education, both before and after I went to school. She was a gifted teacher – as I found to my benefit right up to the point where, many years later, I secured, as a result of her tuition, a university entrance scholarship, with first place in English – a result which neither my school career nor my performance in examinations had suggested would ever be possible.

She also took on the whole burden of my religious education, despite the fact that she was not then a Roman Catholic and that my father was a devout and highly intellectual, as well as orthodox, member of the Catholic Church. Her remarkable commitment to teaching me a faith to which she herself did not then adhere, backed by my father's undemonstrative piety, provided me with a religious foundation that saw me through into early middle age; only then did I begin to understand what religious doubt means, and by then I was better equipped to cope with such problems.

My reading as a child was in some degree Victorian or, at latest, Edwardian. English and American children's books, the names of which are for the most part unknown today, featured strongly: *Dora's Dolls House*, *Helen's Babies and Other People's Children*, the Elsie Dinsmore stories, *Bashful Fifteen* and *Little Lord Fauntleroy*. The *Gem* and the *Magnet* magazines (some of them copies going back to the early twenties) introduced me to Billy Bunter, Harry Wharton et al. Later there was Rider Haggard, Andrew Lang, Jules Vernes and Talbot Barnes Reed. More modern works included Richmal Crompton's *Just William* books, Hugh Lofting's Dr Doolittle stories, and Arthur Ransome's *Swallows and Amazons* series.

My father made his own contribution to my literary education in two ways: first, by reading aloud to me in the evenings both his own unpublished fairy stories and works by authors like Dickens, and, second, by placing in 1937 a standing order at a bookshop for early editions of the *Boy's Own Paper*, which, evidently, he had himself read avidly as a child in London. Eventually, all the issues from 1879 to 1897 came my way, bringing with them the authentic aura of late-nineteenth-century British imperialism – which had as little impact on me as it had had on my father.

I suppose this literary diet may seem a slightly eccentric one for the child of two

Irish nationalist revolutionaries. But despite my mother's assurance to Bernard Shaw (for whom she had acted as secretary temporarily in 1909), in one of her letters in 1914, that she would bring my eldest brother, Dem, up to hate the English, and despite the fact that she remained until shortly after my birth a committed republican, neither she nor my father was capable of sustaining a narrow anglophobia. Dedicated Irish patriots all their lives, they nevertheless had a deep love of English literature which they had acquired during their very different childhoods in Belfast and east London of the late Victorian era. Moreover, their moral roots lay deeply embedded in the values of the Victorian period. It would have been inconceivable for either of them to have failed to pass on to their children these values, and the riches of English literature, in parallel with their passionate commitment to Ireland, to Irish nationalism, and to Gaelic culture. They saw no contradiction in transmitting to their children the whole of this rich and varied heritage. Thus my father's readings from Dickens were accompanied unselfconsciously by encouragement to speak Irish with him – especially after I had acquired what turned out to be a temporary fluency in that language at Ring College when I was nine to ten years old; by the instilling of a veneration for the ancient culture of Gaelic Ireland; and by a wealth of anecdotes about the revolutionary period which were no less inspiring for being presented almost always in a humorous vein: my father never failed to see the funny side of everything with which he had ever been engaged.

Moreover, respect for the great figures of the national movement was something which my brothers and I imbibed from our earliest years – in my case all the more profoundly because by the time I became conscious of such issues, those whom my father had most admired and loved were all tragically dead – the O'Rahilly, killed within minutes of parting from my father in the GPO in 1916; Arthur Griffith, dead of a broken heart, it was said (actually a stroke), in the midst of the Civil War; Michael Collins, shot by a tragic chance in an ambush ten days later; Kevin O'Higgins, assassinated by a breakaway IRA group when I was a baby; and Patrick Hogan, killed in a car crash in the mid-1930s.

This rich cultural background was further enhanced by my father's classical education and his deep involvement with and intimate knowledge of French literature and philosophy – although these latter influences reached me only later on, in my teens.

There were vigorous family debates. In 1997, I met Arthur Griffith's daughter at a dinner commemorating the foundation of the Cumann na nGaedheal party in 1923. She told me that my oldest brother, Dem, had described to her a political debate between my father and his four children during which I was sent to bed at 6.30 – which meant that I was aged six. A quarter of an hour later, I reopened the door, announced that I disagreed with all of them, and then returned to bed! It was,

I think, my argumentativeness that led my father later to propose that I became a barrister.

After Easter 1931, I was sent to a small private school called St Brigid's, run by a Miss Lucy Brayden in a large house in Duncairn Terrace, Bray. I recall my first day at school, sitting on the floor, making words out of letters, as Mother had already taught me. Before long, I found myself in a class of eight or nine children, which after a year or two ceased to have amongst its members any boy other than myself. For a boy with three brothers and no sisters, the experience was a strange but not unattractive one. True, the girls tended to gang up against the single boy in their midst – which soon developed my instincts of self-preservation. But I also learned quite early in life that on their own, girls could be gentle and affectionate. By the age of eight, I had reached the conclusion that the right way to deal with 'the girl question' was to select one and marry her as soon as possible. I made my selection then, and persisted with this choice until my second year at university, when it became clear that the affections of the girl in question were engaged elsewhere. But that is to anticipate.

My interest in international affairs also derives from this experience of an otherwise all-female class. One day in October 1934, when we were changing rooms in mid-morning, our teacher, Miss FitzGerald (no relation), referred to the assassination in Marseilles of King Alexander of Yugoslavia and Foreign Minister Barthou of France on the previous day. It was obvious to me that a number of the girls had already heard this news, and I felt that it must have been clear to all of them that I hadn't. I decided never to risk such a humiliation again; thereafter, for the rest of my life I have read the newspapers assiduously every day and have thus avoided any repetition of this shaming experience.

School was a morning affair. In the afternoon, I went for long, trespassing walks with Miss Cuddy. Even when we went to Bray beach in summer, we took a direct route through the grounds of Loreto Convent. Sometimes we dropped in to a house about three miles away in Shankill. This was the home of Dr Michael Tierney, professor of Greek at UCD (and later its president), who from 1927 to 1932 had been a member of the Dáil and was later to be vice-chairman of the Senate, and whose wife, Eibhlín, was a daughter of Eoin MacNeill.

The Tierneys were friends of my parents, and the two eldest children, girls, were at school with me. I spent many happy hours at their house, the more so because in those years it was one of only two houses that I visited regularly – the other being that of Seán and Eileen Ó Faoláin, whose daughter Julie was a couple of years younger than me.

Until 1927, ministers had availed of state transport only for official journeys to rural areas. My father, who never owned a car, travelled to and from his ministry by tram, even in the later stages of, and immediately after, the Civil War. But after Kevin O'Higgins's assassination in July 1927, the army insisted on guarding ministers. From early childhood, therefore, I had been accustomed to accompanying my father in an army-owned saloon car, driven by a soldier and followed by a guard car with three other soldiers. Each car was, I believe, fitted with two sub-machine guns, and each of the four soldiers carried a rifle, two revolvers and a bag of ammunition.

The army guards were, of course, a great addition to the family, and particularly to my life. Companionable men, obviously fond of children, they ate the thickest sandwiches I have ever seen and did their best to help my mother – once digging up the grass bank outside the study window, believing this was her wish, whereas having laboriously planted it with daffodil bulbs, she was in fact furious, but carefully did not reveal the fact. When we went to spend afternoons bathing at Jack's Hole, south of Wicklow, the guards acted as umpires for our game of Manoeuvres, which involved all concerned – including on occasion bemused distinguished guests from abroad crawling towards each other through the bracken, the object being for each to shout an identification of another before being identified himself or herself.

The change of government in February 1932, and my father's loss of ministerial office, had meant little to me at the time – except that happily thenceforth I saw more of my father than had been the case when he was a minister. The dramatic change in my life came over a year later when the new government withdrew the guards from ex-ministers. At one blow, I lost these friends, and my father lost the only car of which he ever had regular use during his life, becoming dependent thereafter on occasional lifts in a minute second-hand Austin Seven with which my eldest brother, Dem, had managed to equip himself two years earlier.

Fergus and I immediately felt our new vulnerability to the IRA, especially because my father was required at the same time to hand over his revolvers – which in fact he had never fired in anger. We immediately equipped ourselves with bows and arrows and spears, which we kept at the ready in the loft over the stable, in case of an IRA attack – which, happily, never occurred.

On the whole, however, politics intruded remarkably little in our lives, although, of course, my parents' friends included a number of politicians – people to whom they had become close during the period of the national movement. Most of these were still active in politics – for example Ernest Blythe (vice-president of the Executive Council, i.e. Minister for Finance, up to 1932), and his wife Annie, who was Fergus's godmother; Tody (Paddy) McGilligan (Minister for Foreign Affairs to 1932) and his wife, also Annie; and – from across the political divide – Sean McEntee (Minister for Finance in the Fianna Fáil government after 1932) and his wife, Margaret, who was my godmother.

Ernest Blythe had been a friend of my parents since their early days in west Kerry in 1913; Tody McGilligan, and his many brothers and sisters, had become friends of my parents during the War of Independence, but his wife (a sister of the British Foreign Office's Soviet expert, Violet Connolly) was a new addition to my parents' circle, for Tody (his own childhood version of his Christian name) had married late, in 1929.

Friendship with the McEntees went back to 1917 and transcended politics; in 1923, my father had helped to have Sean McEntee released on parole from a post-Civil War internment camp so that he could inspect a public lighting scheme in Wexford for which he had acted as consultant. He then arranged his permanent release, providing him and his wife with passports so that they could celebrate with a holiday in Paris. Shortly after the change of government in 1932, Margaret McEntee broke her leg while at Fairy Hill and had to remain in the house for three weeks. News of this stay got out and provoked a 'non-fraternisation' instruction from de Valera – which, however, the McEntees ignored.

Another close friend from earlier days was Dr Richard (Dick) Hayes, who had been with the Volunteers. He had served as medical officer in the Battle of Ashbourne in 1916, and had later been sent from Dartmoor Prison to Maidstone chained to my father and de Valera – an episode to which de Valera frequently referred when I got to know him very much later, in the mid-1970s. Dick was an extraordinarily gentle and humorous person who married late in life, after we had left Fairy Hill.

On the artistic side there were Sarah Purser, the painter and maker of stained glass – then in her mid-eighties, and Edward Longford, elder brother of Frank Longford – and his wife Christine, who together with Hilton Edwards and Micheal MacLiammoir founded the Gate Theatre in 1928 and kept it going for so many decades.

These were all regular visitors. Occasional guests, of whom I have only vestigial memories, included W. B. Yeats, T. S. Eliot, Desmond McCarthy, Frank Pakenham (later Lord Longford), and Jacques Maritain from outside Ireland, as well as John McCormack, Professor Tom Bodkin, Oliver St John Gogarty, Sean Keating, and Bryan Guinness, later Lord Moyne.

But most of the guests were young people – friends of my two elder brothers, who were in their teens and early twenties while we lived in Fairy Hill. Some of them, like Niall Montgomery and Don MacDonagh, had a literary bent; all were stimulated and entertained by my father's literary, philosophical and political conversation and by his endless flow of anecdotes and reminiscence. These at times overflowed into vignettes of the London music-hall songs of the turn of the century, which had been part of his childhood and which he sang with an authentic Cockney accent.

My mother's role at this stage of her life was a less prominent one. She and my father had differed over the Civil War but she ceased to play an active part in politics after rallying to his political position in the late 1920s, and was content to fulfil a more passive family role. But no one was ever in doubt about her strength of character, or about her sympathy for young people and her insight into their problems. These qualities, and her immense and endless hospitality, made her as popular in her own way with the young as was my father. Throughout the year, but above all in summer, the house was open to young and old alike, especially at week-ends. Aunts and uncles, and cousins, and occasionally my Belfast grandmother and cousins-in-law of hers, born in the 1850s and 1860s, were occupants of the two spare rooms, and sometimes additional accommodation for an overflow of relatives was provided by one or more of us evacuating our bedrooms and sleeping on couches or on a chair-bed.

Summer activities centred around tennis and bathing expeditions to County Wicklow beaches; in winter, there were walks, including hill-climbing (which we, exaggerating the size and steepness of the inclines we attacked, called mountain-climbing). Nevertheless, I vividly recall how proud I was when I climbed the Great Sugar Loaf – all of 1,600 feet! – unaided when I was four. Once there was a car treasure-hunt; when, despite tearful distress on my part, the Longfords were not allowed to take me with them because I had earlier asked to join in the laying of the clues, and my parents feared that I might reveal secrets of where clues had been hidden.

The tennis parties were accompanied by tea, home-made lemonade and cakes on the lawn – including my mother's speciality, a three-tier strawberry-and-cream sandwich cake. No alcohol was served either then, at lunch or at 'late dinner' – the latter being a meal in which I did not participate. My father was not an absolute teetotaler, although, apart from a rather unsuccessful attempt to get him to drink stout medicinally after an illness, I cannot recall him drinking anything other than perhaps a glass of sherry at a reception. But he had a deep distrust of alcohol and distaste for drunkenness. He believed that drink had prejudiced many earlier Irish attempts to achieve independence from Britain. Moreover, I believe that his own father, a London stonemason, had been an alcoholic. As a result, the only alcohol – apart from the medicinal Guinness – that I ever saw in the house was a solitary bottle of Benedictine, kept in the pantry off the dining room 'in case a visitor came' (i.e. one with the temerity to ask for a drink). I don't recall the bottle ever being broached. But the absence of alcohol never seemed to constrain the spirits of our guests of all ages, and I saw no signs of any sense of deprivation, even among my elder brothers' university friends. As each summer drew to an end, and the evenings, and later the afternoons, grew shorter, the house itself came into its own. The drawing room and the dining room, and for smaller groups the study, were centres of discussion, debate and anecdote – the latter being the only part I was old enough to enjoy. Sometimes in the evenings there were charades in the drawing room. I was able, and more than willing, to participate in this game, the house being ransacked for dressing-up materials and props. But winter, except for some weekends and, of course, Christmas, was on the whole a quieter time – that is, if you ignored the sound of the family typewriters.

Visits by relatives were not one-way traffic. While my first visit to my London aunts and uncles was in 1936, when I was ten, my parents and my elder brothers had been regular visitors there either on trips to London, or to and from the Continent, passing through London. After my London grandmother's death in 1927, when I was a year old, my father's elder sister, Ciss, her husband, Ted, and their two sons, Gerald and Ulick (the latter of whom was a regular visitor to Fairy Hill) had moved from West Ham to 15 Cornwall Gardens, off Gloucester Road, Kensington. My unmarried aunt, Kate, headmistress of a primary school in Upminster, who came to visit us every holiday period – Easter, summer and Christmas – and my equally unmarried Uncle France, who owned a chemical works in Stratford, lived there with Ciss, the top floor of whose house was used to accommodate paying guests from the Continent. This gave a cosmopolitan air to this spacious house, the large first-floor balcony of which was a family gathering-place on summer evenings.

My brothers and I also visited our relations in Belfast frequently. Unlike my elder brothers, however, I have no recollection of my grandfather's home at College Green House, nor have I any memory of my Aunt Memi's house in Bangor, County Down, where she and her three young daughters looked after me as a baby while my mother was convalescing on the Continent following my birth. But I recall Memi's house in Marlborough Park, where I stayed later; my grandmother's house in Windsor Avenue; and a cousin's house in Crumlin, County Antrim. After my grandmother's death in January 1936, when I was recovering from mumps, my father brought me to join Mother in Belfast, where she and Memi, the only two of their family living in Ireland at the time, were winding up their mother's estate. Visits to Stormont, where Parliament was not in session at the time, and to the shipyard, were features of this visit that I particularly remember.

My only other journey outside the Dublin area during my early childhood was a summer holiday spent with my parents and Fergus at Derrynane in Kerry, shortly after the change of government in 1932. But there were other events that stand out in my memory, such as the Eucharistic Congress in the same year, which involved attendance at a Children's Mass in Phoenix Park – of which I only remember a visit to the latrines! – and an opportunity to see the arrival of the papal legate and scores of bishops at the pro-cathedral. I seem to recall that I was impressed when told that a Rumanian Uniate bishop was said to have been asked to leave his wife behind in London lest he cause scandal in Dublin – a story which may have had no basis. The other excitement on this occasion was being wakened at ten o'clock one night by a

– northern Protestant – cousin to be driven in to Dublin to see the city lit up. I seem to have missed the spiritual aspect of the Congress in the midst of these profane excitements, however.

My own first holiday in London was an occasion for visiting all the usual tourist places, plus some others in which my parents had a particular interest. Thus my mother brought me to Ely Place to see the Mitre Inn, with its cherry-tree beam, telling me of its rural licensing hours as part of the County of Ely and its gates, which were shut at night. She also took me on a tram ride from Southampton Row through the Kingsway train tunnel to Hammersmith. My father brought me for a walk through Epping Forest, which had been familiar to him as a child, and to Westminster, speculating as to whether, as a former abstentionist MP from 1918 to 1922, he had any special rights there!

Fergus initiated me into how to travel underground for one penny from South Kensington to Gloucester Road via Charing Cross, Oxford Circus and Notting Hill Gate. Some years earlier, in anticipation of such a visit, he had made me learn off all the London underground stations and had ensured that I knew (but did not necessarily take!) the shortest route between any two of them. Fergus's own travel ambitions extended far beyond London. At the end of the previous year, when our father was away in the United States, he had run away from home for no very apparent reason. His objective, he had confided in some sceptical school friends, was to join our allegedly rich Uncle Johnnie – my father's eldest brother – in Brazil. Fergus took the boat to Liverpool, walked most of the way to Chester to see the historic city, and then hitched lifts to near Birmingham to call on Ann Bodkin, one of the five daughters of Professor Tom Bodkin, who some months earlier had moved from his post as director of the National Gallery in Dublin to the directorship of the Barber Institute of Fine Arts in Birmingham. (The Bodkins had been friends of ours in Dublin, and Ann in particular had spent a good deal of time with Fergus, her near-contemporary, and myself, at Fairy Hill.)

Fergus waited outside the Bodkin house in Birmingham until Ann came out on her way to school. He asked her to promise not to tell her parents that she had seen him, thus presenting her with a serious dilemma: she knew how much Fergus's disappearance would have upset my mother, to whom she was particularly attached. Meanwhile, Fergus had gone on to Stratford-on-Avon, which he had been anxious to see, rang home, was pleasantly surprised to find Mother would like him to return, got lost again and, after a spell in a poorhouse, where the police lodged him temporarily – the inmates were apparently edified to find a schoolboy in the otherwise empty Casuals Ward reading the *Aeneid* in Latin, aloud to himself – until collected by his two elder brothers.

Ann was so upset by what she felt to have been her betrayal of Fergus through telling of her encounters with him that she did not feel able thereafter to communicate with him again – as I discovered when I met her again almost fifty years later, after Fergus's death.

As for Fergus and Uncle Johnnie, that story reached its denouement in 1963 when Fergus, on a journey to Brazil, visited his house in the country outside Rio de Janeiro. Johnnie had married for a second time when he was in his late eighties, so that there would be 'someone to look after him in his old age', as he had written to my mother! Fergus met his widow, a Brazilian peasant who had never heard of Ireland and thought our uncle was a German. In the village was a church that my uncle had built years earlier, dedicated to St Patrick, in memory of his father. When the parish priest had refused to use the new church, he had gone to the parish church and chased the priest and parishioners out of it with the aid of some shots from a revolver!

The year that Fergus ran away to Birmingham in the hope of reaching South America was also the year I spent at Ring College in County Waterford learning to speak Irish. The school at that time had about eighty pupils, boys and girls. There were no concessions to comfort – perhaps there never are at boarding school. Fergus who, like my elder brothers, had spent a year there, had warned me that when physically punished I must show no signs of my distress, lest the other boys laugh at me. So on the first of many occasions when, with other boys, I had to queue up behind the girls (they received the same six slaps on the hand as the boys with a thick stick, but had the woman's privilege of going first), for punishment after supper by the headmaster – 'An Fear Mor' as he was known. I held back the tears – nobly, as I thought. My reward was to be jeered at by the other boys on my way up to the dormitory for receiving what they assumed, from my lack of apparent emotion, to have been favoured treatment. It is important to learn as early as possible that there is often no justice in life!

During that year I learnt to speak fluent Irish – which subsequently, with the help of three Easter holidays spent at Ring, enabled me to coast through secondary school without making any special effort with the language, but did not provide me with the vocabulary to cope later in life with issues like economics and politics. On the whole I enjoyed the experience – apart from one moment of embarrassment, when I received the only marriage proposal of my life, delivered in the presence of others, and calling for great tact on my part to refuse gently.

For some reason there were no arrangements for sport in Ring that year – the hurley sticks that boys were required to bring with them were not used. Exercise took the form of long walks, supplemented by our own initiative in undertaking the building of huts with stones, sods and pieces of corrugated iron. Mother, having had previous experience of communications problems with her older children in Ring, had devised a foolproof method of securing a reply to her letters; she inserted a bar of chocolate into each letter, with a clear indication that failure to reply would be followed by the omission of chocolate from her next letter. Additional food supplies, unaccompanied by such sanctions, consisted of a pound of iced cake delivered by post each fortnight, and a standing order for a weekly pot of jam at the local shop.

Shortly after my return home from Ring College in June 1936, an event occurred which for the first time forced me to think, and then to rethink, my attitude to foreign-policy issues. Civil war had broken out in Spain in July 1936. My immediate instinct was to side with the Spanish government. This probably reflected an instinctive analogy with the situation in Ireland after the Treaty. Within a few days, however, I discovered that my father, influenced by the failure of the Spanish government to protect churches, convents, priests and nuns from attack in the previous months, supported Franco. In loyalty to him, I changed my position forthwith, but Fergus and Pierce supported the Spanish government throughout the civil war, so that our family was divided on the issue, as were so many others – although not as deeply, of course, as my parents had been divided by our own Civil War thirteen years earlier.

2

~: Secondary School Years :~

I would not have accepted with good grace the period away from home at Ring College if it had been scheduled to last more than a year. Day school suited me better, and I benefited greatly from the stimulus of life at home with my parents during the years of my secondary education at Belvedere College. I was launched into this phase of my life in the summer of 1936 when my mother brought me to be interviewed by Father Rupert Coyle, the Prefect of Studies of Belvedere College, on the north side of Dublin. After a couple of what seemed to me to be rather un-probing questions, he allocated me at the age of ten to the first division (the classes were streamed) of first year in the senior school. There I found myself in a class whose average age was two years older than my age. This kept me on my toes throughout the rest of my secondary schooling.

Six months later, we made the traumatic move from Fairy Hill, which had been inevitable for some time. Without my father's ministerial salary, Fairy Hill had been well beyond our means since 1932, and whatever remained of my mother's inheritance from her father must have been used up, leaving her with a small life-interest in a trust fund, the capital of which would be distributed only when she and her brothers and sisters were all dead. My father's efforts to eke out his small Dáil salary by journalism, and by spending several months as Visiting Professor of Philosophy at Notre Dame University in America in autumn 1935 (extended to a half-semester in each of the following three academic years), had postponed, but could not prevent, the day of reckoning.

He must, moreover, have been aware of the strong possibility that a reduction in the size of his Carlow-Kilkenny constituency, where he had no local roots, combined with his long absences in the United States, could lead to the loss of his Dáil seat in the general election due later in 1937 – as in fact happened. The house to which we moved – pretentiously named 'Montpelier Manor' – was large enough, and with sufficient grounds, to satisfy the needs of a family of two adults and three children – my eldest brother Dem having just got married.

When I was inspecting the house with my mother before we rented it, I was surprised to find that in the tiny three-and-a-half-foot-by-seven-foot bedroom over the porch, the bed was occupied by a large motorbike. The owner of the house, Mrs Mitchell, from whom we were to rent it, explained that one of her two sons – whether Charles, the future TV newsreader, or his brother, Alec, I cannot recall – slept there and kept his motorcycle in the bed with him in order to prevent his mother from selling it!

The grounds comprised a quite substantial garden, a tennis court, stables, and a field of several acres at the back. Despite its odd shape and design, and its forbidding – because window-less – appearance from the road, the house, with its many windows of little diamond panes, though clearly inauthentic, was quite attractive when viewed from the garden and tennis court.

My two other brothers remained at home for a further five years, and their friends, together with my parents' friends, continued to come to parties. True, these were less lavish than previously, as money was short, especially during the year between the 1937 general election and June 1938. At this time, my father, having lost his Dáil seat, was not a member of either House of the Oireachtas and had no income other than whatever he saved from his 1937–38 semester at Notre Dame University, plus some earnings from freelance journalism. In 1938, however, he was elected to the first Senate established under the new Constitution, and his £360 Senate allowance was soon supplemented by a £500-a-year ministerial pension, introduced around that time.

When we moved to our new house, Mother explained our more straitened financial circumstances to us. If we wished to entertain, we must, she said, do all the work ourselves, using the ground-floor kitchenette that she had installed for this purpose. Division of labour was called for: Pierce and Fergus had to undertake roasting and baking respectively, and I was required to provide desserts – mainly a matter of preparing various flavours of ice cream, to be frozen in our newly acquired, capacious refrigerator. (This proved to be consumer-durable in the most literal sense, running non-stop in successive homes I lived in until 1982!)

Like Fairy Hill, Montpelier Manor has long since disappeared, both houses having been replaced by housing estates. I never saw the inside of Montpelier Manor again after we left it following the outbreak of the war, but I visited Fairy Hill once again in 1966, before it was finally demolished. My eldest brother, Dem, and I visited it together when it was then for sale, each of us pretending to believe that the other might buy it! The house was just as we had left it almost thirty years earlier – even down to the wallpaper – and at the age of forty I was able to confirm that my memories of the home when I was eleven were accurate in every detail.

The move to Blackrock brought about an important change in my social life.

For the first time, I was living in an area with other children nearby. Soon I became involved with the boys next door and their friends in the area – all of them school-boys in nearby Blackrock College, Belvedere's great rugby rival. We formed a 'gang' based on my playhouse, re-erected in our large field. Before long we were defending our patch against rivals. Our defence was impregnable and lethal – and in retrospect incredibly irresponsible. Ensconced behind a stone wall with Ned Kelly-type helmets made from large metal sweet-containers, three of us, each aided by a 'loader', could keep up rapid fire from three airguns. Fortunately, some sense of responsibility returned after the leader of the rival group was hit in the lip; hostilities then ceased. The victim became a distinguished radiographer, of whose services my family and myself had occasion to avail more than once.

These immediate pre-war years enlarged my horizons in other ways. In 1937, I went with my mother to stay for some days with her brother, Villiers: he was back from Canada for a couple of years, with his wife and daughter, living in a cottage in the English Lake District. The locale of Arthur Ransome's *Swallows and Amazons*, which I had read during the previous winter, came to life before my eyes.

In 1935 – the year of his attempt to reach South America and the year when he also cracked his skull on a passing tram-pole – Fergus had exchanged with a French family. It had been an eventful exchange. Fergus was going through a 'buried treasure' phase, and became convinced that the house in which he was staying, at Melun, south of Paris, built by a member of Napoleon's entourage from neighbouring Fontainebleau, contained treasure. In search of this, he demolished a cellar wall, which disclosed a deep well under the house. In the attic he also knocked down a wall and, climbing along under the roof, fell into a shaft, where he had to hold himself up by his arms, calling for Irish bacon and eggs as his last meal, before being rescued by other children – the adult members of the family being absent at the time.

The family comprised Madame Camus, the widow of a distinguished doctor whose death a dozen years earlier had deprived him of the Nobel Prize for which he had been designated, and twelve children. When Fergus went there, they ranged in age from twenty-nine to ten. The nearest to Fergus's age amongst the boys was Jean-Pierre. Fergus persuaded him to obtain an authorisation form for the purchase of a revolver and to get his mother to sign it – in ignorance of the nature of the document. He then purchased a revolver, the existence of which came to the notice of Madame Camus and the adult members of the family when Fergus used the letter box in the gate to the grounds as a target – at a time when the postman was delivering letters from the road outside. My mother's first intimation of Fergus's weapon was an anguished telegram from Madame Camus asking her to instruct him to throw it in the nearby Seine.

Against this background, Madame Camus's positive response three years later to a telegram from Mother asking her if she would accept in a few days' time

Fergus's younger brother, Garret, for a further exchange, can only be described as heroic. Mother's late decision to seek an exchange for me arose out of the fact that she had decided to visit Fergus in Italy, where he was to take a pre-university course at the University of Siena. During the previous two years, he had followed the same scholastic route as my two elder brothers – the one which I too would have followed had the war not broken out in 1939, i.e. a year at College St Michel in Fribourg and a year at Colleggio Don Bosco in Marroggia, Lake Lugano, undertaken after early matriculation from Belvedere College.

En route to France in early July occurred an event which was to have far-reaching consequences for my future career. I had already become interested in aviation, having been conscious enough of this new form of transport at the age of five to have been struck by, and to have remembered thereafter, the R 101 airship crash. In February 1936, at Ring College, I had skipped lunch one day in order not to miss a minute of Cobham's Air Circus flying over neighbouring Dungarvan. Eighteen months later, I recall arguing the relative merits of British and American flying boats with the postmaster in Crewe post office, when my mother and I were changing trains there en route to the Lake District. Now, a year after the encounter in Crewe, I found myself in the Italian Tourist Office in Regent Street as my mother bought her tickets and made her reservations for Siena.

Whilst this lengthy process was taking place, a bored child of twelve was collecting from various stands the timetables of the leading European airlines – to which I later added a copy of Cook's Continental Railway Timetable. In subsequent years, these timetables – which I still retain seventy years later – became my most treasured possessions. Whilst Europe was ravaged by war in the early 1940s, much of my class-time was secretly spent working out, for example, the shortest route from Narvik to Malta by rail or air – ignoring the fact that most of the airlines concerned had disappeared, and that many of the routes I was tracing ran across various battle-lines. So was born the interest in air transport that led me in 1947 to join our national airline, Aer Lingus, with which I remained for the first twelve years of my working life.

But to return to my French exchange. At that stage of my life, I had no fluency whatever in the language. At the same time I had a strong predisposition in favour of France and things French, deriving from my father's francophilia. It was thus without any basic linguistic competence, but with considerable goodwill, that I faced the task of finding my feet in the unfamiliar atmosphere of a – very! – extended French family. For by the time I arrived at Le Bercail, Madame Camus's married children had between them produced sixteen grandchildren. At any given time during that summer, a fair proportion of them were staying in the house; I recall that, including friends of the family, forty-five people were there for lunch on one occasion.

They were a boisterous family, inhibited only by their respect and affection for the matriarchal figure of Madame Camus, whose nonagenarian father, born in the mid-1840s, was also part of the household during the first summer I spent with them. But at first they were intimidating for a not-terribly-extrovert twelve-year-old boy. But I soon found my level, trying out my rudimentary French first on small grandchildren in the three-to-seven-year age bracket, and then extending my social intercourse to the older grandchildren and the younger Camus children. In age I fell between the two generations, being a year younger than Madame Camus's youngest daughter, Marie-Paule, and two years older than her eldest granddaughter, Claude, both of whom soon became close friends.

There was an extensive garden with a wood and a stagnant pool, which we enjoyed on fine days. I once fell into the murky and strong-smelling depths of the pool when I overbalanced on a home-made raft. We shot birds with airguns – birds which at home would not have been regarded as fair game. And we drove to other neighbouring houses owned by married children or friends of the family, fishing in their ponds for perch and carp. There were visits to Paris, too, to see the sights and to shop. The same pattern was repeated in the summer of 1939, although in that year I guessed as I returned home, on the day of the announcement of the Nazi-Soviet Pact, which cleared the way for the invasion of Poland, that there would be no third summer at Le Bercail.

It was the quality of French family life, to which I was admitted as a privileged member, that I particularly appreciated. I was Madame Camus's 'petit lapin', accorded the same warm affection as her own children received. I felt that my family life, which had never involved such a wealth of other children, had been enlarged in an unforgettable way. The ties then established, interrupted during the war, have never been broken. Madame Camus herself died in the early 1960s, but all her twelve children, and all but one of her twelve children-in-law, survived into the 1990s. There are now well over three hundred descendants and descendants-in-law, and I still remain in touch with some of them.

Memories of these holidays are by and large more vivid than those of my schooldays. I was happy in Belvedere, and well adjusted, but never – as some of my schoolfellows later attested – very deeply involved. My emotions were engaged by my own family, and by my second family, the Camus, so I did not, as some children do, feel the need to over-identify with my school. Nevertheless, I enjoyed myself at school, and was stimulated by the teaching, which was on the whole good, and by competition from my older classmates, which ensured that I never secured first place in the class and was rarely even in the first four.

Maths – as distinct from arithmetic – I found increasingly difficult as the years passed. Manifest absurdities like the square root of minus one I could not tolerate, however 'useful' I was told this fiction could be. Nor could I accept as reasonable the proposition that dividing a figure by nought produced infinity for, as I painstakingly and unavailingly sought to explain to my maths master, dividing something by nothing must be the same as not dividing it by anything and that – triumphantly! – must leave the figure in question unchanged.

Religion and politics exercised me, however. My resistance on the grounds of orthodoxy to a history teacher's proposition that Savonarola was a saint – how could he be, I asked, in view of the fact that the Pope had arranged for him to be burnt at the stake? – got equally short shrift. For that contestation I was put outside the classroom door; when I was found there by my old friend Father Coyle, Prefect of Studies, I suffered the martyrdom of six strokes of his leather strap as a reward for my stubborn orthodoxy.

In one respect, however, I was heterodox. By the age of fifteen I had come to the conclusion, to which I have since adhered, that the disciplinary decision of the Council of Trent about the invalidity – as indistinct from the illiceity – of a 'clandestine' marriage, viz. one not before a priest (or in modern terms a civil or registry office ceremony) was theologically unsound.

Even before the war began, I was campaigning in the schoolyard against the Nazis, using as my weapon Pius XI's powerful and now largely forgotten Encyclical *Mit Brennender Sorge* (*With Burning Concern*), and other anti-Nazi material. Resistance to my campaign came from boys who simplistically assumed that the Germans must be right if the British were against them. This became a dominant theme when we resumed school in 1939, a couple of days after the outbreak of war. Like my parents, I was passionately pro-Allied; unlike them, I had no time for neutrality, failing to appreciate their concern lest our participation in the war on the Allied side might, without greatly helping the Allied cause, precipitate a renewal of the Civil War which a mere sixteen years earlier had divided them and the country so deeply.

Candour forces me to recall that, with a couple of exceptions, such as the French master, the lay teachers were very anti-British and, accordingly, appeared pro-German, as did a number of the 'clerics' – those preparing for the priesthood – but only one of the actual priests, a German himself. One of the lay masters, an English teacher, was so anti-British, however, that he provoked even the most republican of boys to write essays extolling the merits of the British Commonwealth. The same English teacher once corrected a sentence in one of my depressingly unimaginative essays, which read, 'The distance from London to Rome is 750 miles', by crossing out 'London' and substituting 'Dublin' – without altering the mileage.

The Treaty and the Civil War still loomed large as subjects of controversy. I fought this battle endlessly, neither converting nor being converted. Later, in fifth year, my efforts in this and other political areas attracted the attention of one cleric, however: Ronnie Burke-Savage, then in charge of one of the school debating societies. He suggested to me that at some stage I should envisage a political career, and to my recollection – but not to his! – suggested that I should aim at becoming Taoiseach. Whichever of us was right on my aiming at becoming Taoiseach, my interest in engaging eventually in politics, already latent, was activated at that point, and thereafter I never lost an ultimate political ambition.

Sport did not feature much in my school life. Two appearances on a rugby field for training when I was ten were sufficient to convince me that this particular sport was far too energetic for me. I valued the absence of pressure on me in relation to sport: I was aware that many schools made a fetish of it and that in another school I could have found myself isolated by my lack of sporting skills or interest in participating in organised games. Nonetheless, I enjoyed attending school rugby matches and internationals at Lansdowne Road, and I sometimes kept the score at cricket matches. I was unenthusiastic, however, about the common practice of school prayers for success in schools rugby: it seemed to me that prayers of intercession in such an area were either ineffective, and therefore a waste of time, or, if effective, unfair and unsporting. In this, as in some other areas of religious activity where I challenged the Jesuits, they ignored my theological insights but did not seem to resent my individualistic views.

Tolerance, indeed, was a feature of the school. While discipline was maintained in a manner that was frequently physically painful, and inevitably from time to time unfair, it was not intrusive. On the whole, and within the reasonable limits required by the running of an institution which then contained six hundred boys, one was allowed to do one's own thing. The boys, too, were tolerant of each other; there was no bullying. And no furtive sexuality that I ever came across.

With their usual percipience, and despite my general orthodoxy and commitment to my religion, the Jesuits divined that I was not priest material, and refrained from approaching me on that subject. Although I was by this time on the whole supportive of authority, they also decided that I was not prefect material either – or rather, perhaps, that others were better adapted to this role. I was content to remain thus unrecognised, having little ambition for school office.

It was towards the end of my school career that I developed, under the inspiration of Professor Tom Bodkin's brother, Father Matthew Bodkin, a deep interest in history. By contrast, I never had any command of, or interest in, Greek, nor was I very comfortable with Latin. Science I did not study: at that time in Belvedere, a choice had to be made between Greek and science, and my father chose Greek for me! I was moderately interested in English, although – like Seamus Heaney! – mainly in the grammar and syntax – and I liked and, for reasons already mentioned, was good at French, in which I later calculated that I secured sixth place in Ireland amongst boys in the Leaving Certificate examination –

the nearest I came to any kind of distinction in that national test.

During these later years at school, we lived closer to town than we had done during most of my childhood. After the war started, Mrs Mitchell, who normally travelled a good deal, wanted to return to Montpelier Manor, and for the greater part of the war my parents rented a large house in Temple Road, Rathmines, near where I now live. The house, in half an acre of garden, had a billiard room in the basement, without a table but with a shelf all around the wall upon which to place beer mugs. The floor was ideal for laying out train sets – I had accumulated a reasonable layout based on my older brothers' original purchases – and toy soldiers, of which we had quite a large number, mostly late-nineteenth-century British army redcoats. I also had a study of my own in a distant corner of the house, as well as my own bedroom upstairs, and in various parts of the basement and outbuildings there were, I once counted, eleven rooms used wholly or mainly as storerooms – for this was the apogee of my parents' accumulative period.

We were only the third Catholic family to come to live on the road, which until the 1930s had been an exclusively Protestant upper-middle-class area. We were made welcome, however, by most of our neighbours, who did not seem to resent our presence, even when I and my friends took advantage of the brilliant table-like surface of the road to organise roller-skating hockey during the virtually car-less later years of the war.

Very shortly after our arrival in the house, I answered the doorbell one day to an Englishman who asked to see my father. I discovered later that he was the Marquess of Tavistock, later Duke of Bedford. In pursuit of a peace mission, he had been told by a Northern Ireland family connection to contact my father as a possible channel to the German minister Eduard Hempel. It would have been difficult to find a less suitable channel for this purpose, given my father's views on Germany. However, one way or the other, as history relates, some kind of contact was eventually made – to the considerable embarrassment of some members of the British government, including Lord Halifax, whose name was later brought into the affair.

Family social life became more restrained in this house, partly because my parents were now in their fifties and partly, perhaps, because of the war. New friends, however, were John Betjeman, attached to the British Mission under Sir John Maffey, later Lord Rugby, and his wife Penelope.

The war years were marked by privations that were modest by comparison with those in Britain and on the Continent, such as the rationing of foodstuffs like butter, bread, sugar, tea and clothing, but not of meat or sweets – items which in Britain continued to be rationed well into the 1950s. Petrol was in short supply in the later years of the war; only certain groups of people, such as doctors, diplomats, ministers and key civil servants, had petrol coupons. This had profound social effects, putting almost everyone on an equal footing so far as mobility was concerned. It also involved a late revival of the horse as an agent of transport, albeit on a limited scale.

Bombs were dropped by German aircraft in half a dozen parts of the city. At breakfast one morning, there was a dogfight over the city between British and German aircraft, the sequence of which boys from different parts of the city pieced together by comparing notes later that morning in the schoolyard.

The Irish papers were censored rigorously, but my parents took the *Daily Mail* and, of course, had access to the airwaves, and in particular to the BBC. I listened also to news broadcasts in French from London, Paris, Vichy, Brazzaville and, from the end of 1942, Algiers, thus helping to preserve the spoken French that I had acquired with the Camus family. Occasionally the voices of William Joyce and Ezra Pound were heard from Germany and Italy, but my father disliked listening to Axis radio broadcasts and was so deeply upset that his old friend, Ezra Pound, should be spewing out anti-Semitic and pro-Axis propaganda that these broadcasts were quickly banned in the home. My absorption with the war during those years was in fact almost total, as is evidenced by the many scores of war maps I drew – badly, but in accurate detail – and which survive.

In June 1940, my brother Fergus, then finishing his second year at University College Dublin, together with most of his friends, joined the army, the ranks of which swelled to almost fifty thousand. In so far as the Civil War was still at that time a divisive element in Irish life, the coming together in the army in 1940 of the sons of the leaders of the national movement finally healed that division. With Vivion de Valera and Liam Cosgrave, Eoin Ryan and Fergus FitzGerald serving side by side in the army that seventeen years earlier had defeated the Republicans in the Civil War, and with the leaders of the Fianna Fáil government and the Fine Gael opposition sitting together in the Defence Council, a wartime advisory body – both equally concerned to preserve formal Irish neutrality whilst supporting the Allied cause in many most un-neutral ways – by 1940 the Civil War episode was clearly closed so far as most of the families who had participated in it were concerned.

In January 1942, although not yet sixteen, I joined the Local Defence Force, or LDF – the military arm of the part-time war-service organisation which attracted in all some two hundred thousand volunteers during the war. Advised by Fergus that by joining a Signals Battalion I would learn morse code – which, he said, would be useful to me later in life (it never was!) – and much preferring sedentary to ambulant service (I have always disliked standing, let alone walking), I went to the recruitment sergeant of the 6th Communications Battalion in Parnell Square, a couple of hundred yards from school. I naturally hoped to bluff the question of age, and was disconcerted when the sergeant said: 'Garret, you needn't try to fool me about your age; you don't remember me, but I was one of your father's guards at Fairy Hill. However, you can join anyway.'

The experience of the LDF was a broadening one. I had never had any real experience of four-letter expletives before, neither at home nor at school, and it was something of a culture shock to have to disentangle and make sense of the words that occasionally intervened between the expletives.

Going to Gormanston training camp in summer involved a further educational process. Our captain assembled us before we left and delivered a talk in terms so guarded that I and my sergeant, Padraic Mulcahy (a son of my father's former colleague in government, General Richard Mulcahy, soon to succeed W. T. Cosgrave as leader of Fine Gael), were mystified. His speech seemed to us to suggest that a health risk attached to cows, which, presumably, we would come across in rural Gormanston, but having had experience of cows as a child, this was not convincing. Later on, when I learned of the existence of VD, I realised what this enigmatic health warning was about.

In April 1942, Fergus marred Una Crean – despite my father's opposition. His own early marriage, at about the same age, and with even less means, did not make him tolerant of sons following his example – as I was to find in my turn a few years later. Fergus's marriage was all the more disapproved of because it encouraged our elder brother Pierce to follow suit two months later, at, for our family, the advanced age of twenty-eight – but, like Fergus, with very limited means, and without completing his final accountancy examination.

Pierce's honeymoon later that year coincided with the temporary emergence of something like a menagerie at our house. My mother, who disliked animals, had felt constrained to keep hens in order to ensure a supply of eggs. A cat was also introduced to deal with a mouse problem, and I decided I wanted to keep a guinea pig. (When I asked my father what I should call my new pet, he suggested 'Ezra Pound'; when I pointed out that the guinea pig was a female, he countered with 'Mrs Ezra Pound' – which I accepted.) My mother's dislike of animals received its come-uppance when to this group of animals were added simultaneously a hedgehog, which my father and I had found on the road; a second cat, which arrived to have kittens on top of our coal; and a Shi-Tzu, or Tibetan Lion Hound, which my brother Pierce had acquired and left with us when he went away on his honeymoon.

During the war years, holidays, including honeymoons, were, of course, confined to Ireland. I spent a number of these summers in different parts of County Wicklow – one of them with the McEntees during the dramatic weeks of June 1940 – but in 1941 I was sent to Glengarriff in Cork to look after my brother Pierce, who was convalescing following the removal of a kidney. Mother and Daddy joined us after a while, and I made the acquaintance of the owner of the hotel, a London solicitor called MacDonnell, whom my father had known for many years and who had in fact defended my uncle France when he had been arrested after an arms-collection adventure in London in 1921. MacDonnell was a remarkable and most entertaining man, of considerable wealth, but careful in his habits. His overcoat had been bought for £1 in Bantry in 1924, and his hat had been left in his office by a client who had been hanged – or so, at any rate, MacDonnell said! He was a friend of Herbert Morrison, who came for a break to Glengarriff during the war, where my father was invited to meet him. At the end of my school career, in 1943, I holidayed with my cousin Edna in Belfast, seeing for myself the destruction caused by the air raids of 1941.

I should have left school in 1942, having passed the Leaving Certificate and National University of Ireland matriculation examinations in June of that year, but Father Coyle's decision to put me into the secondary part of the school at the age of ten at last caught up with me. I was too young to enter University College Dublin. And of course, the war made it impossible for me to follow my brothers' example by going to school in Switzerland for two years between secondary school and university.

My mother's solution was to enter me for Trinity College Dublin, which was less concerned than UCD about physical age. I was unenthusiastic, as my brothers had all gone to UCD, but I went along with the idea, as I wanted to leave school. In the event, nothing came of it. In those days, Catholics were supposed to seek the permission of the archbishop before entering Trinity. My father was too orthodox a Catholic to agree to my going there without that permission, but after initially agreeing to seek it, he changed his mind. He had for several years previously been a member of an ecumenical group known as the Mercier Society, which had, however, recently been the subject of an archiepiscopal ban. My father, hurt that his and his friends' efforts to bring Catholics and Protestants together had been thus impugned, and that his own orthodoxy seemed to have been put in question by this action, was, on reflection, not disposed to seek from the Archbishop a dispensation from the ban on Trinity College.

And so I went back to school for another year, an arrangement which involved joining with the new sixth-year pupils for most purposes, but also studying Thomistic philosophy – an experience which I enjoyed, and about which my father, given his deep interest in the subject, was naturally pleased. I was disappointed, however, about having to postpone entry to UCD for a year – all the more so because I knew that the girl whom at the age of eight I had decided I might marry was entering the college that year. In the light of later events, it is, perhaps, worth recording that amongst the seventh-year boys who had shared my sixth-year class had been Dermot Ryan, and amongst the sixth-year boys whose class I shared when I was in seventh year was Des Connell – both later to become archbishops of Dublin.

3

∽: University and Marriage :∽
1943–47

My mother decided that I should sit for the UCD entrance scholarship examination in modern languages although there was nothing in my school career to suggest that this would be other than a waste of time. English, Irish, French and history were the chosen subjects. Mother decided to coach me in English herself – which she did with such success that, despite having been only about 1,500th out of 4,500 in Ireland in that subject in the Leaving Certificate examination, I secured first place in this subject and second place in modern languages, with the double bonus that the financial pressure of my college career on my parents was relieved by the £100 scholarship and that I became imbued with sufficient confidence in my own abilities to aim at a good degree – without, however, doing much actual work until towards the end of my university career.

In those days, five subjects were required for First Arts. I tried out ten, but after several weeks dropped political economy, as economics was then called, because, despite Professor George O'Brien's legendary exposition of the subject, at that stage of my life I found it dull. I continued to attend lectures in politics, Italian and German but did not sit for them in First Arts. My Honours subjects in that exam were English, French, Spanish and history, with Latin and logic as Pass subjects, to meet exam requirements. Emboldened by my unexpected success in English in the entrance scholarship, I was aiming to take my degree in English and French. However, my year was one of fairly spectacular idleness. Even two weeks before the exam, a diary, briefly kept for that period, records for one particular week one day and two early mornings of work, together with seven lectures and two grinds – the rest of the time being spent lounging around college or taking a modest part in my father's last – and unsuccessful – general election campaign in Dublin County.

The result in First Arts was not as disastrous as it should have been, but I secured only Second-class Honours in my chosen subjects, English and French, as well as in Spanish. (Charles J. Haughey had been a fellow student of Spanish, among other subjects, but judging from his exam result in that subject, he must have taken it no more seriously than I took politics, Italian or German!) To my astonishment, and almost irritation, I secured a First in history – an exam which I sat on the day after the distracting invasion of Normandy. This was the Honours subject that I was doing as an extra, on which I had done virtually no work – and none at all on Irish history during the previous six weeks. (Incidentally, two other history Firsts in that exam were Des Connell, later archbishop of Dublin, and Declan Costello, later attorney-general in the government in which I was foreign minister.) This result determined my future course of action: it was clear to me that even the Second-class Honours in English owed more to my mother's tuition than I could safely rely on for my actual degree; I switched to French and history as my main degree subjects, keeping Spanish as an extra, so that I would have three possible degree options: French and history, Spanish and history, and French and Spanish.

Although I had been sent to Spanish as well as German grinds during my last summer at school (the Spanish grind being given by the mother of Paul Keating, later secretary of the Department of Foreign Affairs for the greater part of my period as minister thirty years afterwards), for all practical purposes I, like most other students, effectively started Spanish at the university. The standard we could reach in three years was, objectively speaking, not high, nor was the teaching very inspiring. However, as I found when it came to the final degree, the standard in Spanish was nevertheless slightly higher than I had judged, for I secured a Second in it rather than the First I had presumptuously expected. French was a different matter, however. The standard was set at a high level, and every effort was made to discourage weaker students at an early stage, especially girls – apparently because it was believed by the professor and lecturer that girls 'fancied themselves' at French!

I was particularly involved with the French Society, of which, indeed, I became secretary. In that position, I had the opportunity to set the rules for a competition for a substantial cup, presented by the French ambassador in 1944, on behalf of General de Gaulle, to whom he had recently switched allegiance. I naturally determined that the competition would be in oral French, and won it with a series of imitations (the accuracy of which few present were able to verify) of speeches by de Gaulle, Pétain, Laval – and Churchill in French. Later I represented the society at a rare inter-debate in Queens in Belfast, where we were entertained by a lecturer in French in her apartment in the house that had been my grandfather's up to eighteen years previously – taking tea in my Aunt Eilis's bedroom.

My favourite subject, however, became history. Our professor of modern history, John Marcus O'Sullivan, a distinguished scholar who was one of the members of the staff to have been appointed when the National University of Ireland was founded in 1908, had been a colleague of my father's in government, as Minister for Education from 1925 to 1932. His lectures were entertaining and stimulating. One felt that he had a certain nostalgic affection for the Austro-Hungarian Empire; in any event, he certainly disapproved of such name-changes as that of Lemberg in Poland to Lwow, which he pronounced dismissively, as if it were the bark of a small dog! He also had what I can only describe as a constitutional aversion to consonants. I still recall trying to discover the name of an Austrian statesman which he pronounced as O – A – U; I tracked it down eventually as Kollaruth.

The lecturer in modern Irish history was Robin Dudley Edwards – who, with Theo Moody of Trinity, was the joint founder of professional, as distinct from mythic nationalist, Irish history. He had been taught history by my mother in Miss Louise Gavan Duffy's Scoil Bhride in 1917, and, after lecturing to Joan and myself in the mid-1950s, was my son John's professor when he took history for his degree a quarter of a century later, and examined my daughter Mary for her entrance scholarship. The UCD Archive, which he established towards the end of his career, contains my father's papers and my own, as well as those of many of my father's contemporaries.

The reappraisal of Irish history in which Dudley Edwards played such a large part made a major contribution to the development of more rational and objective attitudes towards the Northern Ireland problem and Anglo-Irish relations. 'Dudley', as he was known to so many generations of Irish students over half a century, also had a slightly malicious sense of humour, which he was never inhibited from employing to take people – including his students – down a peg or two. An ability to cope with this was for history students over many decades a prerequisite for survival! One of his last engagements was his attendance at the handing-over of my father's papers to the UCD Archive, which he had founded. Typically, he heckled me to complain that I had not said enough about my mother, his teacher seventy years earlier.

The professor of mediaeval history was also an outstanding scholar: Father Aubrey Gwynn, SJ, a member of a distinguished academic family long associated with Trinity College. From him I gained a lasting interest in the early Middle Ages, and a sense of the continuities and discontinuities of European history between the Roman Empire and the modern age.

While I enjoyed work at college, study certainly did not absorb much of my energies. I joined a large number of societies and concentrated on helping with the society teas, having observed at an early stage that the preparations for these festivities, which followed language-society meetings in particular, were undertaken by girls. Boys – oddly, I thought, having been brought up in a family of boys where all had to help with meals – regarded this part of a society's activities as being beneath their dignity. The loss was theirs, I felt, especially as after seven years at a single-sex secondary school, the major attraction of university life, it seemed to me, was the company of girls. Before long, I featured in the college magazine with the comment 'among the girls present was Sir Garret FitzGerald Bart. – and there he remained'.

I also joined the main debating societies, the Law Society, the Commerce Society and, the most prestigious, the Literary and Historical Debating Society, or L&H, where I was able to carry on my pro-Allied crusade in an atmosphere of some hostility – for, as at school, the more vocal elements tended to be anti-British and consequently vaguely pro-German. My interest in statistics must already have been evident at that time, as when I rose to speak, the late Niall St John McCarthy – later a Supreme Court judge – used to heckle me with: 'Garret, say a statistic!'

By any conceivable standards, we were an unsophisticated lot, but this didn't prevent me from establishing early in first year an informal 'Anti-Sophistication Society', with a subcommittee dedicated to the identification of the twenty-nine orders of nuns whose varied habits – in the sense of clothing! – provided a challenge akin to trainspotting. When spring came six months later, this society provided the nucleus of a bicycle-picnic group – no cars in those days – which in varying compositions continued throughout our college years.

Our group was only one amongst many, and not particularly prominent at that – as may be seen from the limited attention we received from the college magazine, the *National Student*. Others found their centre of gravity in different aspects of college life: the L&H establishment, the Students' Representative Council, the Dramatic Society, and so on. More remotely for us, there presumably were others whose interest and activities focused on sport. And, of course, the other faculties, and especially those on more distant parts of the campus, like engineering and agriculture, had their own social lives. None of these were completely sealed off from each other, however. Our cycling group, for example, contained engineers and medics – primarily, however, as a carry-over from school friendships.

I was not the only student of that period who later became involved in politics. Declan Costello, son of John A. Costello, attorney-general in the government of which my father had been a member in the 1920s, was a friend, though his activities were centred rather in a law group. Charles J. Haughey was a contemporary whom I knew reasonably well: in first year, we studied several subjects together. Already he was moving in Fianna Fáil circles. I used to see him with, inter alia, Harry Boland, Colm Traynor and Peadar Ward – all sons of Fianna Fáil ministers. His college centre of gravity seemed to be the SRC and Commerce Society; by contrast, mine was the Literary & Historical and Law Societies. He is recorded as not turning up to speak at an L&H in a debate in which I was uncharacteristically awarded ten marks out of ten. Other friends of his – later ministers, like Brian Lenihan and Sean Flanagan – were several years behind, and less familiar to me at the time, but at a later stage, from her vantage point of the cash desk in the students' restaurant, when she had joined the clerical staff of UCD two years after her degree,

Joan got to know them, as well as Paddy Hillery, later to become a member of the European Commission and president of Ireland, who was then in the midst of his medical studies.

An element of student life in that period was the formal dance – most commonly in the Gresham Hotel, and organised by the past pupils of a secondary school or by a charity – which cost twelve shillings and sixpence (just under 80 cents) and included dinner during the evening. White tie and tails were required for these occasions, but only evening dress and black tie for the five-shilling (32 cents) – dinner-less – Saturday-night dances. Over forty years later, President Reagan, at the end of his state visit to Ireland, allowed himself a moment of personal reminiscence, recalling how when he came to Ireland as a fraternal delegate to a trade union conference shortly after the war, he peered through the Gresham ballroom door one evening and saw men in white tie and tails and the girls in white dresses (only a minority in fact wore white), gliding across the floor. This, possibly the only genuinely personal note struck on that official visit, was the one comment of the president's that went completed unreported by the press.

A feature of these dances was that many of us travelled to and from them by bicycle, often with a girl on the crossbar, her ballgown packed away in a carrier basket, for it was necessary for girls to change at the dance in order to ensure a safer bicycle journey in a shorter skirt. Other forms of transport might be used, however. Joan recalls an evening when, emerging from the Gresham, she saw three young men about to take off in a horse-cab: her next morning's nine o'clock lecturer – future Senator Alexis FitzGerald – astride the horse, and the future President of the Supreme Court and Judge of the European Court, Tom O'Higgins, and Tom Crotty, future Kilkenny County Registrar, on top of the vehicle.

I was – and have ever since been – a poor dancer, and cannot say that I greatly enjoyed the dancing itself, but I enjoyed everything else about these evenings – which were, incidentally, alcohol-free for almost all of us. There were waltzes as well as foxtrots, tangos and rumbas – and this, together with the dance-cards upon which we entered the names of the partners we engaged for each dance, was reminiscent of an earlier century.

My partner at a number of these formal dances was Una Tierney, with whom I had been at school in Bray years before and in whom I had retained since the age of eight a romantic interest. Her home in Shankill was too far out for dance evenings, so she based herself at her grandparents' house in Upper Leeson Street. There I used to collect her, being received by her grandparents, Eoin MacNeill (emeritus professor of ancient Irish history and founder both of the Gaelic League in 1895 and of the Irish Volunteers in 1913, and later a member of the first government with my father) and his wife, who tried to make me feel at home while I awaited Una's appearance.

Towards the end of my first year, the war momentarily seemed to threaten to intrude directly on our lives. On Saturday 11 March, word spread that the Allies had handed an ultimatum to the government, demanding that the Axis diplomatic missions in Dublin be closed. Fergus was ordered to deploy his 120-man cavalry unit – on bicycles – to probe a feared thrust by three British and American divisions south across the border. I thought that my Local Defence Force practice next morning might be for real: that night the anti-British elements in the L&H made the most of their opportunity. For me, however, the prospect of having to defend our state against the Allies, soon to launch their invasion of the Continent, was an appalling one. However, the apparent threat passed off: it had suited the government to allow an exaggerated version of an Allied diplomatic move to leak to the public.

Shortly afterwards, the Opposition defeated Fianna Fáil in the Dáil, most unwisely, as it turned out, De Valera gleefully called an election and, greatly helped by the kudos he had secured in March, recovered the overall majority that he had lost in an election in the previous year.

I had worked at Fine Gael election headquarters in 1943, literally licking envelopes. This time, however, my father, having lost his Senate seat in 1943, was for the first time since 1937 a Dáil candidate in Dublin County, which had been his constituency in the 1920s until he had been persuaded by the party to transfer to Carlow-Kilkenny in 1932.

Neither Dem, as a civil servant architect, nor Fergus, as an army officer, could participate in the campaign. So my second-eldest brother Pierce and I accompanied our father to meetings. He lost.

I had one other minor involvement in politics later that year, helping to define the branch areas in the Dublin Townships constituency – after 1969, my own constituency of Dublin South East. Apart from that, I was not politically involved until the February 1948 election, when Joan and I canvassed for Fine Gael in Dublin Townships.

The summer following the general election of May 1944 and my First Arts exam was the first of two delightfully lazy summers. Students had not then adopted the practice of working abroad during the long vacation – that was a post-war phenomenon, when it became possible again for students to travel to other countries, and when further education was opening to a greater number of students, who needed to supplement their parental resources.

I have never regretted these periods of prolonged inactivity, spent mostly with various girls, or in mixed groups. I wasted relatively little time in the exclusive company of other boys. I had met Joan O'Farrell early on in my college career, on 25 November 1943, at a meeting of the French Society at which jazz was debated, in the Music Room in No. 86 St Stephen's Green, formerly part of Cardinal Newman's

Catholic University, and in our time the Students' Union building. After the meeting, I got talking to her and to an architectural student – and, finding that they had never played three-handed auction bridge (which I had learnt to play as a small child with Miss Cuddy and Fergus), I instructed them in this art on the top of a harmonium. Joan, then in her third year, was not impressed with this brash first-year student, and apart from a picnic which she joined early in the following April, our paths did not cross much until the following summer, when there were several encounters at college Sunday-night 'hops' in Belfield – at that time a student sports centre, but now the centre of the college itself. As I recorded, naively, in a diary that I was keeping at the time, 'she was terribly nice and very helpful – lots of tips etc., but not in a condescending way'. (As I have mentioned, I was a rotten dancer.)

Following a further picnic encounter (my diary records that 'she is very witty in a nice quiet way'!), I developed the habit of dropping in to see her in a room in No. 86, where forty years earlier Joyce had attended L&H debates. With one or two other girls, she used to work there in preparation for her September BA. By mid-July, I was lending her an English history book and had prepared for her a genealogical table to illustrate the War of the Spanish Succession.

The relationship remained a casual one, however. She had her own friends, all in their early twenties, and I was conscious of being a fairly juvenile eighteen. Most of my friends were from my own year, or were second-year students whom I had met through my school contemporaries who had gone to college a year before me. Most of that summer was spent with girls from amongst my own group.

Behind all these frivolities was the ever-present background of the war. My diary for the summer of 1944 records hours spent listening to the radio as Rome was liberated and Normandy invaded, and on 25 August there was the final stage of the liberation of Paris. By a happy chance, at 12.15 on that day I picked up the underground radio station in Paris and was able to follow events throughout the day, culminating in de Gaulle's arrival at the Hotel de Ville in the evening. My devotion to the radio was such indeed that in March 1945 my parents sold it in order to remove this distraction from my academic life!

During that autumn, however, as I moved into Second Arts, and simultaneously started my first year of law studies in preparation for the Bar exams, part of my life began to revolve in smaller circles. Although gregarious larger groups remained part of the pattern, especially for dances and of course picnics, going to the pictures as a foursome became a common enough form of entertainment. A couple whom I increasingly began to join on such occasions were Brendan Dillon, later a foreign-affairs official of distinction, and Alice O'Keeffe, who married him some years later. By Christmas 1944, Joan was accompanying me, with Brendan and Alice, on many of these film expeditions, which for a period attained a frequency of ten a week. Both of us continued, however, to circulate with our own sets of friends: Joan had a number of boyfriends, and I had many other interests too, including Una Tierney.

In the spring of 1945, however, it became clear to me that Una's interest had become otherwise engaged, and I was forced to begin to refocus my romantic attentions. When the news of the German surrender was broadcast, on 7 May, it was Joan whom I rang to ask to join me for the celebration, and we spent that dramatic evening together, with a large group of friends. Following Charlie Haughey's burning of the Union Jack outside Trinity, a riot began, and Joan and I escaped from the ensuing baton charge, jumping over bicycles on the ground as we ran into Trinity Street.

Ten days later, I made up my mind that I wanted to marry her. She was quite entertained by this proposition but did not take it too seriously. Such a proposal by a nineteen-year-old second-year student who had hitherto shown an interest in many different girls, and with a very long-standing predilection until quite recently for one in particular, must have seemed a bit frivolous to her. At the same time, she was clearly fond of me and was content to spend much of the following summer in my company. These were strenuous months for me, as my determination grew in the face of her good-humoured resistance to my proposal.

That she was not irrevocably opposed to the idea became clear, however, one day when we were having tea together in the café of the Grafton Cinema. For the first time, she told me her own history. Her mother was one of seven daughters of a Dublin brewer, Charles Brenan, and of Adelaide Wyse, a member of a well-known Waterford family, one of whom had married a daughter of Lucien Bonaparte. Charles Brenan's grandfather, a maltster in Kilkenny, had established the Phoenix Brewery in Dublin early in the nineteenth century. In old age, lacking sons, Charles had sold the Phoenix Brewery and another that he had acquired. The purchasers did not make a success of it and accused him of having sold them a pup. He sued them successfully for slander and then, in a grand gesture, bought the brewery back – but it was too late, and he died a tired and broken man in 1908, leaving virtually nothing for his wife – who died in 1916 – and seven daughters to live on. Joan's mother and aunts grew up in what is often described as 'straitened circumstances'.

In the Great War, her mother had served in the VAD in Britain. After the war, she met and married Charles O'Farrell. A younger sister of hers had married a first cousin of his some years earlier. The O'Farrells were a predominantly medical family, with their roots in east Galway, but Charles had entered the colonial civil service, serving in Ghana, Gambia and Sierra Leone. Joan had been born at Waterloo, near Liverpool, where her mother was staying with Wyse cousins, taking refuge from the Civil War in Ireland. Her father later retired from the colonial service and got a job in Ireland. After a son, Paddy, was born, he had a mental breakdown and, following a period in a mental hospital in Dublin, went with his wife and children to the seaside in Sussex. There, in February 1929, he became insane and tried to drown his son and to kill his wife. Joan, then six, had to run for help to save their lives. Her father admitted himself to a nearby mental hospital, where he still was at the time Joan told me the story. He died there in 1956.

Joan, her mother, and her younger brother then went to live with her mother's younger sister, Emily, Joan's godmother, who, after studying under Pigou in Cambridge, had become an economist with the League of Nations in Geneva. There the family remained for more than four years, returning to Ireland in 1933, when they went to live in a house in Booterstown Avenue which Emily had purchased. It was with her aunt/godmother's help that Joan had been enabled to go to college.

Having recounted this story, Joan explained that she was uncertain as to the cause of her father's illness. It might have been due to his experiences in West Africa – or it might have been congenital. She was, therefore, uncertain as to whether she should get married and have children.

Ill-equipped though I was at that age to face a problem of this kind, I think it deepened my love for Joan – for my feelings, immature at an earlier stage, had begun to ripen into love. During the remaining months of that summer, I pursued my suit with determination and in a manner that gradually broke down Joan's double reticence to commit herself: her reticence about her own possible mental inheritance and her reticence about my youth and immaturity. Early in September, she finally conceded; six weeks later, we fixed the date of our marriage two years ahead – for 10 October 1947 – forgetting even to check what day of the week that would be! (It turned out to be a Friday – an awkward day from the point of view of catering, in view of Friday abstinence at that time!)

There probably isn't much point in trying to identify the reasons we fell in love; certainly I am in no position to say what moved Joan to accept my proposal. In retrospect, I was not alone rather juvenile in manner and character but also somewhat full-up with myself, not very sensitive to others, and a good deal of a prig. (Some would say that I never entirely lost some of these characteristics!) For my part, I can only say that Joan's warmth, vivacity and intelligence were part of the chemistry, together with the intangible element that can never be pinned down in any such relationship.

Whatever the explanation, by the autumn of 1945 we were both deeply in love and very absorbed in each other. We had, indeed, become poor company for our friends, and remained so until some time after our marriage, not becoming sociable people again until a good deal later. I had no problem about this, as I had never developed a bachelor-type existence – had never gone drinking with other men (indeed I had never been in a pub!), and had gone but rarely to sports events or other predominantly male occasions. Seven years at a single-sex school had cured me of any strong predilection for exclusively male company. On Joan's side, the insecurity of her childhood probably encouraged her to establish an equally close, and for a period quite exclusive, relationship with me, once she became convinced that she could rely on me without risking further severe trauma in her life.

My mother had always had a shrewd idea of my romantic activities too. Now when she saw me – uncharacteristically – devoting all my time, month after month, to one girl, she was visibly worried, and especially concerned about what my father would feel when he found out that I was engaging myself to an early marriage, especially as, for some reason, he had decided that he wanted me not merely to take the Bar exams but to practise as a barrister. This career was at that time considered to preclude marriage for five or six years – unless, of course, one had independent means, which I, of course, had not. He had already been deeply upset at a similar commitment by Fergus, which had led to his marriage at the age of twenty-two, when he was a temporary army officer.

Mother could not, however, prevent herself from sympathising with young love, and her concerns about a premature commitment were therefore balanced by a willingness even to finance our romance with occasional supplements to my pocket money. For some months, however, my father remained ignorant of the affair, or at any rate felt it prudent to affect ignorance.

There was also some preliminary planning: how we might perhaps manage to live on £350 a year as a third secretary in the Department of External Affairs or as an administrative officer in the general civil service, or on much more exiguous amounts as a barrister, eking out early penurious years with earnings from journalism, or from the provision of genealogies to Irish-Americans!

At this point I must, however, turn back to developments within my own family. While I had been so deeply engrossed in my own affairs, my parents had been going through a difficult time. In 1943, just before I went to college, my father had lost the seat in the Senate that he had secured in 1936. Despite a somewhat defensive letter from W. T. Cosgrave, then in the closing months of his leadership of Fine Gael, my father felt – perhaps unfairly – that he had been let down by the party in that Senate election. In 1944, as I have recounted, he most unsuccessfully contested a Dáil seat in County Dublin, bringing a political career of more than thirty years to an end at the relatively early age of fifty-six.

In that 1944 election, Fine Gael reached its lowest ebb, winning only 30 out of 138 Dáil seats. De Valera, and Fianna Fáil, already in power for twelve years, seemed likely to be there for ever – a depressing prospect for someone like my father, who had been strongly opposed to de Valera since the Treaty.

The war against the Axis was going better by that time, but to us in neutral Ireland, the Soviet threat was becoming apparent, especially with the deliberate halt of the Soviet army in front of Warsaw, while the Home Army's revolt was being crushed by the Germans. My father found fresh cause for depression in this situation. And at this moment his sister Kate, who was very dear to him, and to my mother, became fatally ill with cancer. Her last eighteen months, from early 1944 to August 1945, during much of which she was in great pain, were spent with us, first in Lonsdale, and later in what had been my eldest brother's flat in Donnybrook, which we took over when he moved to a house in Killiney early in 1945.

To all these reasons for depression were added money worries. Since his defeat in the Senate election of 1943, my parents' only income had been my father's ministerial pension and my mother's small income from her father's estate. Moreover, the chemical works in east London for which my father had been responsible since his brother France's death in 1941 was in financial difficulties. However, by a stroke of luck, he found a buyer for the works during a visit to London in April 1946, and simultaneously my mother won £150 on the spring double – the Grand National and the Lincolnshire. She chose this moment to tell my father that I intended to marry Joan. In the discussion I had with him immediately afterwards, he told me that while he could not welcome this news, he accepted it as a 'fait accompli', but that there could be no question of the marriage taking place for quite a number of years. It seemed better not to disclose that we had decided on a date eighteen months thence!

At least the whole matter was now out in the open, and Joan could be received (if not actually welcomed!) as part of the family. My mother decided that an appropriate occasion for this would be in Kerry in May. With the proceeds of her racing win, she had rented an island, Illaunslea, off Parknasilla, for that month. It had a house that could accommodate the whole family: my parents, my three brothers and their wives, seven young children, and Joan and myself. Moreover, my parents were going to spend ten days at the Eccles Hotel in Glengarriff immediately afterwards, and as I would not be able to join the family on the island until after the middle of the month because of my Junior Victoria exam at the Kings Inns, Joan and I were to go on to the Eccles with them.

The day before we left for the island, the first post-war airline guide was published – revivifying my long-established interest in air transport. Joan had to put up with endless extracts from the timetables during the nine-hour train journey to Kenmare. I do not think that she shared my highly individual sense of the romance of air transport!

After we had got over the initial awkwardness inevitable on such an occasion, we found life on the island enjoyable. Journeys by boat had to be made to four different points on the mainland for the post, telephone calls, the bus service, or to reach my brothers' cars on a nearby pier. The subsequent stay in Glengarriff, which did not involve the same gregarious family life, was more of a strain for Joan.

After that, I settled down to a belated fourteen-hour workday for the following three months of preparation for my BA exam. But first I prepared the ground.

Especially in history, the choice of questions was wide. Given this, and the fact that only part of any course lends itself to questions, together with continuity of examiners and of exam paper structures for some years previously, it should, I reasoned, be possible to list two sets of topics, each of which would cover questions bound to turn up on any paper, but which together would include only a fraction of the whole course. A careful examination of past history papers showed that such a method worked well in this subject, giving me what seemed like 'certainty squared' of being able to answer fully while studying only one-third of the course. In French and Spanish, analogous, but somewhat less satisfactory, results could be obtained from this statistical approach.

Having listed the topics to be covered, I gave Joan half the history topics, part of the French course, and some English translations of Spanish texts to study with a view to producing appropriate essay-type answers. As she had secured Honours in History on the same course two years earlier and had fluent French, she was well equipped to assist me in this way. She was doing part-time work that summer while waiting to secure a clerical post in the college, and so was relatively free at the time. This procedure enabled me to concentrate in a specialised way on about one-sixth of the history course – despite which I never actually reached the French Revolution, and had to chance my arm in that part of the exam! – as well as reducing substantially the work to be done in French and Spanish.

My results eventually validated this statistical approach. I secured a First in History and French – in the latter by virtue of a good oral exam only – and a Second in Spanish. My First-class Honours, and first place, in history caused me some embarrassment, however, because I was awarded a £250 scholarship to finance an MA in history – an award that I did not want to take, as I was anxious to get a job with a view to meeting our wedding deadline of 10 October 1947. (I did, however, prepare a preliminary bibliography for an MA thesis on 'Allied Intervention in the Soviet Union, 1918–1922', in case I lost the argument!) My parents had other views and were with difficulty persuaded by me that as there was some kind of a means test attached to this scholarship, it would be invidious for me to accept it in view of the size of their income! In the circumstances, this was a very dubious argument, involving an unfair reliance on their pride – but it worked. What annoyed me was that because I was awarded this special scholarhip, which I was proposing to refuse, the £100 scholarship that I would otherwise have secured went elsewhere, and I had to be content with a £20 prize – which was a poor financial start to the run-up to our planned wedding.

During the following two months, I applied for jobs in the civil service and in foreign airlines that were flying to, or might fly to, Ireland. This didn't take up much time, and I spent most of the day pottering around the National Library, researching Joan's genealogy – a pastime which she regarded with a jaundiced eye, believing that I could be more actively engaged in the job market. It may seem curious that I did not apply to the national airline, Aer Lingus, for a job. However, my brothers Pierce and Fergus had both done so in the previous year – and had both failed, in circumstances that led our family to delude ourselves into believing that the company simply did not want FitzGeralds! In November, however, my French lecturer, Dr Louis Roche, pointed out to Joan – by then cashier in the student restaurant in UCD – that Aer Lingus were advertising for administrative assistants. She immediately spurred me into action by a courier sent to me in the National Library.

There were thirteen applicants for four places. At the interview, in the Gresham Hotel at the end of November, I was asked a question about Pan American Airways. I recited that company's route network, starting with its routes radiating from Boston, New York and Miami, but when, in my tour of the US coastline, I reached New Orleans, my interviewers – the secretary, James Gorman, and the staff and services manager, Michael Dargan (later chief executive and then chairman) – halted me, indicating that they were satisfied that I was familiar with Pan Am!

I was one of the four appointed, at an annual salary of £300. We started work as administrative assistants on 13 January 1947, on the top floor of 35 Upper O'Connell Street, in a room with a telephone, an electric fire, and no other furniture. We made phone calls sitting on the floor in front of the electric fire. That was the appalling winter of 1947, when Europe froze and much of it ground to a halt until the thaw came in late March.

I also spent a brief period on a familiarisation visit to the staff and services department, where I was given the task of proposing annual-leave allowances for various grades of staff in this rapidly growing company. I naturally started by allocating a generous eighteen days to the new administrative-assistant grade! One staff member posed a problem at first, however, as I did not understand what the job entailed: a seamstress. On enquiry I discovered that she had been kept on the staff despite the fact that her work, repairing rents in the canvas exterior of DH86 aircraft, had ceased with the substitution of metal-winged DC3s six months earlier!

I was naturally delighted to find myself in our national airline – an ambition that I had held for many years, but one which I had foolishly failed to pursue after my two elder brothers' abortive attempts to join the company. Within a couple of months, I was preparing rudimentary route accounts, purporting to break down the global financial figures into profit and loss accounts for each of the company's services and developing ideas for domestic air routes.

At the time that I had been sitting my BA examination, my father, a heavy smoker whose health had deteriorated under the strain of public and private events, had developed angina, suffering considerable pain, and was under threat of a heart attack thereafter. By this time, his natural buoyancy and gaiety, already affected by the cumulation of factors I mentioned earlier, had been seriously undermined. He was thus in no mood to welcome my decision, a couple of months after the onset of his illness, to take up a position in Aer Lingus. He attributed this decision solely to my desire to marry early, and felt that (as he believed had happened with my brothers Pierce and Fergus), I was throwing away the possibility of a distinguished career, in my case because of a frivolous romantic fancy. (None of us ever dared to ask him to reconcile his precepts in this matter with his own example!)

When I went ahead with the Aer Lingus job, he refused to speak to me. Given his precarious state of health at the time, this was a very painful situation for me. I attempted to overcome his objections by calling in aid the priest who at school had aroused my political ambitions – Ronnie Burke-Savage – and who at this point was still engaged in the fourteen-year-long process of preparation for ordination as a Jesuit. He argued my case with my father, but to no effect. Happily, however, within two months of my starting work in Aer Lingus, my father had begun to recognise from my enthusiasm, and from the way I was obviously stimulated by my work, that my interest in air transport was genuine. In mid-March 1947, he relented. To my immense delight, our deeply affectionate relationship was restored. It was a timely reconciliation, for on the morning of 9 April, my mother, returning to their bedroom after an early breakfast, called me frantically. He was dead of a heart attack on the floor beside his bed, at the early age of fifty-nine.

It was a devastating blow for us all, but above all for Mother – one from which she never really recovered. In the eleven years that followed before her own death, she certainly derived considerable pleasure from her children and grandchildren, but never hid from us the fact that she longed to rejoin him as soon as possible.

My brothers and I shared her terrible sense of loss. All of us loved, admired and respected our father, and had found enormous enjoyment and stimulation in his company – drawing in different degrees according to our individual interests on his literary, philosophical and political talents, but all enjoying equally the stimulation of his company, his irrepressible sense of humour, and his extraordinary fund of anecdote. To live up to his standards of integrity, emulate fully his patriotism and sense of public service, or replicate the combination of physical and moral courage for which he was so highly regarded by many of his contemporaries, was impossible, but at least these qualities had given us something towards which to aspire.

Lest this seem unduly hagiographical, it should be added that there were other sides to his character also. He never succeeded – indeed, I do not think he even seriously tried – to be objective about the 1921 Treaty, the Civil War, or its aftermath. While capable of warm friendship with people who had differed politically from him at that time, he never lost his bitterness about these events, and, like many of his contemporaries, was often reluctant to accept the good faith of some of the major political figures on the other side, tending to ascribe base motives to people who at worst may have had mixed motivations, and many of whom had in fact acted with the same good faith as himself. He had little sympathy with or understanding of many aspects of Irish life, and suffered neither fools nor people with less elevated cultural interests very gladly.

His death was a particular blow to me because of my age; I had enjoyed his company for a much shorter period than my brothers, and although our relationship had been fully restored a few weeks before his death, it had been clouded in the preceding year by his opposition to my proposed marriage and to my choice of career. Moreover, I was conscious that I had missed an opportunity to get to know him better by trying to break through his reticence about his childhood and youth – a characteristic of many people of his generation.

It was fortunate for me, however, that at the time of his death I had Joan to console me, and the prospect of marriage and of my future career in Aer Lingus to distract me. The Aer Lingus appointment had made it possible for us to make concrete plans for a wedding on our long-chosen date of 10 October 1947 – a date which ironically, but fortunately, fell one day outside the traditional six months' mourning period.

By August, I had saved £108, which, with £40 promised wedding cheques and two £29 salary cheques to come (our salaries had been revised to £350 a year), and allowing £13 for an army ball to which we were committed, would leave a total of £193 for two months' pre-marriage living expenses, furniture, my wedding expenses, and our honeymoon. In the event, this sum proved inadequate by a margin of £18 – which I had to borrow from Joan on the honeymoon. For a number of years thereafter, all attempts by me to discourage particular expenditures on her part were met by the unanswerable – but, I felt, overplayed – argument: 'It can come out of my £18.'

It had been decided that we would live in a flat in the upper portion of Joan's mother's house on Booterstown Avenue. The flat contained a sitting/dining room and two bedrooms, with a kitchenette and bathroom. We could not afford water heating and depended on Joan's mother's sitting-room back-boiler for hot water for baths and washing during the first five years of our married life. In summer when there was no fire downstairs, we had to depend on kettles and pots of water heated on our ancient gas stove. Because my mother provided us with a bed – one that my grandfather had purchased for £5 second-hand in Bath in 1913, when my parents were coming to live in Ireland – and because we received several armchairs as wedding presents, our purchases of furniture could be limited to a sitting-room carpet, a dining-room table, a couple of kitchen chairs and, later, a dressing table for the bedroom.

The wedding itself, at 9 AM in the morning in Booterstown Church, was a quiet family affair – both because of my father's recent death and because of Joan's mother's very limited means. Only one photograph – a proof copy – survives, because by the time we could afford to pay for the wedding photographs, several years later, the photographer had disappeared.

Like most men on their wedding day, I was appallingly nervous; Joan, by contrast, was calm and radiant. Just after we got back to the house, and as the first guest was about to arrive, the wedding cake fell off its stand onto the floor, and Joan had to receive the guests without me, whilst in the next room I struggled to put it together again. The section of the cake that is customarily retained for the first christening suffered a further disaster when, during our honeymoon, it was eaten by mice.

We had originally planned to go to France, but when the time came, this proved financially impossible. A good excuse for a switch to London was provided by a hitch that arose about Joan's passport. Her birth in Liverpool raised a query as to her entitlement to an Irish passport, which depended upon establishing her father's domicile – intended place of permanent residence – on 6 December 1922. Because of her father's mental condition, this posed a problem that took some months to resolve.

The journey to London was our first experience of air travel. We went by Viking, a civil version of the Wellington bomber which, despite its poor economic characteristics, Aer Lingus had been required by the government to buy as part of the 1946 deal with the British government that had led to Aer Lingus becoming the sole carrier on Anglo-Irish routes. In London, Joan's aunt and godmother, Emily, had paid a thirty-shilling deposit on a service flat in Bayswater. We benefited financially – if not gastronomically – from the post-war regulations that controlled meal prices in England. We were able to eat in places like the Savoy and Simpsons for sums of under £1 for the two of us – although in Simpsons we found that even arriving as early as 12.30 for lunch, the chicken we had come for was already 'off' the menu.

To be truthful, London in 1947 was a fairly depressing place – so much of it destroyed, and the rest dilapidated and unpainted. But there were many plays and shows to see, and some pleasant outings to Epping Forest – to retrace a walk which my father had taken me on, eleven years earlier – and to Hampton Court, and so on. Nevertheless, we came home earlier than we had intended, partly for financial reasons.

4

~: Aer Lingus and Journalism :~
1947–58

Back in Aer Lingus after our honeymoon I set about inventing my work in the sales department to which I had been transferred. As nobody quite knew what a research and analysis officer in an airline-sales department was meant to do, some inventiveness was needed.

I wasn't at that stage of my life much interested in market research in the sense, for example, of establishing what kind of goods might be most suitable for transmission by air cargo, so instead I set about estimating traffic flows, drawing up timetables, assessing the economic viability of routes and so on. Of course there were other people in head office who were doing these things, but judging by what was happening to the company, they didn't seem to me to be doing them very well, so I felt I would try my hand, oblivious, in my youthful naivety, of the tensions that this could create.

Although no one had asked for them, I prepared traffic estimates for our new transatlantic air route, due to start the following spring. I estimated that only 20 percent of the seats would be sold on this service during its first twelve months, and that it would lose £1 million in that year. This gratuitous advice from a twenty-one-year-old member of the sales department was not well received; I was told that my job in sales was to fill empty seats!

The company had bought five fifty-eight-seat Constellation aircraft, any two of which would have provided a daily transatlantic service. It had been intended that the extra Constellations would be operated on the Dublin—London as well as on the transatlantic and Rome routes, and I estimated that the use of several of these long-range aircraft on the short route to London would cost £300,000 more than servicing it with short-haul aircraft. I also estimated that a direct Constellation service to Rome, to be started in December 1947, would have 92 percent of its seats empty in the first two months – which turned out to be about right. It too was cancelled. And when, in early December 1947, I pointed out that in the previous three weeks no paying passenger had travelled in either direction on the new Shannon—Paris twice-weekly service, and that accordingly this route might be reconsidered, it was in fact abruptly terminated, as were other unsuccessful routes that had also been launched without adequate research.

It is my recollection that in January our incompetent board was quietly displaced, albeit only temporarily, by an executive committee of civil servants, who set about tackling the crisis. Then, in February 1948, a new government, led by Fine Gael, was elected, which – wisely – cancelled the transatlantic service. I had nothing whatever to do with this decision. I had not communicated my doubts about the viability of the route to anyone outside the company, but the fact that I had a Fine Gael background probably didn't help me in the company just then.

With the cancellation of the transatlantic route, all the Constellations were sold. I then became involved in the process of arranging for the substitution of the much smaller DC3s on the London route. The truth was that the company was going through a very bad patch. Some 1,500 more staff than were needed had been recruited as part of this ill-considered expansion. The subsequent contraction of fleet, routes and personnel was painful.

However, by mid-1948 the company was again in good shape and I was by now fully involved, although still in a somewhat irregular manner, with the planning process. By 1949 I had persuaded the management to introduce midweek fares to spread traffic demand through the week. These fares were immensely successful: up to half the passengers switched their day of travel on some routes for fare differentials of between 60 and 90 pence. In 1950 I secured agreement to the introduction of special cheap fares on the Dublin—London early-morning and late-night flights, or Dawnflights and Starflights, as we called them, in the busy summer months. There were no problems in those days with night flights into and out of Heathrow! These early and late flights enabled us to carry far more passengers with our small DC3 fleet. At one point we had a Starflight returning to Dublin from London at 4.30 AM, half an hour after the first Dawnflight had left Dublin for London – at a fare of £4.50 one way in midweek.

New routes were also being opened on the basis of my research into traffic volumes: to Birmingham and Jersey in 1949 and to Bristol, Edinburgh and Cardiff in the early 1950s.

In October 1948 I was sent to KLM in The Hague for a week to pick up ideas from them, and to try out concepts that I had developed during the previous two years. Joan and I took the opportunity of travelling on to Paris from The Hague, where we spent a fortnight. I introduced Joan to the Camus family, who welcomed her as they had welcomed me a decade earlier.

It was a particularly interesting time to be in Paris. The United Nations had not yet moved to New York, and Joan and I had both secured accreditation by Irish newspapers, so we had free access to the Palais de Chaillot, where the UN was in session. This had a restaurant in which food could be found that was not easy to get elsewhere in post-war Paris. Joan and I both returned from this trip having lost our taste for milk in our tea, for milk was still available only to babies in the Paris of late 1948. At the UN we saw Pandit Nehru defending the Indian invasion of Hyderabad on precisely opposite grounds to those he employed to vindicate the earlier invasion of Kashmir, and we followed on the ticker tapes the surprise defeat of Dewey by Truman in the US presidential election. In the streets of Paris we watched Communist riots – missing, however, a major riot in the Champs Élysées, as a result of travelling to the Bois de Boulogne by Métro rather than by bus; I had to content myself with taking photographs of the riot-torn street on the following day.

Back in Aer Lingus, I secured recognition in autumn 1949, in the form of an unannounced promotion to superintendent rank. When this was finally made public in April 1950, I was moved to head office in O'Connell Street to carry on my planning work from a more central location. Within a year I was also given the role of advising on rates and fares, which had the merit of requiring me to attend IATA Traffic Conferences in Nice and Naples. Some time was to pass before they could find for my new position a title that wouldn't offend someone, but my (relatively) patient anonymity was rewarded two years later with the title of commercial development superintendent and a further promotion to the top superintendent grade, at a salary of £1,000 a year.

It took several years longer for me to win recognition that I was not just a backroom adviser but that my work was in fact managerial. Finally, in 1957, when the company learned that I was so frustrated by their reluctance to concede this issue that I was thinking of taking on the editorship of a proposed independent liberal Catholic journal (to be financed, improbably, by Archbishop Charles McQuaid, which never in fact appeared), they caved in, appointing me as commercial research and schedules planning manager.

Even when the long-suffering management had accepted my requirements, I still managed to make life difficult for them. In those days, managers were entitled to a car as a fringe benefit, on the basis that they paid £72 a year for petrol. This carried tax benefits which I was too much of a puritan (Jansenist, Joan insisted!) to accept – and we had already acquired a Morris Minor.

At one point my boss, Max Stuart-Shaw, was reduced to banging the table and shouting: 'If I say you'll have a car, you'll bloody well have a car.' Despite this, I won, securing a £250 addition to my salary in lieu of the car. I had carefully calculated this £250 as the appropriate amount to equate to the value to me of a car, excluding the tax benefit! My objection to the company car was not as eccentric as it may sound. I knew that another manager had got into trouble for not driving his car to work but instead leaving it for his wife, so that she could bring the children to and from school, and as far as I was concerned, that was what a car was really for.

I should, perhaps, add to this account of my personal power struggle with Aer Lingus the fact that I rarely sought salary increases, as most of the time I thought I was generously paid. And I was conspicuously not an empire-builder. When I sought to extend my role, for example by getting control of charters and of adding extra flights during the summer season, I never sought additional staff. Instead I left it to my boss, when he felt I was overloaded, to propose staff additions for my department. In this way, the validity of my case for full responsibility over the whole of the planning area could not be – and never was – challenged as an attempt at personal aggrandisement.

The company's general manager through my whole period as a member of its staff was Jerry Dempsey, who had been its secretary when it was launched on 27 May 1936, and was appointed general manager several years later. He was enormously well liked and respected by the staff, to whom he was a kind of father figure, inspiring loyalty and affection. He managed a difficult team skilfully. His mistakes were occasional ones of excessive kindness, which led him at times to place more confidence in some people than they merited. His long experience not only of aviation but of the Irish governmental, civil service, and business scene was invaluable.

In the immediate post-war period, with the rapid development of air-transport technology, he needed people with experience to head the key commercial and technical divisions of the airline. He got them, in the form of two men, each with more than a decade of experience in Imperial Airways: a stout Englishman called Max Stuart-Shaw, and a large Irishman called Jack Kelly Rogers. They brought with them all the traditional incompatibility of the commercial and technical sides of aviation – to which was added a difference in national temperament. It made for exciting management, especially for those of us with front seats. Accompanied as they were on each side by a number of other people with external airline experience, they brought to Aer Lingus a solid basis of professionalism.

Stuart-Shaw was my boss. Impatient and peppery, he inspired terror and affection in equal measure – although not always in the same people! He was determined that Aer Lingus would be an efficiently run and highly professional commercial airline, and he would brook no excuse for sloppiness or incompetence. It was the kind of leadership that the commercial side of the airline needed, and from which it continued to derive benefits long after his departure.

His professional instincts were so well developed that in my new position I could afford to let my imagination rip, proposing initiatives and innovations of all kinds, safe in the knowledge that he would unerringly sort out the possible from the unrealistic. Our relationship remained throughout a combative one, involving constant cut and thrust on both sides, with no holds barred, but beneath the surface there grew up a deep mutual respect and affection. When, early in 1958, he left Aer

Lingus, where I think he sensed that his nationality might be a barrier to his reaching the top, I felt a great sense of loss, and this was one – although, as I shall explain later, by no means the only – reason for my decision to leave the company myself within the year.

Jack Kelly-Rogers was a very different kind of person. He had piloted Churchill across the Atlantic during the war and was understandably proud of this fact. He was less incisive than Stuart-Shaw but could also be terrifying to his subordinates in his own way. He returned Stuart-Shaw's hostility in kind, although perhaps a little less explosively. But whatever Stuart-Shaw's opinion of him, the Technical Division, which developed under his leadership, was extremely efficient and played a major part in securing for Aer Lingus the high reputation for safety and punctuality that it quickly won in the airline world.

Other key figures at that time were the company secretary, James Gorman, and the staff and services manager, Michael Dargan, who interviewed me jointly when I applied for a position in November 1946, and the chief accountant James Moran – a strange man, eccentric and withdrawn, and difficult to come to grips with.

Stuart-Shaw's first line team were Traffic Manager Oliver Hone, also ex-Imperial Airways, as was his wife Muriel, and a member of a well-known Dublin literary and artistic family; Commercial Manager Paddy Brennan, with whom I had worked in my early months in the company, when he had been assistant secretary of Aer Lingus; Publicity and Advertising Manager Major Eamon Rooney, who had suffered from my father's efforts as Minister for Defence some twenty years earlier to tighten discipline in the army, but who, far from holding this against me, had gone to great trouble to help to teach me how to write articles; and Sales Manager Ralph Leonard, who during the war had undertaken liaison duties in Washington as a colonel in the British army. These, together with the operations manager, Bill Scott, and the chief engineer, Paget McCormack, were the bosses.

I had many colleagues at my less-senior level. Two of those who entered with me as administrative assistants were Tony O'Brien, a school and college friend who worked on the legal side until he left for the Irish Red Cross, and later Shell Worldwide; and Gerry Giltrap, Kelly-Rogers's keyman, who later became secretary to Trinity College Dublin.

Because of our fairly key positions on the commercial and technical sides, Giltrap and I worked closely together, taking great care, however, that our two bosses' attention was not unduly drawn to this fact! On his side, there were several other like-minded people of around the same age – Arthur Walls and George Bourke, later both with Guinness Peat Aviation; whilst on my side I had Niall Gleeson, an Economics MA who joined me in 1952, and later became head of the International Air Traffic Association in Geneva. And around the same time, Gerry Dempsey, later chairman of Waterford Glass, joined the accounts department.

The six of us became a de facto planning group, dealing with commercial and technical policy, advising on the selection of new aircraft, planning new routes, and so on. For a group of young people in their twenties it was a great opportunity, and we made the most of it. We convinced ourselves, of course, that we, rather than our bosses, were running the company, and in turn they were probably entertained by our presumption – or, perhaps, at times a little irritated by it!

In my own area – or what I had set out to make my own area from the outset – I was concerned to secure a solid factual basis for decision-making. What share of total traffic across the Irish Sea were we carrying? How did our costs and fares compare with those of other companies, and, to the extent that ours were out of line, why was this so? How much of our problems were due to the extremely cyclical pattern of traffic across the Irish Sea, with a high summer peak, and how much to the short-haul character of our routes? Exactly where were our passengers travelling from – and where were they eventually trying to get to? What was their newspaper-readership pattern? Did it depart from the average pattern in Ireland or Britain to any significant degree, and if so, could we reach them more cheaply by a careful choice of advertising media? How much extra traffic could be generated by lower fares or additional routes? How did passengers react to higher or lower frequencies of services? Which would be more beneficial on our route network: a larger aircraft, bigger than needed for some routes or certain times of year, but with lower seat-mile costs, or a smaller aircraft costing less per flight, but with higher seat-mile costs? What were the natural hinterlands of the places we served, and could part of these hinterlands be better served by additional routes? Why did our planes take forty-five minutes to turn around at airports, and could this be reduced? How could the percentage of aircraft seats sold be increased?

These were among the questions to which I sought answers by various forms of research. Analysis of ticket sales; sample surveys of passengers (one – covering five thousand passengers – was accomplished at a net cost of £60); statistical data from government sources; analysis of the company's financial accounts, distinguishing between direct operating costs, indirect route costs and overheads; experimentation with fares; data on aircraft operating costs – all these had to be employed, and deployed to best effect.

Contacts had to be made with external sources of relevant statistics, with geography researchers, and with other airlines. Working groups had to be organised to analyse airport turnaround times, to see how they might be reduced so as to squeeze more airtime out of the aircraft. Aircraft-seat design had to be studied to see whether, with better design, seats could be set closer together with less rather than more passenger discomfort.

What made it all so interesting was that most of this work was, in effect, pioneering. We were in many cases first in the field. We simply had to be first, because we were operating in less favourable conditions than any other significant airline, and we could survive only if we became more efficient than any other company.

The truth is that the atmosphere in which we worked in those years was extraordinarily stimulating. We were in an industry which was at the edge of current technology and still in the course of incredibly rapid development. The economics of all forms of transport was an underdeveloped discipline, and the very specific sub-discipline of air-transport economics was quite unexplored. There was in fact almost no theoretical underpinning for many of the decisions we had to take.

In 1952 I read a paper on airfares to the Statistical and Social Enquiry Society, in the course of which I estimated the current price elasticity of air transport at two, i.e. a 10 percent fare cut would create a 20 percent extra demand. Later in the 1950s this was validated by much more scientific research than mine. However that may be, my paper led to my being elected to the Council of the Statistical Society despite my youth, and this in turn extended my horizons greatly, as I attended meetings and listened to papers and debates on much wider economic and statistical subjects, and got to know economists and public servants.

I was able to show that changes in costs were almost completely irrelevant to the optimal pricing of cinema and theatre seats, and were relatively unimportant in certain forms of transport. A paper along these lines which I presented in UCD to economics lecturers and students caused some bemusement, as those concerned endeavoured to translate my home-grown economic theory into what they had been taught in their microeconomics classes!

This was not the first time that I had stumbled over the science of economics accidentally. Earlier, my efforts to develop criteria for deciding whether an individual round trip or route would pay had led me not only to insist on a radical reorganisation of the airline's accounts in order to display cost data in a manner meaningful for such decisions, but to invent a concept of marginal costing which I was later both disappointed and relieved to find to be the subject of a book I came across. Relieved, because it confirmed the correctness of my theoretical approach; but disappointed also, because I had naively convinced myself that I had personally invented this particular wheel!

I had started tackling the professional exams of the Institute of Transport in 1949. In 1953 I sat for the associate-membership examination. Our second child, Mary, was born at this time, just as the exams were taking place, and the two drawers of the cupboard in the nursing-home room were filled respectively with baby clothes and my books and papers for the exam. One subject in particular gave me trouble in this exam: transport management and accountancy. My fears were confirmed when I saw the paper. I could not possibly pass it on the questions that were open to me. There was, however, one desperate remedy. An optional additional question was available for 'overseas students', who might not be familiar with some of the more esoteric features of British transport, to which many of the mainstream questions were addressed. I knew, of course, that the word 'overseas' was intended to apply to places like Argentina and Sri Lanka (or Ceylon, as it was then known), and that it was not meant to apply to Ireland. As, however, the optional question for overseas students was the only one to which I could give a full answer (it was about aircraft depreciation, a favourite subject of mine), and as there was so little else that I could employ my time writing about, I answered it comprehensively. I then spent the rest of my time penning a lengthy justification of my course of action, both on the literal grounds that Ireland is 'overseas' vis-à-vis Britain, and on the rational grounds that the reason for having such an optional-extra question was equally valid in the case of Ireland as for other more distant countries – for an Irish student could not, in view of the history of our two countries, reasonably be expected to know all about British transport!

I passed the paper, and the exam, and became an associate member of the institute. Later I learned that my appeal to the difficult history of our two countries had won the day; it was said that some nervous examiners had hesitated about turning down someone whom they judged must be a dangerous extreme nationalist!

I was already lecturing part-time on the economics of transport at Rathmines School of Commerce, and by 1956 was doing so at my own college, UCD, as well. I also became secretary, and later chairman, of the Irish branch of the Institute of Transport.

One of the most demanding tasks I undertook was the scheduling of aircraft. This involved estimating traffic demand on each route and on each of the 180 days of the summer and winter seasons respectively, taking account of such factors as changes in the date of Easter and Whitsun, and of many special demands, such as the rugby internationals in the early part of the year, and the different holiday seasons in various parts of Britain. I found that the exercise of matching available aircraft, air crews and hostesses, each with different constraints, to the fluctuating traffic demands over 180 days and at different hours of the day on a dozen routes could be undertaken only by a continuous thirty-eight-hour period of concentration. This became for me one of the highlights of my year, together with the subsequent conversion of the fluctuating daily provision of flights into a readable timetable, with provision for extra flights over and above those publicly notified in this way, to be committed as and when demand arose for them.

The process of committing these extra flights in response to demand brought me into conflict with the traffic department, to which this task was traditionally allotted, for that department was inevitably preoccupied with its principal commitment, the day-to-day operation of the airline, and this made it in practice impossible for it to respond to booking demands that sometimes arose six months before the summer peak. As a result, passengers trying to book flights for that period were left unsatisfied, the extra flights that I had provided for this purpose being uncommitted for weeks after the demand for them had arisen. After several years of frustration, I eventually secured the transfer to me of the control of this allocation of all flights up to ten days before the week in question, thus achieving effective control of all but last-minute adjustments to flight scheduling.

I deduced from this a principle of administration – that the urgent and the important should not be handled by the same decision-making mechanism, for the urgent always tends to take precedence over the important.

My passion for matching as perfectly as possible supply and demand reached its culmination in 1958, in the months immediately before I left the company. That year was the centenary of the Apparition of Our Lady at Lourdes. Since 1952, we had been building up a lucrative pilgrimage business to Lourdes, where, indeed, we had become by far the largest operator of both charter and scheduled services, with routes not merely from Dublin to Lourdes but onwards, with traffic rights, to Barcelona and Rome. (As the operator of the only Rome—Lourdes scheduled service, I made a bid for the carriage of Pope Pius XII on his 1958 pilgrimage to Lourdes, and I drew from his decision to fly Alitalia the conclusion that the papacy was more Italian and less universal than it was sometimes represented to be!)

In any event, with the Centenary Year coming up, I asked Stuart-Shaw to defer until autumn 1958 the sale of two of our Viscount 700 aircraft, which were being replaced by the larger and more economic Viscount 800 series. I told him I could use them profitably for Lourdes charters during the five months from May to October. He was sceptical – and even seemed to suspect me of a non-commercial religious motivation! I eventually persuaded him to agree, however, and as a result we secured what I still believe to have been the most perfect supply/demand equation ever achieved in air transport. The two aircraft were used on that route twenty hours a day on every single day of that five-month period, and we carried eighty-one of the eighty-two pilgrimages from Ireland and Scotland to Lourdes that summer.

I have mentioned earlier my concern with aircraft-cabin design and seat-design issues. When I joined Aer Lingus, the seating in the DC3s was being raised from eighteen to twenty-one. But this was far below the weight-lifting capacity of the aircraft, and over my period with the company I and other like-minded colleagues secured a gradual increase in seating to thirty-two, with better interior design and improved seats.

In those days, aircraft seats were massive pieces of steel, stressed with a bar low down between the back legs so that passengers could not put their feet under the seat in front of them. With the impending delivery of the Viscounts in 1954, I pressed for and eventually secured a redesigned seat, lighter in weight and adequately stressed, but without the intrusive bar, so that we were able to operate these aircraft with sixty seats, as against the design capacity of forty-eight. The tourist class seat-pitch at that time was 39 inches, but we got it down to 34 inches without discomfort – viz. the seat-pitch, which later became the standard for the new Economy class.

We were effectively forced to be pioneers in many aspects of flight scheduling and aircraft interior design, as we had already become in the area of promotional fares, because the Aer Lingus route network was at that time a high-cost one, competing with relatively low-cost surface transport. Our peak-valley ratio was one of the highest in the world, traffic in the peak week being over eight times the winter valley level. The stage lengths were short – mostly routes to Britain – and correspondingly uneconomic. And the average fare per mile by sea and rail with which we were competing was half that from Britain to the Continent across the English Channel. This was a formidable combination of challenges to face, and success depended quite simply on our being more efficient in all respects than any other European airline. That is why the job was such fun – and why we all tackled it with tremendous enthusiasm.

I might add, in this era of enthusiasm for privatisation, that an extra spur for those of us in management, and for many of the staff, was the fact that this was our national airline. I don't think we could ever have been inspired to work as hard as we did if the airline had been operating for the private profit of anonymous shareholders. Indeed, after my Aer Lingus experience I, for one, would never have been comfortable working as an employee in a private company and committing all my energies to making profits for shareholders – although, of course, I subsequently worked happily as a consultant for many private firms.

Before explaining why, against this background of commitment to the airline and enthusiasm for my work, I decided to leave Aer Lingus, I must first turn back a decade in order to say something of the other activities in which I was engaged during the decade after 1948.

First, politics. In the February 1948 general election, under the direction of Alexis FitzGerald, son-in-law of John A. Costello, who was shortly to become Taoiseach in the 1948-51 coalition government, Joan and I had sought support for Fine Gael canvassing door to door. My understanding – later Alexis was always to deny that he was responsible for this – was that Fine Gael remained supportive of continued Commonwealth membership, and Joan and I had canvassed accordingly; we particularly remember reassuring the inhabitants of Waterloo Road on this point!

After the election, all opposition parties and independents joined together to form a coalition that would replace Fianna Fáil after sixteen years of unbroken rule by that party. A new party, Clann na Poblachta, led by Sean MacBride, was included in this coalition, and MacBride became Minister for External Affairs. I still recall my disillusionment at this development. I had been brought up to regard MacBride with deep hostility; a member of the IRA from the Civil War onwards, he had been its chief of staff in the mid-1930s, at a time when some particularly shocking murders had made a profound impression on me, including one near Ring College when I was at school there. Not having adult memories of the sixteen years of Fianna Fáil government, I did not fully share the conviction of older people in the Opposition parties that an alliance with MacBride and his avowedly republican party was a price worth paying in order to provide an alternative government.

My unhappiness was intensified when, a few months after the 1948 election, John A. Costello announced the government's intention to declare a Republic. At that time, this clearly meant leaving the Commonwealth, for the evolution of which into a body of sovereign, independent states he, as attorney-general, with people like my father, Paddy McGilligan and Kevin O'Higgins, had worked so successfully in the years before 1932. Moreover, in the months that followed that announcement, the government also decided not to join the North Atlantic Alliance and NATO, which were then in course of establishment following the Prague coup of February 1948, which marked the last stage of the absorption of eastern Europe into the Soviet bloc. I attributed the dynamic of this decision to MacBride also. Fergus and I responded by initiating a pro-Alliance correspondence in the *Irish Independent* which eventually ran to more than eighty letters.

Around the same time, provoked by the British Labour government's reaction to the declaration of a Republic, and concerned not to be outflanked politically by de Valera's worldwide campaigning against Partition, the coalition government launched an all-party propaganda campaign on this issue, which I viewed as counter-productive.

These events, together with my progression to a more responsible role in Aer Lingus, led me to drop out of political activity from then until the mid-1960s. At the same time, however, another area of activity, more compatible with my position in Aer Lingus, opened up.

My father's journalistic involvement as editor of the underground *Bulletin* between 1919 and 1921, and his later experience as Irish correspondent of the *Catholic Herald* and the *Tablet* in the 1930s, had predisposed me towards freelance journalism. In 1946 and 1947, I had written for Irish publications a few articles on a remarkably heterogeneous range of subjects – air transport, dietetics, the Aztecs, Azerbaijan, and a Russian adventurer in post-Great War Latvia – as well as university notes, a couple of book reviews and several translations of articles from French and Spanish.

When I moved to the Aer Lingus sales department in Abbey Street in October 1947, which housed Publicity as well as Sales, I found there a vaguely literary atmosphere. Seamus Kelly, the company's PRO, wrote the 'Irishman's Diary' in the

Irish Times as Quidnunc, and the publicity manager, Major Eamon Rooney, was something of a prose stylist, from whom I learnt a good deal.

In February 1948 I was confined to bed for several weeks, ignominiously, with chickenpox, during part of the general election campaign. My mother's – very practical – birthday present was a copy of the current *Writers' and Artists' Yearbook*, which contained details of many newspapers in English-speaking countries. Inspired by this, and by boredom in bed, I wrote several articles on the election campaign and sent them to a number of papers abroad. These articles were published in Bombay and Johannesburg. This galvanised me into action. Within six months I had published articles on Ireland in the *Standard* of Buenos Aires, the *Ottawa Citizen* and the *Montreal Gazette* and had negotiated a weekly column in the *South China Post* of Hong Kong, to be followed within the year by a fortnightly column in the *Montreal Star*, a monthly one in the *East African Standard*, and less frequent contributions in the *Auckland Star, Melbourne Age, Adelaide News, West Australian, Statesman of India* and *Cape Times*, and in Britain in the *Eastern Daily Press* of Norwich, the *Western Mail* of Cardiff, the *Birmingham Post* and the *Glasgow Herald*. Because of the fact that in several countries I was writing for more than one paper, I usually wrote three versions of each article, one after the other. Occasionally I contributed articles on non-Irish subjects such as the Soviet economy, or air strategy in the atomic age. On one occasion, struck by the relative concentration of my ad hoc newspaper 'chain' around the Indian Ocean, I wrote an article on the uninhabited island of Kerguelen in the south of that sea, which netted me the remarkable sum of £28!

This external journalistic success, in which Joan helped me with perceptive critical comments – to which I soon learned to listen – had some repercussions back in Ireland. My unhappiness with the declaration of a Republic, the anti-Partition campaign, and the decision against joining NATO, was apparent in my articles, and came to the notice of the government, which had established in late 1949 an Irish news agency under Conor Cruise O'Brien, who was seconded from the Department of External Affairs for this purpose, and Douglas Gageby, later editor of the *Irish Times*. By the time their news agency got going, I had already 'sewn up' the Commonwealth journalistically, whilst completely failing to penetrate the United States, where the anti-Partition line of the Government News Agency found a more ready response. I recall a parliamentary question about the volume of material published by the Government News Agency which gave column-inch figures for the Commonwealth. I was delighted to find that their coverage in the Commonwealth was one-fifth of mine!

An early conflict arose when in July 1949, unaware of the government's intention, as yet unannounced, to establish a news agency, I sought to register with the Registrar of Business Names the name 'Irish News Agency'. Despite earlier verbal assurances that there was not, and could not be, any objection to this name, I was than refused permission on the – I still think dubious! – ground that the name was now proposed for a government undertaking. My request for compensation for the cost of my headed paper, which I had arranged to have printed on the basis of the oral assurances I had received, was rejected; I was told that the substitute name I had been forced to adopt – 'Irish News Service' – could be overprinted on the paper!

It must have been extremely irritating for the government to find its propaganda efforts blocked in the Commonwealth by a freelancing twenty-three-year-old son of a former Fine Gael minister. My identity emerged when the accumulation of cuttings from various Commonwealth papers under my name caused John A. Costello to enquire who this 'Garret FitzGerald' was. His private secretary, Paddy Lynch (soon to become chairman of Aer Lingus, and later for many years my academic colleague in UCD, and a friend), enlightened him. Mr Costello was then able to place me, as I had in fact been to his house at least once as a child, and his son Declan had been a friend of mine since we had met at an inter-schools debate and later in college.

I had also been spreading my journalistic wings at home during 1948 and 1949, writing on economic subjects for a short-lived trade magazine, and I had started to write on air-transport subjects for specialised journals abroad. A 'coup' which gave me particular satisfaction was the publication in February 1949 by *News Review* in Britain (the equivalent in post-war Britain of today's *Time* magazine) of a piece I had written about the Soviet airline Aeroflot, which was featured as their lead article. In an early and unusual example of 'Glasnost', Aeroflot had published virtually their entire network timetable. Using my knowledge of airline scheduling, I was able to reconstruct the size and location of the company's fleet from this timetable, thus revealing that Aeroflot then had the world's largest fleet, of 250 aircraft, with about nine thousand seats. I ended the article with the challenging statement: 'If their air force bears the same relation to that of Great Britain as their commercial air fleet does, it will certainly be a factor to be reckoned with in any future conflict.'

At about the same time, I broke into the Irish market for articles on foreign affairs. The *Irish Independent* had introduced a foreign-affairs column known as 'World Spotlight'. The paper's assistant editor was a brother of my colleague in the Abbey Street Aer Lingus office, Major Eamon Rooney. A meeting was arranged, and I submitted some articles – which were accepted. Thenceforth for five years I wrote regularly for this column, quickly developing an efficient technique. I would go in the evening from Aer Lingus to the National Library, and consult the *Encyclopaedia Britannica*, from which I would extract any relevant background up to 1945 on the country about which I was going to write. Then I would trace events forward to the present time, using a publication called *Keesing's Contemporary Archives*. My notes taken, I would go home, have a quick meal, and hammer out an authoritative article on wherever it was. By 9.30 PM I would be in Michael Rooney's office with the finished text. My knowledge of foreign affairs must have appeared to the readers, with more justification than they perhaps realised, to be encyclopaedic!

During this period I had remained very much under my brother Fergus's influence. Whatever about his anti-Franco position during the Spanish civil war – about which he had written a play that was produced by the UCD Dramatic Society – his period in the army, and especially in Army Intelligence, had pushed him sharply to the Right. He – and therefore I, at this stage of my life – saw Communists under every bed. In 1949 I wrote an article for the British news magazine *Cavalcade*, in which I imputed Communist leanings to several quite innocent organisations such as the Irish Housewives Association and the Irish Association of Civil Liberties – the foundation meetings of which Fergus and I had attended. Owen Sheehy-Skeffington, a lifelong liberal, was included in my indictment, as was by implication Christo Gore-Grimes, a solicitor who was a brother-in-law of my eldest brother, and whom I described as 'a Communist stooge'! This unforgivable diatribe was intended to be published anonymously. In fact it appeared over my initials.

Some time later, Christo asked me to call to see him, and confronted me with my handiwork. I could not deny the indictment. There followed a series of solicitors' letters threatening libel actions. I settled with apologies. As neither my solicitor, a friend of Joan's family, nor my barrister – from a sense of solidarity with a non-practising fellow-barrister – would take a fee, the experience was thus costless, but was extremely valuable; I learnt a well-deserved lesson that I never forgot. Those whom I had libelled were extremely forgiving. Sheehy-Skeffington in particular was very kind to me later in life when we served in the Senate together. Although avowedly agnostic, his behaviour was of the kind commonly called Christian, albeit not universal amongst people of that faith.

This aberration aside, my freelance journalism proved remarkably successful. From 1950 onwards I could count on about £350 a year from this source; this, together with the income from some Prudential shares my prudent Belfast grandfather had left to his grandchildren, almost doubled my then Aer Lingus salary of £550. This supplementary income was all the more welcome as by mid-1949 our first child was on the way. John was born on 27 October 1949. Like many young parents, we soon wondered how on earth we had put in our time before this event. Both of us were well adapted to parenthood. Joan had intuitive good judgement in relation to the many problems that arise in bringing up children, including an instinct for medical matters: there was no need for Doctor Spock. And John was from the first an easy child. Then and thereafter, parenthood was a joy. As I mentioned earlier, our second child Mary was born in 1953, and the third, and last, Mark, in 1957.

Towards the end of 1954, there was a significant change in the pattern of my journalistic activity. The *Irish Independent* dropped its 'World Spotlight' series, and around the same time they turned down as 'too controversial' an article of mine on the decline in the number of university students taking Irish as a degree subject, and rejected a series I had written on tourism as 'too dull'. I offered these to the *Irish Times*, where they were accepted with alacrity by the features editor, Jack White. He asked me if I could write a series on university finances, which I did; then he sought articles on the government finances, and finally one on the national accounts.

I knew nothing of these subjects but was happy to undertake the necessary research. My ignorance of economics helped me in one important respect: I had to explain these issues in simple language without jargon, because I did not know any economic jargon.

Soon my articles on economic subjects, written under a pseudonym, 'Analyst', were arousing interest. No one else was writing for the press on economic subjects, and the evident failures of economic management by successive alternating governments during this period was creating amongst informed opinion a frustrated interest in economic issues, which I was starting to satisfy.

Whilst I used a pseudonym in order to minimise any possible embarrassment to or objections by Aer Lingus, I made no attempt to hide my light under a bushel. Such is the power of the press that within a couple of years I came to be regarded as an economist. This profoundly affected my future career, by opening up to me possibilities that I had not hitherto dreamed of.

But to return to my decision of March 1958 to leave Aer Lingus. Why did I decide to leave an activity which I found so stimulating? I have already mentioned that some of the stimulus of the job had disappeared with the departure of Max Stuart-Shaw. I think that may have been what started me thinking about a change of career – there is a reference to that in my contemporary correspondence – but the factors that led me to an actual decision to leave six months later related less to a change in my feelings about Aer Lingus and more to an interest in widening my horizons.

I had never abandoned the hope that one day I might be able to enter politics, and clearly that could not be combined with a managerial position in a state company. Moreover, my life had already broadened out considerably beyond Aer Lingus. I was lecturing part-time in the economics of transport at UCD, providing the required course in that subject for the commerce degree. This brought me in touch with students again, a decade after I had left college, and I made the most of this opportunity in order to benefit from the stimulus of younger minds. Each week I took a batch of my students to the Country Shop tea room after my lecture. Academic life was starting to attract me.

Moreover, my modest denials of being an economist, given my quite different academic formation and lack of any grounding in economic theory, were usually brushed aside by people outside academic life in the light of my writings in the *Irish Times*. Even amongst academics I was generously received. In particular Professor George O'Brien, professor of political economy in UCD since 1926, dismissed as irrelevant my lack of qualifications in the subject, pointing out that he himself had no degree in economics, and naming a galaxy of similarly unqualified economists of great fame going back to Adam Smith.

I had no illusions about my capacity, actual or potential, as an economist, however, for I knew I did not have any real grasp of more than the rudiments of economic theory, and that my blind spot in mathematics ruled out even an elementary understanding of econometrics. But the studies I had made of the Irish economy in connection with my *Irish Times* articles had given me some intuitive feeling for the actual working of the economic system in Ireland, and my lack of training in the subject had at least enabled – indeed forced – me to write about it in language correspondingly more comprehensible to the lay reader.

Moreover, by 1957 I had published several serious economic articles in the quarterly journal *Studies*, then edited by my old friend Father Ronnie Burke-Savage, who had encouraged me when at school to think of entering politics later in life, and who had tried to reconcile my father to an early marriage of Joan and myself. One of these articles was the first serious comparative study of the economies of Northern Ireland and the Republic, using national-accounts estimates as well as industrial- and agricultural-output figures, and another was an attempt at a broad-stroke analysis of the Republic's economic problems as they appeared in 1957.

My work in this area convinced me that the Irish economy had an unrealised potential in both the agricultural and industrial areas – the former inhibited by dependence on the cheap-food British economy, which only access to wider markets could cure, and the latter by the continuance of protectionist policies long after their utility in terms of encouraging the initial establishment of infant industries had disappeared.

The establishment of the EEC by the Rome Treaty in March 1957 – when I got around to noticing it, for it made curiously little impact on me until a negotiation began to establish a European Free Trade Association linking the rest of Western Europe with the Community – seemed a providential answer to this particular Irish problem. For, an association with, or membership of, the EEC would entail the abolition of our protective barriers, the continuance of which had inhibited the entry of Irish manufacturers into export markets.

Because of what seemed to me to have been an over-concentration of Irish economists – with the exception of Professor Louden Ryan in TCD – upon the problems of agriculture, there seemed to me to be an opportunity, and indeed an urgent need, for more economic expertise to be made available to Irish manufacturing in order to meet this new challenge. Despite my lack of formal qualifications in economics, I believed that I might have a useful role to play in preparing Irish industry for free trade and re-orientating Irish manufacturing towards export markets, both for its own benefit and to ensure that Irish agriculture would not be prevented from benefiting from the eventual emergence of an EEC Common Agricultural Policy by an inability on the part of manufacturing to adjust to free trade.

It was going to be vital that the inefficiencies inevitable in a highly protected industrial environment should not stand in the way of the freeing of access to the Irish market as a trade-off for the opening up of other European markets to the products of Irish agriculture, as well as of existing, and especially new, Irish industries.

The coincidence of the opening to me of an academic window of opportunity in the area of economics with the emergence of a perceived need for an economic input into Irish industrial policy seemed to point the way ahead for my next career, one which moreover would have the further advantage of being both a good preparation for politics and a far better take-off point for a political career than Aer Lingus.

Accordingly, early in 1958 I started to sketch out an alternative career, involving a complex combination of intensified journalistic activity, economic consultancy directed especially but not exclusively towards the manufacturing sector, and, hopefully, some kind of academic career in the area of economics – with, as a possible eventual outcome, a move into politics.

The problem was the initial transition from a well-paid managerial post in the national airline to what in my circumstances was bound to be a low-paid low-level academic position – if, indeed, I could find such. Given that I had a wife, and three children to support, I would clearly have to secure supplementary income beyond my existing journalistic earnings.

In proposing such a gratuitous leap in the dark from a stimulating and financially rewarding job with excellent prospects of rising at any rate to very near the top, and perhaps even to the top, of my first-chosen profession, I had Joan's willing support. Even though she knew that a political career – a prospect which she disliked intensely – was in my sights, and that this job upheaval might ultimately facilitate a further switch to a political career, she did not demur.

One factor that influenced her to accept, perhaps even favour, a change of career, however, was her growing dislike of flying. She had not flown herself since summer 1956, and her fears for me had led me also to travel by train and boat on occasion when going to Britain on airline business – although this obviously caused some problems with the company. These occupational pressures to fly would disappear if I changed my career, and part of the 'deal' we agreed was that I would in fact travel by sea and land in future – an agreement that I adhered to rigidly for fourteen years. It is fair to say indeed that the fact that a career outside Aer Lingus would enable me to remove from Joan the pressure of anxiety about travel was a further factor, beyond those already mentioned, influencing my own decision to leave the airline at that time.

In the hope of securing additional income in advance of making the move to my proposed new career, I went to London in March 1958, prefacing my visit by letters to various organisations and institutions – including, for reasons that are now completely obscure to me, the London School of Economics, the Central Statistics Office and the Treasury! These three bodies produced nothing of interest, although I kept in touch with the Treasury for a year or two subsequently, my approach to the *Financial Times* proved fruitful. Freddie Fischer, the diplomatic correspondent, interviewed me and, on the strength of some sample contributions I had sent beforehand, appointed me Dublin correspondent on the spot.

Some weeks later, after I had started to send them news items about events in the Republic, the *FT* asked if I could cover Northern Ireland also. I agreed with enthusiasm, and wrote to various bodies and firms in Northern Ireland to ensure that they kept me in touch with developments in their affairs. I received some chilly replies, to the effect that they already had a perfectly good *Financial Times* correspondent, thank you.

I sought clarification of this from the *FT* and received an embarrassed and obscure reply. Some months later, on my next visit to London, I discovered what had happened. The foreign news department, for which I was working, had assumed Northern Ireland to be foreign, and as nothing had in fact appeared in the paper under a Belfast dateline for some time past, they also assumed that the paper had no correspondent there, and that it was their function to appoint one. But in fact there was such a correspondent – reporting, however, to the domestic news desk (when he reported, which he hadn't done recently!) Several years ago, a Belfast researcher found and sent me a copy of the minutes of a meeting of agitated Stormont civil servants, alarmed at the threat of a Dublin republican reporting on Northern Ireland to the *FT*!

Having been appointed *Financial Times* correspondent in Dublin on the morning after my arrival in London, I was appointed in the afternoon as Irish representative of the Economist Intelligence Unit on the strength of my role with the *Financial Times*; I am not sure whether I thought it appropriate to divulge to them the very recent character of my *Financial Times* appointment! I returned to Dublin feeling that I had taken the first tentative steps in the direction I wanted to go.

Six weeks later, the government asked me to accept an appointment to a committee to reform the Seanad. I was keen to accept this new appointment, but when I raised the matter with the general manager, Jerry Dempsey, he responded negatively, saying that I had already taken on too many outside activities and that my health could suffer. Accordingly, he suggested that I turn down the invitation. Faced with this reaction, I decided on the spur of the moment that the only thing to do was to disclose to him my intention to leave the company in September, and that therefore I proposed to take the appointment to the Commission. He was understandably taken aback by this announcement, but I had burned my boats and had no choice but to go ahead with my plan to leave Aer Lingus, although the additional income that I had so far generated represented only a fraction of the salary I was then being paid by Aer Lingus.

Finding further alternative employment immediately became a very urgent priority. I talked to Professor George O'Brien, whom Joan and I had known for many years; he had been her professor of political economy in UCD fifteen years earlier, and in 1957 he had persuaded me to join one of his clubs, the Royal Irish Yacht Club at Dun Laoghaire, so as to be able to add us to his regular Sunday night dinner companions. He dined each night in different clubs with different groups of friends.

George O'Brien said he would be delighted to have me as a member of his staff, adding, however, that the president, Dr Michael Tierney, would have to approve such an appointment, and recommending that I, rather than he, should approach the president, particularly as Michael Tierney was someone I had known since childhood.

The president was well-disposed, but told me that no post would be available in the coming academic year. Shortly afterwards I mentioned my situation to Dr Louden Ryan, lecturer in economics in Dublin University (or Trinity College, as it was more usually called), and he proposed that for the next academic year I seek an appointment there as Junior Rockefeller Research Assistant at £800 a year. I did so with success, my project being a study of the source of inputs into Irish industry as a contribution to input-output analysis, a discipline then in its infancy in Ireland. Apart from its intrinsic value, this project would both enhance my understanding of the working of Irish industry – necessary if I were to undertake my self-appointed task of preparing Irish industry for free trade – and provide me with a valid reason to approach several hundred industrial firms, seeking detailed information on the sources of their inputs. This process, I felt, would alert these firms to my interest in Irish industry – an interest that hitherto only Louden Ryan amongst Irish economists had evinced.

Feeling that Michael Tierney would be pleased to hear that my employment problem was temporarily resolved, I went to see him with the good news. To my surprise, he was deeply upset. I had not sufficiently allowed for his intense, irrational dislike of Trinity College. He announced that I would be absorbed by that institution: they would swallow me up and I would be permanently lost to my own university. I reassured him, in words that I later came to regret, that such was my loyalty to UCD that if a job turned up there, even at the bottom of the lowest salary scale, I would accept it. That, of course, was what happened a year later, when he offered me a post at the bottom of the Assistant Grade III scale, at £650 a year – which I could not turn down after my protestation of loyalty. On that scale – normally applied only to postgraduate students – I was to remain in UCD for ten years thereafter!

The income gap that remained after my departure from Aer Lingus was soon filled as a result of a number of consultancies that I arranged. Aer Lingus decided that they would require my services on a part-time basis for at least another six months. I was also employed by the Export Promotion Board (Coras Trachtala), and the Central Statistics Office, where I was appointed by Eamon de Valera to be an officer of statistics – the first non-civil servant to have received such an appointment, which gives access to confidential statistical material. And the *Irish Times* agreed to take my occasional economic comment weekly.

And so at the end of September 1958, I retired from my position as research and schedules manager in Aer Lingus and started a new and, as it turned out, hectic life comprising basically three careers – in academic life, in consultancy and in journalism – to which, in 1965, I added a fourth: politics.

5

∾ Preparation for Politics ∾

Just before I embarked on this radical change of career, my mother had suffered a stroke in October 1957. For six months she remained in a coma until her death in April 1958. Her life since my father's death eleven years earlier had been centred on her family and a few old friends. She particularly enjoyed visits to Italy, however, where my brother Fergus and his family had been living since he had secured an appointment with the Food and Agriculture Organisation early in 1951. She was the last of her own family, her two brothers and two sisters, all in North America, having died some years before, but, at the other end of the scale, she had lived to see the birth of her sixteenth and last grandchild, Mark.

Throughout these years, she had continued to live in the spacious flat to which she, my father and I had moved just before the end of the war. Her religious faith sustained her, although after her reception into the Catholic Church in 1944 she had found it difficult to take the readjustment from the austere Presbyterianism of her youth to the baroque Catholicism of the pre-Vatican II period. My last conversation with her before she suffered the stroke that led to her admission to a nursing home had been on this subject; I had tried to reassure her that it was not necessary for her salvation to respond to the flowery sentimentality of many Catholic devotions – something she was finding impossible to do.

Her long illness as she lay in a coma for half a year prepared us for her death, which nevertheless, by severing the last link with our childhood, was for all of us a shattering experience. After her death we came to realise, as I at least had not previously done, the full extent of her role in the partnership with my father. In our family reminiscences for decades to come, she was to play a much larger part than she, in her modesty, would ever have thought possible.

Her own estate was not large, apart from her and my father's personal possessions. These we shared between us, taking turns in choosing articles to which we individually attached sentimental interest and also, in my case (being the shortest-married, with the least possessions), objects which would be useful, such as furniture, china, cutlery and her 1937 Frigidaire. Pending a move to a larger dwelling, we packed one room of our small house with furniture and other articles.

My mother's death, the last of her family, also terminated the trust which had continued to hold the bulk of my Belfast grandfather's estate – in which he had left to his irresponsible children (as he saw them!) only a life interest. Robbie Lowry, son of Mother's old friend Ena Lynd, and later Chief Justice of Northern Ireland (in which capacity he features later in this book), helped to unravel the legal complexities of this process.

My share of my grandfather's estate – one-twentieth – was modest but, coming at a time in 1959 when it had become clear that my income in my new career – or careers – was going to exceed my Aer Lingus salary, it encouraged us to move to a much larger dwelling, with an unusually extensive garden for a town house, in Eglinton Road, Donnybrook. This house contained a garden-level flat for Joan's mother, as well as three other rooms on that floor, four reception rooms (one of which I used as an office until 1973) on the middle floor, and six bedrooms on the top floor. There we remained until my appointment as Minister for Foreign Affairs, at a much-reduced income (for ministers were then underpaid, in contrast to the situation in more recent times), forced us to move some time later to a much smaller house in a more distant suburb. The fact is that we had allowed our change of circumstances to lead us into adopting a standard of living which, although unaccompanied by any particular extravagance, was beyond the means that we could reasonably hope to have available to us if I was later to enter politics and attain public office – as in fact happened.

Meanwhile, I had enjoyed my year at Trinity. Junior and temporary as was my status there, I was nevertheless admitted fully to the life of the college – even, indeed, to the almost-sacred rite of wine-tasting, with a view to keeping the college's cellars replenished.

(This arose from the fact that, needing to buy wine for a new-year party in 1952, I had undertaken a statistical investigation of the seven hundred wines available from Dublin's seven wine merchants of that period – my Belfast mother having taught me to be a careful shopper! From this exercise I deduced that there were significant and consistent differences between the prices charged by different wine merchants for identical wines. This was useful market information. Moreover, the great clarets of 1945 and 1947 were all available for not more than £1.8.0 – less than €40 in today's terms – which meant that a dozen-strong wine-tasting group, which I immediately established with some friends, could taste any of these great wines, in conjunction with lesser and much cheaper wines from the same region, once a month for about seven shillings (€10 in today's terms) – per head. This in turn had led me to write several popular articles on how such a wine-tasting group worked. These were intended to be anonymous, but the *Irish Times* mistakenly published them over my name – endowing me with an undeserved reputation as a wine expert, which is why I was mistakenly co-opted by the TCD establishment to their wine-tasting group!)

All my time that year was not spent in Trinity, however. The basic data I needed for my research was available in the Central Statistics Office, then located in a fairly decrepit row of buildings at the back of Dublin Castle, that were said to be part of an old cavalry barracks that had been condemned as unsuitable for men and horses in 1914! The director of the office, Dr Donal MacCarthy, and his immediate predecessor, Dr Roy Geary, were both known to me from my membership of the Council of the Statistical and Social Enquiry Society, to which I had been elected after reading my paper on air-transport rates and fares in 1952. They were well-disposed to me, as by far the most prolific Irish writer on statistical data.

On my resignation from Aer Lingus, Dr MacCarthy had helped me both by commissioning me to undertake a study of Irish external trade from 1933 to 1957 and by having me appointed by Taoiseach Eamon de Valera as an officer of statistics. This gave me access to the confidential Census of Production data on industrial inputs that I needed for my TCD research project. (I think that this was the only such appointment in the history of the state; until long afterwards even civil servants outside the CSO were not so appointed, and several years later the Department of Finance Economic Planning Division considered using me to secure access to confidential statistical data needed for their planning purposes, but this was eventually regarded as too adventurous an extension of my original appointment. In my doctoral thesis on economic planning in Ireland a decade later, I included the principal conclusions of my research.)

For some months I worked in the CSO as if I were a civil servant, sitting in the same office as an official on temporary secondment from the Department of Finance who was working on trade statistics classification systems. As I was as familiar with the current trade figures as he was, I sometimes answered telephone queries if he was out of the room. When I finished my task and moved back to Trinity, my absence from the CSO was, I heard afterwards, noted with regret by some civil servants whose queries I had been answering; they enquired to what department FitzGerald had been transferred!

One event that I particularly recall during my period in the Central Statistics Office was the occasion when Joan and I had to drive one evening to a charity dance at Dunsany Castle in Meath. This was early during my period with the CSO, when I had not yet become familiar with the ins and outs of the place. Working late that day, I found when I emerged from the office that the carriage door into Ship Street through an arch under the building was locked for the night, leaving as the only means of egress for a vehicle a flight of half a dozen steps down to the level of the road through the back gate of the Castle. Without considering the practicability of what I was attempting, I started to drive the Morris Minor down the steps. Of course it got stuck on the top step. I had to ease it over this obstacle by lifting its rear. When it cleared the first step I drove it down gently, if bumpily, to the bottom – where its front, equally naturally, got stuck. Then I had to lift it gingerly so that it would not, as I released it from its position, run over me. I thus discovered why people rarely drive cars down steps!

My growing involvement with the public service, which had started when I joined the Statistical and Social Enquiry Council in 1952, had taken a further turn in 1958 when I was asked to join an informal Economics Club, drawn mainly from the public service, which discussed contemporary economic issues. Arising from these exchanges, Ken Whitaker initiated proposals, under the umbrella of the Statistical and Social Enquiry Society, to establish an Economic Research Institute, in 1960, with the help of Ford Foundation money.

At about the same time, I attended the foundation meeting of another new body, the Institute of Public Administration. I soon found myself a member of its executive committee, nominated, by some process I do not now recall, to represent UCD. Fortunately for me, everyone else also forgot this process, and so I remained a member of the executive committee for twenty years, attending its meetings even when I was Minister for Foreign Affairs. This gave me the opportunity not merely to assist in the development of the institute, where I frequently lectured, but also to get to know many senior, as well as some more junior, civil servants, local authority officials, members of the staff of state bodies and public service trade union officials. For a potential politician, this was of great benefit.

Later on, when I entered politics, I found that many politicians, even some of those who had been ministers, had a curiously limited view of public servants – frequently crediting them with a party-political bias, which is in fact an extremely rare phenomenon. Even where they did not hold this belief, many politicians felt a need to adopt an 'arm's length' approach to civil servants, as if they were some kind of alien beings. Having worked with many of them in and through the Institute of Public Administration, as well as in bodies like the Committee on Industrial Organisation, the National Industrial Economic Council and the Transport Advisory Committee in the 1960s, I had a quite different perspective. As a result, while I had no illusions as to the human perfection of civil servants, and was well aware of the capacity of some public servants to identify with and skilfully defend the interests of the public service and its members rather than the general public interest, I also understood the dedication of so many of them to that general public interest.

Moreover, I learnt to understand something of the positive rationale of bureaucracy – the concept of the importance of preserving equity between beneficiaries of state assistance, this underlies much of the rigidity of the bureaucratic process, and of the resistance by public servants to the exercise of discretionary powers. Civil servants' powerful urge to protect politicians from themselves, albeit somewhat paternalistic, is well-intentioned. Moreover, the commitment to thoroughness in tackling issues, while at times frustrating due to the slow tempo it imposes on change, protects the system against egregious error.

At the same time, this deeper understanding on my part of the ethos of the public service carried with it a heightened sense of the obligations of public servants to maintain the highest standards, and I developed a much more critical attitude to any failure to live up to the principles that I had come to understand and appreciate. I suspect that this made me a more demanding and impatient government member, especially when, as Taoiseach, I had to deal with so many different departments of state, not all of which were of equal calibre.

Although my consultancy work during the years from 1959 onwards brought me into touch with almost every industry in the country, and with many non-industrial business interests, my close involvement with the public service, in and through the Institute and otherwise, ensured that my orientation towards business remained in large measure a public-service-type approach. I never developed the natural empathy with the private-enterprise sector which many politicians, coming themselves from business or farming, instinctively feel. Whilst this certainly ensured that as a politician I did not easily succumb to business pressures, it may also have inhibited me from developing a full understanding of the working of the business mind, which secures for a politician an easier relationship with the private sector.

Another by-product of my involvement with the Institute of Public Administration was a commission to write a short book on semi-state bodies: state enterprises and non-commercial state boards. In retrospect, this book was a naive analysis of the structure and features of this sector of the economy, although in the absence of any other work on the subject in Ireland, it remained for many years the standard text on the subject. I received £15 for the first edition in 1961, and somewhat more for a revised edition two years later.

This small book reflected, I believe, the perhaps over-positive orientation towards state enterprise that I had developed when in Aer Lingus. I later found this to be far from universal amongst politicians, but it ensured that when in government much later, I did not respond spontaneously to ideological, as distinct from pragmatic, arguments for the privatisation of state enterprises.

During the course of this – for me highly significant – academic year, 1958–59, I had also found myself unexpectedly installed as chairman of the Irish Council of the European Movement. The council had been established some years earlier, at two highly entertaining meetings in the Shelbourne Hotel, when a very varied gathering of people, including Joan and myself, had debated a proposed constitution endlessly – as if it was a new constitution for the state! This initial effort to get the European Movement going in Ireland had failed, however, principally because the honorary treasurer forgot to cash the initial subscription cheques.

In April 1959 a young barrister, Denis Corboy, whom I had met at a debate in the Kings Inns, called a meeting to reconstitute the council. As I went in to the meeting, he asked if, as I was a 'neutral' – not a member of a political party, nor an employer, trade unionist or farmer – I would act as temporary chairman for the night – an invitation which I innocently accepted. I thus found myself chairman of the council for the following four years, as well as editor and author of the reconstituted council's monthly news bulletin on European affairs – a heavy task because of my determination to include in it all information on the EEC on which I could lay my hands. It was, however, an activity that I undertook with enthusiasm – an enthusiasm shared by Joan, whose upbringing had made her francophone also, and who shared my interest in Ireland developing a deeper involvement in Europe.

The council's first visitor from Brussels was the Community's first president, Dr Hallstein. When I met him at Dublin Airport, one young journalist present asked a single question, the ignorance behind which clearly disconcerted Hallstein: was Ireland a member of the Common Market? Another early visitor was the agriculture commissioner, Dr Mansholt. I enjoyed looking at the bemused faces of four members of the government sitting in the front row as Mansholt, with a twinkle in his eye, congratulated them on their success in getting farmers off the land!

Two years later, in April 1961, I paid my first visit to Brussels, as an economic journalist on that occasion, representing the *Irish Times*, together with colleagues representing the other two Dublin dailies. In view of the state of the Irish economy after the stagnation of the 1950s, my two friends felt that I was behaving oddly in posing questions about possible Irish *membership* of the Community, as distinct from *association*, with a very long period of transition to membership. The long period of economic stagnation, and the unprepared condition of the protected Irish industrial sector, meant that hitherto all that the Irish government had publicly aspired to had in fact been association.

Before leaving for Brussels, however, I had gone to see Ken Whitaker, secretary of the Department of Finance, and author of the First Programme for Economic Expansion, launched in 1958, whom I had got to know well through the Statistical and Social Enquiry Society. I asked him if there was anything I could usefully do when in Brussels, and he told me that it would be helpful if I were to test reactions to possible full Irish membership. When I raised this question with EEC officials, my two journalist colleagues expressed surprise at what they saw as my naivety. I reported back to Ken Whitaker on the reactions to my queries, and I had the last laugh on my two colleagues when, three months later, the Taoiseach, Sean Lemass, announced to a surprised Dáil Ireland's application for full membership of the

Community. He had decided that the economic progress that had begun following the Whitaker First Programme initiative, and his own emergence as Taoiseach, justified what many then felt to be a gamble.

This first trip to Brussels inaugurated a series of visits to Europe's new capital, and to neighbouring Luxembourg, sometimes three times a year, and never less than annually. During these visits, the number of different hats that I wore bewildered and amused my new Eurocrat friends. After my appearance as a journalist in April 1961, I reappeared as a university lecturer, leading a team of twenty economists; as vice-president of the European Movement (to which honorary position I was elevated after the end of my period as chairman); as an economic consultant; and, somewhat later, in 1966, as a member of the Opposition front bench in the Senate.

But that is to anticipate. In October 1959 I had become a full-time – as distinct from whole-time! – assistant in UCD, at a salary of £650 a year. I enjoyed every moment of this new life: the contacts with the students, and getting to know as colleagues members of the staff, some of whom not so long before had been my teachers, together with the challenge of lecturing on subjects peripheral to economic theory, such as statistical sources and the European Community, as well as on my 'home ground' of transport economics. On one occasion, however, I was required to lecture on economic theory to first year students. This forced me to read up the subject, which was probably a good thing! My main deficiency as a lecturer was my rate of speech. Despite efforts to slow down, I never managed a pace that satisfied students – as ex-students have commented to me ever since! I endeavoured, however, to compensate for this by making each point several times in different ways, at the same time enlivening the lectures and the seminars with anecdotal references.

I was, moreover, genuinely interested in my students, and despite my many other activities tried to ensure that I was accessible to them. I extended to the smaller Honours classes the kind of social arrangement I had introduced for my economics of transport students when I had been a part-time lecturer – but this time I also invited some students in small groups to my home occasionally, as well as, more frequently, to a tea shop. And I invited various members of the economic establishment, like Ken Whitaker, to join us for the 'at homes'.

The benefits of this socialising process were, to say the least, two-way. Whatever impact it may have made on the students, it had a profound effect on me – all the more so, probably, because this was happening during the 1960s, a period when young people were intellectually stimulated – and themselves stimulating. Up to this point in my life, I had been deeply conservative in my attitudes, to social and religious as well as political issues. Between my shift of career in 1958 and the late 1960s, all that changed. No doubt there were several factors at work: the spirit of the times, which for me and for many others proved infectious, and the influence of my own children, all of whom were in their teens during this decade – although it was only later on that I realised that my continuous contact with students was a crucial factor. Many of my conservative attitudes and prejudices simply did not stand up to the challenges the students were posing. When the process of economic growth after the stagnation of the 1950s had barely got under way, some of them were already beginning to ask very pertinent questions about the purpose to which the additional resources thus created would be put.

This latter challenge in particular was a useful one, for there was certainly a danger that those of us engaged in trying to pull our country out of its inertia and economic stagnation and to prepare it to take its place in a wider Europe might become so absorbed in these tasks as to ignore the social implications of growth. By 1964, under this kind of intellectual pressure, I had not only re-examined my own inherited prejudices about the adequacy of our traditional economic and social structure to secure a just distribution of expanding resources but had incorporated this fully into my political frame of reference as I approached the point when entry into politics was starting to become a real issue. Nor was this process of intellectual revisionism – if one can so describe it – confined to issues of social justice. The religious conservatism that I had retained from childhood was also giving way to an acceptance of the positive value of religious pluralism and to a much less conservative personal theology.

Since its foundation in 1908 as a college of the new National University, in succession to Newman's Catholic University of 1854 and the subsequent Jesuit University College, UCD had been a kind of benevolent academic dictatorship, both under its wily first president, Dr Denis Coffey, and then, after a brief interval with Arthur Conway as president, when Joan and I were students, under Michael Tierney. A son-in-law of Eoin MacNeill, he was professor of Greek and had also been a Cumann na nGaedheal member of the Dáil. A scholar, a genial friend, and very much a family man, he had, nevertheless, a gruff exterior and a strong prejudice against Trinity College and the *Irish Times* – the two of which in conversation he seemed at times to confuse. He suffered fools not at all, knew how he wanted the college to develop, and was dismissive of anyone who opposed his regime. No one could dislike him, but few had the courage to argue with him, and many timid souls actually feared, quite without justification, that they would suffer in their careers if they crossed him. It had been the custom of the governing body to agree with his proposals without demur.

As a member of the academic staff coming late to academic life from a quite different work background in Aer Lingus, where decisions had been made through a management structure that was far from authoritarian, and having spent a year in the very different oligarchic atmosphere of Trinity College, this aspect of UCD bothered me. It would, however, have been psychologically very difficult for me to have challenged Michael Tierney because I had known him since childhood and could not easily have faced the hurt he would certainly have felt and expressed at what he would have regarded in his simple – but effective! – way as my 'ingratitude'.

His term of office expired, however, when he reached the age of seventy in 1964. He was replaced by another son-in-law of another professor and education minister, the professor of modern english Literature, Jerry Hogan, who was married to the daughter of the late John Marcus O'Sullivan who had in fact, been my professor of modern history. The tradition of successive authoritarian presidencies imposed itself on Gerry Hogan, but the times, and his own different style, were against him. A growing demand amongst the staff and later (although only for a brief period, amongst the students), for greater involvement in the running of the College were features of the 1960s.

The appointment by the government in 1960 of a commission to report on university education was the precipitating factor in stimulating a staff initiative. Feeling the need to respond to a request for submissions, and also seeing an opportunity to get a staff organisation under way in non-contestatory conditions, a meeting was held to choose a committee to undertake this task, and somehow or other, despite my quite recent appointment to the full-time staff, I was nominated to it, and was subsequently actively involved in the establishment of the Academic Staff Association that developed from this initiative, and later in the foundation of the Irish Federation of Universities. Thenceforward I was actively engaged in college and, later, university politics – an excellent training ground for the much less emotionally strenuous world of national politics!

The new Academic Staff Association was primarily concerned with academic matters and only secondarily with issues such as salaries and conditions of service. Annual weekend conferences were held in nearby Greystones, to supplement routine meetings of the college governing body, to which, despite perennial complaints amongst the staff about the working of that body, only occasional individual dissatisfied staff members had previously sought election. After some lively discussion of our grievances in 1964 I decided to mobilise support for a more organised approach to the forthcoming governing body election and at a staff association seminar within a couple of hours I secured the agreement of a number of those present to contest this election – four professors to seek election from the Academic Council, and another lecturer (Paddy Lynch, lecturer in political economy and former private secretary to John A. Costello as Taoiseach) and myself to seek election by the thirty thousand odd graduates, as part of a panel which was later extended to include several non-academics.

The graduate election was a strenuous affair, involving the preparation and posting of literature to thirty thousand graduates and an attempt to canvass as many of these as possible. In the event, two of our four academic council candidates were elected – Professors Desmond Williams and John O'Donnell, distinguished historian and chemical engineer respectively – as well as four of the five candidates we put forward for the graduate election, including myself, standing on a 'reform' platform. We already knew that our contestatory approach to the establishment was shared by three of the four Fianna Fáil government nominees, Dr Eamon de Valera, son of the president; Judge Brian Walsh of the Supreme Court; and Máirín Bean Uí Dálaigh, wife of the Chief Justice, later to be president of Ireland.

Thereafter the nine of us used to meet in our house before each governing body with a view to concerting tactics. We were not, however, a very effective opposition, at least not during our first period between 1964 and 1967. Our problem was the group dynamic of the governing body – or rather, perhaps, the lack of any group dynamic! The practice was for the president to introduce each item, usually asking the secretary-bursar, Joe McHale, to develop the details of the issue. The president would then seek approval, to which most members immediately nodded. As soon as any of our group sought to speak, most of the traditionalist majority would turn to look in evident, if somewhat exaggerated, astonishment at the impertinent inter-venor. If another of our group supported the first speaker, the remainder would look quite shocked at this evidence of conspiracy. The psychological pressure to accept the establishment view without dissent was thus enormous.

Despite my wide experience of all kinds of other bodies, I found the whole business exhausting and frequently had to retire to bed after governing body meet-ings suffering from a migraine. It was only when I was elected a year later to Seanad Éireann that I realised the enormous benefits of a structured government/opposi-tion confrontation, completely free from the psychological trauma of the governing body of that time.

I was also active within the political economy department itself. As mentioned earlier in 1962 I organised a visit to Brussels by university lecturers in economics. Despite the scepticism of my southern colleagues I extended to the Northern Ireland university economists in Queens University, Belfast and Magee College, Derry, an invitation to join us. I confounded the scepticism of the southerners, because the northern contingent eventually outnumbered that from the Republic! In all we numbered over a score, and the visit was a success – the commission being surprised and impressed to receive a delegation from the whole island. While some individual university economists North and South were already known to each other, there had not previously been any occasion for a general coming-together of all of them and, given the success of the Brussels visit, it seemed a pity not to main-tain the contact. Accordingly I initiated a conference of Irish university economists at Ballymascanlon Hotel outside Dundalk and just south of the border. This became thereafter an annual event, and even after it lapsed for a couple of years it was revived again and has since continued in an enlarged form, including research economists.

In May 1968 the 'events of May' took place in Paris – a student revolution which almost succeeded in overturning General de Gaulle's government. This helped to stimulate student agitation in Ireland also, and in February 1969 a group of socialist students mounted a protest against the move to Belfield before library facilities could be provided there. They occupied the administrative offices in Earlsfort Terrace and mounted mass meetings of three to four thousand students. In order to defuse this I and some students and members of the staff organised large scale support for the election of an MA student, John Maguire (later a professor of philosophy in UCC) to chair the next meeting and we put down several resolutions, one of which proposed that studies be abandoned for three days in order to enable staff and students to discuss issues relating to the university and society.

This infuriated both the socialist students, who walked out, and the university authorities who, perhaps understandably, resented my initiative. I also persuaded a score of members of the Academic Council to meet in the basement of my house and to agree to prevent disciplinary action being taken against the students. Arising from these events a report was prepared on the future of the university, aiming to bring it under the effective control of staff and students – but, not surprisingly perhaps, nothing came of that initiative. These events did not endear me to the university authorities.

In 1960 my objective of securing a role in the formulation of industrial policy in preparation for free trade had begun to be realised. Sean Lemass after his election by the Dáil as Taoiseach had told the Federation of Irish Industries that they should start to study the problems that different sectors of industry would face as trade began to be freed, and in 1960 the federation asked a fellow-economist, Gerry Quinn, and myself to carry out a pilot study of the highly-protected woollen and worsted industry. We visited every firm in the industry over a period of many months, and a year or so after our appointment we presented our report. In it we suggested that this industry would face serious difficulties under free trade conditions, with many firms likely to disappear unless they made drastic improvements in their productive efficiency and above all in their marketing – something which, we suggested, could not be achieved without large-scale rationalisation.

The fact that we had taken a year to complete this study – admittedly on a part-time basis – suggested the need for a much more radical approach if the whole of Irish industry were to be reviewed within any reasonable timescale, and this seemed necessary in view of the fact that the completion of our report almost coincided with Britain's and Ireland's first application for EEC membership. Accordingly we recommended that the government be approached to co-operate in and help to finance such a general review.

An Economic Planning Division of the Department of Finance had been established two years earlier with my TCD friend Louden Ryan as a consultant economist, and in off-the-record discussion with him and his boss, Charlie Murray, it was agreed that Gerry Quinn and I would propose in our report that this review of industry be undertaken jointly with this branch of the Department of Finance. It might have seemed more logical to have proposed a joint effort with the Department of Industry and Commerce, but despite the fact that the former Minister for Industry and Commerce was now a free trade promoting Taoiseach, that department remained then, and for quite a while afterwards protection-orientated, and seemed unlikely to be an adequate partner in the kind of exercise now contemplated. After some initial hesitation – such a close partnership with the state would be breaking new ground for Irish business – the Federation of Irish Industries accepted our proposal, and in order to ensure that it would be well received, I briefed the Secretary of Finance, Ken Whitaker, in advance about what to expect.

The meeting with him thus led to immediate agreement on our proposal, and a Committee of Industrial Organisation was appointed by the government to mobilise the necessary resources and supervise the project, which over the following four years covered the whole of Irish manufacturing industry with the involvement of all the firms in each industry – save where there were a very large number of small firms, as in clothing, when the smaller firms had to be sampled. The only hitch – and it proved of short duration – was a demand by the Irish Congress of Trade Unions to participate in the exercise; both Ken Whitaker and I had overlooked the unions in our anxiety to get the project launched. Union participation was rapidly agreed and they proved to be most constructive partners.

Indeed, in so far as tensions existed within the committee they proved – as I had anticipated – to be between the Department of Industry and Commerce on the one hand and the rest of us – Finance, Federation of Irish Industries and Federated Union of Employers, and ICTU all endeavouring to nudge the Department of Industry and Commerce into psychological acceptance of free trade.

Meanwhile, as I had hoped would be the case from the time in 1958 when I had identified the preparation of Irish industry for free trade as my next pre-political vocation, I had become economic consultant to the Federation of Irish Industries. I held this position until the time when eight years later, my transition from the relatively non-partisan atmosphere of the Senate to the Opposition front bench in the Dáil made my continuance in this role a source of embarrassment to the Federation – as I gathered the Minister for Finance, Charles Haughey, hinted to them!

But long before that stage was reached my federation involvement had developed other dimensions, for in 1963 the government decided even before the Committee on Industrial Organisation had completed its work, to establish, with a not dissimilar composition, a National Industrial Economic Council as an element in a planning process involving the publication of a Second Economic Programme in July 1964. I was appointed as an FII alternate member of the council, the work of which was directed by a general purposes committee, of which I was an active member – and of which Louden Ryan was a most effective chairman.

As a result I became *de facto* a full participant in the planning process, which involved detailed consultations with all sectors of industry to establish quantified targets in each sector for consumption, imports, production, exports and employment. My understanding of Irish industry was greatly enhanced by participating both in the pre-plan consultations with every industrial sector and in the first annual review of performance by each of these sectors.

This planning process was, I believe, valuable for more than one reason. It forced firms to think of themselves, in most cases for the first time, not just as individual production units but as components in an industry within which they had a market share and were competing for this share vis-a-vis quantifiable domestic and external competition. And it forced state enterprises, in many cases also for the first time, to think of themselves as enterprises providing a public service rather than just as institutions with a right to free state capital, and protection against competition. Finally it forced government departments – if not always ministers – to consider seriously the extent to which various impediments to enterprise arising from political considerations were making it difficult for competitive enterprises to succeed in a free market environment.

Planning of this kind had a short life, however. Disconcerted by a relatively minor recession in 1966, as a result of which they feared that the Plan targets for 1970 would not be met (in the event it turned out that they would largely have been achieved had the government not panicked and abandoned them),the Fianna Fáil government dropped the Second Programme in 1967 and substituted a far less detailed Third Programme designed to fudge all the key issues, as a preliminary to dropping altogether the concept of quantified targets at the end of the decade.

I had benefited from these activities in two quite distinct ways. First, I was able to use the insights I had thus gained into the planning process as material for a doctoral thesis, on which I obtained a PhD in 1969. I turned this material into a book,*Planning in Ireland*, published by PEP in Britain and the Institute of Public Administration in Ireland, the six thousand-word introduction to which, outlining Ireland's unhappy economic history up to the 1950s, is still a recommended university text forty years later. Moreover, on the strength of my PhD I secured belated promotion to the college lecturer grade in UCD after ten years as an assistant (My promotion had been held up because I had no degree in economics).

Second, the detailed understanding of Irish industry that I had secured during this period stood to me in Opposition politics and later in government.

At about the same time as the Committee on Industrial Organisation was established, I had made the transition from undertaking economic consultancy on a personal basis, in parallel with representing in Ireland the Economist Intelligence Unit, to becoming managing director of an economic consultancy company in which I and the EIU of Ireland each owned 50 percent. The board comprised Sir Geoffrey Crowther and John Pinder from the EIU. and my UCD colleague James Meenan, Joan and myself, with Professor George O'Brien as chairman. During its eleven-year life the EIU of Ireland undertook consultancy or research work for some one hundred and fifty clients, including a score of state boards or public boards, another score of industrial or trade organisations, over fifty individual firms, fifteen trade unions or bodies representing workers' interests, half a dozen stockbrokers and over a dozen foreign interests. The experience I gained from this wide range of activities touching so many aspects of our national life proved very valuable in my later political career.

In thus merging my consultancy work with EIU representation I had hoped that the new company would develop a life of its own so that it would, in due course, be able to continue without me – and thus provide me, by way of dividends, with the supplementary income that would be needed to maintain our way of life in the event of my entering politics and being appointed to office. The theory was good, but in practice the company remained too dependent on me, and, whilst furnishing me with a good income to supplement my very small salary from UCD up to 1969, it never developed in the way I had hoped. I wound the company up in 1972.

During the period from 1958 to 1961 I had also served on two commissions – the Senate Electoral Law Commission and the Workmens' Compensation Commission. I have already described how the former appointment had precipitated my announcement to Aer Lingus of my intention to resign from that Company.'

I enjoyed my work on the Workmens' Compensation Commission which, when I was appointed by Sean McEntee to it, had been in session – and it would seem in deadlock – for five years. Frustrated by this situation, I persuaded this body to appoint a working group, which I chaired, in order to speed up the work of reporting. As a result of this, the commission in fact reported two years later, providing the basis for subsequent legislation. My method of working as chairman of the working group, which proved effective, was to ask for the opinions of my fellow members of the working group on each point, and then to dictate in their presence an appropriate paragraph taking their views into account. Further comments from the members on that first draft were then incorporated through an iterative process that eventually produced an agreed text. I recommend this procedure to others who may have to face similar tasks!

The Senate Electoral Law Commission reflected de Valera's interest, towards the end of his period in government, in a possible revision of the composition of the Senate. He had abolished the Irish Free State Senate in 1936 but had revived it when he introduced his new Constitution in the following year. Of the sixty members of this new Senate eleven were appointed by the Taoiseach and three each were chosen by the graduates of each of the two universities NUI and TCD. The remainder were given a vocational veneer by being elected on five vocational panels, but as half of these were nominated by the members of the new Dáil and outgoing Senate, and as all of them were elected by a completely political electorate – members of the Dáil and Senate, and County (including County Borough) Councillors – the vocational veneer was thin.

This commission, comprised ten party politicians, ten non-politicians and a judge as chairman. Ralph Sutton, a barrister friend and son-in-law of John A. Costello, suggested to me that the two of us should present a hard man/soft man act. He would be the hard man, proposing that all forty-three panel senators be elected directly by vocational bodies, whilst I would deprecate his extremism and recommend a middle course involving only half being elected directly in that way. We calculated that the party politicians might then panic, fearing that the remainder of the body might support Ralph, and in order to avoid this fate might plump for my 'compromise' proposal.

This ploy proved remarkably successful. The party politicians fell into our trap and almost all signed a report recommending that twenty-three of the forty-three be not directly appointed by vocational bodies. (Brendan Corish did not sign the report and Vivion de Valera dissented from it). Ralph and I derived malicious pleasure from listening to the subsequent Senate debate on the report in the course of which the Fianna Fáil Senate leader, Tommy Mullins, denounced – as politically illiterate and rejected out of hand – the report that we had led him to sign!

Nothing ever came of the report, however. Whilst the commission was meeting Eamon de Valera resigned as Taoiseach in order to stand for the Presidency and his successor, Sean Lemass lacked any interest in Senate reform.

In 1961 I was appointed by Erskine Childers, then Minister for Transport and Power as well as Tánaiste, to be chairman of the Electricity Supply Board General Arbitration Tribunal.

Childers described the appointment to me as a 'sinecure' involving, perhaps, seven meetings a year with a fee of £750 a year. Having followed my new career since I left Aer Lingus (where, as the relevant minister, he had been impressed with the accuracy of my 1957 traffic forecasts for the new Transatlantic air route), Childers felt I deserved some recognition for my engagement with the public sector. He used to refer to me always as 'Dr FitzGerald' long before I completed my PhD.

(My father had been a member of the government that decided that his father, Erskine Childers Snr, should be executed during the Civil War for possession of a pistol that had been given to him by Michael Collins. As a boy in 1942 I had observed the friendly relationship that nevertheless existed between Erskine and my father when they met in Leinster House. The son had taken literally the father's Christian parting injunction to shake the hands of those responsible for his execution).

In fact there turned out to be over twenty meetings a year of the ESB Tribunal; although, even at that the chairmanship was well rewarded by the standards of the time. However, two years after my appointment to this position Joan saw an advertisement for an economic consultant to the Garda Representative Body – the organisation that was officially recognised as representing the basic rank in the police force for negotiating purposes – trade union membership being ruled out for the police. I applied for this position and was appointed.

Shortly afterwards Erskine Childers called me to his office. In the presence of the secretary of his department, Dr Thekla Beere, he told me that they both saw a possible conflict of interest between these two positions because a claim that I might prepare for the police could conceivably be quoted to me in a dispute that I might have to arbitrate in relation to the ESB! Whilst this contingency seemed somewhat remote, I had to admit that it was theoretically possible, and that I had failed to advert to it. I would, therefore, tell the Garda Representative Body immediately that I had to turn down their appointment. Whilst I regretted this outcome, I privately admired the careful concern of both civil servant and minister for the public interest.

However, ten days later I was again called to Childers' office. An embarrassed Tánaiste told me that my refusal of the appointment with the Garda Representative Body had led to a near mutiny. There had been serious industrial relations unrest in the Gardaí in the previous year as the promotion of some key members out of the Garda Representative Body to the rank of sergeant had been interpreted by some members of the force as an attempt by the authorities to weaken their negotiating position. My notification to them that I was turning down the post of economic consultant was now being interpreted as evidence of government interference. Childers went on to say that in the absence abroad of the recently appointed Minister for Justice, Charles Haughey, the Taoiseach, Sean Lemass, was personally handling this crisis and he had told Childers to direct me to take up the position that ten days earlier he had required me to turn down! I would, of course, have to resign from the chairmanship of the ESB Tribunal.

I accepted this direction – as it was somewhat curiously described – as being properly given in the public interest. He went on to say, that the Taoiseach and himself had recognised this would involve some financial loss and accordingly he had arranged with Ken Whitaker that in part compensation, I would be paid £500 for serving on a Transport Advisory Committee to which Childers had some time previously decided to appoint me. Virtue ultimately proved to be its own reward, for the Garda Body, pleased to have down-faced the government on the issue and to have secured my services, were concerned that I should not be at a loss and more than doubled their proposed fee to the same level as that of the ESB Tribunal chairmanship from which I was resigning!

The Transport Advisory Committee proved an interesting and in at least one respect entertaining appointment. It was to prepare the ground for transport policy in the Second Economic Programme, due to be launched in 1964. One of the issues we faced was the appropriate size of the state's strategic shipping fleet which immediately after the war (during which the absence of such a fleet had created grave problems), had been fixed at 250,000 tons of dry tonnage, later reduced to 200,000 tons. The actual dry tonnage at this time was 150,000 tons. I was concerned that this target of 200,000 – the basis for which the civil servants on the committee told me was contained in a file that had been lost – had never had any objective basis and I felt it should be verified before the fleet was further expanded by another 50,000 tons. So I suggested, only semi-frivolously, that our strategic tonnage needs should be calculated on the reasonably stringent assumption that the entire Northern Hemisphere and one third of our fleet was wiped out in a nuclear war, and that all our strategic requirements therefore would have to be brought from the Southern Hemisphere with the surviving two-thirds of the fleet. This calculation was duly made and the conclusion that emerged was that 160,000 tons of dry tonnage could supply our needs in these extreme circumstances so that our existing fleet would be adequate even if one-third of it were destroyed. It was proposed, however, that we should also acquire 80,000 tons of tanker tonnage – a need that had been overlooked when the post-war target had been set.

I was exceptionally fortunate to have had all these opportunities of public service before entering politics – opportunities in such diverse areas as industrial policy, transport policy, industrial relations, and European integration – not to speak of university politics! I suppose few Irish politicians have ever had the opportunity to acquire such a wide experience in public affairs before entering political life. In so far as my subsequent performance in politics may have fallen short of the standard of achievement I should like to have attained, the fault clearly lay with my character rather than with the experience that I brought to politics.

Of course the multiple activities that I was undertaking during these years as a lecturer, journalist and consultant were. demanding – and were to become even more so during the eight subsequent years when I added to these three careers a fourth, in politics. But I was young and energetic enough to take the strain, and I enjoyed the huge variety of activity involved. Moreover much of my work – preparing lectures, writing articles, undertaking research for consultancy clients and writing reports for them – could be undertaken at home; the house to which we had moved in Eglinton Road being within two miles of UCD in Earlsfort Terrace and of my EIU of Ireland office in Fitzwilliam Square and later in Herbert Place. Thus despite the pressures of my work I probably saw more of Joan and the children than previously when I had been working in the Aer Lingus head office in O'Connell Street and living further out of town in Booterstown Avenue. Furthermore when I had to travel on business to different parts of the country, Joan often accompanied me, as did the children from time to time. Indeed by about 1962 the two eldest, then 12 and 9 respectively, could count fifty hotels in different parts of Ireland in which they had stayed – and they applied their own test to distinguish hotels from guest houses. They defined a hotel as a building with at least two staircases that they could run up and down. The frequency of these family-accompanied journeys undoubtedly helped to account for our growing inability to live within our quite ample means during these years, but it helped to maintain the closeness of our family relationships.

We also made one such family-accompanied trip to the Continent around 1961 when I had to address a tourism conference in Lausanne and Montreux on behalf of the Tourist Board. I had hoped to introduce the children to Mme Camus on this occasion when passing through Paris. Almost a decade had passed since Joan and I had last seen her and her family because we had not been able to afford Continental holidays during the intervening years – but unhappily she was too ill and died shortly afterwards. In Geneva, however, Joan was able to show the children where she had passed four years of her childhood.

6

~: The Senate in Opposition :~
1965–69

My life up to 1964 had increasingly become a conscious preparation for politics. But I had no particular plan as to how I would go about becoming a politician. I had not even fully made up my mind as to which party I would join, although this decision may at an unconscious level have been more predetermined than I admitted to myself.

After 1948, for the mixture of reasons I set out in an earlier chapter, I had opted out of political activity, although I did have a peripheral involvement with Fine Gael when I was associated with a political journal the *National Observer*, which was strongly supportive of Fine Gael.

This was one of the periods when Fine Gael was going through a renewal of intellectual vitality, albeit in circumstances of minimal public support for the party. A Research and Information Council had been established which organised a series of public lectures in the Oak Room of the Mansion House. Declan Costello gave one on social policy.

But it seemed to me at that time that Fine Gael in its current incarnation was still not my cup of tea, although I recognised that at least since the end of 1956 it had attempted to approach our economic problems from a new angle, seeking to open our sheltered economy to the outside world by introducing tax reliefs on export earnings and extending industrial promotion grants, as well as initiating a process of tariff reviews.

When Fianna Fáil returned to office in mid-1957, Ken Whittaker who had been appointed secretary of the Department of Finance fourteen months earlier, presented his minister with a short memorandum which said very bluntly that unless they reversed key policies like industrial protection, the country would become such a failed economic entity that it might have no alternative but to apply for re-entry to the United Kingdom. That was an extraordinarily courageous warning to give a government led by Eamon de Valera – but his minister Jim Ryan, Sean Lemass and de Valera himself accepted his advice, reversing Fianna Fáil's quarter of a century old commitment to protection.

When Lemass took over from de Valera two years later he pursued free trade policies thereafter with the same vigour with which he had started the protection of infant industries a quarter-of-a-century earlier. Whatever my prejudices against Fianna Fáil, I had to admit that he was the best Taoiseach available for the purpose of initiating a long overdue process of economic growth. His partnership with Ken Whitaker (who, since his economic development thesis had been publicly adopted as the basis of the First Economic Programme, commanded great authority), was a remarkably constructive one. Reluctantly I felt obliged in 1961 to accord Lemass the support of my vote, giving my No. 1 preference in Dublin South East to my godmother's husband – the only occasion I ever voted Fianna Fáil!

That party failed to secure an overall majority in the 1961 election, although that did not prevent Lemass from governing in an unusually effective manner- despite being dependent for the next four years on the support of independents. Shortly afterwards, Charles Haughey approached me to ask if I would carry out an analysis for Fianna Fáil of why they did not do better in that election. I suspected – rightly I soon found out – that this was an attempt to draw me into the maw of that party, and I responded by proposing a fee of £100 for this consultancy work, thus making it clear that I was determined to maintain my political independence. He responded with a letter saying that this was not what he had in mind! He invited me to join the party, an invitation that I rejected.

The only other contact with Fianna Fáil came two years later when I was asked if I would contribute to a seminar on Irish language policy, to be organised by the party. I welcomed the opportunity to express my strong views in such a forum. I found myself flanked by two enthusiasts who favoured the revival of the language by a continued policy of making Irish essential for school-leaving examinations and public appointment purposes: Seán Ó Tuama and Donal Ó Morain. This stimulated me to an eloquent attack on this policy, not least because it was in my view clearly incompatible with any serious attempt to achieve Irish unity by consent. The Irish language requirement was, I believed, an insurmountable obstacle to Northern unionists, for almost all of whom the language was alien, and to many of whom its promotion appeared as a means of ensuring that they would be excluded, by virtue of their ignorance of its first national language, from full participation in the life of an Irish state comprising the whole island.

My two co-speakers naturally took a completely different stance, Seán Ó Tuama going so far as to say – with what appeared to me to be a lack of logic and/or patriotism – that if he thought the language would not be revived, he would emigrate!

After our speeches, the conference broke up into small working groups. When the time came to report back to the plenary session it quickly became apparent that a significant minority of the participants had, heretically, agreed with me. One working group chairman refused to report on behalf of his group because they had the temerity to favour a change of policy away from compulsion. Two others charged that I was an Orangeman in disguise – a curious reaction, I felt, to my passionate plea for a revision of policy with a view to removing what I saw as a roadblock to Irish unity! At the end I summed up by saying that I was pleasantly surprised that as many as one-third of those present seemed to agree with me; I did not expect, to convert Fianna Fáil in less than twenty years to realistic policies to reunite Ireland! On that aggressively contentious note I left – and was not asked back!

My only other political involvement during these years was in Northern Ireland in 1959. Michael McKeown, the founder of National Unity, a constitutional nationalist party that preceded the National Democrats, themselves a precursor of the SDLP, had invited me to address a party meeting, together with Harry Diamond, a Republican Labour MP for Belfast. As they could not afford to pay a fee for my talk, he offered me honorary membership of the party, which I accepted. It was thus the first political party that I joined.

During these years my childhood ambition to follow in my father's political footsteps, and my longstanding urge to challenge from within the political system the counterproductive irredentist anti-partitionism that defaced our politics, were reinforced by several new political aspirations. My experience of the efforts then in progress to prepare our industrial sector for free trade and to introduce a form of economic planning was bringing home to me increasingly the limits on administrative action, such as through bodies like the National Industrial Economic Council, as a means of effecting radical changes – and I believed that such radical changes were needed in attitudes and policies in order to prepare our society to take its place successfully within a dynamic European Community. I was coming to be convinced that only through politics could the necessary breakthrough to an efficient and open economy be made in Ireland.

Moreover, my social ideas had been undergoing something of a revolution. The conservatism and indeed clericalism of my youth had given way gradually to a much more liberal and progressive outlook. By 1964, instead of rejecting liberalism and socialism I was concerned to incorporate them into an integrated Irish philosophy of life. The views I had come to hold on these issues were set out in late 1964 in the journal *Studies*, edited by my old friend Father Burke-Savage SJ. Part of my motivation in publishing this article was a feeling that I ought before entering politics to give notice to my future colleagues of my basic political stance.

In this article I summed up in a typically long and convoluted sentence the views I had come to hold: 'Whether or not we succeed in developing a healthier and more positive relationship with our history (and in deriving a more positive inspiration from our past than is commonly the case today), the fact remains that we will have to look to more universal philosophies and wider traditions; first of all to the Christian tradition from which we derive the basic structure of our thought; to such traditions as British liberalism (whose emphasis on tolerance provides a new insight into the meaning of Christian charity) and to the socialist tradition which has helped to develop the sense of social consciousness inherent in Christian thought'. I went on to say that two negative features of Irish life particularly concerned me. First, the materialism of a society in which preoccupation with property loomed large, and, second, what I described as 'the strong anti-cultural bias of a large part of the community'.

I criticised the Catholic Church's excessive emphasis on the right to own private property – suggesting that it might be 'more appropriate to emphasise the corrupting power of property whose effects are at times glaringly evident among our farming community and among the middle classes ... Besides these materialistic preoccupations even the bitterness of some members of the working classes – and surprisingly few are bitter – appear in a favourable light'.

In 1968 I was to return to this issue of attitudes to property in an address on socialism. This was later republished in the *Irish Times* supplement commemorating the meeting of the first Dáil in January 1919 and its radical Democratic Programme, in the drafting of which the leader of the Labour Party, Thomas Johnson, had played a leading part. In this speech I raised the question of the compatibility of the accumulation and transmission of substantial volumes of property by inheritance with the attainment of equality of opportunity in society. Recognising the extreme difficulty of tackling this fundamental problem by an evolutionary process, I nevertheless rejected the revolutionary approach, both on the grounds that any benefits in the form of greater equity might be outweighed by the misery such revolutions create, and also because any attempts at radical social change by such methods would disrupt our small open economy, which was dependent upon our ability to compete in world markets and to attract foreign investment. Accordingly, I preferred to rely on education to change social attitudes in the direction of equity. In the meantime moves towards profit sharing and worker participation in industry and the introduction of a wealth tax applicable to perhaps five thousand large estates, as well as of a capital gains tax, would be small steps in the direction of social equity.

On the anti-intellectualism of Irish society I had said in the 1964 *Studies* article that 'this attitude finds expression in the flagrant pressure towards conformism in the schools, the discouragement of original thought or effort, the cult of the second-rate, the recurrent disregard for an instinct to destroy things of beauty', to which I added reference to 'the elevation of sport and drink to leading roles in society; and the lack of any adequate appreciation of the public as against the private interest'.

The Irish culture that I espoused would, I said, reject these attitudes; it 'would draw on the mixed origins of our society, Gaelic, Anglo-Irish and English, and would be neither exclusive nor sectional. It would glory in our mixed inheritance, despising none of it and elevating no part to a position of pre-eminence over the rest .... relations between North and South would be based on wholehearted acceptance of the principle that political unity must be preceded by a unity of hearts; the government of Northern Ireland as a provincial administration would meanwhile receive the unequivocal recognition that is its due'.

My decision to cross the rubicon and enter active politics was taken in April 1964. There was no immediately precipitating factor. It was just that the time had come, I felt, to make up my mind. I considered the choices: Fianna Fáil, Fine Gael or Labour. Whilst I admired Lemass and felt that he was the best person to lead the government at a time when economic growth was still the first priority, I felt that the future of that party was now firmly in the hands of two groups of politicians – conservative materialists and traditional nationalists – neither of whom were in tune with what seemed to me to be the needs of late 20th century Ireland. Those like Charles Haughey, who then seemed most likely eventually to secure the leadership of Fianna Fáil, and who were already providing a tough, hard core within the existing party structure were, it seemed to me, precisely the wrong people for these increasingly urgent tasks.

From my point of view Labour was far more compatible, but it was too closely linked to a sectoral group – the trade unions – to have the freedom to challenge aspects of our economic system, that were inhibiting economic growth, and it also seemed opposed to EEC membership.

That left as a candidate for this role Fine Gael – towards which, of course, for family reasons, my inclinations in any event drew me. In several respects it came closer to my model than either of the other parties: it had a tradition of less aggressive nationalism than Fianna Fáil, even if since 1948 it had fallen under the spell of irredentist anti-partitionism; it had a strong tradition of integrity – its founders having been people inspired primarily by a concern for the public interest as they saw it and by a revulsion against public office being used for private advantage. Thus in contrast to the new Fianna Fáil that was then emerging, there were reasonable grounds for believing that within Fine Gael there was a potential for resistance to both aspects of the materialist/nationalist axes in the government party.

That Fine Gael could become a force for social progress seemed less probable in 1964. Yet there had always been more radical elements within the party – at that time Paddy McGilligan was still a TD, and my contemporary, Declan Costello, committed to social justice, was a potential force within the party. Moreover, the sense of public service which remained strong within it could, I convinced myself, be mobilised in favour of more redistributive policies. And, if this could be achieved, a Fine Gael–Labour coalition might in time emerge to challenge Fianna Fáil on a more radical, more social democratic and more liberal platform.

Finally, with my family background it was clearly more likely that I would be able to influence the future of Fine Gael. Events ultimately justified my analysis, although not before I had gone through some personal trauma within the party in the late 1960s and early 1970s.

Having made my decision, I then pointed out to Joan that before we were married my friend Maurice Kennedy had warned her that if she committed herself to me she would end up in what he satirically described the Royal Box at Croke Park explaining the finer points of the game to the British ambassador – as wife of the Taoiseach – so she had been warned of my political ambition. Having secured Joan's reluctant, and at best, half-hearted concurrence, I took three initiatives.

A first move was to inform Ken Whitaker, who had since the late 1950s become in a sense my mentor. He was shocked, saying that if I entered politics I would lose the considerable power to influence events that I had acquired through my writings and my involvement with public affairs. He did not believe that this loss of influence would be compensated by any corresponding gain through playing a role in party politics or, eventually, in government. (He later admitted that he was wrong on this issue!).

My second contact was with Declan Costello. Our two fathers had been members of the same team at the Imperial Conferences of the 1920s and had served on the Fine Gael front bench together in the 1930s and early 1940s; as a boy I had been at one party at least in Declan's house and had crossed swords with him at a schools inter-debate in 1942; we had been friends in UCD in the mid-1940s, and we had worked together in the *National Observer* experiment in the late 1950s. I knew that he shared some at least of the views I had come to hold, and he was the point of access to me as far as Fine Gael was concerned.

Declan and I met for lunch in the Unicorn Restaurant. I told him of my intentions and he told me that he was at a critical point in his own relationship with Fine Gael. He had recently almost abandoned hope of its becoming a progressive party, but his father, John A. Costello, had said to him that before leaving it and joining Labour he should at least give Fine Gael a chance to decide where it stood, by putting to its leadership the issues which he wished them to adopt as party policy, so that they could make a clear decision for or against his ideas. Accordingly he had listed eight key points, and was now awaiting the party's reaction. He counselled me to postpone a decision until the results of this initiative emerged. I agreed. Shortly afterwards on 26 May 1964, the party, fearful of the effect of Declan's departure, announced its acceptance in principle of his eight points, authorised him to produce policy documents to flesh them out, and appointed a policy committee under the chairmanship of Liam Cosgrave to examine and review the policy documents in question as they emerged. Declan asked me to join the group he was establishing to prepare this material. I did so, happily postponing any decision on joining the party itself until the result of this exercise became clear.

My third contact was with the leader of Fine Gael – James Dillon – to ask him whether, if I joined the party I would be free to continue to reject the irredentist nationalist thesis that the future shape of Ireland should be determined by a majority in the island as a whole without regard to the wishes of a majority in Northern Ireland? On this point he reassured me.

The following nine months were a busy period as our somewhat heterogeneous group, who were bound together by one common factor, viz. admiration for Declan Costello and for his effort to give a new, contemporary relevance to Irish politics, struggled to produce a set of coherent policy documents covering a wide range of issues.

My own principal contribution was a paper favouring the introduction of a wealth tax with the double objective of encouraging a more productive use of capital, (an area in which the Irish economy was notably weak), and of improving, at least marginally, the distribution of wealth. This was not accepted by the party.

When in March 1965 Lemass called an election unexpectedly – partly, we believed, to pre-empt the emergence of a fully-fledged Just Society Policy – it was in effect Declan's proposals that formed the great bulk of the material put to the parliamentary party for adoption. The 30,000 word document eventually published covered economic planning, prices and incomes policy, banking and monetary policy, social capital investment, taxation, social welfare and health and youth policy.

Despite the qualms of many less adventurous spirits, Declan's policies were largely adopted by a party which had nothing else to offer to the electorate; Declan's move filled a policy gap, especially as no other policy initiatives seem to have been undertaken whilst awaiting the outcome of our group's work. On the night before the party decision Declan and I worked late with several others, preparing for typing and publication a concise and reasonably readable version of documents, the more extensive format of which had hitherto been governed by the need to explain the proposals in great detail to the parliamentary party. Even so, they were not terribly digestible in the form in which they emerged, but the novelty of a party producing a policy document of this type was sufficient to ensure a good reception for the Just Society Policy which was unveiled several days later.

Declan was naturally pleased that his policies had been accepted by the party, and that Fine Gael was to fight the election on this basis. But he was also sceptical about the full-hearted character of the party's conversion to his ideas. Some of this scepticism spread to me. I was approached to stand with his father in Dublin South East. Initially I accepted, but then, within 36 hours of the deadline for nomination, and influenced perhaps by Declan's doubts but also by Joan's unhappiness about such an abrupt entry into parliamentary politics, I withdrew.

Having thus pulled back from the brink, I transferred my attention to a different kind of election challenge: the presentation of the results of the election on television for the first time. I had already had some experience of this medium following the launching of Irish television at the beginning of 1962. Indeed Kevin O'Kelly (already in the 1950s a familiar figure to radio listeners and soon to be Religious Affairs Correspondent of RTÉ) and myself had contemplated setting up a TV production company in 1961, but nothing had come of this. I had appeared as an economic commentator in the early 1962 TV news bulletins until I discovered that there was no provision to pay me for appearances under the auspices of the news department! Then I had prepared and presented a series of programmes on the EEC, including interviews with the Taoiseach, Sean Lemass, the leader of Fine Gael, James Dillon, and the leader of the Labour Party, Brendan Corish. These interviews were carried out in the only studio then available in RTÉ, the small Studio 3, pressure on which was, however, so intense that another interview, with a British expert, Nicholas King Harman of the *Economist* had to be carried out in our drawing room in Eglinton Road. All appropriate precautions against interruptions were taken – someone was at the front door to ensure the door-bell was not rung and the phone was taken off the hook. Nevertheless, in the middle of the recorded interview there was an almighty crash. Hungry pigeons had knocked the lid off a dustbin – an event that we had failed to foresee! – and, as there was no spare film, that crash had to reverberate on the airwaves!

I was now anxious to play a full role in the first TV coverage of an Irish general election. I knew that, because of the Irish PR electoral system – which can involve up to fifteen or more counts in a constituency as surpluses are passed on from elected candidates and as the votes of eliminated candidates are distributed – the preparation and presentation of results visually would give rise to special problems. As since 1943 I had kept details not only of election results but also – possibly alone in the country – had also recorded at some past elections the time at which individual counts had been declared, I was in fact unusually well-qualified to undertake this task.

RTÉ agreed to employ me not only to comment on the results but also to help prepare the programme. I drew up 'shadow' results of the first seventy counts, which would bring us from a 5 PM start on the day after the election (when a few early counts would be available), to beyond the peak period for the flow of counts, which is around 6 to 7 PM. (Counting of votes does not start until 9 AM on the morrow of the election, and the first results do not emerge until that afternoon). At 10.30 AM on the day after the election we all gathered in studio to rehearse on the basis of my shadow results. Everything went wrong, including particularly, the computer. Finally at 12.25 PM the first shadow 'result' started to come in and we made our first comments. But at 12.30 PM a loud whistle blew and the staff all rushed to the exits. 'Fire?' I asked, alarmed. 'No, Lunch', said an RTÉ man, moving at high speed towards this repast.

So our rehearsal of commenting on the results never actually took place. Nevertheless, the exercise proved of value, for in those two hours in the morning the 'bugs' had been got out of the system, and from 5 o'clock onwards the results flowed smoothly. This was, however, largely because at a certain points I deliberately absented myself, from the panel of commentators and as at that early stage in its history RTÉ did not seem to have worked out what to do in those circumstances, they had to await my return before resuming the commentary!

Since the start of the 1950s Joan and I had always held a party at home for both Irish and British election results, and I did not want to be absent too long from my own party after my initial TV appearance – of which my guests had known nothing until I suddenly appeared on the TV screens in our drawing-room and study!

That was, I think, the last time that all the counts were shown on television. Most later TV election programmes, on all of which until 1997 I appeared, in a somewhat different, party political, capacity, gave precedence to comment as distinct from results, despite my repeated protests. This has left serious psephologist viewers in a state of perpetual apoplexy as they found themselves deprived of information on crucial counts that would enable them to forecast the likely final outcome in marginal constituencies – and under the Irish PR system a majority of constituencies are marginal for some party.

A week after the 1965 general election Joan and I were dining in a restaurant with Alexis FitzGerald and other friends. During dinner the restaurant's phone rang; it was Declan Costello, in Leinster House to say that at successive front bench and parliamentary party meetings James Dillon had announced his resignation as party leader after his second general election defeat, and that Liam Cosgrave had immediately been elected in his place.

We were all taken aback; in so far as James Dillon's retirement had been anticipated, and most of us had not seriously expected it so soon after the election, it had been assumed that an interval would follow this event in order to give time for candidates for the leadership to emerge, and that in those circumstances Declan Costello would have had a good chance of being elected by the parliamentary party.

When Liam Cosgrave himself resigned twelve years later he proposed a week's delay before the election of his successor, and in a new Constitution I put to the party in 1978 I made provision for a similar procedure that would avoid the criticism to which the 1965 succession procedure was subjected.

Shortly after the general election Declan Costello and his brother-in-law, Alexis FitzGerald, suggested that I should run for the Senate – the election to which occurs about two months after a Dáil general election. I demurred, as my professor,

George O'Brien, would be standing again for one of the three National University of Ireland seats and I would not put his election at risk. For some reason it had not struck me that I could stand for election by another route, but my friends suggested that as a Fine Gael candidate I should seek a nomination from a vocational body, and thus stand on a Nominating Bodies Sub-Panel for election by the members of the incoming Dáil, and the outgoing Senate, and the County and County Borough Councillors – an electorate of some 872 persons at that time, of whom some 300 were Fine Gael. Liam Cosgrave, the new party leader, was in favour of my candidature.

Having discussed this proposal with Joan, and having secured her somewhat unenthusiastic consent, I set about seeking a nomination from a vocational body. I was rather late in the field and most of the organisations with which I had had some contact in the preceding years had either already given their nominations to a candidate or candidates, or else had decided not to make a nomination.

After a couple of days of fruitless contacts I rang the secretary of the Irish Hotels Federation. I had been undertaking some consultancy work for that body during the previous eighteen months, although I had not yet sent them a bill. The secretary, F. X. Burke, was someone I had known for years; he was indeed a somewhat remote family connection – an in-law of an in-law. He told me that the council of the Federation had in fact decided not to make a nomination but that, as I was their consultant, he would call a special meeting forthwith to decide whether to reconsider that decision.

My initiative provoked several reactions within the Federation. Those who were unhappy with the idea of a party candidate put forward the Federation's current president, Barry McDonnell of the Park Hotel, Virginia, as a non-party candidate, in full recognition of the fact that if nominated he would not be elected. And Fianna Fáil in their turn put forward a Tipperary ex-hotelier, Des Hanafin – father of Minister Mary Hanafin.

When this 'field' emerged I did a telephone canvass of the members of the council on the night before the council meeting, taking advantage of the late hours kept by hoteliers to continue this process until 1 am I also rang Todd Andrews, chairman of the Peat Production Board, Bord na Móna – a radical Fianna Fáil republican with whom I had a good relationship despite the antipathy he had felt towards my father since the Civil War. I asked him whether, despite the fact, which could hardly please him, that I was entering politics in the Fine Gael interest, he would approach his hotelier son, Chris, in Limerick to support me. He at once agreed to do so.

At the council meeting an initial vote to reduce the field from three to two led to the elimination of the Fianna Fáil candidate, and I won the 'run-off' by seven votes to six against the non-party candidate, Barry McDonnell. One of those who voted for me was an apolitical hotelier, Billy Kelly of the Strand Hotel, Rosslare, who may have been influenced to do so, against his natural inclination, by virtue of the fact that I had recently become a client. If so, I benefited in a quite unexpected way from our family decision to change our usual summer holiday arrangements in 1964, abandoning the pattern of the previous decade, when we had spent a month every summer in a rented seaside cottage at Bettystown, County Meath, in favour of a more gregarious holiday at Billy Kelly's Strand Hotel in Rosslare.

The nomination secured, I set about canvassing votes, for it is a well-established fact that without personal contact with the individual members of the political electorate throughout the country, a Senate candidate has no hope of securing support. In the following twenty nine days I made ten sorties from Dublin, driving some 4,000 miles backwards and forwards across the country, calling on over 250 Fine Gael county councillors and almost a hundred others. (Most of the TD and senator nominations had already been committed at that stage so that I had to depend mainly on the county council vote for my election).

Whilst working to secure a nomination I had been plotting the dwellings of these county councillors on half-inch-to-a-mile Ordnance Survey maps of the country, pinpointing the precise location of each councillor with the aid of the expert knowledge of local TDs and of a little-known atlas and gazzeteer of Ireland which my father had acquired for the use of his underground Propaganda Department in 1920. This preliminary mapping made it possible to devise route plans that would minimise the amount of driving involved. The canvass was, incidentally, greatly facilitated by the fact that over 80 percent of the voters were at home when I called, regardless of the hour of the day. This reflected the fact that very many of them were farmers, shopkeepers or publicans, living at their places of work – and also, perhaps, a combination of courtesy and curiosity that encouraged them to make themselves as available as possible to the dozens of Senate candidates seeking their votes. Part of my canvass was undertaken in the company of my friend Alexis FitzGerald, who at my counter-suggestion had secured a nomination on another panel. Moreover on some of the journeys Joan and the three children accompanied me.

I did not quite know what to expect on this canvass; I had heard many stories about Senate campaigns, but did not know enough to distinguish fact from fantasy, truth from reality. In the event many of the more alarming stories turned out to be myths; for example although I was offered countless cups of tea, only six alcoholic drinks were pressed on me. One story turned out to be well-founded, however, viz. that the number of first preference votes I would receive would be 90 percent of the number of which I was 'certain' and 50 percent of the number I thought I 'might' get. In the event, I felt hopeful about 130 voters who had not turned me down and 'certain' of just over seventy, both of which suggested an actual vote of sixty-five. In the event I received sixty-four votes!

Towards the end of the campaign I became sufficiently confident of this formula to cease canvassing when I reached that point, because with anything over
fifty-five first preferences I should be reasonably certain of election. I did this
because I had reason to believe that many of my votes were at the expense of a sitting Fine Gael senator, Ned McGuire, and given his importance to the party as a
Senate front-bencher and main party fundraiser, I did not wish to deprive him of
his seat. In the event my act of self-denial proved fruitless, for, securing only forty
votes, he lost his seat – partly, it was said, because he had spent some of the brief
campaign period cruising around the Greek islands.

My success in getting elected to the Senate at a first attempt was due to a combination of factors. I was already relatively well-known because of my journalistic
work. Indeed one Fine Gael councillor spontaneously promised me his vote as soon
as I approached him, when I found him beside the road cutting his hedge. His ready
commitment was on the stated basis of my occasional articles in the Fianna Fáil-
oriented *Sunday Press*. After twenty minutes chat something I said revealed that I
was standing as a Fine Gael candidate. At that he expressed great relief – he would
have voted for me anyway, he said, but now, knowing my party label, he could do
so with a clear conscience!

About twelve of my first preference votes were, I felt, quite clearly the consequence of my ten-hour stint on the Dáil general election TV results programme.
And a small number of votes in Carlow-Kilkenny, where my father had been a TD
from 1932 to 1937, came from older councillors who had known him and had
worked for him there.

But a significant number – enough to make the difference between success and
failure – were the product of a piece of advice given to me at the outset by Liam
Cosgrave. The only likely candidate from the west on my panel was an auctioneer,
the late Miko Brown from Ballina, who was seeking a nomination from the Fine
Gael parliamentary party – a process which for tactical reasons is not undertaken by
any of the parties until all the 'outside' nominations (viz. nominations from the
vocational bodies), are completed. He told me that Miko would almost certainly
not secure an Oireachtas nomination, and he advised that I should therefore start
my campaign in the west, looking for 'No. 2s behind Miko', which might be fairly
willingly conceded. A modest approach of this kind, sensitive to the prior claim of
a regional 'favourite son', would win me sympathy which should ensure the translation of most of any promised second preference votes into first preferences if and
when Miko failed to get past the starting gate. And so it turned out.

I should, perhaps, add that the standard not merely of courtesy but also of honesty of the voters was very high. Half of the Fine Gael voters whom I approached
told me they were committed to other candidates and a further one-quarter, while
courteous enough to enable me to mark them in as 'possibles', had been careful not

to commit themselves unequivocally. Only a quarter were firm promises, and my eventual vote was equal to 90 percent of this latter figure.

I had not confined my canvass to Fine Gael voters. I also canvassed Labour voters for second preferences (there was only one Labour candidate on my panel), and received almost one-third of these preferences – far more than my proportionate share. I also canvassed independents but without much success, I felt. I wrote to most members of the Fianna Fáil government, and to some Fianna Fáil backbenchers whom I knew, suggesting that they might find me less unacceptable than some other more entrenched Fine Gael candidates and, that, if so, they might register this fact in the allocation of their later preferences – for under our proportional representation system even the later preferences of votes of one's opponents can sometimes affect the outcome as between oneself and others of the same party. I received in return some very friendly letters from ministers and other Fianna Fáil TDs and I believe that in a few cases I may have been given a preference by some of these Fianna Fáil voters ahead of some of their own less-favoured party candidates.

However that may be, I was in any event declared elected on 10 June and attended my first Senate meeting several weeks later. In the meantime Liam Cosgrave had appointed me as one of six Senate front bench members, with full participation in Fine Gael front bench meetings. As a result my first time ever to sit on the back benches was after my resignation from the leadership of the party in March 1987, twenty-two years later!

The Fine Gael members of the new Senate were briefed by Liam Cosgrave before the first session. I recall afterwards asking the late Jim Dooge how I could know if I was keeping in line with party policy, given that in many areas this policy seemed unspecific. 'Make it up' was his half-humorous response – as he claimed he had himself done on many an occasion.

My entry into politics through the Senate rather than the Dáil had several advantages. First, the election process brought me into immediate touch with elements of the party – and indeed of other parties – throughout the country. For a Dubliner with limited experience of the rest of the country this was a great bonus; I was sensitised straight away to a whole range of problems and issues with which I was either unfamiliar, or which, if I already knew of them, tuned out to have dimensions that I had not fully appreciated. I also learnt much about regional differences, in temperament and character as well as in interests. And I rapidly came to appreciate the kindness and courtesy of members of the party throughout the country.

Secondly, the less partisan atmosphere of the Senate as compared with the Dáil, suited a political neophyte like myself. I was not required, nor expected, to make propaganda speeches or to spout political rhetoric in the House. In respect of the great bulk of legislation my task was rather to examine it critically but constructively; the former accorded well with my argumentative disposition; the later with my natural instinct as an academic.

During the twelve months between my election to the Senate and the following year's presidential election I came to grips with my membership of the party's front bench. Much to my disappointment my mentor, Declan Costello, had withdrawn from the front bench while I had been campaigning for the Senate. A combination of unhappiness with what he perceived as an inadequate commitment amongst his colleagues to his Just Society policy, and health problems, had prompted this decision, which left me in a somewhat isolated position within the parliamentary party.

I soon found the party's new leader, Liam Cosgrave, open to some of my ideas, however, and before long I was working closely and harmoniously with him, and with progressive elements in the party's leadership. In 1966, when a second attempt to achieve British, Irish and Danish membership of the European Community was initiated, I persuaded him to go with me on a visit to the European Commission in Brussels. We found Commissioner Jean Rey very well informed about the Irish situation: he even quoted from a recent Senate debate on Europe that I had initiated. This debate had persuaded the government to establish a separate diplomatic mission to the EEC, something that the Minister for External Affairs, Frank Aiken, had turned down when proposed at a Fianna Fáil parliamentary meeting a week or two earlier.

I was now beginning to find my feet in the Senate as a member of the Fine Gael front bench in that assembly. The two other active members of this front bench were Ben O'Quigley, the party's leader in that House, who was a barrister, and Jim Dooge, professor of Civil Engineering and a hydrologist of world reputation, who was also vice-chairman of the Senate. Because Jim Dooge had frequently to be in the chair, and because by convention as vice-chairman he was expected to avoid serious controversy, the brunt of opposition fell on Ben O'Quigley and myself. And when, in the month of July every year, the Senate had to handle a rush of legislation from the Dáil after its summer adjournment, Ben O'Quigley was on circuit to Mayo. If, as happened occasionally, Jim Dooge was also away, lecturing in the United States or Australia, I could find myself handling all the legislation coming to the House. On one occasion I dealt with seven different Bills in a single day!

In all this I was accorded a wide discretion. Most legislation does not involve matters of party policy and one is free to tackle the task of constructive opposition, trying simply to improve the quality of the legislation. A common thread tended to run through many of the debates, however. Fianna Fáil, possibly because it had been in office for twenty-seven of the previous thirty-three years, tended to favour an approach that gave maximum power to the Executive – a position that most civil servants also tended to favour. Fine Gael, by contrast had an instinct for a more open and democratic approach and for conceding a greater role to bodies independent of government. Sharing this instinct I found it easy to pursue a fairly consistent opposition line in the Senate, and enjoyed the mild rough and tumble of debates, especially when they centred on this kind of issue.

I soon found the self-confidence to strike out on my own on certain issues – for example arguing in connection with the 1966 Broadcasting Bill, that, if we believed in a united Ireland, RTÉ should be expected to give one-third of its time to Northern Ireland politics and almost a quarter to the views of Northern unionism! This *jeu d'esprit* evoked no response from the government side, but, equally, no one on my own side demurred at my expression of such heterodox views.

There were often lighter moments, too. In a debate on corporal punishment a Fianna Fáil senator repeatedly asserted that although he had frequently been 'bet' (beaten) at school it had never done him any harm. He said it once too often for Senator Bedell Stanford of Trinity College, normally the kindest and most courteous of men, who rose to remark that if corporal punishment had not done the harm to the senator, he wondered what exactly had done it?!

Shortly before Christmas 1967 word came through at lunchtime of King Constantine's attempted coup against the Greek Colonels. I decided on my own initiative to put down a congratulatory motion. When a few minutes later Fine Gael senators came in to our weekly meeting in advance of the Senate session, I invited them to sign my hastily drafted motion, calculating correctly that none of them would query my authority for this action. Our Senate leader, Ben O'Quigley, who I knew would have opposed such a move being made without party authority, was absent at a Christmas lunch given by the Cathaoirleach (Speaker). All went well until I rose in the House after the prayer to propose my motion. Ben O'Quigley, back from lunch, reacted instantly, pulling me down by my coat-tails and hissing 'You can't propose a motion without party authority'. By the time I had pulled a bemused Liam Cosgrave out of his Dáil front bench seat and secured his authority, it was too late for that day. The coup collapsed and all I could do on the following day was to rise to express regret at the failure of the counter-coup.

Next day I gave my last pre-Christmas lecture to the second commerce class in UCD. There was a lot of shouting and singing in the corridor outside, which for a reason that escaped me at the time, caused hilarity in the class, to such a degree that I had to call them to order – something I had not previously needed to do. They subsided, somewhat mutinously. Afterwards I discovered that the song being sung outside was 'The King and I' – a hit at my Senate motion, the point of which I had however missed because of my failure to identify the tune. After Christmas I apologised to the class for my musical deficiencies.

My entry to politics through the Senate had left me ill-prepared for two aspects of politics: making partisan speeches at public meetings out of doors, and involvement with the party organisation. It was, indeed only the approach of a presidential election, in May 1966 that brought me to a realisation of the curious fact that although by then I was a well-established member of the Fine Gael front bench, I had never got around to joining the party itself. Clearly I must, however belatedly, find my local organisation, and through it join the party.

Accordingly I went to see my local TD, former Taoiseach John A. Costello, to ask him how I should go about joining Fine Gael in Dublin South East. His response was, as usual, forceful, blunt and idiosyncratic: 'forty years in Fine Gael, twice Taoiseach; never joined Fine Gael'. Somewhat timorously I suggested that times were changing and that his precedent was not necessarily the best one for me to follow. Reluctantly, and perhaps with a hint of disappointment at my conventional approach to politics, he conceded that there was a Fine Gael organisation in Dublin South East and that if I turned up at the Morehampton Hotel on the following Thursday I would find the Constituency Executive meeting there.

I followed his directions, and so found my local organisation. It was a small meeting of mostly fairly elderly people. But one young man was there; a nephew and namesake of my friend Alexis FitzGerald, who soon afterwards became my director of organisation and set about creating a machine that could fight the next general election. Our efforts at local level in the presidential election a few weeks later were less than impressive, however.

To my dismay I was called on to play a small part in this larger campaign at national level, by joining our presidential candidate, Tom O'Higgins (later to become co-grandfather with me to five grandchildren) on the trail through Wicklow, with speeches in Bray, Wicklow and Arklow, as well as later on at a final rally outside the G.P.O. in O'Connell Street. Whilst during the previous decade I had acquired considerable experience as a public speaker, especially about the EEC, the idea of addressing outdoor meetings as a partisan political speaker terrified me. Indeed I never acquired any facility for this kind of oratory, and throughout my whole political career remained as uncomfortable at outdoor political rallies and meetings as I was happy to speak at indoor meetings, especially those of a non-partisan character.

Whether my unhappiness at outdoor meetings was due to the acoustic problem because of the lack of resonance out of doors, or to the sense of a fugitive and non-captive audience I do not know. But at my very first such meeting my discomfort was magnified by virtue of the fact that the meeting was held outside the Royal Hotel in Bray and that friends of mine – Tony and Eilis McDowell, parents of Michael McDowell – had chosen to come to listen to me whilst dining in comfort at a window table in the hotel dining-room, right beside the platform – which, incidentally was also beside the courthouse where my late father had received his first gaol sentence fifty two years earlier!

This presidential campaign brought into political prominence for the first time two young men: Michael Sweetman and Peter Prendergast. Peter Prendergast was a marketing consultant, active in Tom O'Higgins's Dublin South constituency organisation, who acted as a personal aide-de-camp and unofficial campaign manager, gaining experience that proved relevant to his subsequent career, for in 1977, after I became leader of the party, I appointed him as general secretary and national organiser. He was responsible in very large measure for the remarkable recovery of Fine Gael between 1977 and 1981 which brought me into government as Taoiseach in June 1981.

Michael Sweetman was a cousin of Gerard Sweetman, Fine Gael Minister for Finance in the 1954–57 coalition government and a leading front bench member of the party. Michael was poles apart from his much older cousin, however; he was a liberal intellectual whereas Gerard Sweetman was a pragmatically conservative businessman. A member of the family who had been politically prominent at an earlier period was Michael's grandfather, Roger Sweetman, an MP of the Irish Parliamentary Party who had come to support separatist Sinn Féin after 1916, and whose home at Derrybawn, near Glendalough, had much earlier been a shooting lodge rented by Joan's brewing grandfather in the late nineteenth and early twentieth century.

Michael Sweetman was a somewhat improbable figure in politics, especially because of his deceptively languid manner, which certainly fooled me when I first met him as a representative of the Export Promotion Board, Coras Trachtala, at a hosiery and knitwear conference in Copenhagen in 1963. (I was attending as Chairman of the Hosiery and Knitwear Council, established following the CIO report on that industry to prepare it for free trade conditions).

But in the interval between 1963 and 1966 Joan and I had got to know Michael – and his wife Barbara – well and to admire enormously the skill with which as a policy adviser and speech-writer he had sought to centre the presidential campaign of 1966 around the concept of a pluralist society. He had a markedly original mind, an unselfconscious lack of convention, and a mischievous sense of humour. He had no time for the conventional pieties or sacred cows of Irish politics. He was a unique and very attractive figure – and his premature death in 1972 in the Staines air disaster – together with those of half a dozen key business figures, was a huge loss to Ireland.

The combination of Tom O'Higgins, as candidate, Michael Sweetman as adviser and speech-writer, and Peter Prendergast as campaign organiser presented a major challenge to Eamon de Valera, seeking a second seven-year term of office at the age of eighty-four. As a retiring Taoiseach in 1959 de Valera had achieved a convincing win over General Sean MacEoin, Fine Gael frontbencher and hero of the War of Independence. But seven years in the relative obscurity of the Presidency, with but one major highlight in the form of the visit of President Kennnedy in

1963, had left him more vulnerable, especially with the younger generation, to whom Tom O'Higgins, in his late forties, with a large young family seemed a more attractive candidate. The tone of Tom O'Higgins' speeches, with their emphasis on moving away from a traditional inward-looking nationalism to a more open and pluralist concept of Irish society, also struck a chord with that generation. He was a candidate well-suited to the 1960s.

Tom had one handicap, however. Few people believed that de Valera could be beaten, so, as his campaign prospered, this was seen by many as a merely a bold but inevitably fruitless challenge. Even in the Fine Gael organisation itself – heartened though it was by the unexpected success of the campaign – there were many sceptics, and while in general the effort put forward was remarkable, in some constituencies it fell short of an all-out effort. And it was these patches of scepticism on the political map that eventually cost him the election, in which he came within 0.5 percent of defeating de Valera.

However, this presidential election had a significant impact on Fine Gael. It strengthened the progressive wing within the party, for it showed that more adventurous policies could attract votes, contrary to the conventional wisdom of the old guard. And it added to Declan Costello's social democracy a liberal element that was to remain an enduring factor within the party thenceforward.

This need not have proved divisive. Parties like Fine Gael and Fianna Fáil have a capacity to accommodate significant ideological differences without undue tension. In the event, however, it worked out differently and divisively. One theory prevalent in the party was that in the aftermath of this election, during the summer of 1966, something of a vacuum developed within the top level of Fine Gael. Tom O'Higgins took a well-deserved long holiday. At the same time my close relationship with Liam Cosgrave seemed to alter. There has been speculation that this may have been due to the invention by a political columnist 'Backbencher' (John Healy) in the *Irish Times* – then approaching the height of his career as a commentator on the political scene – of a phrase 'FitzCosgrave' to describe my relationship with my party leader. This phrase, implying that I was now a major influence on him, could have had a negative effect on any politician sensitive about his image – as all politicians have to be to some degree!

I had been talking to Brendan Halligan about the possibility of a coalition between Fine Gael and Labour – without which prospect it was hard to see public opinion swinging away from Fianna Fáil sufficiently to put them in a clear minority and thus enable an alternative government to emerge. Opposition to a coalition was strong in Labour, Brendan Halligan had told me. In the course of a later discussion Brendan said, however, that his soundings were now showing support for the concept of a coalition, but that Labour would not serve under Liam Cosgrave as Taoiseach.

The receipt of this information appeared to me to pose something of a moral dilemma. Loyalty to Liam Cosgrave seemed to require that he be made aware of this assessment, which could reasonably influence his thinking about the relationship with Labour. I recognised, however, that the bringer of such tidings would not make himself very popular, and prudence suggested that I might be better to keep this information to myself.

I decided to seek advice as to what I should do, and accordingly approached James Dillon, the former leader of the party. (Both James Dillon and the former Taoiseach, John A. Costello, were still members of the Dáil at that time, each occupying a room on the Fine Gael corridor).

I told James my story, and asked what he thought I should do. His reply, delivered as sonorously as were all his pronouncements, left me no wiser: 'Remember 1879, Garret', he said. I racked my brains but could not offhand recall any event in that year relevant to my problem. I confessed my puzzlement. He explained that in that year his father, John Dillon, had apparently helped to plot the removal of Isaac Butt as leader of the Irish Parliamentary Party, and his replacement by Parnell. The lesson I was to draw from this event, of which he clearly disapproved, was the importance of loyalty to the party leader; I should tell Liam Cosgrave what I had heard. I took the advice. This may not have helped our subsequent relationship.

Into this temporary vacuum, so the conventional wisdom in Fine Gael ran, stepped a forceful character – Michael Sweetman's cousin, Gerard Sweetman. His relationship with Liam Cosgrave during the preceding decade was said to have been clouded because of some disagreement about the appointment of Liam's father, former government leader, W. T. Cosgrave, to the Racing Board – a matter which had fallen within Gerard Sweetman's competence as Minister for Finance a decade earlier. But now, in the summer of 1966, whatever coolness may have previously existed between the two men seemed to evaporate. Certainly by the autumn of 1966 Gerard Sweetman was firmly installed as organiser of the party – a position for which his forceful personality well fitted him.

Gerard Sweetman was not an ideological right-winger but rather a politician with a business orientation and a practical interest in winning power for his party. He was tough, and had little instinctive sympathy with the younger generation – above all with the liberal youth of the 1960s. He had no malice in him, and did not bear grudges, but in what he conceived to be the interests of the party he could be quite ruthless. My relationship with him was a combative, but not unfriendly, one. When from time to time we were in agreement on an issue he would tell the rest of the front bench that as we two agreed, further argument was pointless!

Thus from autumn 1966 onwards a certain tension began to develop within the party. It would be wrong to exaggerate its significance in this early period. Only in retrospect, when some years later a fairly clear-cut division emerged, were the roots of this division traced back to the autumn of 1966.

It was in November of that year that I had my first experience of a by-election. Teddy Lynch, the Fine Gael TD for Waterford had died and we were contesting the election with a young candidate, Eddie Collins. Waterford City had remained a Redmondite stronghold during the half-century after the 1918 defeat of the Irish Parliamentary Party and the subsequent death of its leader, John Redmond. His son, Willie Redmond, had represented Waterford for some years, followed for many years thereafter by his widow, to be followed in turn by Thady Lynch, also in the Redmondite tradition. Eddie Collins came from the same background.

So strong was the Redmondite factor that when I arrived in Waterford, accompanied by Alexis FitzGerald and a number of UCD students, including Vincent Browne, we were told that in a number of areas we should seek votes for 'Eddie Collins, John Redmond's man', without stressing the Fine Gael connection. I still remember the response in one house when the door was opened by an elderly woman: 'Of course I'll vote for Eddie Collins; haven't I got John Redmond's picture at the top of the stairs, beside the Sacred Heart'!

At that time Vincent Browne was an enthusiastic Fine Gael supporter. On one occasion we were waiting outside a church for the end of Mass, with my car and loudspeaker well-placed, I thought, facing the church door, so that I could in due course address the departing congregation. After Holy Communion some people started to emerge through the open door of the church, Vincent, thinking that Mass had ended, started to introduce me from the bonnet of the car with the aid of the loud speaker, his voice booming right up the aisle to the altar. In an effort to halt his booming eloquence I grabbed his leg – my voice could not reach him over the loud-speaker – with such vigour that, according to him, I tore his trousers!

Alexis FitzGerald, whose father had been superintendent of the mental hospital in Waterford, introduced me to those present after Mass at another church. Unfortunately an FCA (Local Defence Force) parade followed the Mass. Apart from the parade, only seven other people stayed, probably to watch the parade rather than to hear us. Fearful that they would disappear if we didn't address them before the parade marched off, Alexis climbed on the bonnet of my car, and, over the heads of the parading soldiers and the shouts of command, introduced me in jovial terms not calculated to appeal to Waterford's solemn burghers.

'As one born under the mental hospital clock in Waterford, and therefore mad enough to be addressing you here today, I want to introduce Senator Garret FitzGerald'. Not a flicker of a smile from the audience. Humour, as we found elsewhere during this campaign was not appreciated by political audiences.

Later on, at another after-Mass meeting in Ferrybank, my effort to poke fun at the pomposity of the black-overcoated and black-hatted Fianna Fáil team addressing the crowd before us, provoked a furious reaction from a respectable Fine Gael member who must have been chairman of the local branch 'You're destroying Fine Gael in Waterford', he hissed at me. 'Why can't you be like them', pointing to the Fianna Fáil group. 'And you haven't even asked me to chair your meeting' – clearly the ultimate offence.

Incidentally, it was during that by-election that I learnt for the first time, from two women I canvassed in different parts of the city, that my paternal grandfather came from the borders of Tipperary and Limerick – and I also met a third woman who had known my father in London almost sixty years earlier.

In October 1967 I was appointed a member of an electoral strategy committee to make recommendations on the whole field of policy, tactics, organisation, publicity, selection of candidates etc. The most urgent matter seemed to us to be the possible consequences of a Fianna Fáil proposal to attempt to reverse the negative decision of the electorate on Fianna Fáil's 1959 proposal to substitute for proportional representation by preferential voting (1, 2, 3 etc. in order of your choice in multi-seat constituencies), the British X voting system in single-seat constituencies.

Jim Dooge prepared an analysis of the likely electoral effect of such a change. I worked with him on this task. On 13th December the report was presented to a meeting attended only by Jim Dooge, Tom O'Higgins, Gerard Sweetman and myself, together with the party general secretary, Jim Sanfey. In the light of the fact that the report showed that with this new system Fianna Fáil would win 80 of the 144 seats in single-seat constituencies even if the alternative vote were retained – and something like 96 if the British X-vote system were introduced, those present went to Liam Cosgrave to propose the opening of talks with Labour on how to confront this threat. He agreed and said he would seek discussions with the Labour leader, Brendan Corish if, as was then expected, the government announced on that day a decision to hold a referendum on this issue. Preliminary contact was made with Brendan Corish.

During the following weekend I discussed the situation with Brendan Halligan who at that stage felt that the suggestion of a Fine Gael-Labour alliance was premature by several years and that it could lead to a split in Labour, and was therefore unlikely to be accepted. Brendan Corish felt that whatever chance there might be of getting agreement, a short-term link would certainly be of no interest. Only a long-term or permanent link – perhaps even a merger – would have any chance. According to Brendan Halligan those in Labour favouring a merger were Barry Desmond, Noel Browne, Sean Dunne, Stephen Coughlan and Michael Pat Murphy, with Mickie Mullen perhaps persuadable. Jimmy Tully I was told was hostile, but his attitude could change in the event of a referendum on PR.

On 3 January 1968 a crucial meeting of the Fine Gael front bench took place, which continued from eleven in the morning until five in the afternoon. Mark Clinton suggested a merger, although he knew nothing of the views on this subject that had been expressed by Brendan Halligan and Michael O'Leary. Jim Dooge and Tom O'Higgins supported the idea of exploring this possibility. Gerard Sweetman opposed it, adding that as a trustee of the party he would not agree to provide money to fight for PR in a referendum – only to be pulled up by Michael O'Higgins, Tom's brother, who pointed to the impropriety of a trustee seeking to use that position to seek to determine party policy. Three others expressed reservations about such a close link with Labour, but at the end only Maurice Dockrell persisted.

On the separate issue of whether to reject a government proposal to replace PR by a single-seat system with an alternative vote, a private sounding that I carried out at Liam Cosgrave's request during the meeting showed ten members in favour of retaining PR, two not strongly, as against eight favouring the alternative vote in single-seat constituencies – including Liam Cosgrave himself and Gerard Sweetman.

After the front bench I phoned Brendan Halligan, who recommended an immediate meeting between Liam Cosgrave and Brendan Corish. I passed this on to Liam Cosgrave who, however, did not contact Brendan Corish until the following evening when he reached him in his hometown of Wexford. They agreed to meet on Tuesday 9 January when Brendan Corish would be back in Dublin.

'On the following Tuesday Liam Cosgrave phoned me to say that he had talked to Brendan Corish, who was not encouraging, but sought a proposal in writing. However, a few minutes after they had parted, Brendan Corish had rung to withdraw this request, saying that he was making a speech that night which would cut across the proposal for an arrangement between the parties.

I rang Halligan and at his suggestion went to see Brendan Corish in Leinster House. He was discouraging, fearing that word of talks would get out and would damage Labour. He would be glad to see people like Declan Costello, Tom O'Higgins, Paddy Harte, Oliver Flanagan (in my contemporary notes I placed an exclamation mark after that name!), and myself in Labour, but a merger of the two parties would be very difficult. However, he would put it to his front bench on the following day and would ring me afterwards.

He did so the following afternoon, saying 'nothing doing', adding that he hoped there would be no more approaches from us as in that event they would have to issue a denial. Subsequently Jim Downey of the *Irish Times* told me that the proposal had been defeated by a small majority, but I never got confirmation of this.

And so Fine Gael and Labour have ever since gone their separate paths, although they served in coalitions together on several subsequent occasions. Had this move succeeded the political history of the succeeding years would surely have been very different.

Fianna Fáil went on to launch their referendum on the electoral system, hoping to reverse their narrow defeat of 1959 on this issue. During the Dáil debate an amendment to their proposal involving preferential voting in single member constituencies was put down by Pat Norton, a dissident Labour member who was a son of the former Labour leader, William Norton. Fianna Fáil rejected this amendment, which was not supported by the Opposition either.

This proved to be the death-knell of the proposal. A television programme prepared and presented by Professor Basil Chubb and David Thornley of Trinity College showed that, given Ireland's particular political geography, the introduction of the proposed British-type electoral system would enable Fianna Fáil to win a clear majority with only 40 percent of the votes, and that they would win almost 100 of the 144 seats with the kind of share of the vote they normally secured. When the referendum was held in 1968, after a hard-fought campaign in which Fine Gael (despite Liam Cosgrave's own preference for a single-seat system), and Labour defended PR, it was defeated not by the narrow margin of 1959 but by a majority of almost 235,000 out of 1,080,000 valid votes; in other words over 60 percent voted against it.

After the election of 1965 the process of policy formulation had been resumed, widening the core of Just Society policies. I had prepared an extensive education policy with the help of a committee of educational experts, which was published in 1966. The state archives have since revealed a letter from the education minister Donagh O'Malley to Sean Lemass proposing that he pre-empt publication of my education policy by announcing, without seeking the approval of Finance Minister Jack Lynch, the introduction of the secondary education proposal that was in fact included in my document – so forty years later I learnt that I had a vicarious role in this key development! There was also a policy statement I prepared on the Irish language, proposing the removal of the provision, dating back to 1934, that a school Leaving Certificate be awarded only to pupils who passed in Irish, as well as the dropping of the Irish language requirement for entry to the public service – reforms that were effected by our coalition government eight years later.

A policy statement in connection with the 1967 local elections proposed the removal of planning appeals from the political arena, and the making of state appointments on merit alone. Although, following the foundation of the state, political patronage had been eliminated in respect of the vast majority of state appointments through the establishment of the Civil Service Commission and Local Appointment Commission, several categories of appointments, such as rate collectors, and teachers in local authority schools, was not covered by the remit of the Local Appointments Commission, and appointments of Judges had remained political – something that in practice was modified in the late 1970s and 1980s.

As we approached the general election that was expected to be held in 1969 further work on policy was initiated and at the end of 1968 a special front bench meeting was held in the Montrose Hotel to approve a series of policy documents which, with other people, I had been preparing. The range of areas covered was wide: public enterprise, industrial democracy and industrial relations, estate duty, social security, public administration and public morality, agriculture, foreign policy and development aid. Most of them were adopted, with some amendment, and together with the original Just Society policies of 1965 and the education, Irish language and local government policies of 1966/67, they represented a significant corpus of social democratic and reforming proposals. For the second time, however, my proposal for the abolition of estate duty and the substitution of an annual wealth tax was rejected.

During these years from 1965 to 1969 when I was finding my feet in politics, I was also keeping my other activities going – journalism, consultancy and university lecturing. Combining politics with journalism did not create any serious problem for me, although I was conscious that in my determination to retain my journalistic objectivity, I probably pulled punches when writing about issues that involved government policy. Not everyone accepted that this was the case, however. One departmental secretary who had been closely associated with Sean Lemass told me that he had ceased to read my weekly economic column in the *Irish Times* because he knew it was biased. When I asked him innocently how he knew this if, as he said, he had ceased reading it, he said he did not need to read my articles to know this.

By contrast a number of Fianna Fáil politicians approached me individually in Leinster House to ask me to criticise various aspects of government policy in my economic column. I counted seven such approaches during my first six months as a senator, from five Fianna Fáil politicians, including the Tánaiste, Erskine Childers, who had for long been a fan of my economic writings. He wanted me to criticise more vigorously the government's approach to inflation about which he – rightly – was unhappy. Neither he nor his colleagues were at all satisfied when I explained my concern to maintain my reputation for journalistic objectivity by restraining my criticisms of government policy in the *Irish Times*, nor were they impressed by my offer to make the critical comments they sought in the Senate! I have to add that no similar political pressure in relation to my journalism ever came from any of my colleagues in Fine Gael.

Erskine Childers was not completely consistent, however. One day at a cocktail party in the British embassy, when I was talking to Ken Whitaker, he joined us and, addressing Whitaker, demanded to know whether he did not feel that since I had entered politics my column had ceased to be politically unbiased. This was a tricky question for the Tánaiste to put to the Secretary of the Department of Finance in my presence. Whitaker took it in his stride, however, replying to the effect that he always read my articles and agreed with them 80 percent of the time. Erskine Childers's reaction was remarkable. He crushed the glass in his hand, so that it shattered on the floor, although without injury to himself, turned on his heel and walked away. As I moved to join two senior officials from Foreign Affairs, Erskine's wife, Rita, approached and asked 'What did you do to Erskine, Garret?' 'I did nothing', I replied indignantly, going on to explain what had happened. She immediately, and characteristically, turned to the two officials and said, 'Poor Garret. Erskine is always ringing him up about his articles, I don't know how Garret puts up with him'! I have to add that this incident was completely uncharacteristic of Erskine Childers, who may, for once, have had a sherry too many.

In spring 1964 I became BBC correspondent in Ireland, after an interview with Lionel Fleming in the Shelbourne Hotel. I heard nothing from them for some months until, late one morning during August when I was on holidays in a phoneless house in Bettystown, County Meath, the postmistress arrived on her bicycle with a telegram from the BBC instructing me to broadcast at 3 o'clock on Irish reactions to Princess Margaret's first visit to Ireland, which had just been announced. As Joan cooked me a piece of trout for an early lunch, I hammered out on my typewriter what seemed to me to be suitable and hopefully non-controversial, reactions to this event, driving into Dublin to transmit them from the Radio Éireann studio in Henry Street.

I also took on being correspondent for the *Economist* shortly afterwards. It was the only paper with which I ever had trouble. Proud of their 'house style' they rewrote their correspondents' contributions. Up to a point this can be acceptable. But sometimes they go too far. I was moved to protest strongly when they added a first paragraph of their own to a piece they had asked me to write about the Golden Jubilee of the 1916 Rising, which they published over a byline: 'By Our Dublin Correspondent': 'This week fifty years ago a group of hotheads seized the GPO in Dublin', together with a photograph of de Valera being escorted under arrest by two British soldiers, our president being described under the photograph as 'one of the hotheads'! That time I got an apology!

My consultancy business, the EIU of Ireland, also kept me busy. In 1967 I relinquished my position as managing director, hoping that the company would flourish without my involvement at that level. It did not prove possible to sever my active link with the company, however, and as the years passed the pressure of consultancy work became increasingly a drag on my energies, albeit one I had to put up with because of the income I derived from this activity.

My heart remained with UCD, however. In 1967 the college became involved in a major controversy. The issue was a proposed merger of the college with TCD to form a new university. Even today the origins of this proposal remain obscure. It appears, however that the energetic Minister for Education, Donagh O'Malley, decided to embark on this merger, following publication of a summary of the Report of the Commission on Higher Education that had been appointed in

1961 – which itself had made no proposal for a merger. The UCD authorities appear to have got wind of this proposal and, it seems, decided to pre-empt it by publishing merger proposals of their own. These proposals would have had the effect of submerging TCD in UCD by means of a complete merger of every individual faculty and department – for UCD, being the larger college, would have had a majority of staff in almost every merged unit.

When the governing body met, its members knew nothing of all this to-ing and fro-ing. We were faced with a reading of the minister's letter and an account of the shape of the merger as envisaged by the UCD authorities, which was made to appear as if it were reaction to the minister's proposals. We were asked there and then to endorse the president's merger proposal.

The minister's letter proposed 'one University of Dublin, to contain two colleges, each complementary to the other' – a wording which did not fit with the UCD authorities 'total merger' concept. The UCD staff, who since the previous year had been linked with TCD and other colleges in the newly-established Irish Federation of University teachers, were divided on the merits of a merger but overwhelmingly – and generously it must be said – rejected the 'total merger' concept that would effectively have wiped out TCD. The battle within the college went on until the end of October when a resolution was put to the governing body which included the phrase 'the governing body is prepared to explore the principle of unified departments and faculties in one college or the other'

The minority group on the governing body that I had brought into being in 1964 proposed an alternative resolution, citing the divergent views of various faculties and couched so as to make it clear that the unified faculties and departments approach was not necessarily seen as the best solution and that the college would consider other solutions. We were defeated and subsequently submitted to the government a Minority Report setting out our reasoning and our preference for two colleges, each of which would have a core of key Arts subjects together with Physics and Chemistry.

This action was denounced as disloyalty. We were told that there simply could not be such a thing as a Minority Report from the governing body; that only the majority view could be expressed. The atmosphere at subsequent meetings became even more tense than in the past.

In the event the proposed merger was abandoned partly because of the sudden, tragic death of Donagh O'Malley in February of the following year. Consideration was later given to a modified version of a merger involving two colleges within one University of Dublin, with some shared faculties, but by that time there was little support in either college for such a federal university link. Once the impetus of the initial thrust had been spent in the heated debate provoked by the UCD authorities' effort to secure a 'total merger', the desire of the staff of the two colleges to maintain their independence prevailed.

I regretted that we did not succeed in securing a federal link between the two colleges which I felt might have ensured a better balance between them, given the long-term problems that UCD could face in attracting under straight competitive conditions a fair share of the better students to a larger and more anonymous campus on the suburban site to which we were committed to move. For, although at the time that this controversy erupted, the UCD Arts Faculty was still located in the city, at Earlsfort Terrace, it was due to move several miles out to a site to which the Science Faculty had already been relocated.

There had been concern for some time previously that this move was to precede the removal of the Arts Library to the Belfield site, over two miles away. In the aftermath of the student agitation in Paris and elsewhere in 1968, a radical student movement had emerged in UCD which was poised to exploit an issue such as this. On the evening of 25 February, a badly-prepared and quite unconvincing 'teach-in' by the university administration on this library problem provided an opportunity for these socialist Students for Democratic Action to launch a challenge to the college authorities, organising the next day a mass meeting without a chairman which they controlled by dominating the four microphones. They then occupied the administrative offices. I helped six hundred moderate students to hold a meeting on the following day that passed resolutions supporting the aims – not the methods – of the SDA.

By the weekend, meetings of the Academic Council and the Governing Body had been called for early the following week, which I feared might aggravate the situation by instituting disciplinary action against some of the students. So, despite my junior status – after almost a decade on the staff, I was still an Assistant Grade III because, until I completed my PhD, I had no qualification in Economics – I invited thirty members of the two bodies to my house on Sunday evening – two-thirds of whom, all but one professors, came. Seated in our boiler-room – decorated by my teen-age children with posters, including one of Che Guevara – my invitees agreed to block any disciplinary action. Instead, the next day, in opposition to the president, the Academic Council appointed a Committee of Enquiry, seven of whose twelve members had been at my meeting, and two of whom were elected chairman and secretary of the committee. The president complained that some staff – of whom, by his definition, I was certainly one – had joined in the disturbances: he added ominously that this was not going to be forgotten.

I then invited some of the moderate students – who included Ruairi Quinn – to my home, where we considered tactics for the next mass meeting. It was agreed that we would propose John Maguire – a popular PhD student in philosophy who later became Professor of Philosophy in UCC – to chair future mass meetings. On the following night, John Maguire and some other students attended a meeting in our bedroom during which it was agreed that resolutions would be put to the next mass meeting to prepare proposals for the reform of the governing body and for a review of the arrangements for the transfer to Belfield.

The SDA students walked out of the subsequent mass meeting in high dudgeon at our takeover of their revolution, and the moderates who remained decided that we would abandon lectures for three days to discuss the university and society in classes.

Meanwhile, the temporary library problem was resolved at a staff meeting where I refuted the Librarian's claim that the basement rooms of the Arts Block were too small. Jumping from the second row to the floor of the lecture theatre where we were meeting, I paced across the width of the theatre to demonstrate that the basement rooms had exactly the same width as that of the spacious room in which we were meeting! That settled the library problem.

During these days many staff joined these discussions and were deeply impressed with the students' evident concern to have staff participation, views, and guidance. At an ad hoc meeting of staff, the contrast between the almost uncontrollably negative attitudes of the students at the earlier mass meetings, and the constructive approach of all concerned in this new format, was very striking. Many of the students' contributions concentrated on the need to raise standards – with staff members having to head-off students' enthusiasm for measures that, in some cases, would have cost them their degrees! A statement signed by seventy staff at the end of this exercise recorded the emergence of an emotional climate in which traditional barriers to communications between staff and students had disappeared.

Thereafter, the college evolved towards a more open society with a more relaxed relationship between the administration, the staff and the students.

Little else remains save the memory shared by some thousands of elderly people of an exhilarating moment when barriers disappeared and, for a brief instant, a different kind of academic community of students and staff seemed possible. Three months later I was engaged in my first Dáil election campaign.

But before moving back to the political arena I should, perhaps, record a brief excursion into theology in 1968.

At the end of July 1968 we had gone on a family holiday to France – the first time we had taken such a holiday outside Ireland, although in 1961 the family had accompanied me on a business trip to Switzerland. Four other academic families came with us, making a group of 32 in all – enough to make a significant impact on the village of Croix-de-Vie/St Gilles on the coast south of the estuary of the Loire, which was a French family holiday resort rarely visited by foreigners. I had chosen the location as optimal between the less stable climate of Brittany and the heat of the south east or Mediterranean coasts, selecting the particular resort on the basis of a study of a Michelin map of the area, which suggested that it was a well-established village with a harbour and coves along a rocky patch of coast-line, but also with sandy beaches; just the kind of place for teenagers and children.

On the boat as we approached Le Havre we heard of the publication of the encyclical, *Humanae Vitae*, which at once became a topic of conversation amongst us. When we got the text I found that on reading it my reaction was quite negative, as was Joan's. I had always been opposed to artificial contraception on what I had thought were moral grounds, but study of the encyclical convinced me that the moral argument was not sustainable. I came to the conclusion that my objections to artificial birth control had been aesthetic rather than moral!

When we returned home at the end of the month we heard of a conference to be held in County Wexford later in September at which theologians, doctors, academics and others were to discuss the encyclical. I arranged for Joan and myself to attend. It was a stimulating and indeed inspiring occasion as all concerned strove to address the moral and medical issues involved. We eventually produced a report which we submitted to the Irish Bishops. This report stressed the great problems that the encyclical had created for a significant number of people in relation to contraception itself, in relation to authority, and in relation to developing ideas about the nature of the church. We expressed concern that a document which claimed internal and external obedience to its teaching should have contained apparent inadequacies and inconsistencies. It also recorded that the members of the medical profession present stated that the biological premise upon which its recommendation of the safe period was based was scientifically untenable. The reference to 'natural laws and rhythms of fecundity which, of themselves, cause an interruption in the succession of births' (*jam per se ipsa generationes subsequentes intervallent*) was incorrect and could not provide the basis for a sufficiently effective method of regulating births. These methods were frequently disruptive of the harmony of married life, whereas the contraceptive methods condemned by the encyclical had been found to foster conjugal love and help towards the attainment of maturity in marriage relationships, a view which, the report recorded, was endorsed by married couples present.

Reactions by the Hierarchy to this report, transmitted to them by a lay participant, Vincent Grogan (at the time Supreme Knight of the Order of St Columbanus, which was then passing through a brief liberal phase), were varied. One bishop described it as 'most useful', 'understanding' and 'reasonable'; another remarked that we would appear to have had 'a very interesting and stimulating weekend'! The reply from the Archbishop of Dublin, John Charles McQuaid, was characteristically brief and pungent, however!

'I thank you for your manifesto. I feel sure that you would prefer to go to your judgement with the knowledge that you had done all in your power to secure full assent to the teaching of the Vicar of Christ'!

The deeper interest which Joan in particular and I to a lesser extent developed in theology in our later years was considerably stimulated by that remarkable weekend.

7

~: The Dáil :~
1969–73

Although Jack Lynch could have postponed a dissolution until 1970, an election seemed likely in 1969. The prospects for the Opposition were not good. Labour's sharp shift to the Left, in the delusion that the seventies would be Socialist, and its public rejection of a coalition with Fine Gael and private rejection of a union between the two parties, had widened the gap between the two opposition parties. This was a negative factor in an Irish election where preferential voting between the Opposition parties can be an important factor, influencing the outcome of a number of contests in marginal seats. Moreover the swing against the government party, Fianna Fáil, which might, perhaps, be expected in view of the fact that they were now twelve years in office, was likely to be inhibited by what public opinion must perceive as a prospect of instability if they were defeated with, at best, Labour supporting Fine Gael from outside rather than from within a coalition.

Fine Gael had the advantage, however, of a vigorous and quite ruthless organiser in Gerard Sweetman, and the policy work which had continued since 1965, when the first batch of Just Society policies had been published as an election programme at short notice, provided the party with a more solid and extensive platform than any Irish party had possessed in the past.

Since I had found out how to join the Fine Gael organisation at the time of the presidential election in 1966, I had become actively involved in my Dublin South East constituency, and had become accepted as the natural and more or less automatic successor to John A. Costello on his impending retirement. Attention had, indeed, become concentrated there on the question of a second candidate, on the assumption that I would in any event be presenting myself. A possible candidate was Alexis FitzGerald, not my friend the well-known solicitor but his young nephew of the same name, who had joined the local party at the same time as myself and had become an effective organiser in the constituency. He was reluctant to stand in Dublin South East with me, however, believing that it would be a mistake for our two candidates to have the same name, even if not related to each other. He proposed Fergus O'Brien, a salesman in the ESB in his late 30s who was vigorous and energetic. Unfortunately this issue had been faced too late and Fergus O'Brien had had no chance to build up support for himself.

We were also handicapped in Dublin South East by the fact that whilst I had been active in the constituency organisation during the previous three years, I had not yet got down to building up support by establishing clinics and making myself available to the public in the more deprived areas of the constituency. We fought a vigorous campaign nonetheless, undertaking a fairly comprehensive canvass with the additional man and woman-power we had acquired during the previous three years – mainly young people.

My speeches during the campaign – almost all of them scripts delivered to the newspapers and read to election workers in one or other of our election rooms – concentrated on issues of reform, including social reform. Attacking the increasingly materialist climate of politics, I criticised concentration on wealth creation without regard to its distribution, and advocated the many reforms proposed in the Fine Gael policies adopted during the previous four years, which included participation of parents and students in the educational system and of workers in industry; tax-reliefs for profit-sharing; a Speculative Gains Tax; and an expansion of public housing. I criticised our foreign policy as insufficiently European and unduly subservient to Britain and the United States. And I summed up our policy as being based on social democracy, liberal ideas, and Christian principles.

Public meetings were still held in Dublin at that time. I recall a delightful meeting on a Saturday afternoon at Sandymount Green, addressing a friendly crowd of some three hundred in brilliant sunshine – and another meeting in Ringsend at which for the first time I met Noel Browne, speaking from a Labour platform with the aid of a Fine Gael loudspeaker. There was also a final rally at the General Post Office at which I spoke – the last such major outdoor meeting in the city centre. Thereafter the danger of Protestant para-military bombs, the first of which were set off in Dublin in 1972, made such major public meeting too much of a security risk.

When the votes came to be counted I was found to have topped the poll, with Fianna Fáil and Labour securing the other two seats. However, the outcome of the election nationally was, as anticipated, disappointing. True, Fine Gael with a fractional increase in its share of the vote, gained 3 seats – but so did Fianna Fáil, the losers being Labour and independents. Labour's share of the vote had risen slightly because they garnered a small number of votes in – for them – many hopeless constituencies which they contested for the first, and in some cases only, time, but they lost ground and seats in some of the areas where they had done well in 1965 – in part because their 'Socialist' stance lost them Fine Gael preferences. Thus in the new

Dáil Fianna Fáil, after providing the Ceann Comhairle (Speaker Fianna Fáil), had a majority of five.

The election was followed by a brief Dáil session before the summer recess. This opened on 2 July with the re-election of Jack Lynch as Taoiseach and a debate on his new government. I spoke in this debate, which was probably somewhat unusual for a new deputy. Moreover when the Dáil resumed on 9 July there were three Bills that interested me – an Air Companies Bill, a University Bill, and a Decimal Currency Bill. I spoke on all three that day, and at length on the Finance Bill in the following week, as well as putting down questions to the Taoiseach and nine ministers.

Moreover when the House resumed in October I made lengthy contributions, of two to three hours in each case, on foreign affairs, Northern Ireland and on the Department of Labour estimates. Finally towards the end of the year I had a chance to speak on the subject actually allocated to me on the Opposition front bench, viz. education, when a Supplementary Estimate for that department was introduced, and again in April 1970 when I led the Opposition side in the debate on the education estimate for 1970/71, speaking for almost four hours on the forty-odd aspects of education which seemed to me to be matters of concern or controversy at that time!

The frequency, length and variety of my interventions – a product, in part at least, of the Pooh-Bah role I had been required to play in the Senate – but also, I have to say, of a somewhat bumptious conviction that I had something significant to say on all these issues – provoked some comment. The most pointed (and it did have a certain impact on my subsequent Dáil behaviour), took the form of an *Irish Times* cartoon showing a Fine Gael front bench consisting of 21 Garret FitzGeralds! But of the tensions created by my too wide-ranging parliamentary activities I was only partly conscious at the time.

In the educational area itself I also trod on some corns – including some that had not been accustomed previously to such attentions from Fine Gael speakers. My April 1970 education speech was strongly critical of the excessive time given to the Irish language in primary schools, as shown by an academic study in the 1960s, and I also raised the question of parental involvement in the schools – popular neither with teachers nor with the clergy who manage Catholic primary schools. Criticism of the six-fold division of second-level schools between Catholic and Protestant, secondary and vocational, and boys' and girls', was also controversial at that time, as, in a quite different way, was my strong support on educational grounds for the merger of small one and two-teacher national schools in rural areas – for such schools were seen locally as cherished symbols of community identity.

My simultaneous attempts to engage educational organisations in debate on educational reform fell on stony ground. The teachers' organisations seemed completely preoccupied with issues of salary and status, and could not be persuaded to discuss academic matters, although I did have success in engaging smaller groups of teachers in debate on such issues.

Two years later I was moved to the Shadow Finance portfolio – a promotion which, although I had enjoyed dealing with educational issues, I naturally welcomed, and it was in that capacity that I served out my last two years in Opposition.

Meanwhile in my constituency I had been helping to build up a young and lively organisation. Within a short period there were twelve active branches, nine of them covering various geographical areas, while two others were university branches in TCD and UCD and the twelfth was a unique school students' branch. As students were supposed to be, and often were, also members of geographical branches, and as some of them were elected as delegates for their geographical branches, over a number of years about one-third of our constituency executive members were students, which made for lively and good-humoured debate.

At the same time, with my fellow candidate, Fergus O'Brien, I was undertaking a methodical door-to-door canvass of the very many corporation flats and houses in the area, simultaneously establishing weekly clinics in three such areas. The results of all this work became clear four years later when Fergus O'Brien and myself were both elected, winning two of the three seats with the help of between a quarter and a third of the vote in various working class areas.

This increased involvement in politics following my election to the Dáil entailed some reduction in my other activities. I was happy at that stage to be replaced as a correspondent of the *Financial Times* and the BBC, but I kept up my weekly 'Economic Comment' in the *Irish Times*. So far as UCD was concerned my election to the Dáil had no effect, however; I felt obliged, indeed, to increase marginally my lecture load in circumstances that are, perhaps, worth explaining.

Normally one spends election day visiting polling stations and I had started out on this tour before they opened at 9 o'clock. By 11, however, I had developed a migraine, and I returned home to get a couple of hours rest. In the meantime the post had come, and Joan had opened it. One document was the agenda for the next governing body meeting which included a proposal that any staff members elected to the Dáil should be sent on leave of absence without pay!

To say the least, this was a shock. I had never foreseen such a possibility, especially as since the foundation of the state, UCD staff had, without prejudice to their posts, been members of the Dáil, taking leave of absence only when holding ministerial office. The roll-call of such academic politicians was a long one, including some of the most distinguished academics and notable politicians of the period since independence, such as Eoin MacNeill, John Marcus O'Sullivan, Patrick McGilligan, Michael Hayes and Michael Tierney. To propose to change a policy that had permitted such a fruitful relationship between the college and national politics was certainly a startling innovation, and, as I remarked to Joan, to propose it at a moment when it was too late to prevent oneself from being elected seemed particularly unfair!

I rang Alexis FitzGerald, friend, political adviser and solicitor; he said he would do what he could. In the event he rang his father-in-law John A. Costello, to whose former seat I was about to be elected, and he in turn, I discovered later, rang Jack Lynch, who was horrified at this proposal and who said that he would ask the Fianna Fáil county councillors on the governing body to oppose it.

When the governing body met a week later the proposal was low on the agenda, however, – which, whether by design or accident meant that it might not be reached until after the county councillors, almost all from rural Ireland, had left to catch their trains home. When the proposal was eventually reached, however, it provoked reactions that cut across the normal establishment/opposition divide in the governing body. In particular Michael Hayes, former Professor, Cumann na nGaedheal TD, and Ceann Comhairle of the Dáil, who had never hidden his hostility to my anti-establishment role on the governing body, denounced the motion as outrageous – as well he might in view of his own history! He was supported by, among others, the only councillor who had been able to remain, a retired member of Dublin Corporation who, although not himself a Fianna Fáil representative, said that he was speaking not only for himself but also for his colleagues who had had to leave to catch their trains. His comment on the proposal was brief and to the point: 'If yez do this yez will be the laughing stock of the country'.

Faced with this onslaught the Establishment conceded ground, proposing a sub-committee to examine the matter, with, as chairman, a distinguished medical professor. I don't think that either the college authorities or the professor were immediately conscious of the humorous side of appointing a medical professor, himself a practising consultant, as chairman of a sub-committee to investigate academic pluralism!

The subcommittee, having heard my case, and that of an academic colleague who had also been elected to the Dáil (John O'Donovan, a predecessor of mine as a Fine Gael TD for Dublin South East but now a Labour deputy for another constituency), decided that honour would be satisfied if my salary were reduced by 20 percent on account of my absences from the college during part of the working week – absences which would be slightly longer as a deputy than they had been as a senator – and so as to ensure that no one could complain about my service as a lecturer/deputy I arranged to give one more lecture/seminar each week than any of my colleagues in the Department of Political Economy.

Meanwhile since the Derry march of October 1968, Northern Ireland had been casting a shadow over the whole island. Now, with the largescale rioting of mid-August 1969, it threatened the peace of the whole island.

Joan and I were on holidays in France with the children and some friends when these dramatic events occurred. My first thought was to return, but Tom O'Higgins advised me firmly to remain. A dangerous wave of extreme nationalist feeling was sweeping the country, momentarily infecting Fine Gael itself. Tom O'Higgins knew how I would react to some of the unwise things being said, and feared that if I came back I would be unable to keep my head down. I might thus undermine my capacity to exert a constructive influence at a later stage. Alexis FitzGerald shared his view. I found it difficult to accept these counsels of caution, but was glad eventually that I had done so.

When I returned at the end of the month I immediately drafted a Northern Ireland policy document. Despite my long-standing concern about the attitude to Northern Ireland of political parties in the Republic I had not hitherto intervened in this area of policy. I was now disturbed by the extent to which even some moderate-minded people in the party leadership had been moved by the dramatic events of the preceding weeks to react in what seemed to me to be an extreme manner. The absence of any clear framework of party policy in relation to Northern Ireland had, it seemed to me, left a dangerous vacuum, the atavistic filling of which in conditions of great tension carried evident dangers.

For me the crucial issue was to get acceptance of the principle that, whatever we might think of Partition, and however much we might feel that the effects of the division of the island had been damaging to its peace and prosperity, nevertheless-given that the division had become an established fact it could and should be ended only with the consent of a majority in Northern Ireland. This had never been accepted, overtly at any rate, by Fianna Fáil, partly perhaps because of a feeling in that party that to do so would be to weaken their hold on a segment of republican opinion which might then drift towards support for the IRA. However that might be, Fine Gael, I had always believed, had a duty to make an unambiguous stand on this issue, but for two decades past it had failed to do so. The party had participated in – and from its vantage point in government in 1949 had even led – the anti-Partition campaign of that year, echoing the traditional republican slogans 'The North has no right to opt out', 'Ireland has a right to its six north-eastern counties' and so on. This was part of what had put me off politics at that time, and, as I mentioned earlier when I had decided to re-join Fine Gael in 1964, I had done so only after assuring myself that I would not be expected to accept or propagate this particular line.

My convictions on this issue were based on an accumulation of considerations. I did not believe that this irredentist approach would ever succeed in bringing about Irish unity; Britain would neither be cajoled nor intimidated into 'handing over' the North against the wishes of a majority of its inhabitants, and the more we expounded this irredentist thesis, the more we alienated Northern unionists, thus postponing any possibility of re-unification by the only feasible route – that of unionist consent. Moreover this traditional anti-Partition approach was dangerously near to the IRA's thesis, and must, I felt, encourage that body and its supporters to attempt to bring about by force that which Irish constitutional parties were not prepared to say explicitly could be achieved only with consent.

I had welcomed the Civil Rights Movement as a radical departure from republican irredentism, re-focusing the energies of Northern nationalists, and the sympathies of fair-minded people everywhere, on the hitherto neglected legitimate grievances of the Northern minority. This movement, as I saw it, and still see it, represented a belated and realistic opting in to the Northern Ireland system by the minority there, seeking their rightful entitlement to participation on a basis of equality in the society of Northern Ireland. It represented, I felt, the first step towards a normalisation of politics in Northern Ireland, from which might eventually spring a new climate in which the relationship between North and South could be addressed afresh, with some objectivity.

In the event, this proved grossly over-optimistic; unionist opinion was not capable of adjusting constructively to this kind of 'opting in' by the nationalist minority. Their sense of being themselves the real minority in the island as a whole, with all the deep-seated fears of such a permanent minority, was too strong. Apart from a few leaders like the prime minister, Terence O'Neill, they thus lacked the self-confidence to respond positively to this radical change of emphasis by Northern nationalist opinion. And so by August 1969, what could have been a most fruitful development had been converted by intransigent unionist opposition into an inflammatory one.

To damp down these flames seemed urgent. This must involve reforms that might restore normality to the security situation in Northern Ireland and accommodate the legitimate aspirations of the Northern nationalists, excluded for fifty years from any role in the affairs of the part of the island in which they found themselves. But it must also involve reassurance for the unionists, who for half a century had felt threatened by Southern political demands that Britain reunite the North with the rest of the country regardless of the wishes of a majority in Northern Ireland.

These considerations provided the parameters for my draft policy statement. This began by identifying the problem as deriving from the mutual fear of each other by the two sections of the Northern community – by unionist fears that had been intensified by the Republic's pursuit of policies of attempting to persuade or force Britain to 'hand over' the North as well as by plotting by subversive elements in the Republic, and by nationalist fears of attack by Protestant extremists.

Thus, 'Force as a weapon of policy having been rejected by responsible political groups in the Republic, the only way in which the present divided state of this island can or should be modified is with the consent of a majority of the people of Northern Ireland'. This, as I saw it, was the key sentence in the document, although not everyone who read it or who joined in adopting it at the time may have appreciated its full significance.

The policy statement then went on to propose that we should press the British government to reconstitute the RUC as a civil unarmed police force, similar to the Garda Síochána, recruiting it from all groups in the community. It should also support the disbandment of the B Specials and press for the maintenance of order by a genuinely neutral force, and, after appropriate consultation with Northern opinion, ensure representation of the minority in the Northern Ireland government as the sole means of reassuring it as to the full and continued implementation of the proposed reforms, and of fair treatment. Also the government, and the political parties in Dáil Éireann, should assert formally their rejection of force as a solution to the division of Ireland, and should clearly state their intention to work towards a voluntary reunion of the people of both parts of Ireland. And the government should immediately establish an all-party committee for Northern Ireland affairs to secure the implementation of the above policies.

This, I believe, represented the first suggestion of power-sharing made on either side of the border. At that time northern nationalists were not yet able to envisage a process of working with unionists in government. More than a year was to pass before this concept began to be entertained publicly by nationalist politicians in Northern Ireland.

Recognising that in view of domestic divisions in Fine Gael, a draft policy document emanating from me might not receive a warm reception by some members of the front bench – especially as Northern Ireland was outside my area of responsibility – I asked Paddy Harte, the TD for Donegal East, who was known to be deeply concerned about Northern Ireland, to submit it on his own account to the front bench, having first of all, during the weekend of 7/8 September, sought the opinions on it of John Hume, Austin Currie and Ivan Cooper.

Unsure, however, of the impact of these discussions on my colleagues, I awaited with some trepidation the front-bench meeting of 11 September, at which Paddy Harte was to produce the draft policy – which John Hume and Austin Currie had by then approved.

As it happened, two of the four more traditionally anti-partitionist members of the front bench were absent abroad on that day (making anti-Partition speeches!), and when we came to discuss the policy statement in the afternoon, both Liam Cosgrave and Gerry Sweetman also had to leave the meeting for different reasons. The policy went through without difficulty. I wanted it published at once but our PRO, Frank Aylmer, had standing instructions – reasonably enough! – that nothing was to be published unless Liam Cosgrave had an opportunity to see it first. I awaited the outcome of this clearance process like an expectant father. When Frank emerged from his discussion of the document with Liam Cosgrave, he told me that it was cleared, save for one inessential paragraph.

At the instance of Conor Cruise O'Brien, the principle of 'no re-unification without consent' embedded in this policy was soon afterwards also adopted by the Labour Party, and, after the 1970 Arms Crisis had changed fairly radically the composition of the Fianna Fáil government, Jack Lynch edged Fianna Fáil gradually towards a similar stance, so that when the Sunningdale Agreement, incorporating this principle, was signed in December 1973, he was able to get his party to endorse it.

This did not mean, however, that traditional anti-Partition rhetoric vanished overnight in Fine Gael or Labour, let alone in Fianna Fáil. Indeed, two years later this was to cause problems in Fine Gael, as I shall explain later in this chapter.

Several months after this, I made my first personal contact with John Hume. Accompanied by Tom O'Higgins, Alexis FitzGerald and Michael Sweetman, I went to Derry and had a long discussion with him and Ivan Cooper in the latter's house. It was the beginning of a relationship with John Hume which endured thereafter, even when at times some small policy differences emerged between us, as in the late 1970s.

But before coming to the way in which, in May 1970, Northern Ireland exploded into the politics of the Irish state, with shattering consequences for the Fianna Fáil government, I must turn back to the end of August 1969, to describe a series of other events within Fine Gael itself with which I was involved.

When we had returned from the French family holiday on the car ferry from Le Havre, preoccupied with Northern Ireland, I had found myself faced with an evening-newspaper headline at Rosslare announcing that six young members of Fine Gael, friends of mine, had been expelled from Fine Gael by the party's organisational and disciplinary body, the standing committee.

The expulsions arose from a row about candidates in the Dublin South Central constituency in the June general election. The name of Maurice O'Connell, a young candidate chosen by the local convention to contest the constituency with the sitting TD, Richie Ryan, had been deleted by the standing committee before the election, and he had been replaced on the ticket by John Kelly, professor of Roman law and jurisprudence in UCD. Maurice O'Connell had been a member of the committee that had drafted our educational policy under my chairmanship three years earlier, and his summary removal from the ticket and replacement by another candidate, albeit one of great distinction, had been badly received by many in Fine Gael, especially amongst the young. Maurice O'Connell had, however, breached party rules by then standing in the June election as an independent, and before the summer break, disciplinary action had been initiated by the party organiser, Gerard Sweetman, against him and five others who had supported him at the election.

These included John Maguire, the postgraduate student (and subsequently professor of philosophy in University College Cork) who had played a constructive role in the UCD 'Gentle Revolution' some months earlier; Vincent Browne (then editor of a Fine Gael youth magazine); and Henry Kelly, of British television fame.

Their expulsion at the end of August nevertheless came as a shock, and defects in the procedure adopted seemed to me to call for action. The party's standing committee – its organisational executive – was obviously not going to be persuaded by political means to reverse its disciplinary decision; likewise the parliamentary party, which in any event had no role in matters of this kind. The only course open, therefore, was a legal one. We sought legal advice. Within a few days, a letter was on its way to the party's trustees, calling on them to preserve the rights of the six to the party's property by rejecting the decision of the standing committee on the grounds of a series of procedural irregularities. This legal ploy succeeded. Gerard Sweetman had to admit defeat; and on Liam Cosgrave's proposal, the standing committee reversed its decision before the end of September.

The tensions that had arisen in the party at this stage came home to me very forcibly when I was subsequently called to a meeting – it may have been a subcommittee of the standing committee – apparently to account for my support of the six. For two and a half hours I had the eerie experience of listening to myself being referred to exclusively in the third person. 'We all know he's a Communist, don't we', 'Oh, yes, we know all about him', and so on and so on. On 6 December, however, Liam Cosgrave and Gerard Sweetman asked me if I would help to end the discord by inviting Maurice O'Connell to transfer from Dublin South Central, where Richie Ryan apparently still saw him as a threat, to my constituency, Dublin South East. For the sake of peace in the party, I agreed.

This did not solve the problem, however, for Richie Ryan reacted to the news of this transfer by denouncing what he described as an 'anti-party group', which, he said, was trying to take over the party. This allegation was immediately countered by Tom O'Higgins. But on radio the next day, a Saturday, Richie Ryan was asked who this group were. Some of them, he replied, were willing to receive Maurice O'Connell into their area; that clearly implicated me. He added that some people had said that Maurice O'Connell's actions were such that they agreed with them – which was interpreted as a reference to Tom O'Higgins's denials of an anti-party plot. The aim of this group, Richie Ryan went on, was to destroy Fine Gael; some of them believed in confiscation of property, and the Irish people were not going to abandon their property to revolutionaries who wanted to bring into Ireland doctrines rejected by most countries. He added: 'Those of us who have for years – and when I say years, I mean decades – fought for social reform in this country now find ourselves being accused of insincerity by people who have come along at the last moment to pretend that they are more revolutionary than those who have been providing and fighting for this reform.'

We were all taken aback by this extraordinary onslaught. Direct contact with Liam Cosgrave was not possible at weekends, as his phone number was not available to his colleagues. The party general secretary, Jim Sanfey, was contacted; he had the phone number. He was asked to ring Liam Cosgrave to urge him to get in touch with Richie Ryan – they lived within a mile of each other – to explain that I had merely been a passive agent in the transfer of Maurice O'Connell to my constituency, and that the 'anti-party plot' had consisted of the party leader and national organiser trying to solve Richie Ryan's constituency problem for him! We never heard of any outcome of our initiative.

The row blew over eventually, but relationships within the party were damaged. A belief grew up that Liam Cosgrave was surrounding himself with a clique of 'loyalist' supporters. This would not, however, have been in character. A proud and self-sufficient man, he would not, I feel, have demeaned himself – as he would have seen it – by making himself dependent on any clique of supporters. But the fact that he did not appear to deal with the extraordinary misrepresentation of events in December 1969, apparently feeling it better to leave well alone, together with vocal declarations of loyalty to him by a number of his colleagues during the aftermath, gave an impression that he had sided unfairly with one group in the party; party unity suffered as a result.

In justice to Richie Ryan, it should, perhaps be added that the resentment he expressed in his broadcast interview about latecomers outflanking him on issues of social reform was, perhaps, comprehensible. He had joined Fine Gael with a radical reforming approach in the late 1950s, and it must have been galling for him that Declan Costello had seemed to have trumped his card in 1964-65 with the Just Society Policy, and that a newcomer like myself was by 1969 being seen as yet another new radical force in the party.

However, for a period after the traumatic events of May 1970, which demanded and received a united response from Fine Gael, these divisions disappeared. Let me recount these events as I experienced them.

On 5 May 1970, Jack Lynch informed the Dáil that the Minister for Justice, Micheal Ó Morain, had resigned. Liam Cosgrave asked was this the only ministerial resignation the House could expect? The Taoiseach replied: 'I don't know what the deputy is referring to', to which Liam Cosgrave responded: 'Is it only the tip of the iceberg?' He refused, however, to accept Jack Lynch's invitation to enlarge on what was on his mind.

That evening I went into his office shortly before eight o'clock, only to find a number of members of the front bench talking with him in grave tones. The discussion was clearly a confidential one; I left them to it. Two hours later, I walked into the minister's corridor in search of some minister to whom I wished to speak.

He was not there, but the door of his office was open and the BBC television news was on. I stepped in the door to watch; the news item was about the Kent State student massacre. The door at the end of the corridor to the Taoiseach's office opened. A glowering Kevin Boland (Minister for Local Government) came along the corridor, too preoccupied to notice me. I went home to bed.

At 4 AM, the phone rang. It was Muiris MacConghail from RTÉ. Jack Lynch had announced at 2.50 AM that he had sacked Neil Blaney and Charles Haughey, apparently for gun-running. Blaney, I could understand, but Haughey? What on earth was he doing involving himself in an affair of that kind? The last thing I had heard about his attitude to Northern Ireland had been the previous September, when he had been rumoured to have been a moderating influence against Neil Blaney's inflammatory attitude.

And what should I do? I rang Tom O'Higgins and Alexis FitzGerald. They were equally shocked by the news, but neither had any suggestion as to what could or should be done. Eventually, at about 5 AM, I went back to sleep.

The Dáil assembled at 11.30 AM – an hour later than usual because of the 1916 Commemoration at Arbour Hill that morning. There was a brief delay before Jack Lynch entered. He proposed an adjournment until 10 PM so that the government and the Fianna Fáil Party would have time to meet. Questions from Liam Cosgrave revealed that Neil Blaney and Charles Haughey had not yet responded to the Taoiseach's call for their resignations – but, Jack Lynch added, he was entitled to ask the president to terminate their appointments. After a brief exchange between the party leaders on the possibility of an earlier resumption, an adjournment to 10 PM was agreed.

However, when I had seen Kevin Boland the previous evening, he had just submitted his resignation to Jack Lynch. And shortly after the Dáil adjourned that morning, yet another resignation came: Paudge Brennan, Neil Blaney's parliamentary secretary. By contrast, Blaney himself was reported to have said that he might not in fact be leaving the government. Was he hoping to overthrow Jack Lynch before his appointment was terminated by President de Valera?

By 7 PM, rumours of a 'coup' of this kind were dissipated, however. A late-afternoon Fianna Fáil Party meeting had ended in less than an hour, with Jack Lynch in firm control.

A four-and-a-half-hour debate started at 10 PM on the motion to name Desmond O'Malley as Minister for Justice in succession to Micheal Ó Morain, another minister who had resigned shortly before these dramatic events. In his opening speech, the Taoiseach announced that as neither Neil Blaney nor Charles Haughey would comply with his request to submit their resignations, the president had terminated their appointments on his recommendation. He then outlined a sequence of events beginning on Monday 20 April, when, he said, the security forces had submitted to him information about an alleged attempt to import arms, which prima facie involved two members of the government.

Liam Cosgrave followed, describing how at 8 PM on the previous evening he had informed the Taoiseach of information he had received about an attempt to import arms illegally through Dublin Airport, those involved including, in addition to the two ministers, a brother of each of the dismissed ministers and some of their friends. Following the failure of the Minister for Justice to give a directive to the Gardaí in relation to this matter, the Taoiseach had been notified and the attempted importation had been dropped, but although the question of dismissing ministers had arisen, no action had been taken until the resignation of the Minister for Justice, Micheal Ó Morain, on 4 May. When Liam Cosgrave had received information on Garda notepaper supporting information he already possessed, he had decided to put the facts in his possession before the Taoiseach.

I took no part in this relatively brief debate, but by accident I found myself closing on behalf of the Opposition the subsequent debate on the nomination of ministers to replace those who had been dismissed or resigned on the 5th and 6th. This second debate was the longest in the history of the state, lasting for more than thirty-six hours, from 10.30 AM on Friday 8 May to 11 PM on Saturday 9 May.

Initially, no one expected such a long debate. When, in the early evening of Friday, I was nominated to conclude for Fine Gael (by default, because it was realised at this stage that all our leading front-benchers had already spoken), I expected the debate to end late that night. But every time I looked at the list of members wishing to speak, it had got longer, not shorter. All the members of our party now wanted to say their piece!

Around midnight I went home, to work on my speech in more peaceful surroundings. At about 2.30 AM I was rung to come in at once, as it was believed that the government intended to move the closure. This turned out to be a false alarm, but when, after my arrival back in the Dáil, I was standing in the lobby at the back of the Chamber, with my notes in my hand, someone on the Opposition front bench below summoned me. Radio Éireann, I was told, was broadcasting all night, and if I went to the Key Room (which was precisely what the name said, viz. a room with keys hanging up all along the walls, which had been turned into an emergency studio), I might have the opportunity to address whatever fraction of the nation was still awake. I took this advice and found myself on the air for almost an hour and a half, part of the time partnered by Neil Blaney. Next day, I discovered that a significant part of the population had in fact spent the night listening to the radio.

Returning to the Chamber at around 6 AM, I listened to the debate for a time, but then suddenly realised that I had mislaid the notes for my speech. They were not where I was sure I had left them – on a shelf in the lobby immediately behind the back row of Dáil seats. After a while, someone who had been in the gallery told me that he had seen a Fianna Fáil TD, Joe Dowling, appear to pick up some papers from the spot where I had left my notes. I immediately asked the Fianna Fáil chief whip to ask the TD, whom I did not know well, to return them to me – joke over! The chief whip came back a few minutes later, in a furious humour. The TD had denied taking them, and I had embarrassed the chief whip by putting him in an awkward situation with his colleague.

(However, many months later Joe Dowling told me that he had in fact moved my notes to a table in the lobby outside the Chamber as a practical joke. When I failed to find them there, and the chief whip approached him, he had lost his nerve and had denied the charge! And quite recently, Joe Dowling told me that Kevin Boland had asked him what were these papers; when told they were notes for my speech, Boland had thrown them on to the floor.

That was that. I went home and started again at 7.30 AM, working until near lunchtime. My speech probably benefited considerably from being rewritten. It largely took the form of an attempt to reconstruct the extraordinary events of the preceding weeks from an analysis of all the statements and counter-statements that had emerged from those involved – between which there were many contradictions. George Colley, the new Minister for Finance, said in the following week's debate that although I had not got concrete information on which to work, I had shown very accurate insight into what had in fact happened.

The penultimate sentence of my speech – before a final paragraph extolling the responsibility with which our party and its leader, Liam Cosgrave, had handled this issue – was a pointed contrast between the political bitterness displayed by Neil Blaney and the complete lack of resentment of Erskine Childers, the Tánaiste, with his forgiveness of those – including my father – who had been responsible in 1922 for his father's execution. To my astonishment at this, the Fianna Fáil benches erupted in applause, joined, somewhat uncertainly, by some of my colleagues behind me. I should, of course, have had the wit to sit down at that moment; instead I waited till the applause died down and proceeded unimaginatively to my planned final paragraph – and appropriate applause from our own benches.

On the following Tuesday and Wednesday, there was a confidence debate. I was the penultimate Fine Gael speaker, and I allotted much of my speech on this occasion to pinpointing evasions in the various denials of allegations, and to identifying other questions about these extraordinary events that had been raised and needed to be answered. I had many questions, but few were ever answered satisfactorily, and hardly any of the issues involved are likely ever to be resolved. One question that I pressed was whether the money to buy these arms had come from state funds? The Taoiseach had told the House already that there was no question of Secret Service funds having been used, nor was any money missing from the Department of Defence. I said that 'the likely place is the

Department of Finance; there is no denial in respect of there'.

A couple of hours later, replying to the debate, the Taoiseach said that he had made specific enquiries as to whether any monies could have been voted or could have been paid out of Exchequer funds, or out of any public funds, in respect of a consignment of arms of the size in question, 'and was assured that there were not and could not have been' any such payments. It transpired later that this was an accurate, although not verbatim, account of what he had been officially advised he could say.

However, many months afterwards, when the Public Accounts Committee came to investigate the affair, it transpired that the money had, in fact, as I had suggested, come from the Department of Finance, having been 'laundered' through the Irish Red Cross to bank accounts in false names. Moreover, the file on this 'Fund for the Relief of Distress in Northern Ireland', which had been examined as a preliminary to advising the Taoiseach that he could give this assurance, had contained a number of references to the money being needed by 'Jim Kelly's friends' or 'Kelly's people', and for the week before the debate, during which the Taoiseach had been advised that the money could not have come from public funds, an Army Intelligence officer, Captain Jim Kelly, had been featuring as a key person in the whole affair.

Months passed, however, before these facts on the use of funds authorised by the Minister for Finance emerged in the discussion of the Committee on Public Accounts; I was a member of this committee, which was given the task in December 1970 of investigating and reporting on this matter. By that time, the trials of the ministers and others accused of illegal arms importations were over; they had been found not guilty by a jury.

The committee enquiry went on for over eighteen months. Despite lack of co-operation from many of those who were asked to give evidence to the committee, and a successful Supreme Court challenge to its power to compel the attendance of witnesses, and despite the obvious problems posed by such an enquiry for the Fianna Fáil members of the committee, it produced a final report which clarified to a degree the process by which state funds had ended up being used to finance an attempt to import arms illegally. The report concluded that had three ministers, Neil Blaney, Charles Haughey and Jim Gibbons, 'passed on to the Taoiseach their suspicion or knowledge of the proposed arms importation', the misappropriation of part of the money spent on arms might have been avoided – adding that it was not satisfied that the decision of Charles Haughey as Minister for Finance to make available a specific sum of money from the fund was justified. This was as far as we could bring our Fianna Fáil colleagues on the basis of the evidence we had been able to unearth, despite many obstacles put in our way.

But by the time the committee reported, in July 1972, much else had happened

in Northern Ireland. Shortly after the Arms Crisis of May 1970, the British government had changed, and several weeks after that election came the Falls Road curfew,
when the British army carried out mass raids on houses in nationalist areas. This
alienated many nationalists who hitherto had welcomed the army as protection
against unionist pogroms. Throughout 1971, the situation in Northern Ireland
kept on deteriorating, events reaching their climax with internment in September
1971.

Joan and I had decided to take our 1971 summer holiday in Kerry. For the first
week it rained almost continually. Then we woke one morning to the news that several hundred nationalists had been detained in Northern Ireland with a view to
internment. The reaction in nationalist areas was violent – especially as it quickly
emerged that a large number of those interned were innocent of any IRA involvement, being the victims of the collapse of the police-intelligence system after the
RUC had been discredited in 1969. Moreover, it soon became clear that many of
those arrested had been brutalised after their arrest. There was also much bitterness
at the selective character of internment. No loyalist paramilitaries were included –
an omission which I was later authoritatively told by a member of the Northern
Ireland government had been justified by the security authorities on the grounds
that the files on the loyalists had been lost!

On the day internment was introduced, I was called to Dublin for a meeting
with an SDLP delegation, which did not include John Hume, and for a front-bench
meeting. The SDLP representatives foresaw mounting violence and bloodshed following internment; they were proved right in this, as on that day alone twelve died.
But they took what seemed to me, at least, a very hard-line attitude, insisting that
they would now contemplate nothing except the abolition of Stormont. It later
transpired that John Hume was not in full agreement with this; indeed, when I met
him ten days later in Derry, he was very upset to hear the line his colleagues had
taken with us – which, he said, was very different from the position that had been
agreed amongst them beforehand.

Back in Kerry, I received a phone call on the morning of Friday 13 August from
a fairly recently appointed unionist minister, Robin Baillie, whom I had got to
know before he had become a member of the government. He asked me to come
to Belfast on the following day, Saturday 14 August. He met me at Portadown and
drove me to his home. He had joined the government, he said, because he believed
that Brian Faulkner, who had succeeded Robin Chichester-Clark, provided the only
hope of a peaceful solution, and that Faulkner would steer the North towards an
agreement on full participation of the Northern minority in government. He
believed that Faulkner was still prepared for 'proportional government'; despite
the depth of the rift with the nationalist population arising from the form that
internment had taken, he believed that progress on these lines might even now be

possible. In the light of the events of the preceding week, even quite intransigent unionists were looking for a solution.

I told him that in this post-internment situation, I saw little prospect of getting talks going again between the Northern Ireland government and the Opposition, unless the Opposition could be satisfied in advance that a solution along the lines of proportional government would in fact be acceptable to Faulkner and his government, and that internment would also be withdrawn. He said he would make further soundings, and we agreed to meet again in a week or so.

On my way back to Kerry, through Dublin, I went to my home and typed a letter to Liam Cosgrave telling him of my meeting with Robin Baillie, expressing great scepticism about whether anything could come of this initiative, however, and suggesting that the fewer the number of people who knew of my contact with Robin Baillie the better, but that our shadow Minister for Foreign Affairs, Richie Ryan, must, of course, be told.

There was obviously no point in prolonging the holiday in Kerry, which had already been interrupted twice and which was likely to be interrupted again. Moreover ,it had rained every day! During the following week, I brought the family back to Dublin.

On Thursday evening, 19 August, I rang John Hume, and he agreed to see me on the following day. I arrived in midmorning to find the area around his house full of British soilders. John was out, but returned after half an hour. Furious at the army presence, which put his home and family at risk from the IRA, he rang the RUC, who declared themselves impotent in the matter. John then went down to the corner to persuade the British officer in charge to move his men away. I stood in a doorway beside a heavily armed soldier, watching the other soldiers in the little gardens across the street from the houses listening to the argument.

For about a quarter of an hour, John Hume got nowhere. Then he suddenly had a brainwave. 'Do you realize,' he said to the officer, pointing at the soldiers in the gardens, 'that your men are standing on private property.' The officer, overcome with embarrassment at this apparently unanswerable thrust, responded instantly. The men were told to move away at once. I was enormously impressed with the courteous manner in which the officer conveyed his new orders. To the soldier beside me he said: 'I say, please, would you mind moving away'!

John and I went to a hotel. There I put to him proposals that I had worked out following my discussion with Robin Bailey. First, the British government should at the request of Faulkner, call a meeting bringing together government and Opposition in Northern Ireland; this formula would preserve Faulkner's position with the unionists, but would also make it possible for the Opposition to come to a meeting. Second, the meeting should agree to a new parliament being elected by PR, and to a proportionately representative government being chosen either by parliament or by the British government after consultation – but this should not be made a pre-condition. Third, the detainees should be released. And, fourth, a Council of Ireland with economic and consultative functions should be formed following discussions with the Republic. In other words, I proposed much of what actually emerged two years later at Sunningdale. John Hume believed that he could get his colleagues, with the possible exception of Paddy Devlin, to accept this.

I then drove to Belfast and saw Robin Baillie again. He was prepared to try to 'sell' these proposals to his colleagues, of whom only Brian Faulkner knew he had been talking to me. He saw it as a 'long shot' which if sprung on the Cabinet would be overwhelmingly defeated, but which, with judicious preparation, and given that those capable of thinking must see it as the only hope of their survival in government, might have a chance. But first he felt he should talk to Ken Bloomfield, the permanent secretary to the Cabinet who, he believed, would be more influential than himself with Brian Faulkner, and who, he said, had originated the idea of proportional representation as a way out of the governmental impasse in Northern Ireland. Bloomfield would not be back from holidays for a week. In the meantime he wondered whether I could talk to the Home Secretary, Reggie Maudling, with a view to persuading him to put pressure on Brian Faulkner. When I said that I doubted if Maudling would see me, he offered to try to arrange such a meeting through Peter McLachlan of the Conservative Central Office. Returning to Dublin on the following morning I wrote Liam Cosgrave a full account of my latest visit to the North.

On Tuesday 24 August Robin Baillie rang me to say that he had been able to contact Ken Bloomfield who agreed that my proposal was the only hope. Bloomfield had sent a memo to Brian Faulkner about our discussion, and Faulkner had not turned it down but would require persuasion and would need to be sure that it would be accepted by the nationalist minority. I sent Liam Cosgrave a note about this phone call also, adding that I proposed to discuss with John Hume how the nationalist opposition could be lined up in favour of this proposition. On the following night, however, Robin Baillie rang me in a less optimistic mood, seeing many difficulties.

I had a full discussion with Liam Cosgrave and Richie Ryan about these moves, and in the middle of the following week I dropped into Liam Cosgrave's office a copy of a memorandum I had prepared after consultation with John Kelly and Michael Sweetman. I gave other copies to Conor Cruise O'Brien, who was going to a meeting in London on 1 September of the British and Irish Labour Parties, the Northern Ireland Labour Party and the SDLP, for himself, for John Hume, and, if he thought appropriate, for the British Labour Party.

The memo fleshed out my earlier proposal in considerable detail. It added the idea of a deputy prime minister from the Opposition, which was also later a feature of the end-1973 settlement; a suggestion for the eventual establishment of a security force drawn from the whole community; a proposal for a Bill of Rights to be adjudicated by a panel of judges; and a possible procedure for nominating the judiciary which would ensure a balanced court – something not achieved until after the agreement of 1985. It also included detailed proposals for an equitable grouping of the existing single-seat constituencies into three, four and five-seat constituencies as a means of achieving early PR elections without a lengthy process of constituency review. This grouping was designed to ensure both proportionality of representation in each of three main regions of Northern Ireland and also some representation for both communities in every constituency.

On Friday 3 September, following the announcement of a meeting between the Taoiseach and the British prime minister on the following Monday, the Northern Ireland Opposition members were in Dublin to meet Jack Lynch. Gerry Fitt, the SDLP leader had been struck down with a back ailment in Dublin and was in St Vincent's Hospital, but I met John Hume, Austin Currie and Paddy Devlin in the Dáil, where we were joined by Richie Ryan and by Frank Cluskey of the Labour Party. I formed the impression that John Hume was doubtful about being the best person to 'sell' my proposal to his colleagues; disagreement on the issue of making the abolition of Stormont a pre-condition for political progress, upon which Paddy Devlin and Ivan Cooper had been insisting during the previous week, had left him a bit isolated. However I persuaded Austin Currie to accept that talks with Faulkner could take place without the abolition of Stormont, and Richie Ryan argued successfully with him the case for accepting as an alternative to the release of all the internees, the charging of some of them with offenses and the release of the remainder. At John Hume's request I gave Paddy Devlin a copy of my memorandum, which helped to get over John's fears about the reaction if the proposals seemed to come from him. At the end of the evening it was agreed that during the week the SDLP would call a party meeting at which I would present my memorandum.

When the Taoiseach met the British prime minister three days later a new element entered the situation, however. This meeting represented a significant change of position on the part of both Irish and British governments, by comparison with a fortnight earlier when Jack Lynch had sent a telegram to Ted Heath requesting the ending of internment and Ted Heath on television that night had rejected the Irish government's right to intervene in the matter. Now at this meeting the British government recognised the Irish government's legitimate interest in a situation that threatened the security of both parts of the island, and proposed a tri-partite meeting in which Jack Lynch would be involved in discussions with both Ted Heath and Brian Faulkner – a much closer involvement in the affairs of Northern Ireland than had hitherto appeared conceivable.

Jack Lynch's first reaction to this proposal was, however, quite negative. At a subsequent press conference he did not accept that such a tri-partite meeting had actually been proposed, and Irish government briefings suggested that he was reluctant to get involved in discussions with the leader of a provincial government, and that this would be acceptable only if the Northern Opposition were present also, making it a quadri-partite meeting. This, then, was the position when the Taoiseach reported to the Dáil on Tuesday 7 September.

However, in September 1971 the British government were not ready for the type of quadri-partite meeting that took place at Sunningdale two-and-a quarter years later. On the same day they made it clear that they were proposing a tri-partite meeting and that this was the only meeting to which the Irish government was invited. Moreover simultaneously the Home Secretary, Reggie Maudling, proposed separate talks in London with the Northern Ireland government and Opposition.

Whether the Maudling proposal was a response to my earlier initiative I do not know. If it was, then the fact that it was launched simultaneously with a controversy over the British government's unwillingness to allow the participation of the Northern Opposition in the proposed tri-partite intergovernmental talks greatly reduced its chances of acceptance by the SDLP. Their reaction, despite efforts on my part by telephone to John Hume and directly with Gerry Fitt in St Vincent's Nursing Home – he tried by telephone to get his party colleagues to accept a cautiously-worded statement that I had drafted – was to announce a series of pre-conditions to acceptance of the Maudling proposal, including the abolition of the Stormont government, which they wanted replaced by a commission, and the ending of internment.

Brendan Halligan, the Labour Party general secretary and a political friend since 1967, had been with Gerry Fitt when I called on him that evening. After Gerry Fitt's SDLP colleagues had rejected his attempt to get them to adopt my draft statement, and had announced their pre-conditions, Brendan Halligan had pressed Gerry Fitt to ask the Taoiseach, Liam Cosgrave, Brendan Corish and the British ambassador to call on him and had also pressed him to go on radio to water down the negative SDLP statement.

Next morning I called on Gerry Fitt again on my way to a front bench meeting. Brendan Halligan was there again and after I left he succeeded in persuading Gerry Fitt to go on radio at lunchtime along those lines. John Hume, intercepted on his way back from court, where Austin Currie and himself were being charged with obstruction – they had intervened in a British army attempt to arrest one of their colleagues – felt he had no alternative but to endorse Gerry Fitt's statement which he had not in fact heard – and later in the day Austin Currie followed suit, after Gerry Fitt had rung him.

Meanwhile, following through on Brendan Halligan's plan, at my suggestion Liam Cosgrave had called on Gerry Fitt and had also agreed to bring forward to that night a speech on Northern Ireland planned for the following evening, a draft of which Michael Sweetman had prepared following discussions with me at lunchtime. That speech regretted the absence of consultations between government and opposition and described Maudling's proposals for talks between the different parties in Northern Ireland as containing 'positive and constructive elements' – they proposed for example 'talks designed to ensure an active, permanent and guaranteed role for the minority in Northern . Ireland'. That must surely come close to meeting the central objective of the Opposition in Northern Ireland. The speech went on to refer to Liam Cosgrave's meeting with Gerry Fitt in St Vincent's Nursing Home, adding 'I was very reassured to find him quite flexible in his approach to this question of talks. This attitude was also echoed by Mr John Hume in his interview on Radio Éireann. The moment for talks is now'.

Elsewhere in the speech stress was laid on the need for a settlement that would 'protect not only the rights of the present minority within Northern Ireland but the rights of the present majority there'.

Brendan Corish also called on Gerry Fitt. Reggie Maudling had rung Gerry Fitt that morning and Fitt had explained to him that he was trying to modify the hardline SDLP position, and had asked him to get the ambassador to call on him.

Next day, Thursday, a number of developments took place. The Taoiseach too called on Gerry Fitt, who was reported by the press to have urged him to attend the tri-partite meeting. Later that day it emerged that he would accept this invitation after all. Meanwhile in the North the rest of the SDLP held an all-day meeting, of which Gerry Fitt knew nothing, and issued a long and somewhat defensive statement about their attitude to the proposed Maudling talks. They were to meet the Irish government on the following day and it was arranged that they would subsequently have a meeting with Gerry Fitt in the nursing home at 7 o'clock, following a press conference. Meanwhile, I had rung Robin Baillie and it had been agreed that I would meet with him and Peter McLachlan at Robin Baillie's house on the Friday afternoon, and that Ken Bloomfield would come if he were able. Gerry Fitt asked me to sound out Robin Baillie at this meeting on the possibility of an intermediary being nominated between himself and Brian Faulkner – someone like Maurice Hayes – and he asked me to call on him on my return from Belfast with news of my discussions and after his meeting with his colleagues had ended.

Next day I found Robin Baillie and Peter McLachlan very depressed. IRA bombings of the previous weeks had evoked their intended reaction amongst unionists – a hardline attitude. Nevertheless, they went over a redraft of a memorandum I had proposed for our meeting. This raised a large number of issues including the establishment of an administration in which the different groups would be represented proportionally – this administration to be selected by the existing or a new parliament or to be nominated by the governor after consultations with the parties; parliament itself to be elected in future by PR, with a membership of about 75; the administration to be led by a prime minister and deputy prime minister; a possible endorsement of the new government by referendum; a Bill of Rights; and a possible Council of Ireland. I had left a copy of this into Liam Cosgrave's office before leaving Dublin.

Peter McLachlan and Robin Baillie,who had a twenty minute conversation with Ken Bloomfield at one point during our discussion, favoured the Irish PR system – preferential voting in multi-seat constituencies to the list system. They also favoured endorsement of the new structure by a referendum rather than an election, and Opposition involvement in security. Peter McLachlan also said he would report to Maudling who regretted he had not been able to see me, but was very interested.

On my return to Dublin Brendan Halligan and I visited Gerry Fitt after the SDLP members had left. Gerry Fitt reported that there had been no real discussion of the issues.

We seemed to be stuck. After some discussion he agreed, however, to issue a statement denouncing the Provisionals, which Robin Baillie had felt might help to soften unionist attitudes. But on the following Wednesday, just as Robin Baillie and Peter McLachlan were preparing to get positive reactions to this statement from Brian Faulkner and Maudling, Faulkner signed orders converting the detention of 219 men into indefinite internment – something which he had done without consulting London, giving the British government one hour's notice. That at least was the impression I received from the British embassy.

As I reported to Liam Cosgrave (he was just returning from a week's holiday), in a letter telling him that I proposed to attend the Westminster debate at Peter McLachlan's suggestion in the hope of lobbying Tory MPs, this made any further initiative by Gerry Fitt in advance of the debate rather pointless. I added that I had drafted a Commons speech for Gerry Fitt; because of his back problem he had spent much of his time in St Vincent's Nursing Home lying across the bed with his arms and legs dangling on either side, the only posture in which he could secure relief and could not write out a speech for himself, but had given me an outline of what he wanted to say.

On Monday 20 September I mentioned in a speech in my constituency that a group of TDs was going to attend the Westminster debate. Next morning I read that Richie Ryan was also going and I tried fruitlessly throughout the afternoon to contact him to co-ordinate our plans. Then at 6.30 PM I was rung by a journalist to comment on a statement Richie Ryan had issued criticising our visit to Westminster in astringent terms. I issued an explanatory statement, clarifying some misunderstandings. This was to have a sequel a month later.

In London I found that Gerry Fitt could not read my typescript – the type was too small, he said. I wrote out the speech in block capitals – 25,000 of them, finishing at 4 AM!

At Westminster we were told that our group, the SDLP, and the ambassador would all be in different galleries and we were surprised, and amused, to find that we were in fact seated beside each other, with ropes between us! During the debate some of the comments of British speakers gave rise to Irish hilarity in our corner of the gallery and I noticed Ted Heath looking up in puzzlement at our group.

In Maudling's speech there were some signs of a thaw in British attitudes towards the minority in Northern Ireland and of the beginning of movement towards the concept of power-sharing in Northern Ireland. He commented that it was difficult to reconcile a permanent government and a permanent opposition with the concept of democracy. He also indicated an openness to proportional representation as a method of election in Northern Ireland and spoke of the possibility of a sharing of government through some new basis of representation, with a permanent place in public life for the minority.

When Gerry Fitt's turn came to speak, he stuck to my script only for about four or five minutes. Then his feelings got the better of him and the script was abandoned. Although the speech he made was no less powerful than that which we had agreed he would make, nevertheless in its denunciation of the manner in which internment had been carried out and in its statement of the constitutional nationalist position it lacked certain components of the draft speech which had been designed to evoke a response from unionists in the House, at least one of whom had been prepared to respond to the speech as planned.

As we walking out into New Palace Yard after the debate I realised that I had left some papers behind in the cloakroom and returned to fetch them. I found myself completely alone in the part of the building around the chamber. I shouted 'hello' ineffectively, but there was no one to hear me. I eventually found the cloakroom and retrieved the papers. I found the security implications of this experience alarming, as I did on subsequent occasions when I was allowed into the building carrying a large briefcase without any serious attempt at a security check. Twice I went to the Home Office, meeting a junior minister on one occasion and the permanent secretary on another, to suggest some kind of security check, but so far as I could see nothing effective was done until after the IRA had placed a bomb in a building attached to Westminster Hall. No one was injured on that occasion as I recall, but the bomb was more effective than I had been at getting action on the security front, although the action then taken did not prevent the subsequent murder of Airey Neave.

That was effectively the end of this attempt to secure a Sunningdale-type settlement before rather than after the abolition of Stormont – an initiative which, had it succeeded would have saved unionists the trauma of that event. In retrospect, it probably had no chance of success. If Brian Faulkner even considered it seriously (and the involvement, albeit marginal, of Ken Bloomfield suggested that he may have done so), his Cabinet was unlikely to have countenanced a move to power-sharing at that time, and it has to be recognised that in view of the impact of the internment decision on the nationalist community, the SDLP would have found it very difficult to retain their public support if they had entered into discussions with the unionist government at that point. Moreover the tensions between Gerry Fitt, essentially an independent who was never comfortable in the role of party leader, and the rest of his party, which eventually led to his departure from the leadership, was already present, and his attempt to direct events from Dublin far away from the realities of Northern Ireland, and with the aid of two southern politicians, must have been difficult for them to accept.

Moreover, the coincidence of the brief Anglo-Irish controversy over tri-partite or quadri-partite talks, together with Maudling's proposal for separate discussions with the Northern government and Opposition made acceptance of this latter proposal more difficult for the SDLP because at the critical moment there seemed to surface the more attractive possibility of their involvement in talks involving the two sovereign governments as well as the Northern Ireland government.

These events were, however, to have a curious domestic sequel in Fine Gael a month later. When the Dáil came to debate the Northern Ireland situation on its resumption on 20 October, the speeches both of Liam Cosgrave and of Richie Ryan reflected the setback to progress towards a constitutional settlement that internment represented, but also, perhaps their own instinctive attachment to the pre-1969 anti-Partition tradition in Irish politics which the September 1969 Fine Gael policy document the adoption of which by the front bench I had secured – had been designed to replace. Richie Ryan, claiming specifically the authority of Liam Cosgrave, proposed in this debate that following a suspension of the Northern Ireland government. That area should be constituted an international protectorate under the British and Irish governments for a transitional period – a proposal which had never come before the party or the front bench. Liam Cosgrave had made no reference to this proposal in his earlier, opening speech in the debate but he had called for a phased withdrawal of British troops from Northern Ireland, which probably reflected his scepticism from August 1969 onwards about the long-term efficacy of the British army as a peace-keeping force in Northern Ireland. I shared his concern about the performance of the British army at that time, but then and subsequently saw no available substitute to this force as a deterrent to civil war in that part of the island.

Accordingly, at the front bench meeting on 26 October I, together with John Kelly, raised these two speeches and expressed concern about these major departures from what we had agreed to be party policy on Northern Ireland.

Liam Cosgrave's reaction was instantaneous and, to say the least, vigorous. He told the front bench with evident feeling that I had been engaged over a period in discussions in the North about the situation there without his knowledge and that I had produced and given to people two documents, the second of which I had brought to the North before he had seen it.

I reacted as best I could to this unexpected onslaught mentioning the four letters I had written to Liam Cosgrave setting out all the details of my discussions, as well as my various contacts with him during the period from mid-August onwards. Subsequently I circulated to the front bench a detailed account of the events of the period in question, based on my letters to Liam Cosgrave together with a note which for historical purposes I had compiled on 11 September of events up to that time.

This episode did not help the relationship between Liam Cosgrave and myself. In retrospect it seems to me that while on the one hand, he had not been prepared to instruct me to stop what I was doing – he was perhaps more inhibited about confronting me than I (never the most sensitive of people), realised – this very restraint, combined with some pressure from an aggrieved shadow Minister for Foreign Affairs, Richie Ryan, must have built up a head of frustration. And, as was to happen on several other occasions in the next year or so, this eventually exploded.

On Sunday 31 January 1972 Joan and I were dining at the Royal Irish Yacht Club when we heard first reports of a massacre in Derry. We went home at once and listened to various news bulletins. Clearly the death of so many Derry men and boys at the hands of the British army in Derry, whatever the circumstances – and so far as one could judge at that stage there appeared to have been little, if any, justification for the paratroopers' actions – could endanger peace in the island as a whole. To find out whether there had been any provocation before the paratroopers' attack I rang the City Hotel in Derry, which, until some time later it was burnt down by the IRA, was the usual haunt of journalists in Derry. I got Simon Winchester of the *Guardian*, who told me that he had been one of only three journalists on the spot when the paratroopers launched their onslaught and that he had observed no firing on them beforehand.

Racking my brains to think of what I could do to help defuse the situation I decided that with a view to getting support for an enquiry into this appalling event, I would contact the editor of the *Guardian*, Alastair Hetherington whom I had met. First, however, I got through to the *Guardian* newsroom in London to find out whether in fact they were running Simon Winchester's story. They were, and a subeditor read it to me. When I got Alastair Hetherington in Manchester I made the mistake of referring to the fact that their own news story was about an unprovoked attack. I had got off on the wrong foot. 'Where did you get that?', he demanded, and was not pleased to hear that it was from talking to Simon Winchester and to his newsroom. My blundering approach received a correspondingly cool reaction and proved completely abortive.

Three days later I set off with Tom O'Higgins, Alexis FitzGerald, and Michael Sweetman for the funerals in Derry, taking the long way around via Sligo because of concern that if we took the direct route through Northern Ireland we might be prevented by security forces from getting through. John Hume arranged to have us met at the border near Derry and brought into the city in the car of a friend of his. I shan't attempt to describe the occasion; it was shattering. Everyone in the tight knit nationalist community in Derry had lost a relative, a neighbour or a friend. After the funeral we were brought back for a meal to a 'moderate' house. However, when I went into the kitchen after the meal a woman said to me: 'isn't it great that so many are joining?' 'Joining what?' I asked, bemused. 'The IRA, of course', another woman responded. I started the long journey back with my fears for the immediate future heightened; if that was the instinctive reaction of moderate nationalists to the trauma of these events, what hope was there for Northern Ireland?

On the long journey back we stopped several times, timing our halts to coincide with TV news bulletins. The British embassy in Merrion Square was under attack, and before we got back to Dublin it had been burnt out. My forebodings about the impact of the Derry massacre on security in the Republic as well as Northern Ireland seemed justified.

Next day the Dáil debated the situation. The fourth speech after those of the Taoiseach, Liam Cosgrave and Brendan Corish came from Neil Blaney, ensconced high up on the back benches with three other Fianna Fáil dissidents. It was inflammatory, as I had feared it would be, and reminded me forcibly of the kind of speeches made in Germany in the 1930s. But this speech, and those of Neil Blaney's supporters later in the debate, evoked an immediate, instinctive response from both the government and Opposition benches – a response that demonstrated the strength of our democratic system and the ability of our politicians in a crisis to transcend their differences in the interest of the country. Every one of these speeches was directed towards taking the heat out of the situation and reducing the tension. Instinctively, and without concertation, all concerned resisted the temptation to hit out blindly at the authors of this tragedy. Too much was at stake for that – peace itself. There were, it is true, some on the Fianna Fáil benches who were clearly restive at the restrained tones of the government speeches, but party discipline was maintained.

There followed the Widgery Tribunal, which evoked universal cynicism in nationalist Ireland, but, more important, there were signs that, while no one in the British government would admit the truth of what had happened in Derry, behind the scenes a radical review of British policy in Northern Ireland was under way. Twice in less than six months, both at the time of internment when so many of those arrested had been ill-treated (some to a degree that was later described by the

Commission on Human Rights in Strasbourg as 'torture', a phrase subsequently modified by the Court of Human Rights to 'brutal and inhuman treatment'), and now in Derry, the British army had acted in a manner unacceptable to civilised opinion in Britain or elsewhere, in support of a subordinate civil power not under the control of Westminster. This was not something that men like Ted Heath, Willie Whitelaw and Peter Carrington were likely to tolerate any further. The days of Stormont were now clearly numbered, as, indeed, I had already concluded six months earlier, when, after internment, I had endeavoured to secure a transition to a power-sharing administration in advance of what then appeared to me to be an otherwise inevitable, and, for unionists, dangerously traumatic, abolition of the provincial government.

It was at this point that I first met Willie Whitelaw, who within a year I was to find myself dealing with across the table as my opposite number so far as Northern Ireland was concerned. Shortly before the Derry tragedy I had entertained the Liberal leader, Jo Grimond, to dinner in Dublin and he had suggested that it might be useful for me to meet Willie Whitelaw and possibly also Geoffrey Rippon.

As I was going to London on 2 March as part of a delegation to meet the Anglo-Irish group of the British Parliament, it was agreed that he and I should dine with Willie Whitelaw in the Commons that evening, and that I would stay the night with Jo and Laura Grimond.

Like everyone who ever met Willie Whitelaw I was impressed by his openness and bonhomie. Unaware, of course, that the decision had already been taken at that moment to establish direct rule in Northern Ireland if Brian Faulkner refused the British requirement that responsibility for security be transferred back from Stormont to London, and that Willie Whitelaw himself was to be the first Secretary of State for Northern Ireland, I advocated to him government of Northern Ireland by a commission of non-political people as an interim stage before the installation of a power-sharing administration drawn from political representatives of both communities. I also argued against repartition – a solution which often seems to have a fatal attraction for British politicians unfamiliar with Irish affairs – and suggested that in the longer run a system of regional or local police forces on the British model might best meet the needs of Northern Ireland.

Within days Brian Faulkner had rejected a transfer of responsibility for security to London and had resigned, and Willie Whitelaw was installed as secretary of state.

Four months later, after the breakdown of an IRA ceasefire, Willie Whitelaw met the IRA leadership in London. None of us had foreseen such a development, believing naively that no British government would be so foolish as to encourage the IRA to continue their campaign indefinitely by giving them reason to believe that if they went on murdering people long enough, Britain would negotiate with them. We should have been warned by Harold Wilson's visit to Dublin as leader of the Opposition a year earlier when, behind the backs of the members of the Irish government and Opposition whom he was meeting, he arranged to see the leaders of the terrorists who threatened our state as well as Northern Ireland. In retrospect we should, perhaps, have protested more loudly in 1971 at what we saw as an act of treachery towards the democratic politicians of the Irish state on our own territory, and should not have allowed a concern about alienating a past and probable future prime minister of Britain to mute our outrage at an action that would I think have been inconceivable for a British politician anywhere other than in Ireland.

So far as Willie Whitelaw's initiative vis-a-vis the IRA was concerned, it came to an abrupt end following the breakdown of the IRA ceasefire a couple of days later. I believe he recognised in retrospect that it had been a serious mistake. I am not sure that British politicians even today understand the extent to which this and other similar contacts – such as the NIO/Sinn Féin discussions imitated several years later by Merlyn Rees and contacts in 1981 during the Hunger Strike – contributed to the continuation of the IRA campaign over such a long period by enabling that organisation to persuade its members that persistence in their campaign of terror would eventually lead to a British negotiation with the IRA of a withdrawal by Britain from Northern Ireland.

The argument within Fine Gael about the party's Northern Ireland policy had been sidetracked by the row over my activities sparked off by Liam Cosgrave's remarks at the front bench in October 1971. The disagreement simmered on, however, and in July 1972 reports after a front bench meeting suggested, quite incorrectly, that it had endorsed the anti-partitionist view that as an artificially-created area Northern Ireland could not be regarded as a justifiable unit for a decision on whether it should be re-united with the rest of Ireland. This was the old irredentist thesis that I thought had finally been laid to rest by the policy statement on Northern Ireland that I had drafted and that had been adopted by the front bench in September 1969. This episode was followed several days later by a speech by Richie Ryan in which he seemed to advocate British negotiations with illegal bodies such as the IRA. Efforts by me to head off these departures from our agreed policy were not successful and tensions between what seemed to have become two wings of the party, deriving primarily from disagreements on other domestic issues, were thus intensified by different approaches to the Northern Ireland issue. At the end of the year this internal crisis became public property in dramatic circumstances.

In early November 1972 tensions between Liam Cosgrave and his deputy leader, Tom O'Higgins, who was on the social democratic and liberal wing of the party, had become visible at a party meeting. This had led to a very full, and unusually frank, discussion at front bench meetings on 8 and 14 November. Many of those who spoke at these meetings questioned openly for the first time aspects of Liam Cosgrave's leadership of the party and in particular what was perceived amongst his critics as a withdrawal of confidence on his part from some members of the front bench during the immediately preceding years, together with undue reliance on a small group of 'loyalists' on the front bench.

I have already commented that in retrospect the latter suggestion may have been unwarranted, but there certainly were significant differences of style, as well as differences on policy, between the leader of the party and some of his colleagues. These had surfaced from time to time in public references by Liam Cosgrave, at moments of frustration or emotion to, for example, people who 'allowed their humanitarian instincts to lead them to become communist dupes' – that arose from opposition by some of us to the US bombing of Cambodia – as well as in an unscripted *ard fheis* speech reference to 'mongrel foxes' – a somewhat unhappy simile, which came easily to the lips of a hunting man like Liam Cosgrave, but which was received with less than enthusiasm by people, like myself, to whom, the press believed, it was intended to apply!

At the end of that front bench meeting of 14 November Liam Cosgrave had asked for twenty-four hours in which to consider his position. But when the front bench resumed twenty-four hours later, he ignored the discussion of the previous day and proceeded as if it had never happened. If this was intended to disconcert those who had initiated this discussion, it certainly succeeded! After a discussion between a number of those concerned a week later it was decided, however, to leave the matter on one side for the time being, as in the following week we had to face a difficult decision on how to handle a government bill to amend the Offences Against the State Act 1940 so as to include, inter alia, a provision that would constitute as evidence a statement by a Garda superintendent that he believed that a person was a member of the IRA.

When the front bench met for this purpose on Monday 27 November it became clear at once that the differences on this legislation ran very deep. Eventually it was decided to refer to the parliamentary party meeting the next day a decision as to our course of action, without presenting it with (as was the normal practice), a recommendation from the front bench. This meant that the differences within the front bench were to be openly presented to the parliamentary party. When the party met on the following day, Liam Cosgrave was in favour of supporting the legislation, whereas a majority wanted to oppose it on the second stage because they took exception to some of its clauses, including the new provision constituting as evidence a statement by a Garda superintendent about his belief concerning a person's membership of the IRA. Eventually, however, late that night Liam Cosgrave reluctantly agreed to go along with a proposal to oppose the Bill on the basis of a reasoned amendment, the amendment to be proposed by the shadow Minister for Justice and seconded by Liam Cosgrave himself. It was after midnight when the meeting adjourned.

The party thought that, for good or ill, this ended the matter. By Friday, however, as the debate continued in the Dáil, some among the party leadership were concerned as to whether Cosgrave would feel able to vote with his colleagues. As a result, at lunchtime that day, an approach was made to Fianna Fáil to seek agreement to several amendments that would have met our main concerns and enabled a united Fine Gael to support the Bill. These proposals were, however, turned down at an early afternoon government meeting; by this time Fianna Fáil had smelt blood and were, understandably, looking forward to facing a divided and possibly even headless Fine Gael in a 'law and order' election on the issue.

When word of this was received at 4.30 PM Cosgrave called yet a further party meeting in the hope of persuading his colleagues to reverse their twice-taken decision. This proved too much for the members, who, just before eight o'clock, after several hours debate in the party room and with Tom O'Higgins already on his feet in the Dáil for half an hour waiting to hear what line he was to take, voted by 38 to 8 to oppose the Bill. Six of the eight opponents of the Bill immediately rallied to the majority, leaving Liam Cosgrave and Paddy Donegan alone in their dissent. As some members tried to persuade an unyielding Cosgrave to change his mind and vote with his party, I went down to the House to put Tom O'Higgins out of his agony.

As Tom O'Higgins proceeded to reveal the outcome of the discussions with the government that afternoon, accusing Fianna Fáil of arrogance by refusing to consider any amendments to the Bill, word reached us that bombs had just gone off in Dublin. I think I whispered this news to Tom O'Higgins just as a Fianna Fáil deputy, Noel Davern, interrupted him to ask him if he supported the bombings. Tom replied to Davern that he was aware of them and told him not to be a 'bloody ass'.

I went upstairs at once to our party corridor and found a large number of our deputies engaged in heated discussion on the landing outside the party room. After a few minutes there was general agreement, albeit with some dissentient voices, that in view of the bombings, which at that stage some thought might be an IRA provocation (although in the event it transpired that they had been undertaken by loyalist paramilitaries from the North, leaving 2 dead and 127 injured), we should reverse our stand and agree to support the Bill. I returned to the House, where Tom O'Higgins had concluded – inconclusively – and had gone to look for Liam Cosgrave to tell him what had happened.

After consultations with the government, Pat Cooney intervened in the debate at 9.45 to withdraw our reasoned amendment. Following two adjournments the House reconvened at 11.25 and passed the second stage. Two Fine Gael deputies, Oliver Flanagan and Eddie Collins, voted against, together with Labour and independents.

The committee-stage debate continued until 4 AM, however. When the House then adjourned many in Fine Gael, including past supporters of Liam Cosgrave, left for home believing that he would be replaced as leader the following week. But unknown to most deputies he had during the course of the evening appeared on television to great effect, and by Saturday morning he was widely seen as the hero of the hour: the man who had stood firm and had, in tragic circumstances, been proved right.

And so, in retrospect, he had. Our emotional opposition to this Act was not subsequently justified by the use actually made of it. All too soon, indeed, the 'chief superintendent clause', far from proving dangerous to the liberty of innocent people, was rendered ineffective by virtue of a change in IRA policy instructing members to deny on oath allegations of membership by a chief superintendent. If no other evidence of membership was presented to them, the courts came to accept this rebutting evidence. Moreover, in political terms Cosgrave was also right: had we opposed the Bill we would, I believe, have been severely defeated in a post-Christmas law-and-order election.

Why, in the light of this, did a majority of Fine Gael oppose the Bill? After a long period in Opposition – sixteen years in this case – a party tends to become anti-authoritarian, and in this instance there was a belief that Fianna Fáil, some of whose members were ambivalent about the IRA, had not been enforcing existing laws adequately. This had indeed been an insistent refrain of the Opposition for several years previously, and the new legislation was seen by some as a 'cover' for this perceived failure rather than as a genuine attempt to strengthen the existing law.

Moreover, within Fine Gael Liam Cosgrave's position had been weakened by the manner in which he had handled tensions with Tom O'Higgins and myself and in particular by what was seen as his failure to respond at the front bench meeting of 15 November to the criticisms of his leadership made at the two immediately preceding meetings. The unresolved problem thus created, and left in abeyance because of the need to decide how to handle the Offences Against the State (Amendment) Bill, hung over the stormy debates on this measure in the party a fortnight later at which Cosgrave's quite uncharacteristic vacillation, under what admittedly was extreme pressure, unnerved his own strong supporters in the party.

These dramatic events had profound effects on the political fortunes of the Irish state, for, although deprived by a matter of minutes of the opportunity to call a snap 'law and order' election, Jack Lynch nevertheless calculated that the aftermath of these bruising events within Fine Gael provided his best moment to seek and secure a further mandate almost two years before this Dáil had run its term. This proved to be a major miscalculation, which put an end to Fianna Fáil's second sixteen-year period in office and replaced Lynch with the man who had seemed for a brief moment on the evening of 1 December 1972 to be on his way to the back benches: Liam Cosgrave.

The drastic change in Joan's life and mine that these events were to precipitate had been preceded by a major change in our family situation. John and Mary had both married in late 1972. John had secured a good degree in 1970 in economics and history – an extremely difficult combination – and, after completing an MA thesis on an aspect of eighteenth-century Irish economic history, had joined the Department of Finance as an administrative officer. In September 1972 he married Eithne Ingoldsby; that decision had been made several years earlier when they had been classmates in UCD, and Eithne had preceded him into the Department of Finance, where she had soon become an expert on health and social welfare economics.

Mary had followed John into UCD, where her degree choice had been English and Philosophy. In December 1972, when in her final year and aged nineteen, she married a fellow-student, Vincent Deane, whose enduring interest proved to be Joyce studies, in particular Finnegans Wake. After some years teaching in a school Mary became a temporary assistant lecturer in English in Maynooth, and later in UCD. Thus by the time the 1973 election was held only Mark, aged fifteen, remained at home.

Meanwhile, in anticipation of a possible change of government in which I was likely to be involved I had been shifting the emphasis of my mixed career. My burden had been somewhat lightened, to my relief, in 1969 when I had been replaced as correspondent of the *Financial Times* and the BBC. Moreover, following my election to the Dáil, the Confederation of Irish Industry, on the prompting I understood, of the new Minister for Finance, Charles J. Haughey, had indicated to me that the degree of my political involvement as an Opposition front bench spokesman in the Dáil made it inappropriate for me to continue as consultant to the Confederation and as one of its representatives on the General Purposes Committee of the National Industrial Economic Council. I regretted this change but accepted it as an inevitable part of my career development.

However, for several more years I continued my general economic consultancy work but with growing doubts as to the possibility of the Economist Intelligence Unit of Ireland remaining a viable entity after a change of government, in the absence of my continuing involvement. By 1972 it was clear to me that I was becoming more rather than less involved in keeping the company going; since I had ceased to be managing director in 1967 it had tended to stagnate rather than to develop, and while I still derived a useful income from my work for it I could have earned almost as much working on my own without the overhead of the small staff and office premises. Accordingly, in the spring of 1972 an alternative arrangement was made with accountancy and consultancy firm, Stokes Kennedy Crowley, to work with them as an economic and market consultant, an arrangement that naturally ended when I became Minister for Foreign Affairs a year later.

As a result of these changes I was able to make the transition to government in March 1973 without too much trauma and without upsetting too many clients. The fact that the government was formed during the course of an academic year in UCD did pose some problems, but my colleagues in the economics department took over my seminars and, although I was given leave of absence and ceased to be paid by the college from that moment onwards, I returned after Easter to complete my lectures in the Trinity term.

As it happened, the last of my European Community lectures before I was appointed to office had been about the Council of Ministers, and I had the pleasure of starting my first post-Easter lecture in this course as follows: 'The actual operation of the Council of Ministers is somewhat different from what I described in my last lecture'.

This change of career had serious financial implications, however. The ministerial salary added to my Dáil allowance was very much less than, what I had been earning from my combination of academic, consultancy and journalistic careers; indeed our after-tax income fell by some 40 percent.

Expenditure is more difficult to reduce; over the next two years our overdraft rose exponentially. By 1974 a move to a smaller house was inevitable, and with two of our children married was in any event appropriate. Unable to find a suitable house in the locality we had to move farther out of town, but within eighteen months Mark, now an apprentice auctioneer, found us a home in Palmerston Road. As a result of planning permission for a dwelling in the rear half of the back garden the value of the house had been reduced. Mary and Vincent offered to carry one-third of the mortgage in return for the garden flat, where they and the friends with whom they had been sharing an apartment would live. This made the move back into town feasible for us, although we never succeeded in reducing our living standards commensurately with the drop in income.

8

~: Meeting the Challenges of Coalition :~

This dissolution of the Dáil by Jack Lynch two months later had been intended as a surprise move to take advantage of the presumed disarray in Fine Gael following this debacle. It proved to be a disastrous miscalculation – not merely because it threw Fine Gael and the Labour Party together but also because it rallied Fine Gael itself under Liam Cosgrave's leadership. There was an instant dissolution of the tensions in the party that had developed over several years as a result of both personality differences and ideological divergences.

One feature of the 1973 election remains lodged in my mind. Early one evening, I was canvassing the nuns and residents in the Donnybrook Magdalene Asylum – which at that time had farmland that abutted onto our garden in Eglinton Road. (When we moved there in 1959, as we looked towards the city from the bedroom windows at the back of the house, we could sometimes see a man ploughing their land with a horse!). At seven o'clock I received a message to the effect that Fianna Fáil intended to announce the next day how they would spend on social reforms the £30 million in farm subsidies that would in future be payable by the EEC, following our accession to the Community some weeks earlier.

I rushed to my house and my typewriter to produce a Fine Gael £30 million social policy that Liam Cosgrave could announce when he spoke in Rathmines at 8.30 AM – thus avoiding pre-emption by Fianna Fáil on this issue. By eight o'clock I had spent £27.5 million, so, adding an item 'Miscellaneous £2.5 million', I drove to Leinster House to have my social programme copied. At 8.40 AM, Liam Cosgrave was announcing it in Rathmines Town Hall. I feel this may have been one of the fastest cases of policy formulation anywhere!

In Government I was asked by Brendan Corish and Frank Cluskey – who were happy with my proposals – to go to their offices in Aras Mhic Dhiarmada to turn these proposals into a Government memorandum. The original, in my eccentric typing, lies today amongst my papers in the UCD Archive. I think almost everything I proposed was implemented in the years that followed.

For those not involved in politics the apparent transformation of relationships within the party must at the time have been suspect, but politics has its own particular chemistry, including combinative reactions as dramatic as those in physical chemistry that enable gases like oxygen and hydrogen to combine to form water.

Such a reaction required a two-way process: the 'dissidents' had to be prepared to submerge their previous unhappiness with Liam Cosgrave's leadership, and their ability genuinely to do so depended on their leader in turn demonstrating a new trust and confidence in them. He did so, and it worked. For my part – and my differences with him had been deeper than most – I found it was as easy to work with him in government as I had found it difficult in opposition, and I hope that he found the same, Only once in the four-and-a-quarter years that we served together in this administration did any strain arise between us, and that was the result of an accident that was no one's fault. The transformation in our working relationship was all the more striking in view of the fact that traditionally the relationship between a prime minister and a foreign minister is prone to tension. This is so because this particular relationship involves a greater measure of responsibility-sharing by a head of government than with any other department head, for every prime minister must necessarily be involved directly in many aspects of foreign policy especially when within a body like the EU.

The only inkling about my future that I received before the Dáil resumed to elect Liam Cosgrave as Taoiseach came a week later. He asked me, without prejudice, which government post I would prefer. I said I would be happy to continue in Finance, which I had been understudying as shadow minister, but was, of course, prepared to accept whatever he might propose. He responded by saying that it would either be Finance or another senior post. I asked which other senior post he was thinking of; he hesitated, and then said, perhaps understandably, that he would prefer to leave that over. As I waited for the Dáil to meet, I began to take stock of what was involved in becoming a member of the government. Apart from the sharp drop in income, compensated only in part by having a state car and driver, there was another side also: the security implications. All my life I had visited Northern Ireland on and off in order to see my many relatives there, and in latter years to meet members of the SDLP or other people involved less directly in politics. But after 14 March I would no longer be able to travel to the North without protection, and even on that basis access might be difficult. Irish ministers had never been in the habit of visiting Northern Ireland.

I decided to pay one last visit as a free man to the part of Ireland where my roots were deepest – the only part where I had relatives with whom I had maintained close ties. So I arranged to go on a sentimental journey to Belfast on Tuesday

13 March, the day before the Dáil met. I then took a second decision: to turn the trip to practical advantage by making informal contact with unionist leaders, whom I had not previously met. Accordingly I arranged appointments at the Europa Hotel with three Unionist Party leaders and separately with a fourth, independent, unionist politician. The meetings were cordial, and I was encouraged to maintain contact subsequently when in government. I also called in to the SDLP headquarters, where I discussed PR with two members of their Executive.

Next morning, Wednesday 14 March, I was on my way through Leinster House when I passed a friend from the Department of Foreign Affairs, who said out of the corner of her mouth: 'Welcome to Iveagh House'. Shortly afterwards in the restaurant at lunchtime Brendan Corish, the Labour leader, called me over to his table as I passed by and told me not to be too disappointed if I were not appointed to Finance. 'What's the alternative?' I asked him. 'It could be Foreign Affairs,' he replied.

(I now have reason to believe that my appointment to Foreign Affairs was mainly a consequence of a belief on Liam Cosgrave's part that, although I had been shadow Minister of Finance, Richie Ryan's longer and wider experience in the Dáil fitted him better for the Finance post. He may also have had some qualms about the possible impact of some of my more radical views on my actions in Finance – unnecessarily as in that area I was fairly orthodox! At the same time my extensive engagement with the EC – about which I had been lecturing throughout the previous decade – fitted me for the Foreign Affairs portfolio, given that we had just joined the Community ten weeks earlier. As the son of W. T. Cosgrave, head of the first government from 1922 1932, he may also have been attracted to the symmetry involved in having myself and Declan Costello filling the same posts as in his father's administration half a century earlier.

When Joan came into the House I told her of these hints. She was upset. She had not flown since 1956, nor had I since 1958, out of deference to her fears, save once, a year earlier, when I had missed the night boat-train at Euston. She hated the idea that I might have to fly frequently to fulfil my duties in Foreign Affairs.

At three o'clock the Dáil assembled to elect a Taoiseach. Liam Cosgrave was duly chosen and went to Áras an Uachtaráin to receive his appointment from the president, Éamon de Valera. We were told to be in the Taoiseach's office at 5.30 PM – half an hour before the Dáil was due to resume for the announcement of the new government.

I waited in the corridor outside, expecting that we would be called in one by one, but at 5.35 PM I was asked to join others inside. As I entered, Liam Cosgrave stepped forward, shook my hand and said, 'Foreign Affairs. Is that all right?' I assented.

The Cabinet of fifteen had five Labour members, including Brendan Corish as Tánaiste. When the new Taoiseach read out the list of ministers, confirming my nomination to Foreign Affairs, Joan in the gallery burst into tears. Mark, then fifteen, tried to console her, pointing out that in the immediately preceding period the Minister for Finance had had to fly to Brussels more frequently than the foreign minister!

Several hours passed before we made our way to Áras an Uachtaráin to receive our seals of office. Because of uncertainty about when we were leaving most of us had nothing to eat. I was in the last car of the cortege with Pat Cooney. Along the quays we saw a sweet shop; we stopped the car and I dashed in to buy several bars of chocolate from an astonished shopkeeper. We were still dining off them when we arrived at the Áras.

After the formal proceedings we held, in accordance with custom, our first Cabinet meeting at a table in the Áras, which had been that of the first government, of which my father had been a member. The secretary of the Department of Foreign Affairs attended on this occasion, as well as the secretary of the government and told us that the British government was about to approve a White Paper on Northern Ireland, probably on the following morning, and that if we wished to make an input to their deliberations we would have to move very rapidly indeed. The Cabinet decided that we should prepare a message to send to the British, and appointed a subcommittee to meet at 9.30 AM in order to consider a draft that I was to prepare during the night. This was then to be presented to the Cabinet for consideration at eleven o'clock.

On my way home I first had to make some broadcasts and say farewell to the *Irish Times*, for which I had been writing for almost twenty years. When I eventually arrived home it was 2.30 AM. During the next hour or two I prepared a draft message to the British government, which the ad hoc subcommittee approved, with some modifications, before the government met at 11 AM. Our London embassy delivered the message to Downing Street at 11.45 AM, where the British Cabinet had been in session since 10.30 AM, discussing the draft White Paper.

It was then decided that I should fly to London that afternoon to see the prime minister and the foreign secretary in order to explain our point of view more fully. By 2.30 PM I was on my way, and at 6.30, and after a briefing session at the embassy, I was in Downing Street with Ted Heath and Alec Douglas-Home.

Two things remain in my mind about this first contact with the British government. One was my attempt to persuade them of the value in Ireland of a judicial review of human rights. The feature of the constitutional system of the Irish state had existed in Northern Ireland during the Stormont period, when the High Court in Belfast had the power to declare legislative discrimination against the minority community in the North ultra vivres the 1920 Government of Ireland Act – although the power had rarely been invoked. Ted Heath's response to this suggestion was unambiguous: 'Constitutionally impossible! Her Majesty's judges could not possibly overrule Her Majesty in Parliament'. It was the first time, but by no means the last, that I came up against the curious rigidity of Britain's unwritten constitution.

My second memory of this meeting is the initiative I took about visits to Northern Ireland. I told the prime minister and the foreign secretary about my recent visit and informed them that I would be going there regularly in my new capacity.

The allocation of other portfolios between the two parties was governed by considerations that are easy to explain. Some ministers were clearly seen by Liam Cosgrave as natural posts to be held by Fine Gael as the leading party in government: Finance, for obvious reasons; Justice and Defence, as fundamental to public order; Education, because of the sensitivity of relationships with the Catholic Church; Agriculture, because of the party's strong rural base and the traditional farmer hostility to Labour; and Foreign Affairs, which could not credibly have been allocated to the Labour Party less than a year after that party had been leading the referendum campaign against EEC membership. Given a choice of the remaining departments, it was natural that the Labour Party should have opted for the two social ministries – Health (including Social Welfare) and Labour – and for the other major economic department, Industry and Commerce, as well as for Local Government, where an opportunity existed for a Labour Party minister to emulate a predecessor in the 1948-51 coalition government who had expanded the public housing programme rapidly from a low postwar base. The Labour Party's fifth choice of portfolio was Posts and Telegraphs, which included responsibility for radio and television. The remaining three portfolios – Transport and Power, the Gaeltacht, and Lands – fell to Fine Gael, which also held the attorney generalship and, naturally, the post of government chief whip.

Liam Cosgrave's decision to offer the Labour Party a fifth ministry when its parliamentary strength entitled it to only four seats in the government before Labour could even raise the issue was inspired. He thus ensured a smooth start to this new coalition – the first to comprise these two parties only – and, together with his visible commitment to treating his Labour Party colleagues with respect and consideration, this initial move secured their willing loyalty throughout the life of the government.

In the event, Labour's weight in the government was even greater than this one-to-one ratio of Cabinet seats would suggest. In the first place, Brendan Corish's decision to delegate full authority over his Social Welfare department to Frank Cluskey, his parliamentary secretary, virtually gave them a sixth seat, for Frank had to be present whenever Social Welfare matters were discussed – which, given our extensive programme of social reform, was very frequently – and Liam Cosgrave's respect for Frank Cluskey's political judgement led him sometimes to suggest that he remain on afterwards to join in discussion of other matters.

Second, at the very start of the new government Conor Cruise O'Brien persuaded Liam Cosgrave to give him responsibility for the Government Information Service, which had hitherto always answered directly to the Taoiseach of the day through that service's politically appointed head. Third, the combination of the exceptional intellectual calibre of some of the Labour Party ministers and the weight of the portfolios they collectively commanded gave them a higher profile than numbers alone would account for.

This does not mean that the government leaned ideologically to the left, however. Jimmy Tully of Labour was instinctively to the right of most Fine Gael members, and Conor Cruise O'Brien's concern for law and order also tended to pull the government to the right. Liam Cosgrave's own conservatism, the respect in which the Labour Party ministers held him, and the pragmatic manner in which we addressed our agenda as a government, together combined to ensure a balanced approach to most problems, and to minimise ideological tensions.

The determination of all concerned to ensure the solidarity of the government was evident in the way we tackled our business. The Labour Party sought to avoid becoming isolated on potentially contentious issues, and if there were any danger of this happening, at least one Fine Gael minister joined them in the relevant vote – frequently myself (usually by conviction), or in my absence some other Fine Gael minister (sometimes as a matter of political prudence).

Liam Cosgrave proved to be an effective chairman of the government. This was helped by the fact that – as his father had been in the 1920s – he was older than most members, although Conor Cruise O'Brien was his senior by four years. Because of the length of time Fianna Fáil had been in office, he and Brendan Corish were the only ones amongst us who had previous government experience. Moreover, although he could relax and become a warm personality on informal occasions when he found the company congenial, he had an instinct to the exercise of authority, combined with reticence and a certain remoteness, that did not encourage overfamiliarity, with the result that where he clearly had a strongly held view, most ministers were reluctant to challenge him. In opposition, without the extra authority of office, these attributes had not been sufficient to protect him from challenges over issues on which his conservatism tended to isolate him; in government, they proved effective in safeguarding his authority.

Given the disparate personalities involved, remarkably few tensions developed in the government. The main problem was within the Labour wing of the Cabinet. It centred on Justin Keating, who, it eventually transpired, was the object of suspicion or hostility on the part of three of his Labour Party colleagues. In opposition, Conor Cruise O'Brien and he had quarrelled over Northern Ireland; Michael O'Leary feared that he might become his rival for the succession to Brendan Corish as next leader of the Labour Party; and Jimmy Tully disliked his intellectualism – although why this led Jimmy to align himself with Conor against Justin I never fully understood!

I had come to know Justin well during the EEC referendum campaign, as we had travelled the country together, putting the arguments respectively for and against membership. As Minister for Industry and Commerce, he asserted the traditional claim of his department to handle foreign-trade issues – a claim that Foreign Affairs had contested unsuccessfully since the early days of the state. As a result, from the outset Justin accompanied me to meetings of the Council of Foreign Ministers whenever, as was frequently the case, the Community's foreign-trade competence was under discussion.

Rather than contest his right to attend these meetings, an argument that I would inevitable have lost, I concentrated my defensive efforts on repelling, on the whole successfully, attempts by his civil servants to carve out new areas of external responsibility for their department in order to compensate for the transfer of foreign trade from national to Community control. The strength of my personal relationship with Justin, as it had developed during the referendum period, enabled us to work well together at meetings of the Council and to settle, at intervals of six months or so, the regular accumulation of demarcation disputes between our two departments.

It was only in 1975 that I became belatedly aware of the fact that his three Labour Party colleagues believed that, instead of being tolerantly accepted, Justin's attendance at Council meetings in Brussels and Luxembourg had been contrived by me as part of a plot to promote his candidacy for leadership of the Labour Party! I knew (although clearly his Labour fellow-ministers did not) that Justin had in fact decided not to contest the leadership but instead to seek appointment as the next Irish Commissioner in Brussels when the current incumbent – the first Irish appointee, Paddy Hillery – came to the end of his term. By the time I found out the suspicions that these three Labour minister entertained about me, it was too late to convince them that they had got the wrong end of the stick.

Meanwhile, I had come to the conclusion that Justin Keating was in fact the best available Irish candidate for the commissionership, for it soon became evident that the only member of the government interested in the post was Dick Burke, the Fine Gael Minister for Education, who did not seem to me to have the same intellectual capacity as his Labour Party colleague.

This landed me in a further problem with my Fine Gael colleagues. Unknown to me, Dick had sought and secured from them before the end of 1975 agreement to support his candidature for the post of Commissioner if, as was the case, I was not a candidate myself. My support for Justin Keating's nomination in the course of 1976 may well have irritated some of his Labour Party colleagues, who may have felt their hand being forced with a view to making an issue of his appointment, which in the interest of the solidarity of the government they might have preferred not to do. And it certainly annoyed a number of Fine Gael ministers, who regarded my stance as disloyal to my party. In the event Dick Burke's nomination was agreed by nine votes to six, and he served as Commissioner from 1977 to 1980, and again, on Fianna Fáil's nomination, from 1982 to 1984.

The spring and summer of 1973 was a honeymoon period for our government. We had inherited an economy that had been growing rapidly, although wage inflation was running at 20 percent by June, and prices were rising by 12 percent. This we would have to tackle.

On the other hand, emigration had been replaced for the first time in recorded history by net immigration; young Irish people in the twenty-five-to-thirty-nine age bracket were returning from Britain, with skills acquired there, so as to take up employment in the new industries being established throughout the country by foreign investors, and were bringing with them their young children, who unexpectedly swelled the number in our primary schools. This bright picture was further cheered by the new inflow of financial resources accruing to us through the EC budget, modestly estimated at £30 million in that year, which we had decided to allocate to improvements in the social welfare system.

No one could have foreseen, in Ireland any more than elsewhere, that before the year was out all this would be threatened by the oil crisis, sparked off by the Yom Kippur war, in early October.

Despite my heavy commitments in the Department of Foreign Affairs – during the part of 1973 when I was in government I spent the equivalent of two months on fifteen journeys outside Ireland, and I was also deeply involved in the preparations for the Sunningdale conference – I nevertheless participated fully in the work of implementing our many policy reforms at home. I served on three Cabinet bodies that in the early years of that government had an unusually large role in policymaking: the Economic, Social, and Education Subcommittees.

During 1973, the Economic Subcommittee was mainly engaged in assessing the economic prospects, with special reference to likely price trends, as a guide for possible government action on incomes – in view of the inflation explosion, this had to be a priority – and also in implementing the proposals for capital tax reform that I had managed to get inserted at a late stage into the national coalition's election programme. The Social Subcommittee was concerned with our social reforms, the details of which I had incorporated in a speech I had prepared for Liam Cosgrave at short notice in the course of the election campaign.

The Education Subcommittee was – much less successfully – engaged on an attempted reform of the structure in higher education.

The deliberations of the Economic Subcommittee on the proposal to substitute an annual wealth tax for the traditional estate and legacy duties were of particular concern to me. I had first put forward such a reform as part of my contribution to the Just Society policies in 1964–65 before joining the party, and, as I have recorded earlier, had been disappointed, and indeed disconcerted, by the rejection of my proposal by the policy committee of the party under Liam Cosgrave's chairmanship. Given what I suggested could affect adversely less than 1 percent of the electorate – the richest 1 percent – and would alleviate the burden of estate duties on many others, as well as being broadly redistributive in favour of the great majority of taxpayers, I could not understand the rejection of my proposal on the grounds that it would be 'unpopular'.

I had made a further attempt to get the idea accepted at a two-day policy meeting of the Fine Gael front bench in 1969, but with equally little success. It was only when I returned to Leinster House after getting myself nominated as a Fine Gael candidate in Dublin South East that I had successfully added this proposal to what became known as the fourteen points of the national coalition programme: 'With a view to relieving the heavy and unjust burden on house purchases and farmers, the national coalition government will abolish estate duties on property passing on death to widows and their children and replace them with taxation confined to the really wealthy and to property passing on death outside the immediate family.'

It soon became evident that the Department of Finance was vehemently opposed to this reform of capital taxation. Ten days after our appointment to the committee, the department submitted a memorandum to the government arguing in effect for the abandonment of the election commitment on wealth tax; it followed this up with another salvo four weeks later. It put forward a series of difficulties about the wealth-tax proposal, and submitted an alternative involving a gift tax and a capital-gains tax combined with the retention of estate duties in the form of an inheritance tax – in other words, anything and everything except an annual wealth tax.

After some of us had made it clear what we thought of these extraordinary attempts to reverse government policy, Richie withdrew the department's memoranda, on the basis that we would consider all aspects of the wealth tax.

The Department of Finance then put forward a series of questions that sought once again to reopen its proposal for retaining 'some form of inheritance tax'. This provoked a strong ministerial reaction.

Four months of work on our proposals followed. Then, on 17 November, the indefatigable Department of Finance submitted yet another document to the committee, suggesting that the option it had put forward on 27 April – which involved retaining an inheritance tax and not introducing an annual wealth tax – be further considered. We rejected this fourth attempt to sabotage our policy, and continued with our work. The Department of Finance was not, however, prepared to give up:

at our meeting on 20 December, it made a fifth attempt, resubmitting its November proposal in a new form, describing it as 'an alternative system of capital taxation embodying a modified system of estate duty and gift tax, the present legacy/succession duties and a capital gains tax'. At the same time, it produced a draft document called 'Economic Implications of Proposed Changes in Capital Taxation'. We had asked for a document to provide the necessary economic argument in favour of our policy; in effect, what we received confined itself to arguments against the government's proposals. When I pointed this out at a meeting of the subcommittee, the departmental response was to ask sardonically: 'Are there *any* arguments in favour of the government's proposals?'

This piece of sarcasm was the last straw. The committee decided to bring the issue to government, by means of an interim report. I set about preparing a draft of this report during the Christmas break, including an account of the arguments on both sides of the case – after our experience, I was not prepared to leave that task to the Department of Finance – and an appendix showing the way in which the comparisons of yields from the existing capital tax system and the proposed new system had been prepared by the officials. (The officials had persisted at meeting after meeting, despite protests from me, in using two different sets of data, so they were not comparing like with like, as a result of which the relative yields of the two systems were distorted by some millions of pounds in favour of the existing system.)

I sent my report and its appendices to Richie Ryan on 2 January. Throughout the prolonged battle with his officials, he had presided over our discussions in an unbiased manner and had been careful not to reveal his own view of the issues. Now, however, he reacted sharply to my draft, complaining that it was discourteous and disingenuous for a minister to report on the workings of a committee that was the primary responsibility of a colleague, and describing my memorandum as 'tendentious' and containing 'misstatements of fact and unfair imputations'.

What had upset him specifically, because of its impact on his relations with his officials, was a statement in my report that he had told the government that the Finance memoranda of 27 April and 25 May had not been approved by him, together with an assertion that these memoranda had been 'rejected' by the government. This was in fact the only specific criticism he made of my draft.

Accordingly, I modified the draft to meet the particular points he had raised, and, with the agreement of our four colleagues on the committee, handed it out at a government meeting two days later. This was in clear breach of Cabinet procedure, which requires that memoranda with financial implications be submitted to the Department of Finance for comments before being circulated to the government.

Three days later, Richie submitted a counter-memorandum protesting against my actions and making further criticisms of my draft, which did not, however, challenge the validity of almost any of the facts that I have set out above.

The upshot was that the government confirmed its decision, and a White Paper along the lines of its policy was prepared and published three months later. However, the proposals that eventually emerged in legislation involved a higher threshold (£100,000 in 1974 money terms, or almost €1 million today) and a lower rate of wealth tax (1 percent) than we had envisaged, with the result that during our years in government the proceeds of the new capital tax system were less than the yield from the old estate duties.

But when the government changed in 1977, Fianna Fáil abolished the wealth tax in response to what struck me as a most unscrupulous campaign by some among the wealthy people affected by it. This campaign had been designed to arouse irrational fears amongst people of quite modest means who were in no danger of ever being found liable to pay wealth tax. The deeply ironic result was that the net effect of all my efforts over a decade to substitute a more effective method of limiting the accumulation of wealth in too few hands, which would at the same time bear more equitably on those paying it, achieved the exact opposite result: a much lighter burden of capital tax than hitherto.

When we returned to government in 1981 in a new coalition with the Labour Party, the weight of 'popular' opinion amongst middle classes against a reintroduction of wealth tax inhibited my party from responding to continuous pressure from Labour to restore the system that we had succeeded in introducing in 1974 against so many obstacles.

How typical is this affair of relations between government and civil service? I would say that it was untypical. Civil servants rightly conceive it to be their duty to advise ministers fully on the possible adverse consequences of a proposed political decision; they would be failing in their duty were they to do otherwise. It is also humanly understandable that they should often tend to feel that the status quo – the product largely of their own and their predecessors' efforts – has a certain merit and deserves to be preserved unless very cogent arguments are put forward for altering it.

Some resistance to change is thus to be expected from the civil service, each department of which tends to have its own attachment to policies developed in the past – for example the commitment of the Department of Industy to the policy of industrial protection, developed in the late 1930s, which inhibited it from playing a positive role in the movement to free trade in the 1960s. But normally both the process of warning about the dangers inherent in any change and the emotional attachment to traditional policies are kept within reasonable bounds and are not pushed beyond a certain point, which a minister will recognise and appreciate.

However, the opposition to our proposal to replace estate duties with an annual wealth tax went well beyond the normal pattern of civil service resistance to change.

All in all the episode should be seen as an untypical response, demonstrating the distance civil servants can go in challenging government policy rather than the distance they normally do go in warning governments of the consequences of their actions.

I should add, however, that a factor influencing the civil service approach to this issue may well have been the extent to which during the latter part of the previous sixteen years of Fianna Fáil government they had become accustomed to exercising power without much interference from most ministers. A new government coming into office with fresh policies of its own and a determination to implement them may well have come as unexpected and unwelcome shock to a system in which policy had come to evolve through the interaction of politicians and civil servants in a relationship that had obviously become a relatively 'cosy' one. It is worth recording that while the wealth tax battle was unique in the manner in which it was fought, ministers in other departments also found resistance to our policy initiatives in various areas during 1973; but this seemed to die down when the civil service became accustomed to working with a new, reforming government.

By the time the economic subcommittee had completed its work on the reform of capital taxation, Ireland – together with the rest of the industrialised and developing world – was facing into a major economic crisis deriving from the five-fold increase in oil prices engineered by the Arab oil-producing countries as their response to Israel's victory in the Yom Kippur War. As energy prices rocketed, price and wage inflation accelerated sharply, undermining our attempts to restrain pay increases. There was, indeed a rapid escalation of already substantial pay claims, which led to a further sharp rise in inflation.

An inept negotiation between employers and unions, into which, under an arrangement negotiated by our predecessors, we as a government were tied by virtue of being an employer, had produced a national agreement that, if the government took no action to keep the cost of living down, could yield a 26 percent pay increase within the twelve months to November 1975; if we did take such action that would lead to pay rising faster than prices, thus increasing effective demand at a time when demand needed to be curbed rather than expanded!

It seemed to us in government that the most urgent task facing us was to halt this spiralling cycle of price and pay increases. We got little help from the civil service in tackling this, however, because the Department of Finance was so mesmerised by the evident need to reduce public spending that it seemed unprepared to address any other issue.

Happily help was at hand. The National Economic and Social Council, comprising representatives of employers, trade unions and farmers as well as senior civil servants and some independent members appointed by the government, was currently preparing a report on the causes and consequences of inflation in Ireland. A member of the government obtained a copy of the draft of a crucial section of the report, and this became the basis of a much more radical approach to the prices-pay spiral.

This draft said bluntly that unless the government could persuade employers and unions to change the national pay agreement, national output would decline, inflation would rise to 25 percent and the government would have virtually no pay options open to it. If on the other hand the pay agreement could be changed, a policy package could be devised that would reduce inflation, improve employment prospects, and leave those with below-average pay rates better off – all this at no net cost to the Exchequer.

The package they proposed included many of the suggestions I and other members of the economic subcommittee had put forward, but was much more drastic. It included, for example, the subsidisation of sugar as well as subsidies to reduce electricity and gas process and transport fares. Because these measures were estimated to cut the consumer price index by over 4 percent they could provide a basis for a deal involving the cancellation of the next quarterly pay increase and elimination of the 4 percent minimum for pay increases in subsequent quarters.

Encouraged by this document, the very existence of which within a body such as the NESC suggested some willingness by unions to accept a modification of the pay agreement, our economic subcommittee returned to the attack, and we carried the day. On 26 June the government announced a package of measures, including food subsidies, which actually reduced the cost of living slightly in the current quarter, in contrast to average quarterly increases of over 7 percent during the first half of the year. This tactic worked: the unions accepted a renegotiation of the pay agreement; and although inflation was temporarily at a high level in the early part of 1976 it wound down rapidly thereafter, dropping from 24 percent in the twelve months ending May 1975 to 6.5 percent three years later, before starting to rise again as a result of the inflationary measures introduced by Fianna Fáil after their return to office. This breakthrough in 1975 owed little to the Department of Finance, however; the 'mini-budget' of 26 June 1975 was, almost uniquely, the work of the government itself, aided by the social partners within the NECS.

A price, of course, had to be paid for this achievement. The food subsidies we introduced were not phased out in the late 1970s, as they should have been. With poetic injustice it thus fell to us to remove them during the life of the 1982—87 coalition, at the cost of considerable unpopularity, through raising food prices at a time when, in order to reduce the massive rate of borrowing we had inherited from the 1977—81 Fianna Fáil administration, we were also forced to raise taxes and cut public spending.

My membership of a second government subcommittee, that dealing with social affairs, enabled me to play a full part in the massive programme of social reform that this government introduced. The measures implemented by us included all those I had set out in the speech I had drafted for Liam Cosgrave during the election campaign, together with others proposed principally but not exclusively by the Parliamentary Secretary for Social Welfare, Frank Cluskey. The initial measures were in fact put to the government in a memorandum personally typed by me in Brendan Corish's office in the Department of Social Welfare, where I worked on this programme with Brendan and Frank.

Our social reforms increased significantly the purchasing power of social benefits, and especially children's allowances, which were also extended to the age of eighteen for those not in employment, and were made payable to mothers rather than fathers. They also involved the introduction of schemes to cover new categories of beneficiary: unmarried mothers, prisoners' wives, single women over fifty-seven years of age, and old-age pensioners' dependants. Moreover, the pension age was reduced from seventy to sixty-six where it has since remained.

Other measures of social importance included a 50 percent increase in the public housing programme, together with a reform of the differential rent system for such housing and a liberalisation of tenant purchase arrangements. The less well off also benefited significantly from the implementation of our commitment to abolish VAT on food.

At the same time income tax rates were simultaneously reduced, the top rate from 80 to 60 percent, and the lowest rate from 35 to 20 percent; the rate of company tax was also cut; and domestic rates were halved.

Our reform programme extended outside the social and economic spheres. Legislation was also introduced to secure equal rights for women, and other legislation gave workers the right to participate in membership of the boards of the principal state enterprises. Adoption legislation was liberalised, among other things by removing the ban on adoptions by couples of different religions. Parents were given a role on new management bodies established in primary and local authority second-level schools. A Law-Reform Commission was also established.

Another policy change adopted by Fine Gael in the 1960s and included in the coalition's fourteen-point programme in 1973 was the removal of the Irish language requirement for the award of the Leaving Certificate and for entry to the public service.

This took several years to implement, but I got agreement to earlier action in relation to the exceptionally large intake of twenty-nine third secretaries into the Department of Foreign Affairs in 1974, with the result that no fewer than seven of this number came from Northern Ireland, drawn from both communities there. Few of these would have been able to qualify for entry to the foreign service but for this exemption from Irish.

The education subcommittee was less successful than the other two government subcommittees of which I was a member. Our main task was to help Dick Burke, the Minister of Education, to formulate a solution to the problem of university structures, which had been a controversial issue during the previous five years, following the decision of an earlier minister, the late Donagh O'Malley, to break up the NUI and to merge its Dublin college, UCD, with Trinity College. This committee included two other academics, Conor Cruise O'Brien and Justin Keating. Our efforts produced no tangible result; three academics was perhaps too many!

An issue that particularly concerned me in the early period of this government was the revision of constituency boundaries. In the late 1960s a constituency revision had been carried out by Kevin Boland, Minister for Local Government before his 1970 resignation in protest against Jack Lynch's sacking of Neil Blaney and Charles Haughey over the arms importation affair. In the Dublin region, where Fianna Fáil was weak, with around 40 percent of the vote, he had concentrated on four-seat constituencies, giving his party typically half the seats with its two-fifths of the votes. In the west, where Fianna Fáil was then stronger, with over 45 percent of the vote in many areas, he had concentrated on three-seat constituencies. Even with somewhat less than half the votes, his party could usually secure two out of the three seats in such constituencies. The result of this gerrymander was that Fianna Fáil tended to secure a total number of seats disproportionate to its national vote – about 5 to 6 percent more seats than votes overall.

I was opposed to the artificial distortion of the electoral system, which I regarded as disreputable, and I was concerned lest our government be tempted to undertake a tit-for-tat reverse gerrymander. Accordingly, immediately after the election of the government I prepared a memorandum that I sent to Liam Cosgrave and Jimmy Tully, proposing an independent Constituency Commission. I included a detailed analysis of the contemporary political geography of the state, demonstrating that in the current situation a commission operating on the basis of straightforward terms of reference would have little choice but to recommend a redistribution that, as luck would have it, would tend to favour Fine Gael and the Labour Party over Fianna Fáil. A gerrymander was thus superfluous.

The logic of my memorandum (from which, as I recall, I was careful to omit any arguments of principle that might have justified its dismissal on the grounds of political naïveté!) was ignored. Four years later our defeat in June 1977 was all the more overwhelming because of what came to be known as the 'Tullymander' rebound against us: Jimmy Tully's calculations had been too finely judged altogether, and a shift in the voting pattern that he had not foreseen led to our losing more seats than was necessary.

Two years after the Tullymander a memo was submitted from the Department of Finance proposing the cancellation of the 1976 census as an economy measure. Because of the scale of population changes in the postwar period due to large-scale emigration, censuses had since the war been held at five-year rather than ten-year intervals. By 1975 there was considerable indirect evidence that net emigration had been replaced since the late 1960s by net immigration. It was important to have this confirmed and to establish this pattern of immigration for planning purposes: to the extent that the Irish people now coming home were bringing families with them, this had implications for housing and primary education facilities. There could scarcely have been a worse moment to cancel a census.

The government nevertheless decided to consider this memorandum in the absence of the Minister for Finance, who was away, I believe in Brussels. Despite the strong arguments I and several others adduced in favour of going ahead with the census, it was decided to adopt the Finance recommendation; and it became clear in the decision that for some members of the government part at least of the motivation for this discussion was a concern lest publication of data from such a census should raise the question of a further constituency revision that might undo the Tullymander.

Next day, when Richie Ryan heard what had been decided he exploded, telling me that he had allowed the memorandum to go to the government only to demonstrate what daft ideas for economies his department was producing. It was too late to go back on the decision, however, and an alternative that Richie considered, involving a sample census, proved too complex and expensive.

When Fianna Fáil returned to power in 1977 it revived the Census proposal, with the result that Censuses were carried out both in 1979 and also again in 1981. The 1979 census was used as the basis for a constituency revision which Jack Lynch ensured would be carried our by an independent commission with neutral terms of reference. Because the 1970s had been a period of rapid population growth, and because it was decided to maintain Dáil representation at the maximum level permitted by the Constitution (1 seat per 20,000 population), this revision increased the size of the Dáil by eighteen seats, from 148 to 166. This was of enormous assistance to me as leader of Fine Gael at that time, because it enabled me to encourage many Fine Gael deputies in the Dáil to accept the addition of strong candidates to the ticket in their often enlarged constituencies, on the basis that, with extra seats available, they would need to be both lazy and stupid to lose out to other Fine Gael candidates. I was thus, the eventual, if inadvertent, beneficiary of the census postponement decision that I had myself stoutly resisted.

But to return to 1973: after six months in government some of us felt that we should review our progress, and it was decided to hold an informal 'political' meeting of the government away from our usual environment. I suggested that we hold this in Iveagh House, and that was readily agreed. When my officials heard of this proposal they pointed out that the department's funds could not properly be used for the entertainment of the government. Accordingly I had to purchase the food and drink myself, levying the cost on my fellow ministers. This was readily accepted in principle, but it took me the best part of a year to recover ten pounds a head from every member of the government!

An episode during this period in government that caused a considerable stir was the defeat in July 1974 of our Bill to liberalise the law on contraception. When this matter came before us in the spring of 1974 Liam Cosgrave, who was known for his religious conservatism, stayed silent during the discussion on the terms of the Bill. This was not in fact a government Bill but one introduced by the Minister of Justice, Pat Cooney, on his own account, a distinction that I am afraid was fat too subtle for many people to grasp. Three times at this meeting Conor Cruise O'Brien endeavoured to extract from the Taoiseach a reaction to the proposed Bill, but each time he failed. We left the meeting no wiser about his attitude. The final drafting of the Bill and its insertion into the parliamentary calendar took some time, and it was several months later in July 1974, that the second stage debate was held in the Dáil. Fianna Fáil opposed the Bill, in accordance with its consistent policy of supporting the conservative standpoint of the Catholic Church on such issues, and eventually a vote was called.

Curiously, despite Liam Cosgrave's silence, we had managed to convince ourselves that he would support the Bill when the time came, the interval since the discussion in government having insensibly eroded earlier doubts. The chief whip, the late John Kelly, clearly had no qualms on the matter and was busy persuading the small number of anti-contraception government TDs that they should vote for it, as, according to him, Liam Cosgrave was doing. What we did not realise was that John Kelly had no direct assurance from Liam Cosgrave but was, it seems, relying on an impression of his attitude gleaned from his private office, where the Taoiseach's position had apparently been misunderstood.

TDs had already begun passing through the lobbies when John Kelly discovered his error. Appalled at having misled some conservatively-minded deputies into voting for the Bill on a false premise, he immediately urged the Taoiseach to vote without delay – for, unaware of John Kelly's activities, Liam Cosgrave had loyally intended to wait until the end before casting his vote so as not to influence other members of the party. Once urged by John, he voted immediately against the Bill, and some who had not yet passed through the lobbies decided to follow him. By then having voted, I was back on the front bench and, seeing what was happening, I said to Pat Cooney, 'Wouldn't it be funny if he defeated his government?' – not realising yet that this was what in fact had happened.

Naturally the defeat of our Bill in these extraordinary circumstances caused a sensation and damaged the standing of the government. Our insistence that it was not a government Bill binding all government ministers in collective responsibility was regarded as sophistry, and we were accused of having thrown this crucial constitutional doctrine of cabinet responsibility overboard.

Inevitably my absence abroad meant that I missed quite a lot of government meetings and as a result on several occasions was unaware of significant decisions that had been taken, since the practice was to circulate decisions only to those actually responsible for their implementation. In order to avoid possible embarrassment I arranged after a while to get copies of all decisions.

Despite my frequent absences, whenever any matter of particular concern to me was due for decision I usually managed to ensure that I was present, or occasionally to have the decision postponed; and the meetings of the government subcommittees of which I was a member – economic, social, educational, and also, when matters of external concern arose, the security committee – could usually be arranged to coincide with my periods at home.

As I became increasingly involved in my portfolio I found, however, that I often did not have time to study fully the extensive memoranda, before the government on issues of economic importance on which I felt I should contribute, and even where I felt I was able to study them I often did not have time to undertake my own research into the issues at stake. I was not, therefore, contributing as fully as I might have done to government discussion of these matters.

At the same time I was very conscious of the assistance some Labour Party ministers were receiving from economic advisers, some of them former students of mine with whom I had a good relationship. In the spring of 1975 I suggested to some of my Fine Gael colleagues that we should make similar appointments. There was no general enthusiasm for the idea, but I got agreement that I could go ahead on my own. In June 1975 therefore I appointed Brendan Dowling, another of my former students, as my economic adviser to help me to contribute more effectively to government discussion on domestic issues. Given the quality of advice available to me within my own department I did not need assistance in relation to foreign affairs. The department was naturally content with this arrangement. However, I was amused to find after a while that my officials, off their own bat and without mentioning it to me, sometimes sought Brendan's help also on economic issues of concern to the department.

An example of the way in which such advisers can help make things happen that might not otherwise take place, arose later that year. There was a poor potato crop, as a result of which prices rose sharply and, at the time when we were struggling to master inflation, the Consumer Price Index was consequently in danger of being forced up by an additional 1 percent on this account. I got agreement in government to the appointment of a working group comprising Brendan Dowling and Willie Scally (Justin Keating's adviser), together with officials from Agriculture and Finance, with a view to examining the possibility of removing restrictions on the import of potatoes in order to bring prices down. The Department of Agriculture appeared to be so mortally offended at even the suggestion of allowing potatoes to be imported that they did not attend. With their case thus gone by default, and with Finance concerned about inflation, the two advisers succeeded within the space of a single working week in getting the necessary decision taken. The threat of significant imports (clearly supplies had been held back so as to raise prices artificially), together with actual import of a mere 50 tons, halved prices literally overnight! If the normal departmental processes had been employed the authorisation of imports would probably have been effected around the time of the next potato glut!

Security matters absorbed a good deal of our time in government. Within a fortnight of our coming into office the *Claudia* was intercepted by the Naval Service off the Waterford coast, as a result of good intelligence work by the British. Its arms cargo was seized, and several of those involved, including Joe Cahill a senior IRA-man, were arrested and convicted of the attempted import of arms.

In the autumn we were told that members of the government were under threat of kidnapping by a subversive group. Until then our protection had been limited to the carrying of a gun by our official Garda drivers. My understanding of their instructions was that when we left our cars they were not to accompany us but were to remain with the car, so it seemed that the guns were for the protection of state cars rather then the ministers! Now for a time, we were accompanied by two armed detectives in an escort car whose job was to guard us.

At an informal discussion in government of the kidnapping threat we recognised that, even if the armed escorts discouraged efforts to kidnap ministers, our families would remain vulnerable. We agreed that if any member of our families were kidnapped the minister in question would opt out from discussion of the matter and that, regardless of the threats that might be made against the person kidnapped, no concession should be made to the kidnappers. I had already at a much earlier stage had a similar discussion with the Foreign Affairs staff visiting Northern Ireland, and they had similarly asked that no concessions be made if any of them were kidnapped in the North; all they sought was somewhat better compensation arrangements than those provided for their families by the ordinary civil service scheme, which seemed to me eminently reasonable.

When shortly after this we had to fight a by-election in the border constituency of Cavan-Monaghan to fill the seat vacated as a result of Erskine Childer's election to the Presidency, the Gardaí insisted that for security reasons members of the government stay in the same small hotel. In the event the by-election was entirely peaceful. Some months later, however, in mid-March 1974, a Presbyterian Fine Gael senator, Billy Fox, was murdered in this area by the Provisional IRA while he was visiting his fiancée. When he arrived at her parent's house one night a raid was in progress, by a dozen or so Provisionals, the sectarian character of which was demonstrated when they threw family Bibles into the fire. Billy Fox was chased into a field and shot down when cornered. The Provisionals immediately tried to throw a smokescreen over their actions by accusing the UDA of the atrocity and sending a wreath to Billy Fox's funeral, as well as issuing a statement alleging that he was well disposed towards them. Unknown to them, however, several of the murderers had been intercepted after the killing, and as a result all twelve of the gang were arrested, convicted, and given long sentences.

A year later the kidnap threat was carried out but, possibly because of the protection afforded to the members of the government, the victim was Dutch businessman Tiede Herrema, rather than a minister. Joan and I were in Chicago when we heard the news of his discovery and the subsequent siege of the house where he was held and I immediately phoned my Dutch counterpart, Max van der Stoel, but in his absence abroad spoke to the Minister of State, Laurens Brinkhorst. I assured him that we would do all in our power to track down the kidnappers and to release Herrema. Neither then nor later did the Dutch propose to us that we should negotiate with the kidnappers or accede to their demands. Several weeks later, after a debate in UCD, I went into the bar in the nearby Montrose Hotel to have a drink with some students. As I went to order drinks a man beside me said, 'He's out'. I looked blankly at him, and seeing my puzzlement he added, 'Herrema, he's out; they've freed him'.

I dashed to the phone, rang Joan, told her I was going to the Dutch embassy residence in Dundrum, where I was sure he would be brought, and suggested that she drive in her car to meet me there. There followed a chapter of confusion when we found nobody at home in the embassy and, after a Garda car bringing the Herremas arrived, had to trespass on the hospitality of neighbours across the road where Joan and I and Tiede Herrema were eventually joined by Mrs Herrema and the ambassador and his wife. We then retired to the embassy, where we remained until the early hours, listening to Tiede Herrema's account of his experiences after he had had a bath and a meal. I arranged for him to give RTÉ an exclusive interview, which was transmitted throughout the world.

The murder of the British ambassador, Christopher Ewart-Biggs, in July 1976 had provoked widespread demands for tougher action against the IRA. The Irish political system may be somewhat better equipped than that of Britain to resist pressures to respond to the latest atrocity, but it is not immune to such influences. On this occasion we succumbed to public pressures; worse still we did so belatedly. Instead of acting immediately by recalling the Dáil to enact supplementary legislation at once, we allowed the process of preparing the legislation to take a leisurely course over the following months, so that by the time it reached the Dáil after an abbreviated summer recess public opinion had reverted to its normal condition, concerned to balance the need to tackle the IRA effectively against the need to protect individual rights, and, on reflection, suspicious of measures that seemed to be prompted by an emotional reaction to a particular atrocity.

The debate on these measures was, I believe, damaging to our government, reinforcing the unhappiness of a public that was already critical of the economic measure we had had to take during the previous two years in response to the first oil crisis. There was, moreover, public concern at this time about reports by investigative reporters in the *Irish Times* of Garda brutality in the interrogation of suspects by what was described as the 'Heavy Gang'. I was distressed by these reports, which appeared to me to warrant investigation. Several of my colleagues shared my anxiety. Having reflected on the matter during our holiday in France in August, I decided to raise it in the government and if necessary to force the issue to a conclusion by threatening resignation. In the event I was deflected from my purpose by a consensus in the government that we would be sending very conflicting signals to public opinion if at the same time as enacting legislation that, among other things, extended to seven days, the maximum period for which suspects could be held under the Offences Against the State (Amendment) Act, we instituted an inquiry into the interrogation of suspects held by the Gardaí. I allowed myself to be persuaded to leave this sensitive issue over for several months, although my recollection is that I realised it again in the following November and/or January.

In mid-February 1977 I was asked by two responsible members of the Garda Síochána if I could see them privately to discuss a matter of concern to the force. Although they were members of a different representative body from that which I had served as consultant between 1962 and 1973, I knew them from that period and accordingly agreed to meet them. They told me that there was widespread worry among the Garda force about these allegations of brutality. Many of these allegations were false, they said, concocted by subversives to undermine the Gardaí and in the hope of avoiding conviction for offences of which they were guilty. In cases that had come to trial up to that point, brutality had not been employed by Gardaí, despite allegations to this effect. But in some pending cases it was believed by some in the force that confessions had been extracted by improper methods, and Garda morale would be seriously damaged if these cases went ahead and some Gardaí were persuaded to perjure themselves in the process. I told them I would do what I could to get action to deal with the matter.

My problem was how to proceed. From earlier contacts with Pat Cooney, the Minister for Justice, I knew that he was unsympathetic to such allegations, and while at one level the fact that I now had a basis for my concern from within the Force should add credibility to a further attempt by me to raise the matter with him, at another level any reference by me to contacts of mine within the Gardaí would naturally irritate him; I was already aware of his sensitivity to my former involvement with the representative body.

At the same time my persistent but unsuccessful attempts to raise the 'Heavy Gang' issue in government had made it less likely that I could take the issue up again at that level with any hope of a positive result; if I disclosed to the government as a whole that I had been contacted by members of the Garda Síochána it would almost certainly get a very negative reaction from Ministers who would have resented a similar involvement by me in their own areas of responsibility.

I finally decided that the best approach would be to approach Liam Cosgrave directly, but given his intense preoccupation with law and order and his protectiveness vis-à-vis the Defence Forces and Gardaí, it would have to be very carefully judged; indeed it would have to be designed to meet some of his own security preoccupations in a very direct manner as well as addressing the problem of averting any future Garda misconduct.

At this point I fell ill with gastric and throat infections, complicated by general exhaustion, and was told that I would have to rest for a fortnight. Before retiring to my bed I hammered out on my typewriter a letter to Liam Cosgrave. In it I proposed three measures:

First, to institute a review of the 'right to silence', which could, I suggested, be a factor that might tempt a minority of guards to use strong-arm tactics to get a statement – any kind of a statement – out of a suspect.

Second, to trade off representation of guards (e.g. by a barrister) in internal disciplinary inquiries unconnected with brutality to prisoners (a Garda demand at that time) for agreement to the participation of an outsider in inquiries into complaints by the public against members of the force.

And third, to introduce a rule that all arrests under certain types of legislation would have to be notified to the court within six or twelve hours, so that an officer of the court could be sent at any time thereafter to be admitted instantly to see the prisoner.

I added that he should not underestimate the concern of the Gardaí with the situation as it existed. We needed to help them discreetly. I concluded that I hoped the matter could be kept open until my return from my sick-bed, but that if it did come up for discussion before then would he let me know, so that, doctor or no doctor, I could come instantly.

That was the letter I wrote in February. At the present distance in time I cannot be sure – in view of my doubts about the wisdom of pressing the issue when, despite my concluding paragraph, I might not be in a position to follow it up in person in the near future – whether it was sent then or later, but a letter in these terms was certainly sent. However, the election was called before I could pursue the matter further. After the government changed there were reports of a 'shake-up' in the Gardaí by the new Fianna Fáil Minister for Justice, and thereafter complaints of ill-treatment of suspects ceased to be an issue.

But to revert once more to the legislation provoked by the ambassador's murder: in mid-October 1976 it passed both Houses and was sent to the President, Cearbhall Ó Dálaigh. Before describing what followed I should first explain the circumstances in which Cearbhall Ó Dálaigh had become president. He had been a distinguished jurist and had served as Chief Justice for eleven years before his appointment as the Irish member of the EEC court in 1972. He was held in high regard by artists and writers for his cultural interests. In his youth he had held republican views and when he was appointed to the Supreme Court I sent him for his entertainment the police file, found amongst my father's papers, on a public meeting he addressed in 1931 (with, among others, Cyril Cusack) denouncing my father's proposal to establish an Officer Training Corps of the army in UCD, where Ó Dálaigh was then a student. He enjoyed this reminder of his radical past. I had come to know him quite well in the late 1960s, when he used to call to collect his wife, Máirín, a distinguished Gaelic scholar, after caucus meetings of the opposition group on the UCD governing body at my house.

After Erskine Childers's funeral the government had had to consider possible names to be put forward to the Opposition in the hope of securing agreement on a successor and thus avoiding the trouble and expense of a nationwide election for an office that is mainly, albeit not exclusively, honorary in character. Our first choice had been Erskine Childers's widow, Rita Childers, but two other names were added as possible alternatives. When Liam Cosgrave consulted Jack Lynch on the matter he too favoured Rita Childers, but he warned that his chance of securing his party's support for her depended on complete secrecy being maintained.

That evening the Minister for the Gaeltacht, Tom O'Donnell, had to attend a public function in Skibbereen, County Cork. A journalist asked him what he thought of Rita Childers as a candidate, a local council having passed a resolution in her favour. Misunderstanding the basis of the question, and thinking that agreement between Fianna Fáil and the government on her nomination must have been reached and announced, he endorsed her in terms that implied government support. Jack Lynch was furious at what he naturally saw as a leak, and his support and that of his party shifted to another name, Cearbhall Ó Dálaigh, who accepted the nomination and was inaugurated shortly afterwards.

Although he was generally popular, President Ó Dálaigh did not seem entirely happy in the job and did not adjust easily to his new position. It was believed that he and his wife might have regretted taking on the responsibility, although this was never confirmed. Some believe that this might have been a contributory factor to his resignation in October 1976, but if so it can only have been a subordinate consideration.

Under the Constitution, if the president had doubts about the constitutionality of a Bill he may, instead of signing it, refer it to the Supreme Court, having first heard the view of the members of the Council of State. This power is usually exercised when doubts have been expressed in the Oireachtas during the debates on a Bill. In the case of September 1976 anti-subversive legislation such doubts were expressed, not unreasonably in view of the length of time proposed for detention before a person was charged, which seemed to be at or near the margin of what could be considered reasonable given the provisions of the Constitution on the liberty of the person. Since reasonable doubts existed, it seemed wise to me (and I think to some other members of the government) to have it tested then instead of having it found defective at a later stage when challenged by someone in detention.

Paddy Donegan, the Minister for Defence, held a contrary view, however, and held it strongly. He attended a ceremony in Columb Barracks, Mullingar, where he made impromptu remarks in the course of which he attacked the president's referral of the new Bill to the Supreme Court in confused terms.

The other minister present, Pat Cooney, rang the Taoiseach at once to report what had happened. As soon as Paddy Donegan realised fully the implications of what he had said (especially in view of the fact that the president ex officio is titular commander-in-chief of the Defence Forces), he offered his resignation. Liam Cosgrave rejected the resignation, however, and Paddy instead sought an appointment with the president to apologise. This request was not granted, and on the following day, when the matter came before the government at a meeting in Liam's room in Leinster House, we were faced with a letter from the president protesting at the minister's remarks.

I had been away and I arrived after the meeting had begun. Liam had, as I understood it, just read out the letter. I asked to see it, and may have been the only minister who had the opportunity of poring over the text. The letter did not directly threaten resignation but took the form partly of a series of rhetorical questions. Having said that the relationship between president and minister had been 'irreparably breached', the president went on to ask whether the sequence of remarks by the minister could be construed otherwise than as an insinuation that the president did not stand behind the state: Had the minister any conception of his responsibilities as a minister, and in particular as Minister for Defence?

Most of the members of the government, ignoring the words 'irreparably breached', were inclined to draw some comfort from the absence of an unambiguous threat of resignation. With the advantage of actually having read the text I was less sanguine. I did not, however, feel in a good position to challenge the optimistic view formed before my arrival – not least because to have done so would in effect have been to demand Paddy Donegan's resignation, and as my relationship with him had for many years been one of some distance, I felt ill-placed to be the one person pressing the issue. I contented myself therefore with voicing a measure of pessimism about the more generally accepted interpretation, without attempting to take the matter further.

The following afternoon I received a call from the Taoiseach asking me to come to his office at once. I was there within three minutes, as were several other ministers whom he had summoned. He told us he had been informed that a despatch-rider was on his way from the park with a message from the president, which he feared might contain his resignation. I suggested that he phone Paddy Donegan, who was at home, and belatedly accept his resignation, so that, before the message arrived from Áras an Uachtaráin he could inform the president that the minister had resigned. He did so, and Paddy immediately agreed. But the president had laid his plans with care. He had left Áras an Uachtaráin at 2.30 for an engagement on the south side of the city, from which, at that very moment, he was departing to go with his wife to his own house in County Wicklow. His resignation, which arrived a few minutes later, was irretrievable, and the damage done to the government as immense. Liam Cosgrave had been fatally betrayed by his own excessive loyalty to one of his ministers.

Feeling that a new president with political experience was desirable (although it was far from clear that Cearbhall Ó Dálaigh's lack of such experience had been a factor in his precipitate departure), the members of the government came rapidly to a unanimous decision to propose to Fianna Fáil the name of Paddy Hillery, former Fianna Fáil Minister for Education, Labour, and Foreign Affairs, who would shortly be ending his term as Irish member of the European Commission. The proposal could not, we felt, be turned down by the Opposition, and we would thus avoid an expensive presidential election, which in the unhappy circumstances in which we found ourselves we would certainly have lost, whoever might be our candidate. Our suggestion for an agreed candidate was accepted, and in December 1976 President Hillery was inaugurated, and served for two terms until 1990.

Conor Cruise O'Brien had some time previously introduced a Bill to narrow the terms of the order intended to keep the IRA and their supporters off the air and to transfer from the government to the Dáil the power to sack the RTÉ Authority, a power that had been used by the Fianna Fáil government several years earlier to remove an authority that it felt had not enforced this order with sufficient vigour. Conor felt, with some justice, that vagueness in the wording of the order had contributed to the earlier disagreement between the government and the authority. His action in making the wording more specific was clearly in easement of the situation, as was his legislative change to prevent a future government from removing an authority without Dáil approval.

But theses actions, together with the vigour and clarity with which he defended the principle of the ban, had made him the target of libertarian criticism — to such an extent indeed that a myth developed, which still exists in some circles, that he was the original author of this prohibition of IRA appearances, on radio and television!

Of the ban itself it is sufficient today that there are two sides to the argument about it. On its efficacy against subversives there can clearly be legitimate differences of opinion by people opposed to the IRA – leaving on one side the inevitable attacks on it by the IRA itself and its fellow travellers. The case customarily made against it is, however, far from compelling. The claim, frequently made, that if free expression were allowed, the potential damage from the publicising of extreme views would be countered by skilled journalistic handling, including interviews with IRA spokesmen, has no obvious foundation. To take an example of a person expressing extreme views (which, however fell short of incitement to violence), Ian Paisley, I never saw any interviewer 'cutting him down to size', and the same was in my view true of at least some interviews with the IRA or Sinn Féin spokesmen before they were banned on RTÉ. Moreover, as RTÉ is the public broadcasting service of a state that many unionists have traditionally seen as hostile, the Irish government can be argued to have a special duty to restrain expressions of support for the IRA on its air waves that could further inflame the prejudices and fears of extreme unionists.

I do not suggest that these arguments are irrefutable; but neither are the more theoretical arguments against a ban on the IRA having access to the airwaves. And the case for the ban convinced successive Irish governments under four Taoisigh during two decades to maintain the order, despite its unpopularity with liberal opinion and the media, and notwithstanding the many anomalies to which it has given rise.

When it came eventually to the issue of when to call the election Liam Cosgrave at a government meeting asked for the views of the members of the Cabinet.

When we had taken a headcount with a tied result, I remarked to Liam Cosgrave, 'it seems that the decision is back to you, Taoiseach' – fairly confident that, left to himself with no pressure either way, he would, with his customary caution, decide to postpone a dissolution. To my surprise, he decided on a June election; I do not know why, beyond noting that the completion by the government of four-and-a-quarter years in office, longer than any other government since the war, represented for him a target attained, proving that coalitions can survive as long as, or longer than, single party governments.

Our two parties were utterly unprepared. Fine Gael's organisation had run down during our time in office; party morale was low, for much the same reasons as government morale was low; and we had no clear idea of where as a party we should be going next. The amount that we had achieved in terms of social and other reforms and in overcoming the oil crisis successfully was certainly impressive, and gave us, for what it was worth (very little, I am afraid, in view of the shortness of the public memory), a record on which to stand with some pride. But we seemed to have some difficulty in putting together a convincing programme for the years ahead.

By contrast our opponents had no inhibitions about what they were prepared to promise; a programme of tax cuts and public spending that at any time would have been disastrous if implemented, but which was doubly so at a time when the economy was already expanding at an almost record rate of about 6 percent.

It soon became clear that this explosion of Opposition promises was politically superfluous: Fianna Fáil would have won the election if they had promised nothing, for the people were tired of us. Their extravagant commitments, which severely damaged the economy for a period of a decade proved to have been to no political purpose.

9

~: My First Year in Foreign Affairs :~

My first task within twenty four hours of my appointment as Minister of Foreign Affairs had been to meet the British prime minister and foreign secretary in Downing Street.

The EEC foreign ministers were to meet in Brussels on the day following my London visit. By the time the Downing Street meeting finished it was too late to catch the last plane to Brussels, and no seats were available on the night sleeper via Dunkirk. Alec Douglas-Home rose to the occasion, offering me a lift with him in an ancient Andover of the Queen's flight, which took off from a dark corner of London Airport, illuminated by a single light – a departure that reminded me forcibly of films I had seen about contacts with the Resistance in occupied Europe during the war. The flight gave me the opportunity to establish a relationship with Douglas-Home and assured me of a night's sleep in Brussels before my first encounter with the other foreign ministers of the Community.

The occasion was not in fact a meeting of the Council of Ministers of the Community but rather a meeting of the Foreign Ministers of the Nine on Political Co-operation, or foreign policy co-ordination. Among the topics for discussion was whether the Nine should recognise North Vietnam. This was the type of issue that Ireland had not hitherto had to face, because it had always been the Irish practice to recognise states, not governments, which avoided the awkward problem that could arise when one regime replaced another in non-democratic states. Recognition of North Vietnam was thus not an important question for us, and on this occasion I was able, without attracting attention, to remain silent. Nevertheless, it was clear to me from the discussion around the table that a radical shift was required in the traditional narrow focus of Irish foreign policy now that we had joined the Community. Henceforth we would have to fulfil our responsibilities in conjunction with other member states, and for that purpose would have to develop, on the basis of our own information and our own assessments, policy positions on a whole range of global issues that had hitherto been of concern to us only in the more limited context of UN membership. This could not be done credibly without an extension of our representation abroad, in particular by establishing diplomatic relations with the Soviet Union. At that stage, I think we were the only state in the world apart from Portugal and perhaps Spain and the Holy See not to have such relations, reflecting the extent to which Irish politicians had hitherto allowed fear of popular anti-communist prejudice to influence their actions irrationally in relation to foreign policy.

Back in Dublin on the following Monday morning I went into my department, effectively for the first time. I met the senior people, and was then brought on a tour of the building to meet the rest of the staff. Several incidents stand out in my mind. The first is a conversation I had with Sean Donlon walking up the stairs to the Anglo-Irish division, in which he was then a counsellor responsible for relations with Northern Ireland. I asked him what contacts he had with Northern politicians. 'None at present,' he replied. 'We had contact with the SDLP until last November'. I found this somewhat astonishing. Eventually I discovered that contacts with the SDLP had been maintained until the previous November by a senior official in the Anglo-Irish division, Eamon Gallagher, but that Jack Lynch had apparently been dealing with Gallagher without keeping his minister, Paddy Hillery fully informed. Gallagher had thus found himself in an invidious position vis-à-vis his own minister, and in November 1972 had asked to be transferred to the economic division. Because of uncertainties about government policy, contacts with the SDLP had not been maintained after his departure.

I should perhaps add that during the previous three years the whole question of contacts between the Irish government and Northern Ireland had been complicated by the extreme tension in that part of the island and by concern about British reactions to the maintenance of such contacts, especially after the Arms Crisis in 1970. At one period Gallagher had been told that he could go to Northern Ireland only outside office hours – in the evenings or at weekends – so that if his presence were queried by the British, he could claim to be off duty!

I told Sean Donlon that he should resume contact with the SDLP immediately. I then asked him about contacts with the unionists. There had been none, he told me, and I had the impression that such contacts had not been encouraged. I told him that I did not see how we could hope to find a solution to the Northern Ireland problem without such contacts, and that his decision should follow up the informal discussions I had had with unionists in Belfast six days earlier. I told him also that I would be visiting Northern Ireland on a regular basis.

Having met the staff in the Anglo-Irish division I was brought to the Registry and shown the department's very first file, my father's personal file S/1 (S being for 'Staff'). It contained little except income tax demands from the mid-1920s! Jack

Perry, the boilerman, then brought me around the basement. As we explored the cellars, it became evident that he was still distressed about some of the things that had happened after Lord Iveagh had handed the building over to the government in 1939. In this context he referred obscurely to 'Queen Vicotoria's head under the stairs'. I subsequently elucidated this mysterious remark. When de Valera had taken possession of the house, his personal secretary apparently held strong views about remnants of British Imperialism. According to the account I received, she had ordered the destruction of anything containing what she considered to be a symbol of royalty or the British regime. Happily – and this was what Jack Perry had been hinting at – she had failed to observe that the badly lit but quite remarkable wooden carving along the lower edge of a balcony at the top of the main staircase contained at its centre a medallion of Queen Victoria, which had been missed during this clean-out.

My own office on the first floor was a spacious, and gracious, room. It had eighteenth-century tapestries of sylvan scenes inset along one wall, a huge fireplace in which on appropriate occasions a turf fire blazed, and two great windows overlooking the part of the Iveagh Gardens that belonged to the house, the remainder being at the disposal of UCD. In the UCD part of the gardens thirty years earlier I had been lectured on fine days, had organised a children's party, and had lounged around with friends discussing at times the kind of matters for which I now had ministerial responsibility.

In the centre of the lawn outside my office was a small ornamental pool with overhanging shrubs, where in the spring a pair of ducks from Stephen's Green nested and hatched out their offspring. One Sunday, when in conference with several senior officials on an urgent matter, I saw the hatched ducklings struggling unavailingly to get out of the pond along an overhanging branch; I mobilised the officials to help me find a plank in the basement along which the ducklings could proceed with a view to following their parents out the rear entrance and down Earlsfort Terrace to Stephen's Green.

After my initial tour of the building I sat down to discuss foreign affairs with the secretary and assistant secretaries, who constituted a 'management committee', the meetings of which on Mondays I soon arranged to join in mid-morning, after they had had an opportunity to review outstanding issues among themselves and to prepare for discussion with me.

The secretary was Hugh McCann, a diplomat with great experience who had been appointed secretary of the department ten years earlier after a period as Ambassador to the Court of St James. His secretaryship had been extraordinarily fruitful. He had effected a gradual, fairly painless, and notably humane transition from a system of promotion by seniority to promotion on merit. There had, of course, been objections to this important change in personnel policy, but on the whole they had been muted, and only one senior ambassador sought (without success) to persuade me to turn back the tide on this issue.

Of course, such an innovation takes time to yield results, and I was probably the first minister to benefit greatly from it. By the time I arrived at Iveagh House one-quarter of the ambassadors were under fifty and one-quarter of officials of counsellor rank were 'high-fliers' under forty years of age. There were in addition, a number of young first secretaries still in their twenties, on whose talents I was able to draw, promoting them all to counsellor rank within a couple of years.

At the time of my appointment a reshuffle of senior post in the department was, in fact, pending. I knew that Hugh McCann had been hoping after a strenuous decade as secretary to be released for service overseas, but he agreed at my request to remain for a further year to guide me in my responsibilities and to give me time to feel my way in relation to the staff. I found this immensely valuable. During the crucial early period in the job I had the advantage of his exceptional experience and wisdom in all I attempted.

As it happened I already knew personally over one third of the fifty senior officials. Some had been at college with me and others I had come to know mainly through my interest in EC affairs. After my appointment I made it my business to brief myself from other sources on the capabilities of many of those whom I did not know personally. I was therefore far better placed than most ministers in relation to my staff; many politicians have been appointed to departments where they have no prior knowledge of any officials. Happily Hugh McCann and his successors, were disposed to share with me their responsibility for staff promotions and postings, and although, I never sought to impose my views in such matters, it is fair to say that the disposition of staff whilst I was minister was a joint responsibility, and one that absorbed many hours of my time at different periods in conjunction with the secretary of the day.

After my first meeting with the management committee I decided to call a conference of all senior officials and ambassadors to discuss our foreign policy in the light of our very recent entry to the European Community. No such conference had previously been held. Fortunately I was too new in the job to know much about financial constraints or to be inhibited by a lack of precedent from organising such an event.

The conference, which lasted three days, convened in Iveagh House in mid-April. I decided that our initial discussion should deal with the evolution of a closer Union, looking at this question in European terms broader in scope than the narrow national interest or even enlightened self-interest, for we were now members of the European Community, responsible together with our partners for achieving its objectives. Knowing that some other national bureaucracies had tended to take a narrow view, over-protective of their national interest, and that this was holding up progress towards the economic integration that I believed to be in Ireland's long-term interest, I was anxious to face the department bluntly with this issue. In most other areas I would have to learn from them, but on this I wanted to give a personal lead, based on my long familiarity with the European Community as a UCD lecturer.

I directed the attention of the conference to the issues of supra-nationalism and democratisation of the Community, which I felt had been glossed over in the opening exchanges. Was it more important for us to have a veto to stop things happening or to seek support from others to get things done by means of majority voting? Was there anything in the fear that supra-nationalism – which meant less chance to veto decisions – would lead to big-power dominance? (For myself I thought that the opposite danger existed i.e. big-power dominance in the absence of supra-national decision-making). Were we to be inhibited from pursuing economic integration because of a fear that in a fully integrated Community we should eventually be involved in a defence commitment? After all, we had accepted the logic of this commitment in the publicly-stated positions of both the previous government and my own party on EC membership, and that issue was not likely to arise as a practical matter for a long time to come. Finally was an economic and monetary union feasible, and for it to come into existence would the Community not need much stronger democratic controls?

These queries evoked a discussion which, as I had expected, some scepticism about the desirability from Ireland's point of view of giving the European Parliament more powers, and there were mixed opinions on the issue of the veto. But at least this exchange of views had ensured that Foreign Affairs would look afresh at these matters, and I was satisfied in the light of what had been said that I would not face opposition from within the department in pursuing the European policy that I had in mind. In winding up the debate I stressed the need for us to seek out issues on which we could play a constructive role, not just in the narrow interests of Ireland but in such a way as to demonstrate that we had a European philosophy and would not simply be looking for what we could get out of the system.

A lively moment came during the discussion when I was told that Claude Cheysson had just been appointed a French member of the Commission. But I knew that the Rome Treaty provided for the appointment of Commissioners by the common consent of governments, which in my naivety I thought meant what it said, and I had not been asked for the consent of the Irish government. 'How has he been appointed?' I asked.

'By the French government,' replied Eamon Gallagher.

'But we haven't agreed,' I responded.

'It has been agreed,' replied Gallagher.

'By whom?' I enquired.

'By me,' said Gallagher, after a brief hesitation.

'But you aren't the Irish government,' I responded. 'Don't let it happen again.'

The conference participants were highly entertained by this exchange – both by Gallagher's discomfiture and, I presume also, by my assumption that the Rome Treaty had meant what it said on this matter.

The discussion moved on to the other topics on the agenda. I learnt much from the discussion on the Conference on Security and Co-operation in Europe (CSCE), which was due to convene in Helsinki in three months' time. My belief that we had to open diplomatic relations with the Soviet Union, strengthened by my experience at the political co-operation meeting in Brussels two days after my appointment was reinforced.

I then took a poll on the priority to be given to the opening of diplomatic relations with further countries. This provided guidance for the expansion that I undertook during the following four years – an expansion that increased the number of our resident missions from twenty-one to thirty. A subsequent discussion on development co-operation showed the strength of departmental commitment to the expansion of our hitherto minimal volume of overseas aid.

After a brief review of our information and cultural activities, we turned to Northern Ireland. The publication of the British White Paper, to which the government had sought to contribute on our first day in office, provided a focus. It represented a significant shift in British policy, involving a clear commitment to power-sharing in the North and acceptance of the need for an 'Irish dimension': some kind of North-South Council. This development, together with the fact that our government comprised two parties both of which were explicitly and unambiguously committed to seeking Irish unity only on the basis of consent by a majority of the people of Northern Ireland, created a new situation to which our foreign policy had to adjust.

Finally, we had a session in conjunction with the state agencies responsible for the promotion of various interests abroad: exports, industrial promotion, tourism. It emerged that past tensions between the department and Coras Trachtala, of which I had been aware, had been resolved and a good working relationship had been established.

As to the EEC, having reviewed the pros and cons of alternative approaches, I concluded in the memorandum that I then prepared that our long-term interest would be best served by an evolution of the European Community towards a more democratic structure, involving a greater supranational element in the form of a strengthened European Parliament and possibly a move from unanimity to qualified majority voting. I warned against the unwisdom of allowing fear of getting involved in a defence commitment to determine the whole course of our foreign policy for decades ahead, to the possible detriment of our vital economic and social interests.

On the practical side I set out the need for additional staff both at home and abroad to undertake our new responsibilities, and proposed opening embassies in Luxemburg, Moscow, and possibly Vienna and Oslo. The memorandum was approved by the government on 7 May without difficulty. Most ministers may have been too busy in their departments to have read it!

I had already initiated bilateral contacts in Brussels with some of my Community colleagues. I had a brief meeting with the French foreign minister, Michel Jobert. This aroused interest in the Quai d'Orsay, two officials of which approached me separately some weeks later to suggest a further discussion with their minister. One of them referred to Jobert's 'inexperience' causing problems in the Council of Ministers – a remark I listened to with a straight face as a minister of three months' standing myself – and to the officials' hope that Gaston Thorn and I might help to sort out subsequent problems.

More useful at that point were two meetings in Luxembourg in the margin of Council meetings there, first with the Netherlands foreign minister, Max van der Stoel, and later with the Luxembourg foreign minister, Gaston Thron. In these discussions I suggested an early move to direct elections for the European Parliament and a strengthening of that body's powers. Our substantial identity of views suggested to me the desirability of a multilateral concentration of tactics by Ireland and the Benelux countries. Accordingly we agreed to hold luncheon discussions before the start of subsequent Council of Ministers meetings with a view to concerting our approach to the institutional development of the Community.

I believe these meetings were useful. At the end of the year, however, the Benelux countries became concerned about possible negative reactions elsewhere to our 'caucuses'. I had the impression that they might have been 'warned off', possibly by the French. Despite this setback Van der Stoel and I agreed to try to maintain some cohesion among the smaller countries through bilateral Irish-Dutch contacts – he liaising thereafter with the Belgians, and I with the Danes, and both of us with Gaston Thorn. This loose arrangement was less satisfactory than our joint meetings had been, but it enabled the five of us to achieve some measure of cohesion, for example in relation to a Franco-German move to establish some kind of 'Directoire' in 1975.

Joan's fear of flying had persisted, and after my first scheduled visit to London and Brussels I sought to reassure her by travelling to EEC meetings by train and ship, a journey about twenty hours in each direction. When Joan accompanied me on one such trip, to the OECD annual meeting in Paris in June, she found herself at a dinner beside Christopher Soames, the Conservative politician who had become EEC Commissioner. Soames was so absorbed by his conversation with George Schultz that when they next met Soames failed to recognise her, at which Joan said in a pleasant voice: 'You forget, Sir Christopher, that we met before, at a dinner in Paris, when you ignored me. I think you must be the rudest man I have met'. Soames was delighted with this; they became good friends thereafter.

When the trip to Helsinki loomed up, Joan raised the question of accompanying me, as I would be away for a week. I agreed, pointing out, however, that I would have to pay her expenses. (I worked on the principle that unless Joan was invited on a trip, as happens on bilateral official – as distinct from working – visits, or was required to co-host mixed functions, or was attending a conference such as OECD to which all ministers normally brought their wives, I should pay her expenses). While a number of ministers were bringing their wives to Helsinki, it did not seem that this would be the general pattern, because the dinners and lunches, as at the UN, would not include spouses. To reach Helsinki by train and ship would take two-and-a-half days, with four changes between train and ship in each direction. Joan conceded that this was excessive and agreed to fly, for the first time in seventeen years.

The conference at Helsinki provided an opportunity for a wide range of contacts with foreign ministers from non-Community countries. In addition to meeting William Rogers, the US Secretary of State, and Mitchell Sharp, the Canadian foreign minister, I had discussions with all the Eastern European foreign ministers except the Bulgarian, and with Archbishop Casaroli, who represented the Holy See. I shall return in a later chapter to my discussions with him.

The meeting with Czechoslovak minister was in their embassy after dinner; I had another dinner engagement that evening but dropped in for coffee. Most of the guests had left by the time I had arrived, and I recall my surprise at walking past the guards and their dogs into a building that at first seemed empty. I went from room to room shouting ineffective 'hellos' until I finally tracked down the minister, a couple of his guests and some of his officials in an inner room. When the guests left I raised the attempt to smuggle Czechoslovak arms to the IRA through Amsterdam several years earlier. I was told that the Czechoslovak government had been very upset by this affair; the arms had been sold to a dealer with whom they had had a good relationship for the preceding two years and were intended for the Middle East. They had terminated their relationship with him in view of what had happened.

The conference itself, the successful conclusion of which required a consensus of all thirty-five countries present, was deadlocked at the end of the week by a Maltese demand that the decisions reached should also be applied in the Mediterranean region. Outside the air-conditioned conference hall itself the heat and humidity were intense, and at one point on Saturday morning I wandered into the hall in order to cool down. A man ran up the steps to me clutching a scrap of paper. 'Close the conference,' he said. As I looked astonished at this command, he reeled off the names of a number of countries. 'They've all gone home,' he said.

'And you're next. Take the chair and read out this,' pointing to a sentence handwritten on a scrap of paper, 'and close the conference quickly before anyone objects'. As he trotted away I asked someone who he was. 'Mendelevich, the Soviet representative,' I was told. 'He's been trying to break the deadlock'.

I took the chair, enjoying the astonishment of my officials as they entered the hall in answer to the resumption bell. When the conference had assembled I read out the key sentence, asked 'is that agreed?' and after a fractional pause declared; 'Conference adjourned'. There was massive applause, and as I walked up the aisle congratulations showered on me from all sides – as if I had actually been responsible for the breakthrough!

The most important development from an Irish point of view was the meeting I had with Andrei Gromyko about opening diplomatic relations between our two countries. Gromyko was accompanied by a colleague and an interpreter, and he explained to me in English at the outset that, as his colleague did not speak English, he would speak in Russian and have his remarks interpreted.

I then told him that the government wished me to proceed with the proposal for an exchange of embassies, and I suggested that the matter be settled between us at the end of September during the UN General Assembly debate. What we had in mind, I said, would be an exchange of small missions, as we were a small country.

He responded in Russian, very vigorously. My reference to 'small missions' had annoyed him. His remarks, as interpreted, were a denunciation of the British, who had recently expelled over a hundred Soviet officials from London. He attributed my concern for small missions to British influence. The British, the interpreter went on to say, were not clean. At this point Gromyko interrupted in English; what he had said was that the British were 'unclean': they had spread slanders about the Soviet Union, which, he implied, had influenced the shape of our proposal. I responded that I had no representations from Britain on the subject, and that my recommendation of small missions was made entirely of my own initiative.

He calmed down and went on, in English, to ask me if we had a mission in London – had we not withdrawn our ambassador there some time ago? And we had embassies in Paris and Washington? At this and other points in our discussion he struck me as being badly briefed. At the end of our discussion we agreed to meet again at the UN General Assembly session in New York in September and October in order to settle the arrangements for an exchange of diplomatic missions.

The August break was particularly welcome that year. We spent part of it in Donegal, where we stayed with Sean and Paula Donlon and spent much of the time with John and Pat Hume and other SDLP people, and then went to join some friends who had rented a house in the south of France. This was the start of a new cycle of holidaymaking. Up to the early 1970s our summer holidays had all been simply family occasions, but now, with our children effectively grown up, we accepted an invitation from Denis Corboy, a friend of many years' standing who was now the EEC information officer in Dublin, to join a 'house party'; he had rented a house in a restored medieval village of Les Arcs in the Var. Ever since then many of our holidays have taken this form, with one or other of our children together with their spouses and their children often joining our friends and ourselves.

In September we had a hectic fortnight in New York at the 1973 UN autumn session, during which I met over a dozen Foreign Ministers from various parts of the world and delivered my General Assembly speech. Whilst there, I concluded the negotiations with Gromyko for an exchange of diplomatic missions. The signing ceremony was much more jovial than our initial encounter had been. I referred to the loan of twenty thousand dollars given by the underground Dáil government of 1920 to representatives of the infant Soviet Union in New York against a pledge of jewels that had been the property of a member of the former imperial family – a loan redeemed some thirty years later. He enjoyed my comment that the absence of provision for interest on the loan showed what poor capitalists we were!

I was particularly happy to make my debut at the UN under the auspices of our ambassador Con Cremin, then in his final year before retirement. He and his wife had entertained me in Paris in July 1939. Con was a classical scholar of distinction, a litterateur, linguist and raconteur. He was a most charming companion. My only problem with him was his very strong Kerry accent, which at times I found hard to penetrate – although I noticed that his UN ambassadorial colleagues seemed to have no difficulty with it. Fortunately the Cremins' family language was unaccented French, so that at home in the residence with his family Joan and I could understand him easily.

Joan had accompanied me on his trip also; by now she had completely overcome her fear of flying. As we were paying for her journey, and had decided to return by sea (travelling on the *France* (on what turned out to be one of the famous liner's last voyages), we travelled economy class on the way out by air. So, out of courtesy, did Hugh McCann and my personal secretary, Ita McCoy.

A couple of years later when we were on our way to Brussels one day we were discussing another visit to the UN. Joan commented that the wife of the French Foreign Minister had told her that she sometimes reduced the cost of accompanying her husband by travelling on a charter flight. Joan suggested we look in the newspaper to see if there were any charter flights to New York coinciding with the UN. We looked in the *Irish Times* and by a happy chance found a suitably timed charter organised by a Tipperary hurling team and a Limerick football team, and had a most enjoyable flight with them in both directions.

I have mentioned Ita McCoy. She had been present when the IRA murdered her father during the Civil War because of her brother's participation in the Free

State government: her brother was Kevin O'Higgins, who, in turn, was murdered on his way to Sunday Mass by an IRA breakaway group five years later. Ita herself worked for the Fine Gael party and had been personal secretary to Richard Mulcahy as Minister for Education, to John A. Costello as Taoiseach, and later to her nephew Tom O'Higgins as deputy leader of the party. I think she was about to retire when I became minister, but she agreed to come with me to Foreign Affairs as my personal secretary – that is, secretary for political as distinct from official purposes. I have to add that she was also an unofficial adviser, for her long experience and acute political mind were extraordinarily useful to a relative newcomer to politics like myself.

While Joan and I had been on our way back to Ireland from the UN General Assembly session, travelling on the *France*, the Yom Kippur War had broken out.

The subsequent Arab oil boycott threatened the economic life and the financial stability of the industrialised countries; and because of the skilful way in which the Arabs enlisted the sympathies of the Third World, these events also endangered the relationship between the industrialised and developing countries. The, boycott, moreover, led to a deep split in the Community itself, owing to a lack of support amongst some other Community members for Denmark and the Netherlands, which were threatened with an oil boycott by the Arab countries. It led as well to a French decision to opt out of a Western consensus on how to face this crisis.

The split was already looming when the Council of Ministers met in Brussels on 6 November to consider the situation – a meeting which, contrary to the normal practice, was held in complete secrecy, without officials or interpreters. The president for this occasion was a Danish Minister for Foreign Affairs, Ivar Norgaard, who opened the meeting by telling us that if we spoke very slowly, in English or in French, we would understand each other. On his second repetition of this proposition, Jobert remarked, '*C'est de vous qui'il parle, Garret, et en anglais et en français*'. My speed of utterance had already become a byword in the Council.

In Copenhagen the Queen of Denmark gave a luncheon in our honour. As her children peered curiously down from a high balcony, I asked my neighbour, Alec Douglas-Home, what he thought of Nixon. 'Well, Garret,' he responded, 'you and I are very different people, from different backgrounds – you are Irish and I English, you are Roman Catholic and I Anglican – and we would disagree about the rights and wrongs of certain issues. But at least we know right and wrong exist; that man doesn't'!

The Copenhagen summit itself three weeks later proved a disaster. Pompidou was ill; Brandt not at his best. The 'fireside chat' of the heads of government – a real fire had been provided, at which the foreign ministers were allowed to peep – was an occasion of total confusion. My colleagues and I, charged with preparing a declaration, had to spend many hours trying to reconstruct what the heads of government might have said to each other; and a joint meeting of heads of government and foreign ministers proved less than happy; although it was the first of a number of such meetings at which I enjoyed improving the English of drafts prepared by the British delegation.

The most baroque feature of this least successful of summits was the uninvited appearance of a number of Arab Foreign Ministers, towards whom we felt about as welcome as King Herod to the three kings from the east when they brought him news of the birth of a future king of Israel. Given Europe's parlous energy situation, we dared not refuse to hear them, but the only available time was after midnight. Any hopes that the lateness of the hour might encourage brevity were soon dashed. They were not going to let us off lightly in their moment of triumph, and it was almost three in the morning before they allowed us to stagger off to our beds.

The outstanding issue of EEC consultation with the United States was eventually remitted to the first informal meeting of foreign ministers at Gymnich, near Bonn, in April 1974. (In the event no such consultation took place during the French presidency in the second half of the year. It was left to me, in January 1975, to inaugurate this process by undertaking a visit to Washington to meet Henry Kissinger).

Much time at Gymnich was spent on the question of European union, the first discussion of the subject among the members of the enlarged Community. The Paris summit of December 1972, on the eve of our membership, had decided that 'European Union' should be achieved by 1980. Callaghan's rather negative question about what this might mean produced what might be described as a chorus of nescience; Van der Stoel, Scheel, Thorn, Moro and Jobert all agreed that no one knew what European Union meant!

The social side of this meeting included, after dinner, a descent into the dungeons of the castle, where our host, Walter Scheel – who later that year became president of the Federal Republic, and whose singing voice had won him a golden disc – endeavoured to get a sing-song going. Only Jim Callaghan and Joan were prepared to join in, but this did not deter him. The shortage of a common repertoire proved a problem: when 'Tipperary' was proposed Scheel swept to one side Joan's lighthearted query about the suitability of a British Great War song for a German foreign minister, and we had a good rendering of it. I recall that Jobert and the late Aldo Moro, two small, slight figures, were seated on either side of their considerably larger and jolly host, a triptych illustrating gaiety surrounded by gloom. Before long the two of them had slipped off to bed, leaving us to what they clearly regarded as our quite unsuitable musical activities.

Next morning, sadly, Joan and I had to leave at first light; we had been phoned with the news that her mother had fallen gravely ill. She died a fortnight later, to Joan's deep distress and indeed to that of all our family. An extraordinarily reclusive person and very religious, she had been part of my life for almost thirty years, and the children were deeply attached to her. Given the traumatic background of her childhood, Joan had an extremely close relationship with her mother, whose death left a gulf it was impossible to fill.

After Gymnich, with the election of Giscard d'Estaing as president of France, an unsuccessful attempt was made by French ministers, with support from Germany and Britain, to bypass the European Commission and establish a European Directory of these three states, replacing the foreign ministers' role by regular meetings by heads of government. I led the process of blocking this initiative. Nevertheless, we could not prevent the initiation of regular 'orientation meetings' of heads of government. When the heads met in Paris in December, Harold Wilson, who clearly enjoyed consorting with his fellow prime ministers, started the bidding on the frequency of the proposed meetings of heads of government at four a year plus emergency meetings. Liam Cosgrave countered with a bid of two. The remainder proposed three, and that figure was agreed, with the addition of 'and others when necessary'.

On the issue of direct elections a proposal by Liam Cosgrave at my suggestion that they should be held in 1978 was agreed in a slightly modified form, namely 'at any time in or after 1978'. We were happy with the formula, for, while we were anxious to see these quinquennial elections taking place soon, our particular concern had been to have them coincide, if possible, with our own quinquennial local Council elections. It was our belief – which would prove correct – that the coincidence of two different elections would boost the poll for each. Our next local elections were to take place in mid-1979 and we had calculated that, given some inevitable slippage in implementing this decision, we were more likely to achieve our 1979 objective if we named 1978 than if we named the year we really wanted!

All in all these decisions represented a reasonably satisfactory outcome to a situation that had seemed quite threatening three months earlier so far as both the integrity of the Community's institutional structure and the interests of the smaller countries were concerned. For the three larger countries, on the other hand, there had been something of a setback to their hopes of strengthening their position vis-a-vis the supranational institutions of the Community.

10

~: Irish Presidency of the EC :~

From the time we joined the Community the question of the first Irish presidency loomed large in our minds. Given the extent to which we were likely to become net recipients of Community funds and our reticence about sharing in the defence of the Community, it was clearly important that we use the opportunity of this presidency in the first half of 1975 to demonstrate our commitment to the Community and our determination to advance its interests.

In the latter part of 1973 we asked the Danish government if we could send some of our staff to Denmark to find out how they were tackling their presidency, for which they had had only six months to prepare after entering the Community with Britain and ourselves in January of that year. Moreover during 1974 we organised courses in Chairmanship for the hundred or so civil servants who would have to preside over almost two hundred Community committees and working groups during our six month stint.

In August of that year Joan and I were holidaying in the South of France in company with my fellow minister, Justin Keating, Senator Mary Robinson and the EEC representative in Dublin, Denis Corboy. One day the four of us went off for a working lunch in the garden of a restaurant to discuss the presidency, following which I drew up a memorandum, for my department on the Irish presidency.

In this memorandum I pointed out that whatever proposals we might put forward, they would have most impact if visibly accompanied by a visible change in the style of the presidency during our period, including, I suggested, more frequent and regular attendance at the European Parliament by the Irish Presidents of the General (Foreign Affairs) and other Councils; a more free-for-all-question time procedure there; direct presidential contact with the Economic and Social Committee; presidential emphasis at council meetings on recommended actions by parliament committee, and a more open and relaxed relationship with the press.

All these proposals were, in the event, implemented by us – press relations also being much improved during our presidency through the innovation of briefing the press before as well as after council meetings so that journalists would be less easily misled by partisan national briefings following each council meeting. In relation to the parliament, I attended all seven sessions during my term of office and I also initiated a question time for political co-operation (foreign policy) matters. Hitherto the presidency had answered questions only on Community affairs. To these innovations, on the proposal of DFA officials, I subsequently added a meeting with the full European Commission before the start of the presidency, with a view to concerting our approach to the next six months. Previously this process had been confined to a meeting between the incoming president of the council and the president of the Commission. Later on in our presidency at my suggestion, a state visit was also arranged by the president of Ireland to the four principal institutions of the Community: the Council of Ministers, Commission, Court of Justice and Parliament.

It also fell to us to initiate the regular series of informal weekends of foreign ministers, accompanied at the earlier stages by their wives, on the model of the one-off Gymnich weekend of April 1974; to organise the first European Council meeting in Dublin in March 1975; to bring to a successful conclusion the first of the quinquennial series of Lomé negotiations with the African, Caribbean, Indian Ocean and Pacific countries; and to initiate in Washington the process of political consultation with the USA, which was the eventual outcome of the Year of Europe process of 1973-74.

Another innovation in Community practice during our presidency was the introduction on the occasion of the preparatory meetings for the International Energy Conference of joint spokesmanship by the President of the Council and the Commission in international negotiations – a practice that we repeated in the Euro-Arab Dialogue in Cairo in June, and that later developed into a system under which even in matters not strictly within the treaties the Council Presidency and Commission negotiated together on behalf of the Community. All in all, in these and other ways mentioned below, our presidency was, and was seen to be, a period of considerable innovation.

Immediately after the Paris Summit in December 1974 I had also given thought to how I might best implement the heads of government decision 'to renounce the practice of making agreement on all questions conditional on the unanimous consent of the member states'. Accordingly I devised a procedure for each meeting of the General Council under which I would obtain from the legal advisers to the Council a classification of agenda items that would distinguish decisions requiring unanimity under the Treaties from those that should be taken by qualified, or, more rarely, simple, majority vote and distinguishing also items requiring a formal decision under the treaties from those in respect of which the council was really being asked only for an orientation or opinion. I then proposed to read out this annotation of the agenda at the start of each council meeting and to ask the members whether any of them had difficulty because of a vital national interest in accepting that in relation to each of the items where decisions by qualified majority was provided for in the treaties, we would proceed accordingly.

Before the end of the year I rang my colleagues to tell them of my intentions. As I expected, no one except Jim Callaghan, whom I got on the phone at home, demurred at my proposal. He, however, objected strongly. I made a minor change to my wording in response to a valid point of detail that he raised, but I told him that I intended to implement this procedure despite his objections. I did so at our first council meeting in Brussels on 20 January. Callaghan immediately lodged a protest, which I noted, and this pattern was sustained at each meeting throughout the presidency.

As it happened, many of the matters that came before the council during this six months required 'orientations' rather than formal decisions, and at the first five meetings none involved qualified majority decisions. I began to think that my new procedure would never bring the issue of qualified majority voting to a head. But at the very last council meeting of our presidency on 24 June an opportunity to have a qualified majority vote arose quite unexpectedly, and in the most favourable circumstances.

For at that council meeting Jim Callaghan stated that the beef producers of several Southern African countries were suffering severely from the impact of the levy on beef imports to the Community. (So also – and perhaps more significantly for him – were the big British companies which imported this beef!). Callaghan made a strong, and quite emotional, plea that beef from these states be allowed free entry to the Community. Everyone was in principle agreeable to such an exemption but France and Germany could not agree as to whether this should be done by exempting these countries from the levy or by refunding the levy to them. The proposal was thus in danger of foundering on a technical issue of procedure. I saw my chance and, looking down the table towards Jim Callaghan at the far end, I proposed a qualified majority vote on the issue of which method of meeting the British request should be adopted. Jim Callaghan's face was worth seeing as he saw the trap close on him. He had no choice but to concede the issue of qualified majority on this issue in order to secure his immediate objective. Later that night a further qualified majority vote was held on a matter concerning a trade agreement with Sri Lanka.

I urged my Italian successor in the presidency to maintain this practice, but after a couple of half-hearted attempts, he dropped it, and despite the Paris Summit resolution the council – and, of course, the Committee of Permanent Representatives – soon reverted to the practice of deciding all issues, however trivial, on the basis of unanimity – until the Single Market was initiated in 1985.

One of the first engagements of our presidency was a meeting in Washington on 8 January with Henry Kissinger to launch the process of political consultation between the US and the nine member states of the Community which had been agreed over six months previously, but had not been initiated during the intervening French presidency.

Much of the discussion over lunch involved Henry Kissinger expressing his views on various subjects, in part at least for the benefit of two congressmen present, with occasional interpolations from me. I found this interesting and useful but it represented something of a one-way process.

I was asked a number of questions on the European Community and was pressed about the role of the European Parliament. Kissinger asked how one could possibly imagine a common system of direct elections from Jutland to Sicily, but his scepticism seemed based on an inadequate appreciation of what had already been achieved in the Community. He seemed quite unaware of the fact that the existing parliament was already organised on party lines, largely transcending national differences.

On the previous day the EEC finance ministers, meeting in London, had agreed to 'study' a US proposal for a financial facility to soften the economic consequences of the oil crisis. This proposal had followed an IMF proposal on this matter and may have been seen by EEC ministers as a US move to undermine the IMF approach. However that might be, Kissinger was annoyed at the relegation of discussion his proposal by the EEC to the status of a mere 'study' and threatened that unless the US proposal was accepted, the US would not participate in the Producer/Consumer Conference. I pointed out that reports of the EEC reaction in the US press had been quite misleading in several respects, and added that in my view the US and European approaches were complementary, not competitive. But I also added that the US side, for their part, had contributed to the problem by their approach. The American way of putting things was often unfortunate – I would put it no stronger than that. I went on to add that it was a pity that the US had not contributed to the UN Special Fund to help developing countries in the aftermath of the oil crisis as the EEC and Japan had done. The US attitude to that fund was not understood in Europe. Kissinger said defensively that there was some division in the US government on that issue.

This gave me my opportunity to go on the attack, as for tactical reasons I had decided to do during the plane journey. (After reading a biography of my interlocutor during the journey I had decided that if, as foreign minister of a very small European state I was to make any personal impact on him, I should take every opportunity to engage him in argument). I queried the wisdom of the aggressive and contestatory approach by the US towards the Third World during the recent UN session, which had made it unnecessarily difficult for the Americans to get support for their policies. Psychology was important, and they should not underestimate the neuroses of ex-colonies; Ireland had spent the last fifty years working its way out of a neurosis of just this kind. The United States might do better to let countries like Ireland, which understood the psychological problem, influence the Third World in a constructive direction. Even the ex-colonial powers might in some cases be better equipped to deal constructively with their former colonies than the United States.

Kissinger's initial reaction to this onslaught was – as I had hoped! – one of irritation. But somewhat surprisingly, he soon became defensive. American timing in criticising Third World countries at the recent UN sessions might not have been correct, he said, and the words used might have been better chosen. On the other hand there was a real problem, and the softer European approach might be regarded at times as an evasion of the issues. However, the US should perhaps talk to its allies before the next UN session.

Kissinger then asked if I would like to accompany him and his wife Nancy to a memorial service for Walter Lipmann in Washington Cathedral. The drive gave us an opportunity for some further and less formal discussion about Northern Ireland to which I refer in Chapter 14. On his side he took the opportunity also to say that he would be anxious to keep in touch with me not only during our presidency but after it. The ambassador to Ireland recently appointed by incoming President Ford, was not his choice and it might, therefore, be better if the EEC consultation procedure during our presidency were operated through our ambassador in Washington. He added later, in a whispered aside in the cathedral, that he would appoint a really able deputy head of mission in Dublin to facilitate contacts.

It was clear that my decision to 'pick a fight' at our first formal bi-literal session had been well-judged. Kissinger clearly enjoyed our somewhat combative discussions. Several times in later years, including in Dublin and New York in 2010, he contrasted these with his duller meetings with a number of my more cautious European colleagues.

Although I often taxed my officials' nerves by cutting rather fine my arrival time at airports and railway stations, my departure from Washington after these discussions in January 1975 to connect with an Aer Lingus flight in Boston was, in fact, the only occasion when I nearly missed a plane – despite on this occasion arriving at the airport on time. Liam Hourican, then one of RTÉ's ablest correspondents and later my government press secretary, wanted to interview me after my meetings and I said I would talk to him at the airport. Unperceived by my officials after check-in, I moved with him to a coffee shop from which I could see through the glass to the departure lounge – I became so absorbed in the interview that I failed to observe what was going on outside and because the glass was effectively one-way, the officials could not see me. When I eventually emerged I found an agitated ambassador shouting 'minister, the flight is leaving' and taking off at a run in the direction of the departure finger; I followed, also at a run – but the door at the end of the finger was shut. We persuaded a uniformed official to let us down the steps to the tarmac so that I could chase the plane – the pilot of which, as his plane was being towed backwards away from the stand, observed us and halted the aircraft, opened the door and let down the steps. To the hilarity of my own officials on board – who had been debating whether the inconvenience to them of an enforced stopover in Boston to wait for me would be outweighed by the lesson this experience might have taught me for the future – I ran up the steps and took my seat belatedly.

A few days later the first of two final negotiating conferences with the African, Caribbean, Indian Ocean and Pacific countries – former colonies of Britain as well as France – took place in Brussels. At the much earlier initial meeting I had walked around the table before it started introducing myself to the delegates. I was disconcerted when the Kenyan Minister asked me what I was doing there. 'I'm an EEC minister', I responded. 'But Ireland isn't a member of the EEC', he said, and he went through the nine member countries, naming Sweden, however, in place of Ireland. I told him Sweden was not a member, reiterating that Ireland was. His face fell. 'I told my president it was Sweden', he said sadly, adding with, I thought, some trepidation, 'I'll have to tell him I was wrong when I return'.

Unfortunately the negotiations then started had not been completed during the French presidency in the second half of 1974 as had been intended. A new deadline of 31 January had been fixed, which I, as incoming President of the Council, taking over the European leadership in this negotiation, was expected to meet. The task that then remained to be completed within this brief period was a formidable one. Some fifty separate issues, some of them highly controversial, remained to be settled between the nine EC countries and forty-six ACP countries. Initially I despaired of ever grasping this formidable body of negotiating matter.I was, however, extraordinarily fortunate in the official who had been in charge of the negotiations on our behalf up to that point, a young first secretary, Hugh Swift, whom I soon found to have the confidence and trust of the far more senior ambassadors who represented most of the other countries. He inducted me into the mysteries of the negotiation so that after two days I had some grasp of the issues that remained to be settled.

Ireland had a clear advantage in presiding over this negotiation. The ACP countries knew that we were sympathetic to them, and that, as it happened, we had no national interests to defend. Even on the vexed issue of the scale of aid to be provided, I had a free hand, because of our government's commitment to increase rapidly our own aid programme; which enabled me to press for the acceptance by our partners of as high a figure as possible.

At the same time our EEC partners knew me well enough by this time to understand that I would not betray their interests. Finally, given that this negotiation involved the incorporation of former British colonies into a framework (that of an earlier Yaoundé Agreement), which had previously been confined almost exclusively to former French colonies (plus Zaire and the Netherlands Antilles), the fact that I could negotiate in French was an advantage, reassuring the former French colonies linguistically that I was not biased in favour of the former British colonies.

After two days the meeting was adjourned for a fortnight, towards the end of which I flew on Monday 27 January to Abidjan to attend and address a parliamentary conference between the EEC and Yaoundé Agreement countries. I tried to be clever about getting there, using my familiarity with air timetables to reject the through flight from Paris to Abidjan, which stopped at many places enroute, in favour of a direct flight to Lomé in Togo with an overnight stop there to get a night's sleep, and an onward connection from Lomé to Abidjan. The theory was sound but it did not, however, allow for a four hour delay on departure from Paris owing to a bomb-scare. As a result I got barely one hour's sleep in Lomé.

I was impressed with Abidjan, a most attractive mixture of modern and traditional in what was then most prosperous of African states, the Ivory Coast. What remains most strongly in my mind is the president's Guard of Honour all well over six feet tall and dressed in gold and silver helmets and breast-plates, white breeches and scarlet cloaks – Rome's African legions, as I imagined them, come to life. I also liked their pink bananas, which I felt would go down well with Irish children!

In my speech to the Joint Parliamentary Assembly I naturally made the most of the parallel colonial experiences of Ireland and African countries: colonisation involving dilution but also enrichment of our cultural heritage, but also excessively close post-colonial links with the former colonial power: It wasn't the speech the Council Secretariat wanted me to make and it may not have brought joy to the hearts of the French and British ambassadors, but it got a good reception from the audience!

On the following Thursday morning 30 January, we started the final ACP negotiating session – which went on, with one short break on Thursday night until 7 AM. on Saturday morning. The willingness of my Community colleagues to remain available for meetings of the Council at all hours of day and night together with the quite remarkable negotiating skill and judgment of the ACP team, which included amongst others 'Sonny' Ramphal, later Commonwealth Secretary, enabled us to succeed with what was in fact a mammoth task.

The negotiations had to be interrupted occasionally to enable me to refer back to my colleagues. One such meeting was called for 2.30 PM on Friday afternoon. I allowed the usual 15 minutes grace, in accordance with a resolution of the council passed shortly after we joined, which had solemnly declared that meetings should start not more than a quarter of an hour late, but we were still missing several delegations at 2.45 PM. I waited until 2.55 PM and then announced 'With all the new found authority of a grandfather of one-and-a-half hours' standing I call this meeting to order even in the absence of the Danish delegation'. (I had rung home just before the meeting and Joan had told me the news of the birth of a daughter, Doireann, to Eithne, my eldest son John's wife). This announcement was greeted with warm applause; to my knowledge Doireann remains the only baby whose birth has been so greeted by the Council of Ministers of the Community!

(I am not sure if it was during this negotiation or at another Council of Ministers later in the presidency that I allowed myself to give vent to momentary irritation at the prolixity of someone speaking at length and more than once on behalf of the Italian delegation. I was about to sum up the debate and to move towards a conclusion when I observed a hand raised again. 'Not the bloody Italians again' I groaned. The microphone was live, and the interpreters obliged with a multilingual translation. The meeting, Italians included, dissolved in laughter.)

But to return to the final ACP negotiation. I had been advised that if this negotiation were to succeed I must ensure that the question of sugar was not introduced. Despite some agitation from Caribbean participants this was generally accepted. However, at 2.30 AM on the Saturday morning when I called a meeting of the Council of Ministers – the other members of which had been playing bridge in order to keep awake until I needed them – the Commissioner for Agriculture, Lardinois, who had not been involved in the discussions, arrived to find out how things were going, and proceeded to talk about sugar. At that point I lost my temper and, momentarily forgetting my commitment to preserving and enhancing the Commission's role, threw him out – to the entertainment and satisfaction of my Community colleagues. In his absence we narrowed down the outstanding issues and by 8.30 AM had reached agreement – overrunning our 31 January deadline, but only by eight and a half hours. I returned to Dublin, and bed, with a sense of exhilaration and relief.

Five weeks later we embarked for Lomé, the capital of Togo, a fairly nasty dictatorship, to sign the agreement. Togo had been subject to three colonial masters: Germany till 1914, Britain till 1919 and then France. Unlike other German colonies in Africa, it had been benevolently ruled by a Grand Duke of Mecklenburg-Strelitz, who was so well-regarded that a descendant of his was invited to attend Togo's independence celebrations half a century later!

This was perhaps the most exotic moment of my political career, and it had its entertaining side. On arrival we had some time on our hands. That afternoon I was taken to see the port installations and, while there, the bridge of my reading glasses snapped. I rushed back into the town to find an optician. The shop was closed and I explained to a Togolese lounging against the wall why I needed to find the owner urgently. As president of the EEC Council I had to read a speech at the following day's ceremony. He looked at me and said: (I translate) 'But there are a number of speeches before yours. If you give them to him in the morning he'll have new ones for you before your turn comes'. I was impressed by his familiarity with the agenda for the signing ceremony, but unconvinced by his easy optimism about getting new glasses in time.

I went on to an official reception and that evening, joining the receiving line, I asked each person who arrived wearing glasses if I could try them on in order to see if I could read with them. I had no luck until the 6 ft 8in (at least!) prime minister of Fiji arrived. He pointed out to me what in my near-panic I had failed to realise that the glasses people wore when walking around were normally distance glasses, which would scarcely be of much use to me in my dilemma. 'Try my ambassador's' he said. His ambassador produced reading glasses from his pocket. They worked.

The following day's ceremony was spectacular. In the auditorium of party head-quarters, seating some 3,000 people, each signature was greeted by a chant of welcome and a dance by 2,000 Togolese women in long green dresses. When it came to my turn to speak I found that whilst I could read the text with the Fijian ambassador's glasses, they would not stay on my nose unless I held them. In the absence of a rostrum I had to hold my speech in my other hand, juggling with the pages. I felt that this somewhat inelegant performance required an explantion, which I offered to the delight and hilarity of the hitherto staid audience.

When I went to Mass in the cathedral on the following day, I had to await the end of the previous Mass. The closing announcements included an exhortation to attend the Stations of the Cross on Friday and thus to follow the excellent example of the president of the EEC (I had gone to the church that day to make contact with an acquaintance of an Irish friend of mine, and had to wait while the priest conducted the ceremony). When I entered the church for Mass on Sunday a Togolese woman sidled up to me in the pew and whispered to me that there were ten Praesidia (branches) of the Irish lay Catholic organisation the Legion of Mary in Togo. Before I had time to recover from this news I found myself the subject of the sermon, which extolled the essential equality of the human race, based on the fact that my eyes and those of the Fijian ambassador required the same glasses!

The extent to which Togolese television penetrated the interior of the country became clear to me, moreover, when at a barbecue in a forest upcountry several days later, elderly chieftains performing a ritual dance for our benefit called to me as they danced past: 'Did you get your glasses fixed yet?'

At the formal open-air banquet in Lomé itself after the signature we were enter-tained by part of the choir who had enlivened the signature ceremony. I noticed that when their repertoire moved from songs extolling the merits of the ruler to their own traditional songs, they became much more relaxed and joyous. I recall, however, the words of one of the official songs, sung, I should add, to a very catchy rhythm:

Heureux le people togolais
Heureux les paysans
Pas de taxes nouveaux
Heureux les fonctionnaires
Pas de taxes nouveux
Heureux le people togolais
Dix pour cent par an.

We were invited to dance to this music. Having first established that there was an EC qualified majority in favour of doing so, I authorised my colleagues to join in!

After this episode it was not easy to settle down to meeting Merlyn Rees in London on the following day and presiding over yet another ministerial council in Brussels two days later.

Back in Dublin for the weekend I was deep into preparations, for the first meeting of the European Council, which, ironically in view of my opposition to the establishment of this institution, was now to be held in Dublin. We took considerable trouble with the preparations for this event. In contrast to the somewhat dispersed arrangements for the Paris Summit, where the press facilities were several miles away from the conference venue, we located premiers and press in the same location; indeed the press room was directly underneath St Patrick's Hall where the council met – which led me to suggest frivolously that we arrange a hole in the floor beside my seat so that I could brief the press directly by dropping notes to them.

St Patrick's Hall, where presidents are now inaugurated, is the great hall of the Castle, where formerly the Knights of St Patrick (an order created in the eighteenth century but now extinct) were inaugurated. Banners of the Knights hang overhead, and I noticed that Giscard d'Estaing was to be seated under the Sovereign's Banner, the Royal Standard. My officials restrained me from suggesting to the photographers that they take an angled shot of the French president under a British monarch's standard. Unfortunately the photographers did not think of it themselves!

The effort we put into the physical preparations for the European Council paid off. The press were enthusiastic about the telecommunications arrangements, which gave them instant direct contact with most of their capitals – something which in those days was far from universal as I knew from visiting capitals like Paris and Rome, and indeed the diplomatic quarter of Washington. Amongst the many letters we received after the meeting I recall particularly one from Mark Arnold Foster remarking that he had never previously been asked so politely to stop smoking: 'Would you be of the *Guardian* upset if I asked you if you would ever mind not smoking?' contrasted favourably, he thought, with the harsh brevity of 'Nicht Rauchen'!

Whilst the agenda for the European Council contained a portentous list of subjects it did not in fact involve much of substance apart from the meat of the session which lay in the first items: The Budgetary Corrective Mechanism, and New Zealand.

Since Jim Callaghan's somewhat aggressive launch of British re-negotiation of its EC membership twelve months earlier, Britan's demands had been substantially narrowed down to those two issues and it was fairly clear by this time that it would be possible to meet the British government's political requirement for some concessions in these areas in advance of the rather belated referendum they intended to hold on EEC membership two-and-a-half years after joining the Community. However, there was still some gap to be bridged between Britain's demands and the concessions that the rest of the Community had felt able to make thus far.

Wilson sought to create a positive atmosphere at the outset by stressing in his opening remarks that if these problems were settled, Britain would no longer be a reluctant partner in the Community but would play her part in its development and have a vested interest in its cohesion. Later, in response to a direct question from Giscard d'Estaing about economic and monetary union, Callaghan responded somewhat evasively, but cleverly, by saying that Britain did not retract its commitment to economic and monetary union as expressed in the communiqué from the Paris Summit, adding that no one else had gone any further than that!

I observed with some fascination the ritual dance of negotiation between the heads of government of the three largest states. A happy outcome was clearly pre-ordained, but before arriving at it honour had to be satisfied by various solutions being put forward and rejected. In my naïveté I was disturbed at the fact that the initial proposals from the French and Germans made no arithmetic sense; quite simply they did not add up! When I pointed this out to the French, it was explained to me that this did not matter – the proposals in question were only 'fliers', not seriously intended, and would never have to face such a sophisticated arithmetic test! I subsided, amused at the games the major countries play with each other. When this negotiating dance came to its happy end a formula was found within the financial limits that Helmut Schmidt had laid down at the outset as the maximum his Cabinet would accept. And another formula was found to serve later as a resolution of the New Zealand butter issue.

This meeting, over which Liam Cosgrave presided with dignity, was adjudged a success – and indeed was subsequently contrasted with the immediately following European Councils which did not have to deal with such a key issue as a British re-negotiation. I naturally did nothing to disturb this assessment although privately I believed that this issue could, and would, have been settled by foreign ministers if the European Council had not come into existence.

As on many subsequent occasions I was struck by the fact that the after-dinner discussion on such matters by heads of government seemed to be informed by relatively little hard information, and to be frankly somewhat amateurish, but perhaps on relaxed occasions like these, without papers, it could hardly be otherwise.

The next meeting during our presidency was to be the first of the series of six-monthly informal weekend meetings of foreign ministers that have continued since then. The meeting in Paris on Monday 16 September 1974 at which the ideas that later took shape as the European Council had been discussed by foreign ministers was not seen as having fallen into this category but rather as a restricted session of the council without officials, so it fell to us to inaugurate decisions to hold such informal meetings.

I decided that to make it really informal I would follow the Gymnich pattern by inviting the minister's wives – most of whom had not met each other. (That practice which, however, fell into abeyance during the following couple of years). Finding a suitable location posed a problem as the only government-owned house suitable for entertaining, Barrettstown Castle in County Kildare, was too small for our purposes. Benjamin and Miranda Iveagh generously offered us the use of their home, Farmleigh, at Castleknock near Dublin, since purchased by the state for such occasions. It was eminently suitable in location, accommodation and privacy and Miranda Iveagh joined with Joan in hosting the occasion.

Our preparations were meticulous including seating arrangements for the meals designed to ensure that people had different neighbours on each occasion, and that these neighbours would in all cases have a common language. Meeting these pre-conditions posed a challenge of some mathematical complexity! An expedition to County Wicklow was arranged for the wives on the Sunday, from which they returned in very good form, finding common ground in singing the tune whose words in different languages are Tannenbaum, Mon Beau Sapin and the Red Flag!

Jean Sauvagnargues, who had been accompanying Giscard d'Estaing on a visit to Algeria, had arrived late, just before dinner, having stopped off in Paris to pick up his wife. Miranda Iveagh greeted them on arrival and showed them to their room. When they came down to dinner, Sauvagnargues, indicating Miranda, enquired: 'Qui est cette dame la?' Joan replied that she was our hostess, Lady Iveagh. Sauvagnargues exclaimed: 'Mais elle n'est pas respectable!' meaning 'But she is too young and pretty to be the chatelaine of such a great house' a classic example, I have always thought, of the danger of literal translations of French into English!

After dinner we convened again for an urgent discussion of problems that had arisen at the preparatory conference in Paris between industrialised and developing countries. As we were in the presidency, an Irish senior official the late Eamon Gallagher, in conjunction with the Commission, was leading the Community delegation there. After we adjourned this discussion at midnight we agreed to resume the debates on our agenda at 11 AM on Sunday morning. But shortly afterwards I learnt from Gallagher that matters had reached crisis point there. Instructions from ministers were needed by mid-morning to enable him, if not to save the conference, at least to bring it to a soft landing. I brought this news to three of my colleagues with whom I had been having a night-cap and they agreed that an early morning meeting was necessary wishing me luck with my task of knocking on doors at an early hour to summon sleepy ministers to a discussion they had decided not to have till much later that morning!

When we got back to our agenda next morning we talked through lunch until mid-afternoon. We discussed the Middle East problem, agreeing that diplomatic activity was to be preferred to public declarations at that stage and that I should sign an agreement between the EEC and Israel even though internal differences in the Community were still holding up a parallel series of agreements with the Maghreb countries (Tunisia, Algeria and Morocco).

We then turned to the question of Portugal, where the first election campaign after the April 1974 Revolution, for a Constituent Assembly, was in its final stages. It was then agreed that I should go to Portugal in early June as President of the Council with a view to seeing what we could do to encourage a democratic evolution in that country, where at that stage the revolutionary socialist Armed Forces Movement still remained in control of the situation.

Although I have no written record of this, it is my recollection that I had raised the question of Portugal with Henry Kissinger in February and that he had been sceptical about any initiative at that time. However that may be, I certainly did so in Paris at the end of May, when I attended the meetings of the International Energy Agency and the OECD. He was quite negative, expressing deep pessimism about the Portuguese situation. He seemed to feel fatalistically that Portugal was likely to emerge from its post-revolutionary trauma as, at best, a non-aligned country like Algeria and at worst as a Soviet satellite, and that nothing could be done about it. However, without enthusiasm, he said that we Europeans were welcome to make the attempt.

The omens were not too good as Joan and I left Paris for Lisbon. The Portuguese left-wing press had been featuring false reports about a NATO fleet assembling near Lisbon, and there was evident hostility towards Western Europe amongst the extreme left, amongst whom the Communists had won less than a quarter of the assembly seats in the elections at the end of April, but who still seemed to be the dominant force within the ruling revolutionary Armed Forces Movement.

My first engagement in Lisbon was to host a dinner at the Irish embassy for the foreign minister, Antunes, and some other ministers. I asked Antunes to come early so that we could have a private discussion before the others arrived. I started by reiterating what I had said to him during a brief encounter at the airport: there was general goodwill in the Community towards Portugal and no desire to interfere with Portugal's choice of economic system but there was strong concern for the preservation of freedom and a democratic system there.

Antunes responded by saying that he and the moderates, who, he said, were now in control in the Armed Forces Movement, were concerned to prevent any communist domination. They wanted to ensure the preservation of the rights of man and of individual freedom whilst finding a third way (by implication neither communist nor social democratic) towards socialism

From my point of view the principal purpose of this preliminary private discussion was to enable me to sound out how in the discussions about to begin I could avoid irritating the Portuguese whilst nevertheless getting across the message that the Community would aid only a democratic Portugal. Accordingly I now put the question directly to him: how should I phrase this condition clearly, but sensitively? Without hesitation he replied: 'Il faut dire qu'une aide communautaire sera dans l'optique d'un dévelopment démocratique pluralists en Portugal'. 'You should say that Community aid will be in the perspective of a pluralist democratic development in Portugal'. That was what I needed; I stuck to this formula rigorously during the next couple of days, although I later found that the Socialist leader, Mario Soares, would have preferred more explicit conditionality.

At the subsequent dinner Antunes said that he was favourable to the idea of an agreement with the Community and hoped that impending discussions between himself and Giscard d'Estaing would go well. I encouraged him to visit Italy also during the next few weeks as I felt he would find the Italians sympathetic. He went on to say that Kissinger seemed to have a rather closed mind on Portugal although he felt he had made some progress with him. I refrained from comment on this.

Later that night firing could be heard near the embassy, coming from a near-by barracks. We never heard who was firing at whom.

Next day I met President Costa Gomes – whom Antunes had described as a sensible man, with considerable wisdom (Later I was to hear him described as an 'opportunist'). He told me of his intention that action be taken to deal with the excessive level of communist control of the media, possibly tackling the problem in the state radio and television service by putting a military officer in charge of it!

Prime Minister Goncalves was another matter altogether. He gave me a prolonged but most unimpressive lecture on the aims and objectives of the Armed Forces Movement which was to provide the basic dynamism for Portugal's 'third way' to 'democratic socialism'.According to him this would involve the political parties having the role of forming a kind of 'sounding board'! He was reluctant to accept that the communists posed any kind of danger. He refrained, however, from repeating to me his public references to 'capitalist plots' against Portugal, and it emerged that he was quite unaware of the fact that members of his government had made concrete proposals to me for Community aid. 'Surely that could not be correct?' he asked one of his ministers present, who, however, confirmed what I had said.

At a dinner for Joan and myself given by the Armed Forces Movement I was seated between two young and enthusiastically socialist officers who seemed to disapprove of the formality of the occasion and even of the venue, the Palacio das Necessidades. However after dinner the wife of one of them sought to reassure me; she was strongly anti-communist, she said, and she did not want to lose her car and her house, which she seemed to think would happen if left-wing policies were pursued!

In the margin of these official discussions, I was asked by at least one minister to let him know if I found out who the members of the Armed Forces Movement were; he would like to know who was running the country!

In the margin of one meeting a very left wing minister privately made a special request to me; Portugal's exports of port to Germany and France, to the value of €200 million,were at risk. Portugal had experienced severe droughts over a period of three years and, having insufficient grapes to make brandy to fortify the port, had imported brandy from Yugoslavia. Now the Germans, after testing their port chemically, were claiming that the fortifying spirit could not have been genuine brandy because the port was insufficiently radioactive! The spirit which they had bought from Yugoslavia must have been made synthetically, they said, rather than from grapes exposed to the atmosphere and thus to radioactivity. Consequently this port did not meet the German, or apparently French, customs definition of port wine! Could I ask these two countries to treat the question as still being open by going on testing until they had sold their port to these two countries? I promised to ask Sauvagnargues and Genscher on my return to take whatever steps might be necessary to allow this inadequately radioactive port into their countries. I did so on my return, and, as I heard no more about it, I hoped that my representations had succeeded!

I also met a number of political leaders not in government, including the Socialist leader, Soares who first enquired cautiously about my political bona fides, was I a social democrat? Reassured that I was at the social democratic end of the Christian Democrat spectrum, he spoke freely about the way in which fear was starting to grow again in Portugal a year after the peaceful revolution against Salazar's dictatorship: fear of being bugged, fear of losing one's job, and so on. Opportunists were jumping on the extreme left-wing bandwagon, and an internal coup had just taken place in the centre PPD Party.

I was struck by the fact that Antunes and himself, with a good deal in common, and in key positions respectively in the Armed Forces Movement and the Socialist

Party, did not seem to be in touch with each other. I suggested to Soares that such contact might be fruitful and made the same point to Antunes on my departure.

Soares and I agreed to keep in touch and six weeks later a Portuguese Socialist politician came, at Soares's request, to see me at home. He had been asked by Soares to contact me. Earlier that week the assembly of the Armed Forces Movement had met and at 4.30 in the morning, with half the members present, had passed a resolution in favour of sovietisation. But two days later at a meeting of the Council of the Revolution, Antunes (with whom as I had suggested he was now in contact) had called for the resignation of Prime Minister Goncalves, who no longer hid even from his ministerial colleagues his communist involvement. In doing so Antunes felt strengthened by the disillusionment of the Left in the Armed Forces Movement with the Soviet Union, which had recently told them that Portugal was a Western European country whose problems must be settled in that context: no Cuba in Portugal. Antunes had told Soares that he would have won the vote against Goncalves but for a last-minute intervention by left-wing Admiral Coutinho saying that this was a personal battle between two men, not an ideological confrontation. Goncalves had survived for the moment, and President Costa Gomes had refused Antunes' resignation – thus leaving a stalemate.

Soares was anxious to convey on behalf of what was now a very united Socialist Party that in this situation it was important that the European Community should not react by giving Portugal an unconditionally negative answer. A hard and brutal line in negotiations would not have a good effect but a strong pro-pluralist position should be adopted in private contacts with the regime. Europe was now in a very strong position, as the Left in the Armed Forces Movement now knew that they would get no help from the USSR and that Portugal had to negotiate with Europe. Meanwhile the Socialists had established a firm alliance with the church, and would support Antunes 'au bout'. The Opposition would provide a democratic alternative to the regime.

All this I passed on to my colleagues in the Community, who took due note of it. Four months later the crunch came in dramatic circumstances and a fully democratic system finally emerged, with Mario Soares as prime minister.

In the following years there were a number of changes of government in Portugal but when the closing stages of the Community enlargement negotiation was reached in the autumn of 1984 he and I were in charge of our respective governments and once again I was in the presidency of the Community, this time chairing the European Council. In October of that year at a moment when the Spanish negotiation was bogged down by a wine problem (which was resolved at our European Council meeting in Dublin at the end of the year), Soares asked me if I could help to consolidate Portugal's position in relation to the Community by signing with him in Dublin a couple of days later a 'Constat d'Accord' viz a statement that Portugal and the Community had reached agreement. Our partners had no objection and I immediately agreed; I even succeeded in broadcasting a brief message in Portuguese at the televised signature ceremony! Some time later Soares invited me on an official visit to Portugal during which he invested me with the Order of Christ. And in April 1985, with other Community leaders, I signed Portugal's Treaty of Accession in Lisbon.

In the latter part of our presidency I also undertook a series of visits in the Middle East. In mid-May I went to Jordan, Syria, the Lebanon and Egypt and some weeks later, in June, to Israel and Turkey. I also attended an EEC – Greece parliamentary session in Athens at the end of June.

A week before leaving for the Middle East with Joan I had signed the EEC/Israel supplementary agreement that had been discussed at Farmleigh several weeks earlier. The only convenient date from my point of view was Sunday 11 May because I was in Paris in connection with the celebration of the centenary of Robert Schuman's birth and could make a brief sortie by train to Brussels for the signature ceremony.

Some adverse reaction to this event from the Arab countries was to be expected, but the storm that burst was much more severe than anything that had been anticipated. The Euro-Arab dialogue, a hitch in which earlier in the year had already been resolved by Ireland in the presidency, was again threatened by an Algerian call for its postponement on account of the signature of the agreement with Israel, and while this dialogue had not achieved much, and was not the subject of any great optimism, or enthusiasm, on the European side, it would not be desirable that it should be allowed to founder. Whilst from the bilateral Irish viewpoint these developments did not augur well for my visits it seemed possible that even without wearing my Community 'hat', my visit might enable me to do something to calm the storm. I told the European Parliament, where I answered questions before leaving for the Middle East, that I would seek to alleviate Arab worries about the agreement in the course of my visit as Irish foreign minister.

En route to Jordan we over-nighted at Beirut. The situation there was tense. There had been a brief outbreak of fighting between the Phalangists and the Palestinians five weeks earlier, and six days before our arrival the prime minister had tendered his resignation following the earlier resignation of eleven members of the Cabinet. However, our stay in Beirut was undisturbed although the morning papers reported that firing had broken out again during the night. After a press conference at the airport we flew on the next morning to Amman.

There (as in each of the capitals we visited), we found in discussions with Prime Minister Rifad that the EEC/Israel Agreement was in fact a very contentious issue which had apparently been aggravated by what the Arabs felt to have been Israeli triumphalism. I was taken aback to find that even the fact that as a matter of convenience to me the signature ceremony had taken place on a Sunday was a source of concern. It was alleged that in our anxiety to please the Israelis we had even desecrated our own Sabbath! The agreement, with its provisions for stimulating investment and for access to Community financial institutions, would, it was claimed without any justification extend to the occupied territories. I did my best to remove these misconceptions, with reasonable success in Jordan, less so in Syria.

Before leaving Jordan, Joan and I were invited to breakfast with Crown Prince Hassan and his wife who apologised for eating on the terrace rather than in the dining-room, where the table had been set for a children's party. To enable us to catch up with the rest of our group, which had already left by car for the Syrian border, he lent us a helicopter in which we flew to the Dead Sea and, after a sharp turn that I felt brought us alarmingly close to Israel, up the left bank of the Jordan to a point where we joined the Irish road convoy en route to Damascus. There I met the foreign minister, Khaddam. The discussions with him were a good deal less relaxed than those in Jordan. I had the impression, however, that my explanations about the agreement with Israel were welcomed as providing arguments to persuade others not to make too much of a fuss about it.

On the following morning, Thursday 22 May, we drove to Beirut. The journey seemed uneventful, although I noticed that at the border our Lebanese hosts evinced no enthusiasm for a suggestion that we try to fit in enroute a visit to Ba'albek. We later discovered that the party that had greeted us at the frontline had been ambushed on the way up, and one member had been wounded. When we arrived there Beirut appeared quiet. The streets were surprisingly empty as I drove from our hotel to meet the foreign minister and later President Franjieh, and in the afternoon to a meeting with the EEC ambassadors. In the evening I gave a reception. I was aware that fighting between the Phalangists and the Palestinians had broken out again two days earlier when we had flown out of Beirut to Amman, but the fact that we were in the midst of what turned out later to have been effectively the start of the Lebanese Civil War was not immediately apparent. Joan and I were indeed somewhat taken aback early on the following morning to hear on the BBC World Service that 1,500 shells had fallen in Beirut during the night. The lapping of the waves on the shore in front of our hotel had apparently drowned out the noise of this bombardment a mile and a half away.

Our host in Cairo was the foreign minister and deputy prime minister, Ismail Fahmy, but on the following day I also had meetings with Prime Minister Salem and President Sadat. Once again I explained that the agreement with Israel represented no deviation from the principles of the Community's statement of 6 November 1973 on the Middle East situation and that there was no political motivation involved in the agreement. In fact it was narrower in its provisions than agreements currently under negotiation with a number of Arab countries.

A crucial Cairo meeting was that on Saturday with Mahmoud Riad, secretary-general of the Arab League, which earlier that week had failed in three days of talks to decide on the continuation of the Euro/Arab dialogue. I told him that the EEC/Israel agreement did not apply to the occupied Israeli territories. He asked me was I speaking as president of the Council. I said that I had no authority to speak for the Council as I was visiting the Middle East as Minister of Foreign Affairs of Ireland, but that in my national capacity I could state my government's position on the agreement and that I believed that no other government would disagree with what I had said. He said that an oral assurance on behalf of Ireland would not satisfy the Arab League. I agreed to commit it to writing and did so on the spot in a text which included the following: 'The area of application of the new agreement in relation to Israel is exactly the same as that covered by earlier Agreements'.

He thanked me for this text but said that it would have to be confirmed as being the position of the Community. I said that to put this issue back into the Community decision-making procedure could be time consuming and cumbersome. 'But aren't you meeting your fellow ministers at a political co-operation meeting in Dublin on Monday?' he asked. I agreed that I was. 'Then this is what I propose', he said. 'I'll put this piece of paper in my safe and show it to no one. If at your meeting on Monday you tell them that you've given it to me and that you regard it as being the view of the Community, and if they don't tell you to go to hell, send me a wire to that effect and I'll tell my Arab League colleagues that it's all right'.

This somewhat informal approach to resolving the crisis appealed to me. I agreed to his proposal. On Sunday we flew home.

Quite apart from the political contacts and the somewhat dramatic circumstances of our visit to Beirut it had been a fascinating trip; Joan and I had had a kaleidoscopic view of the countries around Israel during five crowded days, although as a result of a sudden, very sharp, but fortunately brief gastric attack which prostrated her, she had missed a good deal in Cairo – although not the Pyramids where we had enjoyed a 'Son et Lumiere' performance on the night of our arrival. On her sick bed she was attended simultaneously by two doctors, one sent by the Egyptian government and the other by the Arab League, whilst at the other side of the bed two of our officials had been simultaneously engaged in urgent telephone conversations in Irish with Dublin and Brussels.

On Monday I reported to my colleagues at our meeting in the Bermingham Tower in Dublin Castle. Most of them were delighted at the neat solution that Mahmoud Riad and myself had agreed. An exception was Roy Hattersley, standing in for Jim Callaghan. He said that I had purported to act for the Community because in the presidency I could not divorce that role from my position as Irish foreign minister. I responded briskly to this intervention, remarking that it was fifty three years too late for a British minister to be telling a member of an Irish government in Dublin Castle what he could or could not do. I went on to ask him was he seriously suggesting that in two years time, when Britain held the presidency, her foreign secretary would be inhibited by his Community role from any bilateral action? And I said I was perfectly happy to wire Riad to tell him Britain had told me, in his words, 'to go to hell'. Hattersley subsided. After the meeting I gave Riad the 'all-clear'; the Arab League dropped their objections; and the Euro/Arab dialogue resumed, unhappily without ever leading to any significant positive results, however.

Having in the meantime attended the International Energy Agency and OECD meetings in Paris I left again for the Middle East a fortnight later to visit Israel and Turkey. The visit to Israel was bound to be somewhat difficult because to a greater extent than other Community countries except France and Italy we had been sympathetic to the Palestinians' claim to a homeland in Palestine.

I had in fact originally intended to visit Israel before going to its neighbours, but the Israelis had not been able to arrange an appropriate date. In the event the reordering of the visits proved beneficial because as a result we were in a position to give the Israelis a very full picture of what we had learned during our visits to the nearby Arab countries. The foreign minister, Allon, clearly appreciated this feature of our discussion, intervening frequently in my account in order to clarify points.

On the following day we went south to the Weizmann Institute and to a kibbutz near Beersheba. I should have much preferred to see the Old City of Jerusalem, but on an official visit I could not go to any part of the occupied territories. A visit to Nazareth was on offer but we could not be sure that if we went there we would not be brought along the direct road that runs through part of these territories. The journalists who accompanied us south, where the temperature was up to 35 degrees, referred to it privately as official punishment for having turned down a northern trip for political reasons!

Turkey was next; my discussions there were with the foreign minister, Ceylangil. We broke for lunch after a morning session and on the way back to the conference room he brought me into his office, to wait till the officials had settled down, he said. We had been talking about Cyprus. He rummaged in a cupboard, looking for a map of Cyprus, failed to find one, and rang to ask an aide to get one for him. A large relief map was brought in and he proceeded to trace on it the line which, he said, the Turkish army would accept as a dividing line in a negotiation – a line some distance back at most points from the existing ceasefire line following the previous year's invasion. Three times he traced what he felt to be an acceptable line each time moving his finger a little further north. He added that the line he envisaged would leave the Turkish Cypriots with 32 percent of the territory and 40 percent of the economy of the island.

On reflection it seemed to me that the only logical reason for doing this must have been the hope that I would pass it on to the Greek government, which I did three weeks later at an outdoor reception given by Karamanlis, then prime minister, for an EEC/Greece parliamentary meeting that I was attending at the very end of my presidency. Karamanlis asked me to go into his office with his foreign minister, Bitsios, to show him on a map the line his Turkish opposite number had drawn with his finger. Fortunately I am a 'map person' and was able to reproduce it faithfully. My hope that this transfer of information might help towards a solution of the Cyprus problem was not fulfilled, however, although the failure of later negotiations was, I think, brought about primarily by disagreement on other factors.

Joan and I had in fact visited Turkey informally seven weeks before the official visit in June that had brought us to Ankara and Istanbul. Towards the end of April, between addressing a Council of Europe and a European Parliament session in Luxembourg five days later, we had flown on a special charter flight from Zurich to Izmir to attend a meeting of the Bildeberg group at Cesme, on the Turkish coast opposite Chios. There I met a number of people whom I was later to come to know much better, among them Margaret Thatcher, recently elected as leader of the Opposition, whom I had met for the first time at Westminster six weeks earlier.

During a break in the conference I climbed a neighbouring headland to see the Greek island of Chios, a couple of miles away. Tension between Greece and Turkey was high at that moment and we had been told that on the island there was artillery directed at the Turkish coast which, however, we were reassured, was unlikely to open fire until after we had left! Climbing down again across ditches and fences I saw people going on board three police launches that were guarding our meeting; we had been offered trips on the bay on these launches. As I approached I saw Margaret Thatcher on her own boarding one, and decided to join her. We sat together in the open at the stern of the launch, as I made appropriate conversation. After some time she asked me if I thought that we should move into the cabin as the sea, she thought, was getting more choppy. With my usual optimism I said I felt all would be well. At that point the launch turned to go back to the harbour and waves, broke on the stern, ruining I feared, her pastel shaded coat. I cursed my stupidity. Had my optimism led me to wreck any prospect of doing business with her later on Anglo-Irish relations? She took it well, however; and this did not seem to affect our subsequent relationship!

Shortly afterwards Andrew Knight, then with the *Daily Telagraph*, and I had tea with her during an afternoon break. I was particularly interested in her views because it was quite likely that at some point in the years ahead we would find ourselves on opposite sides of the table as representatives of our two countries with their long history of conflict and mistrust, perhaps tackling a still unresolved Northern Ireland problem.

She spoke of the undesirability of the kind of artificial polarisation that she felt had emerged in the economic debates at the conference. She had, however, learnt a good deal from the discussions, for example, about the inadequacy of the money supply approach, because so much had to be done by way of supportive action to make the money supply work. If inflation were very high, an incomes policy was necessary, but there should be a statutory policy only for a very short time. She favoured a political consensus so long as it was of people who agreed on a free society and a mixed economy. When inflation was low politicians would not give it priority, but if it were high priorities had to shift, and then it was no use saying that public expenditure could not be cut. As a spending minister she knew the problem of the unpopularity that came from making such cuts.

Some of these views did not correspond with the picture that Andrew Knight and I had formed of the new Opposition leader. Consequently we quizzed her vigorously and expressed some incredulity when she insisted that her aim was to create a centre force in British politics thus attracting social democrats from Labour. This latter point is not recorded in my contemporary note of her remarks but my recollection of it was confirmed some time later by Andrew Knight when he and I were recalling our astonishment on that occasion – justified as we felt it had been by later events. He told me then that she had said much the same in a discussion at Izmir Airport with the Labour MP, Dick Mabon.

The six months of the presidency had been an exciting period and, I felt, a fruitful one. Ireland's position in the Community had been firmly established; we were seen by our partners as a positive force – not, as could easily have been the case as a 'demandeur', taking substantial material benefits from our partners through the Community budget without putting anything back. Moreover our presidency was generally seen as having been unusually successful and was, indeed, in later years frequently referred to in such terms – successful both at the level of concrete results and also at the technical level, in terms of practical efficiency. Our ministers had chaired their councils successfully, and the civil servants from all departments had risen to the challenge magnificently.

We had, of course, been fortunate in several respects. During that six month period we had not found ourselves having to protect any major national interests, whilst on the other hand there were important tasks to undertake, both internally and externally.

11

~: Protecting Irish Interests in the EC :~

As indeed had been foreseeable when we joined the Community, Ireland in relation to its size quickly became the largest net beneficiary of Community membership in financial terms. This was a consequence of its position as a Northern European country, benefiting from the orientation of the Common Agricultural Policy in favour of products such as meat, milk and grain, but also having a much lower level of income per head than the rest of Northern Europe. As a result of this we also became a major beneficiary from the Regional and Social Funds. So, for several decades after joining the Community net receipts from the Community budget added more than 5 percent to the value of Irish national output.

Sectoral issues are normally dealt with by other ministers in their specialist Councils, but sometimes when a policy is being initiated, as in the case of regional policy, the General Council of Foreign Ministers may become, directly involved. This may also happen if an issue involves relations with other states, as was the case when in the mid-1970s fishing limits of member states were extended to 200 miles.

In my term of office as foreign minister, both regional and fishery policy were major economic issues involving important Irish interests that fell to be dealt with by the General Council. However, another issue, which I had not foreseen, was the highly political question of the number and proportion of seats that each country was to have in a directly-elected European Parliament.

The first of these three issues to come up for decision by our Council was the regional fund. In mid-July 1973 we heard that George Thomson, the British commissioner in charge of regional policy, whom I had known for some time previously as a fellow-member of the executive committee of the European Movement, had proposed to the Commission a regional fund for the three-year period from 1974 to 1976, with a 3.9 percent share for Ireland. That would involve an average annual figure of £16 million for Ireland – as against the £100 million figure that we had identified as representing our needs. Italy, the only other country with problems of underdevelopment, was to get 33 percent of the fund. The remaining 63.1 percent, we heard was to be allocated to the countries which, apart from Northern Ireland as part of the United Kingdom, did not have major regional problems. Britain and France were to share equally half of the total fund!

This came as a great shock. Although proposals by commissioners may sometimes be influenced at the margin by some sensitivity to their home state's national needs, such proposals are normally reasonably objective. There was no precedent for a distortion of this magnitude in favour of a commissioner's home country.

On 26 July, the Commission's decision on George Thomson's proposals was announced. The size of the fund now proposed was one-quarter smaller than he had earlier suggested. No reference was made to quotas; instead 'criteria' were proposed for allocating the fund – criteria that we believed were designed to justify ultimately the distribution of the fund along the lines we knew were contemplated by George Thomson.

This situation was so disturbing that I felt I should visit the capitals of our partners to express my concern and seek a fairer distribution of the fund. Accordingly in September 1973, immediately after a political co-operation meeting in Copenhagen, I initiated a series of visits by flying first to Rome to see the Italian minister for special investments in the Mezzogiorno, and the new foreign minister, Aldo Moro. As Italy was the other country with greatest need for regional aid, it was important if at all possible to ensure that our respective approaches to the forthcoming debate would as far as possible be in harmony with each other, and if possible be actively co-ordinated. We should get nowhere with our other partners if Italy and ourselves contradicted each other's position in making our respective cases.

The approach I proposed was one that would offer Italy as well as ourselves a prospect of a much larger share than had been proposed, and although the Italians did not seem as upset as we were at the implications of the Commission's approach, they were happy to go along with my suggested line of attack. After leaving Rome (where I also saw Cardinal Casaroli on church-state affairs), I spent a busy day visiting three countries: Luxembourg to explain our position to Gaston Thorn; Bonn, where I met Walter Scheel then German foreign minister, and Brussels where I met George Thomson between flights at the airport in order to give him an indication of the strength of our feelings.

Three days later I set off to visit London, The Hague, Paris and Brussels on a similar mission, before attending two ministerial meetings in the latter city.

It was mid-October before the issue came before the council. When my turn came I addressed my colleagues vigorously. I said that the Commission had failed without explanation to observe one of its own guidelines of five months earlier, to the effect that the fund should be concentrated 'very largely in those regions which are most in need in relation to the Community as a whole'. Far from designating the regions most in need they had proposed that the fund be made available to assist areas comprising over half the total geographical area of the Community and containing one-third of its population! Within these areas the range of GDP per head varied by a factor of 3 or 4 – 1, but the Commission had not made any proposal to relate the volume of aid to the widely varying intensity of need within the designated area.

I went on to say that on the Commission's own admission the whole of Ireland qualified for participation in the fund, which meant that unlike any other Community country there was no developed part of the country the resources of which could be drawn upon to support the rest. Ireland was thus uniquely dependent on Community aid for regional development.

While I did not refer in my remarks to the Council to the map that had emerged from the Commission showing the areas to be covered by the fund, I pointed out to the press off-the-record that as well as Ireland and Southern Italy it included all of Scotland (George Thomson's home country) and Wales, as well as most of the northern and south-western parts of England, half of France and Denmark and significant parts of Germany and the Benelux countries!

My address to the council was referred to by the *Financial Times* as 'impassioned' and 'refreshing' and by other papers as 'most vigorous' and 'forthright'. It had its effect. Two days later George Thomson met the Irish journalists in Brussels, and under pressure admitted that the criteria had been 'drawn on a political basis, and on the basis that each member country is entitled to feel it is getting some treatment for its special problems out of the Fund'. (The *Daily Telegraph* had put the point even more graphically by referring to his proposal as offering 'a clawback of the Danegeld' which it saw Britain paying to the EEC budget!)

The journalists gained the impression from George Thomson's remarks that the Irish share might be increased. And so it was to 6 percent over a year later, for the negotiations dragged on until near the end of 1974. At the end of November in that year, shortly before the Paris Summit, I received a phone call from George Thomson. The Commission were about to start this final discussion on a proposal of his that would give us 6 percent of what was now to be a much smaller fund, following the impact of the first oil crisis on Europe during 1974. We should immediately take direct diplomatic action in Bonn, and also in Paris and London.

Following this somewhat surprising initiative on his part we took further action in these capitals, which at the Paris Summit secured an increase in our share to 6.5 percent.

A happy ending? Yes and no. Because of the post-oil crisis reduction in the overall size of fund whilst the argument had been dragging on, the absolute amount secured by Ireland had not in fact been raised – but every other country had see its allocation sharply reduced, so that the battle I had fought aggressively turned out retrospectively to have been a good defensive action that protected us, uniquely, from the financial pressures on the fund during this post-oil crisis period.

The next issue affecting Irish interests that arose in the General Council was in relation to the representation of member states in a directly-elected European Parliament. This arose from the decision of the Paris Summit at our initiative to initiate direct elections to the European Parliament, 'in or after 1978'.

In the existing parliament, the members of which were appointed by national parliaments, there was a weighted system of representation, which had generously given Ireland just over 5 percent of the seats for a population that was about 1.25 percent of that of the Community at the time. We were naturally anxious as far as possible to maintain this disproportion in a directly-elected parliament

Wilson both puzzled and amused other members by saying that in fixing the date of the European election we should have regard not only to church opposition in Britain to Sunday elections but also to 'religious festivals and spring holidays'. 'What was he getting at?' one of my continental colleagues asked me afterwards. 'We didn't think Britain was such a very religious country'. Recalling my experience in Aer Lingus when I had had to make provisions for seasonal fluctuations in holiday air traffic between Lancashire and Ireland, I explained that I believed Wilson was concerned that the election, which was contemplated for May or June, should not coincide with Whitsun (the religious festival in question), with which the local Wakes Week in Lancashire coincided, as a number of his constituents in Huyton and neighbouring areas might then be on holidays! Sabbatarianism being a factor in the Netherlands as well as Britain, Den Uyl shared Wilson's concern about Sunday elections.

When we met in Luxembourg on 1 April 1976 we discussed the day of the week on which the election should be held. Most countries wanted Sunday but Callaghan, now prime minister, wanted Thursday – thus giving a four-day spread. When Moro said that in Italy Sunday elections continued until 2 PM on Monday so as to allow people to vote who might have been away at the weekend, Giscard d'Estaing remarked that the discussion was now becoming somewhat absurd. He was proposing to change the whole French electoral system, which involved two separate rounds a couple of weeks apart, in order to facilitate the European election being held on a single day, and yet Britain was not prepared to drop its insistence on having its election on a Thursday. Why had it to be on Thursday in Britain? Liam Cosgrave remarked sarcastically that the British position was really quite open: it could be held on any day of the week as long as it was Thursday! Jim Callaghan's response to Giscard d'Estaing was majestic in its simplicity, demonstrating, I felt, the delightful conservatism of the British Labour Party: 'Because elections in Britain have always been on Thursday'. And so in order to meet the divergent demands of the British and Italians it was agreed that these elections would be spread over four and half days – from Thursday morning till lunchtime on Monday!

There ensued an apparently endless series of meetings about the size of the directly-elected parliament and the number of seats each country should have. The French, who were unenthusiastic about the parliament (or assembly as they called it), wanted to leave its size unchanged. For our part we wanted 15 seats – 4 percent of an enlarged parliament, and a figure large enough to facilitate the creation, of multi-seat constituencies. The main British concern was that, because it was accepted that smaller countries should be over-represented, Ireland and Denmark would have several times more seats than more populous Scotland. Every country had its own axe to grind.

The thirteen seats originally proposed for Ireland was eventually raised to fifteen – but only on the basis that every other country would also see its number of seats increased by the same proportion, viz. two-thirteenths! This added over fifty seats to the parliament. Then, after Britain (and therefore the other three larger states, for they insisted on parity between the four of them), had secured a further increase in its seat allocation, it emerged that despite all this, the British government was not prepared to allocate more than two of its increased allocation to Northern Ireland. Fearful that this might in certain circumstances leave the nationalist population unrepresented, we persuaded the council to agree that Britain (and therefore the other three major states), should have three extra seats, in order that that Northern Ireland and also Scotland and Wales should each have one extra seat! By the time this crazy bidding game had ended, the Irish delegation's requirements for the two parts of our island had added almost seventy seats to the new parliament's size!

At the time I made a personal good resolution to write after the first European election to those members of the European Parliament who would not have secured seats but for our efforts, in order to let them know how greatly indebted they were to Ireland – but, like many good resolutions, that one fell by the wayside in 1979.

I should, perhaps, add that the British government later tried to divert all three of these extra Celtic seats to England. Liam Cosgrave successfully faced down Callaghan on the issue of the third Northern Ireland seat, but we could not reasonably also defend the interests of Scotland or Wales!

The third issue that came to the General Council of Foreign Ministers during my period as foreign minister involving significant Irish interests was the negotiation concerning a revision of the Common Fisheries Policy in 1976.

In the nineteenth century, Ireland had had a substantial inshore fishing industry, by the standards of that time, but this had declined in the earlier part of the twentieth century, and efforts to revive it after independence had achieved only limited success. Then in 1970, at a moment when serious efforts were starting to be made belatedly to develop the industry in Ireland, the original six member states, anticipating the enlargement of the Community to include three countries with much greater fishing resources than they had, introduced a fishery policy that extended Community competences to this sector. Thus part of the price of EEC membership for new members became the vesting in the Community of Irish, British and Danish fishing rights up to their shorelines. We three had no option but to accept this fait accompli if we wanted to join the Community.

However, in the middle of the decade this Community Fisheries Policy had to be reviewed in the light of Icelandic and Norwegian moves to establish 200-mile zones off their coasts. This created a unique opportunity for Ireland to recover some of the ground that had to be conceded in 1972 in order to secure accession to the Community. For, unlike the UK and Denmark, we had no interest in fishing in Norwegian or Icelandic waters, and could therefore concentrate single-mindedly on using this negotiation to improve our position in relation to waters nearer to our shores, by seeking increased fishing quotas at a time when other states were facing EC limits on their catches due to over-fishing. We found ourselves unexpectedly with considerable bargaining power because under the Community fishery regime our consent would be needed for any agreement with Iceland and Norway to preserve EC countries' fishing rights in the new 200-mile zones proclaimed by those two states.

Britain was in a particularly invidious position because of a domestic conflict of interests. As an island country it had an interest in securing a similar national zone – but it lacked Ireland's unique bargaining position because, unlike Ireland, it also had an interest in access to other waters, specifically those of Iceland and Norway. Thus it could not afford, like Ireland, to use a veto on these latter negotiations in order to secure concessions in respect of its own coastal waters. Britain's best chance – perhaps its only chance – of securing positive results on both fronts was to seek to 'piggy-back' on Ireland's negotiating strength, seeking to get for herself whatever concessions Ireland might secure in respect of its coastal fishing while at the same time concentrating its negotiating efforts on preserving its access to Icelandic and Norwegian waters.

Our officials were pessimistic about our prospects of achieving a major break-through in this negotiation and our sources in the Commission services were no more encouraging. Indeed I was advised of the danger of seeking unrealistically large concessions that might prove unattainable. Should my efforts fail, as I was told was likely, I was warned that my political reputation could suffer.

Several years later as Taoiseach I received the same advice from officials in relation to a precisely parallel situation with respect to proposed milk quotas. It is right that officials should advise caution in such cases; certainly politicians would not thank officials if they allowed their ministers without warning to fall into political traps by launching over-ambitious high-profile campaigns on the international stage. Moreover officials are very aware of the resistance of their colleagues in other administrations to attempts to secure potentially precedent-setting concessions of an exceptional nature.

However, the buck stops with the politician, not with the civil servant. Politicians who always play safe in such circumstances might as well not be in office at all – whilst, of course, if they stick their necks out too far, they will be chopped off, and they may find themselves, perhaps deservedly, out of office!

In this instance I felt I had to take a risk. Too much was at stake for us to play safe. Moreover – and this is a vitally important factor in such matters – the case that we could make was objectively a strong one. Admittedly, because of our own past failure of domestic policy, our fishing industry was in fact grossly under-developed vis-a-vis those of other member states. And, so far as our partners were concerned, the cost of making concessions that would be of great value to us would be marginal for them.

The European Council made a fairly anodyne announcement that it was determined to protect the legitimate interests of Community fisherman. It was left to the Council of Ministers a week or so later to declare its intention to introduce a 200-mile Community fishery zone. Unsurprisingly, the Commission's proposals published towards the end of September 1976 reflected continental rather than insular interests; there was a marked unwillingness to move away from the stranglehold on Irish, British and Danish fish stocks secured by the original Six through their pre-emptive Common Fisheries Policy of 1970. The only concessions to Irish and British interests that were offered were a provision for a 12-mile inshore band, subject to 'historic' rights for traditional fishermen, and an unspecific 'special priority' for Ireland, Northern Britain and Greenland in the distribution of Community Total Allowable Catches.

I made an uncompromising response to this Commission proposal, describing it as 'unacceptable to the Irish government' and as reflecting the interests of the original six member states and being 'clearly inappropriate to the needs and interests of the enlarged Community'. The 12-mile coastal band proposal was, in my view, 'inadequate'.

As the weeks passed the situation became tense. The Germans in particular were impatient. Eventually in desperation they threatened that if agreement was not reached on a mandate to negotiate with Iceland and Norway they would go ahead with such negotiations bilaterally. Bilateral negotiations with external countries were of course incompatible with Community laws and this threat weakened their claim to continued Community control in an extended zone. I was under no illusion, that the Commission would easily capitulate on the key ideological issue of Community control of fishing rights – but they would, I believed, have to propose some substantial concession to us in order to break the deadlock. This calculation proved correct.

The crucial meeting of the Council was fixed for Saturday 30 October, exceptionally in The Hague. Earlier that week I got a call from Finn Gundelach, the commissioner responsible for fishery policy. Could he see me on Wednesday? I agreed. When we met he proposed that on top of the general provision for Northern Britain, Ireland and Greenland, which provided that account be taken of the 'vital needs' of local communities particularly dependent on fishing and allied industries (which came to be known as the 'Hague Preferences'), there would be a special regime for Ireland. The Common Fisheries Policy would be applied so as 'to secure the continued and progressive development of the Irish fishing industry on the basis of the Irish government's fisheries development programme for the development of coastal fisheries'.

This programme was something that I had recently persuaded our Fisheries Department to devise so as to lend credibility to our expressed concern for the development of the industry in the context of the new 200-mile Community fishery zone. It involved a proposal to develop the Irish catch from 75,000 tons in 1975 to 150,000 in 1979, with further increases thereafter. Gundelach's proposal thus guaranteed that whereas other member states' catches would be constrained by catch limitations in order to preserve stocks, Ireland would be able to double its catch within three years and to increase it further after 1979. In addition, he proposed that in recognition of the fact that our small state would be responsible for protecting 23 percent of the Community's waters; the Community would finance 75 percent of the cost of building two modern fishery protection vessels for our naval service.

I believed I could 'sell' this proposal to our fishermen – with whom I had kept in the closest touch throughout the whole negotiation, even bringing their representatives up to our delegation room on the 13th floor of the Charlemagne Building in Brussels where the Council meetings were held, and persuading them on at least one occasion to criticise me for allegedly weakening in the negotiation – so as to strengthen my hand with the Commission and the Council!

Accordingly I went to The Hague on Friday evening 29 October with a light heart. I had an appointment for dinner with my Dutch colleagues, then in the presidency, but during the day a message had come from Tony Crosland proposing a meeting of the British and Irish delegations after dinner. Courtesy required that we meet him for what I knew would be a round of fruitless arm-twisting on his part.

The restaurant where I was to meet my Dutch colleagues was about a hundred yards down the street from the hotel where a number of the delegations, including ours, were staying. As we approached it by car I saw Finn Gundelach approaching the hotel and I decided to suggest to him that we meet later in the evening. The

Dutch ministers, Van der Stoel and Brinkhorst, standing on the steps of the restaurant to greet me were taken aback when I emerged from the car, waved a greeting to them, and tore back up the street to the hotel to catch Gundelach!

After my dinner with them I went to the British embassy. Crosland and his delegation had just arrived, quite late owing to a car accident as they were going to the airport in London. He suggested that I sit at table while they ate, the discussion to be afterwards, but I said I had another engagement that I could fit in. Returning to the hotel I joined Brinkhorst at the bar where he was having a drink with Wischnewski, the Germany secretary of state who was dealing with both development co-operation and fish. I wanted to mend fences with him as he had been furious when at the Council meeting two weeks earlier I alone amongst those present had supported a Commission proposal for 120 million units of account aid to the Machrek countries (Israel's neighbours); The others all voted for 30 million or 40 million, and Wischnewski had expressed publicly his irritation at a poor country like Ireland purporting to be so much more generous to the Third World than its richer partners – backed by EC financial transfers.

At the bar in the hotel I explained to him that our action had not been as he, I think, suspected, an insincere gesture made for publicity reasons in the belief that the votes of the others would ensure that we would not have to pay the price. It had derived from the fact that the decision I had secured from the government on a quantified annual expansion of our very low levels of development aid had given us, until we developed our own Bilateral Aid Programme, a unique temporary capacity to accept proposals for increased multilateral aid through the EEC. Wischnewski accepted my rather complicated explanation and I returned to the British embassy.

There I was greeted by Crosland who proposed that we walk around the drawing-room whilst our officials settled in. He then proceeded to try to attempt to put me on the defensive by telling me that I should content myself with a verbal rather than written reprimand to our ambassador in London. I stopped in my tracks and asked him what on earth he was talking about. 'This disgraceful business of his attempt to interfere with Parliament' he responded. I still looked blank. 'You are probably unaware', he went on, 'that he approached the Opposition to press the government in Parliament about an answer to be given to a parliamentary question on power-sharing in Northern Ireland, the terms of which the Irish government had been made aware of. The Opposition protested to us about the fact that you seemed to have fore-knowledge of the proposed parliamentary answer'.

'Oh, that', I responded, enlightened at last. 'He did that on my instruction; I can hardly reprimand him on that account'. And I suggested we join the officials for the meeting.

An irritated Crosland and I sat together on a couch, with the officials on chairs in a circle around us. He opened by saying that the British government had noted the concessions made to Ireland in the Commission's fishery policy proposals which they had received that morning. They wished to secure similar concessions for the United Kingdom and felt that the best approach would be for us to propose that what had been conceded to us should extend also to the UK! I burst out laughing at the effrontery of this proposal. 'If I did that, I'd be out of a job by ll o'clock on Monday morning' I responded. At this he became quite cross. It would be intolerable, he said, that Irish fishermen should have such advantages and that Scottish fishermen. (I noted that he was careful not to mention his own fishing constituency, Grimsby!), who were similarly placed should not have the same treatment. The relationship between Ireland and Britain would be fundamentally affected if I would not co-operate in this matter; the British people would not forget our unhelpfulness. I ought to remember that we had interests to pursue in Northern Ireland.

I riposted that England had often been described in Ireland as 'our ancient enemy' but that I was beginning to think that perhaps Scotland was being groomed to fill the bill. A Scottish member of the European Commission had proposed a regional policy that had seemed to us to sacrifice Ireland's legitimate interests to Scotland's needs; our share of seats in the European Parliament had been reduced from almost 5 percent to 3.65 percent partly because of British objections to Ireland having too many more seats than Scotland; and now we were being asked to put at risk, for Scotland's sake, what had been secured for Ireland in the form of the Commission's revised proposals for fish catches and fishery protection.

My semi-humorous remarks about Scotland were not well received. Crosland thrust into my hand a typed sheet which contained the text of the Commission's proposals for Ireland with an underlined 'and the United Kingdom' added wherever 'Ireland' appeared! I took it from him so as to have a record of his impertinent proposal, telling him once again, however, that he was wasting his time. I thought that it would be a memento of the occasion, and anyway I wanted to show it to Finn Gundelach.

Back in the hotel I went up to Gundelach's room. Laurens Brinkhorst of the Netherlands joined me on the way up, curious as to what had happened at my meeting with Crosland. They were both highly entertained by the extraordinary British proposal. Gundelach was thus well-prepared when, after my departure, the British deputy permanent representative, who had arrived at his door hot on my heels, presented him with their demarche. Gundelach told me next day that he had suggested to the British official that Crosland be advised not to press such a noncredible proposal.

Next morning Crosland briefly mentioned at the start of our meeting his suggestion of Britain getting the same terms as Ireland. When Denmark, Germany and Italy chimed in to say that they, too, had special claims, a 'stand-off' ensued between all these countries, and agreement was eventually reached that the right to expand fishing catches should apply to Ireland only.

The Commission's proposals were eventually adopted. The Irish Fishermen's Organisation paid a welcome tribute to my efforts, remarking that I had had to overcome immense obstacles to achieve this result. As a result of this negotiation Ireland's fish catch today is four times what it was before we joined the Community.

As to the subsidy for two fishery protection vessels, the subsequent Fianna Fáil government insisted that the first of these be built at the Verolme dockyard in Cork and the cost went up so much that there was no subsidy left for the second!

There is a footnote I should record, however – at a dinner with Tony Crosland to discuss fish after the Hague Conference I was accompanied by Mark Clinton, Minister for Agriculture and Fisheries, and Michael Pat Murphy, parliamentary secretary for fisheries. Towards the end of the meal, Michael Pat had followed Crosland's example by lighting up – in his case a pipe. The foreign secretary was moved to remark that we had not toasted the Queen – an event which on formal occasions in Britain (this was not one), signals permission to smoke. I, followed by my two ministerial colleagues, together with the British and Irish officials present, immediately stood to offer this courtesy. But Crosland, perhaps piqued by the fact that I had taken seriously what he probably had intended as a frivolous comment, did not rise. We remained on our feet for quite a few moments, waiting for him to join us, for at that stage I felt he should not be encouraged in discourtesy to his own monarch, but we failed to move him!

That dinner ended somewhat unhappily shortly afterwards. Mark Clinton, irritated by Crosland's aggressive approach to the issues under discussion, finally got up and left the room. It was not clear if he had walked out or merely gone to the lavatory. We remained standing for a long time before he clarified this ambiguity by returning belatedly, and we then left without much ceremony. It was an unhappy occasion and subsequent distorted press reports of the smoking incident which were unfair to us could not be contradicted without seriously damaging the foreign secretary, which would not have helped the Anglo-Irish relationship.

I should perhaps add that I had had another interesting dinner with Tony Crosland, shortly before the decisive Hague meeting. The genesis of this first dinner had lain in the friendly relationship that I had established with Michael Palliser the UK permanent representative in Brussels. As British ministers often went home early from Council meetings to vote in the House of Commons (they seemed to have much greater problems about pairing than I did!), leaving their permanent representative to take their place, I had had a good deal of direct contact with Michael Palliser there. He had, indeed, written me a very kind personal note of congratulations at the end of my presidency. So, after his move to London as head of the Foreign Office I invited him to breakfast at the embassy. We discussed direct elections to the Parliament and Britain's role in Europe since the war.

On the latter issue I went over familiar ground – the difficulty Britain had had in adapting to the post-imperial era, and I argued the case for Britain playing a more active European role. Ireland, like the Benelux countries, I said, would welcome this as in the absence of a more positive British role we had feared the prospect of indefinite Franco-German hegemony. With Franco-German relations then fraying a bit at the edges, and Giscard d'Estaing currently irritated with Schmidt (as I knew from Gaston Thorn's account of a recent discussion with Giscard), this would be a good moment for Britain to make a fresh start in the Community by adopting a markedly more positive stance.

Michael Palliser welcomed my views as being close to his own and those of the Foreign Office. He added that it could be very useful for me to put this viewpoint forward to the new foreign secretary, Tony Crosland, who might take them more seriously from me than from the Foreign Office. Perhaps I could find an opportunity to talk informally to Tony Crosland?

Accordingly I endeavoured to arrange a meeting with Crosland in London. Many messages went backwards and forwards between Tony Crosland and myself before this meeting was arranged, but several months later I received a message: 'Thursday, 8 o'clock, Carlton House Gardens. With or without civil servants?'. I replied immediately. 'Agreed. Without'. Ten minutes later he responded 'With'. What led to this change of mind I never discovered.

At an appropriate moment at this dinner I broached, circumspectly, the subject of British foreign policy. Traditionally Ireland's primary foreign policy objective had, I said, been the achievement of independence of Britain and full sovereignty. After 1922 the government in which my father had been Minister for External Affairs had pursued this objective through multilateral diplomatic activity within the Commonwealth, culminating in the Statute of Westminster in 1931, which made the Dominions, including Ireland, sovereign independent states. Subsequently de Valera had taken matters further through his new Constitution, and in 1949 a Republic had been declared. This, however, had not given us economic independence of Britain: which had been achieved through entry to the Community within which we were now on an equal footing with our neighbour.

Of course the problem of Northern Ireland remained between us, but within the Community itself our relationship with Britain was now quite different. As had been the case with the Benelux countries for centuries, our interest now lay in ensuring that a balance of power was maintained within the Community between the three major states; it was contrary to our interest that any one, or even two, of these should be dominant. The delay in Britain's entry to the Community and the subsequent British re-negotiation that had been settled in Dublin in the previous year had, however, left something of a power vacuum, with France and Germany still taking the lead and tending to dominate in Community affairs. A more active

British role in the Community would be in our interest, not because we had any particular preference for Britain as against France and Germany, but because we needed a better balance between the three powers than had so far existed.

At that point I stopped, and invited Crosland to comment, hoping in this way to engage a constructive dialogue on British foreign policy. I failed. He looked across at Michael Butler, the British political director, who subsequently became permanent representative in Brussels, and said. 'Michael, would you like to respond to that?'

So I had to tell Michael Palliser that I had had no more success than the Foreign Office in attempting to persuade Tony Crosland to address himself to the issue of Britain's role in Europe! Crosland had been a powerful minister in the Labour governments of the 1960s and 1970s, but his sudden death in early 1977, less than a year after his appointment, makes it impossible to judge how he would have turned out as foreign secretary in the longer run. It could well be that after what seemed to me to have been an uncertain start, the application of his undoubted intelligence to his new office might in time have enabled him to become a major figure on the European stage.

A decade later his widow, Susan Crosland a journalist, came to interview me as Taoiseach. I was delighted to meet her but disconcerted at her first question: 'Dr FitzGerald, what criteria do you and your wife apply in deciding what ministers and civil servants you receive in your bedroom?' Clearly, as a good journalist, she had done her homework!

12

~: Relations with Countries Outside the Community, and Development Aid :~

It was in the summer of 1976 that I indicated my willingness to take up an invitation issued three years earlier to visit the Soviet Union. Some time later the ambassador, Kaplin, asked to see me; I had no doubt about the purpose of his call and I prepared myself suitably for the occasion. When the formalities had been gone through, Kaplin asked where else I would like to go outside Moscow.

'Leningrad,' I replied.

'Anywhere else?' he asked.

'It will be very cold in December,' I responded.

'Somewhere further south?' he ventured.

'Yes,' I replied.

'One of our Republics in the Caucasus?' he suggested.

'Yes,' I said again.

'Which?' he asked.

'Georgia,' I replied. 'We should be finished our business in Moscow by Thursday lunchtime, and if we took the 15.00 flight to Tbilisi we would have Thursday evening and Friday there, after which, if we left by the 06.25 to Leningrad we could have most of Saturday and all of Sunday there. We shall have to take the 23.55 train to Moscow on Sunday night because the first flight from Leningrad to Moscow does not get there in time for the flight that I shall have to catch to get back to Amsterdam for a meeting in the Hague on Monday evening.'

Diplomats are trained not to show any emotion, including surprise. He didn't bat an eyelid, but noted down my suggestions. However my suggestion that we travel on scheduled Aeroflot flights was not adopted; in the event a special plane was laid on for the Moscow-Tbilisi-Leningrad part of the journey.

The discussions in Moscow with President Podgorny and with Gromyko – I did not meet Brezhnev – were fairly stilted and formal. Behind the rhetoric and the well-tried formulae, so carefully designed to obscure meaning, I thought I detected two points of possible significance in my discussion with Gromyko. The first was his apparent disillusionment with the Arab countries and his unqualified commitment to Israel's right to existence; the second was his ready acceptance of the rights of the minority White as well as majority African population not merely in South Africa but also – he volunteered, in supplementation of the interpretation of his remarks – in Namibia and also Rhodesia, soon to be Zimbabwe.

At the end of our discussions I handed to him a list of human rights cases I had been asked to raise. He accepted them without demur – or commitment.

At the luncheon that he and his wife offered in honour of Joan and myself I saw the interpreter approach him after the formal speeches to show him some papers; some telegrams that had come in during the meal, I presumed. But he looked up from them and addressed me across the table in his accented English: 'I see that Joyce and Yeats and Shaw are all Irishmen. Why do you allow the English to steal your great writers?' My impression, formed at our first meeting, that he did not like the English, was confirmed!

The briefing to the other EU ambassadors on my contacts took place at the German embassy, which had a small room that seemed to float in the air, surrounded by a space filled with music, which apparently enabled us to talk to each other without being overheard by the Russians, the assumption being that everywhere else in the embassy was bugged.

We enjoyed our visit to Georgia – the scenery, the antiquities and the people. On the way from there to Leningrad we were in the front cabin of the aircraft, our hosts behind. As we crossed the Caucasus range, with a marvellous view from the Sea of Azov to the Caspian, the interpreter, who had dropped in to our cabin, saw our interest in the view and lent us a map. When the descent began, one of our officials, knowing that most Soviet maps were supposed to be deliberately flawed, but presuming that maps in aircraft must be accurate, slipped the map quietly into his briefcase, but the interpreter who was standing in the door of the cabin was alert. 'I'm afraid we need that,' he remarked, putting out his hand and withdrawing the map.

When we were in Moscow one of our Foreign Office hosts named Suslov had criticised our ambassador, Ned Brennan, a Russian speaker who was a voracious reader of even quite recondite Soviet publications from which he derived much information not otherwise available. 'He reads too much, he knows too much, he asks too many questions,' Suslov grumbled. 'Why don't you tell him go look for trade instead?' Now at dinner in the residence in Leningrad, sitting beside me, Suslov began to criticise the Soviet ambassador to Ireland, Kaplin, who was sitting opposite, beside Joan. In his hearing he accused Kaplin of being a failure, because he did not take a drink and mix well with people – which Suslov certainly did. This act of gross discourtesy shocked us, and Joan and I, backed by our officials, strongly defended Kaplin. If they wanted to know who might usefully be subjected to some scrutiny, we said, what about their Trade Representative, who had moved house, we believed because he wanted to set up secret radio contact with Moscow! A quite remarkably frank and un-diplomatic exchange! (True, Kaplin was a reserved man: at the airport on our departure from Moscow I noted that he held himself back from the embraces being exchanged – but he was respected in Dublin as being, as far as we could judge, an honourable diplomat.)

Our brief stay in Leningrad ended with a dinner given by the Leningrad Soviet – presumably descended in apostolic succession from the body that had launched the Bolshevik Revolution. In my speech at the dinner I referred to Czar Peter the Great, who might not, I suggested, have been a socialist in the strictest sense of the word, but who had been a great planner! After what we had seen and heard in Leningrad during those two days, I knew that this line would go down well, and it was in fact greeted with warm applause! I then concluded my remarks, however, by congratulating my hosts on Russian conservatism, because the train we were taking to Moscow in an hour or so left at the same time – 23.55 – as it had in 1914. (It still does!) The audience was unamused. But, I went on, I also wanted to congratulate them on Soviet progress; it now got to Moscow five-and-a-half hours earlier! On that note we left to warm applause!

On the train back to Moscow we had a drawing-room car, where we entertained Suslov with Irish whiskey. Judging by the results he was unaccustomed to this form of alcohol. By the early hours he was telling us apologetically that he knew what we thought of the way things were run in the Soviet Union, but that we should not be too hard on them as it was a very large and difficult country to manage.

Like so many other visitors we could not but like what we saw of the people and we looked forward to the time when they would have a chance to express themselves freely and to find a way of participating more fully in the running of their own affairs. We were put off, however, by the rigidity of what seemed to have become a hereditary caste system that had grown up as a result of the way in which untrammelled power had corrupted their society. The openly expressed contempt of members of this ruling elite for what they often described as 'the common working people' was particularly offensive to our democratic sensitivities; it seemed as if the attitudes of the rulers of Tsarist Russia had been transferred holus-bolus to their successors two generations later, in defiance of what had been happening to society elsewhere in the world.

Our relationship with the other superpower, the United States, was, of course, qualitatively different. Following my conviction that we would make a more lasting and ultimately more favourable impression if each time we were in Washington I challenged some aspect of US policy, in Washington in October 1975 I next took an opportunity to challenge Kissinger about the recent agreement with General Franco's government, renewing US bases in Spain. I pointed out first of all that, unlike our Community partners, we had not withdrawn our ambassador from Spain following the recent executions of Basques convicted of killing policemen. We too had experience of our police being murdered by the IRA, and while no executions had taken place in Ireland for twenty years, and all death sentences for the capital murder of policemen were automatically commuted to forty-year gaol sentences, the death penalty remained theoretically on our statute book. We did not wish to appear even notionally hypocritical about the Spanish executions. More important, however, was the fact we felt that the withdrawal of ambassadors was bound to be counter-productive. Their inevitable return after a short period would be presented as a victory for the regime.

Having explained all that – and I felt that the Irish position on this issue strengthened my hand in criticising US policy in relation to Spain – I went on to suggest that the signature of the bases agreement with the Franco regime in what were clearly its closing stages of the dictatorship (Franco was known to be dying), could have counter-productive consequences as Spain moved back to democracy, just as had happened in Greece after the overthrow of the Colonels, with whose regime the US had appeared to identify. Kissinger's reaction was satisfyingly heated. 'What did we do in Greece?' he exclaimed. It was an over-rhetorical question; I was given no opportunity to answer it as he went on to describe the European reaction to the Spanish executions as 'European countries taking a free ride and making mock-heroic decisions so long as they did not have to pay for them'. The Europeans had been 'hypocritical in the extreme', he added. Why should the execution of 'convicted cop-killers' be turned into a moral issue? While he could understand that the Franco regime was anathema to Europe, he felt that Europeans were living in the past so far as Spain was concerned, with their mythic memories of the Civil War as a struggle of democracy against fascism.

I managed to intervene at this point to remind him of my opening remarks. My comments related solely to the real-politik of the situation: the un-wisdom of the US following a course of action that might be damaging to its longer-term interest in having a positive relationship with a future democratic Spain.

At that he calmed down and somewhat defensively described the efforts the US was making to establish good relations with democratic forces within Spain. They had delayed work on the Bases Agreement for five weeks longer than could be justified, but if it had expired without formal renewal, their bases could have been dependent solely on oral agreement – a risk that they could not justify.

On Greece he said that America's policy had been 'passive'. Somewhat defensively he added that if they had not been so pre-occupied with Vietnam, they might have paid more attention to Greece. I replied that the European countries had disassociated themselves from the Colonels' regime and thus had a good relationship with their democratic successors; the US had not similarly disassociated itself, and as a result US-Greece relations had suffered, with negative consequences for European security. He did not contest this. Reverting to Spain, his aide, Helmut Sonnenfeldt, commented that it would be helpful if I explained the US position on Spain in the 'sophisticated foreign offices of the EEC capitals'.

I closed this part of the discussion by remarking that however much the US might see European attitudes as being based on myths arising from the Spanish Civil War, the emotions behind these European attitudes were a political fact the US had to reckon with. We then passed on to Portugal, but my last comment on Spain must have made some impact, for an hour later, as I was leaving, I hear him repeat to himself my final remark on the Spanish issue as he turned away 'A myth, if widely believed, is a reality to be reckoned with'.

On Portugal I said that while the situation there remained dangerous (it was only some weeks later that the breakthrough to democracy was finally achieved. with a successful challenge to the left-wing of the Armed Forces Movement), nevertheless I had always been, and remained, fairly confident about the outcome. The strength of popular Portuguese feeling in favour of a democratic evolution could be relied upon and it had been, I felt, quite simply psychologically impossible for the Portuguese army to evolve within the short space of a year or two from being the spearhead of a revolution against a dictatorship into the kind of repressive force that would be necessary to withstand popular pressure. Kissinger conceded that this judgement had proved correct. Discussion of EEC aid to Portugal, upon which the Community had decided earlier that week, revealed that the corresponding US aid offer had got held up within the State Department; Kissinger, visibly irritated by this delay, ordered in my presence that it be go out that evening.

We concluded our discussions with a briefing by me on Northern Ireland.

On this, as on later visits to the US, I travelled to various cities to address meetings on Northern Ireland as well as to deliver academic addresses on aspects of foreign policy. The Northern Ireland meetings were often stormy as groups of IRA supporters sought to disrupt them not merely by external picketing but also in some cases by attending my meetings in strength and attempting to shout me down.

One in particular, in the Biltmore Hotel in New York in 1974, remains in my mind. Three groups of IRA supporters in different parts of the hall drowned out my remarks, which I insisted on completing, but which no one can have heard. When I had concluded I invited questions and, dividing in order to conquer, I successfully called on two of these three groups to be silent so that I could hear and answer questions from the third. Each in turn addressed me with abusive questions which, together with my answers were, however, largely audible as a result of my tactic of getting the other two groups to remain silent.

The security people present were visibly nervous, however. Having failed to persuade me to leave after my address they kept on trying to get me to end my question time. After a while, as the IRA supporters started a series of mini-rushes towards the platform, I saw Joan being reluctantly led out by a woman security officer. Only after irate members of the audience showed signs of throwing punches at the disrupters did I terminate the meeting and leave. I did not, after all wish the event to end with my invited guests being charged with assault!

In the car to which I was led by the security people a bemused New York policeman sat beside me in the back seat. 'Jeeze,' he said, 'I t'ought de IRA was de good guys. Ain't dey fighting de British? But when I went to de old country last summer, everyone tole me dey were [expletive deleted]. I don't understand it all anymore.'

When I arrived at the flat of our Vice-Consul, where we were invited for supper, Joan was not there. I didn't like to make a fuss, so I refrained for some time from making the anxious enquiries that were forming in my mind. After a while, however, she appeared. Escorted downstairs by the woman security officer, they had found no car awaiting them. The officer was nonplussed. Joan suggested they return to the hotel foyer and wait for us. They did so, but we missed them on our way out through the discreet side entrance chosen by my escort. The woman officer had been clearly upset, even in tears. It was only the second time she had been on duty with a gun, which she had in her handbag. Joan had sought to console her until someone eventually turned up who knew where to find us.

During my frequent encounters with these bands of protesters I noticed that they usually included a few vociferous recent immigrants from Northern Ireland, whilst the rest seemed to be second or third-generation Irish who had inherited parental or grand-parental memories of what they saw as having been a colonial war, and who, with their curious frozen-in-aspic concept of Irish nationalism, saw democratically-elected Irish governments, whatever their composition, as quislings.

Even Irish representatives of some of our own state bodies seemed afraid of the IRA. I recall that on one occasion when I was leaving Boston on an Aer Lingus flight I was told that the VIP room was not available for me – because they had thought it wise to lodge the local IRA head there. I raised that with the company when I got home.

Nevertheless, the process of challenging the IRA myth in the US, which had been started by Jack Lynch and his Minister for Justice, Des O'Malley, in 1972, made considerable progress during our term of office. There is reason to believe that the flow of funds from Noraid to the IRA diminished over that period, and by 1977 we had succeeded in rallying all leading Irish-American politicians to give vocal leadership to our cause in the US.

The official visit by Liam Cosgrave to the United States in March 1976 was an important stage in this process. This was one of the first European official or state visits of the Bi-Centennial Year and, coinciding with St Patrick's Day, it was given considerable publicity, which was helpful to our cause. Almost fifty years had passed since his father, as president of the Executive Council of the Irish Free State i.e. prime minister, accompanied by my father, then Minister for Defence, had made the first Irish official visit to that country, and this appearance of a second-generation Irish leadership added spice to the bi-centennial Irish visit.

Liam Cosgrave's speech to a joint session of Congress was the highlight of the trip, which had begun at Williamsburg. The speech had posed a problem, however. Shortly before our departure I had visited the Taoiseach's office to discuss a draft. It was much too long, he said: cut it in half. In vain I tried to explain that Congress had allocated half-an-hour for the address and that failure to fill this 'spot' might cause problems – even, perhaps, offence. He would have none of it. The idea that he could offend anyone by too short a speech simply made no sense to him.

In despair I called in to the office of the assistant secretary to the Cabinet, Dermot Nally. I had first met Dermot Nally many years before when, as an official of the Department of Local Government he had been secretary to the Commission on Senate Electoral Reform. He it was, indeed, who had asked me at lunch one day during a session of the Commission whether I was interested in politics, and if so, of what department I should like to be minister? We had both been somewhat taken aback when my choice of the Department of Education had been greeted from across the table by the Senate Opposition leader, Michael Hayes – a former Ceann Comhairle (Speaker) of the Dáil and Fine Gael front bench colleague of my father – with a somewhat cynical laugh and the comment: 'You'll find there are no votes in that department'. That was, of course, before Donagh O'Malley's announcement of free education!

Dermot Nally had been transferred to the Taoiseach's department as assistant secretary to the Cabinet shortly before we had entered government in 1973, and I had established a good relationship with him there.

Now I posed the question to him: What were we to do about the speech to Congress? He went through the text carefully, deleted a couple of less important paragraphs and proposed that the margins be narrowed and that the spacing between lines be reduced. Presented in this way, the speech went back to Liam Cosgrave, the number of pages virtually halved. He accepted it without further demur – whether because he actually thought we had halved its length or because on second thoughts he had decided to accept the need for a half-hour speech, I do not know. In any event he had the last laugh on us when in actual delivery he added a 'punchline' plug for Irish whiskey which I am sure we should have advised against had we been asked. We would have been wrong; the punchline was a hit!

During my period as foreign minister I visited a score of countries outside the Community, a number of them on Community business during our presidency as I have already related. These included the Maghreb countries of North Africa with which the Community signed agreements in April 1976

President Bourguiba was clearly delighted to greet an Irish minister; he recalled to the Community delegation the death of Terence McSwiney after a prolonged hunger strike in 1921. He and his fellow advocates of Tunisian independence would have followed this example, he said, but for the fact that the French had imprisoned them in forts in the desert and no one would have known they were on hunger strike, which would have removed the point of the exercise. And anyway, he added, rubbing his stomach meaningfully with both hands, it would have been bad for the digestion!

Our visits to all three countries were confined to a precise period of twenty-four hours. That period had been suggested by the Algerians who were concerned that we spend exactly the same period in each of the other two countries.

In Algeria I learnt that my British colleague had asked for bilateral meetings with the foreign minister, Bouteflika, much later the country's president. I added my name to the list, without much conviction that anything would come of it. Bouteflika, however, chose to come to our hotel to see me but, most pointedly, not the British Minister, just before our departure. After some initial general discussion, I took the opportunity to explain our positions with respect to both Northern Ireland and the PLO, because of the belief that elements in the PLO had at one stage helped the IRA. He quizzed me on the point, saying that many Third World governments (clearly including Algeria itself) had assumed that the IRA was broadly operating on behalf of the Irish government and with its tacit support. Algeria had at one point been approached by the IRA for arms but no action had been taken in response to this request.

I asked him if he thought there was any way in which we could influence Gadaffi in this matter. He felt this would be very difficult; he seemed to share the general view that Gadaffi was impossible, extremely opinionated and not willing to listen to others. He added that if we could convince the Palestinians – they and the IRA had done jobs for each other from time to time – that they were barking up the wrong tree and that the IRA were really a right-wing group without popular support, then they might be able to influence Gadaffi – as the PLO were the only people he listened to. He added that he himself would do what he could to explain the true position about the IRA to other Third World countries.

Referring back to our earlier more general discussion he remarked in conclusion that I was the first minister from Europe who had ever spoken about neo-colonialism in terms that showed an understanding of that phenomenon!

My first contact with the Holy See had been at Helsinki in July 1973 when I had had a long discussion with Archbishop Casaroli. I had explained to him the concern of our government to establish a positive relationship with unionists as well as nationalists in Northern Ireland and my own belief that this constructive process might be aided if some features of our state which they found unattractive could be modified. These included the legal ban on contraception and the constitutional ban on divorce. But the most negative feature of all from the point of view of Northern Protestants appeared to be the Roman Catholic Church's position on mixed marriages. I also mentioned the absence of integrated education which helped to reinforce divisions within Northern Ireland itself. He seemed interested in these points and even encouraging. It was agreed that I should put my views in writing and send a document on the subject to him prior to a further meeting in the autumn.

On my return home I prepared a memorandum on these subjects for transmission to him, sending it first, however, to the Taoiseach, Liam Cosgrave, whose views on these subjects I knew to be much more conservative than mine. There was no negative reaction from him, however, and my memorandum was accordingly sent to Rome in early August.

Both the memorandum and my covering letter had been carefully studied, Casaroli now told me. Certain points which touched on doctrinal matters had been referred to the Sacred Congregation for the Doctrine of the Faith and he was considering the remainder carefully himself. He had already received comments from the Nuncio, Archbishop Alibrandi, to whom I had spoken about the points raised in my memorandum.

I stressed that we needed appropriate reforms if we were ever to shift the opinions of a sufficiently large minority of unionists to bring about a majority within Northern Ireland in favour of unity. I emphasised the psychological blockage of Northern unionists who fear being swallowed up by the Catholic South. They feared the possible loss, in a united Ireland, of their present right to divorce through the imposition on them of the ban in our Constitution on divorce. Moreover our laws made a criminal offence out of what Protestants regarded as a right: contraception.

But the most important area of all was that of mixed marriages, where the problem was church, not state, law. While since Vatican II there had been considerable progress in this area at the pastoral level, the halving of the Protestant population of our state in half a century, due primarily to the Catholic parent in mixed marriages almost always fulfilling the church's requirement about the faith in which children should be brought up, had a disproportionate impact on Northern Protestant opinion, which wrongly attributed this massive demographic change to more sinister causes – viz. repression leading to a form of forced emigration. This was a unique aspect of the mixed marriage phenomenon that did not exist anywhere else and which justified, I suggested, a special church regime for mixed marriages in Ireland. Casaroli kicked for touch at this point, suggesting discussions with the Nuncio, Cardinal Conway and some of the Bishops.

(A decade later I smiled to myself when I heard Bishop Cassidy at the New Ireland Forum kicking that ball back to Rome, saying that the Irish bishops had considered appealing to Rome for a derogation from the requirement that the Catholic partner promise orally to do his or her best to have the children brought up as Catholics, but that they had not gone ahead with this as they did not feel there was even a slight chance that Rome would accede to such an appeal! Two government departments seeking to shift a bureaucratic onus to each other could not have been more skilful.)

Casaroli did, however, go so far as to say that he was now of the opinion having heard my case that the Nuncio had given him the wrong slant; his (Casaroli's) comprehension of the complexities of the problem had been changed by our discussion. I wondered – not for the last time in my political career – just what the Nuncio had been saying to him.

Nothing more was heard of my initiative. However around February 1977 in Strasbourg I happened to meet Archbishop Benelli who at that time seemed to have the role of prime minister, whereas Casaroli was effectively Foreign Minister of the Holy See. He suggested that I speak to the Pope Paul VI about Northern Ireland. A couple of weeks later I took him at his word, seeking an interview with the Pope as well as with himself after the Rome European Council of 25—26 March.

As I waited in the open doorway of the Pope's study I could hear someone talking continuously, as if giving a prolonged briefing. When I entered, however, there was no one else there. I realised then as I sat at the desk opposite to him that he had been reading aloud to himself the address in French that he was to make to me. It lasted some six or seven minutes. The theme was uncompromising. Ireland was a Catholic country – perhaps the only one left. It should stay that way. Laws should not be changed in a way that would make it less Catholic.

As he spoke I began to wonder how on earth to respond to his statement. Given his age and frailty, and the respect due to him, as well as the short residue of my brief audience that would remain to me when he eventually finished, I could hardly launch into an argumentative response to all the points he was making. Accordingly, when he finished I said quite simply that there was an appallingly tragic situation in Northern Ireland to which we in our state were trying to respond in a positive and Christian way.

Before I could go any further he intervened. He knew how tragic the situation was in that area, he said, but that could not be a reason to change any of our laws that kept us as a Catholic state. At that I more or less gave up. I left the audience in a somewhat shell-shocked condition. It seemed evident from the tone and content of his remarks that he had been briefed that I was a dangerous liberal bent on destroying Catholicism in Ireland – someone who had to be admonished in no uncertain terms, and whose expressed concerns about the Northern Ireland tragedy should not be taken seriously.

All in all this meeting and subsequent ones with Cardinals Benelli and Casaroli were a depressing experience. I had presented the problem in terms of the need to create conditions that might favour peace and reconciliation – which was how I saw it. I had not expected my suggestions towards this end to be welcomed, but had thought that some discussion of the problem on the basis of a shared Christian concern might be possible and that what I believed to be the evident genuineness of my commitment might provide an antidote to some of the misleading advice the Holy See had been receiving from their nuncio in Ireland. Instead I had been faced with a combination of what appeared to me to be diplomatic evasion and arguments based on power rather than charity.

There was, however, to be another twist to the relationship between Ireland and the Holy See before our government's term of office came to an end. It had been clear throughout our period in power that the Holy See was being briefed from Ireland by conservative forces in the church; that I suppose was to be expected. But there had also been disturbing signs of attempts to persuade the Holy See that our approach to the IRA threat was in some way to be deplored.

There was one area where it could be alleged that we were vulnerable to criticism; there had been allegations of police brutality connected with interrogations. But this was not the subject of the communication we now received from the Holy See; a quite different issue was raised, concerning IRA hunger strikes in two prisons.

Irish government policy on hunger strikes for decades past had been directed towards minimising the risk of deaths from such demonstrations, both by trying – of course not always with success – to avoid allowing circumstances to arise that would precipitate such events, and also by leaving no doubt in anyone's mind about the possibility of the government being persuaded by the blackmail of such hunger strikes to depart from their settled policy of prison management. This approach had been pursued by successive governments with such success that since 1946 no hunger strike in the Irish state has been pursued to a fatal conclusion. By contrast in the 1970s and early 1980s the British government, pursuing a less carefully considered and more uncertain policy, had lost two prisoners in Britain and ten in Northern Ireland through hunger strikes. Irish governments are convinced that their approach has not only been more effective, but also in the long run more humane.

The decision of the Holy See to respond to pressure from some Irish church sources and, we believed, from the Nuncio, by presenting a note to the Irish government about these hunger strikes thus evoked a strong reaction from our government and in particular from Liam Cosgrave as Taoiseach. No more loyal son of the church was to be found in Ireland, but Liam Cosgrave was not prepared to take lessons from anyone – even the Pope! – on how to deal with the IRA.

His reaction was foreseeable by anyone who knew anything about him – and was foreseen by our ambassador to whom Benelli handed an official note. The ambassador turned it round on the desk so that it faced Benelli again – a traditional hint that a protest is not acceptable, and would be better not pressed. Benelli ignored the hint, turning it back again. The ambassador then warned him about the Taoiseach's probable reaction.

The delivery of the note on Tuesday 25 April when I was away in Britain, came shortly after a public statement on the hunger strikes and on prison conditions in the state made by Bishop Daly of Derry just before the strikes were ended. There had also, I think, been a direct approach from the Nuncio to our government which had been rejected. Bishop Daly's statement was considered by the government on Wednesday 26 April, at which point the existence of Benelli's note had not come to its attention. As a message to me from Liam Cosgrave on the following day made clear, there was concern and resentment amongst ministers at Bishop Daly's public intervention which it was feared might even have had fatal results if it had encouraged the hunger strikers to continue a protest which we believed – rightly, as it turned out – had a good chance of being halted because of the way the government was handling the issue.

The government had suggested that I should convey our concern at this untimely intervention by taking the matter up with the Holy See through our ambassador – unaware, of course, that the Holy See had already taken it up with us! As a result of a conversation with Liam Cosgrave on Saturday, after my return, with both of us still unaware of the Benelli note, this proposed intervention was dropped.

When in my absence (in Brussels) the government learnt that their proposed protest had in fact been not only abandoned but had also been pre-empted by Rome some days earlier, there was an explosion. A note was drafted, the text of which was phoned to me in Reykjavik, where I was on an official visit, by my officials in Iveagh House, who wanted to know what they should do with it.

The proposed Irish note certainly pulled no punches. The Holy See was to be told uncompromisingly that the hunger strike had been organised by persons convicted of murder and other crimes committed in the course of a campaign in which almost two thousand Irish people had been killed and nearly ten thousand injured. Government policy on the strike had been frequently and unequivocally stated by the Taoiseach and other ministers. It was based on the rule of law.

There was a sting in the tail, moreover. The government wished to make known their concern at the timing and content of the Holy See's note – which, it was pointed out, had been given to our ambassador when the hunger strike had been over for some days!

I could see why my officials had decided to phone me for instructions – but I could not conceivably tell them not to deliver the note. Instead I drafted on the spot an aide memoire to be presented in explanation of the strength of the Taoiseach and government's reactions. I said that the government had been particularly disturbed by the fact that in the wording of its note the Holy See should have used language that seemed to accept propaganda statements of convicted criminals engaged in a campaign to discredit the government. The government was all the more concerned because it had believed that its dedication to policies of moderation and Christian reconciliation in the difficult situation created by the Northern Ireland crisis were appreciated by the Holy See. It had hoped that my recent visit during which I had explained our policies in relation to Northern Ireland and the whole problem of violence in Ireland would have dispelled any misunderstanding that might have existed. (I thought I was entitled to this reminder of my fruitless efforts to persuade them to help us with our efforts to create conditions for reconciliation!)

A final explanatory comment of mine to the effect that the government could not but wonder about the reliability and impartiality of the sources of information upon which the Holy See had drawn in preparing their demarche was, at our ambassador's suggestion, incorporated in the note itself – as was a reference to annexed statements by the Minister for Justice on the hunger strike.

Benelli's reaction to our communication was defensive on the issue of the reliability of his sources. It had not been the intention of the Holy See to intervene but merely to bring to our attention letters that they had been receiving. I think that the strength of our reaction and the fact that the Taoiseach was involved, and not just me, had its effect.

The episode, taken together with my experience in the Vatican some six weeks earlier, illustrated, however, the difficulties of an Irish government's relationship with the Holy See – difficulties which I have to say seemed to have been aggravated by the activities of the Nuncio, Mgr Alibrandi, who was left for almost twenty years in Ireland despite clear indications by the Irish government of its unhappiness with his intervention in affairs of this kind in which he appeared to some of us at times to confuse Catholicism and some native versions of Irish republicanism.

The 1977 general election was held on Thursday 19 June. Under the Irish system, however, an interval of several weeks elapses after an election before the new Dáil meets to elect a Taoiseach. In this instance the date for the assembly of the new Dáil had been fixed for 5 July. But on the Wednesday after the election, in circumstances that I shall describe elsewhere, Liam Cosgrave announced his resignation as leader of Fine Gael. So when I left a meeting of the Council of Ministers in Luxembourg four days later, to be followed immediately by a European Council in

London, I already knew that I was likely to become leader of the party and thus, if and when we returned to government, Taoiseach rather than Minister for Foreign Affairs.

The ministerial council meeting in Luxembourg was consequently an emotional occasion for me. I had been visiting the European institutions in Brussels and Luxembourg regularly since 1961 and in the previous four-and-a-quarter years had attended some seventy Council of Ministers meetings in these two capitals – as well as over twenty other EEC ministerial meetings in other capitals. These meetings of EEC foreign ministers were occasions at which I had felt entirely at home and where I believed I had been able to contribute to the future of both Ireland and Europe. Now it seemed clear that this would be the last such meeting that I should be able to attend.

Liam Cosgrave had asked me to invite Jack Lynch, who would become Taoiseach a few days later, to accompany us to London European Council meeting but Jack Lynch had declined, saying that he thought this would be an awkward arrangement, and anyway he was busy forming his Cabinet.

The London meeting itself was a dull one but it was a social occasion of some brilliance, for it coincided with the Queen's Silver Jubilee celebration and we were invited to dinner in Buckingham Palace rather than the usual luncheon given to European Councils by heads of state. Moreover it had been arranged that after dinner there would be a Tattoo by the massed bands of the Brigade of Guards on the floodlit lawn at the back of the Palace.

Although Joan was not feeling her best it was nevertheless an enjoyable evening. When the Royal party appeared – somewhat unexpectedly, as Schmidt and Genscher had not yet arrived – in the ante-room where we awaited them, we formed ourselves into a rough-and-ready line, introducing ourselves as they came to each of us. By chance Joan was ahead of me in the line and she was somewhat taken aback when, as the Queen passed on from Joan to me, Prince Philip, shaking hands, asked her: 'Do you always put yourself in front of your husband?' Fortunately, whether through tact or otherwise, she failed to make the obvious response! At table she was seated beside Captain Mark Phillips and was amused to be pressed after dinner by several of the ladies-in-waiting as to whether he had talked to her. When she replied that of course he had, one of them said triumphantly to the Queen's Equerry 'I told you he could talk!'

After dinner, as we walked from the dining room to three large balconies at the back of the Palace to watch the Tattoo, Prince Charles fell in beside me and asked a series of highly relevant questions about Northern Ireland. The Tattoo itself was impressive. As the flags of the Nine, floodlit, were lowered at the end one after another I thought of Ian Paisley and wondered what he would have felt had he (improbably) been there to see the honour paid in this place to the Irish flag. I thought also of my father who had once told me how when he had attended his first function here as Minister for External Affairs in 1923, he had had to make diplomatic excuses to King George V and Queen Mary for the absence of his anti-Treaty wife.

After the Tattoo the Queen Mother asked me to sit down and talk to her in the gallery behind the balcony from which some of us had been watching the display. There Joan found us some time later, alone in the vast room – and there the Queen in turn found the three of us when she came looking for her mother to join in the farewells. She told us that Helmut Schmidt (who, as Roy Jenkins has recalled in his *European Diary*, had that evening arrived late) wanted to leave before Giscard d'Estaing, who, as the only head of state present amongst the guests, should have been allowed to go first. Schmidt had already upstaged Giscard, and shown discourtesy to his hostess by his late arrival, and the Queen's light-hearted comments in our presence to her mother on this latest faux pas disguised an evident annoyance at this performance. As Joan and I descended the great staircase beside Jim Callaghan, he asked me if the Queen had found me; apparently she had been looking for me earlier to discuss Northern Ireland. 'I must have got the wrong Queen,' I replied.

On the way back to Dublin I was sitting beside a relaxed Liam Cosgrave in the aircraft. We found we had something in common of which we had not previously known – both of us as children had had our tonsils removed by Oliver St John Gogarty, and neither of us had been given sufficient anaesthetic!

Before passing on to my period as leader of Fine Gael and of the Opposition in the Dáil I should say something about development aid, and finally about the Department of Foreign Affairs itself.

At the conference of ambassadors and senior staff that I had called in April 1973 I had been impressed by the commitment of the department to development aid. In my foreign policy speech in the Dáil on 9 May I was able to announce that with government approval of my foreign policy memorandum two days earlier, we proposed to increase in a planned manner over a period of years the annual level of assistance to developing countries in absolute terms and as a percentage of GNP. Shortly afterwards I secured agreement to the allocation of £100,000 in the current year to finance the establishment of an Interim Agency for Personal Service in Developing Countries (APSO) which was designed to mobilise skills available in Ireland for voluntary work in these countries. Later thousands of Irish volunteers served under its auspices in Third World countries.

Then in November 1973 I brought to government a memorandum on aid to developing countries which proposed a specific target for the expansion of our development aid 'aiming at an annual increase of the order of .05 percent of GNP taking one year with another over a five-year period'. The memorandum came up for discussion at the end of a Cabinet meeting when, exceptionally, only seven ministers remained. Despite strong opposition from the Minister for Finance – the heady optimism of our early months in government had been punctured several weeks earlier by the Yom Kippur War and the resultant oil crisis – the memorandum was finally agreed by four votes to three, the balance being swung by the late Tom Fitzpatrick saying: 'If we are Christians at all, we must do this!'

This decision enabled me to enter into an international commitment along these lines at a meeting of the Council of Development Ministers at the end of April 1974. At that meeting I recorded the Irish government's concern at the fact that when it came to office the level of Irish development aid had been negligible, and our new commitment to raise this level in absolute terms and as a proportion of GNP. We had in fact doubled it in 1973 and again in 1974 in current money terms so that the share of GNP devoted to development aid had already been trebled.

Some part of this increase was necessary in order to cater for increased multilateral commitments to UN agencies and through the European Community, but the residual which we envisaged as growing rapidly, would fund a new Bilateral Aid Programme. Nevertheless, in absolute terms the amounts available for bilateral aid would remain small and we soon decided to concentrate it on four countries, Tanzania, Lesotho, and the Sudan, which were among the poorest countries in the world, and Zambia, which we had already helped in the 1960s at its request with training for their army and civil service.

In July 1974 I had to attend for 24 hours an Aid Conference in Jamaica. Returning by Air Jamaica to New York I found myself sitting beside two Africans. One of them pointed out to me that the zip on my trousers needed adjustment, as a result of which we got into conversation. They were from Lesotho – a minister and a permanent secretary. I told them of our plans and said that if they were in Europe later in the year, they should come to see us as we might be able to offer them some modest help through our new Bilateral Aid Programme. Several months later representatives of Lesotho arrived in Dublin to take up this offer. Much later I learnt from some Irish people engaged in our new aid programme there that the story circulated in Lesotho was that the minister and permanent secretary had met a drunken Irish minister whom they had persuaded to give aid to Lesotho!

As to the Department of Foreign Affairs itself, it is in the nature of autobiography to be self-centred and the account I have given in this and previous chapters of my period as Minister for Foreign Affairs inevitably fails to place these events adequately in their context – and in particular in the context of the Department of Foreign Affairs within which I was working. I could not conceivably have had any measure of success as a minister without the extraordinary back-up that I had received from this department. At the very least, such successes as I had would have been overshadowed by accompanying failures if my enthusiasms had not been restrained and channelled by wise officials, and many of these successes might not have been achieved at all but for the groundwork undertaken at official level.

Foreign offices are rarely popular institutions. They are often seen as stuffy, elitist and largely parasitical. Their staffs suffer from jealousy on the part of officials in other less high-profile departments, and other ministers resent and frequently seek to undermine the absolutely essential co-ordinating role of foreign affairs in relation to external policies. In many cases the admirers of foreign offices are confined to a small band of academics and diplomatic journalists, who know what foreign affairs is about – plus the rare politician who gets a chance to serve in the department. Ireland is no exception to this almost universal rule. As one with first-hand experience at a very testing time, I have the duty to do my bit to set the record straight.

First of all in the Irish Department of Foreign Affairs the quality of officials is generally high. Of course, there are weak links – in some cases because of faulty initial selection but more often, perhaps, because either the strains of a series of postings, mostly abroad, have taken their toll on the officials themselves, or perhaps on their spouses and children. Finally there is a minority upon whom the physical and mental strain of performing at a high level under pressure over a prolonged period has taken a severe toll, leading to mediocre performance at the end of what sometimes may in its earlier phase have been a brilliant start to a career.

The spouses of diplomats have a particularly hard time – especially, but not exclusively, when serving abroad where they, represent a state that imposes on them a demanding role which has few parallels elsewhere in the public service – and which is not compensated, or even recognised officially. And their family lives are completely disrupted every three or four years when they have to uproot themselves, moving to a different country.

In my experience the high calibre of the staff was attested by the almost universally high quality of reporting and drafting and the unfailing accuracy of the material presented to me as minister – something which from my experience as Taoiseach I know not to be universally true elsewhere in the public service although in the Irish civil service standards in this respect are generally high. Moreover the advice offered to me – which I did not always accept! – was excellent, showing subtlety, insight, and humanity.

Finally, during my period at least, the energy, enthusiasm and commitment of the staff was outstanding. Morale was, of course, high because of the challenge of our entry to the Community, and, for a number of officials, the challenge also of working for peace in Northern Ireland against the malevolent efforts of the IRA and Protestant paramilitaries, and the often uncomprehending and misguided approach of some – although by no means all – British ministers and officials.

In human terms the rapid expansion of the department – which during my relatively brief period in office grew by two-fifths to a strength of almost 200 diplomats, while the number of missions abroad increased by almost half – provided unique opportunities fro promotion. Three-fifths of the ambassadors when I left office had been promoted to that rank during my term which meant that effectively all officials of counsellor rank had become ambassadors, or assistant secretaries in Iveagh House. The same was true of the forty-odd third secretaries who were on the strength when I became minister, almost all of whom were promoted. Of course the relatively large influx of staff during this period – over sixty new entrants, almost half of them in 1974 alone – created subsequent promotional blockages which inevitably later affected morale.

I have already referred to Hugh McCann, secretary of the department for the first year of my period as minister and subsequently a most distinguished ambassador to France. As his successor I had appointed Paul Keating – a cousin as it happened of Justin Keating's and a brilliant diplomat, still just short of fifty, who for some time previously had been political director, viz. the official in charge of the political as distinct from economic aspects of foreign policy. Paul had a subtle mind, a quick and puckish sense of humour, and a pungent and very characteristic style. He combined a refreshing sense of irony, that was in no way destructive, with a very deeply-ingrained idealism.

Paul Keating's home team during his period as secretary was a brilliant one including Noel Dorr (later secretary of the department), in Paul's old post of political director; Sean Donlon in charge of relations with Britain and Northern Ireland; and Eamon Gallagher in charge of the economic division – until, quite exceptionally, the European Commission requested his transfer several years later to the key external relations directorate-general. It was a remarkably talented group, ably backed up on the legal side by Mahon Hayes.

Joan's relationship with the department was more intimate than has normally been the case – although all ministers' wives in foreign affairs are required by the nature of the job to play a larger role than in other departments. Once she had got over her fear of flying she accompanied me on many trips, getting to know our diplomatic staff overseas and their wives, whilst at home she threw herself into the official entertaining, applying her skills and energies to all the problems that this entails. She was notably considerate of and supportive of the staff and their spouses and identified with the department as much as I did. From her point of view as well as mine the years in foreign affairs were the high-point of our joint career.

13

~: Sunningdale :~

At 3.30 PM on Wednesday 5 December 1973, I took off from Dublin Airport on the first of two flights carrying the forty-odd members of the Irish delegation to the Sunningdale Conference. The Conference was to start at 10.30 on the following morning and was provisionally planned to conclude at lunchtime on Saturday, 8 December. In the event it over-ran its schedule by more than twenty-four hours.

Sunningdale Park in Berkshire is a civil service college. The conference itself was to take place in the principal block, Northcote House, and the participants (other than Liam Cosgrave, who was to stay at the Irish embassy, and the members of the British Cabinet), were accommodated in residences on the estate some 500 yards away.

Northcote House, a 1930s mansion (which we were told had been built by a newspaper baron for his mistress), is constructed around a mock 'great hall'. From the balcony which at first-floor level surrounds the hall, and off which the offices of the Irish and British delegations were housed, the floor of the hall below is like a stage set; from this vantage point on the balcony we could observe the entrances and exits of other participants, and speculate about why and concerning what 'A' was talking to 'B', or 'C' sedulously avoiding 'D'. The heavy armchairs appeared permanently occupied mainly by anonymous figures who never seemed to move and who were, we speculated, British civil servants attending in case (as never happened so far as I could see), some special problem should require their particular expertise. On couches around the fireplace sat (or in some instances lay!) politicians awaiting their next call to action. In corners of the hall knotty problems were the subject of intense discussion amongst active participants. The impermanent air of this stage-set atmosphere lent a degree of unreality to our proceedings contrasting with the seriousness of the issues that we were tackling together.

For this conference was, of course, a unique occasion. Never before had the leaders of the British and Irish states and of the two communities in Northern

Ireland, been gathered together in one place. Some 120 people attended, including a dozen members of the Irish and British Cabinets and a score of politicians representing the Ulster Unionists, Alliance and SDLP Parties in Northern Ireland.

On Thursday morning we met a number of our colleagues at breakfast. I was sitting with Brian Faulkner when Liam Cosgrave arrived and joined our table. The two of them already knew each other from hunting, I gathered, and within minutes they were chatting away about mutual friends and acquaintances. They were quickly on good terms with each other, strolling around the grounds together during breaks in the meetings.

At 9.45 AM the participants met for coffee in the hall, before filing into the conference room for the formal opening session. At that point we still did not know what were to be the arrangements for chairing the sessions; nor was it clear how much of the conference Ted Heath would be attending. In the event these two issues solved themselves and each other; the prime minister took the chair at the outset, reasonably enough as the host, and it gradually became clear that he intended to be present at all plenary sessions. He chaired the initial meeting so successfully and fairly that the issue of chairmanship simply evaporated. In retrospect this outcome should, perhaps, have been foreseeable once Willie Whitelaw had been replaced as secretary of state (rather unfairly, we thought) by Francis Pym a few days earlier.

A new Secretary of State for Northern Ireland with no previous experience of the problem could scarcely have been expected to lead the British delegation and despite Alec Douglas-Home's status as a former prime minister, there could have been some internal protocol problems on the British side about the foreign secretary leading the British delegation at a conference on an area that was part of the UK. A decade later a similar British protocol problem led to the British civil service team in the 1984-85 Irish-Britain negotiation being led by their Cabinet secretary, Sir Robert Armstrong (now Lord Armstrong).

The extent of Ted Heath's commitment to the Sunningdale negotiation became clear several days later when the Italian prime minister of the day, Mariano Rumor, paid an official visit to Britain, staying at Chequers. By that time our Conference was over-running its allotted timetable but rather than leave it to meet his official guest, he told his people at Chequers to give Rumor tea and send him for a siesta – subsequently making a hasty helicopter trip to Chequers to meet him during an interval between plenary sessions.

In his opening speech to the conference Ted Heath said that the conclusions would be incorporated in a communiqué, and that, following appointment of the power-sharing executive and devolution powers to it, a formal conference would be held to ratify the agreements reached at Sunningdale. Then Ted Heath listed the main subjects for discussion as: Council of Ireland, structure and functions, law and order, common law enforcement area, extradition, human rights etc., status of Northern Ireland.

It was already common ground that all decisions of the North-South Ministerial Council should be by unanimity. It was also agreed that the Secretariat of the Council would be independent of the Northern and Southern civil services and would be headed by a secretary-general.

On the functions of the Council it was agreed that in addition to having the function of harmonising laws as between North and South, as proposed by Paddy Devlin, it would from the outset have certain executive functions in areas where there was at present North/South duplication, e.g. tourist promotion, electricity generation and agricultural and industrial research. I was one of those who pressed this issue of executive functions for the Council and when a group was established to list the executive functions that should be devolved to the Council I was appointed as the 'lead' member of this group on behalf of the Irish government.

By lunchtime the issues at stake had been fairly clearly identified – except perhaps in relation to policing, which had been touched on only lightly and which later emerged as a crucial issue for some participants. Moreover preliminary agreement had been reached on some aspects of the Council of Ireland.

The afternoon discussion focussed first on further issues relating to the Council of Ireland, which Ted Heath identified as the financing of the Council, and the composition and functions of the proposed Ministerial Council and Assembly. On the number of members of the Ministerial Council, the unionists said they had an open mind, and John Hume's proposal of five from each part of Ireland, was agreed without much difficulty, provision being made for the attendance of other ministers as required.

Unfortunately due to a misunderstanding the provisional agreement reached on this point was conveyed to journalists that evening by our government press officer, Muiris MacConghail. This was quite contrary to what had been decided at the conference, viz. that all agreements were tentative until a whole 'package' had been worked out and that accordingly nothing should be conveyed to the press in advance of the conclusion of the conference. All hell broke out on the following morning when this 'leak' became known; confidence amongst the participants was shaken, and the tentative agreement to the composition of the Ministerial Council was withdrawn, throwing this issue – itself of relatively little intrinsic importance – back into the melting-pot.

We then agreed on equal representation of both parts of the island in the North-South consultative assembly, despite the two-to-one population ratio in favour of the Republic, whilst on the unionist side there was agreement that the assembly could evolve by agreement.

After the teabreak we moved on to the thorny issue of the status of Northern

Ireland. Brian Faulkner raised the question of a possible amendment of the Irish Constitution to delete Articles 2 and 3, to which Conor Cruise O'Brien responded that a simple proposal for their deletion would certainly be rejected in a referendum. The Irish government should not be pushed on this issue, he said. The discussion that followed was inconclusive, but the alternative of reciprocal declarations by the two governments was raised, with the possibility – mentioned by John Hume – that such declarations could be registered with the United Nations.

We moved on to the law and order area. Our attorney general, Declan Costello, led on this subject, outlining in more detail the common law enforcement area that had been touched on earlier. What he put forward was a proposal, to circumvent the problems posed as a result of the rejection by the High Court on constitutional grounds of extradition for 'political' offences. We had felt this rejection to be so conclusive that we had not pursued it on appeal to the Supreme Count – which must in retrospect seem surprising in view of the manner in which that court, admittedly with different membership, re-interpreted the 'political offence' issue in 1982. Our acceptance of the High Court's view on this issue, which determined the attitude of successive Irish governments for some years thereafter, was certainly not motivated by any political consideration; we would have been very happy to have been able to extradite freely to Northern Ireland and would have had no problem about ignoring the inevitable protests from IRA sympathisers.

Given what appeared to us at the time to be the impossibility of pursuing successfully the extradition route, and given the favourable reactions that our common law enforcement area proposal appeared to have evoked when mentioned to the British government before the conference, we found it hard to take the negative attitude of the Alliance Party and of the British attorney general, Sir Peter Rawlinson on this issue. Between them they raised apparently endless obstacles to our proposal, which we were convinced would resolve once and for all this problem of fugitive offenders. They sought instead a way out by means of proposals for changes to the extradition law which, on the basis of the decision against us in the High Court, seemed to us to be quite impracticable. We would have had sympathy with unionist objections in view of their intense frustration about extradition, combined with their evident political need for clear progress on this issue, but given the less vulnerable political position of the Alliance Party and what seemed to us to be deliberate unwillingness on the part of Rawlingson to understand the constitutional issues involved, the objections we faced from these quarters were badly received on our side.

When I referred to the problems posed by our written Constitution (the existence of which Rawlinson had shown no signs of being aware), Ted Heath then said that the problem should be tackled by a legal advisory panel in the morning, but warned against over-optimism about the timescale for implementation of any decisions which, he said, would probably take a minimum of nine months to get through Westminster.

We moved on to policing, on which the Minister for Justice, Pat Cooney, presented in more detail the proposals we had outlined in the first morning session, adding that if the council were to have responsibility for the two Police Authorities, it would need to be an effective decision-making body, or else safeguards would be needed to ensure effective policing in the event of deadlock. This somewhat negative formulation may have reflected his own and his department's reticence about the proposals he had been mandated to put forward. After the disappearance of the Council of Ireland as a practical proposition following the Ulster Workers' Strike, the police authority for the republic agreed at Sunningdale was dropped with remarkable alacrity by the Department of Justice.

The arrangements for participation in the working groups had been left vague; it seemed to be expected that mine, on the executive functions of the Council, would comprise representatives of the Irish government and the unionists. I was unhappy about this and after dinner I tried but failed to make contact with Paddy Devlin, who I understood to be the SDLP representative concerned with the question of executive functions. The British government had not nominated anyone to this working group. I suggested to Ken Bloomfield, former assistant Cabinet secretary to the Stormont government, listed on the strength of the Northern Ireland Office delegation, that he should attend on their behalf, which he agreed to do – with some amusement, I felt.

Next morning I made further fruitless efforts to contact Paddy Devlin, both before and after breakfast. Eventually shortly after 10 o'clock our working group assembled without SDLP representation. We made rapid progress, reaching agreement on a significant list of areas in respect of which studies were to be carried out with a view to identifying aspects suitable for executive action by the Council of Ireland. Then the door opened suddenly and Paddy Devlin appeared. What were we doing meeting in the absence of the SDLP? he demanded. I explained that I had repeatedly tried to contact him about the meeting. What had we agreed? With some pride I showed him our list of functions to be devolved to the Council that had just been agreed. 'Out of the question', he asserted, after a quick glance at the list. He was not going to have his friends – gesturing towards the somewhat bemused unionists present – hung from lampposts on their return to Belfast, as they assuredly would be, he asserted, if the long list of executive functions we had just agreed were published. And he went on to tackle the list vigorously – combining some items and eliminating others so that it was reduced to half its original length. Some further compression at a later stage reduced the resultant thirteen items to the eight that finally appeared in the Sunningdale Communiqué.

By the time we met again briefly in plenary session at 6.00 PM. a more or less agreed draft of an agreement was available that covered a large part, but by no means all, of the areas under discussion. The matters outstanding at that point included: the 'status' declarations by the two governments, in respect of which reservations remained; the financing of the Council (which, however, was covered by a separate draft still under negotiation); and the common law enforcement area and extradition, in respect of which an incomplete and only partially agreed text existed, with the British attorney general still referring to the proposed new court as 'that botched-up court'.

After an adjournment for a meal the conference resumed. The unionists were unhappy about the proposed 'status' declarations, because our proposed Irish declaration 'accepted and solemnly declared that there could be no change in the status of Northern Ireland until a majority of the people of Northern Ireland desired a change in that status', without defining 'status'. It was John Hume who at a much later stage on Friday night, I think, pointed the way ahead by suggesting the inclusion in the British declaration of the phrase 'the present status of Northern Ireland is that it is part of the United Kingdom'. This, however, posed a possible constitutional problem for us because in the draft text the British declaration preceded ours and this statement could thus be held legally to govern the meaning of the word 'status' in our declaration, thus putting at risk the constitutionality of the agreement in our state.

An attempt to resolve this by reversing the order of the British and Irish declarations failed in the face of unionist opposition. The dilemma was resolved, however, during Friday night. Sometime after 2 AM I dropped in to the office used by Francis Pym, a couple of doors along the gallery from our office for a chat with a couple of senior Northern Ireland Office officials, who were using it at the time. I assumed Pym was in bed but at one stage his head popped around the door, and seeing me with his officials, he immediately said 'Sorry' and withdrew – which considering we were sitting in his office was distinctly odd! However the officials seemed quite unmoved by this incident. (It should, perhaps, be added that because of his very recent appointment and unfamiliarity with the issues, Pym was like a fish out of water at Sunningdale, tending to button-hole other participants to ask anxiously: 'What's happening?')

Suddenly I had a brainwave. 'Why not put the declarations side-by-side?' I exclaimed, and, using schoolboy language I added, 'And I bags the left-hand side!' viz. the prime position, reading from left to right which should avoid any suggestion of the British interpretation of 'status' governing its meaning in the Irish declaration. They agreed. I went to Conor Cruise O'Brien, our spokesman on status, to tell him this tentative agreement, and he was happy with my solution. Some hours later in the early morning Conor met one of the British civil servants with whom I had discussed the matter, Philip Woodfield, who told him that the new arrangement of the declarations had been agreed by the unionists, but on the basis of a version in which the British text was on the left! Conor got quite upset and had to be reassured that Philip Woodfield had merely been pulling his leg.

By 11.15 on Friday agreement had been reached on the text dealing with the financing of the Council – Patrick Jenkin, financial secretary to the Treasury had arrived during the evening and had overruled his officials' objections to some aspects of the proposals. Progress was also reported in other areas – except for policing, which by this time was emerging as the principal obstacle to agreement. However, this was left until 9.15 on the following Saturday morning, in the hope that single-minded concentration on it after a night's sleep for those concerned would enable a breakthrough to be made in time to conclude the conference by lunchtime, as originally planned. It was agreed in any event that the conference resume in plenary session as soon as possible after the working group on policing made progress.

Next morning the Irish delegation reviewed the position at 10 AM. We were told that agreement had effectively been reached during the previous night on a text on extradition and the common law enforcement area concept, but that the Alliance Party had 'reneged' on it. Final agreement by all the delegations on the order of the declarations on 'status' was still outstanding at that point but appeared likely. There was no progress to report on policing. We met again at 11.30; extradition was still a problem but Declan Costello believed that a proposal of his that would enable trials for murders in Northern Ireland to take place in the Republic without the need for legislation. He had discovered a provision in an Act of 1861 that would enable this to be achieved by means of an Order rather than a Bill.

Policing, however, seemed irretrievably stuck, with the SDLP requiring a major role for the Council in this area; the unionists resisting this proposal and demanding the transfer of control of policing to the power-sharing Executive; and the British refusing to contemplate transfer of control over policing either to the Executive or to the Council.

At 1.30 PM the SDLP delegation came to see us about the deadlock. John Hume's strongly held view was that if the SDLP could not support policing wholeheartedly, they should not be in government at all, and that the political reality was that they could support it only by having the police associated with the Council. I agreed with him. During the afternoon as we awaited developments we watched racing on television – both Liam Cosgrave and Pat Cooney being racing enthusiasts. The rest of us were amused to see the expression on Liam Cosgrave's face when in the middle of a race he was told that Ted Heath, whose sporting interests were known to lie elsewhere, was anxious to have a word with him. I think, but cannot be certain, that he watched the end of the race before responding to this request.

At six o'clock the policing working group broke up to consult their principals.

At a meeting of the Irish delegation some hours later it became clear that the problem of a role for the Council in policing was now complicated by a clear division between the unionists, the British government and the SDLP, on the transfer of real policing powers to the Executive. The unionists were insistent on this, because Brian Faulkner was convinced that only if control of security returned to Northern Ireland could he 'sell' the rest of the agreement to unionist opinion in Northern Ireland. On the other hand the SDLP, and in particular John Hume, were resistant to this proposal because of their memories of how this power had been used by the former unionist government, culminating in the Derry massacre of 31 January 1972 that had precipitated the abolition of Stormont.

The British government had no particular sympathy with this second aspect of the SDLP position; indeed failure to grasp the psychological importance of securing for the police in Northern Ireland by some means the necessary moral authority within the Nationalist community to defeat the IRA remained unresolved for many years thereafter. But Ted Heath himself shared with the SDLP, and in particular with John Hume, a determination never to allow a recurrence of what he clearly saw – without ever admitting it publicly – as the fatal error of allowing control of security, including ultimately decisions that involved the British army as a back-up force, to fall into the hands of a provincial administration.

It was the complexity of these issues, dividing deeply in different ways three of the participants to the conference, including its chairman, that emerged as the stumbling block to agreement, holding up the successful conclusion of the conference by some thirty hours.

Our position on policing was clear. Despite qualms in some quarters, a government decision favoured in principle 'a common form of policing for the island' But when we had communicated this proposal to the British government, their reaction had been conclusively negative. They had seen no possibility of committing themselves in any way to the achievement at any time in the future of a common form of policing for the whole of Ireland.

The most we could hope for, therefore, as a way of securing nationalist acceptance of policing in Northern Ireland was an arrangement under which Police Authorities North and South would both be responsible to an effective Council in Ireland. We had therefore supported the SDLP position, being willing, however, to leave it to them to determine what variations on an arrangement of this kind would not damage the impact, such as it might be, of such a limited link upon the acceptability of the RUC in Nationalist areas.

During all the coffee and tea breaks Ted Heath had stood beside the refreshment area, sometimes alone. A combination of his status and his shyness left him somewhat isolated. Once or twice I had taken the opportunity to go over to him to exchange a few words. Now I decided to use this opportunity to test his sentiment on this key issue. I found him almost implacably opposed to any devolution of authority over security. Without ever referring to Derry, or any other specific incident, he made it clear that neither he, nor he believed Parliament, would be prepared to agree to such a devolution of security functions, involving ultimately, as it must, the back-up role of the British army. It seemed to me as I talked to him that there should be room for some kind of compromise at least in relation to normal policing as distinct from security, but he showed no sign of being willing to make a distinction of this kind on any of the several occasions when I took the matter up with him informally.

In the face of this deadlock it was decided that the best that could be done before Saturday drew to a close was to hold a plenary session to consolidate the agreement that had by that time been reached on the remaining issues in the hope that this would concentrate the minds of those concerned on the policing issue and would give them an added incentive to reach agreement on some compromise later in the night. This plenary meeting concluded at 11.20 PM.

The final confrontation – as we hoped it would prove to be – between Ted Heath, Brian Faulkner and John Hume (who had effectively taken over the leadership of the SDLP delegation at any rate on this issue), then began in Ted Heath's room, diagonally across the well of the great hall from our delegation room. We stood by, awaiting a signal that would require us to consider, and hopefully agree a compromise on this key issue; we believed that any solution to which John Hume could agree would be likely to be acceptable to us, for this issue was essentially an internal Northern Ireland matter, with, of course, obvious direct implications for the British government as the sovereign power.

As the night wore on the scene in the hall below as seen from the gallery provided us with some entertainment. Various politicians and officials sat or lay around in varying degrees of somnolence. Gerry Fitt was unambiguously asleep on a couch – indeed I seem to recall him performing the impressively athletic feat of sleeping perched along the top edge of a couch, but my memory of this could be enhanced by time. One British civil servant – so at least we judged him to be by a process of elimination, for by this time we knew all the other delegates – was equally fast asleep in a huge leather armchair. We judged that he would gradually slip forward until eventually he would be lying flat on the carpet in front of the arm-chair and we took bets amongst ourselves as to the time at which this logical outcome would be achieved. I think the final stage was accomplished around 4 AM.

Much of the time was spent, of course, in our delegation room, sitting around the fireplace with the assistant Cabinet secretary, Dermot Nally, behind us. Some time around 4 AM he asked us if we would like to play a game, a suggestion to which we responded positively. He distributed pieces of paper and told us to give marks to each of the governments and to the unionists and the SDLP on the basis of what each had secured from the conference so far under the main headings: Council of Ireland functions, law enforcement, human rights and so on. (The Alliance Party were omitted, I think on the basis that they had a less demanding constituency to satisfy than each of the other four delegations.) These marks were then given to me anonymously – although I could identify Conor Cruise O'Brien's marks as well as my own – to be added up I retained that piece of paper, out of, I think, a possible 3,200 marks it was our collective judgment that the UK government had on the outcome thus far secured 1,835, the Irish government 1,755, the SDLP 1,580 and the unionists only 1,205. The game achieved its purpose by identifying which delegation most needed to gain something from the outstanding issue of policing. Reflecting Conor's consistent view, he like I had given the unionists a much lower mark for achievement than any other delegation and only one amongst us had given them anything other than the lowest, or a joint lowest, mark.

It was against this background that we received a very agitated SDLP delegation of John Hume and Austin Currie just before 6 AM. They said that the unionists had decided to wreck the conference by demands that were in contravention of the Irish Constitution; we were all, they said, in real trouble. And so it seemed all the more so because the unionists who late the previous night had raised difficulties on Sabbatarian grounds about continuing beyond midnight on Saturday night, were now saying that an adjourned session could not resume before 12.15 AM on Monday morning!

I asked a Scottish Presbyterian Counsellor from the foreign office when in his view the Sabbath began; his reply, although humorous in intent, to the effect that it began when one got up on Sunday having been in bed, boded ill for an early resumption if we adjourned, as was now absolutely necessary in view of the evident exhaustion of so many of the key participants. I was downstairs in the SDLP room discussing with them this dilemma when Peter McLachlan, a unionist adviser, came in. 'We're meeting again at 2' he said. '2 AM?' I asked – meaning on Monday morning. 'No', he said, '2 PM.'

And so at about 8.30 AM we went to bed for four hours or so. When I woke at about 12.30 PM my mind was as clear as it had been fogged when I had retired earlier. No doubt I had been reflecting subconsciously in my sleep on the result of our 'game' in the middle of the night. I dressed, walked back to Northcote House, found a typewriter, and hammered out the following:

'Put emotion on one side.

Who should give in a negotiation of this kind when it is at the crunch?

The parties who have gained most to the parties who have gained least. On any objective assessment the Irish government and the SDLP have gained most and the unionists least.

Which direction should give in any negotiation at the crunch?

By adding something to the package that will help a party rather than by taking something away that will damage another.

Who will have best balance e.g. gain/loss from a breakdown at this point?

The unionists, who will avoid the immediate and terrible political risks of being destroyed.

What type of concession is most likely to reduce violence post talks?

One to the unionists, which could reduce danger of loyalist violence and above all save Catholic lives.

What is involved in a concession to the unionists?

Merely putting into words what all are agreed would and should happen eventually – devolution of power over normal policing back to Executive'.

To this I appended a possible draft statement on policing which I felt could provide a possible basis for a compromise.

'The British Government envisages that, without prejudice to the question of security, control of normal policing should in due course be vested in the new Executive. This is not possible at the present time. When security conditions permit, and when such a course of action would no longer create a danger of political instability within the system of government of Northern Ireland, it is, therefore, the intention of the British government to transfer normal police powers to the Executive. The position in this respect will be reviewed in six months' time and annually thereafter'.

This done, I watched for Paddy Devlin along the path from the residences; by this time he and others were due to arrive for lunch. As he approached the hall door, I swung it open, and said 'Paddy, I want you to read this'. 'Come down to our room', he replied. I did so. He read my analysis and my draft, and said 'Right, I'll try to persuade John'.

The Heath/Faulkner/Hume session resumed several hours later at 3 PM. I was on the gallery near Ted Heath's room when the door opened and John emerged, smiling, followed by Brian Faulkner and Ted Heath, also smiling. As John passed me he said something like 'we've settled' and gave the thumbs up sign to those on the floor below. There was a cheer. I slipped into a delegation room and rang Joan. She was thus the first outside Sunningdale to know that we had reached agreement, although my emotion was such that I had difficulty in telling her the news.

What had finally been agreed on policing, following my intervention, was the following. On the one hand the British government grudgingly agreed to meet Brian Faulkner's requirement by conceding that 'as soon as the security problems were resolved and the new institutions were seen to be working effectively, they would wish to discuss the devolution of responsibility for normal policing and how this might be achieved with the Northern Ireland Executive and the Police.'

On the other hand an attempt was made to meet the SDLP's requirements by providing that the two governments would co-operate 'under the auspices of the Council of Ireland' through their respective police authorities. Moreover members of the Police Authority of the Republic were to be appointed by the Irish government after consultation with the Ministerial Council of the Council of Ireland, and appointments of the members of the Northern Ireland Police Authority were to be made by the British government after consultation with the Northern Ireland power-sharing Executive – which in turn would consult with the Ministerial Council of Ireland.

It was thin enough, as a means of securing the loyalty of the minority to the police, but it was the most that could be extracted from a very reluctant British government, and the most that SDLP and unionists could concede to each other. From the SDLP's point of view it was a far cry, however, from the proposal that had featured in the draft that had been under consideration as far back as Thursday afternoon.

It took some time to put the agreement including the new policing clauses into a shape appropriate for signature, but after our delegation had met and formally endorsed it, five minutes later the final plenary session took place to hear concluding statements after which the agreement was signed. There followed our farewells to fellow participants, which were quite emotional; then the press conferences and the flight home. The mood on the aircraft was euphoric, as was the case at Dublin Airport when late that night we arrived there.

There was nothing inevitable about the collapse six months later of the carefully-constructed edifice of which Sunningdale was intended to be the coping-stone. Nevertheless, it is fair to reflect on whether this collapse might have been more readily avoided if the outcome of Sunningdale had been somewhat different.

Two reflections occurred to me at some remove from the event, in the early 1990s.

First, the issue that held up for thirty hours the conclusion of the conference proved almost irrelevant to the outcome. The agreement on policing that Brian Faulkner had eventually extracted from Ted Heath and John Hume, and to which I had endeavoured towards the end to contribute, never seemed to feature in the heated debates within Unionism that followed Sunningdale – nor did it do so in the discussion of the agreement in the nationalist camp. Both sides at the conference seemed to have greatly exaggerated the importance of the formulae for policing that they put forward.

Second, in retrospect I believe that we all – Brian Faulkner included – underestimated the significance of the status issue. We, the Irish government representatives, were, of course, handicapped by our concern lest any formulation we agreed be struck down as unconstitutional by our courts. And the constitutional action taken by former TD, Kevin Boland, against the agreement a week after its signature, together, I feel, the terms of the judgments of the High Court and Supreme Court dismissing that action, showed that we were right to have been concerned about this issue.

It is true, however, that once that action had been finally disposed of three months later, we felt able in the light of the terms of the Supreme Court judgment to improve on the Sunningdale working by defining our view of status in terms of the factual position of Northern Ireland being 'of course, that it is within the United Kingdom and the government accepts this and solemnly re-affirms that the factual position of Northern Ireland within the United Kingdom cannot be changed except by a decision of a majority of the people of Northern Ireland'. At the time some said that had we felt able at Sunningdale to state our stance in these stark terms, Faulkner's post-Sunningdale position would have been strengthened, but there was little evidence that our 'clarification' made much impact when it eventually was made.

At the time we ruled out without much discussion, so far as I can recall, the possibility of successfully amending the Constitution along these lines in the immediate aftermath of Sunningdale. Should we have given such a move more serious consideration? There is a case to answer, I feel. Sunnningdale, like the Anglo-Irish Agreement twelve years later-proved much more popular with public opinion in the Republic than those of us in government had foreseen. But Fine Gael and Labour in government tended for historical reasons to feel more vulnerable on the 'national issue' than they need be, and thus too underestimated the potential public groundswell in favour of 'moderate' stances on the Northern Ireland issue, especially stances that offer a prospect of reducing or ending violence in Northern Ireland.

Certainly the chances of successfully launching a campaign to amend the relevant Articles of the Constitution were much better in December 1973 than we had believed possible before Sunningdale. And I should, perhaps, add that a moderate nationalist supporter of Fianna Fáil who was deeply concerned about Northern Ireland, and who was also quite close to Jack Lynch, reminded me years later that before Sunningdale he had told me that we should 'go for' a constitutional referendum immediately after the conference and had given it as his view then that Fianna Fáil would not have opposed such a move.

So much for that side of the argument. On the other side it has to be said that the stakes were very high, for if we had tried a referendum on this issue and had failed, by the action we would have destroyed the Sunningdale settlement which the British government, the three Northern Ireland parties that were proposing to participate in the power-sharing Executive, and ourselves, had done so much to achieve. It must be recalled, moreover, that whilst, Jack Lynch would have wished to facilitate such a constitutional move, his position in his party was not then such as to give us confidence that his viewpoint would carry the day. His victory over more extreme elements in Fianna Fáil three and a half years earlier, when the Arms Crisis had broken had been as much a matter of luck as anything else.

Moreover while several of his extreme nationalist opponents had by December 1973 left the party – Neil Blaney and Kevin Boland – Charles Haughey was still within the fold, smarting from his removal from office in May 1973 and beginning already to build up the grassroots support within Fianna Fáil that enabled him to succeed Jack Lynch as leader six years later. Finally Jack Lynch had lost the general election only ten months earlier and was correspondingly very vulnerable – a condition that had been visibly aggravated by his lapse of memory the previous August over the Littlejohn Affair, the impact of which on his standing in the party had been aggravated by his own unfortunate defensive reference to possibly reconsidering his leadership position because of this memory lapse.

Against this background a decision to propose a constitutional amendment immediately after Sunningdale could easily have had the effect of destroying the consensus between government and Opposition on the agreement itself – a consensus which we rightly believed Jack Lynch to be concerned to establish – and might indeed have brought him down and have replaced him with someone else who, by virtue of the circumstances of his the coming to power within Fianna Fáil on this issue, would have been likely to be a prisoner of extreme elements in his own party. In other words a constitutional referendum in the aftermath of Sunningdale carried with it a risk not alone of destroying the agreement but of putting at risk the consensus within our democratic system upon which, less than two years after the riots that had led to the burning of the British embassy, the peace of our own state arguably depended.

I recite the two sides of the argument on this issue in order to place these events in their historical perspective, lest the hindsight view that it might have been worth attempting the gamble of a constitutional referendum on Articles 2 and 3 be given undue weight.

14

~: Northern Ireland :~
1974–77

Following the publication at the end of January 1975 of the Gardiner Report on interment, Merlyn Rees had set about gradually releasing the internees – a process that was certainly facilitated by the existence of the ceasefire, and which may, indeed, have been a major consideration on the British side in arranging the ceasefire in the first instance and in encouraging its continuance throughout the year.

In mid-February I paid a further visit to Northern Ireland, during which I lectured in Queen's University on the Irish presidency of the European Community, which had begun seven weeks previously. In my lecture I mentioned that during these six months, Dublin would be the francophone capital of the Community – for we were determined, as the first English-speaking country holding the presidency, not to weaken the hitherto exclusive role of French as the working language of political co-operation at official level. This decision had a very positive effect on subsequent Franco-Irish relations. I was amused to be told by a member of the audience, Professor Con O'Leary, that I was reversing what Garrett Mór FitzGerald, Earl of Kildare, had done in 1487 as lord deputy after Henry VII's usurpation of the throne, when he had sought to win favour with the new king by substituting English for Norman-French as the official language of Ireland for legal purposes.

Incidentally, our decision to retain French as the sole language for EU foreign-policy co-ordination forced the British to follow suit in 1977. Later on, we were told by a Foreign Office official that some of the tension between Tony Crosland and his permanent secretary, Michael Palliser, had derived from Palliser's insistence that they must follow our precedent – which was described by Crosland as 'an unwarranted break with the tradition of Palmerston, who established the practice at the Foreign Office of transacting all business and communications in English'.

Early in March, I was in London again; I availed of the opportunity to call on the newly elected leader of the Conservative Party, Margaret Thatcher, at the House of Commons. When I arrived, Willie Whitelaw took me aside. He wanted to assure me of his commitment to the principle that there could be no devolution without power-sharing in government. If his new leader went back on this, he would resign as deputy leader. He would also oppose any deal with loyalist groups in Northern Ireland, and believed that his position in the party was still such that he could prevent any such deals. I thanked him for what he said – which, however, did not reassure me as to Margaret Thatcher's likely attitude towards Northern Ireland.

Willie Whitelaw did not remain for the meeting, at which Margaret Thatcher was accompanied by Airey Neave and an official from Conservative Central Office. As was to be my practice at future meeting with her in the Commons or over breakfast at the embassy whilst I was Minister for Foreign Affairs, I opened the discussion with some comments on the current position in the European Community. I calculated that, if I could be useful to her by way of such briefings, she would be willing to see me in the future and thus give me the opportunity to get across to her from time to time our position on Northern Ireland.

Looking forward to the British EC renegotiation, due to be concluded in Dublin at the first European Council meeting in five days' time, she expressed the hope that a 'one and indivisible' British government would come out and campaign for continued British membership. It was, she said, an appalling aspect of the whole affair that Britain had lost respect and support by so blatantly dishonouring an international-treaty obligation. This comment on the 1974–75 renegotiation was to come back to me some years later when she herself initiated the second renegotiation of British accession.

When we turned to the subject of Northern Ireland, she and Airey Neave listened without much comment. I said that whilst the ceasefire was welcome, the circumstances in which it had come about, involving discussions with the IRA through intermediaries, gave cause for worry – as did the associated 'incident centres'. We had found the British government's attitude to loyalist violence, especially during the Ulster Workers' Strike, most unhelpful, and would like to see it confronted.

Airey Neave wondered if the Opposition should call for the abolition of the incident centres, but I said that once they had been established, however unwisely, their abolition would certainly threaten the ceasefire. The mistake had been in talking to the IRA in the first instance – something that successive Irish governments had always refused to do, instead of undermining them by stepping up the release of internees.

I said that we were generally pessimistic about the convention, in which the loyalists would have an absolute majority and which would, we believed, remain opposed to power-sharing. I went on to describe the contacts we had established with all constitutional parties in the North, which I believed to be helpful in easing unionist fears of the Republic and in keeping us sensitive to unionist preoccupations. This had a drawback from the point of view of our domestic opinion, but in prevailing circumstances it was the best way in which we could contribute to the situation.

Finally I stressed the importance of boosting the SDLP as far as possible; their morale was currently low because of the impact upon their position of British dealings with the IRA. Airey Neave said he hoped to visit Northern Ireland soon and would make a special point of spending time with the SDLP. And there we left matters.

As it happened, some weeks later Margaret Thatcher's path and mine crossed again in more relaxed surroundings, at a meeting of the Bildeberg group of public figures in Turkey. Our informal contacts there helped to strengthen the relationship that I had endeavoured to establish, on a constructive foundation, in her office.

Andrew Knight and I had tea with her during an afternoon break. I was particularly interested in her views, because it seemed likely that at some point in the years ahead we would find ourselves on opposite sides of the table as representatives of our two countries, with their long history of conflict and mistrust, and perhaps tackling the still-unresolved Northern Ireland problem.

She spoke about the undesirability of the kind of artificial polarisation that she felt had emerged in the economic debates at our conference. On the other hand, she had learnt a good deal from the discussions – for example, the inadequacy of the money-supply approach, because so much had to be done by way of supportive action to make the money supply work. If inflation were very high, an incomes policy was necessary, but there should be a statutory policy only for a very short time. She favoured a political consensus so long as it was of people who agreed on a free society and a mixed economy. When inflation was low, politicians would not give it priority, but if it were high, priorities had to shift, and then it was no use saying that public expenditure could not be cut. As a spending minister, she knew the unpopularity that came from making such cuts.

Some of these views did not correspond to the picture that Knight and I had formed of the new Opposition leader. Consequently we quizzed her vigorously, and expressed some incredulity when she insisted that her aim was to create a centre force in British politics, thus attracting social democrats from Labour. This latter point is not recorded in my contemporary note of her remarks, but my recollection of this was confirmed some time later by Knight, when he and I were recalling our astonishment on that occasion – justified as we felt it had been by later events. He told me then that she had said much the same thing in a discussion at Izmir Airport with the Labour MP Dick Mabon.

We now know from the British Cabinet Papers for 1974 that after his return to office in early 1974, Harold Wilson had directed that the option of British withdrawal from Northern Ireland be examined. And, although in retrospect the danger of such a withdrawal may have been greatest in 1974, we know from the published diaries of Bernard Donoghue, who was special assistant to Harold Wilson in 1974–76, that this option, in conjunction with an attempted negotiated independence for Northern Ireland as a Dominion of the Commonwealth, continued to be favoured by Wilson (and, it would appear, also by Roy Jenkins) until it was finally rejected by the Cabinet committee on Northern Ireland in November 1975. But we were not, of course, aware of all this at the time. It is also clear from the British Cabinet papers that Harold Wilson's principal private secretary, Robert Armstrong, now Lord Armstrong of Ilminster (who was later the principal British negotiator of the Anglo-Irish Agreement of 1985) had sought to dissuade his prime minister from pursuing the proposal to withdraw from Northern Ireland.

From mid-1974 until the latter part of 1975 we suspected that Wilson was contemplating such a British withdrawal from Northern Ireland. Irish politicians had been very wary of Wilson following his 1971 visit to Ireland as Leader of the Opposition in Britain, when – through the agaency of John O'Connell TD – he had arranged secretly to meet IRA leaders, under the cover of his discussions with the Irish government and Opposition. The strength of the feelings of our democratic leaders about this episode was not, however, publicly ventilated at the time because of a concern not to alienate a past – and possible future – British prime minister.

Moreover, there seemed to be a hint of a possible British withdrawal from what Bernard Donoghue once said to assistant Cabinet secretary Dermot Nally. And Harold Wilson, in his first inter-governmental meeting with Liam Cosgrave, just after the former's return to power in April 1974, had placed so much emphasis on British political and public pressure for withdrawal as to suggest that he might be thinking along these lines.

As the year 1975 dawned, bringing with it the first Irish presidency of the European Community, my concern as Minister for Foreign Affairs about the possibility of a British withdrawal from Northern Ireland prompted me to raise the issue privately with Henry Kissinger, on 8 January, in the margins of a meeting in Washington, DC, at which my EU colleagues had given me the task of launching the first EU–US foreign-policy discussion. Although Kissinger had already made clear to me that he had a policy of non-involvement in Irish affairs – a stance that he attributed to the influence of his Irish-American wife, Nancy – he nevertheless responded that in the event of such a grave development as a threatened British withdrawal, he would be open to an approach from me.

During my brief stay in Washington, rumours had begun to circulate about British contacts with Sinn Féin (which of course meant the IRA) regarding the possible continuation of the ceasefire by that organisation that had been initiated before Christmas 1974. Over the next six weeks, Liam Cosgrave and I received a series of briefings from the British ambassador on these contacts. These briefings were deeply disturbing, especially as each successive encounter revealed the misleading character of the ambassador's earlier briefing.

Moreover, in the only direct contact ever made to us by Sinn Féin (at a casual encounter in a hotel lobby in Belfast), a Department of Foreign Affairs official was told by that organisation's Belfast organiser that the British government and the IRA were planning negotiations abroad, in connection with which the IRA wanted our government to give free passes to three of their leaders who were on the run – a proposal that we ignored!

In contemplating this possible scenario, my department was clear that our small Irish army of 12,500, part of which was already engaged on border duties, would be quite inadequate to cope with the resultant crisis and anarchy in Northern Ireland. However, if we were to attempt to strengthen the army to prepare for such a crisis, this could create serious unrest and a threat to public order within our state. (We had already been unable to prevent the Provisional IRA from burning down the British embassy in Merrion Square in 1972.) Furthermore, action to strengthen the army might well be interpreted by Northern unionists as a threat to them, rather than as a measure designed to protect our own security. And that, in turn, could precipitate a crisis in the North of the very kind we were trying to avoid. Accordingly, it was felt that such a strengthening of the army had to be ruled out. In this situation, we in the Department of Foreign Affairs decided to seek to ensure that informed British opinion recognised the dangers of any weakening of British resolve, thus creating pressure against any British withdrawal – without, however, being seen to raise the issue ourselves.

Accordingly, in early June, in London, I briefed two responsible British journalists on the Northern Ireland situation – Keith Kyle of the BBC and John Cole of the *Guardian*. Over the next couple of months, reports deriving from this briefing seemed to produce the desired result. But in the meantime, with the report on possible British withdrawal complete, I judged that the moment had come to alert the government as a whole to the dangers we faced.

On 11 June 1975, as sought by the Cabinet some time earlier, I submitted to the Cabinet secretariat a memorandum from my department, together with an accompanying report by an Inter-Departmental Unit on the three 'worst-case scenarios' that had been identified, viz. negotiated independence, negotiated repartition and a collapse of Northern Ireland into anarchy.

This memorandum was naturally directed towards avoiding at all cost the third of these scenarios. It drew the conclusion that, because of the huge disruption that repartition would cause, and the extent to which such an outcome would be likely to consolidate permanently the political division of the island, the least dangerous outcome of a possible British withdrawal – if we should, after all, fail to head it off – would be negotiated independence. (We were aware that some unionist politi-cians, as well as some in the SDLP, favoured such a solution.)

Moreover, it is also now clear – although I do not think this was ever raised directly with me, and I cannot now recall to what extent I was aware of it at the time – that aspects of my briefing of the two British journalists had deeply dis-turbed Taoiseach Liam Cosgrave. It appears that he took a very negative view of any reference being made outside our administration to the vulnerability of our state to the consequences of a possible collapse of Northern Ireland into anarchy – a vul-nerability that I had thought it necessary to refer to in my briefing.

To understand reactions within government to this memorandum, it is neces-sary, first, to say something about the relationship between the SDLP and the Irish state and government. Since the foundation of the SDLP in 1971, we in the Republic had an important common interest with this Northern Ireland political party, which was a powerful barrier against the IRA – the openly stated agenda of which at that time was the destruction of the democratic Irish state and the substi-tution by force of an all-Ireland 'socialist republic'.

But whilst the SDLP and the Irish government shared a certain common inter-est vis-à-vis the IRA, our, and their, concerns were not, and could not be, identical. The primary duty of an Irish government (to which, because of my family back-ground, I have always been very sensitive) has to be to preserve the security of the Irish state; the interests of this state also require that it seek a balanced outcome in Northern Ireland that would command the support of both communities there. The SDLP, on the other hand, was then the main voice of the Northern nationalist community in the struggle against unionist domination.

For much of the time, these two sets of distinct interests could be, and were, met by a similar stance – but there were bound to be some tensions between their and our approaches, and a clash between our interests and theirs could in certain circumstances arise. Consequently, the extent to which it would be appropriate or wise for the Irish government to disclose its hand in this matter to the leaders of that party – an issue that was raised by the memorandum – was potentially contro-versial.

Within the Irish political system, this situation was also complicated by an emotional factor that has rarely surfaced publicly, or been identified by political commentators. This is the existence from the mid-1970s to the 1990s of an element of resentment amongst many politicians in all parties in the Republic regarding the extent to which the common interests of the SDLP and the Irish state in relation to most, but not all, issues have often tied us into a closer relationship with that party than some people in our state have felt comfortable with. Amongst those who were particularly unhappy about our relationship with the SDLP was Conor Cruise O'Brien.

Because, at times, my commitment to keeping lines open to unionists created tensions with some of the SDLP leadership, I had more reason than most of my colleagues to be conscious of the fact that the particular interests of that party and those of our government were far from identical. But because I also shared the view of my professional staff in the Department of Foreign Affairs that negative emotions have no useful role to play in politics or diplomacy, I never came to share some of my colleagues' muted hostility towards that party.

When Conor Cruise O'Brien received his copy of my 11 June memorandum, he responded six days later with a counter-memorandum, which Professor Ronan Fanning has been led to see as 'a vigorous repudiation' of our memorandum. This was because Conor treated the memorandum not as a basis for reflection by the government on how we might prepare in strict confidence for possible outcomes of a British withdrawal – i.e. negotiated independence, a negotiated repartition, or civil war and anarchy in the North – but rather as if I had proposed a public ventilation of this issue! For example, he argued that a confidential exploration by the Cabinet of how we might deal with a British attempt to negotiate independence for Northern Ireland 'would diminish the prospect of continued direct rule and would in effect let the British "off the hook", by enabling them to withdrew in a favourable international climate' – and so on. And – as if this were in some way a contradiction of the policy being pursued by the Department of Foreign Affairs rather than a cogent restatement of that very policy – he concluded that 'the choice lies between British rule and Protestant rule' and that it was 'quite clearly in our interest to do everything possible – which may not be very much – to try to ensure that the British stay'.

That, of course, was exactly what we in the Department of Foreign Affairs had been working to achieve. Conor's counter-memorandum was in fact a classic example of his capacity to invent, and then vigorously denounce, a disagreement where little or none existed.

My recollection is that a similarly negative approach to the original memorandum was taken by some others in government who preferred not to discuss the unpalatable alternatives with which I feared we might in certain circumstances be faced. Like Conor, some of them also seemed to feel that for the Cabinet to have a confidential discussion of these issues would in some unexplained way risk creating public alarm and weakening international confidence in our state and our economy.

For his part, assistant secretary to the Cabinet Dermot Nally – although he had chaired the Inter-Departmental Unit that had prepared the memorandum that had posed the question of whether we should discuss possible British withdrawal with the SDLP – recorded on 17 June 1975 his view that the possible consequences of Northern Ireland becoming independent were so 'horrific' that 'we should on no account give any support to, or engage in any open analysis or discussion of, the subject . . . including any analysis or discussion, with even the semblance of official backing, with the SDLP'. And on 7 July, following a discussion with Taoiseach Liam Cosgrave, he added that 'it would be well to disillusion the SDLP of any ideas they may have that this country, or any other external force, could or would provide worthwhile guarantees of civil rights etc in an independent Northern Ireland', as well as dispelling 'any illusions they may have as to the capacity of the Irish army in any situation of confrontation in Northern Ireland'.

I completely agreed that we should not encourage Northern illusions that we had the capacity to intervene successfully in a 'doomsday situation' in the North, and still vividly recall my horror at a radio interview given by Minister for Defence Paddy Donegan in, I think, 1974, in the course of which he had seemed to offer a prospect of successful Irish military intervention in a Northern Ireland 'doomsday' situation. I had always known that to be quite impossible – and to be an initiative that would put at risk the lives of many thousands of nationalists, especially in Belfast.

But whilst I might share Conor Cruise O'Brien's doubts about external guarantees of human rights in an independent Northern Ireland, rather than face repartition, potential civil war and anarchy there, a 'least bad' alternative would be to join with Britain in attempting to secure an agreed power-sharing government in an independent Northern Ireland, backed by any external guarantees that we could secure.

The reactions evoked by this memorandum suggest that it would have been wiser never to have raised in it the potentially controversial issue of possible consultation with the SDLP. Moreover, it might have been wiser to have circulated the memorandum, at least initially, to a smaller group: the security committee of the Cabinet was such a group, but there was the problem that I was not then a member of that body – although I was occasionally asked to attend meetings dealing with specific topics considered by the committee.

In the event, our concerns about a possible British withdrawal were eased in the following months. Our efforts to alert informed British opinion indirectly on the dangers involved seem to have paid off. The last occasion when independence for Northern Ireland was officially discussed was at a meeting of the Wilson government's Cabinet committee on Northern Ireland on 11 November 1975. In respect of that occasion, Bernard Donoghue records in his published diary, with obvious regret, that 'The politicians were not interested. Rees, Healy and Callaghan all said "do nothing". . . . It was impossible to make progress with reluctant ministers. Especially Jim Callaghan, who has experience in Ulster.'

Callaghan's opposition followed my discussions with him in Cork in the summer of 1975 – the background to which I should explain. Prior to that November meeting, Bernard Donoghue does not record him as having played any part in discussions on independence for Northern Ireland: his duties as Foreign Secretary may have made it impossible for him to attend some or all of these meetings.

In July 1975, we decided to holiday in west Cork with some friends. During the two previous summers, we had spent some time staying with them in the village of Les Arcs near Draguignan in the Var, but 1975 had to be a year of retrenchment. (In what turned out to be a vain hope of clearing our debts and living within my reduced means on a minister's salary, we had just moved from our house in Eglinton Road to a smaller house several miles further out of town.) Belatedly, during July, we picked, quite arbitrarily, Schull in West Cork as our holiday centre – the nearest thing to a rationale for this choice being the fact that Keith Kyle, the BBC journalist known to some amongst us, would be holidaying there, celebrating his fiftieth birthday.

This choice made, Joan rang the auctioneer in the village, Jim O'Keeffe, who was known as 'Jim Schull' to distinguish him from his cousin Jim O'Keeffe, solicitor in Skibbereen – 'Jim Skib'. (Two years later, 'Jim Skib' was elected as a Fine Gael TD for the area.) Jim Schull expressed scepticism about finding us a house at such a late stage, but said that he would ring Joan back on Tuesday. When Joan said that, unfortunately, she would be in Brussels on Tuesday, Jim Schull responded: 'Oh, you're *that* Mrs FitzGerald! I'll be back with something for you tomorrow.' True to his word, he found us a beautiful house, with its own beach and pier, from which one could swim. The only disadvantage of the proprty was its collection of Burmese antiques – to the survival of which holidaying children might be a hazard.

During the course of the month of August, over a score of people stayed with us, including Frank Cluskey, later to be leader of the Labour Party, and his wife and son, and we had almost forty other visitors, including the Tánaiste, Brendan Corish, and his wife Phyllis, and Conor and Maire Cruise O'Brien, as well as the Danish foreign minister, K. B. Andersen, and his wife, who dropped in during the course of a farmhouse tour of Ireland.

But in the context of this chapter, the most significant visitors were Jim and Audrey Callaghan, who were staying with their daughter, Margaret Jay, and her husband, Peter, at their house in nearby Glandore. We had two meetings with the Callaghans: one a dinner engagement at the Jays' together with Jack and Mairin Lynch, and the other a lunch at our house a few days later, with Brendan and Phyllis Corish. (Jack and Mairin Lynch, to whose house we had been invited earlier in the month for their traditional August party, were to have been with us on the second occasion also, but he had to go unexpectedly to Dublin to pay a last visit to Eamon de Valera, who was dying.) In preparation for these two social occasions, I asked my department to prepare suggestions of points I should make if I got the opportunity to do so. I arranged for Conor Cruise O'Brien, with whom I had discussed the proposed Callaghan meeting, to make an input to this briefing.

Early on in the after-dinner discussion on the first of these occasions, Jim Callaghan disclosed that he had disagreed with the handling of the Workers' Strike. His view was that the British government should not have given in to the strikers but should have sat it out.

I stressed the gravity of the problem that would be created for us should there be another failure on the part of the British government to control the situation and to protect the minority. It would not be within our power to resolve the situation that would then have been created, and such a failure could threaten democratic government in our state. When Jim Callaghan suggested that this was too pessimistic a view, I pointed to the situation that had arisen after the massacre at Derry in early 1972, when the government of the day had not been able to prevent the burning of the British embassy. Jack Lynch supported me, pointing also to the problems that he had faced in 1969–70. I emphasised the danger of a political vacuum being created in Ireland, in which extra-European powers, such as the Soviet Union, China or Libya, could be tempted to meddle.

When Peter Jay asked whether, in a hypothetical doomsday situation, there was a possibility of joint action by the Irish and British armies in Northern Ireland, Jim Callaghan said that this was a possibility in certain circumstances, but that the British government would not abdicate its responsibilities and would take the necessary action to deal with a doomsday situation. I then moved on to point out the imbalance of armed forces in Ireland at that time. When I said that our army was only 12,500 strong and could not be increased to a level that would afford us security without such an action appearing provocative to unionists, Jim Callaghan challenged this, saying that we could raise it to 20,000 without having this effect. Eventually, however, when I pointed out that such an increase would require the calling up of reserves or the introduction of conscription, he did not further contest the point.

I went on to remark that the British army's strength in the North had been sharply reduced. On the other hand, the strength of the UDR and the RUC Reserve (which could not be relied on in a doomsday situation, and which had been allowed to grow to 14,000) would be likely to support the 20,000-to-25,000-strong loyalist paramilitaries. Even on the assumption that the RUC remained neutral until it saw who won, there was now a dangerous imbalance between the strength of the regular armies and that of other forces in Ireland. Jim Callaghan did not contest thisl and said that it had been a mistake to allow the new security forces established in Northern Ireland to exceed 4,000.

The discussion then turned to internment. When Jack Lynch and I were pressed on whether it would be possible for us to introduce internment in a crisis, we explained that the abuse of this weapon by the British and Northern Ireland governments in 1971 had discredited internment in Irish eyes, but it was Mairin Lynch who said that even in circumstances in which a British government was seen to be tackling a doomsday situation in the North, Fianna Fáil might not accept the introduction of internment in our state. But when she mentioned the idea of a British declaration of intent to withdraw from Northern Ireland after a period, her husband said that in the present unstable and emotional atmosphere, such a declaration would be highly dangerous – a view with which I wholeheartedly concurred.

At the end of the discussion, Jim Callaghan referred to his membership of the Irish Committee of the Cabinet in terms that suggested that he was a bit unhappy either about his own inability to attend it or about it not having met. He also speculated semi-humorously as to whether it might not have been better for him to have been Secretary of State for Northern Ireland – a suggestion that Jack Lynch and I warmly endorsed.

In my report on this discussion, I commented that Jim Callaghan had seemed genuinely convinced of the importance of Britain staying in Northern Ireland and making a stand against the loyalist paramilitaries, and that I thought we had significantly reinforced his view about the danger to Britain as well as Ireland of Britain not fulfilling its responsibilities there – but there could be a danger that, as a last resort, he might be prepared to consider repartition, with an exchange of populations.

When he came to lunch with us three days later, he was very taken with the house we had rented: as we walked down to the pier together, he wondered whether it might be for sale. Harold Wilson had told him that he would give him three months' notice if he intended to retire, so that Jim Callaghan might prepare to succeed him, but he did not think that Wilson would take this step in the foreseeable future, and accordingly, as he was older than Wilson, he was contemplating retiring, possibly in 1976. The house we had rented was the kind of place he would love to be able to stay in after retiring.

After lunch, he reverted to the discussion we had had three nights earlier. He wondered whether Jack Lynch might not have expressed a less negative view on internment if Mairin Lynch had not intervened first to give her own view of Fianna Fáil's likely reaction to the introduction of internment in our state in the event of a doomsday situation in the North being tackled firmly by the British government. I had wondered the same thing myself. He went on to ask a number of questions, including some designed to verify his recollection of the figures I had given for the strength of various forces in Northern Ireland, as well as questions about various political leaders in the North.

He went on to say that in a doomsday situation, Harold Wilson would be 'all right', but there would be a number of people on the Labour benches who would support disengagement, and a number of Tories who would support the loyalists. For his own part, he attached great importance to the relationship between Britain and Ireland, which he recognised as depending essentially on Britain taking on its full responsibilities in Northern Ireland.

I said that the Anglo-Irish relationship had been less close since the Ulster Workers' Strike. Was this because they had failed to act, he asked. I replied that this was in part the reason but that the problem derived more from continuing uncertainty about British policy, aggravated by the discussions taking place with Sinn Féin. We did not feel that we had been brought fully into the confidence of the British government during the course of the current year and, to put it very mildly, the information given to us on these talks had at times been in arrear of events. It was a matter of deep concern to us that talks with Sinn Féin that had begun on the basis of 'clarifying' aspects of British policy that had allegedly been misunderstood by the IRA should have gone on to include discussion of a declaration of intent to withdraw – as even the British account of the talks had ultimately made clear. At the very least, there now seemed to be reason to think that officials had allowed the IRA to continue to believe that a declaration of intent to withdraw would be considered by Britain if and when the convention talks broke down.

Jim Callaghan said that he doubted whether British officials would have acted in this way. They sometimes acted beyond their authority, but this was a rare event. He went on to ask whether Merlyn Rees – who was, he said, a close friend of his – had been made aware of our feeling of uncertainty and of not being in the full confidence of the British government. Had we spoken to Merlyn Rees as bluntly as we had spoken to him? I said that we had not, adding diplomatically that Merlyn Rees was, we knew, under very great pressure. I thought it better at that stage not to press the point about Merlyn Rees's refusal to meet us during the life of the Convention.

My caution was immediately rewarded. Did I think that a joint meeting between Merlyn Rees, himself and myself would be a good thing, he asked. That could be very valuable, I responded, with an inward sigh of relief: we had made a breakthrough – or at least so I hoped! He would try to arrange this, he said, taking it up at the next meeting of the Irish committee of the Cabinet, whenever that would be.

There the matter was left. In the analysis of the current situation that I prepared two days after this second discussion with Jim Callaghan, I noted that there seemed now to be a real possibility of pursuing more actively our policy of seeking to ensure that Britain took its responsibilities in Northern Ireland, protecting the minority against any loyalist assault and not conceding a declaration of intent to withdraw. A frank discussion between the two secretaries of state and myself, followed possibly by a further Cosgrave/Wilson meeting, might, I believed, re-establish confidence between the two governments and open the possibility of our pursuing a joint policy in the event of an autumn breakdown of the Convention discussions.

About ten days later, when Jim Callaghan and myself met again in New York on the occasion of a UN special session, he was still keen on a joint meeting involving Merlyn Rees, himself and myself. But a week after that, I had a further discussion with him in Venice, in the margin of a European Political Co-operation meeting, at which it became clear that Merlyn Rees had taken amiss his proposal for a joint meeting. I formed the impression that Jim Callaghan may have decided that it was more tactful in terms of his relations with Merlyn Rees to turn his suggestion for such a joint meeting into a request from me – with predictable consequences!

It was indeed clear that Jim Callaghan had not merely met resistance to his idea of a joint meeting between Merlyn Rees, himself and myself but had been told to head off the idea of any meeting whilst the Convention continued. The possibility of restoring some kind of trust and confidence between the two governments, never mind developing a common strategy towards the post-Convention situation, had been aborted by Merlyn Rees's determination to avoid any contact with us.

It soon became clear, however, that despite his claim not to have talked 'seriously' to Merlyn Rees since Schull, Jim Callaghan had in fact been fully briefed by him. For he went on to say that he had checked on the matters raised by me on several occasions in Schull – whether the British government had been allowing an impression to arise that it might contemplate a 'pull-out' from Northern Ireland – and Merlyn Rees had told him that he was quite clear that there had been 'no such statement' by Sir Frank Cooper or anyone else. Jim Callaghan wanted to assure me that such a proposal had not come before the Cabinet – and he was in a privileged position to know this – nor had it been before any 'official committee', nor had there been any such statement to anyone. This was as categorical a denial as he could make, he added, for he wanted to remove any lingering doubts as to the British government's attitude – 'to date'. The last two words were stressed but were accompanied by the slightly humorous smile that was often a feature of his delivery – as if to say that the British government's conscience was clear so far, but that the future was never wholly predictable. That at any rate was the impression of the official accompanying me on that occasion.

Of course I had never said that there had been a statement to Provisional Sinn Féin about a possible British declaration of intent to withdraw, but only that British officials might have allowed the IRA to derive such an impression and to continue to believe that such a declaration might be made in the event of a breakdown of the Convention. I pointed this out to him, but there the matter was left, apart from an additional comment by him that British policy after the probable break-up of the Convention would be direct rule – although he added, worryingly, I thought, that they would then 'look at whatever forces may emerge'.

However, as we now know from Bernard Donoghue's book, when the British Cabinet committee on Northern Ireland met on 25 November, Jim Callaghan, backed by Denis Healey and Merlyn Rees, faced down Harold Wilson on his

Northern Ireland withdrawal project, and that was the end of the matter – even though when he resigned from the premiership a few months later, Wilson left behind a personal document recommending such a policy to a future government!

In 1976 we became worried about the attitude of the Conservatives under Margaret Thatcher to Northern Ireland. I decided to tackle her on this issue. When I arrived in her room in the Commons, she was not yet there. Willie Whitelaw and Reggie Maudling were waiting for me, however, and I had to head off discussion until she arrived. I then started by suggesting that it might be better if our meeting were kept private lest it be connected in the public mind with the controversy about the Strasbourg case that had just been making the headlines. It was immediately clear that while Willie Whitelaw knew of the row, neither Margaret Thatcher nor Reggie Maudling had heard anything about this exchange of fire. Recovering from my astonishment at their ignorance of what had been happening, I pointed out that two successive British governments had committed themselves to power-sharing in any devolved government in Northern Ireland, adding that a new situation had now arisen.

Both Margaret Thatcher and Willie Whitelaw immediately challenged me, asking what on earth I could mean: how could there be a new situation? Was I referring to their party conference, she went on to ask? No, I replied, the problem that needed attention antedated the conference. The SDLP had been seriously demoralised by the circumstances of the breakdown of their talks with the OUP at the end of the Convention, and there was a real danger of their moving to the position of calling for a declaration of intent by Britain to withdraw from Northern Ireland. Given the shift in Fianna Fáil policy forced on Jack Lynch a year earlier, a movement also by the SDLP to such a policy position would endanger the joint policy of the two states. Firm action was needed to restore the situation.

What action, asked Margaret Thatcher and Willie Whitelaw. The minimum needed, I replied, was for the British government and Opposition to reassert in unequivocal terms their adherence to the policy of no devolution without power-sharing. This would steady the SDLP and at the same time weaken the more intransigent elements on the unionist side by removing their belief that a change of government in Britain would give them back majority rule.

How could anyone think that this could happen, enquired my two interlocutors. (Reggie Maudling had remained silent throughout our discussion.) Their policy had not changed one iota.

They might feel that, I responded, but unfortunately that was not how people in Ireland saw the position – especially the unionists. Speeches by the Conservative spokesman on Northern Ireland, Airey Neave, had either omitted any reference to power-sharing, when such a reference would have been relevant, or had seemed to modify or water down this commitment.

They demurred at this. I had expected this reaction and, before going to see them, had asked my officials to boil down the six-thousand-word brief they had given me on the matter into a summary listing all of Airey Neave's score of recorded statements since his appointment as shadow spokesman on Northern Ireland – none of which had contained any positive reference to power-sharing in government and a number of which had been dismissive of the concept. I handed a copy of this to Margaret Thatcher. I could see that the presentation of this document was unwelcome to her, but there had been no other way in which I could prove conclusively my point about Airey Neave.

I went on to tell her and her colleagues that in my own personal contacts with a unionist leader during the year, he had repeatedly insisted that he was confident that the Conservative policy would change and that they would restore majority rule – and in my most recent encounter I felt that he now believed what, earlier, he had merely hoped. It was our clear impression that this, amongst other factors, had influenced the decision by the Official Unionist Party to terminate their talks with the SDLP.

The reality of the unionist illusions about Tory policy was now beginning to impinge on my listeners, even though they were careful not to admit this. What should be done, I was again asked. I replied that if the government, which we believed was now convinced of the seriousness of the problem, took an opportunity to clarify their position, it was essential that this should be unambiguously and immediately endorsed by the Conservative Opposition. It would be helpful if this could be followed by a major speech by Margaret Thatcher herself on Northern Ireland.

She replied that she had hitherto avoided talking about political aspects of Northern Ireland; she was impressed by the sense of fear of people living in Northern Ireland and had accordingly confined herself to security matters. But she did not exclude making such a speech. However she could not, of course, commit herself to any course of action until she had had an opportunity to talk to Airey Neave. I said that I fully understood this.

I then moved the discussion on to other aspects of Northern Ireland policy – security policy, in relation to which I said humorously that it would help if we were not praised more than twice a week by British politicians. She responded that she could arrange to keep it down to once a week!

Margaret Thatcher then asked me why politicians in Northern Ireland could not reach agreement with each other. As I tried to explain the depth of the differences between them, it became clear that she was labouring under the delusion that the majority Convention Report had involved a proposal for emergency power-sharing over a five-year period! Willie Whitelaw and I patiently put her right on this, to which she said, oh, yes, she remembered now that this had been a proposal of Bill Craig's, but she was clearly unaware of the context of Craig's proposal, and I went back and explained just what had happened, and why his initiative had failed. When I said that Paisley was a major problem, she expressed surprise. Willie Whitelaw emphatically agreed with me, however, and I went on to explain Paisley's dominant position, deriving in part at least from the fact that he was perceived amongst unionists as having brought down successive leaders of their party who had been prepared to try to accommodate the minority in some degree.

At the end of our discussion, I renewed my earlier invitation to her to visit Dublin, but from the tone of her response I knew that she had no intention of coming in the near future. As I left, I was torn between dismay at the fact that even after eighteen months of party leadership she was still so poorly briefed on Northern Ireland, and a measure of hope that I might have made sufficient impact to reverse the drift in Conservative policy under Airey Neave's shadow-spokesman-ship.

My representations paid off. Shortly afterwards, Airey Neave wrote to the OUP leader, Harry West, reaffirming Conservative support for power-sharing.

Early in 1976, a serious problem had arisen in connection with the funeral of Frank Stagg. Our government was very conscious of what had happened in 1974, when Michael Gaughan had died in Parkhurst Prison following a sixty-five-day hunger strike in support of a claim for political status. His funeral in both Britain and Ireland was the occasion for demonstrations of support by IRA adherents, which caused concern in both islands. Following that funeral, a fellow hunger striker, Frank Stagg, had been ordered by the IRA to take food. But after a further hunger strike later that year, he had embarked on a third attempt; he died in prison on 12 February 1976.

The IRA wanted to repeat the propaganda exercise of the Gaughan funeral, despite the fact that Frank Stagg's widow, who lived in England, desired a private funeral. She was threatened by the IRA with being shot through the head if she pressed her view. We were told that the authorities in Britain had refused to accord her a police guard on her home and had entered into a deal under which it had been agreed to ignore her right to her husband's remains, and to hand them over to the IRA to bring to Ireland in return for agreement by the IRA to confine their demonstrations to our island. That organisation proposed to parade the coffin through Dublin and various other towns before bringing it to Ballina, County Mayo, for internment.

Stagg's widow approached us on the matter. I was appalled at the British actions, whoever had authorised them, and sent an immediate message to Roy Jenkins that unless he assured me within three hours that Mrs Stagg's wishes would be respected, and the deal with the IRA repudiated, I would call a press conference to expose this macabre plot between authorities in Britain and the IRA.

I got an immediate response. The body was brought to London Airport, where it was handed over to us, and we arranged for the aircraft bringing it back to Ireland to be diverted from Dublin to Shannon. Meanwhile Mrs Stagg flew to Dublin from Birmingham on a flight on which IRA supporters, including other relatives of Frank Stagg, were also travelling. At Dublin Airport, she was met and brought to a different hotel from that in which the others were staying, and was provided with Garda protection.

At six o'clock the following morning, she was brought to Garda Headquarters, where Pat Cooney and I met her. We were appalled to hear that, despite the precautions taken, her room had been invaded during the night and for three hours she had been subjected to intimidation designed to 'persuade' her to hand over her husband's remains to the IRA – intimidation that, with great courage, she had resisted.

We told her that we would respect her wishes and that in view of the pressure she was under, we would understand if she decided to release her husband's body to the IRA – although we would not allow them to bring it to Dublin or on a tour of the country. She said she wanted her husband's body to be brought to Ballina under escort for a funeral Mass there, after which, if the IRA wanted to take charge of the interment locally, she would not resist this. We accepted this, but when the IRA heard that they were not to be allowed to bring the body on a tour of the country, they refused to accept this proposal and took no part in the funeral. Although we took the precaution of placing a concrete slab over the grave to prevent desecration, and guarded the grave for a period after the funeral, the IRA later exhumed the coffin and reburied it in a 'republican plot'. From that dreadful episode, I retain the memory of a remarkably courageous and dignified woman, who was supported throughout by her husband's brother, Emmet Stagg, later to be elected as a left-wing Labour TD.

Early in July I had attended, as I had done most years since its establishment, the annual conference of the British-Irish Association in Britain. There I met the newly appointed British ambassador to Ireland, Christopher Ewart-Biggs. I found him charming and unconventional: we would, I felt, be able to establish a good personal relationship.

He was to pay his first official visit to me at 10 AM on 21 July. As I had finished clearing my desk to receive him, I was told that there had been an explosion near his residence. Soon word arrived that he and a secretary had been killed by a bomb detonated under his car. The permanent secretary to the Northern Ireland Office, Brian Cubbon, and the driver had been seriously injured. Merlyn Rees would have been in the car as well but for a vote in the House of Commons the previous night that had unexpectedly detained him.

I was filled with horror at the atrocity, with shame that Irishmen had murdered the envoy of a neighbouring country, and with shock at our failure to protect him. During a phone call with the British embassy, I was told that his widow, whom I had also met at the British-Irish conference, had heard the news of the explosion in

London on her car radio and was shortly leaving for Dublin on a special flight. As soon as I heard the expected time of her arrival, Joan and I drove to Baldonnell to meet her. Because the British embassy staff were slightly delayed, we were in fact the only people there when she and Mrs Cubbon stepped off the plane.

During the days that followed, we did what we could to comfort her and her children. And at the memorial service in St Patrick's Cathedral, it fell to me to express the horror and shame of the Irish people. It was one of the most difficult moments I had experienced; I am not good at controlling my emotions on such occasions, but fortunately I succeeded – although I do not think anyone could have been in doubt as to how deeply I felt this tragedy.

The reaction of Jane Ewart-Biggs was – and remained thereafter – a noble demonstration of Christian charity. She might, forgivably, have turned against Ireland and everything Irish; instead, she took to her heart the country that had deprived her of her husband, and worked thenceforward for reconciliation amongst Irish people and between Ireland and Britain. Our two countries are deeply in her debt.

Another issue that tested the Anglo-Irish relationship during these months was the case we had taken to the European Commission on Human Rights at Strasbourg regarding the brutalisation of many of those interned in 1971. We had hoped that a friendly settlement might have been reached, but the British government had not felt able to respond in a manner that we could accept.

To minimise tension between the two countries, it was agreed that neither side would brief the press in advance of the publication of the report of the European Commission on Human Rights on 2 September and the announcement of our decision on the next step in the case. To my fury, and that of our government, this agreement was breached on our side a week or so earlier, in circumstances that were never clarified. Naturally enough, the British felt justified in retaliating. Their briefing to their press very successfully diverted attention from the finding of the report: that the combined use of five interrogation techniques, developed by the British army in Aden and introduced by them to the RUC's Special Branch, constituted 'not only inhuman and degrading treatment but also torture'.

In particular, we were accused of bringing the matter unnecessarily before the European Court of Human Rights. The fact was – as I pointed out, unavailingly, to the British media – that once the friendly settlement procedure had failed, we were *required* by the Strasbourg procedures to bring the commissions's report either before the Committee of Ministers of the Council of Europe or before the European Court of Human Rights. We chose the latter in order to avoid unnecessary damage to the Anglo-Irish relationships through a politicisation of our differences in the Committee of Ministers of the Council. The British knew, of course, why we had chosen this course, and some at least on the British side appreciated our motivation; but this did not prevent the misrepresentation of our position by the British government to the press – a misrepresentation that, as the editorials in the British papers showed, proved highly successful.

With the defeat of our government in 1977, my direct involvement with Northern Ireland ended for the time being. I summed up my feelings about this period of my life in the course of my first speech as Fine Gael leader in Dáil Éireann on 6 July, in these words: 'My greatest source of pride is a remark by a Northern politician [John Hume] that our government had won more respect from both sections in the North than any previous government had won from either'.

15

~: Leading the Opposition :~

In the immediate aftermath of the June 1977 election, there was a Thursday party meeting to review the national results. Liam Cosgrave chose this occasion to announce his resignation as leader. He paid tribute to his Fine Gael colleagues in government, mentioning only one by name, myself. Given our difficult relationship in the past and the fact that I was obviously going to be a candidate for the succession, this caused some comment.

When he finished speaking, there were moves from the parliamentary party to persuade him to change his mind. These did not take off: almost everyone knew that Liam Cosgrave was not the man to use a resignation offer as a ploy to get himself drafted back into the leadership. Once he had decided to go, he was not going to be shifted from his decision; he made this bluntly clear in his inimitable, uncompromising manner. These were followed by valedictory speeches. Then he proposed that the election of his successor take place in eight days' time, on Friday 1 July. He clearly did not wish a repetition of the procedure by which he had himself been proposed without warning to a party meeting that had endorsed him without time for reflection.

When the meeting ended, at around five o'clock, I was due to leave for the annual OECD meeting in Paris. Joan was in the car outside, with our luggage, ready to leave for the airport. I went down to her and told her what had happened; we must abandon the Paris visit and I would join her later at home.

I then had discussions with some of the other possible candidates for the leadership, with a view to agreeing a tentative modus operandi. Richie Ryan, the Minister for Finance, was at a meeting in Washington and was then due to travel to Luxemburg; he was not expected back in Ireland until the following Tuesday. It was agreed that any of us who decided to contest the leadership should not canvas for support until Tuesday; otherwise, if Richie were a candidate – as then seemed likely – he would be at a disadvantage vis-à-vis those of us at home. Shortly afterwards, John Kelly indicated that he would be available but would not seek the position. This offer was not pursued; for although until his unexpectedly and untimely death in early 1991, he was extraordinarily popular and greatly admired both inside and outside the party, his individualistic temperament did not attract support for him as a leader of the party.

Returning home, I rang Richie in Washington; he had already heard the news of Liam's resignation. I told him of our 'no canvassing' agreement, but urged him to return as soon as possible; it would be hard to hold this line for long as far as the potential candidate supporters were concerned. He said he could not get out of his Luxemburg commitment but would travel there via Ireland. Joan and I then took advantage of an invitation to dine with Mary and Nick Robinson in Roundwood, County Wicklow, which we had earlier turned down, because of our Paris commitment.

Next day the papers reported that I was the favourite in the Fine Gael leadership stakes. A group of TDs came to see me to tell me that they supported my candidature and that from initial soundings they believed I would have majority support. I was grateful for their initiative but told them that, as had been agreed amongst the potential candidates, I would not be approaching anyone before Tuesday, and I asked them – without, as it turned out, much success – to limit themselves to soundings, as distinct from seeking support for me.

At the weekend, Richie Ryan passed through Ireland en route from Washington to Luxembourg, saying only briefly in Dublin and then stopping in Cork to meet Peter Barry.

I remained in daily amicable contact with Peter Barry during this period. I recall one discussion in the course of which he said that he thought that I would be a better leader than he in Opposition but that he might be better able to cope with government. By Monday, he had emerged as the only other candidate in the field, subject to Richie Ryan's still-unknown intentions. He believed that in any event I would win but that in order to avoid what had happened in 1965, it was important to have a contest.

On Tuesday I methodically phoned the members of the party. One phone call sticks in my mind particularly: John Boland. He cross-examined me for almost half an hour on my intentions as leader. We had never been close, and he can hardly have thought that this somewhat aggressive approach would endear him to me, but in fact I was impressed, and decided that he should be on my front bench if I were chosen as leader.

That night I rang Peter Barry to compare notes. The total electorate – the Fine Gael members of the new Dáil and those Fine Gael members of the old Seanad who had not been elected to the Dáil in the recent election – was sixty-two. I reckoned that I had the support of something like forty-three, leaving Peter with just under twenty. He, on the other hand, believed he had twenty-five supporters, and was slightly upset that our figures did not tally. I told him that if only half a dozen members of the party – less than 10 percent – had allowed both of us to believe they were our supporters, that showed a remarkably high level of political honesty!

Given that there had been ample time for reflection by the party, he felt that my authority would be undisputed even if on Friday I were chosen without a vote; so he announced his withdrawal. And on Richie's return from Luxembourg, it emerged that he too was unlikely to stand.

On Friday the party met, and on the proposing of Peter Barry I was chosen as leader without a contest. Simultaneously the Labour Party was also meeting to elect a leader, for Brendan Corish had resigned on the previous Sunday. The Labour TDs (only Fine Gael accords a say to senators in such matters) elected Frank Cluskey as a leader by nine votes to seven for Michael O'Leary.

After my election, I paid tribute to the generous and considerate way in which Liam Cosgrave had led his government. And I told the party that if my performance commended itself to them, I would serve for a decade. In the event, I remained leader for nine and three-quarter years – close enough! In case there should be any doubt on the matter, in view of my pre-1973 record of multiple careers, I added that I would be a full-time leader. Finally I told them that I would appoint my front bench in September, and in the meantime the eight Fine Gael ex-ministers re-elected to the Dáil would constitute an ad hoc front bench.

Later, I met the press. Foreshadowing the changes I envisaged in our party's role, but also anxious to reassure more traditional supporters, I said that if a new emphasis were needed to preserve or improve our society, this must be explored, but a consensus must be sought and secured in order to avoid a polarisation of the generations. I saw this as a potential danger of the 1980s, given that at the next election, due in 1981 or 1982, one-third of the electorate would be under thirty-two years of age and that our older population was very conservative. The energies of this young electorate – much larger in relation to the population as a whole than in any other industrial country – must, I said, be constructively channelled. There was a need also for a reintroduction of idealism and of a sense of the overall interest of society as against the dominance of sectoral interests fighting with each other for scarce resources. I went on to assert that Fine Gael was the party best equipped to tackle these tasks and should combine its traditional concern for personal independence and freedom with concern for those in our society who were unable to provide for themselves.

Having thus reasserted the social-democratic principles of the Just Society policies of the 1960s, I went on to stress the importance of not weakening the coalition option with Labour, so that at all times an alternative government would be available, and to assert also that the friendship and contacts between our two parties would endure – a sentiment that was given visible form in the next day's papers, which published photographs of Frank Cluskey and myself together after our respective elections. I took the opportunity moreover of a television interview following the press conference to appeal directly to people to join our party.

Next day I wrote a message to the party organisation, emphasising my determination to strengthen links between the constituencies and the party, which had inevitably been weakened during our period in government. I told them that I proposed to visit all the constituencies at weekends during the winter and the spring ahead, for business rather than social purposes, in order to have serious discussions with the local organisation, and also to hold public meetings in every area. (This was a new concept in Irish politics, with which I had experimented when in Opposition in the early 1970s.) And I asked our activists to welcome new members who might join in response to my television appeal.

That done, I had to turn my attention briefly back to government affairs – for we were still in government, and Liam Cosgrave was still Taoiseach. During this period, the government had been making appointments to fill various vacancies in the judiciary and on the boards of state enterprises. I was unhappy with his procedure; it seemed to me that, without prejudice to the quality of these appointments, if a government had failed to fill such vacancies before or during an election campaign, it should refrain from making good this failure after it had clearly lost the confidence of the electorate at the polls. This view was not popular with some of my colleagues. Nevertheless, I resolved that in any government that I led, this inappropriate practice would not be followed. On Tuesday 5 July, the new Dáil assembled and elected Jack Lynch as Taoiseach by eighty-two votes to sixty-one.

At an early stage in the life of the new government, I arranged with Jack Lynch an increase in the state allowance to the parties and a new transport allowance for Opposition leaders. My own financial needs as a full-time leader were met by a decision of the ad hoc front bench at its first meeting to recommend to the party trustees that I be paid an allowance equivalent to that received by a minister.

The advent of the summer recess enabled me to concentrate on my preparations for reorganising the party. The general secretary, Commandant Jim Sanfey, had decided to retire, enabling me to broaden the scope of the job by recruiting a national organiser who would also carry out the functions of general secretary. From 1966 to his tragic death in a car accident in February 1970, Gerry Sweetman, a man of exceptional energy, had combined his parliamentary duties with the role of national organiser. Thereafter the post had in effect been vacant, and the party had suffered accordingly. I was convinced that we needed a national organiser from outside the parliamentary party, as well as a full-time press and public relations officer; and with the approval of the ad hoc front bench, I advertised these two posts.

The successful applicant for the post of national organiser was Peter

Prendergast, who in 1973 had been selected as a candidate in my constituency and had stood again in the recent election – unsuccessfully on both occasions. Ted Nealon, the television presenter and commentator, had, to my great pleasure, applied for the PRO position, and was appointed. They were a formidable pair who worked well together, Ted Nealon in Leinster House and Peter Prendergast in our head office in nearby Hume Street.

Ted benefited from being already a national figure. The party was delighted that he had thrown in his lot with us, and he was greeted with enthusiasm throughout our organisation. Highly regarded in journalistic circles, he had easy access to the media, where his established reputation as a political commentator was a major asset.

Peter had been a member at different times both of the National Council, comprising representatives of constituencies, and the National Executive, the body responsible for party organisation. As a result he was widely known to Fine Gael people throughout the country. This had disadvantages as well as advantages, for he had made enemies as well as friends, and while he had the confidence of some key people in almost every constituency, others were more negative towards him. However, it is more important for a party organiser to be widely feared than universally liked, and the important thing was that he already knew intimately our organisation at local level – and knew whom he could, or could not, trust.

At no point in the past had our party organisation ever matched the professionalism of Fianna Fáil, and in opposition in the 1930s and 1940s it had declined rather than developed. Peter Prendergast's ambition was, by hook or by crook, to remedy this defect. Under his skilful, subtle – some would say Machiavellian! – guidance, Fine Gael was to reach and surpass in sheer professionalism its hitherto dominant rival. Such an achievement was not attained without trauma.

When Peter and I sat down to review what had to be done, we found ourselves in immediate and instinctive agreement. During my years in the party I had observed, as he had, the disastrous effects in many constituencies of the dominance of the local deputy over the organisation in his area. In the Irish multi-seat constituency system, deputies feel threatened more by their colleagues than by their political opponents. Many of ours had been unable to resist the temptation to use their position as the only Fine Gael deputy in a constituency to dominate their local organisation and, consciously or otherwise, to discourage or prevent the emergence of a strong second candidate, who might perhaps win a seat, but who, alternatively, might in the attempt to do so succeed only in displacing the sitting TD.

Extracting the branches in each constituency from under the thumb of the local TDs was only one of our urgent needs. A replacement had also to be found for our poky head office in Hume Street, which contrasted so badly with the relatively impressive Fianna Fáil building in Upper Mount Street. And, far more vital, the base of the party's support had to be broadened. I determined to attract as large a proportion as possible of the younger generation, whose voting strength was currently being greatly increased by the upsurge in the birth rate of the 1960s and the lowering of the voting age to eighteen in 1972. At the same time, I believed that we should try to unleash the political potential of women, whose consciousness of their own worth and rights had been aroused by the non-political – even at times anti-political – feminist movement of the early 1970s. Such objectives as these demanded radical change, and radical change required a new approach to decision-making within the party. My tour of the constituencies would provide the opportunity for rallying support behind my ideas, which hopefully would result in approval for a revised party constitution at my first party conference or *ard fheis*.

On 14 September, before embarking on my tour, I announced my front bench. My plan had been to appoint Mark Clinton as deputy leader. He was a senior and respected party member who had been a very popular Minister for Agriculture from 1973 to 1977 and came from the more conservative wing of the party. He turned down my suggestion firmly, on grounds of age: he was sixty-two. (Two years later, he was elected to the European Parliament, where he served with distinction for a full decade!)

In these circumstances, I appointed to this position Peter Barry, from the centre of the party; in July, he had emerged as my main potential rival for the leadership. He filled the key shadow portfolio of Economic Affairs, including Finance and the Public Service. Almost all the available former ministers were included, with Ritchie Ryan in Foreign Affairs and Pat Cooney, defeated in the Dáil election and now in the Seanad, as Leader of that House. Alexis FitzGerald was his deputy. John Bruton held the Agriculture shadow portfolio, John Kelly that of Industry and Commerce. Two new deputies, Jim Mitchell and Jim O'Keeffe, were given responsibility for Labour and for Law Reform and Human Rights, respectively – which I separated out from the security-dominated Justice portfolio. While I retained overall responsibility for Northern Ireland affairs, Paddy Harte took responsibility under me for this area, and for the security side of Justice.

These appointments made, I set out on my tour of constituencies. I decided that each visit should normally comprise a meeting with the constituency organisation to elicit their views on organisational matters and to encourage them to think radically about these issues; a meeting with the local Fine Gael councillors, who seemed to me to be very loosely linked to the party at national level; and a public meeting, which I would address for half an hour about my vision for Ireland's future, followed by a question-and-answer session for about an hour and a half. As our efforts to interest more young people in politics began to bear fruit, I later added a separate meeting for this group. I excluded attendance at social functions, which in the Irish political system do not start until 11 PM or later and often continue till 3 or 4 AM, during which time one is expected to talk seriously to everyone against blaring music on the dance floor. I hate loud noise, and find such occasions physically exhausting – something that inevitably becomes evident to my hosts.

Following this pattern, I visited about half the constituencies between September and December 1977. I was well, indeed enthusiastically, received. Following our sweeping defeat, a new leader was bound to be a source of hope, and my more relaxed and open style by comparison with that of my predecessor suited the mood of the late 1970s. By Christmas it was clear that my assessment of the need for radical organisational change was quite widely shared – although not, of course, by many TDs, some of whom were beginning to rumble what I was at. The process of reform in which I was engaged was helped by the fact that, in contrast to myself, Peter Prendergast knew a vast number of members of our organisation locally and could quickly identify those who were open to change – and those who were likely to oppose the necessary reforms.

The scale and consistency of support for the kind of changes I had in mind was, however, such that by Christmas I decided to take a short cut. Rather than waiting for the end of my constituency visits before putting forward a draft new party constitution, I decided to launch it in February as a basis for discussion during the second half of my tour.

The most important single change I proposed in our party constitution was in the method of electing the national executive. Hitherto this body had tended to represent the interests of TDs rather than the party as a whole, because the National Council – a body representative of constituency organisations, many of which were in effect controlled by a local TD – elected twelve members, and the parliamentary party a further eight. Even the national officer posts – four vice-presidents and two honorary secretaries – had until the early 1970s normally being held by prominent TDs, whose nominations for election by the *ard fheis* had until the early 1970s rarely been contested.

My new Constitution proposed to transfer to the *ard fheis* the power to elect most of those hitherto chosen by the National Council. The general members represented at the *ard fheis* would tend to be more interested in the future of Fine Gael than in the fate of individual TDs.

As I had anticipated, the party members found this proposal so attractive that when the new Constitution came before the *ard fheis* in May, that body voted to increase its representation from my modest suggestion of eight to twelve. Some three dozen other amendments to my initial draft, some proposed by me as a result of comments made during the second part of my tour, but most put forward by the *ard fheis* itself, were adopted, with the result that the members of Fine Gael could legitimately feel that the final document was their Constitution as well as mine.

Among the important new features accepted by the *ard fheis* was a provision for a Young Fine Gael organisation, independent of, but of course linked to, the senior party, which was given substantial voting strength at constituency level, despite the qualms of many older members. Women members of the party, incidentally, turned down my offer to establish a Fine Gael women's organisation, preferring at that time to rely on the momentum of the national women's movement and on my own support and encouragement. To overcome the excessive rural bias in our structure, I made provision for weighting branch representation by reference to the electorate in a branch area; and so as to encourage new talent to come forward at organisational level, I introduced a maximum of three years for tenure of officerships. And I introduced new posts of constituency organiser and public-relations officer.

The *ard fheis* also approved a provision that within two months of any general election that did not result in the party taking office, the parliamentary party would hold a vote by secret ballot on the leadership. This was designed to reduce tension in the party after an electoral defeat by ensuring that TDs and senators could vote secretly against the leader without having to challenge him or her overtly.

Meanwhile Peter Prendergast and I found suitable premises for our head office. As chance would have it, the building was just opposite Fianna Fáil's headquarters in Upper Mount Street. Having checked that our house was marginally higher (and that therefore we would be able to look down on Fianna Fáil!), I went ahead with the purchase for a sum of £250,000, about twice what the recent general election had cost the party at national level. To finance the ambitious move, we launched a 'Buy a brick' campaign throughout the party organisation, which raised the greater part, although not all, of the purchase price.

The *ard fheis* in May was a huge success. Fianna Fáil had recently moved its *ard fheis* from the traditional venue of both parties – the Round Room of the Mansion in Dublin – to the Great Hall of the Royal Dublin Society, which easily accommodated four thousand people. We had never had more than about half this number at our *ard fheiseanna*, so that to follow Fianna Fáil successfully to this venue would be an immense challenge. The time to take it on was now, when the excitement of radical changes, the debate on the new party Constitution, and proposed policy debates on a wide range of topics, some controversial, would be likely to attract large numbers.

We took the gamble. It paid off. The hall was packed for my first presidential address: there were, I thought, about five thousand people there. Moreover, and more significant perhaps, the attendance at other times was substantial, and the experiment of arranging simultaneous debates in different halls succeeded on this occasion, although it did not prove possible to maintain this conference structure in the years that followed.

My concentration on party organisation and domestic policy matters during this period did not preclude a continued close involvement with Northern Ireland.

At the end of October 1977 I had paid a first visit to Belfast as leader of the Opposition, meeting members of all parties other than the DUP. I was sufficiently encouraged by these contacts to write to Jim Callaghan, Roy Mason and Margaret Thatcher about what seemed to me to be a tentative consensus in principle on the idea of a devolution of executive and legislative authority, subject to withholding the transfer of the final word on legislation until a widely representative executive emerged; but from the replies I received, I had not got the impression that this information about potential common ground was received with much enthusiasm by Roy Mason.

I raised with Jack Lynch at this time the importance of our diplomatic representation in the United States. As a counsellor in our Washington embassy, Michael Lillis had established a relationship with the political leaders on Capitol Hill that had no parallel amongst other EC missions. This was of major importance in relation to Northern Ireland, but it would also be extremely valuable during our next EC presidency, in the second half of the following year. At the time of the change of government a year earlier, I had suggested to the new Taoiseach that the retention of Sean Donlon for a year or so as assistant secretary in the Anglo-Irish division of Foreign Affairs could be very valuable to him, but I now felt that Sean was by far the best-equipped person to exploit to the full, as ambassador to Washington, the spectacular opening that Michael Lillis had achieved. Jack Lynch said that he was inclined to agree; Sean was needed either in Washington or in London, and in the event he appointed him to Washington shortly afterwards. The combination of Sean Donlon and Michael Lillis in that posting was to prove extraordinarily effective.

Throughout these years from 1977 to 1979, I kept in close touch with Jack Lynch as Taoiseach on Northern Ireland affairs. While there were, inevitably, some differences in emphasis between our approaches, we were much closer in our views than he was to the 'rhetorical republicans' of his own party, some of whom had in 1975 secured a shift towards the 'British withdrawal' theme, from which he was clearly most anxious to pull back. I knew that so long as he was in charge, any information I passed on as a result of my contacts in Northern Ireland or with British politicians would be used for constructive purpose, and accordingly I kept the Department of Foreign Affairs, and, where appropriate, Jack himself, fully informed of anything I learnt on these matters.

In mid-February 1978 I had secured the support of my front bench for a public commitment to publish a Fine Gael 'White Paper' on Northern Ireland and for the appointment of a steering committee to assist me with this task. The front-bench members involved were Peter Barry, Paddy Harte, Richie Ryan and Jim O'Keeffe, because of their front-bench positions, as well as John Kelly and Alexis FitzGerald, because of their special knowledge of the problem; Mark Clinton was also asked, and agreed, to join. Work on this policy document went on throughout the following twelve months.

The 'White Paper' based itself firmly on the principle of 'no reunification without consent', which had been fundamental to the policy the party had adopted in 1969, when it also set out the benefits Northern Ireland might secure through a political association with our state. It went on to argue that independence was not a realistic option for Northern Ireland, and it presented an analysis of various political models leading to the conclusion that amongst possible alternatives, the best from Northern Ireland's point of view would be a confederal arrangement. Each part of the island would retain control of its own affairs, save for security, foreign policy (including representation in the EC) and monetary policy, as well as aspects of fiscal policy inextricably related to monetary policy. As the Republic would not be in a position to continue the subsidies currently received from the UK government, provision would be needed within such a confederal structure for a continuance of these subsidies for a number of years, and US and EC aid for Northern Ireland would also be desirable, and might, it was suggested, be available.

The document emphasised the need for Northern Ireland and the Republic to be on a basis of complete equality within this structure, despite the two-to-one population ratio in favour of the Republic. It also stressed the need to ensure that in this new situation, the long-standing relationship that existed between Northern Ireland and Great Britain be respected. An element in this could be the retention of two heads of state of the confederation, to both of whom, and by both of whom, ambassadors could be accredited.

The steering committee and the parliamentary party approved the 'White Paper'. There was only one amendment, which I had rather expected: a specific reference to the monarchy in the context of the suggestion for the possible retention of two heads of state was omitted. This did not matter, as the very concept of two heads of state opened up this possibility.

The document was very favourably received. Fianna Fáil described it in a statement issued to Jack Lynch's instructions as 'well researched and worthy of careful attention'. Even amongst unionists the reaction was not completely negative. Harry West said that 'although it was of no interest, the OUP would be willing to have talks on the document', and on television Martin Smyth took a similar line. Ernest Baird of the VUUP, a unionist splinter group, said that 'it would be less than fair to dismiss it out of hand'. The *Irish Times* described it as 'a message of love, hope and fellowship'. A week later I went to Belfast and spoke about our proposals to a meeting of the East Belfast branch of the SDLP and also in a neutral forum, the non-political Irish Association, where David Trimble gave a unionist reaction.

Following Jack Lynch's resignation, possibly because of the rumours of a Fianna Fáil split that might prevent Charles Haughey's election by the Dáil, on Tuesday

11 December, but also, I think, to allow me time to consult my front bench, I did not start to prepare my speech for the Dáil debate on his election as Taoiseach until the night before the event. I found this a very difficult task. Charles Haughey and I had known each other since the autumn of 1943, when we had met while studying several first-arts and commerce subjects together in UCD; although there were deep differences of personality and outlook, our personal relationship had always been friendly, although never close. In 1961 he had tried to involve me in Fianna Fáil, and in the summer of 1968 we had met on the steps of Government Buildings, and he had confided to me his health worries at the time. A virus infection that he had suffered from in 1967 had now returned, leaving him without enough energy even to go on holiday. (This encounter antedated by some months the car accident to which some have attributed the start of his health problems.) In autumn 1970, after the Arms Crisis, we had met one day on Leinster Lawn, and I was struck by the warmth with which he responded to my greeting. I got the impression that because of recent events he had expected me to pass by without acknowledging him. Later, at the time of the Public Accounts Committee inquiry into that affair, I was accused by some people of 'going easy' in my examination of him as a witness because of our long relationship. In fact this was unfair; I was testing the ground for a much tougher grilling on a subsequent occasion, which never took place, because his brother, Jock, whom we had asked to give evidence, successfully challenged in the Supreme Court our power to compel the attendance of witnesses, and the committee's inquiry was unexpectedly cut short as a result.

The long acquaintance between us could not, however, be allowed to inhibit me from stating in the Dáil before his election as Taoiseach why at that moment I and so many others in all parties regarded him as unsuitable to be head of the Irish government. This, we felt, had to be put firmly on the record. Thereafter, if, as seemed almost certain, he was chosen as Taoiseach, he would have to be accorded the respect due to his office. The task was not made any easier by the knowledge that what I had to say would, because of its necessarily personal character, be badly received by many who would be much more scathing privately than I intended to be about the Taoiseach-designate.

I opened my remarks in the Dáil next day by explaining that because of the inhibitions that would necessarily limit what members of the government party opposed to Charles Haughey could say publicly, I knew that I would have to speak for them as well as for the Opposition. (A number of Fianna Fáil members later thanked me privately for having done so.) Then, having explained the background of my long relationship with Charles Haughey and having acknowledged his talents – the political skills and competence he had shown in the departments in which he had served as minister, which were important qualities in a Taoiseach – I said that in this role these were not enough. All his six predecessors – three of his party and three of mine – had been united by a common bond. They had all come into public life to serve their country, and even their severest enemies had never accused any of them of taking up politics for any motive other than the highest. All had thus commanded the trust of those close to them. Charles Haughey came to the job of Taoiseach, I went on to say, with a flawed pedigree, because he differed from all his predecessors in that his motives had been and were widely impugned, most notably, although not exclusively, by people close to him within his own party. Having observed his actions for many years, these people had made their human interim judgement on him, and they attributed to him an overwhelming ambition not simply to serve the state but to dominate it, and even to own it.

The phrase 'flawed pedigree', an oratorical embellishment that must have owed something to the hour of the night at which I had finally drafted my remarks, achieved lasting fame, being described almost invariably since then as 'that infamous comment'. Although the contrast between him and his predecessors that I had been making was justifiable, I should of course have recognised the danger of using a colourful phrase that could easily be distorted by being taken completely out of the specific context of a comparison between Charles Haughey's and his predecessors' repute among their peers.

The second point I made was that he clearly did not command the genuine confidence of even one-third of the Dáil, although formally he would secure a majority of votes. Many of those who would vote for him, including a clear majority of those who had served with him in government, were withholding their consent in the interior forum, consoling themselves with the hope that they might not have long to serve under a man whom they did not respect. I named many of the ministers who were known to have voted against him and to be bitterly opposed to his leadership, expressing the hope that no one would feel slighted at the omission of his or her honourable name from my list. Of those who had supported him, not all were people ambitious for office, I said; some were inspired rather by a narrow and dangerous nationalism: a patriotism that excluded from the nation as they conceived it one million Irish men and women. They did not believe in seeking unity by consent, but craved unity by constraint. I went on to say that Charles Haughey as Taoiseach would be an uncovenanted bonus for Fine Gael: a precipitating factor that would bring to our support many good and patriotic people who had previously voted Fianna Fáil.

Given the Taoiseach-designate's political skill and energy, why, I asked rhetorically, would the Dáil be taking a chance by electing him to this office? First, I said, because a question mark remained over a man who, having been found not guilty of importing arms for the IRA, had chosen to seek the plaudits of the crowd outside the court for a fellow-accused who represented that organisation, and because for nine long years thereafter, until his election as leader, he had refused to utter one word of condemnation of the IRA, on the extraordinary grounds that he was not responsible for Northern Ireland policy in the government.

Secondly, this long-practised deliberate ambiguity would make him, as Taoiseach, an obstacle to the achievement of Irish unity by agreement. Moreover, as Minister for Health he had brought in a Bill on contraception, the language of which was denominational and therefore damaging to the cause of Irish unity. Finally, he had failed to articulate any idealism that might inspire the younger generation. In conclusion, I made it clear that in speaking as I had done, I had deliberately chosen to reject advice tendered to me to refrain from such a course, and was prepared to take any criticism that might come as a result.

The criticism came, hot and heavy. Although most other Opposition speeches in the debate took a similar line – Noel Browne was particularly trenchant – condemnation was directed primarily at me as the lead speaker. I could see that I had unnerved some of my party colleagues. It will be for historians to judge whether placing my view bluntly on the record at that point was counter-productive or whether it may have contributed to my opponent's failure to secure an overall majority at any of the five subsequent general elections.

Six months later, in connection with an article on 11 May 1980 on the Arms Trial, we put down a motion, seeking clarification of matters raised there. Shortly afterwards I was approached on behalf of George Colley by a mutual friend, with the suggestion that we amend our motion so as to include a more direct reference to the clash of sworn testimony of the Arms Trial, in such a form that the motion would have to be rejected by the Taoiseach. If we did this, George Colley and a number of others would, I was told, abstain, and the motion would be carried. Those concerned felt that such an amendment would provide the last possible opportunity to show their feelings. If it were not provided, many of them might leave politics altogether. Because the issue was not one of collective responsibility but involved a personal matter, they took the view that he could abstain on it without breach of the whip, or that the whip could not properly be applied.

Whilst the prospect of winning such a vote naturally interested me, I saw many difficulties, which I put to the intermediary. On 19 November I met George Colley at a party, and he confirmed the proposal, saying that about twenty members would abstain.

There followed further contacts through Alexis FitzGerald, but when, at Alexis's suggestion, I put the matter to the test by inviting George Colley to draft the amendment himself – which seemed to me the best way of ensuring that the abstentions would in fact occur – he backed away from the proposal. I felt that my caution had been justified, and I turned my attention back to the immediate preparations for the general election, which, although not statutorily due until mid-1982, seemed certain to be called at some point during the twelve months ahead.

In the parliamentary party (as distinct from the party organisation throughout the country), concern about the impact that the strengthening of our panels of candidates of candidates would have on the electoral prospects of existing TDs had been accompanied by unhappiness at the substantial shift in the party's policies that I had effected. A minority was actively opposed to the new liberal and social-democratic thrust; others who had no strong personal views feared that the new policy emphasis would lose the party more support than it would generate. (Politicians know whence their existing support comes, but find it hard to envisage additional votes being secured from new sources. Not losing votes thus tends to loom much larger than gaining them.)

These concerns, aggravated by worries about media reactions to my Haughey speech, had created strains between the parliamentary party and myself – strains that by mid-1980 seemed to me to have become quite acute. At a special party meeting I told my colleagues bluntly that I was not happy with the situation. I felt that I was seen by some as being a useful vote-getter, but only so long as I refrained from voicing what I believed Fine Gael should stand for. I could not, I said, be an effective leader of a party if I had to be looking over my shoulder, not knowing where I stood. If I knew the party was fully behind me in what I was doing, I would get on with the job with renewed vigour. If not, now was the time to face the problem and draw the obvious conclusion.

This had the desired effect. Whilst I knew that some remained unenthusiastic, or secretly hostile, the overt grumbling was stilled. My relationship with Fine Gael TDs at this time was incidentally helped by the fact that the independent Constituency Commission established by Jack Lynch had proposed that the size of the Dáil be increased from 148 to 166 seats, as a result of the dramatic population rise that had been revealed when a postponed census had eventually been held, in April 1979. These recommendations were adopted, and this meant, as I pointed out to the Fine Gael parliamentary party, that unless a TD was very lazy or exceptionally stupid, none need fear losing a seat either to a Fine Gael colleague or to Fianna Fáil.

During this period, my involvement was the European Community had continued through the Christian Democratic movement, in which Fine Gael was on the left wing, with the Benelux parties and with some of the French and Italians. The German Christian Democrats, by contrast, tended to see themselves as conservative and had to be headed off from forming an alliance with, among others, the British Tories.

The proposal in 1978 to establish a European Monetary System with an exchange-rate mechanism, together with the British decision to keep sterling outside the ERM, posed a dilemma for the Irish government, in the resolution of which I was able to play some part. Ireland was by this time less dependent on the United Kingdom than before we joined the Community, but in 1978, 47 percent of our exports were still sold in the British market. An Irish currency linked in the ERM to the deutschmark, when almost half our exports were still being bought by the UK in sterling, with barely 30 percent sold to ERM countries, would be very delicately balanced.

At the negotiations in Brussels, the Irish representatives sought, reasonably enough, to secure some financial support from the European Community to assist the transition from one currency link to another. They seemed to have misjudged their negotiating strength. As a result, at a crucial European Council meeting, a decision to establish the ERM was taken, with Ireland sidelined, its representatives having refused, perhaps because of some confusion within their ranks, the 'best offer' made. Jack Lynch returned home at the weekend in a state of evident confusion, with Martin O'Donoghue, the economics minister, and himself offering conflicting accounts of what this offer had been.

This was humiliating and potentially disastrous for Ireland. After careful reflection, but consulting no one, I decided to see if I could help to find a solution. It was Saturday, but I rang the French ambassador and arranged to see him. I told him that I wanted to get a message through to Giscard d'Estaing to ask him to arrange, in conjunction with Helmut Schmidt, some face-saving additional offer to help our government off the hook on which it had impaled itself. Knowing that the secretary general of the Quai d'Orsay, Jean-Marie Soutou, had ready access to the president, I asked the ambassador to track him down for me. He found that Soutou was spending the weekend in a cottage somewhere in France, and on the phone I put my suggestion to him. He said he would pass my message on to the president, and that he thought that in view of my position as Opposition leader, it would carry particular weight. On the following Tuesday, an offer of additional bilateral aid came from France and Germany; this enabled the government to announce that we would join the ERM after all. Much later, I asked Jack Lynch if he thought my action had influenced the outcome; he said he believed that it had.

My range of international contacts continued to broaden. In 1980, Joan and I made a journey to the Middle East with an Italian journalist and a former Japanese ambassador, to prepare a report on the problems of the region for the Trilateral Commission, of which I was a member. This commission comprises politicians, academics and journalists, businessmen and trade unionists from Europe, North America and Japan. I also wrote a book on Development Co-operation for UNCTAD and gave lectures in the United States and in various European cities. Also in 1978, I lectured in Hong Kong, where the reporter who interviewed me for the *South China Morning Post* was suitably disconcerted when I asked her to tell her editor I was still waiting for the £78 they owed me since they had terminated my weekly column on Irish affairs without notice twenty years earlier!

But the task that absorbed even more of my spare time in these early years of party leadership, keeping me sane by distracting my mind in leisure moments from the cares of politics, was analysing the geographical pattern of the decline in the use of Irish between 1770 and 1870. I found the data I wanted in the nineteenth-century censuses of population, and each weekend, as I was driven around the country on my constituency visits, I propped up the old census volumes on the dashboard and embarked on the hundreds of thousands of calculations required to produce a comprehensive geographic picture of what had happened to the language during this period. I completed my first draft in the autumn of 1979, but it was some years before I was able, whilst Taoiseach, to publish the results of my work, as a Royal Irish Academy paper, illustrated by detailed maps prepared by my brother Fergus.

I also visited the United States several times during these years, lecturing and maintaining my political contacts. One in particular of these American visits I recall vividly. It was in January 1980, just after Charles Haughey had become Taoiseach. Sean Donlon, ambassador to the United States, invited me to stay in the embassy residence, as I had done in various capitals since becoming leader of the Opposition. Jack Lynch had always insisted that every courtesy be extended to me in that position. One minister who had objected to the treatment accorded respectively to himself and to me by embassy officials when our arrivals coincided at an airport received short shrift from his Taoiseach!

On this occasion, however, I thanked Sean but told him it would be wiser for Joan and me to stay elsewhere on this occasion. He objected strenuously, ringing me back later to say that he had asked for and been given ministerial authority for his invitation. I still refused, saying that when we met I would explain why. A day or two later, he rang again, crestfallen, to say that, as I had expected, the authority had been withdrawn, on a direction from higher up!

The visit itself, I believe, proved a particularly interesting one from an Irish point of view. Amongst the engagements arranged for me was a meeting at the State Department with officials from various American agencies. Never while in office as a minister had I met so many people at this level: some forty people from well over a dozen different parts of the administration turned up. Their questions were nearly all about the new Taoiseach, and his likely attitude to Northern Ireland and to Britain. I told them that I believed he would take a constructive line on Northern Ireland and would seek a better relationship with Britain. There was some surprise, perhaps a little incredulity, but also some acceptance that such an analysis coming from me was worthy of a certain amount of credit.

In what I said at that meeting I did not, of course, foresee in any detail the actual approach that Charles Haughey was to adopt in his negotiations with Britain some months later. Nor, on the other hand, did I foresee the clumsiness with which he was to handle the remarkable relationship that had been built up with the US Congress and administration during the previous couple of years.

To explain how the United States had come once again to be an important factor in the Anglo-Irish equation, I must go back a few years. During most of my
period as Minister of Foreign Affairs, our diplomatic efforts in the United States
had been defensive, and directed primarily towards limiting the damage that Irish-
American elements could do to our interests by their support for the IRA. Since at
least 1972, when Jack Lynch and Desmond O'Malley had confronted this issue,
two successive Irish governments had been struggling, in conjunction with the
SDLP to win as much as we could of Irish America back from its tendency to sympathise with the IRA as an atavistic expression of inherited anti-British feeling.
Together with John Hume, we had achieved a good deal in this field by 1976, successfully countering pro-IRA influence in Congress and starting to reduce the flow
of contributions to the IRA front organisation Noraid, some of whose members
were engaged in the purchase and dispatch of arms and explosives to the IRA.

In undertaking this work, the SDLP and ourselves were at times inhibited by
the counterproductive impact on the Irish community in the United States, and
especially on Irish-American members of Congress, of the extensive British propaganda effort there. Much of this British effort was inevitably directed towards trying
to explain away aspects of British rule in Northern Ireland that were not readily
defensible, and which Irish governments spent much of their time trying to get
changed, such as British army harassment, directed almost exclusively against the
nationalist community, and maltreatment of suspects, which had been condemned
in the mid-1970s by the European Commission and Court of Human Rights and
further exposed in the Bennett Report in 1979. And from time to time, the British
diplomatic service abroad, which tended to be much more aggressive towards
Ireland than was often the case with the Foreign Office itself, also launched unjustified attacks on the seriousness of our commitment against the IRA – which had
to be countered. The credibility in the United States of Irish governments espousing
moderate policies and seeking to undermine support for the IRA required that we
face there, just as we had to do at home and in Strasbourg, thorny issues of this
kind.

However, by the end of the Ford administration in January 1977, we had built
up, with John Hume's powerful assistance, strong support for our position in
Congress. Tip O'Neill, Ted Kennedy and Pat Moynihan, supported outside
Congress by Governor Hugh Carey of New York (collectively known as 'the Four
Horsemen'), were holding a firm line against the IRA-sympathising Ad Hoc
Committee on Irish Affairs, chaired by Congressman Mario Biaggi, not to speak of
Sean MacManus's Irish National Caucus and the IRA organisation Noraid.

With the transfer to Washington of Michael Lillis, the sounsellor who had been
serving previously as our information officer in the United States, based in New
York, a new phase in Irish-American relations had begun. Michael brought our

contacts with the Irish congressional leadership to a stage of intimacy never previously achieved, the results of which were demonstrated in the joint statement of the 'Four Horsemen' on St Patrick's Day 1977, which launched the Friends of Ireland movement in Congress. He successfully countered an attempt by Biaggi and the Irish National Caucus to win Jimmy Carter's support during the later stages of his election campaign, and persuaded the White House to adopt the Carter iniative, which was launched in July 1977, just after Jack Lynch took over from Liam Cosgrave. This initiative promised substantial aid to Northern Ireland in the event of progress being made towards a political situation there. (This cheque was cashed eight years later under a different administration, with the establishment of the International Fund for Northern Ireland to back up the Anglo-Irish Agreement of that year.)

As second counsellor in the Irish embassy, Michael Lillis had shown how, with John Hume's help, we could move from what had hitherto been essentially a defensive position, fighting IRA propaganda and also frequently the British Information Service, to one in which we held the initiative and could influence Congress, and even the administration, in our interests. To secure the full benefits of this breakthrough, the level of activity needed to be raised to an even higher plane. This was the background to my suggestion to Jack Lynch in June 1978 that Sean Donlon, although then still under forty, be moved from his position as head of the Anglo-Irish division of the Department of Foreign Affairs to be ambassador to the United States. Like Michael Lillis, Sean had the unique combination of qualities required for the Washington post: the intellectual capacity and diplomatic skill needed to deal with the White House, National Security Council and State Department at an appropriate level, and the personal and human qualities needed to penetrate and command the attention of Congress.

The remarkable success of Michael Lillis and Sean Donlon on Capitol Hill and with the administration had infuriated the Irish 'republican' lobby in the United States, who had been effectively marginalised by their efforts. These groups looked to a new leader of Fianna Fáil and head of the Irish government – whose progression from dismissed minister accused of importing arms for the IRA to Taoiseach they had followed with enthusiasm – to vindicate their cause by getting rid of the ambassador who had so effectively opposed their efforts.

There was no room for Charles Haughey to make a hard-line gesture to his backbenchers on any matter of substance related to Northern Ireland. That would destroy the possibility of a negotiation with Britain, which had to be his primary target. Perhaps, however, he could provide his followers, and above all his external Dáil ally, Neil Blaney, with the short-term satisfaction they sought by throwing them a morsel in a quite different and, as he may have seen it, subordinate theatre: the United States. Fianna Fáil supporters had for long been assiduously courted by extremist 'republican' elements in America – elements that both the Fianna Fáil government under Jack Lynch up to 1973 and from 1977 to 1979, and our national coalition government from 1973 to 1977 had sought to marginalise, because of the sympathy shown by them to the IRA. Quite apart from the expectations of his supporters within Fianna Fáil, he may have been under pressure on this issue from Neil Blaney.

So it was that at the end of June 1980 Sean Donlon was called back to Dublin and told that he was being moved to the post of permanent representative to the United Nations in New York. On Friday 4 July he returned to the United States, stopping in New York for the weekend to prepare the ground for his new posting. But the *Daily Telegraph* correspondent in Washington had got word of the proposed move, and his story was picked up by the Irish Sunday papers that weekend. By Wednesday 9 July, our papers were reporting the fury of the 'Four Horsemen' at this proposed move. They were said to be scathing in their criticism of the proposed removal of Ambassador Donlon, which a government spokesman had in the interval sought to justify as a 'peripheral matter . . . removing a pawn to gain a knight' (that is, Neil Blaney). O'Neill, Kennedy, Moynihan and Carey were reported to be 'deeply hurt'; they had 'received no thanks for their efforts in the past', which were not even 'tolerated'. Despite the Four Horsemen's success in getting the goal of Irish unity inserted in the Democratic election programme, the Irish government had 'decided to align itself with other forces in the US'. In particular, the Four Horsemen resented the apparent support of the new government for Congressman Biaggi, whom they saw as an instrument of Noraid and its offshoot, the Irish National Caucus.

Before this storm, the Haughey reed broke. On the following day it was announced that the report of Sean Donlon's transfer was 'totally without foundation'. At this point Frank Cluskey and I demanded that the Taoiseach also disassociate himself from the Irish National Caucus and Noraid, a call supported by John Hume, whose normal anxiety to maintain good relations with the current Irish government took second place on this occasion to his concern to retain the powerful support he had helped to build up in the US Congress. In order that all shades of suspicion be removed and this unfortunate affair be closed, said John Hume, 'it is necessary that it be made absolutely clear that the activity of the Biaggi committee enjoyed no support whatsoever from any substantial section of opinion'.

Very foolishly from his own point of view, the Taoiseach, smarting from the rebuff he had suffered in relation to Sean Donlon, at first ignored this demand, and the situation was not improved by his minister Michael O'Kennedy, who, while condemning 'any organisation associated with the pursuit of violent methods to deal with the Northern Ireland problem', replied ambivalently to the question whether this referred to Congressman Biaggi's committee, the Irish National Caucus or Noraid, by saying: 'That is open to interpretation.' Accordingly, on

21 July in a letter to the Taoiseach, the publication of which I postponed to give him an opportunity to make a public statement on the matter, I asked him formally whether he maintained the position of all governments during the previous decade in relation to these organisations.

My letter achieved its purpose: at the end of the week, the Taoiseach belatedly provided the necessary clear repudiation of the groups in question, condemning Noraid and adding that this organisation's links with the Irish National Caucus cast grave suspicions on that organisation. The caucus's leader, Sean McManus, responded that the Taoiseach's statement was a 'response to threats and blackmail' from me, and that I had 'once again dictated policy to Mr Haughey' – a statement that I did not feel necessary to deny!

This unfortunate affair had come in the middle of the negotiations that had been opened in the late spring between Charles Haughey's government and that of Margaret Thatcher. One day in May 1980, the Taoiseach had asked me to come and see him in his room. He raised with me a parliamentary matter that hardly seemed to warrant a special meeting. Then he said: 'You know I'm meeting Margaret Thatcher next Tuesday!' 'I knew you were meeting her soon,' I replied, 'but I didn't know the day.' He started to say something, stopped, hesitated, and with an obvious change of gear said lamely: 'Well, if you think of anything I should say to her, let me know.' Politely I said I would, but it did not seem to me appropriate to take up this invitation.

Following an official briefing in Dublin, the *Sunday Times* had reported that the Taoiseach intended during his meeting with Margaret Thatcher to propose 'Anglo-Irish co-operation on defence and foreign policy'. I was not therefore too surprised to be told some time later that at a meeting to prepare for the London summit he had speculated on the possibility of consulting Frank Cluskey and myself about proposing to the British prime minister some form of bilateral defence agreement, but that on reflection he had decided that the Labour Party's commitment to military neutrality made it impractical to consult Frank Cluskey on this issue. This, I thought, might explain what had happened at our meeting: he might have intended to raise this defence proposal with me, but had had last-minute second thoughts. Although there seems to be no record of the tête-à-tête between the British prime minister and Haughey on the occasion of this first meeting between them, the defence issue was, I believe, raised by him on that occasion.

Apparent confirmation of this exists in three respects. First, at his press conference after this bilateral meeting the Taoiseach flatly rejected the idea of Irish membership of the Commonwealth, but – pointedly, I thought – did *not* reject in similar blunt terms a possible defence agreement. Second, months later, in the course of a Dáil debate on defence and neutrality, his government voted *against* a statement that there had been no such proposal. Finally, at about the same time, the British prime minister rejected publicly the idea of such a bilateral arrangement, adding that if Ireland wanted to join in defence, it should do so through multilateral arrangements, i.e. through membership of NATO.

A second Anglo-Irish summit meeting of 1980 took place in Dublin on Monday 8 December, at a time when the first H-block hunger strike was at its peak. The communiqué on that occasion included reference to 'institutional arrangements' and to 'the totality of the relationship' between Ireland and Britain'. In his press conference after this summit meeting, the Taoiseach said that, in joint studies the two governments had agreed to undertake on the relationship between the two states in the context of this 'historic breakthrough', he did not set any limits on the arrangements that might be agreed. 'A government spokesman put a gloss on this by talking of the possibility of 'federal, confederal or other innovative structures'. Only Commonwealth membership was, once again, ruled out. But, asked about the reference to confederation in particular, Mrs Thatcher in her press conference was completely dismissive: 'absolutely no possibility', she responded, and the Northern Ireland secretary said that constitutional changes were ruled out.

Despite the British prime minister's obvious discomfort when questioned in Parliament on this issue, and despite attacks by Ian Paisley in particular about the Irish government's claims in relation to the constitutional position of Northern Ireland, these warning notes were not heeded by the Fianna Fáil government.

True, pressed by me and others in the Dáil on the issue, the Taoiseach became visibly more cautious. Tongue in cheek, I thanked him for clarifying the fact that the constitutional position of Northern Ireland was not at issue – to which he responded that he did not accept what I said. On the following day, however, the Minister for Foreign Affairs, Brian Lenihan, reiterated that 'all options are open' and that 'everything is on the table'. He also said that the next meeting between the Taoiseach and prime minister could be a decision-making one.

The Haughey–Thatcher relationship never recovered from this affair. Indeed, thereafter on Irish affairs the British prime minister became extremely wary of her own advisers as well as of Irish Taoisigh – a problem I had to reckon with in due course. At the time, however, this aftermath of the second Haughey–Thatcher summit meeting was obscured by the ending of the first H-Block hunger strike just a week after the Dublin meeting.

This concluded Charles Haughey's Northern Ireland initiative, on which he had placed great hopes. In retrospect it can be seen that these hopes had been built on sand. It became even more clear to me later, when I became Taoiseach, that there had never been any possibility that a constitutional change in the position of Northern Ireland could have emerged from these negotiations. However, by his fostering the illusion that something of the kind might be on the cards, unionist fears had been fanned to a dangerous level, which made rational discussions with them about devolution much more difficult thereafter and may have contributed to their later hostility towards the Anglo-Irish Agreement of 1985.

For its part, the SDLP, whose hopes had been unreasonably raised by these events, found itself ill-placed after this debacle to cope with the tensions created by the subsequent 1981 hunger strike. In accordance with its policy of working with the government of the day whilst maintaining its own identity and policy stance, it had gone along with Charles Haughey's initiative. At the same time, faced with pressure from Haughey to espouse the demand for British withdrawal, John Hume had cleverly avoided this issue.

I knew that the superficial alignment between the Fianna Fáil and SDLP stances worried John, just as he had been disturbed when we were in office by equivalent Fianna Fáil paranoia about the SDLP's relationship at that time with Fine Gael and, to a lesser extent, the Labour Party. Late in 1980, I suggested to a member of the SDLP who spoke to me about John's concern on this score that if he wanted to reassure Fine Gael (although I did not myself feel this was necessary), all he had to do was tip off the 'Backchat' column in the *Sunday Independent* about his holiday with Joan and myself in the south of France that summer. When this idea was put to John shortly afterwards, I was told that he had immediately rejected it; but within a fortnight the story appeared in 'Backchat' – and it was not I who leaked it!

Throughout these years in Opposition, we had been very critical of Fianna Fáil's handling of the economy and of the government finances. Despite the enormous problems created for Ireland, as for so many other countries, by the first oil crisis in 1973, the national coalition government had left the economy in very good shape four years later, a fact generously recognised by the incoming Taoiseach, Jack Lynch, in the end-of-year adjournment debate six months after the June 1977 change of government. On that occasion he recorded that in 1977 our growth rate, at 5 percent, had been near the top of the league internationally; investment had been dynamic: exports had risen at three times the average rate for industrialised countries; and there had been a rise of seven thousand in manufacturing employment during the year. The volume of agricultural output was up 9 percent, he added; he summoned up the whole picture by saying that 'this is the kind of foundation on which we can build'. He could have added that inflation, which had momentarily attained 25 percent at the height of the oil crisis, was down to an annual rate of 6.75 percent in the second half of 1977.

However, by the time Charles Haughey succeeded Jack Lynch as Taoiseach in December 1979, the rate of Exchequer borrowing had doubled, and the national debt was more than two-thirds higher than when Fianna Fáil had taken over from us two and a half years earlier. Thereafter the situation deteriorated at an accelerating rate. Far from any corrective action being taken, the position was further aggravated by a campaign undertaken by Charles Haughey's new government to increase the number of public servants, regardless of need. And pay claims were settled with such abandon that the average pay rates in the public service rose by almost 30 percent in 1980. The planned current deficit in that year was exceeded by no less than 60 percent, and Exchequer borrowing rose by a further 50 percent.

Against this background, the 1981 budget presentation was treated with a scepticism that in the event proved to be fully warranted. Exchequer spending was officially forecast to rise by no more than one-sixth – the rate that inflation had now attained – and a marginal fall in the current budget deficit to just over £500 million was projected. We believed the deficit would exceed by a considerable margin this published estimate, which we thought had been deliberately held at unrealistic levels, unattainable on the basis of the policy decisions taken (or, rather, not taken) by the government with respect to spending programmes. We were right.

All in all, the Fianna Fáil governments led by Jack Lynch and Charles Haughey between them increased the volume of current public spending by almost half, more than doubled in real terms the annual level of borrowing, and almost trebled the national debt, as well as the rate of inflation, and the Central Bank rediscount rate virtually doubled.

In early 1981 the accelerating speed at which this deterioration was taking place was not, however, known to the public – or to us in Opposition. The presentation of the financial returns to financial journalists during this period was later to be the subject of severe criticism. The undermining of confidence in the public administration was, with that of security, the aspect of the events of this period that most concerned me in 1981, and in 1982. I gave corresponding attention to restoring the public confidence in the process of government when I became Taoiseach. In preparing our manifesto for the election which we believed would be called in the first half of 1981, we had to face the reality of this appalling financial crisis – as far as we knew it. We made this explicit in our manifesto, and proposed to eliminate the soaring deficit over a period of four or five years, giving preference in this process to reductions in public expenditure as against tax increases.

Other proposals in our manifesto were implemented by one or other of the governments I led, such as, for example, the establishment of a Youth Employment Agency; tax allowances for elderly tenants of rented accommodation; the provision through a new Housing Finance Agency of housing loans, with repayments limited to a fixed share of income; and the establishment of an independent Examinations and Curriculum Board to take over important functions from the Department of Education – although this board was later abolished by Fianna Fáil. Moreover, at the insistence of Young Fine Gael, we initiated legislation abolishing the concept of illegitimacy.

Meanwhile we had prepared our election campaign in great detail, with a precise day-by-day programme for the early part of the campaign, including the timing of the launch of our manifesto, and arrangements for my tour by special train – an innovation in Irish electoral history.

I also put in place a strategy committee comprising both frontbenchers and non-Oireachtas members, the latter element of which would, together with several senators, become our election committee the moment the Dáil was dissolved and TDs had to return to their constituencies. My experience before becoming leader had convinced me that deputies trying to get themselves re-elected could not run a general-election campaign effectively. What we needed were people from outside the party structure with a wide range of management and public-relations skills who would have learnt to work with the party in the run-up to the election and who, given this experience, could then take on this task in conjunction with a small number of senators and others with political experience, and with the professionals, Peter Prendergast and Ted Nealon.

This new form of election organisation proved its worth when the election was called in May, and in the two further elections that took place at nine-month intervals thereafter. Indeed I believe this structure was one of the most successful organisational systems devised by a political party in independent Ireland.

The director of elections was the late Sean O'Leary, a Cork accountant and barrister who had himself been a Dáil candidate, and whose qualities of warmth and vitality, political gut instinct, natural authority, toughness and *joie de vivre*, together with his excellent relationship with our national organiser, Peter Prendergast, equipped him ideally for this task. Derry Hussey, Gemma Hussey's businessman husband, provided a key element of calm, stability and order as chairman of the team. The late Alexis FitzGerald and a former senator, Jim Dooge, each with a third of a century of accumulated political wisdom, looked after policy issues and guided the work of a scriptwriting team of young professional people.

Ted Nealon had organised a team of experts, who brought first-rate marketing skills to bear on this campaign. He was not available for the campaign itself, however, because of his nomination as a candidate for Sligo-Leitrim, which he subsequently represented in the Dáil for many years, and his place was taken at short notice by Liam Hourican, the former RTÉ journalist, who had played a distinguished role as correspondent in Belfast at an important juncture in the 1970s and who had recently completed a term in Dick Burke's Cabinet in Brussels. After the election I appointed him government press officer.

A perennial problem with election financing is ensuring that no matter what the political pressure during the campaign, expenditure is not allowed to outrun revenue. In our case, this was ensured by combining the responsibilities of fundraising and expenditure authorisation in one person: Sean Murray, a hard-nosed accountant who had the combination of dynamism and toughness necessary to undertake this dual responsibility. He brought us through these three elections of the early 1980s in most difficult circumstances, balancing the books each time.

By the time the 1981 election was called, this team was well prepared for the task ahead, and during the campaign needed only minimal guidance from front-benchers seeking re-election – although, of course, I kept in touch with them myself day by day and, when in Dublin, joined their meetings, as did some of my colleagues.

Because of the tragic fire in the Stardust ballroom in the Taoiseach's own North Dublin constituency in February, in which forty-eight young people lost their lives and scores of others were maimed, the election was postponed until May. Well signalled in advance, the dissolution was announced on the evening of Wednesday 20 May. The Taoiseach stated that he was seeking a clear mandate because of the grave situation in Northern Ireland, where the renewal of the 1980 hunger strike had already led to two deaths. Two more of the hunger strikers died shortly after the dissolution of the Dáil.

Although public-opinion polls, published some weeks earlier, had shown support for the Fine Gael and Labour Party exceeding that for Fianna Fáil by about ten points, Charles Haughey was at this point more popular than I was, reversing my earlier ten-point advantage over him. We were thus starting the campaign from behind.

Thirty-six hours after the dissolution, however, I launched our own programme, which immediately became the focal point of the campaign and provided a basis for a co-operative relationship with the Labour Party. Michael O'Leary for that party immediately characterised the general thrust of our programme as 'acceptable'.

On Sunday Joan and I started a two-day countrywide tour by special train. This electoral innovation, organised by a member of our election committee, Joe Jennings, who worked in CIÉ, was a well-kept secret. It secured us good initial publicity, both at national and regional level. In two days we visited nine provincial cities or towns – I with one arm in a sling as a result of a domestic accident. I made speeches or gave press conferences, and accepted a proposal for a television debate with the Taoiseach. As the days passed, Fianna Fáil was increasingly being drawn into criticising – and thus further publicising – our programme, in the process losing credibility by alleging that its implementation would cost £800 million.

By the second weekend it was clear that we were pulling in the floating voters – a fact confirmed by the pollsters, who early in the following week showed both Fine Gael and myself closing the gap with Fianna Fáil and its leader. At the same time the press reports of the leaders' tours suggested that Charles Haughey was more at home in this kind of environment and that I was less than comfortable with crowds and the trappings of populism. In part this was a stereotyping exercise –

woolly-headed academic versus practised professional – but there was an element of truth in it, for I have always been chary of all forms of populism and have perhaps been inordinately fastidious about the kind of artificial adulation of the leader that seems to be an inseparable element of party set pieces, including party conferences and election meetings. Moreover, whilst usually comfortable addressing non-political audiences, I have never been happy making political speeches at outdoor meetings, to listeners whose attention to my remarks I cannot help feeling to be governed by considerations of loyalty or courtesy rather than by any actual interest in my necessarily partisan observations on such occasions.

But I was very often moved by the enthusiasm of so many of our party workers engaged in the patriotic work of electioneering and in other less dramatic tasks to be performed between elections. Their efforts – and, of course, those of activists of other parties – which ensure the alternation of governments so vital to the preservation of democracy from corruption and the abuse of power, deserve far more recognition than they ever receive from the general public. And I could not fail to be heartened by the warmth of so many ordinary Irish people, not involved in politics, who frequently feel moved to express their appreciation of those who take part in the democratic process. Without the reward of such enthusiasm and such sporadic public gratitude, the political process would often seem thankless.

During the first general-election campaign that I undertook as party leader, the journalists accompanying me were, initially at least, more conscious of my reticences than of my positive reactions; in particular they missed my exhilaration at the youth of the people who thronged to our meetings, many of them young parents with their children and babies, and at the warmth of the welcome they gave to my reforming ideas.

It was indeed a blissful dawn to what turned out to be a most gloomy decade. I could not but be cheered by finding that at least for that brief moment, there was a genuine appetite for social reform and for more liberal and pluralist attitudes. Many of the new generation that had grown up in the 1960s and 1970s clearly wanted to turn their backs on the sterile, inward-looking form of nationalism that had dominated post-revolutionary Ireland for so long. Above all, when the sun shone, as it did for at least part of the time during what turned out to be a rather showery early summer, there was a mood of gaiety and warmth, and an evident belief that politics *could* be constructive. Somehow this had not come across in the media during the first half of the campaign. However, as the tide visibly turned, I was reported to be 'good-humoured and relaxed' – albeit 'polite to the point of self-effacement'!

The tour was, of course, physically exhausting. At one point Joan remarked, as one journalist recorded, that she had never seen me so weary in my life. However, physical tiredness is a sort-lived phenomenon, from which I recover easily, and I had wisely insisted on building into the process of electioneering at least one rest period during the day. Even forty-five minutes lying down was enough to enable me to go full speed ahead again afterwards.

I should add that on this and other such campaigns, the fact that Joan, despite her severe arthritis, accompanied me, bringing her cheerfulness and wit to bear on our enterprise, made a huge difference to my morale and, I believe, to that of the rest of the team also. At the same time, the clear-sighted objectivity of her comments, especially on my own performance, helped to keep my feet on the ground.

As more and more floating voters were coming our way, three days from the end of the campaign the polls were suggesting a very close outcome indeed between Fine Gael–Labour and Fianna Fáil, and the bookmakers' odds shifted in our favour. It was at this stage that an RTÉ compromise was finally arrived at to get around Charles Haughey's reluctance to undertake a face-to-face confrontation with me on television. It involved each of the three party leaders being interviewed by a group of political correspondents – a clumsy arrangement with which I was not at all comfortable. This must have been evident. The Taoiseach was adjudged to have been more relaxed, and I 'hesitant and slightly nervous'.

Polling was on Thursday 11 June. As the reports of the party 'tallymen' watching the checking of the ballot papers came in during Friday morning, it was clear that the result was likely to be indecisive. And so it turned out. By late Saturday afternoon it was clear that neither Fianna Fáil, with seventy-eight seats, nor Fine Gael plus the Labour Party, with eighty seats between them (sixty-five Fine Gael and fifteen Labour), had a majority. Two abstentionist IRA candidates had been elected in Border constituencies, and there were six independents or representatives of small parties, who were going to hold the balance of power.

Nevertheless, while the absence of a clear majority for a possible alternative Fine Gael–Labour government was disappointing, it seemed likely that I would be elected Taoiseach when the Dáil met in three weeks' time. And by any standard the scale of our achievement was impressive. We had increased Fine Gael's share of the vote by one-fifth, to the highest level attained in over half a century, taking virtually all those votes from Fianna Fáil. We had increased our Dáil representation by over half, from forty-three to sixty-five, in effect winning all eighteen additional Dáil seats and four others besides, so that Fianna Fáil, which had also lost two seats to IRA candidates, had six fewer seats than in the previous, much smaller Dáil. Only one of our former deputies who had contested the election had lost his seat. Over half the Fine Gael deputies elected had not been members for the previous Dáil: an unprecedented influx of new blood into our political system. Many were in their twenties or thirties; and six were women, as against one in 1977. (Five other women were later elected or appointed to the Seanad in the Fine Gael interest, thus increasing overnight the number of Fine Gael women in the Oireachtas from two to eleven.)

One of the casualties of the campaign, however, was the Labour Party leader, Frank Cluskey, with whom I had worked closely for the previous four years. Six days after the election, the Labour parliamentary party met and chose Michael O'Leary as its new leader. During the days that followed, he rejected advances from Charles Haughey, despite pressure from elements within his own party, especially in Dublin. He and I then embarked on talks at the home of a mutual friend. We were later joined by our deputy leaders, Peter Barry for Fine Gael and Jimmy Tully for Labour.

Michael and I had been friends for years. However, as leader of Fine Gael, I had had to give priority to maintaining a good relationship with Frank Cluskey as Labour Party leader; considering the tension that existed between him and Michael O'Leary, I had to keep my distance from Michael to some extent during the years from 1977 to 1981. Joan, however, not being subject to the same political inhibitions, had kept in touch with him during this period. Michael and I were now faced with the task of devising together a joint programme for government that our respective parties could accept. For this purpose, the very comprehensive Fine Gael policy document provided a basic framework, the essential elements of which could be developed or supplemented along lines that could reflect specific Labour Party concerns.

The idea of presenting our joint programme in the context of a four-year national plan to be drawn up in consultation with various sectors was helpful to the Labour Party, as was the concept of a National Planning Board, which in any event I favoured. The Fine Gael proposal for a Public Enterprise Board was transmuted into a National Development Corporation. A new commitment was given to capital taxation, involving as an objective the restoration of the yield from these taxes to the 1972/73 level, which seemed reasonable. The Fine Gael commitment to the re-establishment and funding of a national poverty committee, which Fianna Fáil had abolished, was placed within a framework involving an anti-poverty plan. A proposal for a national income-related pension scheme, contained in a green paper published by Frank Cluskey when he had been a minister of state in the 1973–77 national coalition, was reintroduced.

The social-democratic orientation of the Fine Gael programme facilitated the marrying of our two parties' objectives, because Fine Gael policy contained nothing with which the Labour Party disagreed. At the same time, as few in Labour had actually read our programme, and as most Labour Party members had been conditioned to assume that Fine Gael was a right-wing party, the inclusion of large parts of the Fine Gael document in the joint programme was seen by many in the Labour Party, quite erroneously, to be a victory for Labour over Fine Gael!

By Saturday 27 June, the joint programme was agreed, as was the allocation to the Labour Party of four of the fifteen government posts, together with three junior ministerial appointments. As in the 1973–77 coalition, this gave Labour more than its share of portfolios in proportion to its Dáil seats.

The joint programme was to be put to our respective parties on the following Sunday. In our case, this involved our parliamentary party, but in the case of the Labour Party, a special conference of more than 1,200 delegates was held in the Gaiety Theatre, Dublin – hence the name 'Gaiety Programme', by which the joint policy, somewhat incongruously, came to be known. I had no qualms about what my own party's decision would be, but the Labour Party's special conference was very far from being a foregone conclusion. However in the event, the document was adopted by both parties – in the case of Labour by a less-than-overwhelming majority of 737 votes to 487.

The first business of the new Dáil when it met on the afternoon of Tuesday 30 June would be the election of the Ceann Comhairle. Neither Fianna Fáil nor Fine Gael–Labour was prepared to forfeit a vote in such a delicately balanced situation by nominating a party member for this position. One of the independents, John O'Connell, was a former Labour Party member of some standing who currently had a Fianna Fáil – or at any rate Haughey – orientation. Although Labour was somewhat reluctant, we proposed him for the post, and he was elected.

As two of the eight independents were IRA abstentionists, that left five. Neil Blaney supported Charles Haughey, thus giving the latter a total of seventy-nine votes when he was proposed as Taoiseach. Three of the others – two left-wing independents, Noel Browne and Jim Kemmy, and a single representative of the Workers Party, Joe Sherlock – voted with the Labour Party and ourselves, thus defeating the former Taoiseach by a margin of four votes. I was then elected by eighty-one votes to seventy-eight, Jim Kemmy alone of the independents joining with the Fine Gael and Labour members for this purpose.

On a subsequent visit to Northern Ireland, in June 1978, I discussed with political contacts other approaches to power-sharing and also met the current leaders of the Presbyterian Church. The Presbyterians told me that the maltreatment of prisoners under interrogation, which they said had ceased in the autumn of 1977 as a result of representations by the churches, had begun again. A group of loyalist paramilitaries had recently been beaten up in Castlereagh as part of an interrogation procedure. They asked me to do what I could to have this stopped.

Shortly afterwards I went to London with Paddy Harte to meet Margaret Thatcher as well as Roy Mason. I explained to Margaret Thatcher our concern abut this report from the Presbyterian leaders, adding that British army tactics vis-à-vis the nationalist community were also proving counter-productive in the context of our joint concern to isolate and defeat the IRA. The Opposition leader's reaction was quite negative. She embarked on a prolonged lecture about law and order, in the course of which she seemed to imply that it was 'bad form' for me to have raised the brutality issue in view of the 1976–77 'Heavy Gang' allegations about the Gardaí. When I met Jack Lynch some time later, to discuss Northern Ireland affairs, I described her attitude on this occasion as 'unyielding and unsympathetic'.

Our subsequent lunch with Roy Mason was less abrasive, and ranged much more widely, but I did not feel that we made much impact on the Castlereagh issue. Had there been a more receptive approach to our representations at that time, Britain might have been spared the subsequent embarrassment of the Bennett Inquiry and Report into Castlereagh interrogation.

In the course of the British general election that year, an American congressional delegation, led by Speaker Tip O'Neill, visited Britain and Ireland. The Speaker in particular was unimpressed with British politicians' approach to Northern Ireland. When the delegation arrived in the Republic, a dinner was given for them by Jack Lynch in Dublin Castle. Tip O'Neill made an impressive and moving speech, which showed sympathy and understanding for the unionist as well as nationalist community in Northern Ireland. His irritation with his recent British interlocutors showed through, in a reference he made to the North becoming a political football in Britain.

This isolated remark provoked a political and media storm in Britain; politicians and newspapers attacked Speaker O'Neill and other congressional leaders of Irish extraction in terms that seemed to suggest that these were IRA sympathisers. In view of the solid support these leaders had given to us in the propaganda war we had been waging against the IRA in the United States, this was unjust to the point of absurdity. I was so incensed that I could not sleep that night, and eventually got up and hammered out a furious letter to the *Daily Telegraph* – of which the Speaker was subsequently very appreciative. His attitude to Margaret Thatcher, however, was soured by this episode.

In June, after the British election that brought the Tories to power under Margaret Thatcher, I was able to present the Fine Gael Northern Ireland policy document to an audience at the Royal Institute of International Affairs in London, taking the opportunity to meet the Labour Party leaders, now in Opposition, starting with David Owen, then shadow Minister for Energy. He told me that when he and Jim Callaghan had met Ted Kennedy some time previously with Peter Jay, Callaghan's son-in-law and Britain's ambassador to Washington, Callaghan had frankly admitted that his government had no policy on Northern Ireland. Jay, who had spent two years trying to assure Ted Kennedy and other members of Congress that the British government had such a policy, had been shaken by this admission, he said.

In my subsequent discussion with Jim Callaghan, it quickly became evident that he too was very concerned about the attitude of congressional leaders. I explained to him diplomatically that the Americans had been unfavourably impressed by their discussions in London, suggesting that Callaghan might not have appreciated how strongly they felt about the Northern Ireland tragedy and how upset they had been to find that Peter Jay's account of British policy-making on Northern Ireland, which they had believed, had been lacking in foundation. Callaghan responded irritably that if the Speaker was as naive as that, he should not have the job he held. For the future, he recognised that the Labour Party would have to adopt a somewhat more positive position, but he added emphatically, twice, that they could not be led by the nose by the SDLP. Labour policy would not be settled by Gerry Fitt or Kevin Mcnamara – whom he seemed to regard as an Irish politician who had nothing to do with the British Labour Party.

A few weeks later Jack Lynch arranged for me to have a brief discussion with the British foreign secretary, Peter Carrington, when he visited Dublin. He suggested that I wait in my old room in the Department of Foreign Affairs, where the Carrington dinner was being held. At 9.15 he sent Peter to meet me in my room. As he entered, he greeted me humorously with the words: 'Garret! How do we unite Ireland?!' After speaking favourably of Fine Gael's Northern Ireland policy document, he added that if the Northern Ireland question were not resolved within a year or two, it would have a very serious effect on Anglo-American relations as well as on British relations with the Irish government.

Ten days after meeting him, I also met the new Secretary of State for Northern Ireland, Humphry Atkins, in London, with the new permanent secretary of the Northern Ireland Office, Ken Stowe, who had just been transferred from the Cabinet Office. Atkins was concerned to demonstrate his commitment to the replacement of direct rule with a power-sharing devolved government in the North. Given this commitment, and the fact that it was our first encounter, I did not go into the issue in detail with him. I was amused, however, to be asked by Ken Stowe on one point: 'How do you think we could get around the prime minister on that matter, Dr FitzGerald?' Already, within weeks of the formation of the Thatcher government, I was hearing this theme, which was to be repeated so often thereafter by British ministers and civil servants.

Later that day, at the British-Irish Association conference, I had a much fuller discussion with the Northern Ireland minister of state, Hugh Rossi, and I raised with him the failure of his government, following the Bennett Inquiry, to remove those implicated in acts of brutality at Castelreagh. I pointed out that if Roy Mason and Margaret Thatcher had listened to me a year earlier, the need for the Bennett Inquiry could have been avoided. Rossi promised to take this matter up, but no follow-up action seems to have been taken.

In August came the appalling murder in Sligo of Lord Mountbatten and the son of a friend of his from Northern Ireland. Two of those involved were subsequently charged and convicted of the offence on forensic evidence. In September, with Jack Lynch and Frank Cluskey, I attended the Mountbatten Memorial service in Westminster Abbey.

On a later visit to Northern Ireland in early 1981, Joan and I stayed with Lord Brookeborough in Fermanagh, and with him we visited a number of Protestant farmers who had lost relatives or friends in the course of the IRA's murderous campaign in this Border area. On the same occasion, I spoke at Portora Royal School to pupils from all the secondary schools in Enniskillen. (Before the meeting, the late Dowager Duchess of Westminster, who had lived there for decades, confided in me that 'these people [the unionists attending the reception] are not British at all; I thought they were when I came here first, but they aren't; they're all Irish'!)

At the end of September 1979 the Pope visited Ireland; Joan and I returned from a French holiday just before the visit began. At London Airport we encountered Lord Longford, whom I had first met in 1933 when, as Frank Pakenham, he had come to see my father in the course of writing a book on the Anglo-Irish Treaty of 1921. He enquired of me anxiously whether there would be room at the site at Knock in County Mayo, where the Pope was to say Mass, for him to use a folding chair he was carrying. Not wishing to disturb his faith in my omniscience, I assured him that all would be well. I never heard afterwards whether he got to sit down.

After the impressive Mass in Phoenix Park, we were able to get home for a rest before going to the Nunciature to meet the Pope. While waiting in a small room, with Joan and the Labour Party leader, Frank Cluskey, it struck me, somewhat belatedly, that the occasion of this visit should be used to raise with the Pope the need to modify the operation in Ireland of the Catholic Church's mixed-marriage code. I crossed the corridor to the room in which the members of the government were awaiting the Pope's arrival and spoke to Jack Lynch about this matter – unaware that our discussion was being televised – but without sound, thus arousing some public curiosity, as I afterwards learnt. He told me that he had exactly the same idea, and that President Hillery had also intended to raise the matter if he had a chance. In the event, however, the Pope was so far behind schedule that all these encounters were too rushed to enable us to take this matter up with him.

16

~: Revolving-door Taoiseach :~

Immediately after my election in the Dáil as Taoiseach on 30 June 1981, the secretary to the government, Dermot Nally, with whom I had worked closely when he had been assistant secretary during the 1973–77 government, accompanied me when I drove to Áras an Uachtaráin to receive my seal of office from President Hillery. During the journey, he told me that the financial situation of the state was far worse than we had realised; next morning, I would have to meet the Finance officials with my new Minister for Finance to consider emergency action.

On returning to Leinster House, I summoned my government nominees and, meeting them individually, offered them portfolios. I saw them individually (rather than collectively, as Liam Cosgrave had done), so that I might have the opportunity of having a private word with each of them. I was concerned in particular to ensure that none of them was a member of any organisation of which membership was not a matter of public knowledge. In our state, as distinct from in the United Kingdom (where, in Belfast, my grandfather had been, as I understood it, a high-ranking Freemason and representative of the Grand Lodge of Alabama), it was highly unlikely that Freemasonry played any role in politics; but there are comparable Roman Catholic organisations, membership of which may similarly not be a matter of public knowledge, and I believed that ministers should not be members of any such organisation, because no one should ever feel they had reason to fear that either their legitimate interests or the common good might be adversely affected because any member of a government led by me owed private allegiance to such a body.

I then announced my government to the Dáil. Michael O'Leary, as Labour Party leader, was, of course, Tánaiste. Unwisely, in my view, he also took on responsibility for Energy, as well as for the industrial side of Industry and Commerce. This was far too heavy a load for a newly elected leader of the Labour Party, who would have his work cut out to rally the support of the 40 percent of his party who had opposed participation in government. Moreover, the splitting of a department in which responsibility for Industry and for Trade had been combined since the foundation of the state was disruptive, and John Kelly, whom I asked to take charge of Commerce and also Tourism, was understandably unhappy at this division of responsibility.

The other Labour Party portfolios were the Department of Labour, placed in the steady hands of Liam Kavanagh; Health and Social Welfare, a double load that was, I think, a burden for Eileen Desmond, whose own health was not robust; and Defence, which went to the party's deputy leader, Jimmy Tully. (Jimmy's new career as Minister for Defence almost came to an abrupt end some months later during a visit to Egypt in connection with our UN peace-keeping involvement, when he found himself on the reviewing platform with President Sadat at the moment of the president's assassination, and lost some of his teeth to a ricochet bullet.) On the whole, this did not seem to me to be a particularly successful choice of portfolios from the Labour Party's point of view.

When I offered the Fine Gael deputy leader, Peter Barry, a choice of portfolios, he opted for Environment, which includes Local Government. For the key Finance appointment, which was clearly going to be of crucial importance, I selected thirty-four-year-old John Bruton, who had been an honours student of mine in the late 1960s and a junior minister in the 1973–77 government. He was young for the job by any standards, but was a very serious and principled politician as well as being imaginative and innovative, and also both generous and strong-willed. Two survivors from the 1973–77 government, Tom Fitzpatrick and Pat Cooney, I appointed to Fisheries and Forestry and to Transport and Posts and Telegraphs, respectively.

New to the office as Minister for Justice, but with the experience of a Dáil term behind him, was the late Jim Mitchell. He had shown his mettle – and his extraordinary generosity of spirit – over the previous decade, when on several occasions, once successfully, he had pressed Declan Costello to re-enter the Dáil as a representative of Jim's local area of Inchicore, Ballyfermot in west Dublin, at the expense of his own candidature. I believed he would be sound on security and liberal on law reform. What I did not allow for was his unbounded enthusiasm, which prompted him sometimes to arrive in our bedroom at all hours of the night to brief me on urgent security matters. But Joan and I soon became accustomed to these incursions.

To the Education post I nominated thirty-four-year-old John Boland, whose political intuition and ability to see around corners outweighed in my view his abrasive manner and somewhat negative attitude to myself. And Paddy O'Toole, a gentle westerner and Irish-speaker, became Minister for the Gaeltacht.

That left Agriculture and Foreign Affairs. To the former I appointed thirty-six-

year-old Alan Dukes – like John Bruton a student of mine in the 1960s – who had
been adviser to the Irish Farmers' Association in Dublin and Brussels. Later he had
become a member of the Cabinet of Dick Burke, then the Irish member of the
European Commission in Brussels, until I persuaded him to stand for election, first
for the European Parliament in 1979 and then for the Dáil. I was of course aware
that some past appointments of deputies to the government on their first day in the
Dáil were regarded as unfortunate; but I needed someone in the Agriculture portfolio who would have the confidence of the farming community whilst never
becoming a prisoner of their sectional interest; and Alan, despite his lack of political
experience, seemed – and indeed proved – ideally suited for this role.

Because of my personal experience of Foreign Affairs and my recognition of its
key importance in view of the crisis in Northern Ireland and our involvement in the
European Community, I had been very exercised about who to put into that department. Joan had come up with the answer. She suggested that the late Jim Dooge
was the one man to whom I would certainly be willing to delegate responsibility in
this sensitive area – having wisely identified the risk that, with anyone else, I could
be tempted to adopt an unduly 'hands on' approach to foreign affairs. A scientist of
world reputation in the field of hydrology, and with political experience extending
back to an early stint in local government between 1948 and 1954, followed by a
return to politics in 1961 in the Seanad, where he had been both Cathaoirleach and
Leas-Cathaoirleach, Jim Dooge had one of the wisest political heads in the country.
The only problem was that he had left politics in 1977 for a second time in order
to concentrate on his academic career. I was, however, entitled under the
Constitution to appoint up to two ministers from the Seanad – although this provision had only once been employed in the almost half-century of the
Constitution's existence, and most people had probably forgotten that it existed.
However, by using in Jim Dooge's favour one of my eleven nominations to the
Seanad, I could have him constitutionally qualified for the Foreign Affairs portfolio
within two months; and in the interim, John Kelly could act additionally as foreign
minister. It was with some difficulty, however, that I persuaded Jim Dooge to enter
politics for the third time in his life, in order to give me the support I felt I needed
in this key area.

Another innovation was the appointment of Senator Alexis FitzGerald as special adviser to the government, with the provision that, like the attorney general, he
would attend Cabinet meetings. I had known Alexis – who had been one of Joan's
lecturers in UCD – for a third of a century. He was the founder and senior partner
of one of Dublin's largest and most highly regarded firms of solicitors, and was also
an economist and in later life a student of theology. He had acted informally as
adviser to his father-in-law, John A. Costello, the head of the coalition governments
of 1948–51 and 1954–57. In that capacity, Alexis, together with his close friend

Paddy Lynch (until 1951 a civil servant in the Department of the Taoiseach who, in the interval between those two governments, had joined the Economics Department in UCD, where he had a most distinguished career), had been responsible for the initiatives in late 1956 that started the reorientation of the inward-looking post-revolutionary Irish economy to the world outside. This was the process that, under Sean Lemass's leadership, was brought to fruition in the years after 1958 through the efforts of T. K. Whitaker's First Programme for Economic Expansion.

In the Seanad, where he had served since 1969, Alexis's talents had been deployed to such effect that even when he was in Opposition, his objective criticism of legislation was taken extremely seriously by ministers and their civil servants – even to the point of halting the proceedings on at least one occasion in order to get his help in re-drafting! I did not think that I could reasonably appoint two members of the Seanad to ministerial office – that would have been too big a mouthful for my Dáil colleagues to swallow – but by this alternative arrangement I hoped to be able to avail myself fully of Alexis's legal skills, economic expertise, business experience and immense political wisdom.

His appointment to this novel position nevertheless caused quite a stir. Some of the Labour members of the government feared that he would in effect be a twelfth Fine Gael minister. Charles Haughey described his appointment as 'cronyism', as if I had in some way conferred a benefit on Alexis, whereas in fact he was giving up his Seanad seat and his leading role in his firm for an underpaid and undefined appointment of uncertain (and, as it turned out, very brief) duration.

Finally, as attorney general I appointed Peter Sutherland, a barrister in his mid-thirties whose energy and enthusiasm was already a byword and who accepted without hesitation an appointment that cut his earnings to a small fraction of their previous level.

With four key departments and the attorney generalship placed in the hands of men in their mid-thirties, another key ministerial position allocated to someone who was not then a member of either House, and the creation of the new post of special adviser, it is fair to say that my government caused something of a sensation. This was all the more the case because I had omitted former ministers who by virtue of their seniority – traditionally a dominant consideration in forming an Irish government – had been expected by many in the party and in the media to be included. But I wanted my government to break new ground by bringing in fresh and younger faces rather than to be a virtual replica of the Cosgrave government of the mid-1970s.

As it turned out, the feature of my government that seemed to stir up most controversy was quite a different aspect, which in a country other than Ireland might not even have been noticed: the geographical distribution of the ministers. Perhaps because the establishment of elected local authorities preceded the institution of an Irish national parliament by a quarter of a century, national politics has some curiously parochial features. Many people outside Dublin seem to see each government not as the government of a state but as a kind of federal super-parliament in which their particular county needs to be represented in order to secure its interests vis-à-vis the rest of the country – and in particular vis-à-vis Dublin, which is still widely perceived in rural Ireland as if it were even today a centre of alien colonial rule.

Because six members of my government represented Dublin constituencies and four more had been elected in constituencies bordering Dublin – and above all because only one was from the west – I came under immediate attack, both within my own party and more widely. At no stage was it suggested that more competent candidates were available: the issue of competence seemed to be almost universally regarded as quite irrelevant.

I was more amused than irritated at this reaction. There were far more serious matters to attend to: the financial crisis at home and the hunger strike in Northern Ireland, which together completely dominated our hectic first month in government.

To tackle these two problems I would be drawing respectively on the skills of the Departments of Finance and Foreign Affairs. I would need, however, a personal 'Cabinet' to assist me with this and my other tasks of government. In the latter part of my period in Opposition, I had strengthened my office by the appointment of a young graduate, Katherine Meenan, as my personal aide, with particular responsibility for our relations with the Christian Democratic movement in Europe, of which we were part, but also to assist in handling relations with members of our parliamentary party. She came with me into government to continue this work.

As government press officer I appointed Liam Hourican, the former RTÉ correspondent who had served in Dick Burke's Cabinet in Brussels and who had stepped into Ted Nealon's shoes during the election campaign. And CIÉ seconded to me Joe Jennings (who had been responsible for the launch of my campaign by special train) to head the Government Information Service.

With a view to ensuring effective liaison with Foreign Affairs, I appointed Michael Lillis as my diplomatic adviser. His performance in the United States as information officer, and later as counsellor at the Washington embassy, had impressed me enormously, and more recently he had acquired European experience in Commissioner Dick Burke's Brussels Cabinet. Moreover, he had a rapport – if occasionally of a combative nature! – with our ambassador in the United States, Sean Donlon, whom I intended to bring back as secretary of the Department of Foreign Affairs.

As private secretary I appointed Declan Kelly from Foreign Affairs, who had been my assistant private secretary in that department. Since then he had served as private secretary to two other Ministers for Foreign Affairs and to two ministers of state in that department, one of these Fine Gael and three Fianna Fáil. This appointment caused a storm in the Department of the Taoiseach. Whereas in Foreign Affairs the private office was vacated when a new minister was appointed – even if he be from the same party – so as to enable the minister to choose his own private-office staff, it transpired that in the Department of the Taoiseach the tradition was completely different. The practice had been hitherto that the private secretary and the staff of the Taoiseach's private office remained, even when there was a change of administration. I had been quite unaware of this, and when the displaced private secretary of many years later became secretary-general of the Department of Justice, I apologised to him for my inadvertent intervention in his earlier career!

My decision on this matter clearly came as a bombshell to my new department, and was the subject of strong protests on behalf of the staff. Even though the terms in which this reaction was expressed appeared inappropriate to me, I could understand the feelings of those concerned when I came to realise how far I was departing from precedent. Nevertheless, I held to my decision; and indeed when I returned to office at the end of 1982, I reappointed Declan Kelly, who had in the meantime served as private secretary to yet another Fianna Fáil Minister for Foreign Affairs; he remained in this position until 1985.

Quite apart from Declan Kelly's own outstanding personal qualities of discretion and judgement, I believe that, given the potential tension between a private secretary, whose task it is to look after his political master's interests, and the secretary of the department, who may have a different and, as he would see it, more long-term view (compare the role of these two civil servants in the television programme Yes, Minister), there is in any event a good case in principle for ministers being free to draw private secretaries from other departments. In fairness, however, I should say that I am not personally aware of cases where tension of this kind has caused problems in the Irish system of government. However that may be, the team thus assembled (which, partly by virtue of his physical location on the floor below my office, included the attorney general, Peter Sutherland) proved to be a 'happy ship'.

The Department of the Taoiseach itself posed some problems. During the Haughey administration from 1979 to 1981, the short-lived Department of Economic Planning and Development, established by Jack Lynch in 1977, was abolished, and its functions were effectively merged with those of the Department of the Taoiseach, which thus overnight grew from a small and compact Cabinet secretariat to a full-blown department with a staff of two hundred and with two departmental secretaries: the secretary to the government, Dermot Nally, and the secretary of the department. I was never happy with the resultant dual structure, which seemed to me to be top-heavy, although both parts of the department had some able staff.

From the moment of my appointment, I found myself deeply involved with the new Minister for Finance, John Bruton, in tackling the disastrous financial crisis. The Exchequer borrowing level, which, after peaking in 1975 as a result of the oil crisis, had been reduced by the national coalition government to a little over 10 percent of GNP in 1977, had risen to almost 15 percent by 1980. The 1981 budget had purported to reduce it to 13 percent of GNP, but when John Bruton and I met the Finance officials on the morning of 1 July, they told us that current spending had been running almost one-sixth ahead of the budgeted level – in addition to which, a number of the state enterprises that had been allowed to run into a loss-making phase were demanding substantial capital injections, for which no provision had been made.

During these three traumatic weeks of July, however, I had to give much of my attention to the evolution of the hunger-strike crisis. Our position on this was that, in accordance with the traditional policy of Irish governments on such strikes within their own jurisdiction, we would not press the British government to concede to paramilitary prisoners the political status demanded by the IRA. We had, however, noted proposals made by the Commission for Justice and Peace of the Roman Catholic hierarchy on 3 June involving the extension to male prisoners in the Maze Prison of the arrangements for the use of their own clothes that applied to women prisoners in Armagh Jail, as well as greater freedom of association, not involving military-type activities, and orientation of work towards cultural and educational activities. Even though these proposals did not meet their five demands, the prisoners had expressed appreciation of the commission's proposals. This sounded hopeful.

Immediately before the Dáil reassembled, Charles Haughey had called in the British ambassador and had issued a statement saying that the time to find a solution to prevent further deaths was now. The British government had responded to this with a long statement saying that there was scope for development in the prison regime but that this process of improvement could not proceed further under the duress of a hunger strike.

The IRA reaction, allegedly on behalf of the prisoners, had been to describe this response as 'arrogant'. Nevertheless, the Commission for Justice and Peace saw the British statement as encouraging – as did we – and sought further clarification. Our information from the prison was that, despite the IRA statement purporting to speak for them, the prisoners wanted the commission to continue its involvement. We were also aware that some of the relatives of the prisoners on hunger strike were becoming increasingly restive at the IRA's intransigent approach.

On 1 July, Michael O'Leary and I communicated our view on these points to the British ambassador and urged that the NIO meet the commission again and allow the commission to meet the prisoners. We also warned against any policy of brinkmanship, which – especially in view of the nearness to death of one hunger striker, Joe McDonnell – could harden attitudes, including in particular the attitudes of the relatives, who had the power to influence developments. That night I rang Margaret Thatcher to make these points directly to her.

At this point, the relatives of the hunger strikers asked to see me. Despite the fact that I believe it generally undesirable in an issue of this kind to become involved in potentially emotional situations with the relatives of those concerned, I agreed to see them, in view of their crucial role and the fact that almost all of them were known to want a settlement – as indeed, it seemed, did most of the prisoners at that point. This meeting, on 3 July, was, as I had expected, intensely distressing, but it enabled me to see for myself that while there were those among them who took a straight IRA line, many of them were indeed primarily concerned to end the hunger strike.

The minister of state at the NIO, Michael Allison, then met the commission again. He gave the impression that he wanted to be more conciliatory, but referred to 'the lady behind the veil', namely the prime minister. As we had proposed, he cleared a visit by the Commission for Justice and Peace to the prisoners, who then issued a statement that, as we had thought likely, was much more conciliatory than the one which had been published by the IRA on their behalf three days earlier. They said they were not looking for any special privileges as against other prisoners, and that the British government could meet their requirements without any sacrifice of principle. It looked as if the commission would now be able to resolve the crisis with Michael Allison, who seemed close to accepting their proposals.

Several days were to elapse before we heard that, authorised by Margaret Thatcher, direct contact was made with the IRA by the British government, through an intermediary. The proposals made by the intermediary were close to what the prisoners and Allison, through the commission, were near to agreeing, but went further in one respect. Not unnaturally, the IRA preferred this somewhat wider offer, and above all the opportunity to be directly involved in discussions with the British government. They were then allowed by the British authorities to send Danny Morrison secretly into the prison for discussions with the hunger strikers and with the IRA leader there, Brendan McFarlane. This visit was later described by the IRA as a test of the authority of the British government representative in touch with them to bypass the NIO.

The commission, unaware of all this, was preparing its document, which was to be the basis for an agreement involving the ending of the hunger strike. On Monday 6 July at 3.30 PM, according to the account given to me shortly after these events, Gerry Adams phoned the commission seeking a meeting, revealing the

British government's indirect contact with them. An hour and a half later, two members of the commission met Adams and Morrison, who demanded that the commission phone the NIO to cancel their meeting.

Members of the commission, furious at this development, then met Allison and four of his officials. They asked him if he had been in communication with the hunger strikers or with those with authority over them. He said that no member of his office had been in contact, and, when pressed, repeated this line.

When the commission contacted us immediately after this meeting, they told us nothing about the London contact with Adams and Morrison – understandably, given that this was a telephone call. In any event, this did not loom large in their eyes at that point beside the agreement they believed they had reached, which seemed to them to be about to end the hunger strike. The commission had produced to Allison the statement on which they had been working, which they described as 'a true summary of the essential points of prison reform that had emerged.' They told Allison that this statement was considered by the hunger strikers to be 'the formation [*sic*] of a resolution of the hunger strike', provided that they received 'satisfactory clarification of detail and confirmation by an NIO official to the prisoners personally of the commitment of the British government to act according to the spirit and the letter' of the statement. Allison went out to make a phone call and then came back to say that he had approval. He proposed that an NIO official would see the prisoners with the governor by mid-morning the following day, Tuesday. When we received this information, Dermot Nally phoned the British ambassador to urge that this confirmatory visit take place as soon as possible.

Late that night, however, the commission was phoned by Danny Morrison seeking a meeting, which they refused; but half an hour later, he arrived at the hotel, saying that the Sinn Féin-IRA contacts with the British were continuing through the night and that he needed to see the actual commission proposals. This request was refused, although he was given the general gist of them. Twelve hours later, on Tuesday afternoon, Gerry Adams rang to say that the British had now made an offer but that it was not enough.

Meanwhile, the commission had spent an agonising day, for while London had been negotiating with the IRA, Allison and the NIO had prevaricated about the prison visit, repeatedly promising that the official was about to go to the prison. But at ten o'clock that night, Allison phoned to say that the official would not now be going to the prison until the following morning – adding, however, that this delay would be to the prisoners' benefit.

At 8.30 PM, however, Morrison and a companion had come without warning to the hotel where the commission had its base. Their attitude was threatening. Morrison said their contact had been put in jeopardy as a result of the commission revealing its existence at its meeting with Allison; the officials present with Allison had not known of the contact. Despite this onslaught, the commission refused to keep Morrison informed of their actions.

Just before 5 AM that night, Joe McDonnell died. At 6.30, the governor, in the presence of an NIO official, read a statement to the prisoners that differed markedly from the one that had been prepared by the commission and that had, in their view, been approved by Allison thirty-six hours earlier. Fifteen minutes later, Adams rang the commission to say that at 5.30 AM the contact with London had been terminated without explanation.

When we heard the news of Joe McDonnell's death, and of the last-minute hardening of the British position, we were shattered. We had been quite unprepared for this volte-face, for at this stage we, of course, had known nothing whatever of the disastrous British approach to Adams and Morrison. Nor had we known of what seemed to have been an IRA attempt – regardless of the threat this posed to the lives of the prisoners, and especially to that of Joe McDonnell – to raise the ante by seeking concessions beyond what the prisoners had said they could accept. We had believed that the IRA had been in effect bypassed by the commission's direct contact with the prisoners at the weekend, which we had helped to arrange.

That afternoon, the Commission for Justice and Peace issued a statement setting out the discussions they had had with Allison leading to the agreement reached on Monday evening. I then issued a statement recalling that I had repeatedly said that a solution could be reached through a flexibility of approach that need not sacrifice any principle. While the onus to show this flexibility rested with both sides, the greater responsibility must, as always, rest on those with the greater power.

I have given a full account of these events (some of them unknown to us at the time they took place) because in retrospect I think that the shock of learning that a solution seemed to have been sabotaged by yet another and, as it seemed to us, astonishingly ham-fisted approach on behalf of the British government to the IRA, and by what subsequently was an IRA decision to prevent a settlement for their own political reasons, influenced the extent and intensity of the efforts I deployed in the weeks that followed, in the hope – vain, as it turned out – of bringing the British government back to the point it had appeared to reach on Monday 6 July.

During these weeks in July and early August, I may also have been influenced more than I realised at the time by the frustration I felt at having to deal thereafter with the British government while I had, in a sense, one hand tied behind my back. For I would naturally have liked to have confronted them with – and would have liked even more to be able to make public – my knowledge of the furtive contacts on behalf of the British government with the IRA. But careful reflection led me to conclude that any revelation to the British of our knowledge of these activities would be likely to render a solution less rather than more likely. Disclosure of this knowledge could have driven the British government, and the prime minister in particular, into a state of embarrassed intransigence possibly accompanied by denials, which – if we had refused to accept them, as in honesty we would have had to do – would have made impossible the development of any kind of reasonable relationship between that government and ourselves. The fact, moreover, that our information, while absolutely convincing in its detail, was necessarily second-hand (it was what a member of the commission told us Adams and Morrison had said to them) reinforced the need for caution.

My frustration became all the more intense when a week later the IRA, with which an organ of the British government had chosen to deal behind our backs, launched a demonstration on our streets that threatened public order in our own state. Foreseeing the emergence of such a threat, I had written on 10 July to Margaret Thatcher telling her that a rising tide of sympathy for the hunger strikers was threatening the stability of the Republic. I urged her, in order to avoid a serious and progressive deterioration in bilateral relations, to accept as the foundation of a solution the detailed description of a possible future prison regime set out by the commission; I added that the ending of the hunger strike would deprive the IRA of its most potent weapon and would restore a climate in which our efforts could again be directed to more positive and constructive endeavours in pursuance of the process initiated by her and my predecessor in December 1980, to the continuance of which I attached great importance.

During a telephone conversation with John Hume on the following Friday, Atkins told him that as a result of my letter to the prime minister and the ministerial meeting in London, 'the whole matter is under reconsideration' – a remark that temporarily raised our hopes. Nevertheless, it seemed desirable to exert whatever pressure we could at this crucial point. Accordingly, I wrote to President Reagan to ask him, in view of the increased support accruing to the IRA as a result of the situation, which was threatening our security, to use his influence with the British prime minister to secure the implementation of what I described as 'an already existing understanding' mediated by the Commission for Justice and Peace.'

Arising from my letter about the hunger strike, the president said to our ambassador, Sean Donlon, that several days previously he had conveyed to Margaret Thatcher the concern of Tip O'Neill and Ted Kennedy in relation to the matter – which would not, I felt, have had much impact on her if, as seemed to be the case, he had not indicated that he himself shared this concern. He added, not very encouragingly, that he had a difficulty, as he did not wish to aid prisoners detained for terrorism.

Sean's easy access to the key US policy-makers, including, informally, to the president, which many far larger countries would envy, reflected the extraordinary success of our diplomatic efforts in Washington during the previous five years. On this occasion, however, we were asking the Americans to jeopardise their relationship with Britain on an issue they did not fully understand and on which, because convicted terrorists were concerned, they were not instinctively sympathetic. This intervention of mine was perhaps a mistake, born of frustration with the British handling of the hunger strike, but it did not prejudice the success of our later efforts to secure US support after Margaret Thatcher's 'Out, out, out' remarks in November 1984, when we were seeking $250 million in US aid for Northern Ireland in conjunction with the 1985 Anglo-Irish Agreement.

Three days later, the IRA-dominated H-Block committee organised a demonstration and march to the British embassy in Dublin. There were five thousand people on the march, many of them from Northern Ireland. They repeatedly attacked Gardaí along the route with stones, and many carried pickaxe handles or stakes. In Ballsbridge, five hundred of the two thousand Gardaí on duty were deployed behind barriers blocking the main road leading to the embassy.

At one point, the line nearly broke under this sustained assault. Fortunately it held, for if the mob had swept through and on to the embassy, they would eventually have faced the last line of defence, a unit of the army. That was a confrontation we were most anxious to avoid. Eventually the Gardaí moved to disperse the mob with a baton charge. Within five minutes the demonstration was over; but on their way back to the city, the marchers broke scores of windows and stoned Gardaí along the route. Houses near the scene of the riot suffered severely, many of their gardens having been ransacked for missiles to throw at the Gardaí. On the following day, Joan, on her own initiative, visited the area to sympathise with the occupants.

These events were reviewed by the government during the following week. Although deeply concerned about the possible consequences of a conflict between soldiers and the mob, we eventually concluded that we had no choice but to maintain an army presence at the embassy for a further march that was threatened for the following Saturday. However, on my suggestion, arrangements were made to take pressure off the Gardaí manning the barrier by having a second group available to take the mob in the flank and rear on the next occasion. This tactic proved successful; the second march was in any event on a much smaller scale.

17

∿ Second Term:
Picking Up the Pieces ∿

Before embarking on an account of my final term of office, I should perhaps say something about how Joan's and my personal life had been affected by the changes in my political fortunes.

For since my appointment as minister in March 1973, our pattern of living had been significantly altered. During the years to 1973, I had been under great pressure as I tried to juggle my four careers of university lecturer, economic consultant, journalist and front-bench opposition politician. For me, the change to a single, if highly demanding, job, as Minister for Foreign Affairs, had been something of a relief, but for Joan the change had been traumatic: she had had to adjust to travelling by air after seventeen years of avoiding that form of transport, as well as to my frequent absences from home. However, once she had overcome the air-travel barrier, in July 1973, she had found a new and positive role as a participant in diplomatic activities.

My subsequent transformation from Minister for Foreign Affairs to Leader of the Opposition in 1977 had involved a further hiatus in her life. Whilst at election time the wife of a party leader can play a significant role, this is much less the case between elections. Joan disliked my frequent absences during the years from 1977 to 1981, as at weekends I toured the forty-one constituencies, most of them twice; and whilst, as always, she identified with my new career, domestic politics on this scale was certainly less interesting for her than foreign affairs had been.

A new dimension had also entered our lives since 1975. Doireann and Iseult, John and Eithne's two eldest children, had been born whilst I was foreign minister, and their sister Aoife arrived in 1980, in the later part of my stint as leader of the Opposition. The new and welcome role of grandmother helped Joan to adjust. For my part, ten years were to elapse – and several more grandchildren were to arrive – before I was able to give as much time as I would have wished to being a grandfather.

We were both very distressed when in August 1981 our daughter, Mary, and her husband, Vincent Deane, had to emigrate to Tromsø in Norway, well north of the Artic Circle, where the sun does not shine for two months in the winter. Mary had spent several years as a temporary lecturer in English in Maynooth, where she had been very happy; but despite the efforts of her professor, Father Peter Connolly, because of opposition in a university that was still under the control of the Catholic hierarchy, she was dismissed. Whilst she was judged by the Labour Court to have been wrongfully dismissed, she was awarded no compensation. Then, after two years as a temporary lecturer in UCD, following Professor Denis Donoghue's departure to the US, she found herself unemployed again. The only work she could find that year, in addition to some part-time lecturing, was designing furniture for a factory in County Donegal – which entailed travelling through Derry. In 1981, as the hunger-strike situation deteriorated, this became a hazardous journey for the daughter of such a prominent enemy of the IRA, and after a disturbing experience in Derry, and on Garda advice, she had to abandon this work.

The only academic post then available was a senior lectureship in English at Tromsø University. She found that her students were not much stimulated by English literature but were fascinated by Ireland, so when she went back to Norway after the 1981 Christmas holiday, she took a library of books on contemporary Ireland, and inaugurated courses on Irish politics and economics. Joan and I visited Mary and Vincent in Norway at Easter 1982, when I took up an invitation to give a lecture there on Northern Ireland.

Her mother was determined that if Mary had to be an emigrant, she should be a more accessible one; by dint of pursuing every relevant advertisement in the *Times Higher Education Supplement*, Joan eventually tracked down a post as head of the English Department at the Crewe-Alsager Higher Education College in Cheshire, a mere 150 miles from Dublin. There Mary remained for seven years, until a back problem forced her to retire on health grounds, and she returned to Ireland to start a new career in painting. Vincent, a scholar specialising in *Finnegans Wake*, was fortunately able to carry on his work wherever Mary happened to be.

During my years as Taoiseach, Mary's house in the Elizabethan market town of Sandbach in Cheshire became a place of refuge for Joan and myself. We stayed there frequently, enjoying the tranquillity of the Cheshire countryside and the freedom to move about among the uninquisitive Cheshire people. Until 1985, when the impending Anglo-Irish Agreement heightened my profile in Britain, I was not encumbered by security there, and was glad to be able to wander the town on foot, or occasionally on Vincent's bicycle.

In December 1985, just after the signing of the agreement, we had the joy of acquiring two more granddaughters: Réachbha, born to Mary, and Ciara, born to Mark's wife Derval O'Higgins. In 1975 Mark had fulfilled his ambition to enter an auctioneering firm as an apprentice. By 1982, at the age of twenty-five, he had become the managing director of the firm, Sherry FitzGerald; before the end of the decade, he had developed it into one of Ireland's leading real-estate agencies. During most of my period as Taoiseach, he and Derval lived in a flat in our Palmerston Road home, where, on their marriage in 1983, they had replaced Mary and Vincent as co-owners of the house with Mary and myself. Thus it was only in 1988, after more than forty years of marriage, that Joan and I, for the first time, found ourselves without offspring in the house; but Mark, and shortly afterwards Mary, settled within a few hundred yards of us, and John's home is only four miles away, so we saw a lot of our children and grandchildren. This expanding family enriched our lives, and provided Joan with new interests, as my involvement in politics became more demanding.

When we could, we liked to spend some hours dining with our closer friends, almost all of them from outside politics – for, like many politicians, I endeavoured to keep my personal life separate from my political one. Whilst I enjoyed the company of many of my political colleagues during the working day, I preferred in spare moments to relax with old friends. Moreover, after becoming leader of the party, and later Taoiseach, it also became important to avoid being more friendly with some members of the party and government than others, lest this create suspicions of favouritism. Some, although perhaps not all, of what has been seen as a certain detachment from personal relationships in my political life reflected this factor.

Turning back to politics, I must describe the political atmosphere in which we were operating, and the spirit in which we approached our task of governance. Naturally enough, like any government anywhere in the world, we were concerned that our parties should emerge successfully from this endeavour, with a fair prospect of being re-elected to office. That was sufficient motivation for sticking together in the face of adversity – and we had no illusions about the amount of adversity we were going to face. But in our case, this motivation was reinforced by three considerations that went well beyond the normal concerns of party politicians; all these related to the dangers that we felt the country would face if Fianna Fáil were to return to power.

First, the experience of two Haughey governments, and particularly that of 1982, raised in our minds serious concerns about the future of the country if such a government were to be re-elected in the near future with an overall majority. I had moved, some would argue too hastily, to bring down the second Haughey government in November 1982 because of the urgency of restoring the non-political character of the Garda Síochána, which had been put under threat by the Haughey government's abuse of phone tapping, and neither I nor my colleagues could easily contemplate allowing, through any default of ours, the circumstances to recur that had led to the GUBU events of 1982.

Second, whilst I recognised, as did some at least of my colleagues, that there had been a reversal of the disastrous financial approach of the Fianna Fáil government in July 1982, when the Minister for Finance, Ray MacSharry, had asserted himself, it was not clear that Charles Haughey's conversion to prudent financial policies was genuine and irreversible. Ray MacSharry had disappeared from the Fianna Fáil front bench after the revelation that he had secretly tape-recorded a conversation with a colleague, Martin O'Donoghue. And our suspicions of Charles Haughey's own economic predilections were confirmed when in September 1983 he advocated a reflation of the economy at a time when Exchequer borrowing was still, despite our initial measures, running at 14 percent of GNP.

Third, in my mind at least (in the early stages of our government this may have been less true of some of my colleagues), there was a possibility that we might make some progress towards eliminating the danger of IRA political success in Northern Ireland and laying the foundation for future progress towards peace and stability there by concluding an agreement with the British government. Following the events of 1980, and more particularly Charles Haughey's actions in 1982 at the time of the Falklands war, this I felt would be politically impossible for a Fianna Fáil government to achieve, at any rate as long as Margaret Thatcher remained British prime minister.

The combination of these considerations meant that it was vital not alone for our party but also for the national interest that Fine Gael and the Labour Party should maintain their unity in government for the four years or so ahead. Against this background, I simply did not have the option that as Taoiseach I might have had in other circumstances, of bringing the government to an end by a dissolution in order to resolve differences that might arise between Fine Gael and Labour.

This carried implications for the manner in which the government was to operate. Although for my own part I was prepared in respect of most domestic affairs to have decisions in government taken by a majority vote, even if this meant (as it often did!) that I was myself left in a minority, such majority decisions could not without great risk be taken on a basis that would involve Fine Gael overruling Labour. Where the Labour Party ministers as a group, as distinct from individual ministers, saw a particular issue as one of vital importance to their own party, it had to be resolved by discussion, and where necessary compromise, rather than by a vote or by a ruling by me. In either of these cases, if the decision went against Labour, we would risk a split that could have disastrous consequences not just for one or other (or both) of our parties but, in our estimation, for the country itself.

The onus for getting the necessary decisions taken against this background fell primarily on me, and required that I exercise my authority judiciously and in close concert with Dick Spring – who, it must be said, recognised fully his responsibility in maintaining the cohesion of the government in the circumstances in which we found ourselves. In a sense, what resulted was a threefold system of decision-making. In the area of Northern Ireland policy, and in certain limited areas of particular concern to me, such as preserving the volume of development aid, I operated rather as a chief than a chairman. Most matters of domestic policy, however, were determined by government by consensus, or where necessary by a vote. But in a third category of decisions, where such a vote could clearly have divided the government along party lines on an issue that either party saw as vital, the calling of such a vote clearly had to give way to settlement by discussion – and discussion of this kind could often be extremely prolonged.

Such sensitive issues were relatively few in number, but, because there was no clear-cut method of resolving them, they tended to take up a lot of time. They included a small number of financial questions in each budget, and an even smaller number of other legislative matters on which the parties were divided (for example, the terms of reference of a new National Development Corporation and a proposed Local Broadcasting Bill). It must be added, however, that as in any other government, decisions on departmental estimates, regardless of party, were also inclined to lead to prolonged discussion, because of ministers' reluctance to vote down a colleague on some expenditure item of particular concern to him or her, lest they be voted down on a similar matter when their turn came. Perhaps in this area I allowed more latitude for discussion than was desirable in the interests of efficient government – so some of my colleagues clearly felt! – but some of these were sensitive issues for the Labour Party, and my Fine Gael ministers might not have appreciated being overruled when this would not have been possible in cases involving Labour Party ministers.

I was conscious at times of the frustration felt, by some of my Fine Gael colleagues in particular, at the length of time taken to resolve certain delicate questions. They were not always as conscious as I was of the danger of taking the easy path of calling a vote, which could have precipitated serious problems between the parties.

There was another element in my own approach to government that I should perhaps mention at this stage. From the outset, it seemed to me that the scale of financial problems we had inherited made it possible that no effort of ours could bring our economy back to a growth phase in time for this happy outcome to influence voters at the next election. My experience both as an economist and as a politician had led me to the conclusion that even when economic recovery has begun after a period of recession, at least a further eighteen months have to elapse before this begins to impinge on public consciousness. That meant that in order to be well placed to win the next election, we would need to complete the adjustment within two and a half years – which seemed improbable.

It is of course conceivable that had we taken much more severe measures at the outset, bringing the public finances under control more rapidly, we might have faced a somewhat more favourable political situation in 1987; I suspect that this may today be the 'conventional wisdom' on this issue – and, of course, it may be right. But the scale of deflation that would have been involved if we had sought to resolve the problem of public finances within two and a half or three years would, I believe, have been of a severity unknown until recently in Western Europe or the United States, and it is at least equally possible that the result of this would have been an even longer recession, with the economy simply unable to recover from such a tremendous shock. (I should perhaps add that I may have been unduly influenced by memories of damage done by excessively deflationary action in 1952 and 1956.)

I am content to leave that debate to economic historians; it is for them rather than for me to attempt to judge the merits of the approach we adopted. The political reality, however, was that from the outset, a serious doubt existed as to whether, regardless of what course we adopted, our government would be re-elected in 1987; and for me it became a primary aim of policy to work towards a situation in which, if a change of government did take place in that year, it would happen in circumstances in which our Fianna Fáil successors would be less likely to repeat the errors of that party's recent administration. If we could achieve a sufficient degree of progress with the public finances by 1987, a Fianna Fáil government coming to power at that time might be able to see a clear advantage in continuing on the same lines, creating a reasonable prospect that the difficult and unpopular task we were undertaking would not again, as in 1982, be undone.

So far as Northern Ireland policy was concerned, the best way of ensuring the survival of whatever arrangements we might be able to put in place during our term of office was, I felt, to have these brought into effect as early as possible, so that there would be time for any initial Fianna Fáil Pavlovian opposition to them to be replaced by a more rational acceptance of our achievements as a basis for further progress by that party in government. If we could also achieve a sufficient degree of progress with the public finances by 1987, a Fianna Fáil government coming to power at that time might see a clear advantage in continuing on the same lines, with a reasonable prospect that the difficult and unpopular task we were undertaking would not again, as in 1982, be undone.

The economic task ahead of our new government was indeed formidable. In tackling the public finances, we would be starting from a position notably worse than that which we had left behind a year earlier. This was so for two reasons. First, the level of economic activity in 1982, and thus of tax revenue, had been far lower than forecast at the start of the year by the Department of Finance. And second, as I mentioned earlier, Fianna Fáil in its post-election March budget in that year had increased both current and capital spending above the level proposed by

John Bruton, while at the same time eliminating a number of taxes introduced by him. The resultant enlarged financial gap had been temporarily filled by a once-off transfer of tax revenue back from the following year, 1983. As a result of these factors, the opening borrowing requirement for 1983 was far higher than that which, a year earlier, it could reasonably have expected to have been at this point, on the basis of our January 1982 budget.

Against this background, it was clear in late 1982 and early 1983 that, despite two years of falling living standards and rising unemployment, further stringent and prolonged budgetary action would have to be taken, involving a continuing deflation of the economy, which was bound to create tensions both within and between parties in our new government. Moreover, the common ground between Fine Gael and the Labour Party lay in the commitment of both parties to reforms in our social and legal systems, which, while in most cases not involving large expenditure, would almost inevitably involve the deployment of *some* additional resources. And such additional funds were clearly unlikely to be available on any significant scale during the lifetime of our administration. The fact that as a government we would thus be inhibited from undertaking many of the initiatives that would reflect our joint aspirations would not be helpful to our cohesion.

In tackling the financial crisis left by Fianna Fáil, we could expect no assistance from that party in Opposition. I knew that they would oppose ruthlessly and opportunistically all the unpleasant measures that their past actions in government would now force us to take. Furthermore, the steps that I saw as necessary to salvage the Anglo-Irish relationship would be unlikely to commend themselves to Charles Haughey, and, whilst I knew that he shared my concern about the threat posed by the growth of support for the IRA in Northern Ireland, it was far from certain that he would support the kind of political action that I contemplated with a view to tackling this problem. Anything we might achieve in this area – even if it exceeded what Fianna Fáil might have secured – would be attacked by that party as falling short of its rhetorical aspirations.

Much would obviously depend on the kind of relationship that would develop between Fine Gael and Labour segments of the government team. I had been heartened by my experience of negotiating the formation of the government with Dick Spring, and I believed that at a personal level he and I could work well together. It was clear to me that he was a serious politician. We shared many of the same values; my own instinctive sympathy with the younger generation, derived from my years as a university teacher and from what I had learnt from my own children, would, I believed, help me to overcome the age gap between Dick and myself, although it might take some time for him to feel entirely comfortable with someone so much older.

When he and I discussed portfolios, he had decided that he himself would take

Environment – which I thought rather heavy, given his other responsibilities as Tánaiste and leader of his party. He proposed the Labour portfolio again for Liam Kavanagh, and we agreed on Health and Social Welfare for Barry Desmond, and Trade, Commerce and Tourism (the truncated department that had been the by-product of Michael O'Leary's choice of Industry as well as Energy in the 1981–82 government) for Frank Cluskey.

Barry Desmond I had known for almost twenty years. As minister of state in the Department of Finance in the 1981–82 government, he had found inadequate outlets for his frustrated energies – which had led to some friction with his minister, John Bruton. But as a minister in charge of two major departments, he would find full scope for his remarkable capacity for work and his ability to command the most complex of briefs. Liam Kavanagh I had come to know well during the period of the 1981–82 government, when his calmness, cool judgement, and trade union experience had proved a great strength to us. The friendly working relationship I had established in the 1973–77 period with the fourth Labour Party minister, Frank Cluskey, had continued throughout the period when we had been the leaders of two Opposition parties. Joan and I had been particularly close to him when his wife, Eileen, had died. I looked forward to working with him again, not foreseeing the differences over the Dublin Gas issue that were to mark his brief period as a minister before he resigned at the end of 1983.

Three of the Fine Gael ministers in my previous government were not available at this time. John Kelly had opted out because of his unhappiness over a coalition with the Labour Party; Jim Dooge sadly did not feel able, for health reasons, to serve again; and Tom FitzPatrick had accepted nomination as Ceann Comhairle. To replace them, I chose Austin Deasy, my severest critic after the January election, whose independence of mind and sense of 'grass roots' feeling would, I felt, be valuable; Michael Noonan, whose parliamentary performance since his election to the Dáil eighteen months earlier had been impressive, both as a government back-bencher and later in Opposition; and Gemma Hussey, who, although with limited Dáil experience, seemed to me to have the capacity to be an effective minister in a reforming portfolio.

Peter Barry was one of the more 'nationalist' members of Fine Gael. I felt that he could play a very important role in maintaining a strong link with the SDLP during the difficult period ahead. It was at that time far from clear that the SDLP would accept my idea of a New Ireland Forum open to unionists and to the Alliance Party, and tensions could also arise with the leadership of that party during the nec-essarily confidential negotiations with the British government that I hoped to initi-ate after the Forum had reported. Accordingly, to strengthen our links with the SDLP and Northern nationalists generally, I asked Peter to take the foreign-affairs portfolio, which included responsibility for implementing government policy on

Northern Ireland, the initiation of which is the Taoiseach's responsibility.

In allocating the remaining portfolios to other Fine Gael ex-ministers – only one of whom had government experience pre-dating 1981 and most of whom were likely to remain prominent in politics long after I would retire, I was concerned – perhaps excessively so – to ensure that during my leadership they would each have experience of more than one department.

Accordingly, except for Paddy O'Toole, whose command of Irish justified his retaining the Gaeltacht portfolio, but to whom I allocated additional responsibility for Forestry and Fisheries, I switched all the others. I appointed Alan Dukes to Finance – like John Bruton, he had been a student of mind and had an economics degree – and gave John the major Industry portfolio, which involved responsibility both for industrial policy and for some of our ailing state enterprises. The other department responsible for a large number of state enterprises was Communications, to which I appointed Jim Mitchell, whose dynamism and deter-mination would, I believed – correctly, as it turned out – make a major impact on many of these loss-making bodies.

I was particularly concerned about the need for public-service reform, which I felt had been neglected because the Department of Public Service had been com-bined with the Department of Finance under a single minister. Given the state of the public finances, no Minister for Finance, however competent, was going to be able both to restore financial stability and at the same time bring about the neces-sary reforms in the public service. Accordingly, against the conventional wisdom, I decided to give the Department of the Public Service a separate minister, at least for this term in government; and John Boland seemed to have the necessary qualities for this demanding job. I knew that he would not allow himself to be bullied or cajoled by the civil service into backing off from what needed to be done. He was, I have to say, most unenthusiastic about taking on the task, partly because he had hoped to return to Education and partly, I think, because up to that moment he had not given much thought to the need for public-service reform.

To the other former minister, Pat Cooney, I offered Defence; and I asked Austin Deasy to take Agriculture – much to his astonishment. He objected that he had no special knowledge of the area, but I told him that, in view of the pressure of the Common Agricultural Policy, what we needed in this department in the period immediately ahead was a tough negotiator, and that I felt he had the requisite qual-ifications. Gemma Hussey was equally astonished to be offered Education; I believed, however, that she would tackle it with vigour and imagination, initiating reforms that were long overdue.

Finally I asked Michael Noonan to take the Justice portfolio. I judged that he had the combination of qualities needed to tackle sensitively and successfully the recent subversion of our security system for party purposes, of which I had become aware in recent weeks, and to restore the independence of the Garda Síochána by securing the force against the kind of political interference that had become a source of public concern during the previous nine months. He too was taken aback at the offer of this portfolio, more particularly when I told him that I had reason to believe there was substance in reports that had recently appeared in the press about the improper phone-tapping of two political journalists, Bruce Arnold and Geraldine Kennedy. The unravelling of this would be bound to involve him at the very outset in a painful confrontation with the top level of the Garda Síochána.

The interval before the formation of this government had given me an opportunity to prepare a letter to each of the members of my Cabinet, setting out in some detail a number of matters relating to their duties and to the general running of the government. Much of this had to do with working arrangements for the government as a whole, and relations between departments, but I took the opportunity to raise some other points. For example, I insisted that differences on points of *fact* between departments be reconciled before memoranda came to government. In my previous administration, it had seemed to me absurd that we appeared to be expected to reconcile such factual differences at the Cabinet table. And I also insisted on the co-ordinating role of the Department of Foreign Affairs in relation to external policies. This was something that domestic departments often ignored, especially in the EC framework.

I took this opportunity to raise a number of other points with my new ministers. I required those who had to travel outside the state for purposes other than EC Council meetings to inform my office and the Department of Foreign Affairs as soon as such a visit was mooted, and to keep that department posted on any changes of plan; on occasion, I added, our ambassadors in certain capitals had found themselves handling simultaneously as many as three quite separate ministerial visits, one or more of them without notice.

On a further practical point, having discovered as Minister for Foreign Affairs how the concern of civil servants that their ministers be well treated could lead to greater expenditure on visits abroad than ministers themselves, if appraised of what was involved, might wish to incur, I said that the hiring of limousines be avoided unless for a stated reason they were essential, and that rooms rather than suites be booked in hotels unless it was the intention to hold an official meeting in the minister's room – as is, in fact, often necessary on such occasions.

I also put in writing the view that I had put verbally to ministers in my previous government before appointing them – that membership of any organisation in which participation was by policy not a matter of public knowledge would be incompatible with membership of the government. Word of this must have leaked out, for one day in the Dáil I was asked by the backbencher Oliver Flanagan if I had imposed such a requirement in order to rule out participation in government by members of the Knights of Columbanus, of which he was himself a declared member. I replied diplomatically that as I had not seen the rules of that organisation, I could not say whether this decision applied to it – which foxed him!

Other matters I dealt with in this letter of appointment were the arrangements for ministers' private offices, the making of appointments by ministers to the boards of state bodies, the roles of ministers of state, and the briefing of the press after government meetings. I ensured a measure of control over the appointment of special advisers in ministers' private offices – which in principle I favoured if they were people with relevant expertise rather than PR people – by requiring that prior to any such engagement, I be informed of the reasons and of the expert qualification of the person concerned. At the same time, I asked that until a study of past practices in relation to employment of civil servants to deal with ministers' constituency correspondence (as distinct from correspondence with deputies and senators) had been completed, in a few days' time, such work should not be allocated to civil servants. This enabled me to ensure shortly afterwards that there would be no repetition in my administration of the excessive use of civil servants to deal with constituency matters – something that was reported to have been a feature of the government we had just replaced.

(It had been suggested that some ministers in that government had engaged a dozen or more civil servants on this kind of work. Indeed, when I became Taoiseach I had noted with some amusement the discreet disappearance of a 'general section' of my own department, comprising sixteen people, who I gathered had been looking after my predecessor's constituency work. In my case the personal secretary who, in accordance with custom, had accompanied me from Opposition took care of this side of my activities.)

During my earlier term of office as Taoiseach, I had come to realise that although it was the practice for ministers to inform their colleagues of intended appointments to the boards of state bodies for which they were responsible, and sometimes to invite comments on their proposed nominations, it was in fact difficult at such a late stage in the appointment process to influence their choices. Accordingly I laid down that each minister was to notify me in advance of his or her intentions in relation to all such appointments once 'a preliminary view' had been arrived at about who might be nominated, so that I might have 'an opportunity to consult with him or her before any initiative is taken in the matter'.

This arrangement enabled me to consult Dick Spring about proposed appointments – as I did in relation to everything of consequence coming to government – before discussing the suggested names privately with the minister concerned in advance of the relevant government meeting. This process proved an effective deterrent to an excessive number of appointments based on political allegiance – overindulgence in which, often without adequate regard to the capacity of the individuals concerned, had in my view been in part responsible for the deterioration over the years in the performance of a number of state bodies, including some key enterprises.

It is my recollection that during the four and a quarter years of the government, this procedure ensured that with only two exceptions, no more than one 'political' appointment was made to any given state body, and that those thus appointed were people capable of contributing significantly to the success of the organisations concerned. Together with the contribution made to the work of state bodies by ministers responsible for a number of them, such as Jim Mitchell and John Bruton, this approach helped to secure the recovery of many of the institutions involved from the unhappy and in some instances disastrous situation prevailing in them when I took over the reins of government.

I should incidentally add, lest what I have written give a contrary impression, that most of my ministers were as concerned as I was to make effective appointments. One minister indeed went so far as to spend two days interviewing individuals for a single vacancy on one board in order to make the best possible appointment – which I have to say seemed to me a case of excessive conscientiousness!

Some boards are appointed by the government as a whole, and this responsibility was taken very seriously by our Cabinet, especially in the case of the RTÉ Authority. One member of the outgoing Authority was an active supporter, indeed an adviser, of Fine Gael, but he was also an extremely able participant in the work of the Authority. When the time came to appoint a new Authority, I decided that he should be retained but that all the other appointments to the Authority should be non-political. The members of the Authority we eventually selected were chosen specifically by the Cabinet collectively, so as to secure a board that would stand up to pressure from *any* government – our own included. However, only one of these was reappointed by our successors in 1989; there was clearly no inclination on their part to follow our example of ensuring a strong and politically independent Authority.

Another area of appointments with which I was involved was that of judges. In the late 1970s, Jack Lynch had broken away from the practice of making appointments of judges on a purely party-political basis, and I was determined that we should not revert to it. No vacancy in the Supreme Court occurred in our time, but we had to make a number of appointments to the High Court and Circuit Court, and in each case we sought to appoint on merit, as best we could judge it. In a number of cases, however, our first or even second choice was not available; judges' salaries are far lower than the earnings of many senior barristers, some of whom feel that they cannot afford to accept a judicial appointment, especially while they have children to educate. We were, for example, particularly anxious to maintain the tradition of having at least one Protestant judge in the High Court; but none of the senior Protestant barristers we approached was able to accept appointment when the occasion arose. We did, however, appoint the first Jewish High Court judge, Henry Barron.

The appointment of district justices pose a particular problem, because a very large number of lawyers seek these appointments. The great majority of those concerned would be unknown to most members of the government. In the absence of any rational system of placing applicants in some kind of order of merit, such appointments tended to be quite haphazard. One or other candidate might be known to a particular minister, and in the absence of any other rationale, his recommendation might carry the day. The wonder is not that some district justices are eccentric or unsatisfactory but that so many of them perform so well. Towards the end of our period in office, I proposed the introduction of a rational system designed to place the candidates for the District Court in order of merit, taking account of their qualifications and experience, but unfortunately the government fell before owe were able to give effect to this reform.

But to return to December 1982: I was concerned that all ministers of state should have specific tasks formally delegated to them by their ministers – something that in the past had often not been the case. Accordingly I had decided in each instance the duties of the junior minister, and asked that the formal assignment of these functions be made by the member of the government concerned.

In addition to the chief whip, Seán Barrett, I appointed two other ministers of state to my own department. I gave responsibility for Arts and Culture to Ted Nealon. For some decades past, government involvement in this area, including the appointment and financing of an Arts Council, had been the responsibility of the Taoiseach, and I knew that I would not have the time to give detailed attention to this area of activity. Ted proved an energetic and creative arts minister.

I asked the late Nuala Fennell, one of the best-known amongst the group of mainly feminist women who had been elected in the Fine Gael interest in the contests of 1981–82, to undertake the co-ordination of women's affairs across various departments that handle issues affecting women's rights and interests. She tackled this assignment with energy and enthusiasm, but found it frustrating, because many of the civil servants, and some of the ministers, upon whose area of responsibility her co-ordinating function impinged were notably unwilling to allow her the freedom of action she needed. In some cases, this reflected a measure of male chauvinism, but for the most part it was simply the instinctive response of ministers and departments to any attempt at co-ordination that impinged upon their responsibilities. All in all, she had a thankless task, and she found it particularly frustrating when some of her former colleagues in the women's movement criticised her for not doing things she would have loved to do, and might have been able to do had her effort been better received in some key departments.

At government meetings, Dick Spring initially sat in the traditional Tánaiste's position, to the left of the secretary to the government, Dermot Nally, who was himself on my left. This is not in fact a good position for contact between Taoiseach and Tánaiste: while each can lean across behind or in front of the government secretary to speak to the other, there is no possibility of eye contact, which can facilitate sensitive handling of difficult situations. Accordingly, some weeks later, when Dick returned from treatment in hospital for his back, with his agreement I moved him to a position at the centre of the long side of the oval table directly opposite myself. This new position put him on Alan Dukes's left, which also had possible advantages when difficult financial issues were being discussed. (Incidentally, I was amused by the manner in which ministers always sat in whatever place they chose by chance at their first government meeting – sometimes forging surprising ad hoc alliances with neighbours they found themselves sitting beside.)

The first issue our new government had to face was in fact the financial situation. Rightly or wrongly, we had set a five-year budget target in terms of a reduction in the current deficit. The difficulty was that the Department of Finance was by this time single-mindedly determined to cut the deficit by the maximum amount possible, almost regardless of any economic consequences. They seemed to feel that unless the current deficit was reduced to a figure close to £750 million in 1983, external confidence in our economy might wither, and our ability to borrow this sum, plus our capital needs, might thus be prejudiced. Alan Dukes, pitchforked into the Finance portfolio in the most adverse circumstances conceivable, was in no position to challenge this rather apocalyptic view of his officials.

In these difficult circumstances, it seemed to me that we needed some kind of cross-check on the Department of Finance's assessment that in international financial markets we would not 'get away' with a current deficit significantly in excess of £750 million. Accordingly, I decided to attempt an independent verification of this Finance view. I knew that, after his replacement as Secretary of State by Zbig Brzezinski in 1977, Henry Kissinger had set up a politico-economic consultancy service – of a fairly expensive kind. My personal relationship with him was such, however, that I knew that if I asked him to check something for me, he would do it without a fee. Early in January, therefore, I rang him and asked if he could check in New York financial markets how decisions on our part to achieve current budget deficits or either £750 million or £900 million would be viewed.

On the afternoon of Monday 10 January, he rang me back. He said that the New York financial markets were more concerned that we should have a programme to which we would stick rather than a more ambitious one that would fall apart. The expectation – he could almost say prediction – in New York was that we would be going for 'the moderate programme', namely a current budget deficit of around 7 percent of GNP (just over £900 million) and total Exchequer borrowing of 12 percent of GNP (about £1,600 million). This assessment had been based on contacts with the research departments of the leading New York banks. He asked if we had any idea of going to the IMF. I told him that we had no such intention, and he responded that he strongly agreed with this; the feeling in New York was that at this stage we had the possibility of solving our own problems.

This conversation, which seemed to confirm my suspicion that Finance had been overstating the case, provided me with good grounds for rejecting its demand for a £750 million current deficit. The department, which presumably had not previously had its advice challenged by a cross-check of any kind, was, not surprisingly, furious. Within hours, Alan Dukes – under pressure from his advisers, I assumed – came out publicly in favour of a £750 million deficit.

Dick Spring, with whom of course I had also been in continuous touch on these matters, and who was about to go into hospital for treatment for his back, wrote to me at once to protest formally at Alan's public statement, urging that there be no further comment on budgetary matters until decisions were taken by the government. The matter was discussed that Tuesday afternoon, following which a statement was issued saying that the government had not yet decided on the appropriate level of the current budget deficit and that there had been concern on the part of the Taoiseach and a number of ministers of both parties lest the figure of £750 million, which the Minister for Finance had mentioned as a target to aim at, should be taken as reflecting a government decision.

Having established our key parameter of a £900 million current deficit, we went to work to achieve it. It was a painful exercise, but with the aid of large tax increases, an increase in non-tax revenue and some cuts in proposed expenditure (which nevertheless left budgeted spending in 1983 above the 1982 level), we were able to meet the current deficit target while making provision for social-welfare increases going beyond the forecast cost-of-living increase. Helped by a £200 million, or 20 percent, cut in capital spending, these measures brought total Exchequer borrowing down from 16.5 to 13.5 percent of GNP – some seven points lower than the figure we had faced for 1982 when we had first taken office eighteen hectic months before.

In December I had sent Alan Dukes a note of a number of proposals Dick Spring and I had discussed in the course of our negotiations on the formation of the government. These were measures that Dick had recognised required further consideration and were to be examined with a view to possible implementation 'unless they give rise to technical or administrative obstacles that cannot be overcome or would have adverse economic effects which in the Finance Department's view would make them seriously inadvisable'. These proposals included an increase in the top income-tax rate to 65 percent; increases in taxes on luxuries, such as video recorders, cosmetics and furs; and an increase in the ceiling for PRSI contributions

– all of which in fact were introduced in this budget. Moreover, an income-related residential property tax was announced in the budget, and was brought into effect by legislation later that year. Other measures on this list were introduced in later budgets during our term of office.

The income-related property tax was an idea of mine on which I had worked during 1982 with my daughter-in-law Eithne, a social economist who was a Labour Party county councillor and was subsequently a Labour junior minster. While it could be argued that people with limited means who live in small dwellings should not have to pay local-authority rates, it seemed absurd that since 1977 well-off people in larger houses also made no contribution to local services. There is an economic case against very high income-tax rates even on large incomes – they certainly lead to large-scale avoidance and evasion by many wealthy people – but similar arguments do not apply to taxes on fixed property, in particular residential property, which by definition cannot be moved elsewhere. The impact of a residential property tax is, in my view, both economically and socially beneficial, because it discourages a wasteful use of residential accommodation, which is normally in short supply. By introducing such a tax, which was eventually fixed at a rate of 1.5 percent but was limited to houses worth £60,000 or more in 1983 (€320,000 today) and whose occupiers had incomes of £20,000 or more (€55,000 today), with indexation in subsequent years, I felt we would be raising some additional income in a way that would not be open to criticism either on economic or social grounds.

Naturally enough, when I had put this to Dick Spring during our post-election discussions, he had been happy to accept my proposal, which came to be seen in due course as a 'Labour' tax, despite the fact that I never made any secret of the fact that it was my idea. I have to say that I was quite unimpressed by subsequent middle-class criticism of this tax, which became more acute in the late 1980s, when house prices, which had for years lagged behind the cost of living, belatedly adjusted upwards into line with the trend of consumer prices.

Whilst the government had been engaged in the laborious and painful task of preparing this budget, Michael Noonan had reported to an astonished Cabinet the results of his inquiry into the telephone-tapping affair. The tale of what followed is long and complicated. I will merely summarise it here.

Because of suspicions about leaks from the Fianna Fáil Cabinet of 1982, the Minister for Justice, Sean Doherty, had directed the head of the Special Branch, on grounds of 'national security', to tap the phones of two journalists: the present editor of the *Irish Times*, Geraldine Kennedy, and Bruce Arnold of the *Irish Independent*. Both phone-taps had very properly been queried by the relevant official in the Department of Justice, who had also made a negative recommendation on the grounds given for the phone-taps, but the minister had nevertheless directed that they go ahead.

The Gardaí involved in the phone-tapping had been unhappy that they were being asked improperly to do work of a purely political nature, and had been pressed almost daily as to whether anything 'useful' was coming from the intercepts. Their dissatisfaction had come to the ears of former justice minister Jim Mitchell, who had informed me of what was happening. My concern at these events had contributed to my decision to attempt to bring down the government in November, instead of waiting until or after the January 1983 budget.

Unconnected with those events was a separate request by the minister to the head of the Special Branch to deliver a tape recorder with a sensitive microphone to the Minister for Finance, Ray MacSharry, and subsequently to have typed up the material recorded on it. It later transpired that this recording was of a conversation between the minister and a former minister, Martin MacDonagh.

The commissioner and the head of the Special Branch both resigned, and Ray MacSharry was excluded from the Fianna Fáil front bench during our term in government, but returned as Minister for Finance and between 1987 and 1989 completed the process of fiscal adjustment upon which we embarked in 1981.

Meanwhile our government had its own problems. One of these was the constitutional amendment on abortion to which I had committed Fine Gael before we took office.

One evening towards the end of January, as I was about to leave for home, Peter Sutherland came to my room and handed to me his formal legal opinion on the wording of the proposal Fianna Fáil abortion amendment. This opinion was to the effect that this amendment was ambiguous in ways that I had not appreciated. Whilst it was possible that these ambiguities might never give rise to a problem if the wording were not tested in the courts, it was, I felt, morally impossible for us to propose to the people a formula that the Supreme Court at some time in the future might feel obliged to interpret in such a way as either to exclude the preservation of the life of the mother in certain cases where it was currently safeguarded, or, at the opposite pole, actually to permit abortion in the early months of pregnancy.

The Labour Party ministers had already indicated that they would not support the Fianna Fáil amendment. Accordingly, before bringing the attorney general's opinion formally before the government, I called a meeting of the Fine Gael ministers in my room. The dilemma facing us was painful. We were under no illusion about the consequences of rejecting the amendment as it was phrased. We would be accused by Fianna Fáil of going back on our pre-election commitment to support their wording and, unscrupulously, of being 'soft on abortion'. The damage to our party would be considerable, and it was far from certain that we could secure a majority either in the Dáil or in the country for an alternative wording, which Peter

Sutherland warned us might in any event prove very difficult to draft. Yet my colleagues did not hesitate. The possibility that the Fianna Fáil wording could be interpreted in the ways Peter Sutherland had suggested was enough for them. Within twenty minutes, they had reached a unanimous decision to withdraw our support for his dangerously ambiguous wording and to seek a safer alternative formulation.

The fact that, faced with a clear moral issue of this kind, none of my colleagues hesitated about taking a decision that was bound to arouse deep – and dangerous – controversy was, and remains today, for me a source of great pride. I am conscious also of the irony of the fact that it was this profoundly moral decision that precipitated one of the worst confrontations in Ireland between the state and the Catholic Church.

Immediately afterwards, on the morning of budget day (and my birthday), 9 February, the second-stage debate on the Amendment Bill opened in the Dáil. Michael Noonan explained the background to the amendment, making it clear that he himself had an open mind on an appropriate wording. There had been, he said, many other drafts before this particular one had been adopted by Fianna Fáil on the eve of the November 1982 general election. This comment alerted public opinion to the possibility of a change in the wording.

I was naturally anxious that the rationale of our decision to amend the wording be understood by public opinion. I knew that there were groups of extreme right-wing Catholics, deeply hostile to us because of our stance on issues like contraception and divorce, who would welcome any opportunity of denouncing our attitude on this issue. Our change of position on the wording would triumphantly be misrepresented by them as 'proof' that we were 'soft on abortion'. Some of those involved would have neither the capacity nor the willingness to understand the moral basis of the decision we had taken. The hierarchy of the Catholic Church was, I knew, under constant pressure from these groups, whose members seemed to feel that they themselves rather than the bishops were the true guardians of the Roman Catholic faith. It was important therefore that the bishops should understand the reasons that had impelled us to review the wording of the proposed amendment, before they came under pressure from the right-wing extremists to attack our decision.

Accordingly, I rang Bishop Cassidy of Clonfert, whose house in Ballinasloe I would be passing on my way to a Young Fine Gael conference in Galway (at which this whole issue was passionately debated), to ask if I could have a word with him. When we met, I told him of the decision we had been forced to take, as a result of the moral imperative of concern for human life, and also of my anxiety that our action, when announced, should not be misunderstood by the Catholic hierarchy. How could we best convey this directly to the bishops and keep in touch with them so that they would know what alternative wording we were likely to put forward?

He expressed his understanding of our dilemma and said he would consult his colleagues and come back to me about a channel of communication.

Bishop Cassidy rang me shortly afterwards. The bishops, he told me, would not meet the government but would appoint a representative to whom we could talk. I was astonished and deeply disturbed at this reaction. It was unprecedented for any group or organisation to refuse contact with the elected government of the state. Was it possible that the Hierarchy, or some influential group within it, was planning to exploit the moral problem we faced in order to engineer a confrontation, or, at best, was seeking to avoid facing, as we had done unhesitatingly, the moral issue posed by the ambiguity of the draft amendment? Or was their unwillingness to meet us due to fear of a reaction to such a meeting from the right-wing lay Catholic lobby, from which I knew some bishops felt themselves to be under pressure? I had heard rumours that some of them feared, or had even experienced, denunciation to Rome by some of these extremists.

Whatever the reason, this refusal boded ill; it would make it difficult to convey to the Catholic hierarchy, individually and collectively, as personal contact would have enabled us to do, our sincerity in facing this problem. And there was always the danger of misunderstandings arising when communication had to be carried through an intermediary. These fears proved fully justified.

Meanwhile, however, Peter Sutherland and Michael Noonan were wrestling with the task of finding an alternative to the Fianna Fáil wording that they could in conscience recommend to the Oireachtas and to the electorate. It soon became clear that there was no way in which both the Oireachtas and the Supreme Court could be excluded simultaneously from having a future role in the matter, as it now transpired the authors of this proposal had intended. Any wording designed to tie the hands of the Oireachtas would have to be fairly specific in order to deal with the complexities of the problem, and the intricacies of that very precise wording would then necessarily be subject to interpretation by the Supreme Court. On the other hand, if a wording were to be employed that sought to preclude the Supreme Court from intervening to rule a law against abortion to be unconstitutional, as the United States Supreme Court had done, such a provision would necessarily leave the issue to the Oireachtas.

When we brought the matter to the Fine Gael parliamentary party, the party members demanded a full debate, and, after insisting that they hear Peter Sutherland's opinion in person, persuaded by this view, opted by a large majority for a simple formula designed to exclude intervention by the Supreme Court – namely, 'Nothing in the Constitution shall be invoked invalidating a provision of a law on the grounds that it prohibits abortion'. This was subsequently amended on technical grounds to: 'Nothing in this Constitution shall be invoked to invalidate or to deprive of force or effect a provision of the law on the grounds that it prohibits abortion.' This wording was endorsed as being preferable by the main churches other than the Roman Catholic Church.

The eventual vote in the Dáil was extremely confused, with members of both Fine Gael and Labour splitting three ways on the wording of the Bill: some voting for, some against, and some abstaining. The net result however was that, with the support of eight Fine Gael deputies and four Labour Party members, the ambiguous Fianna Fáil wording was eventually adopted. Following a legal challenge that got nowhere, it was decided that the referendum be held on 7 September. The Fine Gael party as such did not campaign, although a number of us made our positions clear, setting out the grounds on which we rejected the Fianna Fáil amendment, and urging the people to vote against it because of its dangers.

The campaign for the amendment was conducted on emotional lines and almost completely without regard to the actual issues at stake as set out in Peter Sutherland's opinion – issues that I presented in a speech on the subject during the campaign. The ambiguities of the Fianna Fáil wording were either ignored or were rejected without serious discussion by its supporters, apart form one intervention by the Bishop of Kerry (later the Archbishop of Dublin), the late Dr Kevin McNamara. He dismissed our fears on the grounds that a form of words could 'be devised which by any reasonable interpretation would render highly unlikely a court judgement that was compatible with legalised abortion'. On the danger that the Fianna Fáil amendment might be interpreted to prohibit surgical operations of a kind currently being carried out, the bishop contented himself with the comment that the fact that such practices were possible *under existing law* seemed a sufficient answer. These comments completely missed the constitutional points at issue.

In a speech on 12 April I described the evasion of the legal issues involved as 'astonishing'. Bishop McNamara's response to this was that I was 'ascribing to the law a kind of rigidity that was totally irreconcilable with the idea that the law is a flexible and developing science'. The reference to the flexibility of law ignored the fact that the whole issue arose from the manner in which the law had been flexibly interpreted in the United States and from a fear that it might be interpreted in the same way in Ireland.

This defensive attitude on behalf of the Catholic hierarchy did, however, suggest a certain amount of unhappiness on their part at the way they had handled the matter. I was left with the impression that they recognised that there was no intellectual basis on which to challenge the criticisms of the amendment put forward by Peter Sutherland but that, faced with pressure from right-wing lay Catholics, they had adjudged it safer to support the proposed amendment than risk being accused by unscrupulous elements in the anti-abortion camp of themselves being 'soft' on the issue.

However that may be, on 22 August the Hierarchy issued a statement that gave it as their considered opinion that the amendment would safeguard the life of both the mother and her unborn child – a remarkable excursion by the bishops into the field of constitutional law, in the course of which they clearly had no qualms about flatly contradicting the view of the attorney general, which by this time had been reinforced by that of the Director of Public Prosecutions. The Bishops' statement said: 'While some conscientiously hold a different opinion, we are convinced that a clear majority in favour of the amendment will greatly contribute to the continued protection of human life in the laws of our country'. This seemed at odds with their 1973 statement that 'it is not a matter for bishops to decide whether the law should be changed or not. This is a matter for the legislators'.

The amendment was carried by a two-to-one majority in a 54 percent poll.

In the end of the day, no one came well out of the affair. The Catholic hierarchy was, at best, weak in the face of extremist pressure. Fianna Fáil for its part was completely opportunistic in wooing the pro-life lobby. Even the Labour Party, the leaders of which had from the beginning taken up a wiser position than I had on the issue, was at the end of the day even more divided than Fine Gael, with over a quarter of its deputies voting with Fianna Fáil, as did one-ninth of ours, for the amendment that had originally been proposed by the Haughey government.

For my part, I should never have accepted the original referendum proposal put to me, however harmless it may have appeared at the time, for that commitment to introduce a constitutional amendment on the issue led me eventually into a position that, while intellectually defensible, was much too complicated to secure public understanding or acceptance.

However, the truth is of course that, given the attitude of such a substantial minority of the members of both government parties, no tactics of mine could have prevented the amendment from being forced through by Fianna Fáil, whatever I had proposed or failed to propose. As long as simplistic attitudes to complex moral issues persist in Ireland, and as long as unscrupulous politicians are prepared to exploit religious feeling for party purposes, our society may remain vulnerable to 'crawthumpers'.

Several months after the formation of the government, whilst we were immersed in this referendum issue, a number of backbenchers, one of whom was herself a biochemist, approached me about an alleged industrial-pollution problem in County Tipperary. It was suggested that toxic emissions from a chemical factory had affected human and animal health on a nearby farm. The issue was a complex one, and when I raised it in government in late March it was agreed that an interdepartmental report be prepared for us to consider at an early date. (A proposal of mine that Justin Keating, a former lecturer in veterinary medicine, examine the problem on our behalf was rejected by the government.) Despite various promises, this report was not produced until July, and when I received it I found it most unsatisfactory, leaving so many loose ends that I had to raise some fifty further queries on it. The response to these further queries of mine still left outstanding some score of issues, which I sought to probe further, but because the farmer had initiated a legal process against the company that owned the factory, and was not in a position to furnish us with further information until the case was heard, I could not take the matter any further.

Why did I involve myself so deeply on this issue? Because I was worried about the possibility that undue concern about the negative impact on industrial development or agricultural exports of the establishment of a link between the factory and the farm health record might have unconsciously influenced officials into taking up an overdefensive attitude on the matter. If this *had* happened, the rights of the farmer involved could have been jeopardised by our administration. A politician's job, as I have always conceived it, is to make sure that such individual rights are protected, not undermined, by the machinery of government.

It was clear that the officials from the departments involved were extremely irritated by my approach, although they did their best to hide it. They asserted that there was no evidence to link the problem at the farm with emissions from the factory, and that cross-referencing of the dates on which the incinerator at the factory was operated with the dates on which odours were reported, and when the animals were reported to be suffering respiratory difficulties, did not indicate such a link.

Yet five years later, the Supreme Court found that on the balance of probabilities the farmer's lung disease *was* caused by toxic emissions from the factory and that there was *uncontroverted evidence* that animals had been seen and heard to be in distress at the time the emissions had taken place. Moreover, five veterinary surgeons were of the firm opinion that what the animals were suffering from was caused by toxic emissions from the factory.

Whilst I recognise that in such a case it is impossible to arrive at objective truth with scientific certainty – the court case hinged on issues of the burden of proof, and eventually the issue was decided on the basis of *probable* causes – nevertheless it was disturbing that the farmer won his case partly on the grounds of facts as to the relationship of the timing of emissions and the timing of animals being in distress that directly and flatly contradicted what I had been told by the officials whom I had asked to examine the matter. My concern at the time lest officials' concepts of the public interest in relation to industrial promotion and the reputation of our farm exports clouded their judgement about the only real public interest – that of justice – seemed to me to have been validated in this instance.

Another case several years later in relation to which I found myself concerned about the rights of the individual being damaged by his relationship with the public service involved drug smuggling in Spain. I learnt that an Irishman charged with a drugs offence in Spain claimed to have been acting as an undercover agent for our Customs service. When I sought information about this case, I found that he was telling the truth, despite which he was now facing a sentence of up to twenty years, because the Customs officials who had been using him in the hope of trapping a member of a Tamil drug-smuggling ring had failed to tell either the Gardaí or the Spanish police about their plan.

When I discovered this during a weekend, I immediately summoned the heads of the relevant government departments to my home to see what could be done for this hapless tool of our Customs service, galvanising all concerned into approaching the Spanish authorities at the highest level to secure his release – which, with great difficulty, we eventually achieved. Because his life and that of his wife were now known to be at risk – a danger of which inadequate account seemed to me to have been taken by those who initiated this scheme – we subsequently had to help him start a new life in another country, a project upon which John Rogers, the attorney general, had to spend many weeks.

To the establishment, if I may call it that, my involvement in cases like these must have seemed quixotic and destabilising. I think they had become accustomed to a more passive and less interventionist political leadership so far as human-rights issues of this kind were concerned.

In the Department of Foreign Affairs, which had a strong human-rights basis, I had found less of a problem about issues of this kind, although even there I experienced some reticence about a case in which I authorised the Dutch wife of an Irishman in a mental hospital to have her two children put on her passport without her husband's consent (which he was then incapable of giving), so that she could take them with her to the Netherlands, where she could get employment more readily. However, departmental caution was vindicated in that case, for later on, when I was in Opposition, the husband sued the department, and the court found that I had acted incorrectly in exercising what had always been believed to be an unfettered ministerial discretion to decide passport issues of this kind. Apparently I ought to have asked the courts to decide the issue.

There had been no legal repercussions in yet another foreign-affairs case, however, where a woman whose American husband had succeeded in taking their child to the United States, in defiance of an Irish custody order in her favour, asked me to add the child's name to her passport without her husband's consent, so that when she had saved enough money, she could go there to take the child back to Ireland. She succeeded in this venture, escaping from her husband's Californian dwelling with the child and, with assistance from our local consul-general, returning to Ireland. I had no compunction in assisting in this enterprise, given that our public administration, through defects of procedure, had failed to protect her legal rights in the first instance; and the secretary of the department, Paul Keating, sharing my concern, was quite unperturbed when a newspaper headlined the mother's successful enterprise.

But to return to our early months in office in 1983. We found ourselves faced with the need to reform An Bord Pleanála. For as they had done in June 1981, Fianna Fáil in December 1982 had made a number of public appointments between the time of their election defeat and the transfer of power – something I had ruled out when my first government fell. As a result, five of the nine members of An Bord Pleanála were now political appointees of Fianna Fáil who had no apparent relevant qualifications or experience. Dick Spring, Minister for the Environment as well as Tánaiste, was gravely concerned at this, especially in view of information that suggested that some appeals were in effect being delegated to groups of board members that might include no non-political appointees. A huge backlog of three thousand cases had also accumulated.

Dick brought this matter to government, and we authorised him to prepare a Bill that would limit the ministerial power to make appointments to the boards. The Bill confined the choice of chairman to a person nominated by a committee consisting of six ex-officio holders of prominent positions in the public and private sector. It also limited the choice of four other members of the board to panels of names to be proposed by groups of organisations representing professional, environmental, development and community interests; and one member was to be a civil servant. Word of our review of the board's position had reached the press on 4 March, and then, days later, our decision to replace the board emerged, its current members being given the option of resigning or being dismissed.

This reform was of course bitterly fought by Fianna Fáil, but was equally firmly insisted on by our government, because of the vital importance of sealing off the physical-planning aspects of the appeals system from political influence – which, given the amounts of money at stake, could be open to accusations of corrupt use. Irish politics, for most of the life of the state, had been mostly free of any suspicion of financial corruption; but since the institution of physical-planning controls in 1963, doubts had been expressed as to whether this happy situation had continued.

It is fair to add that the number of national politicians about whom there has been serious suspicion can be counted on the fingers of one hand. Nevertheless, the scale of the pressure on the physical-planning system from interested parties with a major financial stake in the outcome of planning decisions and appeals has clearly led to significant corruption at local level, requiring a long-drawn-out tribunal enquiry.

Whilst we were tackling this delicate issue of Board Pleanála, I was establishing a quite different kind of planning board, one that would produce proposals for a National Economic Plan covering the difficult deflationary years ahead. The idea of establishing such a board had been present in my mind for some time before I returned to power at the end of 1982, for during my earlier nine-month government I had been concerned to observe how far the Department of Finance had moved from the innovative developmental role it had played under T. K. Whitaker's leadership in the late 1950s and 1960s. Faced with the enormous increase in public spending since 1977, the department's preoccupation with the need for expenditure cuts was understandable and laudable, but its concern was concentrated so much on each separate year's budget that there did not seem to me to be a sufficient sense of direction even for the medium term, let alone the long term.

Accordingly, when I came to form my second government at the end of 1982, I consulted several people who had played a key role in the 1960s, including Ken Whitaker himself and Louden Ryan. (Louden Ryan, who had been responsible for my year's research stint at Trinity in 1958-59, had subsequently been involved in the process of economic development, both when he had been seconded to the Department of Finance for a number of years, and later when he had been chairman of the National Industrial Economic Council and its more broadly based successor, the National Economic and Social Council.)

Following these consultations, I moved to establish on 18 March 1983 the National Planning Board, with Louden Ryan as chairman and six other members drawn from industry, the trade union movement, and academic life. The board's objective was to report to the government through a task force of ministers on how to maximise output and employment in competitive conditions and how to undertake and finance infrastructural works at minimum net cost over and above unemployment payments, as well as how best to reconcile social equity and the efficient use of public resources.

I was particularly concerned that the board should operate independently of the government machine, because it seemed to me that a late-1982 attempt by Fianna Fáil at planning had suffered greatly from being undertaken – with outside assistance, it is true – within the government framework. The text of the document they then published bore all the marks of having being filtered through processes designed to ensure that it said nothing that would be either politically embarrassing or contrary to Department of Finance orthodoxy.

The speed with which the new board submitted to the task force of ministers their initial 'Programme for Recovery' was impressive. We needed an early contribution from them so that we could build their initial recommendations into our departmental estimates for 1984, and we had their programme before us three months after the establishment of the board. The final version of this document, incorporating their reactions to departmental comments, was with us in September. They then went on to prepare their 'Proposals for a Plan', which they completed in March 1984. This in turn provided much of the basis for the government's plan *Building on Reality*, published in October 1984.

This was as fast a pace of work as could possibly have been expected. But the fact that the government's plan, based on the board's proposals, was eventually published almost two years into its term of office – and terms of office of govern-ments rarely exceed four years in practice – must in retrospect raise a question as to whether, given the urgency of the problems we faced in late 1982, it had been wise to proceed by this rather circuitous route. By the autumn of 1984, not alone was the government almost halfway through its effective life but by that time some at least of the possible field of action had been pre-empted by events. Also, because the board had been established initially to help us tackle a particular situation, its role was not adequately built into the permanent administrative structure for deci-sion-making. It did not therefore leave as enduring a mark on public administration as I had hoped.

Nevertheless, quite a number of important recommendations were imple-mented. Thus we adopted their proposal to limit the burden of tax to 36.5 percent of GNP, as well as some of their suggestions for public-service reform. Other rec-ommendations adopted included the abolition of the newly introduced 65 percent top income-tax rate, the substitution of a higher rate of children's allowances for the child allowance in the income-tax code, the introduction of changes in the Farm Advisory Service, and the abolition of the Land Commission. We also set about introducing a land tax, as proposed by the board, but the complex administrative arrangements for this had not been completed in early 1987, when Fianna Fáil suc-ceeded us in office and abolished this form of farm taxation. Another recommen-dation of the board that we adopted and that Fianna Fáil also reversed (only to reverse that reversal again several years later) was for a much higher level of invest-ment in roads.

The implementation of proposals such as these provided the core of *Building on Reality*, which was launched with some style in the ballroom of Iveagh House in the autumn of 1984. There were several other features of the plan in relation to which I took initiatives of my own. For example, one of the board's proposals was to put to work some of the 110,000 long-term unemployed on schemes to be organised by or through local authorities. The proposal would be expensive to implement: including overheads and supervision, it would cost perhaps £156 million a year over and above the saving on unemployment payments involved. The board said that this sum should be found through spending cuts beyond those the board itself had recommended. But as we were experiencing great difficulty in making even the rec-ommended cuts, this did not seem very realistic.

Thinking over this dilemma one morning when I had woken up early – as sometimes happened to me when I was under pressure – it suddenly struck me that, half a loaf being better than no bread, this financial constraint could be overcome if each unemployed person were put to work for *part* of a week. For each week's work involved, the heavy overhead of materials and supervision would thus be spread over two workers. I put this to our government Task Force on Employment,

346

on the basis that each long-term unemployed person taken on would work for twelve months, and that the number of days worked per week would be scaled in relation to the marital status and number of children of those involved. The task force judged this latter aspect to be too complex, however, and decided instead on a flat half-week's work for each long-term unemployed person, with a rate of pay that varied with family commitments – but not by enough to be attractive to people with families, whom I had been particularly anxious to help through the scheme. Another feature of my proposal that was adopted, however, was that people would be free to undertake other work during the half of each week when they were not working under the scheme. I also secured a provision that the services of those concerned be made available to voluntary bodies as well as to local authorities. Unfortunately, in Dublin, where the city council had already laid off workers because of cuts in its rates-support grant, the trade unions refused to allow the council to use the scheme to give work to unemployed people.

Nevertheless, an enormous amount of useful work was done through this Social Employment Scheme, which was intended to provide a year's break in the cycle of long-term unemployment for people who found themselves out of work for a prolonged period. However, when the twelve months was up, most of those involved naturally wanted to remain at work, and where community organisations or other voluntary bodies were involved, they in their turn normally preferred to keep the people they had become used to and had trained, rather than start again with a new temporary employee. But as the whole idea of this revolving scheme had been to provide a *temporary* break for as many long-term unemployed as possible, this aspect was not open to review.

Another element of the government's plan in which I had a direct involvement was the decision, despite the massive cuts being made in most forms of public investment other than roads, to increase investment in higher education, where in the 1980s we had to cater for a rapidly expanding number of young people. I knew from our discussions in government that some of my colleagues were unsympathetic to priority being given to this. They took the view that in time of financial crisis, we simply could not afford to expand significantly the most expensive sector of education, especially as we already had far more graduates than we could employ at home – with the result that such an expansion would involve educating people for jobs in other countries.

I had always rejected this utilitarian, manpower-related approach to education. It seemed to me that if (in large measure because of past political mismanagement) a high proportion of those now in primary and secondary education were not going to be able to find employment in Ireland, we owed it to that generation at least to offer as many as possible of those who sought higher education, and were capable of benefiting from it, the opportunity to qualify themselves for a more rewarding career abroad. Moreover, a far higher proportion of graduates than the proportion of those who left the educational system after second level secured employment at home, and some at least of this reflected an unfulfilled demand, especially by new foreign industries, for people with a high standard of education. If we educated more people to this level, fewer would emigrate in the long run.

In a government in which a major part of my role had to be to urge my colleagues to reduce spending, and the members of which were constantly watching each other's performance in this economy campaign, I was not well placed to argue the case for more expenditure on higher education – especially as I myself was a university lecturer on extended leave of absence, and therefore suspected of being partisan.

However, my chance to achieve my objective came when Alan Dukes asked me, because of his absence abroad, to stand in for him as Minister for Finance in discussions on the provisions to be made in the *Building of Reality* medium-term proposals for certain departments, including education. When Gemma Hussey and I came to discuss this matter – she along with her officials and I accompanied by the Finance officials – I disconcerted the latter by accepting the demographic basis of her argument, and her view that this need should be met, whilst proceeding to counter-argue strenuously that half of this need could be met by more intensive use of physical space and a reduction in the ratio of staff to students. The resultant increase in provision for higher education contributed notably to the eventual 38 percent rise in educational investment in our plan. (An increase of 50 percent in the number of third-level enrolments took place between 1980 and 1987, the years of economic crisis.)

Unhappily, some of the expansion of facilities thus planned was still to be implemented when the government changed early in 1987, and in their vigorous attack on public spending in that year's budget, a reformed and frugal Fianna Fáil cancelled many of our plans – only, once again, to reinstate some of them later.

Finally, in another area to which I was personally committed, I got agreement to a continued expansion in the share of our GNP devoted to development assistance to the Third World during the period of our plan, a decision that was in part at least implemented during our tern of office, although (not for the first or last time) the new Fianna Fáil government subsequently cut by almost two-fifths the share of GNP devoted to this purpose. I noted wryly at the time that this slashing of our aid programme to a level below that of any other Western European country was agreed with far less public protest than I had met for not *increasing* more rapidly the share of GNP devoted to this purpose.

How did our national plan fare? In the three-year period of the plan, GNP grew, albeit by 5 percent, as against the plan figure of 7.5 percent; our external payments and inflation rate performed much better than we had foreseen; and living standards rose much faster than expected. Industrial output, boosted by foreign investment, had been rising rapidly since our first year in office; but although redundancies, which were mainly in indigenous industries, fell sharply after the autumn of 1984, employment failed to respond. The rise in unemployment was, however, slowed by the various schemes we introduced, but the number of people out of work did not begin to decline until the end of our period in office.

One of the most notable economic achievements of our term of office was the winding down of inflation. When Fianna Fáil had left government in mid-1981, inflation was approaching 20 percent. Whilst this owed much to the sharp rise in import prices following the second oil crisis, the situation had been aggravated by runaway pay increases in the public sector, where the average level of earnings had been allowed to jump by 29 percent in the single year of 1980. The public-sector pay round that we negotiated during our first term had brought the annualised increase in pay rates down to 10 percent. In the first half of 1983, we had a further very tough negotiation with the public-service unions, which brought the increase down further to 6.5 percent; and by the end of our term of office, the figure was below 5 percent. A combination of this public-service pay moderation with government 'guidelines' helped to wind down pay rises in the private sector to the same levels, albeit with a time lag of a year or so vis-à-vis the pay trend in the public sector.

This achievement was hard-won. The trade unions, which had had such an easy time of it with Fianna Fáil in the two years before we had taken over in 1981, were clearly unhappy with our determined stand; they may have particularly resented it in view of the Labour Party's participation in our government. Meetings between us and the ICTU were formal, often tense, and on the whole unproductive throughout our term. Indeed, the only personal recollection I have of a genuine worthwhile discussion with the unions is of an encounter between the ICTU and the Fine Gael ministers that took place in the Fine Gael party office. However that may be, Fianna Fáil inherited from us in 1987 an industrial-relations situation that had been transformed, and the fruits of this were soon to be seen in the three-year national agreement for annual pay increases of around 2.5 percent that they were able to negotiate later that year, and in the future national pay agreement of early 1991.

Some reforms that I pressed on my colleagues at this time were, however, successfully resisted at civil-service level. Proposals for tackling the problem of arrears of tax were dismissed by Finance officials as inspired by 'ill-informed comments suggesting that vast sums of unpaid taxes are there for the asking' – words that came back to me when, following an initial, limited tax amnesty by our government, our successors in office launched a large-scale amnesty that yielded several billion euro. And my proposal to extend normal PRSI to the hitherto exempt category of the civil service was met by an extraordinary defensive memorandum claiming that this would cost more than it would bring in, because civil servants would have to have their pay increased to compensate them for such a change and would also have to be given the opportunity to draw double pensions, both occupational and social-welfare ones!

I had more immediate success in the area of the reform of the public service itself, where for the first time there was a minister – and an energetic one at that – whose sole task was to tackle this issue. During the Easter break in 1983, I wrote to John Boland at some length on a range of issues, including the appointment of secretaries of departments for a limited period rather than until retirement, and the introduction of mobility between departments. The initial response from the Department of Public Service on the issue of mobility between professional and administrative grades and between departments of the civil service was discouraging. Several years previously, they had put a great effort into this, and despite resistance from the civil-service unions, they had made some progress at the level of assistant principal officer, although in order to overcome what they described as 'the known opposition of departments to interdepartmental promotion schemes' they had conceded that only 20 percent of existing posts at this level would be open to competition from other departments.

They had, however, apparently given up on the issue of mobility at higher levels, which I felt was of crucial importance, both in order to extend to that level the principle of promotion on merit rather than on seniority and also to bring fresh attitudes and ideas into various departments from other areas of the civil service – as well as, hopefully, from outside it. Partly at least because of the effects of the internal promotions system, many departments had in the absence of fresh thinking from outside become very conservative and defensive in their attitudes, pursuing traditional departmental policies long after they had ceased to be relevant.

The lack of momentum on this issue seemed to me to be a product of trade union pressure to extend mobility beyond the home civil service to diplomatic postings. It was clear that the Department of the Public Service was itself in sympathy with this approach, with the result that its officials seemed unwilling to proceed further with the mobility issue unless Foreign Affairs was first forced to accept that diplomatic postings be covered by the new arrangement. Foreign Affairs had, in my view, been absolutely right in resisting this demand, which, if conceded, would have been seriously damaging to the effectiveness of our foreign policy. Our success in foreign relations since the early days of the state had depended to a high degree on the development of a corps of skilled and very experienced diplomats, whose ranks had in practice frequently been strengthened by a substantial, but always selective, inflow of able officials from other departments.

In subsequent discussions I told John Boland, who on this issue seemed to share the view of his department about Foreign Affairs, that he should not allow the whole mobility issue at higher levels of the civil service to get bogged down by a kind of dog-in-the-manger attitude towards the Department of Foreign Affairs. He eventually accepted this, but, I later discovered, not before he had spent a whole day trying to put pressure on the Secretary of Foreign Affairs, Seán Donlon, to concede on the issue, Seán, knowing the strength of my views on this matter, had given him no satisfaction, however.

There remained the problem of getting through the government a scheme combining mobility at the higher levels of the civil service on a basis of merit with a new system of appointing departmental secretaries for seven-year terms rather than until retirement. There was bound to be resistance to these proposals from ministers, many of whom would have an instinctive personal preference for the appointment to senior posts of officials whom they had come to know from within their own departments, as against people from other departments of whom they may never have heard. And the senior civil servants would, I feared, if they learnt of the proposal in advance, try to brainwash their ministers against what I saw as a long-overdue reform. Accordingly, I encouraged John to bring the proposal to the government without circulating a memorandum in advance. While objections to the proposal were indeed raised by a number of ministers, it eventually got through at a second meeting – some ministers asked for a few days to reflect – by a narrow majority: a margin of a single vote, as I recall it.

At about this time, I also initiated collective government 'brainstorming' sessions to review progress and to plan ahead. Several of these meetings were held, the state-owned Barrettstown Castle in County Kildare being the location for all but one. Although in attractive grounds, the castle is quite a small building, with a drawing room and a dining room that can just accommodate fifteen ministers and a government secretary, and one other reception room: a small study that can be used as a communications room. There are, however, nine bedrooms of varying size and comfort, in which ministers from places distant from Dublin could stay overnight.

Experience showed, however, that policy initiatives arising from unstructured discussion without written policy documents on occasions like these sometimes fail to mature into action. Account was taken of this in arranging the agenda for future sessions in this location, at the next of which I succeeded in substituting a transport allowance for junior ministers in place of state cars and Garda drivers; the saving was some £750,000 a year, and thirty to forty Gardaí were released for other duties. Needless to saym this reform, announced after this July Barrettstown meeting, was at the time unpopular with many junior ministers!

The Barrettstown conferences nevertheless had, I believe, a very positive psychological effect on the solidarity of the government. From the outset it had been clear that we were in for a very rough ride; the financial crisis we had inherited was, as I had foreseen, putting our coalition under great pressure. While this was especially true at the level of our parliamentary parties, at government level too there was tension, especially between Dick Spring on the one hand and John Bruton and Alan Dukes on the other. Although for the most part this tension was institutional rather than personal, both Dick and John, as distinct from Alan, had short fuses, and this occasionally led to fireworks at the Cabinet table. However, these clashes, and the less emotional ones between Dick and Alan, were tempered by the mutual respect felt for each other by Dick and his two Fine Gael colleagues; the opportunity to meet in the more relaxed atmosphere of Barretttstown, as well as from time to time for a post-Cabinet drink in Seán Barrett's office beside the Cabinet room, helped to keep things on an even keel.

Indeed, these informal encounters developed a sense of camaraderie and warmth between members of the government that balanced underlying tensions which never completely disappeared. The Labour ministers clearly feared that at some point a misjudgement on the Fine Gael side might push them over the brink, making it impossible for them to remain in government. At the same time, among Fine Gael ministers there was a persistent concern that the problems faced by the Labour ministers might at some point precipitate a split. There was, moreover, frequently irritation and at times alarm at the leaks by the Labour ministers' aides to the press, which seemed to be designed to keep their more restless TDs and non-parliamentary left wing happy. The apparent implication of many of these leaks – that only constant vigilance on the part of the Labour ministers saved the country from savage cuts in public services – was particularly galling for Fine Gael ministers, whose concern for the preservation of these services and for minimising the impact of spending cuts and tax increases on the less well-off was in fact just as great as that of their Labour Party colleagues.

The frustration of some Fine Gael ministers with this aspect of Labour's participation in government was intensified by the self-defeating dogmatic ideological position of the Labour Party on a small number of issues. One of these was the development of local broadcasting, where the short-sighted opposition to our proposals by one Labour backbencher close to the unions in RTÉ prevented any progress being made throughout the life of the government with a scheme that would have given RTÉ the right to a significant minority share in all local commercial stations. As I feared at the time, this recalcitrance gave Fianna Fáil in government in the late 1980s the opportunity to introduce legislation for commercial broadcasting, including television, that put RTÉ's longer-term viability at some risk. In the face of so many pressures, our government would scarcely have survived if the personal relations between its members had not been so good, and if my own relationship with Dick Spring had not been solidly based.

By the time the Barrettstown meeting of July 1983 took place, this fundamental solidarity of our government had been well established. I was happy enough with our situation when, shortly after this meeting, Joan and I went to Schull in County Cork for a few weeks' holiday. Friends of ours, Gay and Jacinta Hogan, who had stayed with us in Schull in 1975, had been so attracted to the area that in 1992 they had bought a house there, near the end of a boreen that was sometimes submerged at high tide. The house was secluded; the ever-changing view from it over a tidal inlet was satisfying. Throughout this period in government, they frequently gave us refuge there.

That summer, Joan was quite ill. Since June, she had been suffering from a gastric complaint that was not resolved for well over a year and which in 1984 became life-threatening. Fortunately, August 1983 was a glorious month in west Cork, and the Hogans arranged for Joan to spend the days in bed on the lawn overlooking the inlet. I had always had an ambition myself to lie comfortably out of doors between sheets, my head resting on pillows, and before long we were spending many of the summer days head to head in two beds, our faces sheltered from the sun by a huge parasol.

Our relaxation was interrupted in sad circumstances. My next brother, Fergus, had been very ill during the previous twelve months. Since childhood we had been very close, despite the six-year age difference, and he had been a major influence on me in my youth. During his long period as an official of the FAO in Rome after 1951, we had seen less of each other: we had been able to visit Rome on only a couple of occasions, and he got home on leave only every second year; but we had kept in close touch throughout this period.

After the death of his wife, Una, he moved to the EC in Luxembourg, where I saw him quite frequently. He retired from that post in 1976, however, following his remarriage to Eilis Johnston, chief hostess supervisor with Aer Lingus, and came back to Ireland, settling with undisguised sentimentality in Bray, a few hundred yards from our childhood house, Fairy Hill, which was by then buried beneath a modern housing estate. There he had become an active member of Fine Gael – the only one of my brothers to involve himself politically. For the year before his death, he had faced with remarkable courage the fatal consequences of lung cancer. His last engagement, linking past and future, had been my son Mark's wedding, two weeks before his death. Since my parents' death, he had been my strongest link with childhood; we had been able to share many pre-war memories of our parents. Now we heard that he was close to death. We broke our holiday to see him for a last time; he died the next day.

Mark's wedding, though in the shadow of Fergus's impending death, had been a great joy to us. He had met his wife, Derval O'Higgins, at the presidential inauguration in 1976, at which her father, Tom O'Higgins, officiated as Chief Justice. Mark had then been accompanying Joan on that occasion, as I was absent abroad at the time, and Derval had been replacing her mother, who was unwell. In the intervening years, Derval had already become part of our family.

The marriage linked two families whose members had been friends for over sixty years: Derval's great-uncle Kevin, murdered by an IRA breakaway group in 1927, had for years before been my father's greatest and most admired friend. Kevin O'Higgins's brother, Tom, had been a member of the second coalition of 1954–57, and Tom himself had been deputy leader of Fine Gael, on the front bench with me from 1965 to 1973, when our views on policy and on the party had been closely aligned.

On his marriage, Mark purchased Mary's share in our house. We had already moved from the top to the two lower floors, converting Mary's flat there into living accommodation for ourselves, because Joan's disablement as a result of arthritis had made it impossible for her to continue to climb the stairs. The top floor was simultaneously converted into a separate flat for Mark and Derval, in which they lived throughout my period as Taoiseach. On the middle floor, the dining room became a bedroom for Mary and Vincent when they were in Ireland during holiday periods, leaving us with the drawing room on that floor as a reception area – rarely used, because of Joan's disability.

This arrangement was the best we could manage during those years. It meant that our accommodation was fairly cramped: basically two rooms on the garden level, with the corridor serving as a kitchen. On this floor, we never succeeded in overcoming the problem of rising damp, which we combated with a noisy dehumidifier in our bedroom, where even in summer artificial light was needed for reading because of overhanging shrubs in front. I think it was the most modest accommodation ever occupied by an Irish prime minister, but it saw us through this period until I was in Opposition again. With the aid of the gratuity paid on my simultaneous belated retirement from UCD, we were able then to install a lift. We thus recovered the use of the whole house, Mark and Derval having at this stage purchased a home of their own nearby.

The question of an official Taoiseach's residence had occasionally been raised; indeed Jack Lynch had planned to build one for his successors in office in the Phoenix Park, on the site of what had for many years been the Papal Nunciature. But I have to say that even if such a residence had existed, and despite the limitations of our own accommodation at this time, I think we would have been reluctant to move there.

18

∾ New Ireland Forum and the Anglo-Irish Agreement ∾

In my earlier, more historical autobiography of two decades ago, the negotiation of the Anglo-Irish Agreement of 1985 absorbs some forty thousand words. Here I shall simply concentrate on some of the highlights of this process.

In opposition during 1982, I had had the opportunity to reflect on recent developments in Northern Ireland. I came to the conclusion that there was now a real danger of a major destabilisation of the situation there following the gain in support for Sinn Féin and the IRA as a result of the hunger strike. This could lead to a heightening of IRA violence and even perhaps to civil war, the effects of which might then overflow to our state. In these circumstances, would it be right for me to persist with my policy of pursuing an accommodation with a persistently intransigent unionist bloc, rather than, as I had always wished to avoid doing, negotiating a deal with the British government behind the backs of these stubborn fellow-Irishmen? With this in mind, in a speech on Northern Ireland during the November 1982 election campaign, I said that a 'complete and radical rethinking of British policy was now needed quickly' if we were to avoid the situation drifting into chaos.

At a meeting of the Northern Ireland committee of my new Cabinet in mid-January, I found strong support both at ministerial and civil-service-adviser level for the view that we should in fact switch the thrust of our policy towards seeking an agreement with the British government that could not be sabotaged by unionist intransigence, but when I brought a proposal to Cabinet to launch a forum to prepare the way for such a negotiation, I was completely taken aback by the fact that twelve of my fourteen Cabinet colleagues opposed the idea, fearing, I think, that my deep concern about Northern Ireland could distract me from what they saw – with very good reason – as exceptionally pressing domestic financial problems. Together with my chief whip, the next day I set about persuading my colleagues individually to reverse their negative votes on this issue, using the political argument, which I had perhaps not sufficiently emphasised at the previous day's meeting, that if we did not move at once with my proposal, Fianna Fáil, at their *ard fheis* later that week, would put us on the spot by announcing acceptance of John Hume's concept of an exclusively nationalist Council for a New Ireland. By this means I secured the Cabinet's belated agreement to a forum, and before the Fianna Fáil *ard fheis* began I had written to Charles Haughey and the leader of the Workers Party to invite their participation in talks on this basis.

I asked John Hume to come to Dublin on his way back from Strasbourg, and persuaded him to accept my wider version of a New Ireland Forum, open to all political parties in the island, and to press Charles Haughey to agree to join in this project. This John did, with immediate success, and by lunchtime that day, my terms of reference for the New Ireland Forum, deliberately excluding any reference to Irish unity, had, somewhat surprisingly, been accepted by Charles Haughey. (The exclusion of such reference had been designed to leave open, at least in principle, the participation of unionists and, less improbably, of the Alliance Party in the Forum.) We agreed with Fianna Fáil on the appointment of Colm O'hEocha as chairman – a schoolmate of mine at Colaiste na Rinne near Dungarvan, fifty years earlier, when his father had been headmaster of the school.

I had two main objectives for the Forum – first to secure agreement on a set of principles which could be acceptable to the British government and that would contain nothing objectionable to unionists – these principles to be incorporated into the report of the Forum; and also to incorporate in its conclusions not merely models involving different forms of Irish unity, but also some form of British/Irish Authority in Northern Ireland. In particular I wished the report to include a paragraph along the lines of 'the parties to the Forum remained open to discuss views on solutions other than forms of Irish unity which might contribute to political development'.

Such a joint-sovereignty proposal for Northern Ireland was designed to leave open a solution involving continued British sovereignty over Northern Ireland, which I knew that Margaret Thatcher would not be willing to relinquish. But with respect to this issue, I told Dick Spring and John Hume privately that at an early stage of discussions by the four party leaders, I would propose that an economic study be undertaken based on alternative political models. For my part, I would then propose building into these alternative models an economic variant based on the confederation proposal that my party had put forward in 1979, whilst Dick and John should propose a joint-sovereignty model. In fact, these different models would never have had much impact on the economic study, but I guessed that Charles Haughey would not appreciate this, and by approaching the issue via this economic route I could ensure that the joint-sovereignty ('Brits in' rather than 'Brits out') model would work its way into our political conclusions.

Subsequently, realising that Margaret Thatcher would not wear joint sovereignty, I sought the agreement of my three colleagues to modifying this term. Far from Charles Haughey demurring at any weakening of this term for this model, as I had been concerned might happen, it was in fact he who eventually proposed that it be changed to 'joint authority'!

During the meetings of the Forum, Fianna Fáil concentrated on introducing into the report a crude nationalist interpretation of history. Fine Gael representatives in particular had great difficulty with this, and inter-party battles on this issue led to the Forum taking eighteen months to complete its work, rather than the nine months I had originally envisaged.

It was agreed that each party to the Forum could invite two individuals or groups to give evidence to it in public. Groups of Northern Protestants were invited by Fine Gael to do so.

A curious episode in the course of the Forum was an occasion when Dick Spring (who was still in a very combative mood after having just arrived from the Dáil, where he had been attacking Fianna Fáil on domestic policy issues) asserted that a recent leak from its work had come from the Fianna Fáil delegation. Charles Haughey angrily described this as an unjustified and outrageous attack on his delegation; he threatened that unless Dick Spring withdrew this allegation, he would lead his party out of the Forum. He then broke down and was escorted from the room by Ray MacSharry, his finance minister in the recent GUBU government. It transpired that, earlier that day, he and his family had been very upset by a biographical book on him, *The Boss*.

The Forum was immediately adjourned, and Dick Spring made his peace with Charles Haughey, but following the afternoon session, I realised that I had earlier responded to a query from Vincent Browne, editor of the *Sunday Tribune*, about my Christmas reading, saying that *The Boss* was something that I would want to read during the break. I then found that Dick Spring had also mentioned the book to Vincent in this way. I rang Vincent – who I found already knew what had happened that morning – and he agreed not to publicise the traumatic event in the Forum and to substitute other works in place of *The Boss* on my list, and in Dick's.

A highlight of the Forum was the appearance of a delegation from the Roman Catholic Church hierarchy, but owing to a mistake by the Forum's administration it was not until December that we learnt that there would be a positive response to our invitation to the church authorities to appear. Eventually the delegation appeared before the Forum on 9 February – which happened to be my birthday. I would have liked to have been the person questioning them on their submissions, but my Fine Gael group preferred that this be done by John Kelly, to whom I made extensive suggestions as to questions he might put. However, he reduced my list of questions drastically and when I came back with yet more suggestions, I am told he threw his hands up in horror, saying: 'It's like one of those bloody biological specimens put under a microscope: take your eye away from it for a minute and it subdivides itself sixty million times!'

One question was related to the handling of mixed marriages, in relation to which Bishop Cassidy said that the Irish Episcopal Conference had considered appealing to Rome on this issue, for a derogation from the church's general provisions in relation to this matter, but had not done so, as they did not feel that there was even a slight chance that Rome would accede to such an appeal. I should love to have been able to point out in reply that six years earlier, when I was Minister for Foreign Affairs, I had raised this matter in Rome, only to be told that I should take it up with the Irish hierarchy!

In mid-February, after a morning session in which Charles Haughey had been in a very constructive mood, he returned after lunch to insist that there should be only one recommendation from the Forum – for 'a unitary state'. He could not 'sell' the other models to his colleagues, saying that if he tried to do so 'we'd have two Fianna Fáils'.

At a private meeting of the four party leaders, he explained that his sudden change of stance was due to opposition within his own delegation; this was reinforced by the extreme stance of Ray MacSharry in the subsequent public session. Fianna Fáil were insisting that the only solution was a unitary state. (I believe that this was because at the outset I had proposed a confederal solution, so that John Hume and Dick Spring could put forward what became the joint-authority model, thus distracting attention from my concern to ensure the inclusion of this latter model. My ploy had been too successful!) I was not happy with the emphasis thus given to the 'unitary state' model, but succeeded in having the word 'would' inserted into a proposed wording describing a unitary state, achieved by agreement as 'the particular structure of political unity which the Forum would wish to see established'. This amendment was eventually accepted by Charles Haughey.

Despite strong reservations from the Labour and Fine Gael delegations about the historical section of the report, shared by members of the government, and despite the fact that I myself recognised the danger that there could be hostile British reaction to the propagandistic tone of the chapter, I felt that, given that the report covered my two initial requirements, it should be accepted.

Despite objections from the Fianna Fáil delegation, Charles Haughey finally accepted the principle of consent by agreeing that a solution to the Northern Ireland problem should be 'agreed to by the people of the North and by the people of the South' – which left no doubt about the need to secure the consent of a majority in Northern Ireland to unification.

When it came to the public launching of the report, Charles Haughey told us, the three other leaders, that at his press conference, immediately after mine, he would be presenting his own view of the report, reading to us from a note of what he proposed to say. We could not reasonably quarrel with what we understood from a quick hearing to be the content of his proposed remarks on Fianna Fáil's position. In my opening remarks for the media, referring to the report's nationalist analysis of past history, I said that the full report had 'transcended this analysis and interpretation of past events' and that it sought to raise its sights to new horizons and to set out ideals that could provide common ground for the two traditions, and a basis for common action by the two governments seeking to reconcile these traditions.

Charles Haughey followed me. In his opening remarks, he largely confined himself to generalities, but in replies to somewhat hostile questions at his press conference, he frequently misquoted the report, culminating with a statement that 'the only solution as stated in the report, is 'a unitary state with a new Constitution'. He also rejected the concept of a majority in Northern Ireland being a precondition for Irish unity, which had of course been clearly established in the report, with his agreement.

The role of the report as an agreed position of the four parties was clearly damaged by this episode, but its text nevertheless provided a basis for a new approach to the British government. My first meeting with Margaret Thatcher, following my re-election as Taoiseach, had been in the margin of a European Council meeting in Brussels in March 1983. I told her then that one of my hopes was that a New Ireland Forum, having been set up on a basis that was open to presentations of a unionist position, would develop in such a way that their British identity could be accepted by nationalists so that unionists would feel less threatened. Nevertheless, it was clear that, following Charles Haughey's reaction to the Falklands crisis, I would need to work hard if I was to restore the kind of relationship that I had achieved with her in November 1981.

In July I had authorised Michael Lillis, the head of the Anglo-Irish division in the Department of Foreign Affairs, to make contact with the British to urge our view that from their point of view, as well as ours, political authority in Northern Ireland must receive a visible Irish as well as British legitimacy. He soon struck up a friendship with David Goodall, a descendant of a County Wexford family, one of whose ancestors, as a member of the Irish Parliament in the middle of the eighteenth century, had been involved in one of the earliest challenges from within the Anglo-Irish community to the Dublin Castle establishment. David, a Roman Catholic, had a strong interest in theology, which he shared with the newly appointed British ambassador to Ireland, Alan Goodison. (Joan and I had met Alan Goodison, even before he presented his credentials – at the first of a series of 'theology weekends', the establishment of which Joan had prompted shortly before this.)

The Anglo-Irish Intergovernmental Council structure, which I had established with Margaret Thatcher in November 1981, had as its joint chairmen Sir Robert Armstrong and Dermot Nally, our two Cabinet secretaries, with Michael Lillis and David Goodall as joint chairmen of the subsidiary co-ordinating committee. Meanwhile I had appointed Noel Dorr, one of our most distinguished diplomats, as ambassador to London and had later appointed Richard Ryan as his number two in London to establish close contacts with Conservative members of the British Parliament, whose support we would need to win over for any agreement that might emerge in due course. As a poet and a good shot, I felt he could establish good relationships with both Labour and Conservative mps! In this way, the two negotiating teams had emerged which I hoped would provide at civil-service level the negotiating team for a new Anglo-Irish Agreement in the post-Forum period.

By the end of September, Michael Lillis had been told authoritatively that the problem of the alienation of nationalists was now being taken very seriously by the prime minister. So at that stage it was clear that we had interested Margaret Thatcher in the possibility of a major initiative during her second term of office. In November 1983, at a meeting in Chequers involving both Northern Ireland Secretary Jim Prior and Foreign Secretary Geoffrey Howe, I raised the question of whether, in advance of the publication of the Forum report, the British prime minister might see merit in the matters in question being pursued informally between officials?

As I had been told by the British side that Margaret Thatcher was more likely to respond in a less inhibited way if no one else were present at that part of our meeting, I explained to her in private the thinking behind the establishment of the Forum. However, she said that she could not authorise such discussions because, if she was questioned in Parliament at that stage, she must be in a position to say that no negotiations were taking place.

Meanwhile Dick Spring and Peter Barry, who had accompanied me, had been told by the two British ministers that it might be possible for our government to have a particular involvement in the administration of Northern Ireland, with a right to be consulted. Some form of joint authority might be possible, but not joint sovereignty.

Much to my surprise, in March 1984 a British delegation, led by the Cabinet secretary, Sir Robert Armstrong, arrived in Dublin with quite radical proposals that had been approved at British Cabinet level. These proposals would involve creating a 'security band' along the border, to be overseen by a joint Security Commission and policed by joint crime squads, which could develop later into a common police force. They also proposed a Law Commission for the whole island, with the possibility of a Northern Ireland mixed court then or later, as well as more equitable franchise arrangements in Northern Ireland and symbolic measures, such as changes in the flags-and-emblems legislation. These proposals could be used as building blocks for future political arrangements, and there might be a parliamentary tier.

After these discussions, Dermot Nally came to tell me what had been proposed. I was taken aback by the proposal for a Joint Border Zone, which, I felt, would create two new borders not to be crossed by security forces in pursuit of the IRA – instead of, at present, one such border. Accordingly, I asked Dermot Nally to contact the British delegation and tell them that I saw difficulties about this.

Quite recently, one of our officials then involved in the negotiations has said to me that it had perhaps been a mistake on my part to sound such a negative note immediately about such radical proposals, which had the authority of the British Cabinet. However that may be, once the Forum report was agreed and published, we learned that whilst the prime minister had reacted negatively to it, the foreign secretary, Geoffrey Howe, had a more positive attitude, and the Northern Ireland secretary, Jim Prior, said that if Articles 2 and 3 could be changed, a lot of things might open up.

As a result, I came to the conclusion that we should review our tactics on Articles 2 and 3, as otherwise there didn't seem to be much possibility of significant movement. After discussion with Peter Barry and John Hume at my home, it was agreed that we would indicate at official level that if an adequate settlement were agreed, we would be disposed to put that package to the electorate by way of a plebiscite or referendum, as provided for by our Constitution.

At that stage a curious thing happened. Separate proposals came to us from Jim Prior, apparently without the knowledge of Margaret Thatcher. By mistake, these had been transmitted to us by a telex from our London embassy, because of the absence through illness of our number two in London, Richard Ryan. This message seems to have been picked up by the British monitoring centre in Cheltenham, which created problems for Prior and his number two, Richard Needham, who had delivered them to our London embassy. We had to give our assurance that nothing said privately to us by ministers or civil servants would be transmitted in future by telex, and thereafter I had to send a courier to London regularly to bring back such private information. The US embassy in London complained that as a result they were no longer able to find out what was happening in the negotiations, and a member of the US administration suggested that if we wanted to communicate confidentially with them, we should send someone to see them personally in Washington, as telex messages could be intercepted.

When I confirmed to Margaret Thatcher our willingness to move to amend Articles 2 and 3 of the Constitution, it was pointed out by the British that if such a referendum failed, both countries would be in a far worse position. I agreed, but said the problem would never be solved unless we were prepared to take some risks.

However, I was told that the prime minister remained very well disposed towards me and felt that our discussions in the margin of the Fontainebleau European Council in June 1984 had been very useful indeed. She was now committed to doing something rather than nothing, but had doubts about our capacity to act, and also about her own capacity to carry a major initiative vis-à-vis her own party and the unionists.

A key meeting between the two sides took place in Chequers in November 1984. When we arrived there, I once again saw Margaret Thatcher privately, without advisers or note-takers. I told her that I believed that a satisfactory agreement could enable me to achieve an amendment of Articles 2 and 3, which would be of immense value to relationships with the unionists. These articles were seen by members of the unionist population in Northern Ireland as a threat to their position and, however unjustified that might be, in their present form they represented major obstacles in the way of a better North–South relationship and a reconciliation between the two communities in Northern Ireland. We had a chance now to make a historic breakthrough by tackling with one blow both the growing alienation of the Northern minority and the siege mentality of the unionists. She and I had a unique opportunity that had not previously existed and might not readily reoccur. We should take our courage in our hands and together make this breakthrough. I was prepared to do my part by calling the people of the Republic to amend their Constitution, if she could agree to changes in Northern Ireland that would end the alienation of the minority, especially from the security forces, and would enable the minority to identify with the system of government in Northern Ireland in which we would be playing a part.

She listened carefully, quizzed me on various aspects of what I was proposing, and promised to reflect overnight on all that I had said. Next morning the two of us resumed our discussion – on this occasion, however, with note-takers present. She was obviously sceptical about my proposal to amend Articles 2 and 3 in return for a deal sufficiently substantial to give me a chance of securing the support of our electorate for such a change. After I went over again the points I had made the previous night, she said she did not understand why nationalists in Northern Ireland sought such special treatment, which Macedonians, Croats, Serbs and Sudeten Germans did not enjoy! Might a possible answer to the problem not be a redrawing of the boundaries? That would be a fatal mistake, I replied. 'Who was really being alienated in the North?' she asked: some 2,500 people had lost their lives there in the security forces. The vast majority of deaths, I countered, were not in the security forces but were civilians, a great number of them being amongst the nationalist minority.

And so it went on. After a long discursive argument ranging over a whole series of problems, she said that while the consultation process that she was willing to envisage would be genuine, the judgement of the secretary of state could not be fettered for she, as prime minister, was answerable to Parliament, which was answerable for Northern Ireland. I couldn't resist pointing out that for fifty years Parliament had not regarded itself as answerable for Northern Ireland and had refused to allow questions about the North to be raised there. That was part of the reason for the present trouble.

It did not seem that I had made much progress as a result of our discussion the previous night. We then rejoined our ministerial colleagues. She asked me to open the discussion, saying I looked depressed. I said that frankly I was very worried. The political problem was being sidelined by an exclusively security-oriented approach. Unless a political solution was found that would enable the minority to identify with the system of government in Northern Ireland, it would be impossible to solve the security problem. The British side should face the fact that there had to be a political context were anything significant to be done on the security side. Yes, I was depressed.

The discussion soon reverted to the issue of the exclusion of the minority from power in the North. I said that we needed more than an advisory role, for example in relation to appointments and complaints. She replied: 'We can't have that, Garret. That's joint authority, that's out.'

From the long and discursive discussion that followed, it became clear that both she and Douglas Hurd were unhappy with the idea of a referendum on Articles 2 and 3, partly because they recognised that for us to be able to approach such a referendum with any hope of success, they would need to concede more than they were willing to do – and partly because of genuine doubts as to whether we could get electoral support for such a change. Eventually she said 'It looks as if we won't have any communiqué' but added that it had been a good meeting, as it was the first time we had come to grips with the problem and talked about the real issues. 'We need to keep meeting and maybe we should say something in the communiqué [which she had just abolished!] about meeting again in the spring.'

'That,' I responded, 'would be disastrously dampening. We need to meet again very early in the new year, not in the spring.'

When Geoffrey Howe proposed that the communiqué should say that both of us recognised our need to find a way of enabling us to make a serious input into security matters, Margaret Thatcher intervened at once to say that they should be careful: they did not want to cause problems for me back home. She said once again 'Garret, you look depressed. Is it that bad? I'm not depressed. We are now tackling the problem in detail for the first time. This was the best discussion we have ever had.'

Then I returned one last time to the constitutional-amendment issue, telling her not to underestimate the effect of such an amendment. It would release positive forces in unionism and at the same time would enable us to solidify the moderate ground in our state in a way that could not be easily undone by a subsequent government. I added that we had asked the British government not to exclude anything in these talks; logically, therefore, we for our part could not exclude anything. 'Then I could say that you are not excluding anything?' the prime minister asked quickly. 'Yes,' I replied, 'but only at the same time you say that you are not excluding anything.' 'I'd better stick to what you say' was her answer.

Before we left, after lunch, a communiqué had been agreed. Despite the combative tone of much of the discussion, it was positive, and left the way open for further progress. It described our exchanges in Northern Ireland as 'extensive', which was certainly true, and 'constructive', which was more arguable.

We drove back to London with very mixed feelings. It seemed clear to us that the British ministers had decided to scale down the scope of any agreement to an extent that would provide no basis for an attempt to amend Articles 2 and 3, to which I had become strongly committed. Moreover, what they had in mind would have a completely inadequate impact upon the alienation of the nationalist minority in Northern Ireland.

It was agreed that at five o'clock Margaret Thatcher would give a press conference on our meeting and I would follow at six o'clock with a similar event at the Irish embassy. There would not, I felt, be much for me to say. I would have to stick closely to the communiqué, emphasising the positive parts of it. One of our officials would attend the British press conference and report to me before I went in my turn to meet the press. He had to return to brief me before Margaret Thatcher's longer-then-expected press conference had ended, but what he had heard of it was, with one exception, very encouraging. She had described our meeting as 'the fullest, frankest and most realistic bilateral meeting I have ever had with the Taoiseach'. She had agreed that the two identities in Northern Ireland merited equal respect and recognised that the minority did not think that their identity was fully reflected in the structures and processes of Northern Ireland. She had also volunteered that the security issues we discussed included prisons and judicial issues as well as policing. On neutrality, she said that the Irish were proud of it, and it was a matter for us.

This seemed to me to have been a heartening presentation: she had gone out of her way to be as helpful as possible. I said I would like to hear the Radio Éireann news headlines before going to my press conference. But because of interference by a pirate radio station, I was not able to catch much of what was said about our meeting in the opening minutes of the news, and I went to my press conference, a few minutes later, somewhat less happy than I had been before listening to Radio Éireann. I was, however, completely unprepared for the hurricane that was about to hit me. It very quickly became apparent that the positive comments that the prime minister had gone out of her way to make, up to a late point in her press conference, as well as the positive elements in the communiqué itself, had been rendered completely irrelevant by the manner in which she seemed to have dealt with the three Forum models. As I had not heard her actual remarks, I was completely thrown by the questions hurled at me by the assembled media. Things were made all the more difficult to handle because it became clear that the journalists had never grasped the full significance of the enabling clause in paragraph 5.10 of the Forum report, the basis upon which we had been negotiating since the formal rejection of the three models in the early stages of the negotiations in July – of which, of course, the journalists knew nothing. As the three models, as such, had ceased to be relevant to the negotiation at that stage, I was disconcerted at their sudden reappearance as controversial issues at this point, and could not – as I did not know the context of her remarks – deal with her rebuttal as robustly as the press clearly expected me to do, without risking a complete breakdown in the negotiations. As a result I was completely at cross purposes with the journalists, who had missed the whole point of what had, admittedly, been a subtle negotiating stance on our part. To them I seemed to be ineffectively trying to obscure the reality of what they saw as a humiliating rebuff. 'Out, Out, Out' being her response to a question about the three models in the Forum report – a response which it appeared she had delivered in a very emphatic way.

It was a glum party of ministers and officials who returned home from London that night; things were made even worse by the fact that Douglas Hurd had disregarded the carefully framed communiqué, revealing instead some of the proposals put to us by the British at the Chequers meeting and dismissing any possibility of an executive role for the Irish government in Northern Ireland – a breach of confidence against which we launched a strong protest.

The next day, however, I began to realise that the impact of Margaret Thatcher's 'Out, out, out' could be turned to our advantage. If we, for our part, could avoid any hostile comment. The critical reaction that I believed her apparently over-the-top performance would evoke in Britain might eventually help us to get the negotiations back on a constructive path. Of course, this left us at a serious disadvantage in the face of the scathing attacks on me by a jubilant Fianna Fáil Opposition, but that short-term price seemed worth paying for a possible long-term advantage.

A subsequent Fine Gael meeting was, however, one of the most difficult I had to face as leader. In reply to a mass of critical comments, I said that I recognised that the remarks were seen by the party as 'gratuitously offensive', and I called on them to support my efforts for peace. Most unhappily, the term 'gratuitously offensive' was torn from its context and attributed to me as my own comment. When these words leaked out, it partly undid my efforts to hold the line so as to ensure for us any moral advantage the situation had created.

I wrote to Margaret Thatcher to explain just how damaging had been the impact of this part of her press conference, and received from her a conciliatory response. Moreover, when we met shortly afterwards in the margin of the European Council in Dublin, she opened a tête-à-tête on Northern Ireland by saying that she had been doing everything she could – smiling all day at the Dublin meeting! She thought that her press conference had been all sweetness and light. 'What had gone wrong?' she asked me. In her press conference after the European Council, she tried to undo some of the damage of two weeks earlier, emphasising that in the margin of this European Council meeting 'we had had a very successful talk'.

Knowing that Margaret Thatcher valued her relationship with President Reagan, we decided to approach the president on the issue through Bill Clark, the former national security adviser, who was a close friend of Reagan's, and who had a house in Malahide. We suggested that when Margaret Thatcher visited Washington just before Christmas, the president might find an opportunity to express his concern about the Anglo-Irish situation. He did so – surprising, I believe, his State Department advisers – and telling her that he looked forward to hearing when they met again in February how the Anglo-Irish relationship was going. Clearly this had a profound impact on Margaret Thatcher and the British government, for on 21 January we received new proposals, on the basis of which serious negotiations could take place, without any quid pro quo from us in the form of an amendment to Articles 2 and 3.

The key meeting with Margaret Thatcher, halfway through that year, took place in the margin of the Milan European Council meeting in June. An outstanding issue at that point was the set of 'associated measures', designed to provide reassurance to the nationalist minority. These were to involve a review of prison sentences following a sustained period of peace; the announcement of a new code of conduct for the RUC; the accompaniment of army patrols by the RUC save in the most exceptional circumstances; and a possibility of mixed courts in both parts of the island, in each case involving a judge from the other jurisdiction. She seemed very hesitant on all these issues, which, from our point of view, were all of crucial importance.

On the mixed-courts idea, I said that, as she knew, I had met the Lord Chief Justice of Northern Ireland socially some time ago (our mothers had been friends, and as a barrister he had represented our family in a case in Belfast thirty-five years earlier), and that I had outlined to him in a very broad way the mixed-courts proposal. He had immediately said that if that idea were pursued, he would write to the prime minister, the lord chancellor and the Northern Ireland secretary to say that in those circumstances he would resign – as, he believed, would the rest of the court. However, it appeared that the judges of the higher court of Northern Ireland had come together to ask what all this was about and, it seemed, in the end, had confronted Lowry, saying that they would do whatever their constitutional duty was, and that there was no question of them resigning. A letter had been written to her on behalf of the higher judiciary – which I understood she had not yet received. I knew that she would not be pleased to learn that I knew of this letter before she received it herself, but the issues we had to address were of such importance that I did not think I could let this opportunity to settle the associated measures pass without dealing fully with the mixed-court issue.

She said that she had received no such letter and that there could be acute difficulties if I told her about what went on in her territory in relation to the court system! All that could be done was that the agreement would say that consideration would be given to the possibility of setting up a mixed-court system. She went on to say that it was hard to believe that if announcements of associated measures were not made at the same time as the agreement, the agreement would be jeopardised. She would hope to implement them over time, but with her responsibilities she had to consider unionist reactions.

I replied that unless the nationalist minority supported the new arrangements from the very first moment, it would all just be worthless. There was no way that the minority could stand up to the IRA without these measures.

I had put my personal authority on the line here in the face of the deepest scepticism towards our negotiation on the part of very many people in the Republic, but it had now become clear to me that I was getting nowhere on these associated measures and that the only course open to me at this point was, I felt, a make-or-break one. I must now go in with all guns blazing, using more forceful language than I had ever previously used. At the worst, this would lead to a break in the negotiation, but given the way our discussion had been going, that seemed inevitable anyway. There was always the possibility that I could shock her into modifying the 'stone-wall' attitude that I had met so far in the course of our discussion. I was not seeking these things to the benefit or our people in the South; in fact, our people did not want to be involved in the North. But it seemed to me to be vital to try to break out of the cycle of violence in Northern Ireland, even if it involved taking risks.

So I told her that this whole business would never have started if the right thing had been done at the right time. In 1969, when the Troubles had started, all the minority community had wanted had been a right to be represented in Parliament as a constructive opposition with equal rights, but there had been fierce opposition from unionists in Northern Ireland even to that minimal reform, and then in 1974 a British government – not hers – had walked away from an agreement that had been made at Sunningdale, and things that could well have worked had collapsed, again in the face of unionist opposition. We had always been faced with half-solutions: too little too late.

The consequences of doing nothing now would be to force supporters of the

SDLP into the arms of Sinn Féin. With all the moral authority I possessed I had to campaign for a settlement that would stop this from happening. There was a deliberate campaign being waged by the IRA in Northern Ireland to create instability; Gaddafi was deeply involved, and was willing to put millions of pounds into destabilising efforts both North and South. He was backing the IRA politically and trying to manipulate the Irish state in that way.

For eight hundred years, English realpolitik had taken it as a fundamental element of policy that Ireland must not be allowed to be a base for attacking Britain. Now Britain could be allowing that very thing to happen; its government could be doing just what British policy over those centuries had spent every effort to prevent – at great cost to Ireland.

This was a historic opportunity. I did not know what history would say if we missed it. It was something that she and I could do together; no one else could do this, now or for the foreseeable future.

As I reached this point in my extempory address, I glanced across at Dermot Nally, taking notes. I could see from the look on his face that he thought that I had gone over the top, with probably fatal results.

Regardless, I ploughed on. But at this stage Margaret Thatcher intervened to say that she saw what I was getting at: I wanted something visible. We should not call these moves 'associated measures'; rather, they should be described as 'confidence-building measures'.

I went on to say that one of the highest offices in the Northern Ireland police force had recently been filled by the appointment of a man who had been involved in a machine-gun attack on flats which had killed a child, as well as in a second incident in which whole streets of Catholics had been burned out without intervention by the RUC. Both instances had been described in the Scarman report.

She was clearly shocked at this. She started to say that Douglas Hurd would never have approved such an act. 'But that's the very point,' I interrupted. 'Someone is not telling him the facts.' We had fullest confidence in the Cabinet Office and the Foreign and Commonwealth Office, but there were serious doubts about what was getting to the secretary of state from the Northern Ireland Office.

Disturbed at what I had just said, she asked me to tell her more: were there any other similar instances of which I knew, she asked me. I replied that I was using these instances simply as an illustration and did not want to go into details: we were not engaging in a witch-hunt. 'What you're talking about,' she replied, 'is a code of conduct.' 'Not just a code of conduct,' I replied. 'A declaration that the police would uphold the rights of both communities'. If some people in the RUC did not like this and decided to go, then that opportunity should be used to pick other suitable people from both sections of the community. What we were looking for was a declaration by the UDR and the police that in their activities they would be fair to both communities. 'Go on,' she replied. 'I want to hear all about this.' Encouraged by her response, and by the remarkable change in atmosphere that had followed my impromptu address, I went on to discuss the UDR, which in some areas harassed local Catholic boys, many of them neighbours of theirs, and people with whom they had grown up. This harassment went on and on, and had become a problem that in Northern Ireland tended to have the sort of end that we all knew.

We then moved on to discuss the possible timing of a summit meeting at which an agreement could be signed. 'What about October?' she asked. 'That meeting should be in Dublin,' I said. 'Not in Dublin,' she replied, 'and there would be difficulties about Belfast.' She was not objecting to a place in the South, but not Dublin: that would heighten the profile too much. I told her that as far as location of the summit meeting was concerned, Belfast posed no problem for me, but it must in any event be in Ireland. As for the 'associated measures', I didn't mind what they were called so long as they were implemented, and attracted and sustained the confidence of the minority.

There our discussion ended, as the session of the European Council was about to start. I left much relieved. My onslaught seemed to have produced the desired result. At least she was now converted in principle to the need for certain confidence-building measures, and if these were to be described as part of the implementation of the agreement, so much the better. A key element in the agreement that emerged was the creation of a joint secretariat in Belfast.

Thereafter the Armstrong/Nally meetings took place at intervals of a week to ten days: there were in fact more than a dozen meetings between 9 July and 12 November. In addition, there were a number of ministerial meetings. At the first of these, it became clear that the 'associated measures' were now accepted in principle on the British side. The proposal that the RUC accompany, the army or UDR on patrols was agreed on the basis of 'the principle that the military [which included the UDR] operated only in support of civil power, so that there would be a police presence in all operations which involved direct contact with the community, 'save in the most exceptional of circumstances' – a phrase which was explained by the British side as covering cases when an RUC man might fail to turn up for a patrol, or where there was a major security crisis that prevented the RUC from providing police officers to service a patrol.

With regard to the mixed courts, it was agreed that the joint bodies to be established under the agreement would seek ways of securing public confidence in the administration of justice, considering among other things the possibility of mixed courts in both jurisdictions for the trial of certain offences. As I had told Margaret Thatcher, the letter she had received from the Northern Ireland judiciary had said they would do whatever Parliament wanted – despite Chief Justices Lowry's objections.

In connection with the courts, we pursued the question of their composition. The Northern Ireland Office stood by the under-representation of Catholic judges by claiming that Catholic QCs were unwilling to become judges – which we contested, having established that a number of Catholic QCs of a calibre that would be acceptable to the lord chancellor in the British context had been repeatedly passed over for senior judicial appointments. Moreover, one of the judges claimed by the NIO to be a Catholic was in fact a well-known member of the synod of the Church of Ireland! We were then told that there were no vacancies to enable this religious imbalance to be addressed, but we were able to point out that under their legislation, there was a vacancy in the High Court. The NIO then objected that there wasn't sufficient work for a further judge! But eventually, after long argument, this problem was finally addressed. The chairman of the Northern Ireland Bar Council, Michael Nicholson, was then appointed to the High Court, as was a further Catholic judge later.

I had the clear impression that at both the Cabinet Office and the Foreign Office, some of the senior ministers involved, including Margaret Thatcher herself, had been extremely unhappy with the situations that our probing had eventually revealed.

(However, after we had left government, the only change made in the crucial Court of Appeal was the replacement of a retiring Catholic judge by a Protestant unionist barrister, thus producing for the first time in many years an all-Protestant court of appeal. When this move had been forecast to us by senior Catholic barristers in 1985, I had been unwilling to believe that the British government would ever allow this to happen – or that an Irish government would fail to address the problem – but happen it did, exactly as we had been told it would on year earlier.)

A crucial element in the agreement was, of course, the establishment of a joint secretariat in Belfast where Irish and British officials could work together and be available twenty-four hours a day to deal with any crisis that might arise. From a security point of view, this proved a very valuable innovation. Up to then, if a security problem arose – for example, misbehaviour by a British patrol in some area – we had to address this through diplomatic channels, whereas with the secretariat in Belfast, a complaint from any part of Northern Ireland relayed to the Department of Foreign Affairs was immediately conveyed to the secretariat, where the Irish and British officials could at once deal with the situation, contacting the Chief Constable of the RUC or the General Officer commanding the British Forces in Northern Ireland, as appropriate. The existence of the secretariat, which, as it happened, was located right beside the UDR barracks to the east of Belfast, immediately became the object of huge unionist resentment, and it had to be protected against attack.

An agreement was finally reached on the issue of where the signing was to take place. Margaret Thatcher was said to wish this to happen in a British military base in Northern Ireland, which clearly was unacceptable to us. Eventually, agreement was reached that it would be signed in Hillsborough Castle, the former seat of the governor of Northern Ireland, but provision was made that if for any reason that location became an object of unionist demonstrations when word leaked out about it, an alternative site was available at Dromoland Castle in County Clare. In the event, on the previous day, the unionists did get wind of our intentions to use Hillsborough, and demonstrations were mounted there. At ten o'clock the previous night, I accordingly suggested to our Cabinet secretary that we use Dromoland instead, but the British believed that they should maintain the Hillsborough location and that it could be protected from attack.

For my part, I would have preferred to have had the agreement signed in the Royal Hospital in Kilmainham, where by shifting a couple of portraits it could have been signed immediately under the portraits of King William III and Queen Mary, as a gesture to unionists. But Margaret Thatcher was determined that it should not be signed in Dublin.

On the day in question, we flew by helicopter to Hillsborough. Officials had prepared a 'catechism' of fifty-nine questions with which Margaret Thatcher and I were both to familiarise ourselves, so that whatever question might be asked, we would give the same answer to it. So, at a preparatory session, Margaret Thatcher asked Dermot Nally to pose some questions to her, and Robert Armstrong was to pose some to me, so as to test our preparedness for questions that might be put to us at the press conference after the signature of the agreement. This worked well, and we then went down to the conference room. After the signature of the agreement, and the press conference, we went upstairs together to drink a glass of champagne. It emerged that Margaret Thatcher was quite upset because she had just heard that Ian Gow, a close friend and aide, had resigned in protest at the signature of the agreement.

When I mentioned to her the arrangement under which it had been agreed that our ambassadors to the European Union should jointly raise the question of financial support by other European states to Northern Ireland in support of the agreement, she demurred, saying, as she gestured towards the country outside: 'More money for these people? Look at their schools! Look at their roads! I used it for my people!' in England. This arrangement had been settled quite a while previously and I had in fact spoken to all the heads of government – except the Danish prime minister, whom I was unable to contact – to secure their support for supplementing the $250 million that the United States and some Commonwealth countries had agreed to provide for the benefit of Northern Ireland. As a result of her reaction, the substantial aid that we might have secured for the North from Europe was not sought, until several years later, when a much smaller sum then I had expected was raised from this source.

Despite unionist fury at the signing of the agreement, and the huge demonstrations organised in protest against it, I subsequently received the present of a Hillsborough Castle tie – which I have since occasionally worn – from a unionist in Hillsborough who, in contrast to the bulk of the population, approved of the agreement! Meanwhile, in Parliament, despite Ian Gow's resignation, only twenty-one Conservative members, on the extreme right, and a small number of left-wing Labour members, voted against the agreement – reflecting the hard work put in by Richard Ryan during the previous two years. With his delightful Korean wife, he had charmed many members of the Conservative Party into a more positive attitude towards the agreement than they might have adopted if left to themselves. As a result when, before the signing of the agreement, the Conservative whips came to make an assessment of the likely reaction of their party to an agreement of the kind then contemplated, I was told that they had found a much more positive reaction then would have been the case had the issue arisen a year or two earlier.

When Margaret Thatcher and I met eighteen days later in the margins of the European Council in Brussels, it was clear that she had been shaken by the scale of the unionist reaction, which she described as 'much worse than expected'. She felt that I had all the glory and she had all the problems. I told her that I had already met two groups of unionists who had come to Dublin, and had been encouraged by their attitude following what I had told them about the agreement. 'But they will not speak – they dare not speak,' she replied. I told her that nobody in the South had said 'this is a step towards a united Ireland': over a three-day debate in the Dáil, this point had been made by no one. There was no triumphalism on our side. I pointed out that between two-thirds and three-quarters of the people in the South openly supported the agreement, with its assurance on the status of Northern Ireland, and she agreed that she had been relieved that the unionists had reacted constitutionally. There were no strikes and no bombs, and she seemed to calm down somewhat at that stage.

Events were not helped, however, by a statement by Northern Ireland secretary of state Tom King at a luncheon in Brussels that we had in fact accepted that for practical purposes, and in perpetuity, there never would be a united Ireland. I immediately challenged these inaccurate and inappropriate remarks. That row took some time to die down.

Meanwhile, the secretariat had moved into Maryfield – a building which the British government had identified as a possible seat of the joint secretariat. The first meeting of the conference provided for by the agreement was held in Belfast and was attended by the Chief Constable of the RUC and the Commissioner of An Garda Síochána. Thus, less than four weeks after signing the agreement, the structures it established were in place and were operating as we had intended.

During 1986, many issues were successfully addressed by the joint secretariat. As a result of speedy action through that body, many security flashpoints were successfully resolved, and a major programme of change involving legislative and administrative provisions was under way, designed to remove or mitigate many of the disadvantages under which the nationalist population in Northern Ireland had laboured, in some cases since 1920.

The Flags and Emblems Act, which discriminated against the symbols of the nationalist minority, was repealed. Criteria were established for decisions on the routing of controversial parades and marches. The law on incitement to hatred was strengthened. New and improved guidelines for fair employment were introduced, and there was a commitment to strengthen the legislation in this area, which was later implemented – with the result that during the 1990s discrimination gradually ceased to be a problem in the North. Decisions were also taken to abolish and replace three nationalist blocks of flats – the Divis, Unity and Rossboro flats – decisions that had been sought for more than a decade, without success. And recognition was given to the use of Irish for place-names, which had been banned for some decades previously. Moreover, a Police Complaints Commission was established, and a document was published summarising complaints procedures in relation to the army.

But there was little or no progress on the army and UDR being accompanied by the RUC on patrols. One-third of patrols remained unaccompanied, despite the fact that the Ministry of Defence had accepted the provisions of the agreement on this matter. We never received any satisfactory explanation for this.

However, this was balanced in the short term at least by the manner in which the RUC handled unionist demonstrations against the agreement, displaying by their firmness their capacity for even-handed action, and showing the extent to which, under the leadership of Jack Herman, the force had become non-political.

In relation to prisoners, there were improvements in arrangements for parole and compassionate leave, and standards of proof in relation to bail applications, together with guidelines on the admissibility of confessions, were revised to make clear that if they had been obtained by the use of threats of violence, they were not admissible. Suspects in police custody also became entitled to have a person outside informed of their arrest and of their whereabouts, and were given automatic access to a solicitor after forty-eight hours. The waiting time for trial was reduced by the appointment of three additional judges and by an increase in the size of the Senior Bar, as well as by a new power for scheduled cases to be heard outside Belfast.

Moreover, the controversial 'supergrass' cases, which involved the joint trial of large numbers of suspects on the evidence of a single accessory, were abandoned. However, provision for a RUC code of conduct was postponed for two years – after which, contrary to what had been agreed, it was introduced privately, without any publicity. And the announcement of the possibility of prisoner releases in the event of a reduction in violence was also postponed for a year, and the mixed-courts proposal was never implemented.

In the event, nationalists accepted the agreement overwhelmingly, leading, as we had intended, to a significant swing in support from Sinn Féin to the SDLP. However, this was probably due not so much to the many changes produced by the agreement, which I have just outlined, but rather to the scale of unionist protests against the agreement, which convinced the nationalist population that it represented a major step forward.

19

~: Final Years in Politics :~

My return from our August 1983 holiday in west Cork coincided with the shooting down of a South Korean airliner by the Soviet air force off the coast of Siberia. Like the rest of the world, our government reacted with a vigorous denunciation of this atrocity. The US government, however, wanted something more from friendly states than a condemnation of this act. We came under strong pressure to close down Aeroflot's operations at Shannon, where it had established the principal transatlantic stopping-place for its airliners flying to Cuba and other points in Central and South America.

Because of the scale of Aeroflot's operations at the airport and the manner in which Aer Rianta's other activities were facilitated by the availability of Soviet aviation fuel at keen prices, such an action would have imposed a unique burden on us. We decided accordingly to confine ourselves to taking action similar to that of some other countries that were withdrawing temporarily Aeroflot's traffic rights: we did not withdraw the airline's right to make technical stops at Shannon. The US government was clearly annoyed at this response.

As it happened, quite a different action in relation to the Soviet Union was required at this time for other reasons. Our intelligence services reported to me that several members of the small staff at the Soviet embassy had been engaged in improper activities that had involved the use of our territory for the secret transfer of information concerning the military affairs of the United States. A US marine in Helsinki had been approached by a Soviet intelligence agency, and after reporting this to the CIA, had become a double agent agreeing to hand over information – presumably phoney – to Soviet agents in, of all places, the Stillorgan Shopping Centre! In the absence of Foreign Minister Peter Barry, I instructed Jim O'Keeffe, minister of state at the Department of Foreign Affairs, to call in the Soviet ambassador to demand the recall of two Soviet diplomats and the wife of another member of the Soviet embassy staff. This action had the effect of calming American irritation at our refusal to respond to their demand in relation to Aeroflot's operations at Shannon. At the same time the Soviet authorities must have recognised privately that our action in relation to their diplomats was justified, and may also have given us some marks for resisting US pressure in relation to Aeroflot. In any event, there was no retaliatory expulsion of Irish diplomats in Moscow.

I naturally briefed Charles Haughey fully on this spying affair. Indeed, throughout my period as Taoiseach I kept him informed on important security issues, as well as briefing him on other sensitive matters that required the co-operation of the Opposition in order to secure speedy parliamentary action. He was always helpful in matters of this kind.

Charles Haughey and I, with Dick Spring, also co-operated that autumn in persuading President Hillery to serve for a second term. The late Dr Hillery was notably reluctant to continue in office, and several meetings were necessary before he agreed, good-humouredly commenting as he conceded on the issue that this was the only sentence in respect of which apparently one got an additional seven years for good behaviour.

I had always had a good relationship with Paddy Hillery. Joan had known him in college forty years earlier, and even when, before he had assumed the presidential office, he and I had found ourselves on opposite sides politically, we had always got on well. During my official visits to him as president, I kept him well informed of what was happening on the political scene, including my developing plans for an Anglo-Irish Agreement, and I tried to help him with problems that he faced in his office.

It cannot be easy for anyone who has a wish to exchange and communicate ideas publicly to accept the constraints of presidential office, and the actual role the president can play in Irish life offers limited compensation for this deprivation. I should add that I had other, personal reasons – a preference for continuing my own post-government lifestyle and a concern to be freer to look after Joan in the years ahead – for not standing for this office on Paddy Hillary's formal retirement in 1990.

On our return from holiday at the end of August 1983, Frank Cluskey had immediately come to me to say that a major insurance company, the Private Motorists' Protection Association, was near the point of financial collapse. The PMPA offered motorists insurance premiums lower than those of the established insurance companies. Now an official enquiry had given Frank Cluskey good reason to believe that a collapse was imminent.

It was only at the end of October that everything was ready to deal with this. Fortunately the company had survived until this point. When we brought the draft legislation before the government there was immediate approval for our proposed action, and Frank Cluskey was congratulated by all on the manner in which he had tackled the problem and for his success in maintaining complete secrecy throughout. On 30 October, as the crisis in the company reached its climax, we moved without warning, and with complete success.

This almost coincided with another crisis, involving the Alliance and Dublin Consumers' Gas Company, familiarly known as the Dublin Gas Company. Disagreement with his colleagues on this second matter was to be the precipitating factor in Frank Cluskey's resignation from the government.

The Dublin Gas Company, a privately owned public utility, had a reputation for inefficiency and poor management that had permitted the development of unacceptable work practices. The company was, however, a major user of natural gas from the newly developed Kinsale gas field, the product of which was handled by a state enterprise, Bord Gáis Éireann. This state company had an agreement with the Dublin Gas Company to help finance the conversion of its network and its customers' appliances to natural gas. But by the latter half of 1983 it was evident that because of the Dublin Gas Company's problems not alone were the Bord Gáis investments in a pipeline from Cork to Dublin and in the conversion of the Dublin gas network at risk but so also was the continuance of the existing gas supply to several hundred thousand Dublin homes that depended on gas for cooking. This posed the question as to whether and on what conditions the state, through its agent, Bord Gáis, should further subsidise the operation and development of a grossly inefficient gas company. Frank Cluskey was quite clear on his position: Dublin Gas should be nationalised, which in practice meant it being taken over by Bord Gáis.

There could not be, and indeed were not, any serious objections to this on ideological grounds. Moreover, given the efficiency of the state-owned Bord Gáis relative to the inefficiency of the privately owned Dublin Gas Company, the case often made against state ownership made no sense in this instance. There was, however, another consideration that influenced most members of the government, including some of Frank Cluskey's Labour Party colleagues: if Dublin Gas were to be merged with Bord Gáis, might not the Dublin Gas workers, many of whom were felt to have 'milked' that company for years, attempt to use their key position to 'milk' Bord Gáis on an even larger scale. For, as a result of the exceptionally favourable terms of the state's agreement with Marathon, the owners of the Kinsale gas field, this state company enjoyed very large profits indeed. This risk appeared to most of us to be too great, and, despite Frank Cluskey's counter-arguments, the government decided in favour of retaining Dublin Gas in the private sector. This battle within the government was a long-drawn-out one; there was no better man than Frank Cluskey for this kind of rearguard action. But when it was clear that he had lost, he resigned.

There was some speculation amongst his colleagues as to whether Dublin Gas was the real, or any rate the only, reason for his action. As I have related earlier,

Frank Cluskey had been very unhappy at the establishment of the New Ireland Forum. He was also visibly uncomfortable, to an even greater extent than the rest of us, at finding himself part of a government that was being forced by the extravagance of its predecessors to cut spending as well as to increase taxes sharply. This was not Frank Cluskey's 'scene', and it may well have been that his general discomfort with the financial decisions being forced on us influenced him, at least subconsciously, to make the Dublin Gas issue a resigning matter.

I regretted losing a colleague whose courage, social commitment and political skill I had come to appreciate over the years and whom I regarded with affection – albeit tinged at times with frustration at his occasional stubbornness. However, some of my colleagues did not have quite the same feeling for him, and some were visibly relieved that we were now to face the rest of our stormy voyage without him.

The irony of all this was that our attempt to maintain an 'arm's length' relationship between the gas field and the Dublin Gas workers eventually failed. Despite our appointment of a number of directors to its board, the management problems of Dublin Gas were not resolved, and two and a half years later we had to mount a further salvage operation. In the course of this, the company was finally taken over by Bord Gáis, which eventually turned it into a reasonably efficient concern with a reduced workforce.

Dick Spring's choice of successor to Frank Cluskey was Ruairi Quinn, whom I had known since the late 1960s, when he was a student of architecture. Ruairi and I had been involved together in seeking to defuse the 'Gentle Revolution' of 1969 in the college, and I had kept in touch with him after he graduated. Whilst he and I were constituency rivals, we remained friends, and the ideological complexion of much of my Fine Gael constituency organisation at that time favoured a co-operative relationship between us – save when, in the first 1982 election, Ruairi had seemed to take an anti-coalition stance.

Dick Spring proposed that Liam Kavanagh now take over the Environment portfolio from him, with Ruairi Quinn replacing Liam as Minister for Labour, with Dick himself taking over the Department of Energy. Trade, Commerce and Tourism were to be restored to the Department of Industry, where John Bruton was the minister.

Ruairi Quinn proved to be an energetic Minister of Labour, committed to mitigating the impact of unemployment by various schemes designed for those out of work, especially the long-term unemployed. If he was not fully successful in establishing a good relationship between the government and the trade unions, the reasons for this lay at a deeper level than he or any other Labour Party minister could deal with, for in the wake of the Fianna Fáil governments of 1977–81 and 1982, it had fallen to us not merely to cut spending and raise taxes but also to wind down inflation by constantly pressing for more modest pay rounds – without being able during this period of deflation to offer the unions much to compensate for these measures. At the same time, there seemed to me to be a deep irritation on the part of some union leaders with Labour participation in government, which, particularly in relation to the public sector, they appeared to regard as involving a confusion of the clear-cut division between representatives of labour and management with which they were comfortable.

The period during which the Dublin Gas issue had been fought to a conclusion in the government coincided with the early stages of the Don Tidey kidnapping affair. Don Tidey, an executive of the Quinnsworth supermarket group, was kidnapped by the IRA with a view to extorting a large sum from the Canadian owners of the group, the Westons. Almost three weeks were to elapse before he was found and rescued, at the expense of two lives – a Garda recruit and a soldier killed by the IRA in the course of the rescue operation.

We hoped that the foiling of this and other kidnap attempts by the IRA and various breakaway groups would have ensured that this possible source of funds would be barred to them. Unhappily, we discovered fourteen months later that £2 million sterling had been paid to a Swiss bank; the great bulk of this money had been transferred via New York to a branch of an Irish bank in Navan. When we learnt this, on Wednesday 13 February 1985, we set to work at once to draft legislation that would enable us to seize this money in a manner that could not be challenged in the courts on the basis of a claim that the constitutional property rights of an alleged owner had been violated. The Bill went through more than twenty drafts in the course of the intervening weekend before the Dáil was due to meet on Tuesday. The Senate had to be summoned for that day also – it had not been due to meet until the following day – and this caused much speculation. But secrecy was maintained, enabling us to enact the Bill after the close of bank business on Tuesday afternoon, with the president signing it later that night. I had of course briefed Charles Haughey about the legislation and the reason for introducing it, and the Opposition co-operated fully in ensuring the speedy enactment of our Bill.

In October, we appointed the first Ombudsman. An imaginative suggestion, adopted enthusiastically by the government, was the nomination to this post of the late Michael Mills, political correspondent of the *Irish Press*. Although the paper for which he wrote had been the party organ of Fianna Fáil from its foundation fifty years earlier, Michael Mills had won universal respect among politicians for his independent and incisive reporting of political events and for his wise comments on political matters.

In March 1984, when returning from Washington to Brussels for a European Council meeting, I heard that Dominic McGlinchey, leader of a particularly vicious breakaway IRA group, the INLA, had been recaptured by the Gardaí. Having absconded when on bail pending a Supreme Court hearing of an extradition process against him, he had been on the run for many months.

Before leaving the United States I had directed that, if arrested, McGlinchey should be extradited at once on foot of the Supreme Court's decision. Having learnt of his capture, I tried, on landing at London Airport, where I was to change planes, to phone Dublin from a VIP lounge to confirm that the extradition was being carried out as I had directed. To my astonishment I was refused permission to make this call, on the grounds that only local calls could be made from the VIP lounge. I blew up at this lunatic piece of British red tape and told the British Airports Authority representative what I would say to Margaret Thatcher when I met her at lunch in Brussels in a couple of hours' time. This left the official quite unmoved, but fortunately an Irish embassy official who had come to meet me found a coin-box phone and produced a ten-pence piece, which enabled me to contact my office in Dublin.

In the event, before McGlinchey could be got to the border a habeas corpus action was initiated; but an emergency sitting of the Supreme Court that evening reaffirmed its earlier decision, and late that night he was handed over to the RUC at the border. However, that was not to be the end of the story. The evidence in relation to the particular murder for which he was extradited did not stand up in the Northern Ireland courts, and in October 1985 we had to re-extradite him from Northern Ireland in order to try him for another offence in our state, for which he was given a long sentence.

In mid-1984 we faced the European Parliament election. Although Fine Gael's share of the vote dropped slightly, we in fact gained two seats; Fianna Fáil, its vote still under 40 percent, gained three seats, but the Labour Party lost all four of its seats, as did the republican independent Neil Blaney. Whilst this result was demoralising for Labour, and increased anti-coalition sentiment within that party, in the short term it naturally had a beneficial impact upon Fine Gael morale.

In conjunction with the European election, we had initiated a constitutional referendum to enable us to reciprocate the British provision, under which, despite our departure from the Commonwealth in 1949, our citizens had retained the right to vote in elections to Westminster. This was something I had agreed at the time of my first summit meeting with Margaret Thatcher in November 1981. The proposal was adopted by a popular majority in favour of reciprocation, illustrating the unique character of the Anglo-Irish relationship.

This marked the beginning of a period in which some of our reforms began to emerge from the frustratingly long legislative pipeline. For example, the legislation for the establishment of an independent Garda Complaints Tribunal was published on the day after the European election and referendum.

The first fruits of Gemma Hussey's negotiations with the European Community on allocating resources from the Social Fund to the educational sector also emerged: grants of £300 a year were provided for up to one-third of school leavers who undertook courses in preparation for employment at the end of their school careers.

Jim O'Leary, my economic adviser during my period as leader of Fine Gael in 1982, had accompanied me into government at the end of that year. In 1983, however, he had decided to leave to join the National Planning Board. I had heard that Patrick Honohan, new governor of the Central Bank, who had been my economic adviser in 1981–82, was willing to take on his role again, and he rejoined me in the Department of the Taoiseach.

In mid-1984 a new control system on public expenditure that I had introduced, which involved monthly reports on the cumulative total of spending under each departmental vote, revealed that spending was currently running ahead of the level we had provided for. There had to be emergency spending cuts.

The National Planning Board had recommended the abolition of the food subsidies that the national coalition government had introduced in the mid-1970s with a view to securing a renegotiation of a grossly excessive national pay agreement. The government had already decided to accept this recommendation, and at the end of July it was agreed that we should eliminate half of these food subsidies forthwith. This would not alone cut public spending in the current year but would also spread over two years the impact on consumer prices of the removal of the subsidies.

Because of the timing of this decision at the end of July, it was decided that news of it should be released during the August holiday weekend rather than being held over until the following week; this, we thought, might have the advantage of reducing adverse public reaction to the announcement. In the event, it had the opposite effect – and the fact that in the absence of the Minister for Finance it was decided to leave it to the government Information Service to give this news to the media, without ministerial involvement, made matters worse. End-of-term exhaustion explains this error of judgement, which proved to be one of the major public-relations miscalculations of our period in government.

A factor which may have affected my own judgement on this issue was my deep concern about Joan's health. On top of her problem of arthritis, she had been suffering throughout the previous year from a mysterious gastric complaint, and I had just been warned that its persistence for such a prolonged period could have most serious consequences. Happily the complaint was diagnosed some time after our return from holiday and was successfully treated in the months that followed. But at the end of July I was deeply preoccupied with getting her away on holiday.

Part of our holiday that year was spent in the south of France, some of it with friends of ours: Brendan Dowling, my economic adviser as Minister for Foreign Affairs, and his wife Dorrie had taken a house inland. And President Mitterrand had invited Joan and me, with some friends, to stay in the French president's official retreat, the fort of Brégançon, on the coast to the east of Toulon, which had once housed Napoleon at an early stage of his career.

I had accepted this invitation after enquiring from several people who had stayed there whether there were many steps in the front – a matter that concerned me because of Joan's disability. I had been assured that there were only a few steps from the car to the guest accommodation, but in fact when we arrived I counted no fewer than 168! Nevertheless, because the accommodation at the higher level of the fort opened onto lawns surrounded by battlements, once Joan had managed to get there, with considerable difficulty, she was able to remain at that level in comfort during our stay, descending to the formal reception level only once, when President Mitterand and his wife, together with Prime Minister Fabius and Foreign Minister Dumas and their wives, came to dinner.

The dinner was, incidentally, a most entertaining occasion. The fortieth-anniversary celebration of the liberation of Paris had just taken place, and Mitterrand enlivened the evening with many stories of his experiences at that time. His aide-de-camp was named Barry, which happened also to be the name of one of Mary and Vincent's friends, the composer Gerald Barry, who was staying with us but did not speak French. When a phone call came in the middle of the night for the aide-de-camp from the Élysée Palace it was unfortunately put through to Gerald, whom we had coached to explain in French, when addressed in that language, that he did not speak a word of that language. This response, apparently from the president's aide-de-camp, must have had a fairly shattering effect on the caller from the Élysée!

In the autumn of 1984, the relationship between Dick Spring and myself came under unexpected strain. We had to nominate a member of the European Commission for the period 1985–88. I had reflected on whom I should propose from Fine Gael. Conscious of the need to field an outstanding candidate who might become a really influential member of the European Commission, I felt at the same time that I could not spare one of my ministerial 'heavyweights', nor did I wish to face a by-election that we might easily lose.

It was Joan who came up with the answer, when I put the dilemma to her one morning. She suggested Peter Sutherland. He was an ideal choice – someone who could, and did, become a leading member of one of the more successful Commission teams for many years, and who increased immensely our reputation in Europe.

When I brought his name forward, Dick Spring was prepared to agree, but on one condition: that he would nominate Peter's successor as attorney general. Hitherto the attorney general had always been the personal choice of the Taoiseach of the day, for the relationship between Taoiseach and attorney general is a particularly close one, partly because of the delicacy of the legal issues that arise under a

Constitution that so tightly controls the actions of both executive and legislature. The attorney general's office, indeed, was sited on the floor immediately below that of the Taoiseach, and, at any rate in my experience, the attorney general is a frequent and valued visitor to the Taoiseach's office. Despite my close friendship with Dick Spring, to have my attorney general chosen for me was something I instinctively resisted, and Dick's choice, John Rogers, a Junior Counsel, was not known to me – although I soon learnt that before moving to Labour he had been a member of Young Fine Gael!

I reflected for some weeks on this matter and consulted several senior legal people to get their views, before I finally agreed, with some qualms, to Dick's proposal. I need not have worried: John Rogers turned out to be an excellent attorney-general, and enormously helpful to me on political as well as legal matters. Because of the nature of my personal relationship with Dick Spring, no problems of divided loyalty arose, and John Rogers was often able to help smooth over problems between the two parties in government. His relative lack of experience in constitutional matters was fully compensated for by his qualities of judgement and his willingness to draw on the advice of his office or on others with special skills. He shared my commitment to the achievement of an Anglo-Irish Agreement and played an important role in its negotiation.

When, at the end of July, I had talked to Jacques Delors about my possible nomination of Peter Sutherland, I had told him something of Peter's exceptional qualities and legal skills, and had suggested that he might consider him for the Competition portfolio in the Commission. This is a particularly important portfolio, the holder of which has personal power to determine on his own account what state aids governments may give to their industrial sectors. By virtue of this power, the Commissioner for Competition tends to carry considerable weight in the Commission, and Peter's appointment to this portfolio, together with his own qualities, seemed to me to be likely to provide him with the opportunity to become an outstanding member of the next Commission. Jacques Delors (whose appointment as president of the Commission I had recently secured in my capacity as president of the European Council, overcoming Margaret Thatcher's objections to another French president of the Commission) took my recommendations seriously, and when the time came several months later for him to make his appointments, he eventually nominated Peter Sutherland for this position. Peter's success in this appointment, and his emergence as one of the key figures in that Commission, and subsequently in the Uruguay trade round, are a matter of record.

The third of the corporate crises that faced us during this term of office declared itself in November 1984. This time it was a state company, Irish Shipping, which had been established in 1941 to provide us with a wartime strategic shipping fleet and which had been retained in state ownership thereafter, operating on the whole with success over the intervening decades. Unhappily, the key posts of chairman, chief executive and chief accountant had been allowed by a board containing too many political appointees by successive governments to be accumulated in the hands of one person, who made a grave error of judgement in chartering vessels on a long-term basis at rates that proved unsustainable outside periods of strong shipping demand.

With the recent collapse of shipping rates, this entire operation became immensely vulnerable. We now found ourselves faced with an insolvent company whose debts were state-guaranteed to the tune of £40 million but which also had long-term liabilities of over £140 million. We had no alternative but to allow the company to go into liquidation and its staff, of almost four hundred people, to be made redundant. The most tragic part of the affair was that we were unable to supplement the meagre statutory-redundancy payments for the staff without risking an extension of our legal liability to include the additional £140 million of debts, for which the state simply could not afford to take responsibility. Understandably, the staff and their dependants could not grasp why they alone of those found redundant in the state sector during these years had to be confined to statutory-redundancy payments, receiving no adequate compensation for their loyal service to the company. This was one of the most painful decisions that we had to take while in government, and one that has bothered me ever since.

Four months later, we were yet to face another corporate crisis that, although this time in the private sector, was of such a character that we could not avoid becoming involved in its resolution. Associated with Irish Shipping throughout much of its life had been an insurance company, the Insurance Corporation of Ireland, which was originally established to provide cover for the shipping fleet. However, this company had developed a much wider range of business and had eventually been privatised. Allied Irish Banks had acquired ownership of the Insurance Corporation of Ireland in September 1983.

In the week beginning 4 March 1984, it was discovered that the ICI had incurred huge and, in the short term at least, unquantifiable liabilities in the London insurance market as a result of the activities of its London manager. These losses were known to be so great that they appeared to endanger the stability of Allied Irish Banks, which accordingly approached the government to seek help to save the bank.

In mid-March, when the matter was brought to the attention of the government, I was temporarily laid up. It was Alan Dukes, as Minister of Finance, and John Bruton, as Minister for Industry and Commerce, who had to deal with the crisis, together with their civil servants and the Central Bank. The advice the two ministers received was that unless the government acted to relieve AIB of the liabilities of ICI, the bank itself might nor survive, and the collapse of AIB could endanger the other major banking group, the Bank of Ireland, and indeed the credit of the state and the stability of the currency. If this crisis were to be avoided, not merely would the state have to act in an unprecedented way, but it would be necessary not to disclose the full rationale for this action, lest such a disclosure precipitate financial panic.

When Alan Dukes and John Bruton came to tell me this at home, I was horrified at the scale of the disaster and shocked that the banking system, of which I had made an intensive study in 1965, could since then have been allowed to become so vulnerable to mismanagement in a single subsidiary. I was told that this extraordinary situation had arisen because, since I had undertaken my study, the arrangements for bank equity had been modified so as to treat as equity certain loans from other banking institutions, loans which could be withdrawn without notice if any subsidiary of the bank became insolvent. I could not understand, and have never since had explained to me, how such an element of inherent instability had been allowed to creep into the banking system without the government being alerted to this dangerous development. We were informed that the Department of Industry and Commerce had been assured that all was well with ICI by the British Department of Trade and Industry, which apparently had responsibility for supervision of the company's activities in London. In other words, nobody in Ireland appeared to be to blame, but our government had to carry the can.

The Opposition supported in the Dáil the necessary legislative provisions to deal with the crisis, involving the acquisition of the ICI by a company established by the Department of Industry and Commerce for this purpose, together with the funding of the deficit by the Central Bank out of its reserves. But Fianna Fáil soon began to criticise us severely for our handling of the affair. We could not respond adequately to this criticism at the time without causing dangerous doubts about the state of the whole banking system.

However, I insisted that the Central Bank should return to this problem later in the year, working out a scheme under which the temporary assistance it was providing would over time be refunded by AIB, with some assistance from other banks and insurance companies. This was eventually done, so that the taxpayer was ultimately protected from carrying any part of this burden. Unhappily, we never succeeded in convincing public opinion of this, and as a result the myth has persisted ever since that the Exchequer, i.e. the taxpayer, has carried the burden of bailing out AIB.

I shared to the full the sense of frustration and indignation about the manner in which this affair had been handled by AIB, and was frankly shocked at the provocative way in which the bank shortly afterwards announced that its results for the year would be unaffected by this development and that no reduction would be made in the dividend payable to shareholders. Its concern to reassure its shareholders seemed to me, and to many other people in public life, to take precedence over any sense of public responsibility; the effect on the credibility of the banking system with the broader public was certainly very negative.

Shortly before the AIB-ICI crisis broke, we had put through the Dáil a Bill reforming the law on contraception. In 1979 Charles Haughey, then Minister for Health, had produced what he had described as 'an Irish solution to an Irish problem': the legalisation of the sale of contraceptives on prescription, for family-planning purposes only, viz. to married woman. This had followed a judgement of the European Court of Human Rights in Strasbourg that had impugned the ban on contraception in the case of a married woman whose health would have been in jeopardy in the event of a further pregnancy.

I was determined to replace this anachronistic and disreputable piece of legislation, which sounded like a late flowering of medieval canon law, with a straightforward legalisation of the open sale of contraceptives by pharmacies and health boards, although I recognised that to get this through the Dáil – which was certainly not going to be easy – there would have to be a (somewhat theoretical) limitation on the sale of contraceptives to people of eighteen years and over.

A few days later I had the pleasure of seeing published the only substantial Bill that I had the opportunity of personally introducing and steering through the Oireachtas during my time in government: the National Archives Bill. This Bill provided for merger of the Public Record Office and the State Papers Office to form the National Archives, and made provision for the lodging therein of the papers of central government, at the end of thirty years. Up to that time, there had been no provision of this kind, although in the 1970s Liam Cosgrave had lodged papers from the Department of the Taoiseach for the first quarter of a century of the existence of the state in the Public Record Office, where they had been made accessible.

In drafting this legislation, I had been concerned to make it as liberal as possible, limiting very strictly indeed the categories of papers that could be withheld, and setting up a system of checks designed to ensure that these liberal provisions would be adhered to. In January 1991 the great bulk of pre-1960 central-government records were released to historians – an estimated one million files. Unhappily, this archive has been seriously neglected by the present government.

In June 1985 I lost a valued friend, Alexis FitzGerald, who had been ill for some time previously. We had known each other for almost forty years, sharing many common interests, although often having differing viewpoints, and I had drawn heavily on his advice and assistance throughout my political career, both when he had been a senator and also when he had been a special adviser to my first short-lived government of 1981–82. In the closing years of my premiership, I greatly missed his advice and support.

A few days after his death, local elections were held – elections which, against my advice, had been postponed from the previous year. During the preceding twelve months, the continuing deflation of the economy had, as I had warned, reduced our popularity, and in these elections, for the first time since the 1960s, Fine Gael lost a significant amount of ground in many city and county councils. The inevitable weakening of morale in Fine Gael was temporarily mitigated by the signing of the Anglo-Irish Agreement in November.

One of the short-term domestic political consequences of this agreement was the resignation of Mary Harney from Fianna Fáil. A year earlier she had told me that she was very disillusioned with the party under Charles Haughey and was thinking of leaving, and possibly joining Fine Gael. I had suggested to her at the time that the announcement of the Anglo-Irish Agreement, which I believed Haughey would oppose, would provide an appropriate occasion for such a move. The consequence of this delay, however, was that, with such a prominent member of Fianna Fáil as Des O'Malley already 'on the loose' as an independent, Mary Harney did not in fact join our party after the signature of the agreement but instead, at the end of that year, joined with him in the establishment of the Progressive Democrats. For myself, I would have preferred it if Des O'Malley and she had joined Fine Gael, as I had told Des the establishment of a new political party was, I felt, a second-best. But whatever the short-term consequences for Fine Gael – and I have to say I never contemplated a drift of our voters to the new party on the scale that actually occurred in 1987 – it seemed a good thing at the time that a new rallying point be established against Fianna Fáil under Charles Haughey – one that would ensure that he would not become leader of a government with an absolute majority in Dáil Éireann.

The closing months of 1985 saw the emergence of two other issues that were to loom very large in 1986, our last year in government. These were the early stages of the teachers' pay dispute, and growing pressure for the introduction of divorce.

The teacher's unions have always been a powerful force, and their efforts had led to a higher value being placed on the work of teachers in Ireland than in many other countries. I believe that over the years this high level of teachers' pay has been one of a number of factors contributing to the high quality of Irish education. We were now, however, faced with a serious dilemma. We were experiencing great difficulty in reducing the level of the budget deficit, and of government borrowing, below that to which we had cut them quite sharply between 1981 and 1983, and the Exchequer was certainly in no position to take on the burden of a very large increase in teachers' pay – which, it was proposed, should be backdated, and which could all too easily prove a headline for similar claims from other groups in the public sector. Accordingly we felt we had no alternative but to plead inability to pay the proposed award, and by mid-January 1986 talks on the issue had collapsed.

Gemma Hussey had been actively pursuing a whole range of reforms in the educational sector – a number of which were, however, being frustrated by lack of resources. She was distressed at the idea that sums many times in excess of those needed to provide the resources for a significant improvement in the quality of education in various sectors were now being sought to improve the already high level of teachers' pay at a time when the community as a whole was going through intensive belt-tightening.

I had always envisaged a reshuffle of the government in the second half of our term of office. The delay in the conclusion of the Anglo-Irish Agreement had led me to postpone consideration of such a move until early in 1986. Whether we won the next election or not, I intended to retire as party leader in the early part of the next Dáil. I was concerned to leave behind me a party in which the leading figures would have as wide a range of experience as I could manage to secure for them, and would thus as far as possible find themselves well equipped to face a leadership contest. I wanted to make sure that none would be disadvantaged by virtue of the roles they had been required to play in my government. I was convinced that it would be wrong of me to try to influence in any way the outcome of this contest; on the contrary, my duty to the party was simply to ensure the widest and most open choice. I was also concerned, as I had been in December 1982, when I did not reappoint some of the junior ministers who had served in my previous brief administration, to give an opportunity to several younger backbenchers to serve in government for a time before the next general election.

To these considerations was now added concern lest several ministers find their future political prospects damaged by being identified in the public mind with financial cuts made necessary by our extremely difficult economic situation. I was anxious that those concerned would have an opportunity to recover ground in other, less controversial departments before our government came to the end of its term in 1987. These various worthy motivations led me now into a reshuffle whose consequences proved damaging to me personally and to our government.

The two ministers whom I had decided some time previously to move, with a view to minimising the political damage that participation in this government might have done for them, were Alan Dukes, who had the most unpopular job of all in Finance, and Barry Desmond, who had handled the Health portfolio with great skill but at the cost of considerable unpopularity because of the cuts he had had to make. Dick Spring agreed with me about his party colleague, Barry Desmond, who had a marginal seat.

Gemma Hussey also had a very marginal seat; for her to remain in her post while the teachers' dispute continued to rage would, I felt, put her re-election at risk too. On the pay issue itself, I was completely supportive of her stand, and in moving her I had no intention whatever of easing the way for a government climbdown.

As to the others, John Bruton had, I knew, been very upset about not having been reappointed to Finance in December 1982, but this had given him an opportunity to widen his experience, and he could, I felt, now return to the job to which I knew he aspired, without the danger of being typecast as the man who had taken all the unpopular decisions over a six-year period.

Michael Noonan had done an excellent job in Justice and was entitled to be given experience in some other major post. John Boland had carried through a number of key reforms that I had wanted to see implemented in the structure of the civil service, and deserved a chance to apply his talents to a 'heavy' department, where his toughness and drive might achieve worthwhile results in the year ahead.

Peter Barry, my deputy leader, had told me that if I wished to move him from Foreign Affairs he would go. However, he clearly preferred to stay where he was, and there was a case for maintaining continuity here in the early stages of the implementation of the Anglo-Irish Agreement.

That is a rough outline of the main features of the reshuffle I initiated on the evening of Wednesday 12 February. Most of the changes were accepted without too much demur by those concerned, although Gemma Hussey was clearly, and understandably, upset by being asked to move from Education. However, she was obviously attracted by my proposal to make her Cabinet Minister for Europe.

Two problems then arose. First, Barry Desmond refused to move, preferring, he said, to lose his seat, if that were the price to be paid, rather than to abandon his portfolio. And Dermot Nally that morning informed me that if I appointed Gemma Hussey as European affairs minister in the Cabinet, I would have to divide the Department of Foreign Affairs in two and to appoint a separate secretary of a new Department of European Affairs.

The Barry Desmond crisis, which soon began to leak to the media, prevented me from probing this latter advice as deeply as I might otherwise have done. By midday, Dick Spring, who had supported my proposal to move Barry Desmond, was in my office telling me that he had been unable to resolve that problem and that in the circumstances he felt he must resign from the government together with his colleagues. I should prepare to establish a Fine Gael government without the Labour Party, he said.

Shattered by this completely unexpected consequence of my concern, and Dick's, for Barry Desmond's political future, and aware of the growing atmosphere of rumour outside, I sat down to prepare a Fine Gael alternative government. However, within half an hour Dick Spring was back with the news that Barry Desmond would relinquish his Social Welfare portfolio if he could keep Health; he had always given most of his time to health matters.

The outcome was not really satisfactory. Gemma Hussey was deeply distressed at being moved from Education and then losing the proposed European affairs portfolio, to the prospect of which she had begun to look forward. She saw Social Welfare as a bed of nails rather than as an opportunity to initiate a fundamental reform of income redistribution – for which, indeed, there would be very little time before the already impending election. While Pat Cooney was happy to move to Education, being of a conservative bent he did not have Gemma Hussey's deep commitment to educational reform. Moreover, in my view he turned out to be too easily convinced by his civil servants of the need to concede to some of the teachers' unions demands – although in fairness I should add that they ended up persuading me also, against my better judgement, to agree to these concessions, on the very dubious basis that the cost would be covered by a combination of savings on the salaries of teachers who had been on strike and a claim for a graduates' allowance that was due to be settled but could be subsumed within the settlement of the dispute.

Moreover, quite apart from the Hussey/Cooney dimension of the reshuffle, the public impact of what was seen as a badly executed move was damaging, and the mess was made worse by a subsequent error of mine with respect to the reshuffling of the Fine Gael junior ministers. When I had appointed the junior ministers in 1982, I had made it clear to them that I indented to reshuffle them at some point, and that I would be introducing some new blood during the lifetime of this government. In line with this policy, I decided to replace two of my older ministers of state with two backbenchers in their mid-thirties. I was given to understand that one of the ministers of state to be replaced already expected to return to the back benches; when I saw him, he accepted my decision without demur. The other protested. Not wishing to rub salt in their wounds, however, I did not (as Dermot Nally had warned me I should do) specifically ask them to put their resignations in writing; I foolishly assumed that they would do this automatically. I suffered the consequences of this moment of unwise compassion, for when they returned to their constituencies after I had announced their resignations and the names of their replacements in the Dáil, they repudiated my statement, declaring that they had not resigned – as, technically, they had not. I was then forced to implement the procedure for termination of their appointments, and also to apologise to the Dáil the next time it met for having inadvertently misled it.

Two further changes of junior ministers took place subsequently. One Labour minister of state resigned and was replaced by a colleague, and I had to replace a Fine Gael junior minister in unhappy circumstances. Through inadvertence, and clearly without any improper intent, Eddie Collins, a minister of state in the Department of Industry and Commerce, who was an exceptionally hard-working and effective member of our team, had attended some meetings of the board of a family company, from which he had quite properly resigned on appointment to his ministerial post. He was present in the room at one such meeting when an application for assistance from a state financial institution was discussed.

My request for his resignation was a painful decision, taken after a personal examination by me of the events in question. He clearly found my decision hard to accept. I felt, however, that if I were to uphold integrity in public life, I must ensure not only that no impropriety occurred – which in my view was clearly the case – but that no suspicion of impropriety be allowed to exist. Justice, in terms of integrity in public life, must be seen to be done, as well as actually being done. Some of my colleagues, I believe, felt that I was acting more strictly than necessary in this case; for my own part, it was perhaps the most painful personal decision I had to take as Taoiseach, and one that has left me most unhappy ever since.

The issue of divorce had been a live one within Fine Gael since 1978, when, at a very well-attended meting during my first *ard fheis* as leader, the participants had given strong support to the removal of the constitutional ban on the dissolution of marriage. During my first period in government, I had sought to have this matter discussed by an all-party committee, but this had been rejected by Fianna Fáil.

It would have been possible, I suppose, to stall more or less indefinitely on this issue, but that carried the risk that divorce would feature largely in the eventual general election, to be held in 1987. This seemed to me highly undesirable: that election should, I believed, be fought as clearly as possible on the issue of fiscal policy, with a view to pinning Fianna Fáil down to facing the need for continued action to reduce borrowing should they, as seemed possible, return to power at that election. If the issue of divorce were not faced now, we could find ourselves facing an election in which the crucial economic issue might be sidelined by a campaign in which we would be under attack both from liberals, for not having initiated a divorce referendum, and from Fianna Fáil, for allegedly intending, on re-election, to introduce divorce on demand. My feeling that this matter should be addressed without further delay was reinforced by the fact that public opinion, as recorded by various polls, appeared to favour a move to introduce a restricted form of divorce, although I would have preferred the margin in favour of this to have been somewhat larger.

Irish marriage law as it evolved in the nineteenth century, with some amendments in 1972, is uniquely complex, with quite different provisions for different religious denominations, as well as provision for civil marriages before a registrar. Clearly, as the great majority of marriages were solemnised in churches of one denomination or another, with a subsequent civil registration of the marriage, any move to modify the provision in relation to the indissolubility of such marriages must involve consultation with the churches in question. Moreover, other issues in relation to marriage itself needed to be addressed.

Accordingly, on 14 February 1986 I wrote to the heads of the various churches to tell them that in view of the common interest of the state and the churches in the stability of marriage – and more specifically in view of the fact that the vast majority of marriages were solemnised in churches and were registered as civil marriages by the clergyman concerned – I was anxious to have the views of the principal churches on the recommendations of the Joint Oireachtas Committee on Marriage Breakdown and on matters that might arise from these recommendations, before bringing to the government proposals in relation to these matters.

I went on to list the issues on which I was particularly anxious to have the views of the churches, namely the minimum age of marriage; the possible desirability of providing for a minimum period of notice before marriage; counselling for married couples having matrimonial difficulties; the legal grounds for separation; the enforcement of the law proscribing bigamy; possible changes in the law of nullity; the possible establishment of Family Tribunals to deal with all types of marriage cases; and, in cases where a marriage had irretrievably broken down, the question of divorce and remarriage.

I also told them that I would prefer to arrange these consultations generally on a joint basis should this prove acceptable to all the churches concerned – although even if this were acceptable, I recognised that on particular points, separate consultations with an individual church or churches might be considered desirable. However, most of the churches preferred not to participate in a joint consultation, asking me to receive them separately. Moreover, the Irish Episcopal Conference of the Roman Catholic Church asked to add several items to the agenda, namely better financial support for the family in marriage; the rights of the parents vis-à-vis their own children in the light of proposals to safeguard children from abuse and neglect; and the Domicile and Recognition of Foreign Divorces Act, which we had introduced some time previously.

The meetings with most of the churches were in fact very constructive, and contributed significantly to the proposals we subsequently produced. Thus our decision to propose a minimum age of eighteen for marriage, subject to the possibility of authorisation of marriage in exceptional circumstances by a proposed Family Court for people between the ages of sixteen and eighteen, reflected the thinking of most of the churches; and our proposal to introduce a new requirement of a minimum of three months' notice for marriage was influenced by our discussions with representatives of the Catholic hierarchy in particular. The decision to allow divorce only where a marriage has failed and the failure has continued for a period or periods of at least five years reflected the thinking of several churches, including in particular the Church of Ireland.

It had been expected that the discussions with representatives of the Roman Catholic hierarchy would be the most difficult, because of their objection to the introduction of any form of divorce, but in fact that part of our discussion proved relatively straightforward, in that we agreed to differ on that issue. Some tension did arise, however, in the course of this meeting on a different issue, which requires some background explanation.

The Irish civil law of nullity derives from the ecclesiastical law of the Established Anglican Church of Ireland, which had always remained very restrictive by comparison with the developing provisions for declarations of nullity by ecclesiastical tribunals of the Roman Catholic Church. This produced the uncomfortable situation where a certain number of Irish marriages that have been annulled by the Roman Catholic Church in circumstances that permit of remarriage in that church remain valid marriages in the eyes of the state. In these cases, remarriage in a Catholic Church constitutes bigamy, although because of the difficulty in securing evidence of the second marriage, prosecutions for bigamy have not taken place. This is an uncomfortable position for both church and state, and it was a matter that had to be addressed in the context of our discussions – which, in conjunction with Alan Dukes, the new Minister for Justice, I undertook with the representatives of the Roman Catholic hierarchy.

When we reached this point on the agenda, I remarked that the problem could be tackled by separating the civil and religious ceremonies but that I was reluctant to contemplate such a separation, if it could be avoided, in view of what I believed to be the attachment of most Irish people to the traditional joint ceremony. The member of the Hierarchy allocated by their delegation to deal with this matter than raised the possibility of a new arrangement under which a church remarriage of someone who had benefited from a church decree of nullity would constitute a purely religious event, which would make no claim to be, and give no appearance of being, a civilly valid marriage. It was suggested that the Hierarchy and the government might co-operate in the development of such a new arrangement.

In retrospect, I think that perhaps, in their concern to find a solution to the conflict of laws that would enable the Catholic Church to continue with its existing practice of making declarations of nullity, the representatives of the Hierarchy may not have considered the implications of this proposal for Alan Dukes and myself. As a result they were, I think, taken aback by the strength of our reaction to a proposal that appeared to us to suggest that, instead of amending the Constitution to provide a means for dealing with this as well as other marriage-breakdown problems (which the representatives of the Hierarchy were strongly opposing), we should collaborate in undermining the existing constitutional protection of marriage. For, as long as this clause remained in the Constitution, we were committed as officers under the Constitution to uphold it. In the face of our very negative reaction to their initial suggestion, the representatives of the Hierarchy did not proceed to elaborate the suggestions they had in mind about how such an arrangement might be implemented on their side; instead, we passed on to other matters.

However, some years later, this matter surfaced publicly when, in an interview as leader of Fine Gael, Alan Dukes expressed forcibly – and, it must be said, in inappropriate language – his feelings about the proposal made to us by the Hierarchy. For my part, in December 1989 in an article in the magazine *Alpha* I wrote: 'there was even a suggestion by the Hierarchy delegation that we "bend" our civil marriage laws so as to accommodate these bigamous marriages, a suggestion that was, in my view, quite improper'.

This comment evoked a letter to me from the late Cardinal O'Fiaich in which he took issue with my comments. He went on to explain that what the representatives of the Hierarchy had been intending to propose to us at that meeting was that, in the case of Catholics whose earlier marriage had been annulled in the ecclesiastical court, they be remarried either by way of a religious marriage accompanied by a disclaimer of any civil significance for the ceremony, or by way of a marriage ceremony in the absence of an episcopally ordained minister, with a lay person delegated instead to assist at the marriage, or perhaps even by a marriage taking place in the presence of witnesses alone and without any representative of the Catholic Church present!

I responded to this letter several months later, pointing our that from our point of view what the Hierarchy delegation had started to propose to us would have involved an arrangement between the government and the Hierarchy of one church designed to facilitate the entry by some people into arrangements that at the very least would in the eyes of the public purport to displace the existing joint civil-religious marriage, which enjoyed the protection of the Constitution. And I went on to raise a number of other aspects of the matter that concerned me. At the end of the letter, I suggested that the publication of this exchange of letters, on a matter of considerable interest, would be appropriate, with a view to clarifying for the public the complex issues at stake, but because of Cardinal O'Fiaich's tragic death some time later, possibly before he had an opportunity to read my letter, I did not pursue this matter. The two letters were, however, reproduced as an appendix to my 1991 autobiography, but, surprisingly, evoked no comment then or since.

A fortnight after this series of meetings with the churches, Dick Spring, Alan Dukes and myself launched our proposals for a referendum on an amendment to the Constitution to remove the ban on the dissolution of marriage. In conjunction with the press conference, we published the text of the Bill and a statement of our intentions with regard to separation and divorce. This statement was designed to meet a genuine and widely held concern that, in introducing a restricted form of divorce, we might be starting on a slippery slope towards 'easy divorce'. The proposed constitutional amendment itself provided that a dissolution could be granted only where certain conditions were fulfilled, 'that the marriage had failed and that the failure had continued for a period or periods amounting to at least five years'; that there was no possibility of reconciliation between the parties to the marriage; and that, moreover, the court was satisfied that adequate and proper provision, having regard to the circumstances, would be made for any dependent spouse or for any child who was dependent on either spouse.

In the Bill that we announced simultaneously with the proposed constitutional amendment, we also proposed that a divorce would have to be preceded by a judicial separation at least two years previously, and new grounds were introduced for such separations – namely desertion, including constructive desertion, separation for up to three years, or separation for up to one year with the consent of the respondent. Separation and divorce cases were to be heard by a Family Court, to be presided over by a judge or judges of the Circuit Court especially assigned for this purpose, and this court would have the power to adjourn proceedings for a separation if it thought it necessary or appropriate that a mediation process, to be conducted by a registered counselling agency, should be undergone before the legal proceedings.

In the course of our press conference, I made it clear that our two parties would be supporting the amendment to the Constitution in the Dáil and before the electorate, whilst accepting that individual members might on grounds of conscience not wish to participate in the campaign if they held a contrary view on the amendment.

The basis on which we were proceeding to introduce the provision for divorce was our belief that the balance of social good would be served by making this provision, for whilst it was accepted that any divorce provision might have a negative effect on some existing marriages, on the other hand the number of people now in irregular unions and the number of children adversely affected by this situation was, in the considered view of our parties, even more destabilising of marriage. During the press conference, one journalist remarked that the campaign on the referendum had already been predicted to be a dirty and divisive one, and asked how I would be trying to 'sell' the referendum when I went out to the country to campaign on it – to which I replied: 'Less luridly.' She was right about the campaign being dirty and divisive, however.

A poll was carried out a few days later that showed that at that point 57 percent were in favour of our constitutional amendment and 36 percent against, with 7 percent not holding an opinion. There was a majority in favour in all four regions, in rural as well as urban areas, and in all political parties (although by a small margin in the case of Fianna Fáil supporters); only the oldest age group, and farmers with large holdings contained a majority against the referendum at that point.

The campaign against the proposed amendment was launched on 9 May. A few days later, the Roman Catholic hierarchy set out their opposition to the legislation and their intention to publish and distribute one million copies of a pastoral letter against divorce.

By early June, a poll showed that about one-fifth of those who had previously favoured the amendment had clearly become undecided about it, with no change at that point in the proportion against divorce. However, as the anti-divorce campaign gained momentum, with a formal statement by the Hierarchy on 11 June, support for the amendment eroded rapidly, and a poll taken shortly before the referendum, which was held on 27 June, showed that opinion had by that time swung conclusively against it.

The suddenness and magnitude of this shift in opinion during the first half of June was unexpected. Two factors seem to have played a major part in it. The first was the fact that an earlier commitment by the Catholic hierarchy not to tell people how to vote but to confine themselves to stating the Catholic moral position on the issue was not adhered to. Immense pressure from the pulpit was put on people to oppose the referendum. The second fact was the unscrupulous way in which some opponents of divorce sought to spread alarm about the possible effect on property rights of the introduction of divorce.

These two elements, combined with the strong opposition to the amendment from Fianna Fáil throughout the country, despite that party's stated neutral stance, as well as unenthusiastic campaigning by many supporters of our party in particular, had produced a swing in opinion on the part of something like a quarter of the electorate, which led to a 63 percent majority against the proposed constitutional amendment.

I found the debate itself extremely depressing. Given the Catholic Church's stated position that it did not seek to impose its theological views on the civil law of the state, it seemed to me that the only relevant consideration was whether the balance of social good would or would not be served by a restricted form of divorce – an issue that was never adverted to by either side of the referendum in the campaign.

Quite unconnected with the divorce question was the introduction of legislation at around the same time to abolish the concept of illegitimacy. This was a matter that Young Fine Gael had taken up some years earlier, running a national campaign on the issue that had awoken people's consciences and had stimulated us to address the question in government. It turned out, however, that the legal complexities of the issue were far greater than they, or indeed I, had envisaged. The excellent memorandum for the government on the proposed legislation ran to almost a hundred foolscap pages. This did not include any padding but comprised detailed analysis of many consequential legal effects of the changes that we proposed to make. The Status of Children Bill effected a major and long-overdue reform in our law; while the enactment of the legislation took several years, coming to fruition in the following Dáil, I was happy that we had initiated and drafted such a significant measure of social reform.

The last few months of 1986 proved to be our most traumatic time in government.

Our small majority in the Dáil had effectively evaporated, and our government found itself at the mercy of half a dozen members of our two parties who on one issue or another were threatening to withdraw their support. At the same time, for the first occasion during our period in government expenditure began to exceed the level provided for in the estimates, leading to a sudden sharp rise in interest rates. Moreover, the implementation of EC sex-equality legislation, which had, negative effects on some social-welfare beneficiaries, led to a revolt in our two parties, necessitating a series of climbdowns by the government, with serious financial implications. The ratification of the Single European Act, postponed at Labour's request until after its party conference in early November, was placed in doubt. The highly contentious legislation to ratify the Convention on the Suppression of Terrorism, with a view to strengthening our extradition law, had to be got through a Dáil in which we no longer had a clear majority. And whilst all this was happening, our two parties found themselves unable to agree on budgetary proposals – a development that eventually led to a break-up of the government. I doubt if any other government since the end of the Civil War in 1923 faced such a catalogue of difficulties crowding in on it one after the other in such a short space of time, perhaps with the exception of the present government.

Despite defections by Fine Gael and Labour Party deputies, which eventually eliminated our combined majority in the Dáil, we continued to introduce reforming measures, including an Adoption Bill to extend adoptions to legitimate children who had been abandoned by their parents – a cause to which I had been strongly committed since an experience I had in an orphanage during the 1979 European election, but one that required particularly careful handling because of possible constitutional difficulties.

In mid-October, as part of an effort to steady the markets and to restore confidence in our determination to maintain the process of reducing the deficit and borrowing, I put to the government a proposal that we should announce that the current deficit for 1987 would be held at the current year's budgeted level of 7.4 percent of GNP. I also proposed that we make it clear that we would not increase the burden of taxes.

The clear implication of any such announcement was that significant expenditure cuts would be effected. This naturally presented problems for our Labour partners. Nevertheless, the threat to interest rates in particular posed by the decline in confidence in financial circles was such that I felt it necessary on this occasion to do what I had never previously done: to press for a majority decision, despite the opposition of our Labour Party colleagues.

Whilst warning that this could put at risk their continued participation in the government when we came to take decisions on the estimates for 1987, the Labour Party ministers agreed to accept this majority decision without public dissent in order to deal with the immediate crisis. Nevertheless, the fact that we were forced into this unprecedented course of action made it virtually certain that our government would not survive in its current form to present the 1987 budget.

The final hurdle was the Extradition Bill, on which a serious of votes was decided on the Ceann Comhairle's casting vote after one of our deputies had abstained. It was eventually passed, on the basis that in order to leave time for the various procedures under the Bill to be sorted out, it would not come into effect until 1 December 1987. Two deputies who were ill – David Andrews of Fianna Fáil and Oliver Flanagan on our side – attended; the appearance of Oliver Flanagan, who everyone knew had not long to live and who had been a stormy petrel in Irish politics during his forty-three years in the Dáil, evoked a spontaneous round of applause from the whole Dáil.

We knew that the 1987 pre-election budget would pose serious difficulties for us. If these could be resolved, however, then despite the ground lost because of Fianna Fáil's brief return to power in 1982, when taxes had been cut and spending increased, in comparable terms we would have reduced Exchequer borrowing from the threatened figure of 21.5 percent of GNP for 1982 that had faced us on coming into office in mid-1981 to 9.75 percent five and a half years later. This would have been a remarkable achievement.

But 1986 was to prove thoroughly disappointing. First of all, even though as late as May 1986 the Central Bank was projecting a 3.5 percent rise in GDP, by early 1987 it was clear that there had in fact been no growth at all in the economy during the year. Tourism was having a bad year, because American tourists were avoiding Europe, fearing retaliation for the bombing of Libya; agricultural output was being adversely affected by weather for the second successive year; and the rise in industrial output had been halted as export growth had flagged. A sudden and sharp depreciation of sterling at a time when the dollar had also fallen was clearly beginning to put undue competitive pressure on our already depressed economy.

At the beginning of August, John Bruton, now back in Finance, and myself, decided, on the proposal of my economic adviser Patrick Honohan, to tackle this latter problem by a unilateral devaluation of the Irish pound within the EMS. On a Saturday morning, we sought, by telephone, agreement from our EU partners to a 10 percent devaluation of our punt. By lunchtime they had agreed to 8 percent, but our acceptance of this was delayed for some hours because in those pre-mobile-phone days the Minister for Finance was uncontactable while attending his 'clinics' in County Meath!

This was a controversial decision. Since the formation of the EMS in 1979, the Irish pound had occasionally been allowed to move down with the franc and the lira during the general realignments, but on other occasions it had stayed in the middle of the band. As a result, our currency had strengthened relative to all the

EMS currencies except the deutschmark and the guilder, and substantially also relative to the franc and the lira. This had stood to us in our domestic financial difficulties, helping to maintain international confidence. To reverse this policy now was, to say the least of it, adventurous.

Nevertheless, I was convinced that, although a once-and –for-all devaluation within the EMS band might have a negative short-term effect on confidence, it would put us in a position where, regardless of any future devaluation of sterling or the dollar, we would for years ahead be able without fear of a significant loss of competitiveness to keep our currency in line with the deutchmark and thus gradually command the long-term confidence of the international financial markets. This move produced no significant upward pressure on consumer prices; indeed prices remained stable for some months thereafter, and rose only 3 percent in the whole of the succeeding twelve months. Nor did it have any impact on pay levels.

For five years thereafter, the Irish pound remained closely linked to the deutschmark. This stability contributed to a major influx of funds, which helped to bring Irish interest rates down and to keep them at a level much nearer to the German than the British level. In the spring of 1991, the three-month Euro-currency interest rate was more than seven percentage points nearer to the German rate than in 1982, and four points below the British rate, whereas in 1982 it had been five points higher than in Britain – a relative improvement of nine percentage points.

We recognised of course that we could not now hope to achieve our planned target for 1987, but the Fine Gael members of the government believed that to preserve confidence, the current deficit and borrowing must be reduced by more than 1 percent of GNP. As mentioned earlier, we had announced this in mid-October after a government decision in which for the first and only time the Labour Party members were placed in a minority.

After endless painful meetings, we succeeded in cutting the departmental spending demands by £350 million, reducing the threatened current deficit from 10 percent to just over 8 percent of GNP. To get below that figure required further cuts, however, mainly in the provisions for Health, which Barry Desmond and his Labour colleagues were not prepared to concede. The Fine Gael ministers for their part were not prepared to achieve our deficit and borrowing targets by increasing the burden of tax above the level at which it had been fixed in the National Plan. By mid-December it was clear that the two parties had reached an impasse, that was unlikely to be resolved, although we would continue to make the attempt.

I think that by this time we all knew that the end had come, but there was no point in giving up at that point and precipitating a break before Christmas. We agreed to review the position in January; but when we did so, the conclusion was evident. We agreed amicably that the parting of the ways would be on 20 January, when Labour would leave the government, explaining that they could not accept the proposed health and social-welfare measures. Fine Gael for its part would stand by its determination to reduce the deficit and borrowing to a level significantly below that to which it had risen in 1986 as a result of the recession in that year. Each of us could thus appeal to our constituency.

Shortly before the day came for Labour to leave the government, my eldest brother, Dem, died of Alzheimer's disease. Pierce, who was two years younger, had died in Rome nine months earlier, after a long visit home at Christmas 1985, half of which he had to spend in hospital. With their deaths, the last close family links with my childhood snapped, almost simultaneously with the end of the active phase of my political career.

When the day came for Labour to leave the government, it was a sad moment. We had soldiered together in this government for over four years, restoring confidence in the political independence of the Gardaí and in the integrity of public life, and introducing many social and tax reforms, despite the financial pressures under which we had operated. We had initiated the New Ireland Forum and had negotiated the Anglo-Irish Agreement. We had just passed through the Dáil, by the Ceann Comhairle's casting vote, the extradition legislation. And we had together come very close indeed to the point of halving the borrowing/GNP ratio that Fianna Fáil had left behind in mid-1981. Moreover, although our two parties responded to somewhat different economic constituencies, we shared a deep concern for social justice, liberal values, and integrity in public life.

We knew that in parting thus, it was unlikely that we should find ourselves shoulder to shoulder again in the near future, and I knew that if and when that day came, I would not be leading that government. After Dick had handed me his own and his colleagues' formal resignations, we all shook hands with each other warmly and with considerable emotion; Gemma Hussey was embraced by several of our Labour colleagues. Then, at noon, Dick and his colleagues told the press outside Government Buildings that they had resigned, and they went across to a conference room in the Setanta Building in Kildare Street to explain to the media the reasons for their decision.

After the election, during the interval before the Dáil met to elect a new government, Gemma Hussey suggested that there should be a dinner for 'the real government'. I found that I was entitled to hold such a function, at my own expense, in Barretstown Castle, and there, on 3 March, the coalition ministers of both parties, the attorney general, John Rogers, and the Leader of the House, Seán Barrett, and chief whip, Fergus O'Brien, celebrated until a late hour a government in whose record we all took pride.

As Labour were announcing their departure from the government, I was preparing for our press conference three hours later in Iveagh House. There I presented Fine Gael's uncompromising estimates and budget proposals. They included policy changes involving expenditure cuts of £210 million on top of the pruning of departmental estimates, combined with increases in expenditure taxes and a limit of 3 percent on welfare increases – which were also to take effect from November 1987, much later than usual. The expenditure cuts were set out in the greatest detail: no one could accuse us of fudging any of the issues.

On the basis of the then prevailing forecast of GNP for the year ahead, these measures fulfilled the commitment we had entered into in mid-October with regard to the size of the current deficit and Exchequer borrowing. In the event, as the outturn of the (only marginally different) budget eventually introduced by Fianna Fáil was to demonstrate, the recovery in the economy that occurred during 1987, which the Central Bank had forecast, would have reduced borrowing under our budget to less than half the figure we had faced when we had come to power in June 1981. Thus, contrary to the popular myth – to which even some academic economists have succumbed – well over half the painful financial adjustment effected between mid-1981 and the budget of 1991, with its planned Exchequer borrowing figure of 1.9 percent of GNP, was undertaken by our two governments, operating under very adverse circumstances, especially towards the end of our period in office. (In saying this, I have no desire, however, to minimise the contri-bution made by the subsequent Fianna Fáil administration in its cost-cutting budg-ets of 1988 and 1989.)

In presenting this uncompromising budget to the people, I had two objectives in mind. First of all, I wanted to ensure that in the subsequent election campaign we would be placed firmly on the high ground and in a position to challenge Fianna Fáil day by day to match our approach. My guess, which proved well founded, was that Charles Haughey would be reluctant to face this issue. Accordingly I made pro-vision for an exceptionally long campaign – four weeks instead of three – in order to give plenty of time to hammer home to the electorate the contrast between our approach and his.

My second purpose was to ensure that the budget Fianna Fáil would bring in when they came to power – as I believed they were likely to do – would keep the economy on the right course as the recovery predicted for 1987 was taking place. I felt comfortable fighting an election on a strategy that would in practice determine the shape of Fianna Fáil's first budget but was likely to leave them at a disadvantage during the election campaign, because they would be unwilling to commit them-selves to this strategy before the electorate. Meanwhile, I had allocated to the exist-ing Fine Gael ministers the portfolios relinquished by Labour, appointing Peter Barry as Tánaiste, and had launched the campaign with a helicopter tour of the midlands and the west. John Rogers agreed to remain on as Attorney-General of this interim Fine Gael government.

Particularly for ministers, including former Labour Party ministers, all of them exhausted by the strain of government during such a difficult period, and in particular by the trauma of the last three months, the campaign was a very tiring one, and I think we showed considerable signs of wear and tear. Nevertheless, the tactic of having a long campaign, giving the electorate time to take account of the crucial budgetary issue, proved correct. During the course of the campaign, there was a swing of about 5 percent from Fianna Fáil to Fine Gael.

During the last week of the campaign, I faced the test of a television debate with Charles Haughey. It had been agreed that the discussion on this occasion would follow a certain pattern, opening with 'harmless' questions to be addressed to Haughey and myself by the moderator, Brian Farrell, then moving through various aspects of the economic and financial situation, and finally to the issue of Northern Ireland policy. However, whatever question Brian asked me completely disconcerted me; I lost the thread of the discussion and could not thereafter follow properly the proposed different stages of the debate. All I could do was keep on demanding that the leader of the Opposition explain where he stood on the budgetary issue – which he had avoided throughout the campaign. After what seemed an eternity, the discussion turned to Northern Ireland.

Just before the debate started, I had recalled something Charles Haughey had said on the radio the previous day about renegotiating part of the Anglo-Irish Agreement because of what he saw as its constitutional implications; the words he had used had been hastily scribbled down for me on a piece of paper. Now that we were discussing Northern Ireland, I put it to my opponent that his commitment to renegotiate the agreement would put at risk all that had been achieved. He proceeded to deny that he had ever said anything of the kind, claiming repeatedly that the remarks to which I referred related to emigration – although this made no sense whatever.

I searched for the scrap of paper on which I had written down the words he had actually used. At first I could not find it; but just as Charles Haughey once again repeated his denial, I spotted it on the desk in front of me and, picking it up, proceeded to read it out, unaware of the fact that a camera over my shoulder had focused on it so that the viewers could see the words themselves: 'We would strive by diplomatic and political action to see if we can change these constitutional implications to which we take exception.'

It was now his turn to be disconcerted: the viewers could see that his attempt to suggest that the quotation related to emigration had been utter nonsense. The negative impact of this on his credibility was reinforced visually by the manner in which the camera had focused on the note of his words that I had read out.

Thus when I emerged from the studio, I found to my astonishment that I was widely seen as having been victorious in this debate. Even my panic-driven reiteration over and over again of the demand that my opponent clarify his position on the budget had come across to the viewers as a masterly tactic to put him on the spot, and the collapse of his credibility over his Northern Ireland statement appeared as a climax to what was seen as my successful handling of the debate!

It seems likely that this debate helped to boost fine Gael's fortunes and to damage Fianna Fáil in the closing stages of the campaign, for the vote actually recorded in the election gave us several percentage points more, and Fianna Fáil several points less, than any poll up to that point.

However, there was one further development in the campaign that I think had a significant impact on the result. Two days before election day, my team told me there had been contacts with Des O'Malley's new party, the Progressive Democrats, and that they were willing to engage in a reciprocal exchange of transfers between our two parties. If effective, this could have a significant impact on the eventual result, the Irish electorate being traditionally open to persuasion by their parties about their later-preference votes.

I was willing to accede to this preference-exchange proposal, confidently expecting that in accordance with what had been agreed between our two election teams, an offer of such an arrangement by me would be reciprocated. It wasn't. A number of the former Fianna Fáil members of the PDs immediately phoned in to its head office a demand that my offer be rejected – and rejected it was, to the fury of those in our election headquarters who had negotiated the arrangement. Nevertheless, PD transfers, of which there were a large number (for many of their candidates were eliminated), came to us rather than to Fianna Fáil, in a ratio of three to one, and this disproportion in the transfers gave us four, perhaps even five, additional seats.

I listened to the election results coming in at our headquarters. The figures were better than the polls had led us to expect, and it soon became clear that, as I had hoped, Fianna Fáil was not going to secure the overall majority of which, given the events of the months immediately preceding the election, it had been confident. It was highly unlikely, however, that anyone else but Charles Haughey could form a government. With the outcome still uncertain that evening, I could have taken the line that in its minority position, Fianna Fáil might not be capable of forming a government, but this would have seemed like whistling in the dark, and would have deprived me of the opportunity of ensuring that Fine Gael rather than other parties would control the performance of Fianna Fáil in the next Dáil.

Accordingly, on the television results programme that night, I conceded the election, and announced that we would support Fianna Fáil if they pursued similar fiscal policies to ours, and if they accepted and 'worked' the Anglo-Irish Agreement. By this tactic I hoped to ensure that, even though in order to secure a majority Fianna Fáil would have to get the support of some independent deputies, Charles

Haughey would know that in the government he need not depend on these independents for electoral support or be influenced by mavericks into pursuing the kind
of irresponsible policies he had adopted in 1982, when his minority government
had been at the mercy of the Workers Party. Perhaps on this, his third occasion as
Taoiseach, he would in any event have adopted the strategy I was seeking to impose
on him, but in view of past experience there was no harm in making sure that he
did so, especially as not alone the responsible handling of the economy but the survival of the Anglo-Irish Agreement depended on this.

When the Dáil came to meet on 10 March, the issue of the election of a
Taoiseach was still in doubt. It was clear that my nomination as Taoiseach would be
defeated, but it was not clear that Charles Haughey's nomination would be
endorsed. The possibility of a deadlock existed. Indeed, given the stance adopted by
the socialist independent Tony Gregory, such a result might have been deemed
probable. For that deputy informed four of our backbenchers that he would be voting against Charles Haughey's nomination – which would have led to his defeat. I
judged, however, that the fact that he had taken the trouble to communicate this,
not just by chance to one of our backbenchers but deliberately to four of them,
meant that he was seeking to put tactical pressure on Fine Gael to break the deadlock by abstaining as a party on Charles Haughey's nomination; that was something
I had no intention of doing. I believed that when it came to the point, Tony
Gregory would not vote against my opponent as he saw our party going into the
lobbies against his nomination.

Nevertheless, I could not be certain that this would happen, and I had to consider what steps I would take if a deadlock did in fact emerge. I decided to discuss
the matter with President Hillery, who would have a crucial role to play in resolving
such a deadlock. He suggested to me a course of action that would put maximum
pressure on the Dáil to elect a Taoiseach, if not on this occasion then shortly afterwards. I was to prepare two alternative speeches to be made after the vote on
Charles Haughey's nomination: one to be used in the event of his election to office,
announcing that I was going to Áras an Uachtaráin to present my resignation to the
president, and the other to be used if Charles Haughey were also to be rejected by
the Dáil, saying that I would discuss with the president the situation that had
emerged. Under no circumstances, the president advised, should I suggest that in
the event of a deadlock I would seek a dissolution – although I would of course have
to resign following the defeat of my nomination as Taoiseach.

Then, after visiting him, I was to go back to the Dáil and attempt, by knocking
heads together, to get a resolution of the deadlock. If I failed in this attempt, I was
to return to the president once again – at which point he would publicly instruct
me to make a further effort, acting on his authority. We both hoped that the
mounting pressure thus created would resolve the problem, should it arise.

I was very appreciative of the manner in which President Hillery approached the problem, and I was entertained also by the irony of the situation in which I might find myself: in order to prevent the country becoming leaderless, seeking to cajole the Dáil into electing Charles Haughey as Taoiseach! There was, of course, the possibility that, arising from a deadlock, Charles Haughey might come under pressure to stand down, with a view to another Fianna Fáil nominee being put forward, but this seemed to me extremely unlikely in view of the failure of all earlier attempts to shift him.

In the event, it all worked our as I had expected. Faced with the responsibility for deciding the issue one way or the other, Tony Gregory abstained on the vote, and Charles Haughey thus became Taoiseach for the third time, in a government that depended thereafter for its survival on the support of Fine Gael. This support was subsequently accorded to it on an appropriate conditional basis by my successor, Alan Dukes, implementing my commitment on the night of the election count.

Meanwhile, during the interval between the election and the assembly of the Dáil I had several meetings with Charles Haughey to prepare for the almost certain transfer of power. As had always been the case in relation to our private contacts, these were amicable encounters. During these meetings, we discussed practical matters, and at the end of the first I asked him to let me know if he would wish to have my views on key diplomatic postings related to the Anglo-Irish Agreement. At the second meeting he said he would glad to hear my views on this, and I suggested names to him for three of these posts – two of which featured in the decisions he later made on this matter, although in a slightly different form than I had suggested.

When he had been elected Taoiseach, we had a third brief discussion, during which I explained to him the layout of the Taoiseach's office, which had replaced in 1983 the original office in another part of the building. He remarked on this occasion that any government would have been unlucky to have had to face even one of the commercial crises that had arisen during our term of office (there had been crises in relation to the Dublin Gas Company, the PMPA, Irish Shipping, and the ICI), but that we had had extremely bad luck in having to face all of these in turn.

Meanwhile I had been reflecting on my own personal position. When I had taken on the leadership of Fine Gael in July 1977, I had said then that I would undertake this task for a period of ten years, of which nine and three-quarter years had now elapsed. If, as seemed likely, Charles Haughey were elected Taoiseach, there was a fair chance that his government would run for at least four years; if I sought to remain leader of the party during that period, with a view to the possibility of returning to office at the end of the next Dáil, I would by then have been leader of the party for fourteen years and would be sixty-five years of age. This seemed to me to make no sense, either for me or for the party. I could, of course, remain on for some time after the new government was formed, choosing a moment later in the life of the Dáil to retire from the leadership, but the only result of this would be to shorten my successor's period of preparation for the task of taking on Fianna Fáil at the next election – which in view of the close result might be much less than four years away. Moreover, given the fact that I had found the wear and tear of office fairly gruelling, especially in recent months, I did not think that I had the physical or moral stamina to provide the kind of dynamic leadership the party would need in order to recover from the defeat that it had just suffered.

Finally there was Joan to consider. She had never been enthusiastic about my political career but had supported me loyally throughout, despite the fact that during the whole of the period of my leadership she had been disabled, increasingly so as time went on, by arthritis. It would not, I felt, be fair to impose a further strain on her; at this stage she deserved more of my time and attention, as did my grandchildren.

She raised the question with me shortly after the election, and I asked her to let me reflect on it for a period so that I could satisfy myself that if I retired at this stage it would be the best thing not merely for the two of us but also for the party and the country. I discussed the matter with none of my parliamentary colleagues, although I did speak to one or two other people who were closely involved with me in the political arena. Ten days later I made up my mind. Everything pointed to an immediate resignation once a new government had been formed.

Accordingly, immediately after the election of Charles Haughey I called meetings of the front bench and the parliamentary party for the following morning. Although in the previous couple of weeks there had inevitably been some speculation that I might resign after the election of the new Taoiseach, there had not been time overnight for members of the party to address this issue, and I think almost everyone was taken by surprise when I told first the front bench and then the parliamentary party of my intention to resign, and proposed that the election of my successor take place in eleven days' time.

That afternoon I held a press conference, and was highly entertained to receive from the political correspondents a cartoon from the Richmal Crompton 'Just William' books. It showed a disgruntled William telling his friends: 'I don't want to be Prime Minister. You can keep your old Prime Ministership.'

Some time previously, I had received an invitation to lecture in Tulane University in New Orleans, and I had allowed my acceptance of this engagement to stand, despite the election, feeling that I might want to take it up whether or not I was Taoiseach. I had in fact arranged that Joan and I would leave for the United States on the morning after my resignation, to return on the morning of 22 March, when the election of my successor as leader was to take place. This had the great advantage that I would be absent throughout whatever campaign for the leadership might take place. I had always thought it of crucial importance that I should not attempt to influence the outcome of such an election in any way; indeed, it was in part this concern that had led me to attempt the abortive reshuffle of my government a year earlier. (I had arranged that Joan and I would have dinner with Henry and Nancy Kissinger on the night of our arrival in New York. During the meal we discovered that Henry and I had just been reading the same book on quantum physics on our recent respective journeys across the Pacific and the Atlantic!)

Three candidates had entered the ring: Peter Barry, John Bruton and Alan Dukes. Returning on the morning of Saturday 22 March, I went to the party meeting, curious to see what the outcome of the election would be. I found that the three candidates had agreed that the tellers for the election should be the chairman of the party, Kieran Crotty, and myself, and they proposed that when we announced the winner, we should give no details of the votes cast, lest a narrow majority for whomever was elected might weaken his authority, or a poor vote for one or other candidate might adversely affect his subsequent standing in the party. I agreed to this, and, having counted the votes, simply announced that Alan Dukes had been elected.

Ironically, despite my determined neutrality, reinforced by my absence during the entire campaign, a belief subsequently developed that I had been actively promoting the candidature of Alan Dukes. I never succeeded in dispelling this particular rumour (which soon hardened into an accepted myth), partly because to have attempted to do so with the vigour necessary to carry conviction could have misled people into thinking that I was unhappy with the new leader.

20

∾: Retirement :∾

With the leadership and succession thus sorted out, I found myself for the first time a 'backbencher'. (In fact, I found a seat for myself at the end of the second row, where James Dillon had sat after he had retired from the leadership of the party in 1969.) I attended regularly, except when I was absent from Dublin, and I cleared these absences with the whips to ensure that a pair was provided for me on those occasions. (Some subsequent ex-Taoisigh seem to have become less careful about this.)

It had been my intention to leave politics in 1989, after twenty-four years either on the front bench with Fine Gael or in government. However, when Charles Haughey called that year's election – foolishly, as it seemed to me and to many others – I was faced with the fact that if I could persuade enough people not to vote for me but instead to vote for my colleague, the late Joe Doyle, Fine Gael might actually win a second seat. This appealed particularly to my sense of humour. I hugely enjoyed that campaign and managed to persuade almost half of my voters to switch to Joe Doyle – as a result of which he gained 50 percent more first-preferences than I did. Happily, with the elimination of PD Michael McDowell in that election, most of his votes came to me, which meant that Joe's vote and my own ended up roughly equal – ahead of those of the second and third Fianna Fáil candidates. As a result, we won the seat. However, the fact that I secured so few votes greatly disturbed many of my supporters; it was perfectly clear that if I stood again at the next election, votes would swing back to me and we would lose our second seat. So I decided that I would not stand for re-election in 1992.

Somehow, I became entangled in the presidential election of 1990. I participated in a *Questions and Answers* TV programme at which a student, whom as far as I could recall I had never met, challenged Brian Lenihan about his approach to the president after my January 1982 budget deficit with a view to persuading him to refuse me a dissolution of the Dáil. Brian Lenihan's confused recollection of those events, which I had to challenge on air, led to him losing the election to Mary Robinson. I was wrongly accused of having conspired with the student towards this end, and found it difficult to persuade people that I had not.

I was now able, of course, to give more time now to Joan and the family than had been possible during the fourteen years when I had been foreign minister, leader of the Opposition or Taoiseach. Compared to very many other TDs, I had in fact been lucky during those years, because my constituency, Dublin South East, included within its boundaries my home, the university where I lectured, the Dáil, the Department of Foreign Affairs, and Government Buildings, where the Taoiseach's Office is. So unless there was some luncheon engagement, I had been able to go home to have lunch with Joan daily and to see my children regularly – although of course my daughter Mary was abroad from 1981 to 1989.

I had never become so immersed in politics as to lose contact with the friends I had made outside politics. From 1973 onwards, we had holidayed each year in the south of France or in west Cork, with some of the children and with many friends. Even as Taoiseach, I had insisted on taking an adequate summer holiday of three or four weeks, plus breaks at Christmas and Easter. We had always had our friends to dinner whenever we could arrange that, and since the 1960s had picnicked in the summer with family and friends, normally near the Powerscourt Waterfall. We also had a New Year's Eve party for our friends every year. When we had held the first of these in 1968, we were in a very small flat, with only about eight chairs for people to sit on. To solve the seating problem, we organised competitions for our friends to engage in, posted up on the walls around the living room and hall, so that they wouldn't notice the fact that for most of them, there was nowhere to sit!

By the 1980s, the numbers for these parties had grown to the point where we had to find some way of reducing their size. Joan and I eventually changed them into parties to be attended only by friends who were also grandparents, bringing their grandchildren with them. Now, after 1987, there were fewer constraints on our social life, and we were able to see more of our friends than had been possible while I was in office.

Whether as foreign minister, leader of the Opposition, or during my period as Taoiseach, I never had time to attend to my own financial affairs. Indeed, whilst I had been Taoiseach for the second time, I had not opened a bank statement; when I was defeated in 1987, I did so with some trepidation. I was right to be worried. Because of the fact that I had had no time to look after my finances, I found that we had accumulated an overdraft of horrifying dimensions: £80,000! I had no idea how I was going to be able to pay this off without a complete disruption of our reasonably comfortable way of life. Within some weeks of my liberation from office, however, I was approached on behalf of Guinness Peat Aviation to ask if I would join their board. I was delighted to do so; to get back into the world of air transport, which I had left almost thirty years earlier, at that stage was a very attractive prospect. Moreover, the financial arrangements in connection with the post seemed to offer an eventual way out of the disturbing financial situation in which I now found myself. In taking up membership of the GPA board, I had an opportunity to purchase some shares with a bank loan – shares the dividends from which would supplement my income significantly in the years immediately ahead. As a result, I was able, over a period of a few years, to repay the overdraft and start repaying the bank loan.

I then took out a second loan in order to buy some further shares for the benefit, eventually, of my grandchildren. At that point, the shares were at a very high price indeed. Then, through GPA's efforts to raise $1 billion to expand its aircraft-leasing business, the company collapsed, and effectively had to be wound up. The remains of the first loan, plus the additional one that I had recently taken on, were very substantial. After their marriage in 1983, Mark and Derval had lived at first in a flat upstairs in our Palmerston Road house but had subsequently purchased a house of their own not far away. Now, so as to allow for Joan and myself to remain living in the first floor of the Palmerston Road house, they bought it from me and moved into the lower floors. With us occupying all the bedrooms on the top floor, this was not really suitable accommodation for a family with three children – which in the years immediately following grew further as two more children were born to them. That transaction completed, and my mortgage paid off, what was left went to the bank, who agreed a settlement.

Mark and Derval's extraordinarily generous gesture in abandoning their own house to squat in two floors of ours, without adequate bedroom accommodation, solved the accommodation problem for Joan and myself. Because of her disability, when I left office in 1987 and simultaneously resigned from my post in UCD – from which I had enjoyed leave of absence since March 1973 – I had used my UCD gratuity to install a lift at the side of the house. This made it possible for Joan to live upstairs in the house thereafter. However, by 1995 she was confined to bed, and we used the largest of the upstairs bedrooms as a combined bedroom, living room, dining room, and office for me. Medical equipment – including a drip – was installed in the en suite bathroom. By placing tables right around Joan's bed, we were able to continue to have family and friends to dinner in that room until near the end of her life.

I was most reluctant to move Joan elsewhere, as she hugely enjoyed the company of what eventually became five grandchildren in the house. However, I recognised that it would be unfair for me to continue to occupy this space when I became a widower. Accordingly, when, one day in 1996, we learned that the people who lived in the house beside my daughter Mary in Annavilla, Ranelagh, had bought another house, I went down with Mark the next morning to discuss with them the possibility of our buying the house that they were about to leave.

This was agreed at once. For several years I installed tenants in the property, and eventually moved there in December 1999, six months after Joan's death – thus liberating the bedroom floor in Palmerston Road for Mark, Derval and their family.

The purchase of this Annavilla house was a hugely worthwhile move. It soon became a joint house with interconnecting doors on both floors, and the removal of the fence between the two gardens created a more welcoming space. In my house, I retain a living room, an office, and a bedroom; Mary's two daughters live in my part of the joint dwelling, and I have been able to extend the dining room to accommodate an enlarging family.

Living with my daughter, and close to my two sons, made it easier for me to cope with the loss of Joan eleven years ago. The fact that it had been possible for Joan to remain at home in Palmerston Road throughout the four years of her final illness reflected the fact that during the years after I ceased to be Taoiseach I had developed sufficient earning power, in supplementation of my pensions, to be able to finance what in effect was a one-bed hospital at home. In some of those later years, we employed as many as eighty different nurses or nursing aides to care for her. For in those later years, Joan needed a lot of care: most of the time there were two nurses – or nursing aides – by day, and one at night.

The additional income came partly from a number of boards of which at different times I was a member, partly from lecturing and consultancy work overseas, and from my writings. I've already mentioned my appointment to the GPA board in 1987; for almost twenty years I was also a member of the board of the Trade Development Institute – an Irish export consultancy firm. At the end of the 1990s I was also director of a software company called Point, whilst between 2003 and 2009 I was a director of a Russian investment fund.

Many years later, the Moriarty Tribunal asked if I would allow them to examine my relationship with the AIB so that they could compare it with the relationship that Charles Haughey had had with that bank years earlier; I agreed immediately. Several months later, the tribunal contacted me to tell me that they had discovered that the first of my two loans had been 'non-recourse', which meant that I had had no obligation to repay it when GPA collapsed. But years before, I had told the bank that it would simplify matters if I made a single payment on the two loans; unknown to me, in the process of making this arrangement, they had converted my first loan into one on a recourse basis, thus improperly making it repayable to them. In other words, I had not owed the bank as much as I thought; when account was taken of this non-recourse factor, the amount that I had paid them after the sale of the house had in fact been virtually all I had been due to pay. The write-off of my debt by the bank had in fact been quite insignificant. I gave evidence to the Moriarty Tribunal on all this subsequently, but the fact that I had paid virtually all of the amount I had been due to pay to the bank never got through to the general public.

Throughout much of the two decades following my departure from office, I was asked to undertake lecturing or consultancy in various parts of the world, mainly eastern Europe and Africa but also in Asia. The European Community Organisation known as TACIS provided consultancy services in the former Soviet Union. Whilst in Russia, I worked with a unit of the finance ministry which was run by a young German economist called Jochen Wermuth (who later formed the investment fund of which I became a director). But it was difficult to have much impact in such a large country, so in 1993–95 I took on various assignments for the EU in Kazakhstan.

The capital of that state, Almaty, is on the lower slopes of the Tian Shan Mountains – an extensions of the Himalayas – and in spring of each year, when the snows melt, a hugh volume of water rushes through the city. To avoid flooding, this water is channelled through drains on the side of every street. Some of these drains are quite narrow and easy to jump over; some are wider. In an attempt in 1990 to jump one of the larger ones, I fell, ripping my trousers, losing my glasses, cutting my knee and spraining my ankle. I realised as I took off that perhaps it had been a mistake not to simply walk around the drain! I was well looked after by two German colleagues, who brought me to a nearby bureau de change. They rang for an ambulance, which brought me to a hospital and X-rayed me. I managed to get a new pair of glasses made. These cost $1 for the prescription – showing how low incomes were in Kazakhstan at that time – but more than $50 for the (imported) glasses themselves!

Early on in my post-Taoiseach period, I had visited the Far East for several weeks to generate interest there in investment in Ireland. Although Joan needed a wheelchair for this journey, she was able to travel without too much difficulty, so that it was possible for her to accompany me. A cousin of hers, to whom she had been close all her life, came too, and helped look after her throughout the journey.

We visited Japan, Korea, Taiwan and Hong Kong before going to China, where the government had invited me to spend ten days. When we flew from Hong Kong to Guang Zhou, I was asked on arrival at the airport whether I had any apples: a curious question for Customs to ask. This posed a problem for me, as I cannot cope with Asian cuisine, and was going to be dependent on nine large Japanese apples for sustenance during our visit. I am afraid that, for the only time in my life, I lied to the Customs official and denied the possession of any apples, hoping that, if I was detected, the fact that the Chinese government had invited me would help me avoid going to jail!

The roof of the hotel in Guang Zhou contained a garden with a lake. Trees grew on either side of it, and on an island on the lake. It was a stormy night and, when we woke up in the morning, the wind had blown open the double doors at the entrance to our penthouse, and the floor of the hall was completely covered in leaves, blown from the trees on the island in the lake!

Next day, we were driven to a farm about thirty miles away. On our arrival, we were brought into a five-storey building with balconies all around it. On each floor there was a large living room with a television set, and on all the balconies there were flowers growing. We waited to be brought to the farm, only to discover that this *was* the farm. The flowers grown on the balconies were sold to Hong Kong at prices that enabled the farmer to earn £30,000 a year – just using the balconies of his house! The Beijing representative with us was as astonished as we were at this, and said he looked forward to going back to Beijing to tell them what farms were like in south China!

We had asked to go to Xian to see the Warriors, some of whom had been brought to Ireland when I was in office, and of course we also ended up in Beijing. There we were brought to see the Great Wall of China and the Ming tombs. The weather had been cold; there had been snow and ice not long before we were there. I managed to place my foot on the only patch of ice still left at the Ming tombs: I fell and broke my arm. A doctor attached to the Australian embassy came around to our embassy to put my arm in plaster.

When it came to going home – which in those days you had to do through Tokyo, there being then no direct flights between Europe and Beijing – I began to worry about the problem of excess baggage. Joan's fabric purchases in the course of this long journey had been quite extensive – so much so that we had to buy an extra bag to bring them home. On the basis of the excess-baggage charges we had paid in Hong Kong on the way to Guang Zhou, it seemed that we could end up paying some thousands of pounds in charges for the journey home. However, a combination of an efficient Irish embassy first secretary and a GPA representative in Beijing brought our baggage to the airport and managed to get it dispatched home without excess-baggage charges being levied. I was extremely grateful.

Immediately after leaving office in 1987, I had the good fortune to be offered honorary membership of the Reform Club in London, at a time when I was in fact looking for somewhere that I could stay in that city when I had occasion to visit it. I had been told that there would be a little informal dinner to welcome me to the club. Despite my long experience of British understatement, I took this at face value. But when, on 'Black Monday' 1987, I arrived in London and went to leave my bag in the club, a friend travelling with me went into the club to have a look at it. (The atrium in the centre of the club had been used in the opening scene of the film *Around the World in 80 Days* some decades earlier.) When I came downstairs after leaving my bag in my room, my friend pointed out that a notice in the hall explained that the entire dining room had been booked for my dinner that night.

The dinner was obviously on a much larger scale then I had understood to be the case! Apparently I would have to speak at this dinner. So when we returned to the club at six o'clock, after a busy day in the City, I got down to preparing a suitable speech dealing with Anglo-Irish relations. I was pleased to have been able to put one together in which I managed – for once – to avoid any reference to Northern Ireland; I dealt only with bilateral Anglo-Irish relations.

As honorary membership of the club was soon afterwards offered to the Duke of Gloucester, a cousin of the Queen, I felt that it was right for me, as the immediately preceding honorary member, to attend the dinner for his membership and welcome the Duke to what was now my club, as it were. I had already met the Duke some years earlier, when I had been invited to a dinner in the Middle Temple on the evening of the Fontainebleau European Council of June 1984. The council had overrun its allotted time and did not finish till six o'clock. It took an hour to be driven to the airport in Paris, another hour to get to London, the best part of an hour to get to the embassy – and the best part of another hour to dress in white tie and tails. (Apart from Pope Paul VI's funeral, this was the only white-tie occasion I had encountered since I had attended dinner dances in the Gresham Hotel as a student.) So when I arrived at the Middle Temple – bringing greetings from British foreign secretary Geoffrey Howe to his wife Elspeth, who was among the guests – the dinner was over, and all they had been able to keep for me was five strawberries! But the Duke and Duchess of Gloucester had kindly stayed on to greet me.

A year or two later, I brought Joan to a Chagall exhibition in the Royal Academy in London. Having pushed her in her wheelchair into the building, we were greeted by the Academy officials. Just as they were asking me if I wished to accompany my wife in a lift upstairs, a voice behind me said: 'How are you, Dr FitzGerald? I don't think you will remember me, but I am the Duke of Gloucester. I had difficulty getting in because of the security surrounding your presence here!'

Also in 1987, Roy Jenkins became chancellor of Oxford University and offered me an honorary degree on the occasion of his election as chancellor. When I checked the records, I found that in 1904 there had been thirty-four honorary degrees conferred, on the occasion of a chancellor's inauguration; on the next such occasion, there had been as many as twenty-five. Roy Jenkins managed to get the number down to twelve, four of whom were to be political figures. He had a problem, however: Margaret Thatcher's name had already gone forward for an honorary degree in Oxford, and she had been turned down by the university. So he couldn't ask her again – and nor, in consequence, could he follow the long-established tradition of asking other British politicians. Looking elsewhere for political figures, he chose, amongst others, myself, King Baudouin of Belgium and President Cossiga of Italy.

After the conferring ceremony – carried on exclusively in Latin – there was a dinner in All Souls, at a very long table which accommodated 130 people. As I was near the centre of the table, at the end of the dinner I had to walk the length of it in order to reach the exit. En route, I was approached by somebody whom I took to be the Butler at the college (although I am not sure that this was his exact title). In a very marked Dublin accent, he said to me: 'Come up here to the centre till I show you something.' I followed him. 'There it is,' he said, proudly pointing to a silver centrepiece. 'That piece of silver is the only thing that Cromwell didn't destroy when he came to this college.' After forty years in the college, he had lost neither his Dublin accent nor his Irish aversion to Cromwell!

Incidentally, I had had some difficulty in getting into the conferring ceremony. Joan was with me and, very kindly, Tony Kenny of Balliol had arranged for a car to bring us the few hundred yards from his college, where we had been staying, to the entrance to All Souls, as security was very tight. Indeed, security was so tight that I wasn't able to enter All Souls, despite the fact that I was resplendent in my red doctoral robes. We had to drive right round the city to another entrance; this was inaccessible to Joan's wheelchair, so we returned to the first entrance – where we were finally admitted!

As a non-practising barrister since 1947, it had always been my practice to dine in the Kings Inns several times each year. When I became Taoiseach, however, I felt that it would be awkward to turn up there at a barristers' table, as the Benchers might feel obliged to ask me to join them at their top table. Wishing to avoid this possible embarrassment, I stopped going to dinner at the Inns, feeling that some day perhaps I might be made an Honorary Bencher – as, I believed, had happened with other former Taoisigh before me. However, it was Charles Haughey, having been Taoiseach before me, who had to be accommodated in this respect first, and that took quite a long time to come about. So for something like a decade, I found myself unable to continue my practice of dining at the Inns. Since then, as an Honorary Bencher, I try to attend once a term. The food and wine at the Benchers' table is certainly better than that which I had enjoyed during the war as a student. At that time, we were told that the Inns had had to sell their wine cellar. We got very strange wine indeed; a friend of mine alleged, humorously, that it had been brought in powdered form from Portugal!

In the late 1980s and early 1990s, I was chosen to be deputy European chairman of the Trilateral Commission – a body about which an extraordinary amount of nonsense has been written. The commission was founded by David Rockefeller in 1973 to encourage contact between people in the US and Europe on the one hand, and people in Japan on the other. It meets once a year in plenary session but also has an annual European meeting, at which papers are presented, discussed and published. These papers are normally written by three authors, one from each of these three areas. In 1980, I was asked to become one of a group writing about the

Palestinian problem – as a result of which I travelled to Israel, Jordan, Egypt and Saudi Arabia. Later, in 1990, I was asked on my own account to update our report. I included in it a reference to Israel's nuclear weapons – a subject about which an extraordinary silence has prevailed since the 1960s, when the French, under de Gaulle, assisted Israel to develop a nuclear capacity.

I went to Zimbabwe in 1989 as a consultant. I was very unimpressed by the quality of the Europeans I met there, but impressed by the quality of the Africans I encountered, including in particular the civil servants. Meeting with the Institute of Directors in both Harare and Bulawayo, I noted that no Africans were present.

President Mugabe had been an official guest of our state in the mid-1980s, with his first wife – who was an able woman and, I thought, a good influence on him. She was ill during her visit here, and Joan looked after her. However, she had died a couple of years later. Soon after that, while I was having lunch with two Zimbabweans at a Ballsbridge hotel, the two of them suddenly jumped up and dashed out to the hall in a way that, I have to say, surprised me. It transpired that they had seen Mugabe's secretary in the hall and had gone to ask him if the president was in the hotel. He was in fact resting there incognito to recover from his wife's death. I invited him to dine informally at home with some friends of mine who had connections with Zimbabwe, and we had a very amicable evening. Some of the terrible problems that have arisen in Zimbabwe during the later years of his presidency have been attributed to his second wife.

I also continued my involvement with international affairs through participation in the Institute of International and European Affairs and as a member of the international-affairs committee of the Royal Irish Academy. In addition, throughout the 1990s and during the past decade, I have undertaken a number of lecture tours in the United States, addressing audiences in many American universities.

In September 1991, having completed an earlier version of my autobiography, I moved to resume my weekly column in the *Irish Times*, which I had had to abandon in 1973 when I became foreign minister. In the ten years between 1987 and 1997, I wrote this column every single week. I then discovered that I was entitled to six weeks' holiday every year – which I have taken advantage of since then. Writing a weekly column is certainly a challenge, but one which I hugely enjoy. It gives me an opportunity not merely to comment on many aspects of Irish life, and sometimes on foreign affairs, but also to present much data on the Irish economy and Irish society derived from the study of official statistical material which is otherwise extremely underutilised. Over the last two decades, I have continued to write many papers and chapters of books, as well as several books of essays on Ireland and the world outside.

I mentioned earlier that when I became leader of the Fine Gael Party, I had sought some distraction by analysing nineteenth-century census data on

Irish-speaking. From this data, I was able to construct a picture of the decline in the speaking of Irish from 1770 to 1870 in 320 different parts of the country. I published this when I was Taoiseach and it became, I think, the standard work on this subject. Now, in retirement, I decided to use material from the 1911 census in respect of four thousand different parts of the country, to establish the scale of Irish-speaking in the 60 percent of these areas where the language still survived at the time of the Famine. More recently, I have completed a study of Irish education in 1824, before the introduction of national schools, drawing for this study upon British parliamentary papers. I have been able to identify the relative proportions of boys and girls, and Protestant and Catholics, at school in 320 parts of the country, together with the amounts being paid by parents for their children's education at that time: between six and seven shillings a year, out of an income per head of around £10 per year.

The truth is that I am happiest when undertaking research or writing, and would be very uncomfortable indeed if I did not have some project of this kind to occupy my spare moments. Having spent twenty-seven years in active politics, including fourteen years as a full-time politician either in government or as leader of the Opposition, I have greatly enjoyed being able to return in 'retirement' to the kind of career in which I had been engaged before entering politics in 1965 – viz. lecturing, consultancy work, and writing books and papers.

Once I left the Dáil in 1992, I sought to re-establish my independence of political involvement. This proved to be quite difficult, as people have a tendency to continue to identify me with the political party I once led. I find this somewhat problematic, because my capacity to contribute constructively to public affairs in my post-political period depends upon my being able to establish and maintain an independent position. I cannot write credibly about political economy – to use an old-fashioned phrase – without adverting to the position taken up from time to time by different political parties on economic issues. It would be non-credible, for example, to criticise policies adopted by Fianna Fáil in government in the first decade of this century whilst suppressing the fact that the Opposition parties went along with these policies in the elections of 2002 and 2007. Yet reference to this is not always welcomed by Fine Gael. The truth is that to be an ex-politician is to walk a constant tightrope when dealing with public issues.

Since the early 1990s, I have had some health issues: the onset of a heart problem, Type 2 diabetes, and since 2008 a problem with a greatly reduced lung function, which makes walking any distance or climbing stairs difficult. However, none of these have posed a problem when it comes to intellectual activities. Reduced physical capacity does not bother me very much, because I was never inclined to take much exercise. I recall at the age of ten abandoning the rugby-football field when I discovered that I was meant to run after balls and not just to kick them if they came near me! At the advanced age of ten, running after balls seemed to me a rather childish activity – a view which, however, was regarded as eccentric by many of my associates of that period and since!

Where I have been blessed has been in the quality of my family life. Joan was a wonderful partner to have, and we had just over fifty years together. It was only after 1977 that her health began to deteriorate, and for eighteen of the following twenty-two years we spent most of the time living a normal life. The impact of Joan's death, after four years ill in bed, was softened by the support of my children and grandchildren. We were always a family-oriented pair – even though I was often distracted by other activities.

The fact that since her death I have been able to live with my daughter and spend much time with my two sons has made a huge difference to me. From the time I reached the age of eighty in 2006, members of my family have insisted on accompanying me on my extensive travels as a consultant and lecturer. In my first two years as an octogenarian, this involved 140,000 miles of travel to twenty-seven countries.

In the last couple of years I have travelled much less – but in October 2010 I went on a lecture tour to four US universities, whilst also finishing this book as well as another on Irish education in 1824 (just before the launch of our national school system), when there were almost twelve thousand primary schools in Ireland.

And I've never lost my interest in Irish society, the Irish economy, or Irish politics!

Appendix

Career Map

CAREER MAP

	MAIN CAREER	JOURNALISM	CONSULTANCY & PUBLIC SERVICE
1947–54	Aer Lingus	Fourteen papers abroad *Irish Independent* column on Foreign Affairs	Secretary, Irish Medical Association Committee
1955–58	Aer Lingus	Fourteen papers abroad Aviation journals *Irish Times* – 'Analyst'	Senate Reform Commission
1958–59		*Irish Times* weekly column Correspondent for the *Financial Times*	Workmen's Compensation Commission General Consultancy
1959–61	UCD Lecturer – Political Economy Dept.	*Irish Times* weekly column Correspondent for the *Financial Times*	Chairman – European Movement Study of Woollen & Worsted Industry (co-author)
1961–69	UCD Lecturer – Political Economy Dept.	*Irish Times* weekly column Correspondent for: the *Financial Times*, the BBC and the *Economist*	Economic Advisor to: the Federation of Irish Industries, Construction Industry Federation, Bord Fáilte, Lever Bros, Esso Petroleum, Representative Body for Guards Member of Committee on Industrial Organisation National Industrial Economic Council Transport Advisory Committee Chairman of ESB Arbitration Tribunal
1969–73	UCD Lecturer – Political Economy Dept.	*Irish Times* weekly column	

1947–2010

BUSINESS	ACADEMIC	BOOKS	POLITICS	RESEARCH
	Transport Economics – Rathmines College			
				TCD – Inputs into Industry 1953–56
	UCD Lecturer – Political Economy Dept.	*State Enterprises, 1961*		
Managing Director of *Economist* Intelligence Unit of Ireland	UCD Lecturer – Political Economy Dept. Member of UCD Governing Body	*Planning in Ireland*	Senate: Fine Gael Front Bench from 1965	Input Output Study of Irish Tourism
Board of Industrial & Trade Fairs	UCD Lecturer – Political Economy Dept.	*Towards A New Ireland*	Dáil – Fine Gael Spokesman on Education 1969––71 and Finance 1971–73	

MAIN CAREER	JOURNALISM	CONSULTANCY & PUBLIC SERVICE	
1973–77	Minister for Foreign Affairs		
1977–81	Leader of Fine Gael & of Dáil Opposition		
JUN. 1981 – MAR. 1982	Taoiseach		
MAR. – DEC. 1982	Leader of Opposition		
DEC. 1982 – MAR. 1987	Taoiseach		
MARCH 1987 – 1991	Member of Dáil		Institute of European Affairs
1991– 2010	Retirement	*Irish Times* weekly column	Royal Irish Academy – International Affairs Committee
			Consultancy & Lectures in twenty–one Eastern European, African and Asian countries (some for the World Bank)
			President – Institute of International & European Affairs

BUSINESS	ACADEMIC	BOOKS	POLITICS	RESEARCH
	Member of NUI Senate		Minister for Foreign Affairs	
			President of General Council of Ministers	
			President of Council of Europe	
			Committee of Ministers	
	Member of NUI Senate	*Unequal Partners – First and Third Worlds*	Leader of Fine Gael and of Opposition	
	Member of NUI Senate		Taoiseach	
			Member of Council of State	
	Member of NUI Senate		Leader of Opposition	
			Member of Council of State	
	Member of NUI Senate		Taoiseach	Decline of Irish Languge 1770–1870 in 321 Baronies
			Member of Council of State	
Boards of TDI, Guinness Peat, Point International, GEF	Lectures in UCD, British and US Universities	*The Middle East and Trilateral Countries* (co-author)	Member of Council of State	
Adviser to Integrity Interactive	Member of NUI Senate	*The Israeli–Palestinian Issue*		
		All in a Life (autobiography)		
Boards of Point International, GEF	Lectures in British, US and Canadian Universities	*Reflection on the Irish State*	Member of Council of State	State of the Irish Language in 1840s in 4,000 electoral areas
	Universities Chancellor of NUI 1997–2010	*Further Reflections – Ireland and the World*		Irish Education in 1824 in 321 Baronies including fees paid by pupils (in preparation)
		Desmond's Rising, Just Garret		

~: Index :~